ON THE INTERPRETATION OF TREATIES

Law and Philosophy Library

VOLUME 83

On The Interpretation of Treaties

The Modern International Law as Expressed in the 1969 Vienna Convention on the Law of Treaties

by

ULF LINDERFALK

Lund University, Sweden

Springer

A C.I.P. Catalogue record for this book is available from the Library of Congress.

ISBN 978-1-4020-6361-9 (HB)
ISBN 978-1-4020-6362-6 (e-book)

Published by Springer,
P.O. Box 17, 3300 AA Dordrecht, The Netherlands.

www.springer.com

This book is a revised and fully up-dated version of a Swedish manuscript entitled "Om tolkningen av traktater". This manuscript was translated into English by Peggy Oscarsson (Letrix), Malmö, Sweden, in close co-operation with Ulf Linderfalk, with the exception for Chapter 1, Section 1, and Chapter 12, which were originally written in English.

Printed on acid-free paper

TABLE OF CONTENTS

LIST OF ABBREVIATIONS

Draft Articles With Commentaries (1966)	International Law Commission, "Draft Articles on the Law of Treaties with Commentaries", Report to the United Nations General Assembly, on the work of the second part of its seventeenth session and on its eighteenth session (UN Dec. A/6309/Rev. 1), *ILC Yrbk*, 1966, Vol. 2, §§ 187ff.
Draft Articles With Commentaries (1964)	International Law Commission, "Draft Articles on the Law of Treaties", with commentaries, Report to the United Nations General Assembly, covering the work of its sixteenth session, 11 May-24 July 1964 (UN Doc. A/5809), *ILC Yrbk*, 1964, Vol. 2, §§ 176ff.
ETS	European Treaty Series
HRLJ	Human Rights Law Journal
ICJ Reports	International Court of Justice, *Reports of Judgments, Advisory Opinions and Orders*
ILC Yrbk	Yearbook of the International Law Commission
ILR	International Law Reports
LNTS	League of Nations Treaty Series
PCIJ	Publications of the Permanent Court of International Justice
Publ. ECHR Ser.	Publications of the European Court of Human Rights Series
UNTS	United Nations Treaty Series
VCLT	Vienna Convention on the Law of Treaties, Opened for Signature on 23 March 1969

TABLE OF CASES

"AAPL v. Sri Lanka", Asian Agricultural Products Ltd v. Republic of Sri Lanka, International Centre for the Settlement of Investment Disputes, Arbitration Tribunal, Award of 27 June 1990, *ILR*, Vol. 106, p. 417 et seq.

"Abdulaziz, Cabales and Balkandali", Case of Abdulaziz, Cabales and Balkandali, European Court of Human Rights, Judgment of 28 May 1985, *Publ. ECHR*, Ser. A, Vol. 94

"Administrative Decision No. II", Administrative Decision No. II, Dealing with the Functions of the Commission and the Announcing Fundamental Rules of Decision, Mixed Claims Commission (United States and Germany), Decision of 1 November 1923, *American Journal of International Law*, Vol. 18 (1924), p. 177 et seq.

"Aegean Sea Continental Shelf", Aegean Sea Continental Shelf Case (*Greece v. Turkey*), Jurisdiction, International Court of Justice, Judgment of 19 December 1978, *ILR*, Vol. 60, p. 512 et seq.

"Air France v. Saks", United States, Supreme Court, Judgment of 4 March 1985, *ILR*, Vol. 96, p. 113 et seq.

"Air Transport Services Agreement Arbitration", Air Transport Services Agreement Arbitration (*United States of America v. France*), Arbitration Tribunal, Award of 22 December 1963, *ILR*, Vol. 38, p. 182 et seq.

"Al-Adsani v. United Kingdom", European Court of Human Rights, Grand Chamber, Judgment of 21 November 2001, *ILR*, Vol. 123, p. 24 et seq.

"Alberta Provincial Employees", Re Alberta Union of Provincial Employees *et al* and the Crown in Right of Alberta, Canada, Alberta Court of Queen's Bench, Judgment of 25 July 1980, *ILR*, Vol. 90, p. 181 et seq.

"Ambatielos", Ambatielos Case (*Greece v. United Kingdom*), Preliminary Objection, International Court of Justice, Judgment of 1 July 1952, *ICJ Reports*, 1952, p. 28 et seq.

"Anglo-Iranian Oil", Anglo-Iranian Oil Co. Case (*United Kingdom v. Iran*), Preliminary Objection, International Court of Justice, Judgment of 22 July 1952, *ICJ Reports*, 1952, p. 20 et seq.

"Arbitral Award of 31 July 1989", Case Concerning the Arbitral Award of 31 July 1989 (*Guinea-Bissau v. Senegal*), Merits, Internationxal Court of Justice, Judgment of 12 November 1991, *ILR*, Vol. 92, p. 1 et seq.

"Arena Mexican Nationals", Case Concerning Avena and Other Mexican Nationals (*Mexico v. United States of America*), International Court of Justice, Judgment of 31 March 2004, available through the Court's web-page: <http://www.icj-cij.org>

"Article 3, Paragraph 2, of the Treaty of Lausanne (Frontier Between Turkey and Iraq)", Permanent Court of International Justice, Advisory Opinion of 21 November 1925, *PCIJ*, Ser. B, No. 12

"Artico", Artico Case, European Court of Human Rights, Judgment of 13 May 1980, *Publ. ECHR*, Ser. A, Vol. 37

"Banković", Banković and Others v. Belgium and 16 Other Contracting States, European Court of Human Rights, Grand Chamber, Judgment of 24 October 2001, *ILR*, Vol. 123, p. 94 et seq.

"Beagle Channel Arbitration", Beagle Channel Arbitration (*Argentina v. Chile*), Court of Arbitration established by the British Government pursuant to the Argentina-Chile General Treaty of Arbitration, 1902, Award of 18 February 1977, *ILR*, Vol. 52, p. 93 et seq.

"Belgian Linguistics (Merits)", Case "Relating to Certain Aspects of the Laws on the Use of Languages in Education in Belgium", Merits, European Court of Human Rights, Judgment of 23 July 1968, *Publ. ECHR*, Ser. A, Vol. 6

"Border and Transborder Armed Actions", Case Concerning Border and Transborder Armed Actions (*Nicaragua v. Honduras*), International Court of Justice, Judgment of 20 December 1988, *ILR*, Vol. 84, p. 219 et seq.

"Bosnia Genocide", Case Concerning the Application of the Convention on the Prevention and Punishment of the Crime of Genocide, Merits, International Court of Justice, Judgment of 26 February 2006, available through the Court's web-page: <http://www.icj-cij.org>

"Bouzari v. Islamic Republic of Iran", Bouzari and Others v. Islamic Republic of Iran, Canada, Ontario, Superior Court of Justice, Judgement of 1 May 2002, *ILR*, Vol. 124, p. 428 et seq.

"Brogan and Others", Case of Brogan and Others, European Court of Human Rights, Judgment of 29 November 1988, *Publ. ECHR*, Ser. A, Vol. 145-B

"Buchanan and Co. Ltd v. Babco Ltd.", James Buchanan and Co. Ltd. *v.* Babco Forwarding and Shipping (U.K.) Ltd., England, House of Lords, Opinions of 9 November 1977, *ILR*, Vol. 74, p. 574 et seq.

"Campbell and Fell", Case of Campbell and Fell, European Court of Human Rights, Judgment of 28 June 1984, *Publ. ECHR*, Ser. A, Vol. 80

"Canadian Agricultural Tariffs", In the Matter of Tariffs Applied by Canada to Certain US-origin Agricultural Products (CDA-95-2008-01), Arbitral

Panel Established Pursuant to Article 2008 of the North American Free Trade Agreement, Award of 2 December 1996, *ILR*, Vol. 110, p. 543 et seq.

"Certain Expenses of the United Nations", Certain Expenses of the United Nations (Article 17, Paragraph 2, of the Charter), International Court of Justice, Advisory Opinion of 20 July 1962, *ICJ Reports*, 1962, p. 151 et seq.

"Chamizal", In the Matter of the International Title to the Chamizal Tract (United States and Mexico), International Boundary Commission, Award of 15 June 1911, *American Journal of International Law*, Vol. 5 (1911), p. 785 et seq.

"Colozza", Colozza Case, European Court of Human Rights, Judgment of 12 February 1985, *Publ. ECHR*, Ser. A, Vol. 89

"Competence of the ILO for Agriculture", Advisory opinion given by the Court on August 12th 1922 upon the following question: "Has the International Labour Organisation the competence in regard to international regulation of the conditions of labour of persons employed in agriculture and to examine proposals for the organisation and development of the methods of agricultural production as well as other questions of a like character?", Permanent Court of International Justice, *PCIJ*, Ser. B, No. 2–3

"Compulsory Membership", Compulsory Membership in an Association Prescribed by Law for the Practice of Journalism, Inter-American Court of Human Rights, Advisory Opinion of 13 November 1985, No. OC-5/85, *HRLJ*, Vol. 7, p. 74 et seq.

"Construction of a Wall", Legal Consequences of the Construction of a Wall in the Occupied Palestinian Territory, International Court of Justice, Judgment of 9 July 2004, available through the Court's web-page: <http://www.icj-cij.org>

"Corfu Channel", The Corfu Channel Case, Merits, International Court of Justice, Judgment of 9 April 1949, *ICJ Reports*, 1949, p. 1 et seq.

"De Jong, Baljet and Van den Brink", European Court of Human Rights, Judgment of 22 May 1984, *Publ. ECHR*, Ser. A, Vol. 77

"Delcourt", Delcourt Case, European Court of Human Rights, Judgment of 17 January 1970, *Publ. ECHR*, Ser. A, Vol. 11

"De Wilde, Ooms and Versyp, De Wilde", Ooms and Versyp Cases ("Vagrancy Cases"), European Court of Human Rights, Judgment of 18 June 1971, *Publ. ECHR*, Ser. A, Vol. 12

"Diversion of Water from the Meuse", The Diversion of Water from the Meuse, Permanent Court of International Justice, Judgment of 28 June 1937, *PCIJ*, Ser. A/B, No. 70

"EC-Biotechnical Products", European Communities – Approval and Marketing of Biotechnical Products, complaint by the United States (WT/DS291), Canada (WT/DS292), and Argentina (WT/DS293), Report of a WTO Panel, Report adopted on 21 November 2006, available through the web-page of the WTO: <http://www.wto.org>

"EC-Beef Hormones", European Communities – Measures Affecting Livestock and Meat (Hormones), complaint by Canada (WT/DS26) and the United States (WT/DS48), Appellate Body of the WTO, Report adopted on 13 February 1998, available through the web-page of the WTO: <http://www.wto.org>

"EC-Poultry", European Communities – Measures Affecting Importation of Certain Poultry Products, complaint by Brazil (WT/DS69), Appellate Body of the WTO, Report adopted on 23 July 1998, available through the web-page of the WTO: <http://www.wto.org>

"El Salvador/Honduras", Case Concerning the Land, Island and Maritime Frontier Dispute (El Salvador/Honduras), Merits, International Court of Justice, Judgment of 11 September 1992, *ILR*, Vol. 97, p. 114 et seq.

"ELSI", Case Concerning Elettronica Sicula SpA (ELSI) (*United States v. Italy*), International Court of Justice, Chamber, Judgment of 20 July 1989, *ILR*, Vol. 84, p. 312 et seq.

"EMBL v. Germany", European Molecular Biology Laboratory Arbitration, Arbitration Tribunal, Award of 29 June 1990, *ILR*, Vol. 105, p. 1 et seq.

"European Commission of the Danube", Jurisdiction of the European Commission of the Danube Between Galatz and Braila, Permanent Court of International Justice, Advisory Opinion of 8 December 1927, *PCIJ*, Ser. B, No. 14

"E. v. Norway", Case of E. v. Norway, European Court of Human Rights, Judgment of 29 August 1990, *Publ. ECHR*, Ser. A, Vol. 181-A

"Fisheries Jurisdiction (Spain v. Canada)", Fisheries Jurisdiction Case, International Court of Justice, Judgment of 4 December 1998, *ICJ Reports*, 1998, p. 432 et seq.

"Fogarty v. United Kingdom", European Court of Human Rights, Grand Chamber, Judgment of 21 November 2001, *ILR*, Vol. 123, p. 54 et seq.

"Gabčíkovo-Nagymaros Project", Case Concerning the Gabčíkovo-Nagymaros Project (Hungary/Slovakia), International Court of Justice, Judgment of 25 September 1997, *ILR*, Vol. 116, p. 2 et seq.

"Georges Pinson", Georges Pinson Case (France and Mexico), Mixed Claims Commission, Award of 19 October 1928, *ILR*, Vol. 4, passim

"Golder", Golder Case, European Court of Human Rights, Judgment of 21 February 1975, *Publ. ECHR*, Ser. A, Vol. 18

"Grimm v. Iran", Grimm v. The Government of the Islamic Republic of Iran (Case No. 71), Iran-United States Claims Tribunal, Decision of 18 February 1983, *ILR*, Vol. 71, p. 650 et seq.

"Groppera Radio AG", Case of Groppera Radio AG and Others, European Court of Human Rights, Judgment of 28 March 1990, *Publ. ECHR*, Ser. A, Vol. 173

"Guinea-Bissau v. Senegal", Arbitration Tribunal for the Determination of the Maritime Boundary, Award of 31 July 1989, *ILR*, Vol. 83, p. 1 et seq.

"Guinea – Guinea-Bissau Maritime Delimitation", Guinea – Guinea-Bissau Maritime Delimitation Case, Court of Arbitration constituted under an Agreement of 18 February 1983, Award of 14 February 1985, *ILR*, Vol. 77, p. 636 et seq.

"Guzzardi", Guzzardi Case, European Court of Human Rights, Judgment of 6 November 1980, *Publ. ECHR*, Ser. A, Vol. 39

"Habeas Corpus in Emergency Situations", Inter-American Court of Human Rights, Advisory Opinion of 30 January 1987, No. OC-8/87, *HRLJ*, Vol. 9, p. 94 et seq.

"Hagerman v. United States and Others", Canada, Court of Appeal, Judgment of 24 September 1990, *ILR*, Vol. 92, p. 719 et seq.

"Handyside", Handyside Case, European Court of Human Rights, Judgment of 29 April 1976, *Publ. ECHR*, Ser. A, Vol. 24

"Ijzeren Rijn", Arbitration Regarding the Iron Rhine (Ijzeren Rijn) Railway (The Kingdom of Belgium/The Kingdom of the Netherlands), Arbitration Tribunal, Award of 24 May 2005, available through the web-page of the Permanent Court of Arbitration: <http://www. pca-cpa.org>

"International Commission of the River Oder", Case Relating to the Territorial Jurisdiction of the International Commission of the River Oder, Permanent Court of International Justice, Judgment of 10 September 1929, *PCIJ*, Ser. A, No. 23

"International Status of South-West Africa", International Court of Justice, Advisory Opinion of 11 July 1950, *ICJ Reports*, 1950, p. 128 et seq.

"IMCO", Constitution of the Maritime Safety Committee of the Inter-Governmental Maritime Consultative Organization, International Court of Justice, Advisory Opinion of 8 June 1960, *ICJ Reports*, 1960, p. 150 et seq.

"Iran-United States, Case A/1", Iran-United States Claims Tribunal, Decision of 3 August 1982, *ILR*, Vol. 68, p. 523 et seq.

"Iran-United States, Case No. A/18", Iran-United States Claims Tribunal, Decision of 6 April 1984, *ILR*, Vol. 75, p. 176 et seq.

"Italy-United States Air Transport Arbitration", Arbitral Tribunal, Advisory Opinion of 17 July 1965, *ILR*, Vol. 45, p. 393 et seq.

"James and Others", Case of James and Others, European Court of Human Rights, Judgment of 21 February 1985, *Publ. ECHR*, Ser. A, Vol. 98

"Japan-Alcoholic Beverages", Japan – Taxes on Alcoholic Beverages, Complaints by the EC (WT/DS8), Canada (WT/DS10), and the United States (WT/DS11), Appellate Body of the WTO, Report adopted on 1 November 1996, available through the web-page of the WTO: <http://www.wto.org>

"Johnston and Others", Case of Johnston and Others, European Court of Human Rights, Judgment of 18 December 1986, *Publ. ECHR*, Ser. A, Vol. 112

"Kasikili/Sedudu Island", Case Concerning Kasikili/Sedudu Island (Botswana/Namibia), International Court of Justice, Judgment of 13 December 1999, available through the Court's web-page: <http://www.icj-cij.org>

"Kjeldsen, Busk Madsen and Pedersen", Case of Kjeldsen, Busk Madsen and Pedersen, European Court of Human Rights, Judgment of 7 December 1976, *Publ. ECHR*, Ser. A, Vol. 23

"Kronprins Gustaf Adolf", The Kronprins Gustaf Adolf; The Pacific (United States and Sweden), Borel, Arbitrator, Award of 18 July, 1932, *ILR*, Vol. 6, p. 372 et seq.

"La Bretagne Arbitration", Dispute Concerning Filleting within the Gulf of St Lawrence ("La Bretagne") (Canada/France), Arbitral Tribunal established by Agreement of 23 October 1985, Award of 17 July 1986, *ILR*, Vol. 82, p. 591 et seq.

"La Grand Case", La Grand Case (*Germany v. United States of America*), International Court of Justice, Judgment of 27 June 2001, ICJ Reports, 2001, p. 466 et seq.

"Legal Status of Eastern Greenland", Permanent Court of International Justice, Judgment of 5 April 1935, *PCIJ*, Ser. A/B, No. 53

"Lithgow and Others", Case of Lithgow and Others, European Court of Human Rights, Judgment of 8 July 1986, *Publ. ECHR*, Ser. A, Vol. 102

"Loewen v. United States of America", The Loewen Group Inc. and Raymond L. Loewen v. United States of America, NAFTA Arbitration Tribunal, Award of 26 June 2003, *ILR*, Vol. 128, p. 359 et seq.

"Loizidou v. Turkey", Case of Loizidou v. Turkey, Preliminary Objections, European Court of Human Rights, Judgment of 23 March 1995, *Publ. ECHR*, Ser. A, Vol. 310

"Luedicke, Belkacem and Koç", Case of Luedicke, Belkacem and Koç, European Court of Human Rights, Judgment of 28 November 1978, *Publ. ECHR*, Ser. A, Vol. 29

"Maritime Delimitation: Jan Mayen", Case Concerning Maritime Delimitation in the Area Between Greenland and Jan Mayen (*Denmark v. Norway*), International Court of Justice, Judgment of 14 June 1993, *ILR*, Vol. 99, p. 396 et seq.

"Ministry of Defence v. Ergialli", Italy, Court of Venice, Judgment of 5 February 1958, *ILR*, Vol. 26, p. 732 et seq.

"Minority Schools in Albania", Permanent Court of International Justice, Advisory Opinion of 6 April 1935, *PCIJ*, Series A/B, No. 64

"Mondev v. United States", Mondev International Ltd v. United States of America, ICSID Arbitration Tribunal, Award of 11 October 2002, *ILR*, Vol. 125, p. 110 et seq.

"Müller and Others", Case of Müller and Others, European Court of Human Rights, Judgment of 24 May 1988, *Publ. ECHR*, Ser. A, Vol. 133

"Namibia", Legal Consequences for States of the Continued Presence of South Africa in Namibia (South West Africa) Notwithstanding Security Council Resolution 276 (1970), International Court of Justice, Advisory Opinion of 21 June 1971, *ILR*, Vol. 49, p. 3 et seq.

"National Union of Belgian Police", National Union of Belgian Police Case, European Court of Human Rights, Judgment of 27 October 1975, *ILR*, Vol. 57, p. 262 et seq.

"Nicaragua v. USA (Jurisdiction)", Military and Paramilitary Activities in and Against Nicaragua (*Nicaragua v. United States*), Jurisdiction, International Court of Justice, Judgment of 26 November 1984, *ILR*, Vol. 76, p. 5 et seq.

"Niemetz v. Germany, Case of Niemetz v. Germany, European Court of Human Rights, Judgment of 16 December 1992, *Publ. ECHR*, Ser. A, Vol. 251-B

"Nuclear Weapons – WHO Request", Legality of the Use by a State of Nuclear Weapons in Armed Conflict (Request by the World Health Organization for an Advisory Opinion), International Court of Justice, Decision of 8 July 1996, *ILR*, Vol. 110, p. 1 et seq.

"Oil Platforms", Case Concerning Oil Platforms (Islamic Republic of Iran v. United States), Preliminary Objection, International Court of Justice, Judgment of 12 December 1996, *ICJ Reports*, 1996 (II), p. 803 et seq.

"Oil Platforms (Merits)", Case Concerning Oil Platforms (*Islamic Republic of Iran v. United States*), International Court of Justice, Judgment of 6 November 2003, available through the Court's web-page: <http://www.icj-cij.org>

"OSPAR", "Dispute Concerning Access to Information under Article 9 of the OSPAR Convention (*Ireland v. The United Kingdom*), Arbitration Tribunal, Award of 2 July 2003, available through the web-page of the Permanent Court of Arbitration: <http://www.pca-cpa.org>

"Pakelli", Pakelli Case, European Court of Human Rights, Judgment of 25 April 1983, *Publ. ECHR*, Ser. A, Vol. 64

"Plama", Plama Consortium Ltd. v. Republic of Bulgaria, International Centre for the Settlement of Investment Disputes, Arbitration Tribunal, Award of 8 February 2005, available through the web-page of ICSID: <http://www.worldbank.org/icsid>

"Pope & Talbot v. Canada", Arbitration Tribunal constituted under Chapter 11 of the North American Free Trade Agreement, Award on the Merits Phase 2, Award of 10 April 2001, *ILR*, Vol. 122, p. 294 et seq.

"Proposed Amendments", Amendments to the Naturalization Provisions of the Constitution of Costa Rica, Inter-American Court of Human Rights, Advisory Opinion of 19 January 1984, No. OC-4/84, *HRLJ*, Vol. 5, p. 161 et seq.

"Prosecutor v. Blaskić", International Criminal Tribunal for the Former Yugoslavia, Trial Chamber, Judgment of 3 March 2000, *ILR*, Vol. 122, p. 2 et seq.

"Pulau Ligitan and Pulau Sipadan", Case Concerning Sovereignty over Pulau Ligitan and Pulau Sipadan (Inonesia/Malaysia), International Court of Justice, Judgment of 17 December 2002, available through the web-page of the Court: <http://www.icj-cij.org>

"Quatar v. Bahrain", Case Concerning Maritime Delimitation and Territorial Questions Between Quatar and Bahrain (*Quatar v. Bahrain*), International Court of Justice, Judgment of 1 July 1994, *ILR*, Vol. 102, p. 2 et seq.

"Quazi v. Quazi", England, House of Lords, Opinions of 22 November 1979, *ILR*, Vol. 74, p. 552

"R (Marchiori) v. Environment Agency", England, Court of Appeal, Judgment of 25 January 2002, *ILR*, Vol. 127, p. 620 et seq.

"Railway Traffic Between Lithuania and Poland (Railway Sector Landwarów-Kaisiadorys)", Permanent Court of International Justice, Advisory Opinion of 15 October 1931, *PCIJ*, Ser. A/B, No. 42

"Raimondo v. Italy", Case of Raimondo v. Italy, European Court of Human Rights, Judgment of 22 February 1994, *Publ. ECHR*, Ser. A, Vol. 281-A

"Rainbow Navigation Inc. v. Department of the Navy", United States, Court of Appeals, District of Columbia Circuit, Judgment of 24 August 1990, *ILR*, Vol. 96, p. 97 et seq.

"Rainbow Warrior Arbitration", Rainbow Warrior (*New Zealand v. France*), France-New Zealand Arbitration Tribunal, Award of 30 April 1990, *ILR*, Vol. 82, p. 500 et seq.

"Reparation for Injuries", Reparation for Injuries Suffered in the Service of the United Nations, International Court of Justice, Advisory Opinion of 11 April 1949, *ICJ Reports*, 1949, p. 174 et seq.

"Restrictions to the Death Penalty", Inter-American Court of Human Rights, Advisory Opinion of 8 September 1983, No. OC-3/83, *HRLJ*, Vol. 4, p. 339 et seq.

"Rights of Passage (Preliminary Objections)", Case Concerning Right of Passage Over Indian Territory (*Portugal v. India*), Preliminary Objections, International Court of Justice, Judgment of 26 November 1957, *ICJ Reports*, 1957, p. 125 et seq.

"Rights of US Nationals in Morocco", Case Concerning Rights of Nationals of the United States of America in Morocco (*France v. United States of America*), International Court of Justice, Judgment of 27 August 1952, *ICJ Reports*, 1952, p. 176 et seq.

"Riley and Butler v. The Commonwealth", Australia, High Court, Judgment of 18 December 1985, *ILR*, Vol. 87, p. 144 et seq.

"Salini", Salini Costruttori S.p.A. and Italstrade S.p.A. v. The Hashemite Kingdom of Jordan, International Centre for Settlement of Investment Disputes, Arbitration Tribunal, Award of 29 November 2004, available through the web-page of ICSID: <http://www.worldbank.org/icsid>

"Schiesser", Schiesser Case, European Court of Human Rights, Judgment of 4 December 1979, *Publ. ECHR*, Ser. A, Vol. 34

"S.D. Myers v. Canada", S.D. Myers Inc. v. Canada, NAFTA Arbitration Tribunal, Award of 13 November 2000 (Partial), *ILR*, Vol. 121, p. 73 et seq.

"Social Insurance (Alsace-Lorraine)", Arbitration Tribunal of Interpretation Created under the Provisions of Annex II to the London Agreement of August 9, 1924, Between the Reparation Commission and the German Government, Award of 24 March 1926, *American Journal of International Law*, Vol. 20 (1926), p. 566 et seq.

"Soering", Soering Case, European Court of Human Rights, Judgment of 7 July 1989, *Publ. ECHR*, Ser. A, Vol. 161

"Sovereignty over Pulau Ligitan and Pulau Sipadan", Case Concerning Sovereignty over Pulau Ligitan and Pulau Sipadan (Indonesia/Malaysia),

International Court of Justice, Judgment of 17 December 2002, available through the Court's web-page: <http://www.icj-cij.org>

"S.S. 'Wimbledon' ", The P.P. Wimbledon, Permanent Court of International Justice, Judgment of 17 August 1923, *PCIJ*, Ser. A, No. 1

"Sunday Times (First)", The Sunday Times Case, European Court of Human Rights, Judgment of 26 April 1979, *Publ. ECHR*, Ser. A, Vol 30

"Territorial Dispute (Libya/Chad)", Case Concerning the Territorial Dispute (Libyan Arab Jamahiriya/Chad), International Court of Justice, Judgment of 3 February 1994, *ILR*, Vol. 100, p. 1 et seq.

"United States-United Kingdom Arbitration Concerning Heathrow Airport User Charges", Arbitration Tribunal, Award of 30 November 1992, *ILR*, Vol. 102, p. 216 et seq.

"U.S.-France Air Services Award", Case Concerning the Air Services Agreement of 27 March 1946 (*United States v. France*), Arbitral Tribunal established by the *Compromis* of 11 July 1978, Award of 9 December 1978, *ILR*, Vol. 54, p. 304 et seq.

"US-Gasoline", United States – Standards for Reformulated and Conventional Gasoline, Complaints by Venezuela (WT/DS2), and Brazil (WT/DS4), Appellate Body of the WTO, Report adopted on 20 May 1996, available through the web-page of the WTO: <http://www.wto.org>

"US-Shrimp", United States – Import Prohibition of Certain Shrimp and Shrimp Products, Joint Complaint by India, Pakistan, and Thailand (WT/DS58), Appellate Body of the WTO, Report adopted on 12 October 1998, available through the web-page of the WTO: <http://www.wto.org>

"Van der Mussele", Van der Mussele Case, European Court of Human Rights, Judgment of 23 November 1983, *Publ. ECHR*, Ser. A, Vol. 70

"Vidal v. Belgium", Case of Vidal v. Belgium, European Court of Human Rights, Judgment of 22 April 1992, *Publ. ECHR*, Ser. A, Vol. 235-B

"Yaung Chi Oo Trading v. Myanmar", Yaung Chi OO Trading Pte Ltd v. The Union of Myanmar, Arbitration Tribunal Constituted under Article X of the 1987 ASEAN Agreement for the Promotion and Protection of Investments, Award of 31 March 2003, *ILR*, Vol. 127, p. 42 et seq.

"Young Loan", The Kingdom of Belgium, The French Republic, The Swiss Confederation, The United Kingdom and The United States of America v. The Federal Republic of Germany (Young Loan), Arbitral Tribunal for the Agreement on German External Debts, Award of 16 May 1980, *ILR*, Vol. 59, p. 495 et seq.

"Öztürk", Öztürk Case, European Court of Human Rights, Judgment of 21 February 1984, *Publ. ECHR*, Ser. A, Vol. 73

LIST OF TREATIES

Tratado de Limítes, Argentina and Chile, Signed at Buenos Aires, on 23 July 1881. (It should be noted that the treaty is authenticated in the Spanish language only. The English translation used for this work is the one provided by the court. (See *ILR*, Vol. 52, pp. 127–131. For the authenticated text of the treaty, see ibid.)

Convention on the Delimitation of French and Portuguese Possessions in West Africa, Signed on 12 May 1886. (It should be noted that the treaty is authenticated in the French and Portuguese languages only. The English translation used for this work is the one provided by the court. (See *ILR*, Vol. 77, pp. 659–661. For the authenticated French text of the treaty, see *Archives Diplomatiques*, Vol. 24 (1887), p. 5 et seq.)

Anglo-German Agreement, Signed on 1 July 1890. (For those parts of the treaty discussed in this work, see ICJ Reports, 1999(II), p. 1060.

Treaty of Peace with Germany ("the Treaty of Versailles"), Signed at Versailles, on 28 June 1919, *American Journal of International Law*, Vol. 16 (1922), Supplement, p. 1 et seq.

Covenant of the League of Nations, Signed at Versailles, on 28 June 1919

Convention Concerning the Territory of Memel, Signed at Paris, on 8 May 1924, LNTS, Vol. 29, p. 86 et seq.

Convention and Statute on Freedom of Transit, Signed at Barcelona, on 20 April 1921, LNTS, Vol. 7, p. 11 et seq.

General Act for the Pacific Settlement of International Disputes, Concluded at Geneva, on 26 September 1928, LNTS, Vol. 93, p. 343 et seq.

Convention for the Unification of Certain Rules Relating to International Transportation by Air, Signed at Warzaw, on 12 October 1929, LNTS, Vol. 137, p. 11 et seq.

Charter of the United Nations, Concluded at San Fransisco, on 26 June 1946

Statute of the International Court of Justice, Concluded at San Fransisco, on 26 June 1945

Treaty of Peace with Italy, Signed at Paris, on 10 February 1947, UNTS, Vol. 49, p. 3 et seq.

American Treaty on Pacific Settlement ("the Pact of Bogotá"), Signed at Bogotá, on 30 April 1948, UNTS, Vol. 30, p. 55 et seq.

European Convention for the Protection of Human Rights and Fundamental Freedoms, Concluded at Rome, on 4 November 1950, ETS, No. 5

Protocol No. 1 to the Convention for the Protection of Human Rights and Fundamental Freedoms, securing certain rights and freedoms other than those already included in the Convention, Concluded at Paris, on 20 March 1952, ETS, No. 9

Agreement on German External Debts, Signed at London, on 27 February 1953, UNTS, Vol. 333, p. 4 et seq.

Treaty of Amity, Economic Relations and Consular Rights, United States and Iran, Signed at Tehran, on 15 August 1955, UNTS, Vol. 284, p. 93 et seq.

Exchange of Notes, between France and Portugal, on 26 April 1960, Concerning the Definition of the Maritime Frontier between the Republic of Senegal and the Portuguese territory of Guinea (It should be noted that the treaty is authenticated in the French and Portuguese languages only. The English translation used for this work is the one provided by the court. (See *ILR*, Vol. 92, p. 34. For the authenticated French text of the treaty, see *Revue générale de droit international public*, Vol. 31 (1960), p. 891 et seq.)

Exchange of Notes between the United States of America and the Federal People's Republic of Yugoslavia, on 28 November 1962, UNTS, Vol. 460, pp. 192–194

Protocol No. 4 to the Convention for the Protection of Human Rights and Fundamental Freedoms, securing certain rights and freedoms other than those already included in the Convention and in the first Protocol thereto, Concluded at Strasbourg, on 16 September 1963, ETS, No. 46

Final Act, Agreement and other Acts relating to the establishment and operation of the Iron Gates Water Power and Navigation System on the River Danube, Yugoslavia and Romania, All signed at Belgrade, on 30 November 1963, English translation, UNTS, Vol. 512–513

International Covenant on Economic, Social and Cultural Rights, Adopted at New York, on 16 December 1966, UNTS, Vol. 993, p. 3 et seq.

International Covenant on Civil and Political Rights, Adopted at New York, on 16 December 1966, UNTS, Vol. 999, p. 171 et seq.

Treaty on Principles Governing the Activities of States in the Exploration and Use of Outer Space, Including the Moon and other Celestial Bodies, Opened for Signature at London, Moscow and Washington, on 27 January 1967, UNTS, Vol. 610, p. 205 et seq.

Vienna Convention on the Law of Treaties, Opened for Signature on 23 March 1969, UNTS, Vol. 1155, p. 331 et seq.

Agreement between Canada and France on their Mutual Fishing Relations, Signed at Ottawa, on 27 March 1972, UNTS, Vol. 862, p. 209 et seq.

Treaty Between the Hungarian People's Republic and the Czechoslovak Socialist Republic Concerning the Construction and Operation of the Gabčíkovo-Nagymaros System of Locks, Signed at Budapest, on 16 September 1977, English translation, UNTS, Vol. 1109, p. 236 et seq.

Agreement between the Government of the United Kingdom of Great Britain and Northern Ireland and the Government of Sri Lanka for the Promotion and Protection of Investments, Signed on 13 February 1980. (For the parts relevant to this work, see *ILR*, Vol. 106, pp. 478–479.)

Declaration of the Government of the Democratic and Popular Republic of Algeria Concerning the Settlement of Claims by the Government of the United States of America and the Government of the Islamic Republic of Iran ("the Claims Settlement Declaration"), Initialled on 19 January 1981, *Iran – United States Claims Tribunal Reports*, Vol. 1, pp. 9–12

International Telecommunication Convention, Signed at Nairobi, on 6 November 1982

Special Agreement between the Governments of Guinea and Guinea-Bissau, Signed at Bissau, on 18 February 1983. (It should be noted that the treaty is authenticated in the French and Portuguese languages only. The English translation used for this work is the one provided by the court. (See *ILR*, Vol. 77, pp. 642–645.)

Memorandum of Understanding ("MoU") between the Government of the United States of America and the Government of the United Kingdom of Great Britain and Northern Ireland on Airport User Charges, Signed at Washington, on 6 April 1983. (See *ILR*, Vol. 102, pp. 561–564.)

Vienna Convention on the Law of Treaties between States and International Organizations and between International Organizations, Opened for Signature on 21 March 1986, UN Doc. A/CONF.129/15 1994 års WTO Agreement on Agriculture. (For the parts relevant to this work, see *ILR*, Vol. 110, p. 557.)

CHAPTER 1

INTRODUCTION

1 PURPOSE AND TOPIC

We live in the age of treaties. Increasingly, bilateral and multilateral written agreements are used for the creation of new international legal standards. For political reasons, states are decreasingly less willing to rely upon customary international law for the regulation of legal matters. New technology and growing international exchange have established the need for an ever more precise and flexible international law – a need not satisfactorily met by customary law. In many fields of activity, we can seriously question whether the creation of a rule of custom is at all possible. Considering also that the number of states capable of drafting and concluding treaties seems to be growing, it is not surprising that treaties are concluded far more frequently than ever before. In several ways this is a development that should be met with approval. By entering into written agreements, states avoid the difficulties inherent in customary international law. At the same time, the increasing number of treaties should also be causing concern. The more treaties that are concluded, the more treaties that will have to be applied; and the more treaties that are applied, the more often the question will arise: To what extent, and under what specific conditions, should such an application occur? Naturally, this includes the question of how treaties should be interpreted.

Resolving issues of treaty interpretation demands the time and skills of many different authorities: national courts, police, immigration authorities, civil servants, military officials, diplomatic personnel, international courts and arbitration tribunals, international organisations, and so on – they will henceforth be referred to using the generic term APPLIERS (OF INTERNATIONAL LAW). In quantitative terms, few issues are more important for appliers than the interpretation of treaties.[1] At the same time, the interpretation of treaties is known to be one of the most difficult and contradictory issues on the appliers' agenda.[2] If nowhere else this is evident from the practice of international courts and tribunals. Surprisingly often, when an international court or arbitration tribunal is requested to settle a dispute between two or more states concerning the application of a treaty, it is precisely because these states have different opinions about the meaning conveyed by that instrument. Similarly, it is precisely because judges and arbitrators so often disagree on matters of interpretation, that dissenting and separate opinions are so common in international judicature. To my mind, all such differences of opinion should be avoided. Disagreements between states should be avoided, since they tend to complicate the mutual dealings of states in general. Differences of opinion between judges and arbitrators should be avoided, since they are clearly detrimental to the legitimacy of the judicial decision.

Why is it that the interpretation of treaties causes such great concern among the appliers of international law? Obviously, part of the explanation is that different appliers tend to hold different opinions about the contents of the relevant legal regime currently upheld in international law. Arguably, the situation today is far better that the one prevailing during greater parts of the twentieth century. In retrospect, much of the lively debate on interpretation of treaties and related topics that infused the international law literature of the previous century up until 1960–1970 appears to have had it its origin in the fact that for a long time there was no general treaty governing this field of activity.[3] Since 1969, we benefit from the existence of the *Vienna Convention on the Law of Treaties*.[4] The Convention includes among other things three articles on the interpretation of treaties, all drawn up with the ambition that they would codify the customary international law hitherto applied. They read:

Article 31. General rule of interpretation

1. A treaty shall be interpreted in good faith in accordance with the ordinary meaning to be given to the terms of the treaty in their context and in the light of its object and purpose.
2. The context for the purpose of the interpretation of a treaty shall comprise, in addition to the text, including its preamble and annexes:
   (a) any agreement relating to the treaty which was made between all the parties in connexion with the conclusion of the treaty;
   (b) any instrument which was made by one or more parties in connexion with the conclusion of the treaty and accepted by the other parties as an instrument related to the treaty.
3. There shall be taken into account, together with the context:
   (a) any subsequent agreement between the parties regarding the interpretation of the treaty or the application of its provisions;
   (b) any subsequent practice in the application of the treaty which establishes the agreement of the parties regarding its interpretation;
   (c) any relevant rules of international law applicable in the relations between the parties.
4. A special meaning shall be given to a term if it is established that the parties so intended.

Article 32. Supplementary means of interpretation

Recourse may be had to supplementary means of interpretation, including the preparatory work of the treaty and the circumstances of its conclusion, in order to confirm the meaning

resulting from the application of article 31, or to determine the meaning when the interpretation according to article 31:
(a) leaves the meaning ambiguous or obscure; or
(b) leads to a result which is manifestly absurd or unreasonable.

Article 33. Interpretation of treaties authenticated in two or more languages
1. When a treaty has been authenticated in two or more languages, the text is equally authoritative in each language, unless the treaty provides or the parties agree that, in case of divergence, a particular text shall prevail.
2. A version of the treaty in a language other than one of those in which the text was authenticated shall be considered an authentic text only if the treaty so provides or the parties so agree.
3. The terms of the treaty are presumed to have the same meaning in each authentic text.
4. Except where a particular text prevails in accordance with paragraph 1, when a comparison of the authentic texts discloses a difference of meaning which the application of articles 31 and 32 does not remove, the meaning which best reconciles the texts, having regard to the object and purpose of the treaty, shall be adopted.

Certainly, with the existence of Vienna Convention Articles 31–33 many of the major controversies illustrated by the twentieth century international law literature must be considered as finally resolved. Hence, we can now clearly say of the norms laid down in international law that they are not merely guidelines, as sometimes suggested.[5] The norms *shall* be applied;[6] they establish obligations. Further – despite what certain French authors have suggested[7] – we can easily conclude that according to general international law, separate rules of interpretation do not apply for separate kinds of treaties. The exact same rules shall apply regardless of whether the treaty interpreted can be characterised as a *traité-loi* or as a *traité-contrat*.[8]

On the other hand, the importance of the Vienna Convention should not be exaggerated. Despite the adoption of the Convention and the codification accomplished, it is still far from clear to what content the norms of international law shall be applied.[9] On closer scrutiny, this uncertainty would seem to be due mainly to the way articles 31–33 are designed. Overall, the provisions of the Convention do not address in a direct and straightforward fashion the question of how to understand a treaty in need of interpretation. Rather, they address questions concerning which means of interpretation an applier shall be using in the interpretation process, and in which order. Obviously, such a law-making strategy has the advantage of making the law of the treaty more flexible. To some extent, the process of interpretation may be adjusted to suit the needs of specific treaties or situations, and the adaptation of law over time will be greatly facilitated. Hopefully, when new patterns of interpretative behaviour develop, they can still be accounted for within the framework originally established. On the negative side, the textual cast used for Vienna Convention articles 31–33 has rendered possible a wide variety of opinions as to their normative contents.

As a simple way of illustrating the problem, the various opinions expressed in the international law literature may be placed on a scale, whose two opposing ends would then be seen to represent either one of the two most radical positions. According to the one position – typically expressed by the sentence that interpretation of treaties is a matter of art, and not science – interpretation is a political exercise.[10] I will refer to this as radical legal skepticism. In the conceptual world of radical legal skepticism, legal norms capable of constraining political judgment simply do not exist. Hence, whenever a certain understanding is advanced as the correct interpretation of a certain treaty provision, the only question to be asked is whether the interpretation is legitimate or not. Stated somewhat differently, according to radical legal skepticism, the only aspect to be considered in assessing the interpretation is that of its political correctness.

According to the opposite, equally radical position, treaty interpretation is a field of activity governed entirely by rules of law. I will refer to this as the one-right-answer thesis. In the view of the one-right-answer thesis, the legal regime created in international law for the interpretation of treaties is an absolute one, in the sense that an applier can interpret a treaty by applying a number of legal rules and be perfectly certain of always arriving at a determinate result in a completely value-free way. There is no room for political judgment. Whenever a certain understanding is advanced as the correct interpretation of a certain treaty provision, the only question to be asked is whether the interpretation conforms to the standards laid down in international law or not. Stated differently, according to the one-right-answer thesis, the only aspect to be considered in assessing the interpretation is that of its legal correctness.

It is the purpose of this work to investigate the contents of the currently existing regime established by international law for the interpretation of treaties. In so doing, I will address the two most radical positions just delineated, my conclusion being that in the final analysis neither can be taken as a sound description of the prevailing legal state of affairs.[11] On the one hand – contrary to what radical legal skepticism suggests – in a discussion about the correct interpretation of a treaty, legal rules capable of constraining political judgment certainly do exist. As this work will show, not only does international law provide information on the interpretation data (or means of interpretation) to be used by appliers when interpreting a treaty provision. It also instructs the appliers how, by using each datum, they shall argue to arrive at a conclusion about the meaning of the interpreted provision. Furthermore, international law to some extent also determines what weight the different data of interpretation shall be afforded when appliers discover that, depending on the specific datum they bring to bear on the interpretation process, the conclusion arrived at will be different. In consequence of this, the currently existing regime established in international law for the interpretation of treaties will have to be described as a system of rules. The rules are of two kinds; they will henceforth be referred to as first-order-rules and second-order-rules of interpretation, respectively.[12] A first-order-rule of interpretation tells appliers how they shall understand an interpreted treaty provision, in a case where the provisions have been shown to be unclear. A second-order-rule of interpretation tells appliers how they shall understand an interpreted treaty provision when two first-order rules of interpretation have been shown to be in conflict with one another. Hence, the question investigated in the course of the present work is the following:

> What first- and second-order rules of interpretation can be invoked by an applier, in accordance with the currently existing regime established by international law for the interpretation of treaties?

On the other hand, in almost any process of interpretation questions are bound to arise which concern matters beyond the reach of international law. As this work will show, the rules of interpretation currently existing in international law are far from the self-sufficing regime suggested by the one-right-answer thesis. The rules of interpretation provide a framework for the interpretation process; but within this framework, appliers are often left with what could be called a certain freedom of action. The important question is how this freedom of action should be used.

Obviously, on a scale between radical legal skepticism and the one-right-answer thesis, a correct description of the prevailing legal state of affairs would have to be placed somewhere in the middle. Typically, whether a certain understanding of a treaty will be perceived as correct or not is a matter partly of whether the understanding can be shown to conform to the standards laid down in international law, partly of whether it can be shown to be legitimate. Hence, if appliers of international law wish to improve upon the prevailing state of affairs and make a disagreement on interpretation matters look more the exception than the rule, then clearly, a constructive debate on these matters needs to be concerned with two things. First of all, it needs to be concerned with the purely legal question: What are the contents of the currently existing regime established by international law for the interpretation of treaties? Second on the agenda comes the political question: Given that, according to the prevailing legal regime, certain issues of interpretation are left to be decided upon by appliers on the basis of reasons other than international law, how should that freedom of action be used?

Of course, the answer to the one question depends on the answer given to the other. If appliers are largely uncertain about the contents of the rules of interpretation laid down in international law, then obviously, they are also uncertain about the freedom of action left to them under said rules. As it seems, I have actually two good reasons for investigating the contents of international law. Not only will such investigations contribute to reducing disagreement among appliers with regard to the contents of international law. They will also provide the foundation for a constructive and more rational discussion concerning how the freedom of action left to the appliers under international law should be used. And there you have it, in just two sentences: the motivating idea for this work in a nutshell.

2 THE LEGAL REGIME FOR THE INTERPRETATION OF TREATIES AS A SYSTEM OF RULES

Earlier in this work, I ventured a proposition that will have inevitable effects on how this work will be performed. I suggested that the currently existing legal regime for the interpretation of treaties is best described as a system of rules. This is a proposition I would now like to establish properly. Section 2 will be spent on this task.

As I stated earlier, in the sphere of activities dealt with in this work, we benefit greatly from the existence of the 1969 Vienna Convention on the Law of Treaties. The Vienna Convention – in this work simply referred to as the VCLT – is one of those significant international agreements created during the last 60 years under the aegis of the United Nations. The idea of "a treaty on treaties" was first expressed in 1947, when the International Law Commission (ILC) was created and assigned with the task to "promote the progressive development of international law and its codification".[13] One of the first steps taken by the ILC was to produce a list of areas particularly suited for codification.[14] On this list, the law of treaties was one of the three priorities.[15] Nevertheless, it took years to complete a draft convention that could be used as a basis for an international diplomatic conference, and it was not until 1966 that such a conference could be called by the UN General Assembly.[16] Two sessions were held in Vienna; the first from 26 March to 24 May 1968, and the second from 9 April to 22 May 1969. On 22 May 1969, the Conference completed its work, and the Convention was adopted as definite;[17] the following day, the Vienna Convention on the Law of Treaties was declared open for signature. Another 11 years passed before the Convention entered into force on 27 January 1980.[18] As of 11 June 2007, 108 states were parties to the Vienna Convention.

Whenever appliers set out to interpret a treaty, they should consider VCLT articles 31–33 as a starting-point. Support for this proposition is not so much the Vienna Convention as such, in its capacity of a written international agreement. Formally speaking, the rules laid down in the Convention can rarely be applied. First of all, the provisions of VCLT articles 31–33 are binding only for the parties to the convention. In addition to this, the provisions have no retroactive effect. According to the provisions of VCLT article 4, "the Convention applies only to treaties which are concluded by States after the entry into force of the present Convention with regard to such States".[19] As support for the proposition expressed, I would rather direct the reader's attention to the Vienna Convention in its capacity of a contribution to state practice. Parallel to the rules of interpretation laid down in articles 31–33, customary law also contains a set of rules to be used for this purpose. These rules of international custom are identical to the rules laid down in the Vienna Convention – nowadays, a fact on which not only states,[20] but also authors,[21] as well as international courts and tribunals,[22] seem to be in agreement. Articles 31–33 of the Vienna Convention on the Law of Treaties should therefore be seen as evidence, not only of the rules of interpretation that apply according to the convention between its parties, but also of the rules that apply according to customary international law between states in general.

If it is the purpose of this work to establish the content of the currently existing rules for the interpretation of treaties laid down in international law, the starting-point for this investigation should be articles 31–33 of the Vienna Convention. The question is how the content of these articles should best be described. The provisions of the VCLT articles 31–33 tell appliers how to proceed to determine what they shall regard as the correct meaning of an interpreted treaty provision, considered from the point of view of international law. In principle, this could be done in two different ways. One way is to state the rules of interpretation to be observed by the applier.[23] In this case, VCLT articles 31–33 would indicate, first, the interpretation data to be used by appliers when interpreting a treaty provision; second, how appliers, by using each datum, shall argue to arrive at a conclusion about the meaning of the interpreted provision. Another way is to simply authorise the use of certain interpretation data.[24] In this case, VCLT would only indicate the different interpretation data to be used by appliers when interpreting a treaty provision.[25] How the applier, by using each datum, shall argue to arrive at a conclusion about the meaning of the interpreted treaty provision, would be left to the discretion of the applier.

In order to describe the provisions of VCLT articles 31–33 as simply authorising a set of interpretation data, we must not only identify the relevant set of interpretation data. In addition, we need to establish as a fact that each datum, independently of the other authorised data, and without qualifications attached, on each occasion of use allows appliers to reach an interpretation result, which they can regard as conclusive, considered from the point of view of international law. This seems an impossible task, considering the wording of the Vienna Convention. First, it is evident that the parties to the Vienna Convention have authorised a set of interpretation data, although in the text of the Convention they are termed as MEANS OF INTERPRETATION. These means of interpretation include conventional language ("the ordinary meaning"), the context, the object and purpose, the preparatory work of the treaty, and so forth. However, from the wording of the Convention, it is evident that not every means of interpretation can be used independently of the others; and it is certainly not in every case a question of an unqualified use. Some means of interpretation have no independent function at all; they can be used only relative to other means. Consider for example the case where an applier interprets a treaty using the context, according to the provisions of VCLT article 31. The context can be used only in relation to conventional language. "A treaty shall be interpreted in good faith in accordance with the ordinary meaning to be given to the terms of the treaty in their context" – this is how the text of article 31 § 1 reads. Other means of interpretation can certainly be used independently, but then the usage of them is still qualified in some way or another. For example, the preparatory work of a treaty can be used independently of other means of interpretation, but only to confirm a meaning resulting from the application of article 31, or to determine the meaning of the interpreted treaty when an application of article 31 either leaves the meaning ambiguous or obscure, or leads to a result which is manifestly absurd or unreasonable – this is clearly expressed in VCLT article 32. Apparently, in order to correctly describe the contents of the rules laid down in VCLT articles 31–33, we need to explain in more detail how each and every means of interpretation shall be used in relation to all the others. We need to describe, first, which means are used relative to which. Second, we need to state the particular conditions under which the means shall be brought into relation with one another. And, third, for each and every case where we find that two or more means shall be brought into relation with one another, we need to specify how the different means interrelate. This cannot be done, as long as the provisions of VCLT articles 31–33 are described as simply authorising a set of interpretation data.

Secondly, not all means of interpretation can be used in accordance with the provisions of VCLT articles 31–33 so that on each occasion of use, appliers are able to reach an interpretation result, which they can regard as conclusive, considered from the point of view of international law. We know from experience that when an applier uses more than one means of interpretation, the results obtained will sometimes conflict. If such is the situation, a conclusive result can be obtained only on the assumption that the authority to be conferred on the one means is greater than that to be conferred on the other. The Vienna Convention provides the framework, within which such assumptions shall be made. According to what is provided, given that certain conditions are shown to exist, some means shall be considered to have an authority greater than that possessed by others. For example, conventional language ("the ordinary meaning") shall be considered to have an authority greater than that possessed by the preparatory work of the treaty, lest it can be shown that by using conventional language the applier will be left, either with a meaning which is ambiguous or obscure, or with a result which is manifestly absurd or unreasonable – this follows from the provisions of article 32. Apparently, in order to correctly describe the contents of the rules laid down in VCLT articles 31–33, we need to explain how the different means of interpretation are to be used when they have shown to be in conflict with one another. This cannot be done, as long as the provisions of VCLT articles 31–33 are described as simply authorising a set of interpretation data. All things considered, I have difficulty coming to a conclusion other than this: the contents of VCLT articles 31–33 are laid out in such detail, that we cannot describe them as simply authorising a set of interpretation data. We must accept that in fact, the contents of VCLT articles 31–33 amount to something more, namely a more or less coherent system of rules. The same could then be said about the contents of the identically similar rules of interpretation laid down in customary international law.

3 BASIC CONCEPTS DEFINED

Among the many concepts assumed in this work, two in particular press for attention. I will now make an attempt to define them. A first basic concept is that of a *treaty*. Different meanings can be conveyed by the word TREATY. According to article 2 § 1(a) of the 1969 Vienna Convention, TREATY "means an international agreement concluded between States in written form and governed by international law". What does not fit this description is a group of international agreements, which in recent years have become increasingly more significant (if not nearly as important as the agreements described in VCLT article 2 § 1). The agreements referred to are those concluded between states and other subjects of international law, or between other subjects of international law *inter se*.[26] My guess is that the rules to be applied for the interpretation of treaties concluded between states are exactly the same as those to be applied for the interpretation of treaties concluded between states and other subjects of international law, or between other subjects inter se. An indication of this is the 1986 *Vienna Convention on the Law of Treaties between States and International Organizations or between International Organizations*,[27] which includes provisions for the interpretation of treaties exactly matching those of VCLT articles 31–33. Still, a guess cannot serve as a basis for a work of this kind; and any attempt to find conclusive reasons to support it would simply require too much work. Hence, I have chosen to leave the issue of whether or not my guess is correct, and I will instead strictly limit the subject matter of this work to the interpretation of treaties, in the sense of article 2 § 1(a) of the 1969 Vienna Convention.

A second concept that urges to be defined more precisely is that of *interpretation*. The word INTERPRETATION is ambiguous; and what is more, it is ambiguous with regard to several aspects of its meaning. First of all, INTERPRETATION is ambiguous owing to the distinction between the concepts of *interpreting* a text and *understanding* it. In one sense, we can say that we are engaged in an act of INTERPRETATION each time we are faced with a text, to which we (consciously or unconsciously) attach a certain meaning. Regardless of how carefully the text of a treaty is drafted, no one expression contained in the treaty can be regarded as clear until it has gone through interpretation. In this sense, INTERPRETATION is the only way to an understanding of a treaty. In another sense, it is only when we have already read a text, and the text has shown to be unclear, that we can say that we then INTERPRET it. The text of a treaty does not always have to be interpreted, and when a treaty is interpreted it can be so to a greater or lesser extent, depending upon how much of the text we have earlier considered clear and how much we have considered unclear. In this sense, INTERPRETATION is but one of many ways to understand of the text of a treaty. It has been said that, in the context of reading and understanding laws and legally binding agreements, INTERPRETATION is used in the latter sense.[28] In any case, this is clearly the way the word is used in the 1969 Vienna Convention on the Law of Treaties. This is obvious if nowhere else in article 33 § 4: "...when a comparison of the authentic texts discloses a difference of meaning which the application of articles 31 and 32 does not remove ...".[29] Hence, in this work, whenever I speak about the INTERPRETATION of treaties, the term is used in its more limited sense, meaning the *clarification of an unclear text of a treaty*.

Secondly, the word INTERPRETATION is ambiguous due to the distinction between *the result of a clarifying operation* and *the clarifying operation as such*. INTERPRETATION can be used in the sense of *act of interpretation or interpretation process*; *the activity through which the meaning of a text is supposed to be clarified*. But it can also be used in the sense of *interpretation result; the meaning of a text as clarified through one or more acts of interpretation.* The provisions of Vienna Convention articles 31–33 can be seen to contain rules for the INTERPRETATION of treaties in both senses of the word.[30] Therefore, if someone says he will try to identify the rules of interpretation that can be applied according to present-day international law, then this person has the possibility to approach his task from two completely different perspectives. In the one case, the task is to explain the concept of a correct *interpretation process*, considered from the point of view of international law. The problem we are studying can be described as follows: a person is uncertain over the meaning of a treaty provision; she wishes to know what steps best to take, in order that her line of action will be considered correct from the point of view of international law. The following questions must be answered:

- When shall an interpretation process be initiated?
- What rules of interpretation shall be applied to determine the meaning of an interpreted treaty provision?
- In what order shall the various rules of interpretation be applied?
- At what point shall an interpretation process be ended?

In the second case, the task is to explain the concept of a correct *interpretation result*, considered from the point of view of international law. This is the problem investigated: a person is faced with an assertion concerning the meaning of a treaty provision, what we will henceforth term as an *interpretation proposition*; the person wishes to know whether, from the point of view of international law, the proposition can be regarded as correct or not. The only question that needs to be answered is the following:

- What rules of interpretation shall be applied to determine the meaning of an interpreted treaty provision?

When I investigate the contents of Vienna Convention articles 31–33, and of the identical rules laid down in customary international law, this latter perspective is the one from which I approach my task. My intention is only to explain the concept of a correct interpretation result (or proposition), considered from the point of view of international law. This is not to say that this work cannot be used as a guideline in the event that the reader wishes to learn more about the rules that govern the interpretation process as such. The rules that govern the result of the interpretation process are strongly dependent on those that govern the interpretation process as such; and vice versa. It is impossible to explain the concept of a correct interpretation proposition, considered from the point of view of international law, without indirectly examining the concept of a correct interpretation process. Hence, it is my strong belief that the conclusions drawn from this work – if they indeed relate to the concept of a correct interpretation proposition – may also be used to shed light on the rules that govern the interpretation process. At least, the conclusions can be used as a basis for reconstructing these rules.

Thirdly, the word INTERPRETATION is ambiguous depending upon *who* interprets. In the literature, authors sometimes distinguish between operative and doctrinal interpretation.[31] Operative interpretation is performed by national courts, police, immigration authorities, civil servants, military officials, diplomatic personnel, international courts and arbitration tribunals, international organisations, and other authorities empowered to decide on issues concerning the application of international agreements. Doctrinal interpretation is typically performed by the legal scholar, either in the capacity of an independent researcher, or in the function of a legal adviser to a government. In this work, attention will be focused on operative interpretation of treaties. The idea is to make an attempt to create some assumedly greater certainty among the appliers of international law with regard to the content of the currently existing legal regime for the interpretation of treaties. This is not to say that the conclusions drawn in this work are of no interest to legal scholars; quite the opposite. Certainly, the provisions of VCLT articles 31–33 appear to be designed primarily with the situation of operative interpretation in mind.[32] However, the contents of the provisions have an effect on operative and doctrinal interpretation alike. If a legal scholar assumes the task to determine through interpretation how a state shall (or, alternatively, should) be conducting itself according to some certain written international agreement, and this legal scholar wishes to be taken seriously, then naturally he must be careful not to exceed the legal framework, within which the agreement will have to be *applied*. On the other hand, even if the activity we refer to as operative interpretation is premised on conditions partly identical to those of doctrinal interpretation, we must not forget its unique characteristics. Two such characteristics should be noticed in particular.

My first remark concerns the validity of the interpretation result. When appliers interpret a treaty, and find themselves in a situation of operative interpretation, they are faced with a specific issue concerning the application of the treaty. The task is to determine the legal effects of the treaty on some certain set of facts – a specific case. This places relatively little demand on the validity of the interpretation result. The meaning of the interpreted treaty need not be clarified to a greater extent than that required by the specific case at hand. When a treaty is subjected to doctrinal interpretation, it might be that the interpreter has his mind set on some certain specific situation, but this is not necessarily the case. A legal scholar may interpret a treaty in order to produce an opinion regarding the pending settlement of a specific case, or to criticise some such settlement already decided upon.

But he may also engage in interpretation for the purpose of bringing to order the seemingly contradictory opinions expressed in the literature or in the practice of international courts and tribunals; or he may be set on recommending some sort of measures – for example, the enactment of new law, the issuing of further administrative regulations, or the drawing up of a new foreign policy. If the former is the situation, the demands upon the validity of the interpretation result are just as low as in the case of operative interpretation. The one thing that needs to be clarified is the meaning of the interpreted treaty text in relation to the specific case at hand. If the latter is the situation, the requirements are more exacting. The meaning of the interpreted treaty must be determined in relation to an unspecified number of cases of a similar kind.

My second remark concerns the "precision" of the interpretation results. When appliers interpret a treaty, and find themselves in a situation of operative interpretation, they are faced with a specific question that needs to be solved. They must determine whether a specific line of action of a specific state agree with the obligations incumbent upon that state according to some certain written international agreement, and if not, what consequences arise from breaching the agreement. This places relatively substantial demands on the "precision" of the interpretation results. The meaning of the interpreted treaty must be conclusively determined. The process of interpretation must not lead to a result leaving the meaning of the interpreted treaty unclear, so that the legal effects of the treaty cannot be determined. When a treaty is subjected to doctrinal interpretation, it is because the interpreter wishes to engage in a discourse on the legal effects of the treaty in question. The task is to provide suggestions for how the treaty shall (or, alternatively, should) be applied, either for the settlement of a specific situation of application, or for the settlement of an unspecified number of cases of a similar kind. This means that the requirements put on the "precision" of the interpretation result are relatively low. A legal scholar can opt to conclusively clarify the meaning of the interpreted treaty, but he is never forced to do so. Depending upon the individual policy of the particular scholar, he can always be content with stating the possible interpretation alternatives, together with the various reasons supporting them, and then leave the final choice to the appliers or to the political decision makers.

4 METHOD

Before I introduce my method of research, some further concepts need to be commented upon. In jurisprudence, the concept of *method* is closely related to that of *legal sources*. The problem is that the term LEGAL SOURCE is ambiguous. In one sense, LEGAL SOURCE can be used to refer to the *source from which a legal norm originates*; *the source from which a norm must derive, in order to be considered legally binding*. In another sense, LEGAL SOURCE can be used to refer to *the source to which one resorts to obtain knowledge about the existence of legally binding norms and their contents*. In this work, legal sources in the former sense will be termed as FORMAL SOURCES OF LAW; legal sources in the latter sense will be termed as MATERIAL SOURCES OF LAW.[33] Secondly, the term LEGAL SOURCES in the sense of material sources of law can be used in at least two different ways. Scandinavian legal literature, and perhaps Swedish literature in particular, has traditionally reflected a rather liberal view as to the legitimacy of different material sources of law. In part, this flexible attitude could be explained by the fact that no great division has been made between the use of legal sources for the discovery of legal norms and their justification.[34] LEGAL SOURCE, in the sense of a material source of law, would then seem to be ambiguous depending on whether by this term we mean the material actually used by a judge to discover the contents of law, or the material through which the discovery made by the judge can be justified.[35] To further clarify what has been stated above, I would like to point out that it is in the latter sense that I speak of a MATERIAL SOURCE OF LAW, not the former. The purpose set for this section of the introductory Chapter 1 is not to explain how I actually arrived at conclusions about the contents of international law. The purpose is to explain how I believe the conclusions can be justified.

Two sets of rules for the interpretation of treaties will be examined in this work, deriving from two separate formal sources of law. The first set of rules takes the form of a written, international agreement. I refer to the rules laid down in articles 31–33 of the Vienna Convention. The other set of rules takes the form of an international custom accepted as law: the rules of customary international law, which – as we earlier noted – are identical to those laid down in VCLT articles 31–33. The question is how the investigation should be organised, so that I can be sure to obtain well-founded knowledge about the contents of these two sets of rules. What material sources of law should be used? What authority should be conferred on each source of law in relation to the others? And in what order should the sources be used? These are the questions I will now try to answer.

What material sources of law should be used? To answer this question I will use as my starting-point the *Statute of the International Court of Justice*, article 38 § 1:

The Court, whose function is to decide in accordance with international law such disputes as are submitted to it, shall apply:

(a) international conventions, whether general or particular, establishing rules expressly recognized by the contesting states;
(b) international custom, as evidence of a general practice accepted as law;
(c) the general principles of law recognized by civilized nations;
(d) subject to the provisions of Article 59, judicial decisions and the teachings of the most highly qualified publicists of the various nations, as subsidiary means for the determination of rules of law.

Formally speaking, article 38 § 1 simply contains a list of the material sources of law to be used by the International Court of Justice in settling disputes submitted to it. However, on the more informal level, the article clearly bears a greater significance. Most experts agree that Article 38 § 1 is also reflective of the norms laid down in customary international law: each and every source of law that the International Court of Justice shall use, according to its Statute, shall also be used by appliers in general according to customary international law.[36] We should note that the list contained in article 38 § 1 has been criticised by several authors for being incomplete; the argument is that more sources of law can be used by appliers than those listed in the article.[37] However, none of the alternative lists presented have received any greater recognition. Without taking sides as to whether the list contained in article 38 § 1 should be expanded, and if so, what additional sources should possibly be considered, I have decided to strictly limit myself to the list such as it is.

This means that, all in all, four kinds of sources will be used for this work. To determine the contents of VCLT articles 31–33, I will use the text of the Convention as finally adopted. Further, I will use "judicial decisions", including not only decisions made by international courts and arbitration tribunals, but also decisions made by domestic courts insofar as they are based on rules and principles of international law.[38] And, lastly, I will use "the teachings of the most highly qualified publicists of the various nations", that is, international law literature. To determine the contents of the rules of interpretation laid down in customary international law, I will use general practice, as evidence of an international custom accepted as law;[39] I will use "judicial decisions"; and I will use international law literature.

The Vienna Convention has been authenticated in five languages, of which no one version – according to what the Convention provides – shall have precedence.[40] Of these five language versions, I will only be able to consider those in English, French, and Spanish.[41] Of course, in reading the text of the Convention we will often be faced with the situation that the text is of no use at all until interpreted. When we interpret the text of the Vienna Convention this must be done with consideration for the rules of interpretation established in international law. A legal scholar who interprets a treaty to determine its meaning must always be careful not to exceed the legal framework, within which the agreement will have to be applied; otherwise, he will not be taken seriously. The problem is that the typical reader of this work probably will begin reading it with only a dim picture of what those rules of interpretation contain; indeed, that is the very motive inspiring this work. Naturally, being the author of this work, I have a clearer idea of the subject, having worked with it now for several years. When I write this text, it is in order to justify a series of conclusions, which some way or another I have drawn before commencing to write. In principle, I cannot see why, in a work of this nature, it would not be possible, already at the beginning of *the text*, to presuppose the answer to a question, which – considered the sequence of *the text* – will be answered only later. From a pedagogical perspective, however, this is of course not the best of approaches. Trying to balance these seemingly conflicting considerations, I have organised my inquiry so that in the earlier chapters of the work, I refer to the rules of interpretation laid down in international law, but only when I think this can be done without suffering pedagogical losses disproportionate to what I might gain in terms of a convincing argument. As the work proceeds, references to the rules in questions will be more frequent.

In the area of treaty interpretation, state practice chiefly takes the forms of (1) diplomatic and other official correspondence containing arguments for the resolution of a specific dispute involving questions of interpretation; (2) written memorials submitted in connection with the settlement of a dispute by an international court or tribunal, and records of oral pleadings; (3) decisions made by domestic courts; (4) drafts of statutes, reports and other similar parliamentary material originating from the process of states' ratification of the Vienna Convention; (5) the preparatory work of the Vienna Convention; and (6) the text of the Vienna Convention, as finally adopted.[42] In many respects this collection of material seems rather difficult to handle. The problem with the forms enumerated as (1), (2), (3), and (4) is that practice is scattered over many separate documents, and therefore presents a relatively demanding task to collect. In addition, it is not particularly representative for the international community as a whole. State practice is a conglomerate of acts, to which not all states contribute; and of those that do, some contribute more than others. The problem with the two forms enumerated as (1) and (4) is that they are often difficult to access. In cases where the material is at all accessible for scientific study, it is often difficult to penetrate for linguistic reasons. The forms enumerated as (2) and (3) are accessible via international publications, but only in a limited selection. This further reinforces the argument that practice of this kind lacks the representative characteristics required. Therefore, of all the possible forms of state practice that could be used to determine the contents of the rules of interpretation laid down in international law, I have chosen to use above all those two forms enumerated as (5) and (6), that is, the text of the Vienna Convention and its preparatory work. The forms enumerated as (1) and (4) – official correspondence and parliamentary material – I have chosen not to use at all. The forms enumerated as (2) and (3) – memorials and pleadings, and decisions made by domestic courts – will be used, but only when absolutely necessary and always with greatest caution.

By the PREPARATORY WORK of a treaty (TRAVAUX PRÉPARATOIRES) international lawyers usually mean the documents directly related to the drafting of a treaty.[43] Many documents can be said to have influenced the process leading up to the adoption of the Vienna Convention as definite: (1) summary records from the 1968/69 Diplomatic Conference held in Vienna;[44] (2) reports from meetings of the Sixth Committee of the UN General Assembly;[45] (3) *Draft Articles With Commentaries* adopted by the International Law Commission in 1966 and presented to the UN General Assembly;[46] (4) comments by governments on the ILC Draft Articles;[47] (5) *Summary Records* of ILC meetings;[48] (6) reports prepared by the ILC Special Rapporteur, containing drafts and commentaries;[49] (7) a resolution on the interpretation of treaties, adopted by the Institute for International Law (*l'Institut de droit international*),[50] and an article treating that same subject,[51] written by Gerald Fitzmaurice – both documents, from which the Special Rapporteur expressly stated that he had taken inspiration for his first draft.[52] Not all of these documents can be considered comprised in the extension of the PREPARATORY WORK of the Vienna Convention, at least not in the context of this work – when I speak of the PREPARATORY WORK of the Vienna Convention it is because it is supposed to form part of a state practice.[53] The question is how the concept should be defined. The definition I have chosen to use is rather a broad one. In the preparatory work of the Vienna Convention, I will not only include texts emanating from the states themselves, but also other texts, insofar as states can arguably be said to have had a possibility and a reasonable cause to comment upon them. Therefore, the *preparatory work* of the Vienna Convention will be used to include all those documents denoted by the numbers (1) to (4), but not those denoted by the numbers (5) to (7).[54]

What authority should be conferred on each source of law in relation to the others? The sources I have chosen to use do not all share the same level of authority. First, greater authority will have to be conferred on the text of the Vienna Convention and on state practice than on judicial decisions and international law literature.[55] According to the Statute of the International Court of Justice, article 38 § 1, judicial decisions and legal literature shall be taken into account "as subsidiary means for the determination of rules of law". Primary means are limited to include only "international conventions", "international custom", and "the general principles of law recognized by civilized nations".[56] Secondly, it seems a sound approach that a more recent source should be considered to have greater authority than an older one. The content of a legal norm is not necessarily constant over time; and this applies regardless of whether the norm takes the form of a written, international agreement or an international custom accepted as law. The older the source I consult, the greater the risk that the picture of international law provided by that source is no longer accurate. The purpose set for this work is not to describe the contents of those rules of interpretation that might have existed in international law at some time in the past. The purpose is to make a description of the rules that exist today.

One suggestion voiced in the literature is that as a rule, judicial decisions must be considered to have greater authority than the opinions expressed in the international law literature.[57] To my mind, this is only partially correct. Actually, a great deal must depend upon the volume of the particular source considered and its consistency. In addition, the origins of the particular source are important – some authors and judicial bodies have great authority, others have less.[58] My judgment is that, *generally speaking*, greater authority must be conferred on judicial decisions than on the opinions expressed in the literature, but that, ultimately, the relationship held between two particular sources cannot be determined other than on a case-by-case basis.

In what order should the various sources of law be used? Not all material sources of law used for this work are equally accessible. Naturally, the easiest source to access is the text of the Vienna Convention. Of the remaining sources, it appears that international law literature and the preparatory work of the VCLT are more easily accessible than the judicial opinions expressed in courts and tribunals and the arguments advanced by states in international judicial proceedings. With consideration for the relative accessibility of the sources and their relative authority, I have decided to use them in the following order. As a first step, I will resort to the text of the Vienna Convention. As a second step, I will have recourse to the international law literature and the preparatory work of the Vienna Convention – a more recent material will always be considered prior to an older one. Of course, a condition is that regardless of what can be derived from a particular source, support must be found in the text of the Vienna Convention considered in light of the rules of interpretation laid down in international law. As a third step, I will use the judicial opinions expressed in international courts and tribunals; opinions more recently expressed will be consulted before older ones. The condition laid down for stage two applies to this stage as well. As a fourth and last step, I will have recourse to the judicial opinions expressed in domestic courts, and to the arguments advanced by states in international judicial proceedings. However, I will do so with the limited purpose of lending greater support to a conclusion that, for one or another reason, I deem to be in need of confirmation. Under no circumstances will I make use of more material than necessary. If I pore over a particular selection of sources, and discover that based on these sources, I am fully able to form a satisfactory hypothesis about the answer to the specific question at hand, then I will assume that the answer is correct and that the interpretation process can be concluded. When I find that a particular selection of sources leads to a result, which is either obscure or ambiguous, or manifestly absurd or unreasonable,[59] only then will I draw upon additional sources.

5 ORGANISATION OF WORK

Earlier, I stated that the ultimate purpose of this work is to investigate whether, and to what extent, greater clarity can be achieved with regard to the content of the currently existing regime for the interpretation of treaties established by international law. It is a basic assumption that this legal regime can only be described in terms of a more or less coherent system of rules. What rules of interpretation can be invoked by an applier, in accordance with the currently existing regime for the interpretation of treaties established by international law? This is the question I intend to answer. Up to this point, I have not said a great deal about the concept of the rule of interpretation as such. I have noted that in international law – as in domestic legal systems – we will benefit greatly from distinguishing between first- and second-order rules of interpretation. A first-order-rule of interpretation tells appliers how they shall understand an interpreted treaty provision where it has shown to be unclear. A second-order-rule of interpretation tells appliers how they shall understand an interpreted treaty provision where two first-order rules of interpretation have shown to be in conflict with one another. To my mind this is far from sufficient. If I am to succeed in reconstructing the system of rules laid down in international law for the interpretation of treaties, then I believe it is necessary for me first to establish more closely what a rule of interpretation is. I believe it is necessary for me to establish a model that in general terms describes the contents of the rules of interpretation laid down in international law. This will be the task in Chapter 2.

Chapters 3 through 11 will then be devoted entirely to the more direct investigation of the law. For this part of my work, I have elected to adhere to the outline of the Vienna Convention, as much as possible. Hence, in Chapters 3–6, I will describe what it means to interpret a treaty using the interpretation data described in VCLT article 31, what we will henceforth be terming as PRIMARY MEANS OF INTERPRETATION.[60] In the terminology of this work, describing what it means to interpret a treaty using some certain means of interpretation will then be tantamount to clarifying and putting to words those first-order rules of interpretation, through which the usage has to be effectuated. In Chapter 3 I shall describe what it means to interpret a treaty using conventional language ("the ordinary meaning"). In Chapters 4, 5 and 6, I shall describe what it means to interpret a treaty using "the context": first – in Chapter 4 – I will treat the contextual element termed as "the text" of the treaty; second – in Chapter 5 – I will treat the two elements set out in VCLT article 31 § 2(a) and (b); finally – in Chapter 6 – I will treat the three elements set out in VCLT article 31 § 3. In Chapter 7 I shall describe what it means to interpret a treaty using its "object and purpose".

In Chapters 8 and 9, I shall describe what it means to interpret a treaty using the interpretation data authorised by VCLT article 32, what we will henceforth be terming as SUPPLEMENTARY MEANS OF INTERPRETATION. In Chapter 8, I shall describe what it means to interpret a treaty text using supplementary means of interpretation, in the sense of the *set of elements* that can be used to supplement the means of interpretation listed in VCLT article 31.[61] In Chapter 9, I shall describe what it means to interpret a treaty using supplementary means of interpretation, in the sense of *the rules of interpretation* that can be applied according to VCLT article 32.[62] In Chapter 10, I shall describe the relationship that shall be assumed to hold between the different means of interpretation recognised by the Vienna Convention. Describing the relationship that shall be assumed to hold between any two means of interpretation is tantamount to clarifying and putting to words those second-order rules of interpretation that shall be applied according to international law. Hence, a first task will be to determine the relationship that shall be assumed to hold between primary and supplementary means of interpretation. A second task will be to determine the relationship that shall be assumed to hold among the primary and supplementary means of interpretation, respectively. Lastly, in Chapter 11, I have taken on the task of clarifying and putting to words the contents of the special rules laid down in VCLT article 33 for the interpretation of treaties authenticated in two or more languages.

6 TYPOGRAPHICAL CONVENTIONS ADHERED TO IN THIS WORK

Writing about interpretation is difficult, if we demand that it be done with clarity and precision. Repeatedly, the author finds himself in the situation where he must simultaneously handle various concepts, whose different shades of meaning are difficult to communicate in any adequate manner. It is as if language itself was not sufficient. To improve understanding, I will have recourse to a few typographic conventions. *Expressions* are enclosed by quotation marks.[63] *Words and lexicalised phrases* – where there is a risk that a word or a lexicalised phrase might be misunderstood to represent an expression or the meaning of an expression – will be denoted using capital letters. *The meaning of words and lexicalised phrases* – in those exceptional cases where I think it important to emphasise that what I refer to is not the word or the lexicalised phrase as such – will be denoted using italics. Italics – according to tradition in Anglo-American literature – will also be used for foreign words, phrases, and expressions appearing in the main text. It is hoped that these typographical conventions will enhance clarity and thus make this work easier to read.

NOTES

1. Cf. the following statement by Anthony Aust: "Most disputes submitted to international adjudication involve some problem of treaty interpretation. Just as the interpretation of legislation is the constant concern of any government lawyer, treaty interpretation forms a significant part of the day-to-day work of a foreign ministry legal advisor" (p. 184). See also the 40-year old statement by Robert Jennings: "There are few aspects of international law more important than the interpretation of treaties. A very large proportion indeed of practical problems and disputes have this question at the core of the matter" (p. 544).
2. See e.g. Mehrish: "The interpretation of treaties is among the most confused and controversial subjects in international law" (p. 39). See also Köck: "Die Auslegung völkerrechtlicher Verträge – das tägliche Brot der zur Anwendung Berufenen (grundsätzlich die Außenämter der Vertragsstaaten, daneben vor allem internationale Gerichte und Schiedsgerichte) – macht in der Praxis oft große Schwierigkeiten und gibt auch der Lehre eine bisher noch immer (wie es scheint) nicht völlig bewältigte Problematik auf" (pp. 17–18; footnotes omitted).
3. Examples include: Fenwick, pp. 331–337; Yü, in extenso; Ehrlich, pp. 1–145; Wright, pp. 94–107; McNair, 1930, pp. 100–118; M.O. Hudson, pp. 543–573; Lauterpacht, 1934, pp. 713–815; Jokl, in extenso; Harvard Law Research in International Law, Part 3, pp. 939ff.; Cheng, in extenso; Sørensen, 1946, pp. 210–236; Lauterpacht, 1949, pp. 48–85; Institut de droit international, Session de Bath (1950), Session de Sienne (1952), Session d'Aix-en-Provence (1954), Session de Grenade (1956), *Annuaire de l'Institut de droit international*, Vol. 43:1, pp. 366–460, Vol. 44:1, pp. 197–221, Vol. 44:2, pp. 359–406, Vol. 45:1, pp. 225–230, Vol. 46, pp. 317–368; Fitzmaurice, 1951, pp. 1–28; Hambro, pp. 235–256; Stone, pp. 344–368; Grossen, pp. 102–131; Schwarzenberger, 1957, pp. 488–532; Fitzmaurice, 1957, pp. 205–238; Soubeyrol, pp. 687–759; Favre, 1960, pp. 75–98; Hogg (I), pp. 369–441; Hogg (II), pp. 5–73; McNair, 1961, pp. 364–473; Fitzmaurice, 1963, pp. 136–167; Degan, 1963, in extenso; Bernhardt, 1963, in extenso; De Visscher, 1963, pp. 13–162; Gordon, pp. 794–833; Berlia, pp. 287–331; Tammelo, in extenso; McDougal, pp. 992–1000; Fitzmaurice and Vallat, pp. 302–313; Voïcu, in extenso.

4. UNTS, Vol. 1155, pp. 331ff.
5. For the earlier literature, see e.g. Yü, p. 203; Anzilotti, p. 82; Lauterpacht, 1934, pp. 713–714; Harvard Law Research in International Law, Part III, pp. 939ff.; Sørensen, 1946, pp. 220–222; Kelsen, p. xiv; McNair, 1961, p. 366; Degan, 1963, pp. 162–164. For the more contemporary literature, see e.g. Klabbers, 2002, p. 204; Restatement of the American Law Institute, 1986, p. 196; Favre, 1974, p. 251; Elias, 1974, p. 72.
6. Cf. e.g. the wording of article 31 § 1 of the 1969 Vienna Convention on the Law of Treaties. The word "shall" is not to be perceived as implying that the rules of interpretation laid down in international law are considered to be of a peremptory character. (For a detailed discussion of this issue, see Leonetti, pp. 95–98. For a discussion on the concept of *jus cogens* in general, see e.g. Hannikainen, in extenso; Sztucki, in extenso.) The rules of interpretation laid down in international law are *jus dispositivum* – they apply only on the condition, and to the extent, that the parties to a treaty have not, among themselves, come to agree on something else.
7. The suggestion that separate rules of interpretation apply depending on whether the interpreted treaty is considered a *traité-loi* or a *traité-contrat* has often been made, mainly in the French international law literature. (See e.g. Rousseau, pp. 292ff.; Cavaré, pp. 138–157; Favre, 1960, pp. 75–98; Cheng, pp. 85ff. See also McNair, 1930, pp. 100–118.)
8. Another question is whether the distinction between a *traité-loi* and a *traité-contrat* is even valid. Some authors are inclined to answer in the negative. (See e.g. Lauterpacht, 1950, pp. 374–375.)
9. See e.g. O'Connell (although I do not entirely share his scepticism): "Articles 31–33 of the Vienna Convention on the Law of Treaties are concerned with treaty interpretation, and they have the effect of transforming logical positions into rules of law. However, the priorities inherent in the application of these rules are not clearly indicated, and the rules themselves are in part so general that it is necessary to review traditional methods whenever interpreting a treaty — More controversy is likely to be aroused by them than allayed" (p. 253). See also Torres Bernárdez: "*[T]he Vienna rules on treaty interpretation are not susceptible of being inscribed or enrolled in any one of the schools or doctrines on treaty interpretation that existed prior to the 1969 Vienna Convention and ... consequently, their* mise en ouevre *requires new practical methods of application which are yet to be fully developed* " (p. 734).
10. For an analysis of the statement that treaty interpretation is a matter of art and not science, see Linderfalk, forthcoming, 2007(b).
11. See infra, Chapter 12.
12. I draw entirely on the terminology established by Wróblewski. (See Wróblewski, 1963, p. 414; for more detail, Wróblewski, 1969, pp. 9–10.) Today, the distinction between first- and second-order rules of interpretation seems to be widely accepted. (See e.g. Ost and Van der Kerchove, p. 39; McCormick and Summers, pp. 511–544; Simon, pp. 133–134, cit. Ziembinski, p. 241.)
13. The decision to establish the International Law Commission was taken by the UN General Assembly on 21 November 1947 by adoption of res. 174 (II). The mandate of the commission is stated in the Statute of the ILC. (See the annex to said resolution, especially article 1 paragraph 1.)
14. See the *ILC Yrbk*, 1949, p. 58.
15. Loc. cit.

16. The Diplomatic Conference on the Law of Treaties was held in accordance with GA res. 2166 (XXI) of 5 December 1966, and GA res. 2287 (XXII) of 6 December 1967. For a more detailed description of the conference, see Rosenne, 1989, pp. 364–376; Neuhold, 1971/1972, pp. 1–55; Rosenne, 1970(a), pp. 30–94; Reuter, 1970, in extenso; Nahlik, pp. 24–53; Sinclair, 1970, pp. 47–69; Neuhold, 1969, pp. 59ff.
17. Of those states present, 79 voted for and 1 (France) against the proposal; 19 states (including the entire Eastern Bloc) abstained.
18. According to VCLT article 84, the Convention shall come into effect on the thirtieth day after the 35th ratification or accession instrument is deposited at the office of the UN General Secretary.
19. It should be noted that different opinions have been expressed as to how this provision should be interpreted. According to some authors, the article shall be considered to contain a *general participation clause.* The provisions of the Convention – this is the suggestion – are applicable in the relationship between states, with regard to a treaty concluded after the point in time when the VCLT entered into force for those states, but only under the condition that all states, which are parties to that same treaty, are also parties to the VCLT. (See e.g. O'Connell, p. 205; Thirlway, 1972, p. 108). According to others, the provisions of the Convention are applicable in the relationship between states, with regard to a treaty concluded after the point in time when the VCLT entered into force for those states, regardless of whether the other parties to the treaty are parties to the VCLT. (See e.g. Sinclair, 1984, p. 8; Vierdag, 1982, pp. 779–801; McDade, pp. 449–511; Rosenne, 1970(b), pp. 21–22.) I will not further engage in this debate.
20. See e.g. Indonesia and Malaysia, *Sovereignty over Pulau Ligitan and Pulau Sipadan*, § 37 (at the time of writing, the decision is available only through the web-page of the ICJ: http://www.icj-cij.org); Botswana and Namibia, *Kasikili/Sedudu Island*, ICJ Reports, 1999(II), p. 1059, § 18; USA and Canada, *Canadian Agricultural Tariffs, ILR*, Vol. 110, pp. 575–576, § 119; New Zealand and France, *Rainbow Warrior Arbitration, ILR*, Vol. 82, p. 584; USA and Italy, *ELSI, ILR*, Vol. 84, p. 403; Argentina and Chile, *Beagle Channel Arbitration, ILR*, Vol. 52, p. 124; USA and Iran, *Award of the Iran-United States Claims Tribunal in Case No. A/18, ILR*, Vol. 75, p. 187; Canada and France, *La Bretagne Arbitration, ILR*, Vol. 82, pp. 611–612; Guinea and Guinea-Bissau, *Guinea – Guinea-Bissau Maritime Delimitation, ILR*, Vol. 77, p. 658; Belgium, France, Switzerland, Great Britain, USA and The Republic of Germany, *Young Loan Arbitration, ILR*, Vol. 59, p. 529; Sweden, *Swedish Engine Driver's Union, Publ. ECHR*, Ser. B, No. 18, p. 89; Finland, *Namibia, ICJ Pleadings*, 1970, Vol. 2, p. 65; The Netherlands, ibid., p. 124; South Africa, ibid., pp. 191, 194, 197; Ireland, *OSPAR*, § 81, available through the web-page of the PCA: http://www.pca-cpa.org; Canada, *Bouzari, ILR*, Vol. 124, p. 439, § 48.
21. See e.g. Criddle, p. 438 et seq.; Wessel, p. 162; Bernhardt, 1999, p. 13; Torres Bernárdez, p. 747; Ress, p. 30; Golsong, pp. 147–148; Matscher, 1993, p. 63; Ris, pp. 116–117; Davidson, p. 130, n. 6; Sinclair, 1984, p. 19; Jiménez de Aréchaga, p. 42; Elias, 1974, p. 13; Haraszti, p. 206; Sur, p. 285; Reuter, 1970, p. 7; Vallat, p. xxiv.
22. See e.g. the International Court of Justice, *Bosnia Genocide*, § 160, available through the web-page of the ICJ: http://www.icj-cij.org; *Avena Mexican Nationals*, § 83; ibid.; *Construction of a Wall*, § 94, ibid.; *Pulau Ligitan and Pulau Sipadan*, § 37, ibid.; *Oil Platforms (Merits)*, § 41, ibid.; *La Grand Case, ICJ Reports*, 2001, pp. 501–502, §§ 99, 101; *Oil Platforms (Jurisdiction), ICJ Reports*, 1996 (II), p. 812, § 23;

Nuclear Weapons – WHO Request, *ILR*, Vol. 110, p. 15, § 19; *Quatar v. Bahrain, Jurisdiction and Admissibility (Second Decision)*, *ILR*, Vol. 102, p. 59; *Territorial Dispute (Libya/Chad)*, *ILR*, Vol. 100, pp. 20–21; *Guinea-Bissau v. Senegal*, *ILR*, Vol. 92, p. 46; NAFTA Arbitration Panel, *Loewen*, ILR, Vol. 128, p. 351; *Mondev*, ILR, Vol. 125, p. 123; *Canadian Agricultural Tariffs*, *ILR*, Vol. 110, pp. 575–576, § 119; ICSID Arbitration Tribunal, *Salini*, p. 175; *AAPL v. Sri Lanka*, *ILR*, Vol. 106, p. 437; Ireland-United Kingdom Arbitration Tribunal, *Ijzeren Rijn*, § 45, available through the web-page of the PCA: http://www.pca-cpa.org; Arbitral Tribunal, *EMBL v. Germany*, *ILR*, Vol. 105, p. 25; France-New Zealand Arbitration Tribunal, *Rainbow Warrior Arbitration*, *ILR*, Vol. 82, p. 548; Canada-France Arbitration Tribunal, *La Bretagne Arbitration*, *ILR*, Vol. 82, pp. 611–612; Iran-United States Claims Tribunal, *Award of the Iran-United States Claims Tribunal in Case No. A/18*, *ILR*, Vol. 75, p. 187; Guinea – Guinea-Bissau Court of Arbitration, *Guinea – Guinea-Bissau Maritime Delimitation*, *ILR*, Vol. 77, p. 658; Arbitral Tribunal for the Agreement on German External Debts, *Young Loan Arbitration*, *ILR*, Vol. 59, p. 529; Inter-American Court of Human Rights, *Habeas Corpus in Emergency Situations*, *Human Rights Law Journal*, Vol. 9, p. 97; *Restrictions to the Death Penalty*, *Human Rights Law Journal*, Vol. 4, p. 352; European Court of Human Rights, *Bankovic*, § 55; *Golder*, *Publ. ECHR*, Ser. A, Vol. 18, p. 14, § 29; Appellate Body of the WTO, *US-Gasoline*, p. 17; available through the web-page of the WTO: http://www.wto.org; *Japan-Alcoholic Beverages*, pp. 10–12, ibid.

23. Note that in the literature, the terminology is not consistently used. To refer to what I call a RULE (Fr. RÈGLE; GER. REGEL), authors sometimes use terms such as NORM (FR. SCNORME; GER. NORM), PRINCIPLE (FR. PRINCIPE; GER. PRINZIP), MAXIM (FR. MAXIME; GER. MAXIME), DIRECTIVE (FR. DIRECTIVE), AXIOM (FR. AXIOME), and CANON (FR. CANON). I have chosen throughout to speak of RULES of interpretation. In comparison with other terms, the word RULE seems the most neutral and appropriate.
24. This could be categorised as a variant of *topic theory*. (Cf. Alexy, 1989, pp. 20–24.) An outspoken supporter of *topic theory* is professor Tammelo. (See Tammelo, in particular pp. 36–55.)
25. The idea that the contents of VCLT articles 31–33 should be described as simply authorising a set of interpretation data is a view apparently supported by a number of authors. (See e.g. Klabbers, 2002, p. 204; Wolf, p. 1025, n. 11; Tammelo, pp. 36–55.) Other authors seem to assume some sort of mixture, in the sense that the contents of articles 31–33 should partly be described as simply authorising a set of interpretation data, partly as a coherent system of rules. (See e.g. *Starke's International Law*, pp. 435–438; Brownlie, pp. 626–632; Elias, 1974, pp. 71–87; Verzijl, pp. 314–328.) It can be seriously questioned whether this latter approach is at all defensible.
26. Examples of other agreements that also do not fit the description set out in VCLT article 2 § 1(a) Vienna Convention include: (a) international agreements governed by domestic law; (b) instruments which are not agreements, at least not in the sense of the Vienna Convention, e.g. reservations, unilateral declarations, and non-binding agreements.
27. UN Doc. A/CONF.129/15. As of 13 January 2005, the convention has still not entered into force.
28. See Dascal and Wróblewski, pp. 203–205; Alexy, 1995, p. 73.
29. How could a difference in meaning otherwise be disclosed, previous to the application of articles 31 and 32?

30. Clearly, this is fact which does not enjoy sufficient recognition among authors of international law. (See e.g. Klabbers, 2003, p. 272.) I dare say that this is one of the more important reasons why the literature on treaty interpretation sometimes exhibits such a degree of confusion. See e.g. VCLT article 31 § 4: "A special meaning shall be given to a term if it is established that the parties so intended." The sole function of this text is to establish a burden of proof: an expression contained in a treaty shall be understood in accordance with conventional language, as long as there is insufficient reason to believe that the parties to the treaty used the expression in another (i.e. special) meaning. Of course, this rule holds no interest for us when we ask whether, from the point of view of international law, a proposition of interpretation can be considered correct or not. The rule is, however, highly relevant when we ask how appliers should proceed, so that their chosen line of action will be considered correct from the point of view of international law. None of the authors that dwell on the contents of VCLT article 31 § 4 have taken up this issue.
31. See e.g. Wróblewski, 1985, pp. 244–246, cit. Ferrajoli. In the literature, authors sometimes speak of a third type of interpretation, termed as authentic interpretation. An authentic interpretation exists when *all* parties to a treaty reach an agreement, governed by international law, to henceforth understand the treaty in some specific way. However, this is not interpretation in the sense of an activity performed in accordance with the rules of interpretation set forth in international law.
32. Articles 31–33 are included in Part III of the Convention, headlined "Observance, Application and Interpretation of Treaties".
33. Cf. e.g. *Oppenheim's International Law*, p. 23; Danilenko, pp. 16ff.
34. See e.g. Agge: "Alla faktorer som faktiskt påverka domstolarna (och andra myndigheter) att, medvetet eller omedvetet, uppställa och följa en viss modell för sitt handlande, äro att uppfatta som rättskällor" (p. 45). "All factors that truly stimulate the courts (and other authorities) to establish, consciously or unconsciously, and abide by a particular model for their actions are to be considered as sources of law" (authors translation). In parallel to this, we may notice that authors in the international law literature do not always distinguish in a clear fashion between the act of discovering the meaning of a treaty and the act of justifying a meaning already discovered. An example of this is the often used statement that interpretation is to some extent an art, not an exact science. (See e.g. Klabbers, 2003, p. 272; Aust, 184.)
35. Cf. the distinction between *context of discovery* and *context of justification*. For a more detailed discussion of these concepts in the legal context, see e.g. Golding, pp. 124–140; Wróblewski, 1992, pp. 14–16; Wasserstom, pp. 25–31.
36. See e.g. Malanczuk, p. 36; Higgins, 1994, pp. 17–18; *Oppenheim's International Law*, p. 24; Shaw, p. 59; Akehurst, 1987, p. 23; Bos, 1977, p. 18.
37. See e.g. *Oppenheim's International Law*, p. 45; Akehurst, 1987, p. 23; Bos, 1977, p. 18.
38. See e.g. Thirlway, 1991, pp. 127–128; *Oppenheim's International Law*, p. 41; Shaw, p. 91; Akehurst, 1987, p. 37; O'Connell, p. 35.
39. According to article 38 § 1 of the ICJ Statute, the Court shall apply "international custom, as evidence of a general practice accepted as law". However, most authors seem to think of general practice as something that serves as evidence for an international custom, and not the opposite. (See e.g. Higgins, 1994, pp. 18–19; *Oppenheim's International Law*, p. 26; Akehurst, 1987, pp. 25–26; Bos, 1977, p. 25; O'Connell, p. 9; Schwarzenberger, 1957, p. 39.)
40. See VCLT article 85.

41. Apart from English, French, and Spanish, the Convention is authenticated in Chinese and Russian. For whatever it is worth, it may be noted that the Vienna Conference worked with only three languages, namely English, French, and Spanish.
42. Cf. Villiger, pp. 4–5, 334–338.
43. See e.g. Van Hoof, p. 220.
44. Summary records of the plenary meetings and of the meetings of the Committee of the Whole, United Nations Conference on the Law of Treaties, First session, Vienna, 26 March–24 May 1968, *Official Records*, pp. 166–185, 188–190, 441–443; Summary records of the plenary meetings and of the meetings of the Committee of the Whole, United Nations Conference on the Law of Treaties, Second session, Vienna, 9 April–22 May 1969, *Official Records*, pp. 57–59; Documents of the Conference, United Nations Conference on the Law of Treaties, First and second sessions, Vienna, 26 March–24 May 1968 and 9 April–22 May 1969, *Official Records*, pp. 148–152.
45. Report of the Sixth Committee, 4 November 1965 (UN Doc. A/6090), *Official Records of the United Nations General Assembly*, 20th session, Annexes, Agenda item 87, p. 11, §§ 50–52; Report of the Sixth Committee, 21 November 1966 (UN Doc. A/6516), *Official Records of the United Nations General Assembly*, 21st session, Annexes, Agenda item 84, p. 23, § 72; Report of the Sixth Committee, 24 November 1967 (UN Doc. A/6913), 22nd session, Annexes, Agenda item 86, p. 33, § 33.
46. Report of the International Law Commission covering the work of its sixteenth session, *ILC Yrbk*, 1964, Vol. 2, pp. 199–208; Report of the International Law Commission on the second part of its seventeenth session and on its eighteenth session, Part II, *ILC Yrbk*, 1966, Vol. 2, pp. 217–226.
47. Comments by Governments on Parts I, II and III of the draft articles on the law of treaties drawn up by the Commission at its fourteenth, fifteenth and sixteenth sessions (UN Docs. A/CN.4/175 and Add.1–5; A/CN.4/182 and Add. 1–3), *ILC Yrbk* , 1966, Vol. 2, pp. 279–361; Comments on the final draft articles on the law of treaties prepared by the International Law Commission at its eighteenth session, Report of the Secretary General (UN Doc. A/6827 and Add. 1 and 2), *Official Records of the United Nations General Assembly*, 22nd session, Annexes, Agenda item 86, pp. 1–28.
48. Summary records of the sixteenth session, *ILC Yrbk*, 1964, Vol. 1, 726th meeting, §§ 2–39, 765th–766th meeting, 767th meeting, §§ 34–75, 769th meeting, §§ 3–81, 770th meeting, §§ 11–49, 54–68, 774th meeting, §§ 50–57; Summary records of the eighteenth session, 4 May–19 July 1966, *ILC Yrbk*, 1966, Vol. 1, Part 2, 869th meeting, §§ 52–70, 870th–872nd meeting, 873rd meeting, §§ 1–47, 874th meeting, §§ 1–43, 883rd meeting, §§ 90–102, 884th meeting, §§ 1–49, 893rd meeting, §§ 7–43, 894th meeting, §§ 87–94, 162–181.
49. Waldock, Third Report on the Law of Treaties, *ILC Yrbk*, 1964, Vol. 2, pp. 52–65; Waldock, Sixth Report on the Law of Treaties, *ILC Yrbk* , 1966, Vol. 2, pp. 91–103.
50. Résolution adoptée par l'Institut à la Session de Grenade, II. – L'intérpretation des traités, 19 april 1956, *Annuaire de l'Institut de droit international*, Vol. 46, pp. 364–365.
51. Fitzmaurice, 1957, pp. 203ff.
52. "Articles 70–73 take their inspiration from the 1956 resolution of the Institute of International Law and from Sir G. Fitzmaurice's formulation of the 'major principles' of interpretation in an article on the law and procedure of the International Court published in 1957." (Waldock, Third Report on the Law of Treaties, *ILC Yrbk*, 1964, Vol. 2, p. 55; footnotes omitted.)

53. It should be noted that according to VCLT article 32, the preparatory work of the Vienna Convention can also be used as a supplementary means of interpretation. In this case the concept is somewhat extended. For more on this subject, see Chapter 7 of this work.
54. Of course, nothing stops me from using the documents denoted by the numbers (5), (6) and (7) as part of the international law literature.
55. See *Starke's International Law*, p. 54; Shaw, p. 98; Bos, 1977, p. 59; Akehurst, 1974/1975, p. 280; Schwarzenberger, 1957, pp. 26–28.
56. See e.g. Akehurst, 1987, p. 40; Schwarzenberger, 1957, p. 58.
57. See e.g. Van Hoof, p. 177, cit. Fitzmaurice, 1958, pp. 171–172.
58. Cf. Akehurst, 1974/1975, p. 280.
59. Cf. VCLT article 32.
60. Cf. e.g. Ris, p. 117; Villiger, p. 345; Verdross and Simma, p. 493; Jiménez de Aréchaga, p. 46; Elias, 1974, p. 80; Mehrish, p. 62; Sharma, p. 386; Jacobs, p. 326; Tunkin, at the eighteenth session, 872nd meeting of the International Law Commission, *ILC Yrbk*, 1966, Vol. 1, Part 2, p. 201, § 43; Ago, at the same meeting, ibid., p. 202, § 50; Waldock, Third Report on the Law of Treaties, *ILC Yrbk*, 1964, Vol. 2, p. 99, § 19.
61. For further explanations, see the introduction to Chapter 8 of this work.
62. Loc. cit.
63. For a more detailed description of the concept *expression*, see Chapter 2 of this work.

CHAPTER 2

THE RULE OF INTERPRETATION

In this chapter, I will set up a model which describes in general terms the contents of the rules laid down in international law for the interpretation of treaties.[1] To make the task more manageable, I think it suitable at the start of this chapter to establish some sort of definition. As a starting point for discussion of the rules of interpretation laid down in international law, anyone should be able to accept the following uncontroversial statement:

> The rules of interpretation laid down in international law contain a description of the way an applier shall be proceeding to determine the correct meaning of a treaty provision considered from the point of view of international law.

However uncontroversial this definition may be, it is bound to raise the following questions:

(1) What is meant by "the correct meaning of a treaty provision considered from the point of view of international law"?

(2) How can we best describe the way an applier shall proceed to determine the correct meaning of a treaty provision considered from the point of view of international law?

These are the questions I will now try to answer. The chapter is organised so that in Section 1, I begin by answering question (1). In Sections 2–4, I shall then proceed to answer question (2). In the last two sections of the chapter, Sections 5 and 6, drawing upon the observations made in the earlier sections, I shall examine the consequences of these answers. As stated before, the idea is to establish a model that in general terms describes the contents of the rules laid down in international law for the interpretation of treaties.

1 THE CORRECT MEANING

What is meant by "the correct meaning of a treaty provision considered from the point of view of international law"? In principle, we have only three kinds of meanings to choose from whenever we speak about the meaning of a text.[2] First, there is the *utterance meaning* of the text, that is, the contents of the utterance or utterances expressed in the text. By an utterance we mean the use of a specific subject in a specific occurrence of a specific piece of spoken or written language,[3] for example a word or a phrase.[4] The determining factor for the contents of an utterance is the information associated with that utterance according to the intentions of the utterer.[5] Secondly, there is the *sentence meaning* of the text, that is to say, the contents of the sentence or sentences that make up the text. By a sentence we mean an ideal succession of words linked together according to the grammar of the language assumed.[6] The content of a sentence is tantamount to the information associated with that sentence according to the underlying linguistic system.[7] Thirdly, there is the *receiver meaning* of a text – the contents of the text as received. The content of a text as received is much the same as the purely personal associations which the text creates in the reader or listener,[8] who is not necessarily a specific person, but can also be a reader or listener of a specific type.[9]

According to the rules of interpretation laid down in international law, the correct meaning of a treaty does not correspond to the sentence meaning of that treaty – this much is evident from the literature. Nor does the correct meaning of a treaty correspond to its receiver meaning. In the literature, most of the authors who have participated in the discussion about the rules of interpretation and their content express a view on the ultimate purpose of interpretation. These statements are strikingly similar: when an applier interprets a treaty by applying the rules of interpretation laid down in international law, the purpose is to establish *the intention of the parties*.[10] Considering this, I can only draw the conclusion that the correct meaning of a treaty corresponds to the utterance meaning of that treaty. This is not to say that we can consider the issue decided. We can say that the correct meaning of a treaty is a meaning of the kind previously defined as its utterance meaning, but the statement cannot be made without some reservation. For three reasons we are forced to define our positions more precisely.

A first reason is the fact that a treaty is never an expression of a single utterance. A treaty is always an expression of multiple utterances, often derived from a variety of different subjects. Broadly speaking, we can say that a treaty gives voice to utterances derived from each and every individual who participated in the drafting process leading to the adoption of that treaty. Among the individuals who take part in the drafting of a treaty, we will always have to include representatives of states, but sometimes individuals may participate in the capacity of independent experts or representatives of non-governmental organisations.[11] Of course, all these utterances cannot serve as decisive for what is to be considered as the correct meaning of the treaty in question. Clearly, the correct meaning of a treaty does not correspond to the contents of utterances other than those derived from states.

The question is which states we are talking about. In principle, I can think of three alternatives. According to a first alternative, account is taken of any and all states that participated in the drafting of a treaty; consequently, we ignore those states that did *not* participate in the drafting but are nevertheless parties to the treaty – it may be open for accession, for example. According to a second alternative, account is taken of any and all states that participated in the drafting of the treaty and for which the treaty has already entered into force; consequently, we ignore those states that did *not* participate in the drafting, as well as those that are (still) not parties. According to a third alternative, account is taken of any and all states for which the treaty has already entered into force, regardless of whether they participated in the drafting of the treaty or not; consequently, we ignore those states that participated in the drafting but are (still) not parties.

The rules of interpretation laid down in the Vienna Convention contain expressions that can be said to support the third alternative. Article 31 § 2 speaks of "any agreement relating to the treaty which was made between all the *parties* in connexion with the conclusion of the treaty", and of "any instrument, which was made by one or more *parties* in connexion with the conclusion of the treaty and accepted by the other *parties* as an instrument related to the treaty".[12] Article 31 § 3 speaks of "any subsequent agreement between the *parties* regarding the interpretation of the treaty or the application of its provisions"; "subsequent practice in the application of the treaty which establishes the agreement of the *parties* regarding its interpretation"; and "relevant rules of international law applicable in the relations between the *parties*".[13] Further clarity is provided in the provisions of article 31 § 4: "A special meaning shall be given to a term if it is established that the *parties* so intended".[14] PARTY, according to the terminology of the Vienna Convention, means "a state which has consented to be bound by the treaty and for which the treaty is in force".[15] This third alternative also appears to have the support of the literature. Most authors confirm the idea that the correct meaning of a treaty corresponds to the contents of those utterances that derive from "the parties". Some uncertainty remains with regard to the meaning of this expression. Some authors seem to limit the extension of "the parties" to include only those states that participated in the drafting of a treaty.[16] However, The meaning ascribed to the expression in the language of international law in general is the same as the one assumed in the text of the Vienna Convention. Hence, all things considered, I arrive at the following conclusion: the correct meaning of a treaty corresponds to the contents of the utterances expressed by that treaty, excluding from consideration anything but the utterances that derive from states which are parties to the treaty.

A second reason that makes it impossible to unreservedly say of the correct meaning of a treaty, that it corresponds to the utterance meaning conveyed by that treaty, is the fact that it does not necessarily carry information with regard to one, simple matter only. Depending on the intentions held by the parties, there can be many layers of information linked to a treaty.[17] It can be a piece of information concerning the reference of specific expressions; it can be a piece of information concerning the norm content of the treaty; a piece of information concerning the different instruments comprised by the treaty; a piece of information concerning the relationship held between the contents of the treaty and other norms laid down in international law; a piece of information concerning the relationship held between the treaty and some certain values external to the treaty; concerning its object and purpose; and so forth.[18] All this information cannot possibly determine the correct meaning of the treaty; this much is clear. The question is which information we should take into account. At least in this work, the answer must be considered a given. The subject matter of this work is the operative interpretation of treaties.[19] When appliers interpret a treaty, and find themselves in a situation of operative interpretation, they are faced with a specific situation concerning the application of the treaty. The task is to establish a basis that can subsequently be used for the application of the treaty. What the applier uses is the norm content of the treaty. Considering this, the correct meaning of a treaty must be tantamount to the piece of information conveyed by that treaty with regard to its norm content.

A third reason situation that forces us to more precisely define our positions is the fact that a treaty is not only the expression of different utterances, as stated earlier. The different utterances conveyed by a treaty can also be of different content: it may be the case that for different parties the text of a treaty carries different pieces of information. It is a widely known fact that negotiating states, already at the point when a treaty is adopted, can have different views with regard to the contents of that treaty. According to what some authors seem to think, the obligations held by a state under a treaty stem from the single will of that state, as expressed in the treaty.[20] For these authors, the correct meaning of the treaty would be seen to correspond to the piece of information conveyed by a treaty, according to the intentions held by each individual party, *regardless of the information conveyed by the treaty according to the intentions held by other parties*. This is certainly a position I have difficulty accepting. As noted earlier, when appliers interpret a treaty, and find themselves in a situation of operative interpretation, it is their task to establish a basis that can subsequently be used for the application of the treaty. In this case, what is used is the norm content of the interpreted treaty text; that is, the agreement expressed by the text. What the applier uses is the norm content of the treaty, that is to say, the agreement confirmed in the treaty. An agreement concluded between two parties is constituted by an offer followed by a concurring acceptance. Hence, the utterance meaning of a treaty cannot possibly be tantamount to the pieces of information conveyed by a treaty, according to the intentions held by each individual party *separately*. Arguably, the correct meaning of a treaty should be identified with the pieces of information conveyed by the treaty, according to the intentions held by each individual party, but only insofar as they can be considered *mutually* held.[21]

All things considered, it appears we are able to define the correct meaning of a treaty provision, considered from the point of view of international law, as follows:

> The correct meaning of a treaty should be identified with the pieces of information conveyed by that treaty with regard to its norm content, according to the intentions of the treaty parties – all those states, for which the treaty is in force – insofar as these intentions can be considered mutually held.

Thus, the first of the two questions posed at the beginning of this chapter seems to have an answer. We will now move on to the second.

2 HOW TO DETERMINE THE CORRECT MEANING

How can we best describe the way an applier shall proceed to determine the correct meaning of a treaty, considered from the point of view of international law? On the face of it, the answer to this question is rather simple. The correct meaning of a treaty classifies as of the kind earlier defined as its utterance meaning. Hence, it seems a reasonable answer to say that to determine the correct meaning of a treaty, the applier should proceed in the exact same way as any common reader would proceed to determine the utterance meaning of any text. However, on a closer inspection, we must admit the insufficiency of this answer, since the following difficult question remains:

> How can we best describe the way the common reader proceeds to determine the utterance meaning of a text?

Since I want to establish a more definite description of the rules of interpretation laid down in international law, I must seek support in some general theory of verbal communication. Of course, an utterance is not an end in itself. Whenever a written utterance is produced, it is because some specific subject (a writer) has some particular piece of information that he wishes to convey to some other particular subject (a reader). When the writer succeeds, communication is achieved; we can say that the reader understands the utterance expressed by the writer. The question is how a writer and a reader succeed in understanding each other. How is verbal communication achieved?

As an answer to this question, linguistics offers two explanatory models.[22] From antiquity to modern semiotics, scholars have worked with the hypothesis that verbal communication is merely a matter of coding and decoding messages;[23] this is what we can call the *code model*.[24] A fundamental idea is that all acts of communication – regardless of mode – comprise three elements, namely, a message, a signal, and a code.[25] In this instance, a code is defined as a system through which specific kinds of messages can be linked to specific kinds of signals. A message is defined as a piece of information stored in the brain of a human being; it has no existence outside of the internal world of that human being. Lastly, a signal is defined as a modification of the sensory world, whose principal distinctive feature is that it can be produced by an encoder and received by a decoder. According to the code model, the following events occur when two people communicate with one another: a person (X) wishes to convey a message to another person (Y); X encodes the message into a signal using an encoder; the encoder sends the signal over some particular communication channel to a decoder; the decoder decodes the signal into a message, which it passes on to the intended receiver of the message, the person Y.[26]

This general description can be simplified somewhat, if we choose to concentrate on the situation where X and Y communicate in a strictly verbal manner by means of a text. Then the encoder can be described as identical with the original sender of the message (X), and the decoder can be described as identical with its receiver (Y). Coding and decoding occur when X and Y make use of their respective linguistic abilities. The communication channel can be described as identical with a text. The signal can be described as identical with an utterance. Hence, the communication involving the two persons X and Y can be described as follows: a person (X) wishes to convey a message to another person (Y); X encodes the message into an utterance; the utterance is sent to Y using a text, after which Y decodes the utterance and partakes of its content, that is to say, the message from X.[27]

A distinguishing characteristic of the code model is the importance placed on the utterance as a conveyor of messages. In the code model, the utterance is a fact, through which the receiver (in our case the reader) can immediately form a true opinion of what the sender (the writer) wished to convey with that utterance; the only thing required is that the reader has access to the right code. In recent times, philosophers have come to question whether, in the understanding process, the role of the utterance (and perhaps also the role of the writer) has in fact not been exaggerated; as a consequence, some authors have begun developing a different model.[28] In this model, the utterance is just a piece of indirect evidence. The utterance is a fact, from which the receiver-reader can only *infer* what the sender-writer wished to convey. The receiver-reader must insert the utterance into some sort of context. Only by drawing on a context is it possible for the reader to arrive at a conclusion with regard to the content of the utterance; this is what we will call the *inferential model.*[29] According to the inferential model, the following events occur when a writer makes himself understood by a reader using a text: a person (X) has a message, a piece of information, that she wishes to convey to another person (Y); X indicates the message by producing an utterance; the utterance is transferred to Y via a text; Y notice the text, then inserts it into a context, through which the utterance – the message from X – can subsequently be inferred.[30]

The decided difficulty with the inferential model is the concept of context. By a CONTEXT we would have to understand something that belongs exclusively to the intellect of the reader – this much is clear. When trying to understand an utterance, it is not the physical world as such that a reader brings to bear on the understanding process, but the mental representations he makes of the physical world. We would then have to accept that CONTEXT is defined as the entire set of assumptions about the world in general, that a reader – through decoding, through inference, through direct perception or through using his memory – has access to when reading a text.[31] Consider the example of a reader, an insurance adjuster, confronted with the following passage in a written notification of damage: "Anders ran after the dog with false teeth in his mouth". The notification, written by one Britta Andersson, describes how her husband's false teeth came to be damaged. Now, assume that the reader draws the conclusion that the dog and not the man Anders has the false teeth in his mouth, though both alternatives are fully possible from a grammatical point of view. It is then conceivable that the reader (consciously or unconsciously) argues along the following lines:

Premise (1): Either the man Anders or the dog has the false teeth in his mouth.
Premise (2): Somehow the dog has got hold of Anders's false teeth.
Premise (3): If the dog gets Anders's false teeth, he puts them in his mouth.
Conclusion: It is the dog that has the false teeth in his mouth.

The first premise is the result of decoding. It has its basis partly in the reader's perception of existing grammatical rules, and partly in the reader's assumption that Britta expresses herself in accordance with the rules of grammar. The second premise represents the result of inference. It has its basis partly in the reader's assumption that, in some way, Anders's false teeth have become damaged, and partly in the application of a proposition of generalised knowledge; if the dog gets hold of Anders Andersson's false teeth, then the teeth will very likely be damaged.[32] The third premise also represents the application of a proposition of generalised knowledge. It is based partly on the reader's collected experiences of dogs in general, and partly on the reader's assumption that dogs will be dogs.

The problem with describing the understanding of utterances as dependent on a context is that it can only partially explain how understanding is actually achieved. The scope of a context borders on the infinite. Any reader faced with an utterance has access to countless assumptions. In principle, any assumptions could be used as a premise for the reader's inference. Naturally, however, not all of the assumptions will lead the reader to the true content of the utterance. The question arises: considering that a reader has access to thousands and thousands of contextual assumptions, how can she succeed in selecting the ones that lead to understanding? According to the answer offered by linguistics, the reader resorts to a second-order assumption. The reader assumes about the utterer (the writer) that he is communicating in a rational manner. In other words, the utterer is assumed to be conforming to some certain communicative standards.[33] It is this communicative assumption *together* with the context that makes it possible for the reader to successfully establish the content of an utterance.

As a suitable illustration, we can return to the notification of damage and the passage "Anders ran after the dog with false teeth in his mouth". The reader understands the utterance to express that it is the dog and not the man Anders who has the false teeth in his mouth. The reader's premises are those earlier denoted as (1), (2) and (3). Of course, these are not the only premises available to the reader. Among other things, the reader should typically also have access to the two assumptions denoted as (4) and (5) in the syllogism stated below. Used in the manner illustrated in the syllogism, these assumptions lead the reader to the conclusion that it is the man Anders and not the dog who has the false teeth in his mouth.

Premise (1): Either the man Anders or the dog has the false teeth in his mouth.
Premise (4): Anders owns false teeth.
Premise (5): If Anders owns false teeth, then he has them in his mouth.
Conclusion: It is the man Anders who has the false teeth in his mouth.

So what is it that compels the reader to use contextual premises (2) and (3), and not premises (4) and (5)? One possible answer could be that, according to an assumption held by the reader, the writer (Britta) has expressed herself according to the communicative standard stated below:

> If a person produces an utterance taking the form of a written notification of damage, then the notification should be drawn up, so that its entire content appears fully relevant.

For what is the point of uttering the passage "Anders ran after the dog with false teeth in his mouth", if it does not in some way explain the damage to the false teeth?

Now, the question of relevance for this work is how these two models – the code model and the inferential model – should be approached. Both models are intended to offer an explanation of how a writer and a reader succeed in communicating using a text. The problem is that the explanations provided by the two models are different. The code model and the inferential model would then have to be seen as competing models. Given the question I intend to answer in this chapter – How can we best describe the way an applier shall proceed to determine the correct meaning of a treaty provision, considered from the point of view of international law? – and given that I wish to provide a definite answer, it is apparent that I cannot apply both. I need to make a choice. This choice will determine the direction taken in the subsequent chapters of this work, the purpose set for those chapters being to clarify and put to words all those rules laid down in international law for the interpretation of treaties. The question is whether the code model or the inferential model should be seen as the better description of the way an applier shall proceed to determine the correct meaning of a treaty provision, considered from the point of view of international law. If the code model is better, then an important task will be to identify the code presupposed by the rules of interpretation laid down in international law. If the inferential model is better, then the task will be to determine what those rules of interpretation presuppose in terms of communicative assumptions.[34]

In my opinion, the inferential model should be seen as the better description in the sense stated above. Two lines of argument support this conclusion. The first line of argument is one about language in general. Circumstances indicate that only the inferential model could be seen as a correct description of the way the common reader proceeds to determine the utterance meaning of a text. In modern linguistics, the code model has come under so much criticism that it must be questioned whether this model should be regarded at all as valid. In Section 3 of this chapter, I will describe the main points of this criticism, drawing heavily on a piece of work written by the two British linguists Dan Sperber and Deirdre Wilson.[35] The second line of argument that supports my conclusion is an argument about language considered from the point of view of the Vienna Convention. Circumstances indicate that only the inferential model could be seen as a correct description of the way an applier shall proceed to determine the correct meaning of a treaty provision, according to the rules laid down in international law. Regardless of whether the code model should be considered valid or not, strong arguments suggest that this model should at least not be regarded as valid for the very specific purposes we have in mind. In Section 4 of this Chapter, these arguments will be presented in more detail.

3 HOW TO DETERMINE THE CORRECT MEANING (CONT'D)

In order for the code model to be accepted as a valid description of the way the common reader proceeds to determine the utterance meaning of a text, it must be possible to establish the existence of a code – but not just any code. The code must be such that a written utterance can always be paired with what the utterance contains – a specific message. One suggestion is that this code can be identified with the lexicon and grammar of a language – what we call semantics.[36] This is a sound suggestion insofar as the semantics of a language actually can be seen to form a code. The problem is that semantics is not a code in the very sense implied by the code model. The rules of semantics form a code, according to which sentences can be linked with sentence meanings. For the conclusion to be tenable, that a reader is able to use the rules of semantics to pair the production of a written utterance with a specific message, it must be possible first to regard the production of an utterance on a piece of paper as amounting to much the same as the production of a sentence; second, it must be possible to regard the sentence meaning of a text as always corresponding to a specific message. These are conditions that cannot possibly be considered fulfilled. It is conceivable to say that there is a close resemblance between the production of a sentence on a piece of paper and the production of a written utterance.[37] When a written utterance is produced, it is through the production of a sentence or a series of sentences on a piece of paper. What cannot as easily be overcome are the differences between the content of an utterance and the sentence meaning of a text.[38] Let us cite Sperber and Wilson:

> An utterance has a variety of properties, both linguistic and non-linguistic. It may contain the word "shoe", or a reflexive pronoun, or a trisyllabic adjective; it may be spoken on top of a bus, by someone with a heavy cold, addressing a close friend ... [G]rammars abstract out the purely linguistic properties of utterances and describe a common linguistic structure, the sentence, shared by a variety of utterances which differ only in their non-linguistic

properties. By definition, the semantic representation of a sentence, as assigned to it by a ... grammar, can take no account of such non-linguistic properties as, for example, the time and place of utterance, the identity of the speaker, the speaker's intentions, and so on. The semantic representation of a sentence deals with a sort of common core of meaning shared by every utterance of it. However, different utterances of the same sentence may differ in their interpretation; and indeed they usually do.[39]

Of course, it is a possibility that we are dealing with a code, which contains the rules of semantics but only as part of a larger signal system more comprehensive in kind. "Much recent work in pragmatics", state Sperber and Wilson, ...

... [has assumed] that there are rules of pragmatic interpretation much as there are rules of semantic interpretation, and that these rules form a system which is a supplement to a grammar as traditionally understood.[40]

This assumption is only partially correct. Indisputably, rules of pragmatics exist, and among the many kinds of utterances that cannot be fully comprehended by a reader applying the rules of semantics, there are indeed those that can be comprehended using pragmatics. Consider the example of the woman, Mrs. K, who comes home from work one evening and finds a note from her husband on the kitchen table:

(1) "I am at a meeting with the PTA (Parent-Teacher Association)".

Mrs. K can instantly comprehend what Mr. K wishes to express, namely that *Mr. K* is at a meeting with the PTA. The reason is that a basic rule of pragmatics can be brought to bear on the text written, according to which the "I" in an utterance typically refers to the utterer. In order for pragmatics and semantics to function as a code in the sense of the code model, something more is required: each and every one of the great number of utterances that cannot be fully comprehended by a reader applying the rules of semantics, needs to be such that it can be comprehended using pragmatics. Clearly, this is a requirement that pragmatics cannot live up to.[41] Take for example the following utterance:

(2) "Here comes Mrs. K. She has egg on her blouse."

Certainly, everyone can understand that it is Mrs. K who has egg on her blouse. Using English grammar we can easily conclude that the pronoun "she" refers to a person of female gender. But – and this is where utterance (2) differs from utterance (1) – no pragmatic rule can be brought to bear on the utterance that allows us to identify the person being referred to, that is, Mrs. K. Apparently, in order for a reader to understand utterance (2), something more is required than just semantics and pragmatics.

Several linguists have described understanding as an inferential process, while still assuming the code model to provide the framework for a general theory of verbal communication. The underlying assumption is that a process of inference can be part of a larger decoding process.[42] This notion that the understanding of utterances is a process at least partially based on inference squares well with our everyday experiences. The problem with the idea is that it greatly underestimates the difference between a decoding process and a process of inference. A decoding process begins with a signal and results in a message, which is linked to the signal using a code. A process of inference starts with a set of premises and results in a conclusion linked to the premises using ordinary rules of deductive reasoning. For a reader to be able to decode a written utterance and comprehend the message that the writer wishes to convey, it must be possible for the reader to use that very same code, which was earlier used by the writer to encode the message. Hence, whoever assumes that a process of inference can be comprised in a decoding process is forced also to assume that a reader and a writer can be simultaneously working on the basis of an identical set of assumptions. This assumption is obviously difficult to defend.[43] The premises used by a reader for the understanding of a written utterance are drawn from a context.[44] According to what we stated earlier, CONTEXT is the entire set of assumptions about the world in general that a reader has access to when reading a text.[45] Of course, the problem is that it is impossible to find two people who hold two identical sets of assumptions about the world in general. Different people have different experiences, and different experiences inevitably lead to the development of different assumptions. Even in cases where two people happen to share an experience it cannot be taken for granted that they will develop identical assumptions with regard to that common experience. Tests have shown that two people witnessing the same event can still have completely different ideas of what actually happened.[46]

Of course, some assumptions held by two people will always be shared. Hence, if a reader and writer wish to understand one another, they would only have to ensure that nothing but shared assumptions are used.[47] Naturally, the reader and the writer must be able to distinguish the assumptions they share from those that they do not share – a requirement not easily met. For a reader and a writer to be *certain* that they share a given set of assumptions $\{A_1, A_2, A_3\}$, the reader would have to *know* that the writer holds the assumptions $\{A_1, A_2, A_3\}$, and the writer must know that the reader holds those same assumptions; but this is not all. The reader and the writer must *mutually* know that they hold the assumptions $\{A_1, A_2,$ and A3$\}$.[48] The reader must know that the writer knows that the reader holds the assumptions $\{A_1, A_2, A_3\}$, and that the writer knows that the reader knows that the writer holds the assumptions $\{A_1, A_2, A_3\}$, and that the writer knows that the reader knows that the writer knows that the reader holds the assumptions $\{A_1, A_2, A_3\}$, and so forth into infinity. In the same way the writer must know that the reader knows that the writer holds the assumptions $\{A_1, A_2, A_3\}$, and the reader must know that the writer knows that the reader holds the assumptions $\{A_1, A_2, A_3\}$, and that the reader knows that the writer knows that the reader knows that the writer holds the assumptions $\{A_1, A_2, A_3\}$, and so forth into infinity. This condition is impossible to meet.[49] A reader and a writer can never *know for sure*, that they share a given set of assumptions. They can only *assume* that this is the case.[50]

It seems to be the natural way for supporters of the code model who wish to avoid this dilemma, to give up the requirement of mutual knowledge and instead replace it with a requirement of mutual *assumption*: the reader and the writer must mutually *assume* that they share a given set of assumptions.[51] But even this more realistic requirement gives pause. The problem is that the greater the number of assumptions linked together in a chain of the kind discussed here, the less likely the assumption found at the end of the chain.[52] For example, a reader may assume with a probability approaching certainty, that a writer holds a given set of assumptions $\{A_1, A_2, A_3\}$; the reader should be less certain, that the writer assumes that the reader holds the assumptions $\{A_1, A_2, A_3\}$, and even less certain that the writer assumes that the reader assumes that the writer holds the assumptions $\{A_1, A_2, A_3\}$; and so forth. The weakest probability of all should be the one conferred on the assumption that the reader and the writer mutually assume that they share the assumptions $\{A_1, A_2, A_3\}$, being the last link in the reader's chain of assumptions. The reader's and writer's respective chains of assumption are always infinitely long. Considering this, the question arises how it is ever possible for a reader and a writer to even begin meeting the requirement of not using assumptions other than those that are shared. The question remains unanswered.[53]

Let us summarise. A person who advocates the code model as an explanation of the way any common reader would proceed to determine the utterance meaning of a text will quite clearly have difficulties justifying her position. In order for the code model to be considered justified, it must be possible to show the existence of a code, through which a written utterance can be linked with a specific message. The rules of conventional language are themselves incapable of functioning as such a code – this is something that even supporters of the code model have come to realise. Hence, supporters of the code model contend that the rules of conventional language are to be seen as forming only a part of the larger signal system, which also includes the mutual assumptions held by the reader and the writer with regard to the world in general. In order for the mutual assumptions held by reader and writer to perform the functions of a code, reader and writer must be able to distinguish the assumptions they share from those they do not share. As of this date, no one has been able to show how this requirement can ever be met in practice. The conclusion that immediately presents itself is that the code model should be dismissed. If we wish to describe the way any common reader would proceed to determine the utterance meaning of a text, then the inferential model is our only remaining choice.

Nevertheless, the choice of the inferential model also poses certain problems of justification. It cannot be denied, that when a reader understands a written utterance, decoding will be involved to some extent.[54] Decoding occurs whenever the reader takes assistance from the linguistic rules of a language – i.e. from semantics and pragmatics – to pair the utterance with some certain linguistic meaning. Wishing to defend our choice of the inferential model, we are obviously faced with the task of trying to explain how decoding can be a part of a process of inference, despite the fact that a decoding process and a process of inference are two completely different things.[55] The explanation is quite simple. All we need to do is consider the result of decoding as a piece of indirect evidence, based on which a reader can only *infer* what the writer wished to convey.[56] When a reader has noticed an utterance, and she has realised the linguistic system used by the writer, it is only logical that the reader should start by drawing upon the rules of that same system to see how far it gets her. Any of the following two results may be obtained. First, it may be that the linguistic meaning of the text is indeterminate, the conclusion being that the writer's message obviously must be something else than what is shown by a mere application of linguistic rules. To determine conclusively what the writer wishes to convey, the reader would then be forced to continue her efforts, inserting the utterance into a context. Second, it may be that the linguistic meaning of the text is determinate. It is possible that the reader then decides that she has obtained the writer's message, and that the process of understanding can be concluded. The thing is, however, that the reader can never be completely sure of actually having obtained the writer's message. It might be that the writer made a grammatical error, or it might be that something is implied. The reader can only assume that the true message is the one obtained by an application of linguistic rules. In both cases, the reader's understanding of the utterance is a matter of decoding; but in neither case is the linguistic meaning of the utterance itself decisive for the reader's conclusion. The linguistic meaning is nothing but a piece of indirect evidence, based on which the reader can only infer what the writer is trying to convey.[57]

4 HOW TO DETERMINE THE CORRECT MEANING (CONT'D)

Regardless of whether the code model should be considered as valid or not, strong arguments suggest that this model should at least not be regarded as valid for the very specific purposes that we have in mind. It is a fact that the rules of interpretation laid down in international law are not always sufficient to generate a determinate interpretation result.[58] If appliers interpret a treaty, and several rules of interpretation can be applied, the results obtained will sometimes conflict. In international law, there are rules for resolving some of these conflicts. Not only does international law comprise a number of first-order rules of interpretation, but also a few second-order rules are provided.[59] A first-order rule of interpretation tells appliers how an interpreted treaty provision shall be understood, in cases where the provision has shown to be unclear. A second-order rule of interpretation tells appliers how an interpreted treaty provision shall be understood, in cases where two first-order rules of interpretation have shown themselves to be in conflict with one another. However, not every conflict between two first-order rules of interpretation can be resolved merely by applying a legally binding second-order rule of interpretation. We have to accept that, although a treaty may have been interpreted in full accordance with the rules of interpretation laid down in international law, there will nevertheless be situations where two conflicting interpretation results must both be regarded as legally correct. This is a fact that can be reconciled with the inferential model, but hardly with the code model.

Let us assume that the procedure to be used for determining the correct meaning of a treaty provision, according to the rules of interpretation laid down in international law, is the one described by the inferential model. In the inferential model, an interpretation result is always an assumption. The understanding of a written utterance is dependent upon a context. It has been stated earlier that according to the inferential model, the following events occur when a writer (X) and a reader (Y) communicate using a text: a person (X) has a message, a piece of information, that he wishes to convey to another person (Y); X indicates the message by producing an utterance; the utterance is transferred to Y via a text; Y notices the text, then inserts it into a context, through which the utterance – the message from X – can subsequently be inferred.[60] We have also observed that we would have to understand context to represent the entire set of assumptions about the world in general to which a reader has access when reading a text.[61] An assumption is neither true nor false; it is measured in terms of its strength. Hence, given that a conclusion obtained through deduction is never stronger than the weakest premise, then according to the inferential model, an interpretation result can only be described as more or less strong or well-founded. This is a fact that causes little concern. In the situation where two conflicting interpretation results are both to be regarded as correct, considered from the point of view of international law, we can still defend our claim that they are both prima facie warranted.

Now, let us assume instead that the procedure to be used for determining the correct meaning of a treaty provision, according to the rules of interpretation laid down in international law, is the one described by the code model. In the code model, an interpretation result will always have a truth value. The understanding of a written utterance is dependent upon the existence of a specific state of affairs, namely that the reader and the writer have access to the exact same code. According to the code model, the following events occur when a writer (X) and a reader communicate using a text (Y): a person (X) wishes to convey a message to another person (Y); X encodes the message into an utterance; the utterance is sent to Y using a text, after which Y decodes the utterance and partakes of its content, that is to say, the message from X.[62] A state of affairs either exists, or it does not. A writer and a reader either have access to the right code, or not; no other alternatives are available. Therefore, according to the code model, an interpretation result must be either true or false. As earlier stated, there are situations where two conflicting interpretation results will both have to be regarded as correct, considered from the point of view of international law. Given the assumption that the code presupposed by the code model will have to be found in the rules of interpretation laid down in international law, and in those rules alone, it seems we would also be forced to accept the proposition that two conflicting interpretation results can be equally true. Of course, this is a proposition we cannot accept.

Naturally, if someone says that the procedure to be used for determining the correct meaning of a treaty provision, according to the rules of interpretation laid down in international law, is the one described by the code model, then this is not necessarily tantamount to saying that the code presupposed by the code model will have to be found in the rules of interpretation laid down in international law, and in those rules alone. It might be the case that we are speaking of a code of which the rules of interpretation are only a part. The code could be comprised partly by the rules of interpretation laid down in international law, and partly by some other norm or norms of international law. The question is which other norm or norms this could possibly be. One answer could be *the principle of good faith.* According to what is provided in VCLT article 31 § 1, "[a] treaty shall be interpreted in good faith" (Fr. "*de bonne foi*"; Sp. "*de buena fe*").[63] Judging from the literature, this principle of good faith is a norm that guides the entire interpretation process.[64] Consequently, the principle should be seen to influence not only the contents of the rules of interpretation. They should also be seen to play a part *above and beyond these rules*.[65] In the situation where two first-order rules of interpretation are in conflict with one another, and the conflict cannot be resolved through the application of a legally binding second-order rule of interpretation, one should still have to ensure that the treaty in question is interpreted in good faith.

Good faith has been defined in the following manner:

> **Bona fides** (good faith). A person acts in *bona fides* when he acts honestly, not knowing nor having reason to believe that his claim is unjustified ... *Bona fides* ends when the person becomes aware, or should have become aware, of facts which indicate the lack of legal justification for his claim.[66]

Translated to the context of treaty interpretation and to the legal regime laid down in international law, the idea of good faith can be expressed more precisely. An applier can be said to act in good faith, if she chooses to understand a treaty in accordance with a first-order rule of interpretation, as long as the application of that rule does not leave the meaning of the treaty unclear.[67] If an applier chooses to understand a treaty in accordance with a first-order rule of interpretation, although the application of that rule leaves the meaning of the treaty unclear, she cannot be said to have acted in good faith. The concept of clarity assumed for the regime of interpretation laid down in international law is the one expressed in VCLT article 32. Saying that a treaty provision is clear is tantamount to saying that the provision can be understood in such a way that its meaning will neither be considered "ambiguous or obscure", nor will it be regarded as amounting to a result which is "manifestly absurd or unreasonable".[68] The Vienna Convention's call on appliers to always interpret a treaty in good faith could therefore be rephrased in the following manner:

> If it can be shown that a treaty provision, according to whatever first-order rule of interpretation is applied, cannot be understood in such a way that its meaning will not be considered "ambiguous or obscure", or will not amount to a result which is "manifestly absurd or unreasonable", then the provision should not be understood according to this rule.[69]

Saying that the meaning of a treaty is "ambiguous" is tantamount to saying that the first-order rules of interpretation laid down in international law can be used to support two conflicting interpretation results.[70] If a meaning is "obscure", it means that none of the first-order rules of interpretation laid down in international law are applicable.[71] If a meaning is "absurd or unreasonable", it means that it cannot be rationally defended.[72] The expression "manifestly" embodies a requirement on significance.[73] Saying that a treaty provision T cannot be interpreted according to a specified first-order rule of interpretation (R_1), without it leading to a result which is "manifestly absurd or unreasonable", then this would obviously be tantamount to saying the following: the reasons for not understanding treaty provision T in accordance with the rule of interpretation R_1 are significantly stronger than the reasons for the opposite.[74] What we are discussing here is the situation where two first-order rules of interpretation conflict with one another, without there being any legally binding second-order rule of interpretation that can be applied for resolving the conflict. In such a situation, a treaty provision cannot be understood in such a way in accordance with a first-order rule of interpretation, so that its meaning will not be considered "ambiguous or obscure".[75] Obviously, in the situation confronted, the principle of good faith (as it has earlier been described) can then be simplified:

> If a treaty needs to be interpreted, and it can be shown that two first-order rules of interpretation are in conflict with one another, and that the reasons for understanding the treaty in accordance with the one rule are significantly stronger than the reasons for understanding the treaty in accordance with the other, then the treaty should not be understood in accordance with this other rule of interpretation.

It is now clear that the principle of good faith does not fit well with a theory, according to which the rules laid down in international law for the interpretation of treaties are to be given a description based on the code model. Assume that we interpret a treaty (T) by applying two different first-order rules of interpretation (R_1 and R_2). Assume also that the rules R_1 and R_2 have shown themselves to be in conflict with one another, and that no legally binding second-order rule of interpretation can be applied for resolving the conflict. In order for us to be able to resolve the conflict by applying the principle of good faith, the reasons for understanding the treaty T in accordance with either of the rules R_1 or R_2, must be sufficiently stronger than those for understanding the treaty in accordance with the other rule. Two things make this task appear problematic. First, it appears that the principle of good faith would involve questions of an explanatory nature equally difficult to handle as those questions occasioned by the code model in general. Considered the way the principle of good faith has been defined earlier, we are forced to identify the reasons for understanding a treaty in accordance with the rules of interpretation R_1 and R_2. Obviously, these reasons must be other than those represented by the rules themselves. We cannot possibly say about the two rules R_1 and R_2, that the one is significantly stronger than the other; both are part of international law, and as such equally strong. The question is whether we even know what reasons we are speaking about. The principle of good faith appears to be based on an answer to the question, to which even linguistics has been forced to resign: how can the code required by the code model be described?

Secondly, the principle of good faith does not seem enough powerful to be used for the purpose here at hand. If the procedure to be used for determining the correct meaning of a treaty provision, according to the rules of interpretation laid down in international law, is the one described by the code model, then a conflict between two first-order rules of interpretation must be resolved – two conflicting interpretation results cannot both be true. As it appears, this is a requirement that the principle of good faith cannot possibly meet. It is true that at this juncture we cannot really say what the code model implies, when it refers to the reasons for understanding a treaty according to a first-order rule of interpretation. However, from general practical reasoning we know for a fact that a conflict of norms is not always easy to resolve. Situations do arise where two conflicting norms are supported by reasons, of which the reasons supporting the one norm can be said to be significantly stronger than the reasons supporting the other. But we are also often faced with situations where the reasons supporting two conflicting norms will have to be regarded as more or less equally strong. I cannot see why this would not also be the case when the conflict concerns the norms constituted by the rules of interpretation laid down in international law. All things considered, it seems that the principle of good faith can hardly be the missing piece that we need for our explanation, in order to defend a description of the rules laid down in international law for the interpretation of treaties being based on the code model. For the same reason, I maintain that I have good grounds for drawing this conclusion: the procedure to be used for determining the correct meaning of a treaty provision, according to the rules of interpretation laid down in international law, is the one described by the inferential model.

5 THE CONCEPT OF A FIRST-ORDER RULE OF INTERPRETATION

It seems it is time to summarise. Two questions were raised in the introduction to this chapter:

(1) What is meant by "the correct meaning of a treaty provision considered from the point of view of international law"?
(2) How can we best describe the way an applier shall proceed to determine the correct meaning of a treaty provision, considered from the point of view of international law?

We can now consider these questions answered. The first of the two questions was the one I addressed in Section 1 of this chapter. The correct meaning of a treaty, considered from the point of view of international law, must be categorised as of the kind earlier defined as its utterance meaning. The correct meaning of a treaty can be identified with the pieces of information with regard to its norm content, according to the intentions of the treaty parties – all those states, for which the treaty is in force – insofar as these intentions can be considered mutually held. The second question was the one addressed in Sections 2, 3 and 4. To determine the correct meaning of a treaty, appliers should proceed in the exact same way as any common reader would proceed to determine the utterance meaning of any text. According to linguistics, we would then have to choose between two explanatory models.[76] The one is the code model, the other is the inferential model. As I have tried to establish, the procedure to be used for determining the correct meaning of a treaty provision, according to the rules of interpretation laid down in international law, is definitely the one described by the inferential model. When appliers interpret a treaty provision according to the rules laid down in international law, the provision is inserted into a context, from which the meaning of the provision is subsequently inferred. Let us now examine what possible consequences might ensue from these observations.

International law distinguishes between correct and incorrect interpretation results. Not all interpretation results can be considered correct from the point of view of international law. The only results that can be considered correct are those that can be justified by reference to the rules of interpretation laid down in international law. As we stated earlier, when an applier interprets a treaty provision in accordance with the rules of interpretation laid down in international law, she starts by inserting the provision into a context; then, using inference, she draws on the context to arrive at a conclusion about the meaning of the interpreted provision. We also noted that CONTEXT means the entire set of assumptions about the world in general that a reader has access to when reading a text; we have termed these as CONTEXTUAL ASSUMPTIONS. Hence, it appears that in order to distinguish between correct and incorrect interpretation results, we would have to single out some contextual assumptions as being acceptable and some as unacceptable.

If we examine articles 31–33 of the Vienna Convention on the Law of Treaties, the idea is expressed somewhat differently. The provisions of the convention do not address so much the idea of acceptable and unacceptable contextual assumption; rather, they address the idea of acceptable and unacceptable means of interpretation. However, on closer inspection, this must be seen to amount to very much the same thing. When we say that a reader inserts a written utterance – a text – into a context, this is much the same as saying that the reader obtains an idea – that is, he develops an assumption – about the relationship held between the utterance and the world in general. A means of interpretation can be said to correspond to a more or less distinctly defined part of the world in general. The list of acceptable means of interpretation includes conventional language, "the context", the object and purpose of the interpreted treaty, and *travaux préparatoires*. All things considered, it is apparent that when the Vienna Convention categorises means of interpretation as either acceptable or unacceptable, this can be seen indirectly to imply a corresponding categorisation of contextual assumptions. Of all those contextual assumptions that can possibly be made by appliers with regard to the relationship held between an interpreted treaty provision and the world in general, the only ones that *may* be used, according to the convention, are those regarding the relationship held between the provision and the means of interpretation recognised as acceptable.

However, this is not the only limitation international law sets for the use of contextual assumptions. Take for example the following syllogism:

Premise 1: According to what is stated in article 4 § 1 of the *European Convention for the Protection of Human Rights and Fundamental Freedoms*, "[n]o one shall be held in slavery or servitude".

Premise 2: In conventional language, the meaning ascribed to the word PIG is *greedy, dirty or unpleasant person.*

Premise 3: In article 4 § 1 of the European Convention, the meaning conferred on the term NO ONE is the same meaning as the meaning ascribed to the word PIG in conventional language.

Conclusion: According to article 4 § 1 of the European Convention, a greedy, dirty or unpleasant person shall be held in slavery or servitude

Three premises are used for the deduction. The first premise is an assumption about the existence of a written utterance – the text denoted as article 4 § 1 of the European Convention. The second premise is an assumption about the content of a particular means of interpretation recognised as acceptable by international law – the one denoted as conventional language. The third premise is an assumption about the relationship held between a written utterance (article 4 § 1 of the European Convention) and a particular means of interpretation recognised as acceptable by international law (conventional language). All three assumptions cannot be regarded as acceptable, considered from the point of view of international law. Such is the case if we consider the legal regime established by international law for the interpretation of treaties as merely authorising a set of interpretation data. But international law does not just authorise a set of interpretation data. As we stated earlier, the content of the legal regime established by international law amounts to a more or less coherent system of rules. International law indicates for the appliers not only what particular means of interpretation they are allowed to use for the interpretation of a treaty, but also how appliers, by using each means, shall argue to arrive at an acceptable conclusion about the meaning of said treaty. The implications of this are easily seen: of all those assumptions that can possibly be made by appliers with regard to the relationship held between an interpreted treaty provision and a means of interpretation recognised by international law as acceptable, not all can be said to be acceptable considered from the point of view of international law.

The only way to further limit the use of contextual assumptions is to limit the use of *communicative assumptions*. As earlier stated, when a reader selects, from among the many possible contextual assumptions available, those particular assumptions to be used for the interpreting of a text, she does so on the basis of a communicative assumption. The following is an example of a communicative assumption:

> The parties to the European Convention have produced their respective utterances in such a way, that in article 4 § 1 the meaning of the expression "[n]o one" agrees with conventional language.

If it is indeed the case, that international law distinguishes between those contextual assumptions that are acceptable and those that are not, then clearly, the rules of interpretation laid down in international law should best be described as if they were authorising a set of communicative assumptions. The only acceptable communicative assumptions are those that can be categorised as being of certain kinds – simply stated, this is what the rules of interpretation provide.

Considered that we are interested in providing a general description of the contents of the rules of interpretation laid down in international law, it would then appear that we should also be interested in the question of how a general description of the content of a communicative assumption could possibly be provided. That being the case, we need only remind ourselves of what we have already stated. We noted earlier that a communicative assumption is one that limits the use of contextual assumptions. In our case, limits are set on the use of contextual assumptions with regard to the relationship held between an interpreted treaty provision and a means of interpretation recognised as acceptable by international law. A communicative assumption has been defined earlier as the assumption of a particular reader that a particular writer expresses herself in accordance with some particular communicative standard. The type of communicative assumption we wish to identify here must then be an assumption to the effect, that the relationship held between an interpreted treaty provision and some particular means of interpretation is of a particular kind – the relationship held is a kind that conforms to a particular communicative standard. Schematically, this can be described in the following way:

> The parties to the treaty have expressed themselves in such a way, that the relationship held between the interpreted provision and the means of interpretation M conforms to the communicative standard S.

If we wish to establish a model, which describes in general terms the contents of the rules laid down in international law for the interpretation of treaties, it could be stated as follows:

> If it can be shown that between an interpreted treaty provision and any given means of interpretation M, there is a relationship governed by the communicative standard S, then the provision shall be understood as if the relationship conformed to this standard.

This model will be of great help when I address the purposes set for Chapters 3–9. In Chapter 3, I shall describe what it means to interpret a treaty using conventional language ("the ordinary meaning"). In Chapters 4, 5 and 6, I shall describe what it means to interpret a treaty using the context. In Chapter 7, I shall describe what it means to interpret a treaty using its object and purpose. In Chapters 8 and 9, I shall describe what it means to interpret a treaty using what we have earlier termed as supplementary means of interpretation. In the terminology used for this work, describing what it means to interpret a treaty using some specific means of interpretation M is tantamount to clarifying and putting to words those first-order rules of interpretation, through which the usage has to be effectuated.[77] Drawing upon the model stated above, we can now define this task more precisely. Considering my intention to describe what it means to interpret a treaty using some specific means of interpretation M, if I wish to be successful I must determine the contents of the means of interpretation M. (The question is: what is meant by "M"?) Moreover, I must determine the contents of the communicative standard or standards that govern the relationship held between an interpreted treaty and the means of interpretation M. (The question is: what communicative standard or standards shall the parties to a treaty be assumed to have followed, when an applier interprets a treaty using the means of interpretation M?)

This being said, we can now move on to our last task in this chapter. As stated earlier, the rules laid down in international law for the interpretation of treaties include rules of two kinds; they have been termed as first-order rules and second-order rules of interpretation, respectively. A first-order rule of interpretation tells appliers how an interpreted treaty provision shall be understood, in cases where it has shown to be unclear. A second-order rule of interpretation tells appliers how an interpreted treaty provision shall be understood in cases where two first-order rules of interpretation have shown themselves to be in conflict with one another. What I have described in the present Section 5 is only the concept of a first-order rule of interpretation. I have still to describe the concept of the second-order rule of interpretation. This will be the task in Section 6.

6 THE CONCEPT OF A SECOND-ORDER RULE OF INTERPRETATION

First of all, I need to refine the terminology used in Section 5 of this chapter. As we have noted, a first-order rule of interpretation tells appliers how an interpreted treaty provision shall be understood in cases where it has shown to be unclear. It indicates the type of relationship that, according to a specific communicative standard, shall be assumed to hold between an interpreted treaty provision and a given means of interpretation. An assumption to the effect, that the relationship held between an interpreted treaty provision and some particular means of interpretation is of a kind that conforms to a particular communicative standard, is what we have hitherto been terming as a communicative assumption. We shall now be more specific; we shall call this a first-order communicative assumption. Accordingly, a first-order rule of interpretation can be described to authorise a set of first-order communicative assumptions.

A second-order rule of interpretation tells appliers how an interpreted treaty provision shall be understood in cases where two first-order rules of interpretation have shown themselves to be in conflict with one another. Assume that a reader intends to conclusively determine the meaning of treaty provision T. The reader applies the rules of interpretation laid down in international law, but he discovers a conflict exists between two first-order rules of interpretation – the application of the two first-order rules of interpretation leads to different results. In such a situation, the interpretation of the treaty provision T immediately becomes more complicated. If the application of two different first-order rules of interpretation leads to different results, then this is ultimately because different rules of interpretation allow the use of different contextual assumptions – this is something we have already established. As we have also established, if different first-order rules of interpretation allow the use of different contextual assumptions, then this is because different rules of interpretation allow the use of different first-order communicative assumptions. The question is what an applier is to do upon the discovery that, firstly, the rules of interpretation laid down in international law allow the simultaneous use of two different first-order communicative assumptions (A_1 and A_2); and secondly, that the assumptions A_1 and A_2 collide, in the sense that the use of assumption A_1 ultimately leads to a different conclusion about the meaning of the interpreted treaty provision T than does the use of assumption A_2. The answer to the question is that the applier must make an additional assumption – an assumption that further limits the use of contextual assumptions. The applier must make an assumption about the relationship held between the two assumptions A_1 and A_2. Such an assumption will henceforth be termed as a second-order communicative assumption.

If it is the case, that a second-order rule of interpretation tells appliers how an interpreted treaty provision shall be understood in cases where two first-order rules of interpretation are shown to be in conflict with one another, then – just as with a first-order rule of interpretation – a second-order rule of interpretation could be described as authorising a set of communicative assumptions. First-order rules of interpretation have earlier been described as authorising a set of first-order communicative assumptions. By the same token, second-order rules of interpretation can be described as authorising a set of second-order communicative assumptions. The only acceptable second-order communicative assumptions are those that can be categorised as being of certain kinds – simply stated, this is what the rules of interpretation provide. As shown earlier, providing a general description of those first-order rules of interpretation laid down in international law is a question of how to describe in general terms the contents of an acceptable first-order communicative assumption. Similarly, providing a general description of the second-order rules of interpretation must then be a question of how to describe in general terms the contents of an acceptable second-order communicative assumption.

To facilitate such a description, it may be suitable to present an example. Hence, let us once again assume that, during the interpretation of treaty provision T, a reader discovers two things: first, that the rules of interpretation laid down in international law allow the simultaneous use of two different first-order communicative assumptions (A_1 and A_2), and second, that the assumptions A_1 and A_2 collide, in the sense that the use of assumption A_1 ultimately leads to a different conclusion about the meaning of the interpreted treaty provision T than does the use of assumption A_2. Assumption A_1 is allowed by the rule of interpretation R_1:

> If it can be shown that between an interpreted treaty provision and any given means of interpretation M_1, there is a relationship governed by the communicative standard S_1, then the provision shall be understood as if the relationship conformed to this standard.

Assumption A_2 is allowed by the rule of interpretation R_2:

> If it can be shown that between an interpreted treaty provision and any given means of interpretation M_2, there is a relationship governed by the communicative standard S_2, then the provision shall be understood as if the relationship conformed to this standard.

Hence, the assumptions A_1 and A_2 could be schematically described in the following way:

> A_1: The parties to the treaty in question have expressed themselves in such a way, that the relationship held between the interpreted provision T and the means of interpretation M_1, conforms to the communicative standard S_1.
>
> A_2: The parties to the treaty in question have expressed themselves in such a way, that the relationship held between the interpreted provision T and the means of interpretation M_2, conforms to the communicative standard S_2.

In order for the reader to be able to arrive at a definite conclusion about the meaning of the interpreted treaty provision T, she must make a second-order communicative assumption. The reader must make an assumption about the relationship held between the communicative assumption A_1 and the communicative assumption A_2. Now, let us presume that the relationship held between the two assumptions A_1 and A_2, according to what the reader assumes, are such that the reader can use only assumption A_1. In principle, such an assumption can take on four different forms. The reader's assumption can be an *unconditional, conclusive reason*, to use only assumption A_1; the reader's assumption can be a *conditional, conclusive reason*, to use only assumption A_1; the reader's assumption can be an *unconditional reason pro tanto*, to use only assumption A_1; and the reader's assumption can be a *conditional reason pro tanto*, to use only assumption A_1.[78] This can be illustrated in the following manner:

(1) *Regardless of what particular circumstances can be shown to exist*, the parties to the treaty in question have *not* expressed themselves in such a way, that the relationship held between the interpreted treaty provision T and the means of interpretation M_2 will conform to the communicative standard S_2, if this means that the relationship held between provision T and the means of interpretation M_1 will *not* conform to the communicative standard S_1.

(2) *Given that certain particular circumstances can be shown to exist*, the parties to the treaty in question have *not* expressed themselves in such a way, that the relationship held between the interpreted treaty provision T and the means of interpretation M_2 will conform to the communicative standard S_2, if this means that the relationship held between provision T and the means of interpretation M_1 will *not* conform to the communicative standard S_1.

(3) *Regardless of what particular circumstances can be shown to exist*, the parties to the treaty in question, *rather than* expressing themselves in such a way, that the relationship held between the interpreted treaty provision T and the means of interpretation M_2 will conform to the communicative standard S_2, have expressed themselves in such a way that the relationship held between provision T and the means of interpretation M_1 conforms to the communicative standard S_1.

(4) *Given that certain particular circumstances can be shown to exist*, the parties to the treaty in question, *rather than* expressing themselves in such a way, that the relationship held between the interpreted treaty provision T and the means of interpretation M_2 will conform to the communicative standard S_2, have expressed themselves in such a way that the relationship held between provision T and the means of interpretation M_1 conforms to the communicative standard S_1.

If we wish to establish a model, which describes in general terms the contents of the second-order rules laid down in international law for the interpretation of treaties, it seems that this model must be relatively flexible. Several alternative schemes must be allowed. The second-order rules of interpretation would have to be described using one of the following four norm sentences:

(1) If it can be shown that the interpretation of a treaty provision in accordance with a first-order rule of interpretation R_1 leads to a result, which is different from that obtained by interpreting the provision in accordance with the first-order rule of interpretation R_2, then, regardless of what other particular circumstances can be shown to exist, the provision shall *not* be understood in accordance with the rule R_2.

(2) If it can be shown that the interpretation of a treaty provision in accordance with a first-order rule of interpretation R_1 leads to a result, which is different from that obtained by interpreting the provision in accordance with the first-order rule of interpretation R_2, then, given that certain other particular circumstances can be shown to exist, the provision shall *not* be understood in accordance with the rule R_2.

(3) If it can be shown that the interpretation of a treaty provision in accordance with a first-order rule of interpretation R_1 leads to a result, which is different from that obtained by interpreting the provision in accordance with the

first-order rule of interpretation R_2, then rather than with the rule R_2 – and regardless of what other particular circumstances can be shown to exist – the provision shall be understood in accordance with rule R_1.

(4) If it can be shown that the interpretation of a treaty provision in accordance with a first-order rule of interpretation R_1 leads to a result, which is different from that obtained by interpreting the provision in accordance with the first-order rule of interpretation R_2, then rather than with the rule R_2 – given that certain other particular circumstances can be shown to exist – the provision shall be understood in accordance with rule R_1.

This model will be of great help when I address the purposes set for Chapter 10 of this work. As noted earlier, the purpose of Chapter 10 is to describe the relationship that shall be assumed to hold between the means of interpretation recognised as acceptable by the Vienna Convention. This is tantamount to clarifying and putting to words those second-order rules of interpretation that shall be applied according to international law.[79] Drawing upon the model stated above, we can now define this task more precisely. If I wish to succeed in describing the second-order rules of interpretation laid down in international law, I must first define the extent to which conflicts between first-order rules of interpretation can be resolved (if at all) through the application of a second-order rule. Secondly, I must define how each particular second-order rule of interpretation is designed, considered as a reason for action. Shall the rule be considered a conclusive reason for understanding a treaty provision in accordance with some specific first-order rule of interpretation, or only as a reason *pro tanto*? Shall the rule be considered an unconditional reason for understanding a treaty provision in accordance with some specific first-order rule of interpretation, or only as a conditional reason? And if the latter is the case, what are the conditions?

NOTES

1. I wish to extend my warmest thanks to Doctor Marianne Gullberg, of the *Max Planck Institute for Psycholinguistics* in Nijmegen, for her professional review of this chapter and her many valuable comments.
2. Cf. Endicott, p. 454; Marmor, p. 30; Hirsch, pp. 1–6; Williams, 1946, p. 392.
3. See e.g. Lyons, 1977, p. 28.
4. Cf. ibid.: "We can ... distinguish between the sentence as something that can be uttered (i.e. as the product of a bit of) language-behaviour and the sentence as an abstract, theoretical entity in the linguist's model of the language system. When it is necessary to distinguish terminologically between these two senses we will use text-sentence* for the former and system-sentence* for the latter" (p. 29). By the same token, one can define a WORD either as something one uses when writing or speaking, or as a unit in a theoretical model. When I refer to "word" and "sentence", it is in the material sense of *something one uses when writing or speaking*.

5. See e.g. Blakemore, pp. 3–10; Lyons, 1995, pp. 234ff.
6. See e.g. ibid., pp. 131ff.
7. Loc. cit.
8. See e.g. Kittang, pp. 79–106.
9. See e.g. Aarnio, pp. 29–30.
10. See e.g. McLachlan, p. 287; Naigen, p. 203; Ress, p. 30; *Oppenheim's International Law*, p. 1267; Seidl-Hohenveldern, 1992, p. 91; Brownlie, p. 627; Reuter, 1989, p. 74; Dupuy, p. 220; Greig, p. 476; Sinclair, 1984, p. 115; Jiménez de Aréchaga, p. 43; Barile, p. 85; Yasseen, p. 16; Elias, 1974, p. 73; Hummer, p. 97; O'Connell, p. 251; Köck, pp. 26–27; Sharma, p. 367; Jennings, p. 549.
11. See *Review of the Multilateral Treaty-Making Process* (1985), passim.
12. My italics.
13. My italics.
14. My italics.
15. VCLT article 1 § 1(g).
16. See e.g. *Starke's International Law*, pp. 435–436; Haraszti, p. 28. See also, implicit, Amerasinghe, p. 200.
17. It is not entirely clear what it means when we say that a collective institution (such as a state) has intentions. For further a discussion of this topic, see e.g. Hurd, pp. 968–976; McCallum, pp. 247ff.; Radin, pp. 863–885.
18. Cf. Marmor, pp. 165–172; Dickerson, pp. 69–71; McCallum, pp. 239ff. See also Chapters 3–11 of this work.
19. Regarding the concept of *operative interpretation*, see above, Ch. 1, Section 3.
20. See e.g. Shafeiei: "The obligation of States stems uniquely from their own will." (Diss. op. Shafeiei, on the issue of dual nationality, relating to Cases Nos. 157 and 211, *ILR*, Vol. 72, p. 537.)
21. See, explicitly, Seidl-Hohenveldern, 1992, p. 91; Brownlie, p. 627; Yasseen, p. 16; Barile, p. 85; Sharma, p. 367; Bernhardt, 1963, p. 34.
22. Speaking of only two explanatory models can be construed as an oversimplification. Nevertheless, the fact is that in all the attempts of linguistics to come to grips with the problem of communication, two principal approaches can be discerned. These two approaches have in turn resulted in numerous more specific variants. However, I do not see any reason to go into a more detailed discussion of linguistics than is necessary to complete this chapter. The task at hand is to construct a model that describes in general terms the contents of the rules laid down in international law for the interpretation of treaties. In principle, the only thing I need to state is that linguistics offers us explanations that, better than others, describe the way an applier shall proceed to determine the correct meaning of a treaty, considered from the point of view of international law. (For more information about this issue, see p. 41, n. 34.) The British authors Sperber and Wilson use the code and inferential model dichotomy for similar purposes of explanation. (See Sperber and Wilson, Ch. 1.) I intend to do the same.
23. Examples of works often cited in connection with the code model include Saussure, Ogden and Richards, Hjelmslev, Gazdar, and Bach and Harnish. Even Searle seems to follow a line of reasoning that in greater parts must be considered inspired by the code model. (See Searle, passim.)
24. This term has been borrowed from Sperber and Wilson. (See Sperber and Wilson, p. 2 et seq.)

25. A code model description often cited is that originally framed by Shannon and Weaver (See Shannon and Weaver, passim.)
26. Cf. e.g. Lyons, 1977, pp. 38–39.
27. Cf. Sperber and Wilson, p. 5.
28. Examples of works often cited in connection with the inferential model include Grice, 1967; Lewis, 1979; Leech; Sperber and Wilson; Levinson; and Grice, 1989.
29. This term has been borrowed from Sperber and Wilson. (See Sperber and Wilson, pp. 2ff.)
30. Cf. e.g. Blakemore, especially Ch. 1.
31. See Sperber and Wilson, pp. 81 and 81–93; also Blakemore, pp. 18, 87–88, and Blass, pp. 9, 30–31.
32. The term PROPOSITION OF GENERALISED KNOWLEDGE has been borrowed from Ekelöf. According to Ekelöf, PROPOSITION OF GENERALISED KNOWLEDGE means "an assertion about the relationship held between two phenomena, that applies for these phenomena *in general*". (Ekelöf, p. 10; my translation.)
33. According to what is often claimed, it was the linguist Paul Grice who first introduced this idea in his "William James Lectures". (See Grice, 1967.) Of course, Grice had chosen a very special linguistic phenomenon as the topic of his lectures, namely implication or implicative. What he wanted to explain was how a speaker or writer succeeds in communicating more with an utterance, than what the utterance can be said to explicitly express. More contemporary linguists, however, have discovered Grice's observations to have a broader scope of application – they can be applied to verbal communication in general.
34. Once again I wish to emphasise that my division of linguistics into two principal models should definitely be considered a simplification. One basic idea unites the supporters of the code model, namely the idea that verbal communication is something that occurs in accordance with a code. However, we must also admit that different adherents often have different opinions of what should comprise this code. Another basic idea unites supporters of the inferential model: verbal communication is something that occurs according to communicative standards. But again we must note that different supporters maintain different opinions of what these standards contain. In terms of the arguments I present in this chapter, I hold that this simplification is warranted. The only thing I am interested in stating is the following: each time a treaty is interpreted according to a rule of interpretation laid down in international law, the act of interpretation is based on the assumption that parties to the treaty expressed themselves in accordance with some specific communicative standard. Using this idea as the starting-point of my inquiry, and using legal method, I will then try to clarify the various communicative standards presupposed by the rules of interpretation laid down in international law. It is not my intention to take a position regarding whether these communicative standards must also be said to apply with regard to the understanding of (written) utterances *in general.*
35. See Sperber and Wilson, especially Ch. 1.
36. See ibid., pp. 5ff.
37. See ibid., p. 9.
38. See ibid., pp. 9–11.
39. Ibid., p. 9.
40. Ibid., p. 12.
41. See ibid., pp. 11–12.
42. See ibid., p. 14.

43. See ibid., pp. 15–21.
44. See Section 2 of this chapter.
45. Loc. cit.
46. See Sperber and Wilson, p. 16, n. 8, cit. Loftus, in extenso, and Neisser (ed.), in extenso.
47. See ibid., p. 17.
48. See Schiffer; Lewis, 1969. (Note that Lewis uses the term *common* knowledge).
49. See Sperber and Wilson, pp. 18–20. See also Green, passim.
50. See Sperber and Wilson, pp. 19–20.
51. See ibid., p. 20.
52. Loc. cit.
53. Loc. cit.
54. "[C]ases of communication", write Sperber and Wilson, "clearly achieved without the use of a code are rare, and ... the thoughts so communicated tend to be rather simple" (ibid., p. 26).
55. See ibid., pp. 26–27.
56. See ibid., pp. 26–28.
57. Loc. cit.
58. See Ch. 1, Sections 1 and 2 of this work.
59. Loc. cit.
60. See p. 37 of this chapter.
61. See pp. 37–38 of this chapter.
62. See pp. 36–37 of this chapter.
63. My italics.
64. See e.g. Ress, p. 31; Zoller, p. 202; Yasseen, pp. 22–23; Rest, p. 144, n. 1; Müller, p. 127: Schwarzenberger, 1955, p. 301; Bin Cheng, p. 105.
65. See also Tammelo, pp. 33–34.
66. *The Oxford Companion to Law* (1980).
67. Cf. the statement in Ch. 1, Section 3: when an applier engages in interpretation, it is, according to the terminology of the Vienna Convention, in order to clarify the unclear text of a treaty.
68. See, expressly, Ress, p. 37; Thirlway, 1991, pp. 24–25; *Oppenheim's International Law*, pp. 1275–1276; Brownlie, p. 630; Bernhardt, 1984, p. 322; Yasseen, pp. 81–82; Haraszti, pp. 91–102; Favre, 1974, p. 254. See also, more or less implicitly, Amerasinghe, pp. 200–201; Sinclair, 1984, p. 127; Jiménez de Aréchaga, pp. 46–47; Elihu Lauterpacht, p. 417; Köck, p. 86; Hummer, pp. 98–99; Greig, pp. 477–481; Bernhardt, 1967, p. 503.
69. Cf. *Oppenheim's International Law*, p. 1272, n. 7; Sinclair, 1984, p. 120; Rosenne, 1982, p. 356; Rest, p. 27, cit. Ehrlich, pp. 81ff.; Schwarzenberger, 1955, pp. 300–301. Cf. also sep. op. Ajibola, *Territorial Dispute (Libya/Chad)*, *ILR*, Vol. 100, p. 71, cit. Rosenne, 1982, p. 356.
70. See Ch. 10, Section 3 of this work.
71. Loc. cit.
72. See Ch. 10, Sections 4–6 of this work.
73. See Ch. 10, Section 6 of this work.
74. Loc. cit.
75. Theoretically, the only imaginable situation is where the use of conventional language ("the ordinary meaning") leads to two different interpretation results, without the applier

being able to use any other means of interpretation whatsoever. However, from a practical standpoint I have difficulty seeing how such a situation could possibly arise.
76. See the reservation on p. 35, n. 22 of this work.
77. See Ch. 1, Section 5 of this work.
78. By a "conditional", an "unconditional" and a "conclusive" reason, and a reason "*pro tanto*", I mean a reason *assumed* by the reader *to be* conditional, unconditional and conclusive, respectively, or assumed to be a reason *pro tanto* – nothing else. For a more detailed discussion of the rule of interpretation as a conclusive reason and a reason *pro tanto*, see Ch. 10 of this work.
79. See Ch. 1, Section 5 of this work.

CHAPTER 3

USING CONVENTIONAL LANGUAGE ("THE ORDINARY MEANING")

"A treaty shall be interpreted in good faith in accordance with the ordinary meaning to be given to the terms of the treaty in their context and in the light of its object and purpose" – this is provided in VCLT article 31 § 1.

A treaty shall be interpreted in good faith in accordance with the ordinary meaning to be given to the terms of the treaty in their context and in the light of its object and purpose.

Un traité doit être interprété de bonne foi suivant le sens ordinaire à attribuer aux termes du traité dans leur contexte et à la lumière de son objet et de son but.

Un tratado deberá interpretarse de buena fe conforme al sentido corriente que haya de atribuirse a los términos del tratado en el contexto de éstos y teniendo en cuenta su objeto y fin.

The provision can be analysed as actually describing three distinct acts of interpretation. A distinguishing mark of each is the means of interpretation used. Accordingly, it appears we can speak of, in turns, interpretation using conventional language ("the ordinary meaning"); interpretation using the context; and interpretation using the object and purpose of the treaty.[1] The purpose of this chapter is to describe what it means to interpret a treaty using conventional language.

Two questions must be answered before this task can be considered completed. The first question is simple:

> What communicative standard or standards shall the parties to a treaty be assumed to have followed, when an applier interprets the treaty using conventional language ("the ordinary meaning")?

The answer is given already in the text of article 31 § 1:

> If a state makes an utterance taking the form of a treaty provision, then the provision should be drawn up so that every expression in the provision, whose form corresponds to an expression of conventional language, bears a meaning that agrees with that language.

The second question is more difficult:

> What is meant by conventional language ("the ordinary meaning")?

I shall now give what I consider to be the correct answer to this question.

1 INTRODUCTION; IN PARTICULAR, REGARDING THE PROBLEM CAUSED BY SOCIAL VARIATION IN LANGUAGE

By "the ordinary meaning" of the terms of a treaty, the Vienna Convention refers to the meaning ascribed to these terms in conventional language, as opposed to the meaning that can possibly be ascribed to the terms by applying principles of etymology.[2] Conventional language is the means of interpretation used by the applier when he interprets a treaty text "in accordance with the ordinary meaning to be given to the terms of the treaty". Evidently, in order for an applier to be able to interpret a treaty "in accordance with the ordinary meaning to be given to the terms of the treaty", he needs to know the conventions of the language used for the treaty. This implies the applier must be familiar, first, with the *lexicon* of the language, and second, with its underlying system of rules. By the "lexicon" of a language, we shall understand what can simply be called its vocabulary.[3] The rule system of a language can be divided into three categories of rules: morphological, syntactical, and pragmatic.[4] Morphological rules describe how words are inflected and word forms are constructed; syntactical rules describe how phrases and sentences are put together; and pragmatic rules describe how linguistic expressions are used in certain kinds of situations (not dealt with in syntax). Take for example the following passage of the *European Convention for the Protection of Human Rights and Fundamental Freedoms*:

> Everyone who is arrested shall be informed promptly, in a language which he understands, of the reasons for his arrest and of any charge against him.[5]

English morphology, together with the lexical definition of the word ARREST, helps us understand that *"arrested"* refers to an event in the past. English syntax allows us to conclude that *"promptly"* represents a qualification of the expression *"informed"*. Pragmatics makes it clear that *"he"*, *"his"*, and *"him"* all refer back to the expression *"[e]veryone"*.

Many authors use the term GRAMMATICAL INTERPRETATION to define what appliers do when they interpret a treaty "in accordance with the ordinary meaning to be given to the terms of the treaty".[6] This is a term which easilymisleads.[7] The GRAMMAR of a language is what we normally understand to be its morphology and syntax.[8] Accordingly, if someone speaks of grammatical interpretation of a treaty provision, it can first of all be construed as if the applier, in interpreting the provision, shall take no heed of the lexicon of the language. This is of course pure nonsense. It lies in the very nature of morphological and syntactical rules that they cannot be used in isolation; whenever these rules are used, a lexicon is assumed. Second, grammatical interpretation can easily be construed as synonymous with an act of interpretation paying no regard whatsoever to the rules of pragmatics. This is also a distortion of reality. The Vienna Convention speaks of "the ordinary meaning" of the terms of a treaty without in any way qualifying the word ORDINARY. Surely, this implies that all rules of a language must be considered – and not just some of them – no matter how the rules might be classified in linguistics.

It is a distinctive quality of human languages that they change. Among other things, they change with the social context. Many linguistic communities can often be said to exist within the framework of what we would usually call a language – each having its unique set of linguistic conventions. Accordingly, we can speak not only of different languages – Swedish, English, French, and so on – but also of different *varieties* of a language.[9] One such variety is the one we somewhat loosely refer to as EVERYDAY LANGUAGE – the language all people use and most consider generally applicable.[10] In addition to this everyday form, a language possesses many less extensive varieties adapted to specific situations of use, or developed for specific purposes.[11] These more specialised forms of usage are often found within particular occupational groups or among people sharing some similar interest: the language of economists differs from that of lawyers, which in turn differs from that of computer specialists, and so on.[12] Therefore, to refer to them we often use the term TECHNICAL LANGUAGE.

The following question arises: What linguistic variety or varieties are to be taken into account by an applier when he interprets a treaty provision "in accordance with the ordinary meaning to be given to the terms of the treaty"? Obviously, everyday language cannot be left unconsidered. The principal difference between technical and everyday language is the lexicon employed. Normally, a technical language does not have a grammar of its own (i.e. a morphology and syntax), at least not one comprehensive in character.[13] Nor does it have rules of pragmatics. Therefore, it cannot arguably be assumed that "the ordinary meaning" refers to technical language, without at the same time referring to everyday language. The issue is whether it is by reference to everyday language *alone*, or by reference to everyday *as well as* technical language, that "the ordinary meaning" shall be determined. In answering this question, the Vienna Convention is of little help. The word ORDINARY (Fr. ORDINAIRE; Sp. CORRIENTE) is ambiguous. It can be used in the sense of *familiar*, *everyday*, *unexceptional*. But it can also be used in the sense of *customary; usual; regular*. Taken in the former sense, "the ordinary meaning" of a treaty shall be determined by reference to everyday language *alone*. Taken in the latter sense "the ordinary meaning" shall be determined by reference to *both* everyday *and* technical language.

Few authors deal directly with "the ordinary meaning" in the aspect at issue here. Many, however, comment upon the content of *the special meaning* referred to in VCLT article 31 § 4. "A special meaning" – this is provided in VCLT article 31 § 4 – "shall be given to a term if it is established that the parties so intended."

Un terme sera entendu dans un sens particulier s'il est établi que telle était l'intention des parties.

Se dará a un término un sentido especial si consta que tal fue la intención de las partes.

This is something we can exploit. The relationship between the ordinary and the special meaning is converse: a non-ordinary meaning is by definition a special meaning, and a non-special meaning is by definition an ordinary meaning.[14] If we can determine the content of the special meaning, then by exclusion we can also determine the content of the ordinary meaning.

The meaning of the terms of a treaty can be of two kinds. It can be conventional, founded on the language practised in a linguistic community of some sort. Or it can be non-conventional – neological – founded only on the parties' own semantic stipulations: the parties may have felt compelled to introduce a new term in the treaty; or – probably more likely – they may have selected a term that already exists, but for one reason or another – implicitly or explicitly – they have agreed to give the term a new semantic content, better suited to the purposes at hand. To simplify matters, I have divided conventional language into two categories, depending on whether a particular usage can be defined as being of everyday or technical character. This allows us to distinguish between three kinds of meaning: (1) everyday meaning, (2) technical meaning, and (3) neological meaning. It is obvious that everyday meaning falls within "the ordinary meaning" in the sense of VCLT article 31 § 1, and that neological meaning is a kind of SPECIAL meaning, in the sense of article 31 § 4. The question is where technical meaning belongs. Shall it be classified as "ordinary" or "special"?

Several authors refer to the ordinary meaning as a limited concept, treating the special meaning as a correspondingly broad one, so that the ordinary meaning of the terms of a treaty comes to include nothing but its everyday meaning. Haraszti may serve as an example:

[T]he ordinary meaning will not be normative for all terms. There are professional terms which have no *everyday meaning* at all, or, if taken over from the current usage, their *professional meaning* departs from everyday use. If their use in the professional sense can be established, then these terms will have to be understood in their professional meaning. This is expressly permitted by paragraph (4) of Article 31 of the Vienna Convention which agrees to a special meaning being given to a term, if it can be established that the parties have so intended.[15]

Another author to be cited is Yasseen:

"Un terme["], dit le paragraphe 4 de l'article 31, ["]sera entendu dans un sens particulier s'il est établi que telle était l'intention des parties." Il est logique de présumer que ceux qui rédigent le traité emploient les termes dans le sens ordinaire que tout le monde comprend. Mais les parties peuvent employer les termes dans un sens différent, un sens technique ou particulier.[16]

As a member first of the International Law Commission, and later of the Vienna Conference Drafting Committee (as chairman), Yasseen must have had the best possible understanding of the drafting process. His comments can of course be interpreted in different ways. In my opinion *"le sens ordinaire que tout le monde comprend"* must be understood as a reference to everyday meaning and *"un sens technique ou particulier"* as a reference to technical and neological meaning, respectively. Yasseen would then be taking a position identical to that of Haraszti.

Other authors view the issue differently. For instance, in the records of the sixteenth session, 766th meeting, of the International Law Commission, we read the following:

Mr. **RUDA** said that if — the special or extraordinary meaning of a term had been "established conclusively", then the meaning in question was perfectly clear and there should be no need to resort to auxiliary means of interpretation in order to establish that special meaning.[17]

Ruda seems to consider "special meaning" and "extraordinary meaning" as interchangeable expressions; and, in Ruda's terminology, "extraordinary meaning" appears to be the same as what has been termed in this work as neological meaning. So, according to Ruda, it appears that the special meaning is the more limited concept and the ordinary meaning the broader one. In other words, according to Ruda, the ordinary meaning of a treaty would include not only its everyday meaning but also its technical meaning. According to Rest and Gottlieb, the "parlance of lawyers" is decisive for "the ordinary meaning" of a treaty term. "Die 'ordinary meaning' ", Rest writes,

... bestimmt sich danach, welche Bedeutung einem Begriff in der allgemeinen Rechtssprache und nicht in der Laiensphäre zukommt.[18]

In a similar fashion, Gottlieb writes:

When the [International Law] Commission referred to "ordinary meaning" it presumably meant just that – ordinary meaning in the parlance of lawyers.[19]

These two statements might seem somewhat confusing. The ordinary meaning must include the everyday meaning – this is an observation we have we already made; anything else is absurd. As a consequence, I find it difficult to interpret Rest and Gottlieb to mean that legal language be the only thing an applier shall rely upon when interpreting a treaty "in accordance with the ordinary meaning to be given to the terms of the treaty". In my assessment, what these authors wish to comment upon is not really the content of *the ordinary meaning* as such, but rather the possible existence of multiple ordinary meanings, and the rules they assume to exist for dealing with conflicts of this sort. When the terms of a treaty bear one meaning in everyday language, and another in technical language, or different meanings in different technical languages, a conflict arises. Such conflicts can be resolved in various ways. The point that Rest and Gottlieb seem to be making is that legal language *generally* shall take precedence when in conflict with other linguistic varieties, whatever their kind. Whether this is really a correct description of the legal state-of-affairs is something we will have reason to return to in later chapters of this work.[20] The only observation to be made at this juncture is the broad interpretation of "the ordinary meaning" that Rest and Gottlieb seem to imply; for it is only when "the ordinary meaning" in VCLT article 31 § 1 is interpreted as a reference to both everyday and technical meaning that conflicts arise between legal language and other linguistic varieties, already at the point when nothing but conventional language is used.

So, all in all, it seems the language used by legal authors is somewhat unresolved. According to some authors, the technical meaning of an expression is to be characterised as "special", in the sense of VCLT article 31 § 4. According to others, the technical meaning is to be characterized as "ordinary", in the sense of VCLT article 31 § 1. Support for the former group of authors can be found in the preparatory work of the Vienna Convention. The International Law Commission submitted the following short commentary to the text that the Vienna Conference later adopted as article 31 § 4:

> [Paragraph 4] provides for the somewhat exceptional case where, notwithstanding the apparent meaning of a term in its context, it is established that the parties intended it to have a special meaning. Some members doubted the need to include a special provision on this point, although they recognised that parties to a treaty not infrequently employ a term with a technical or other special meaning. They pointed out that technical or special use of the term normally appears from the context and the technical or special meaning becomes, as it were, the ordinary meaning in the particular context. Other members, while not disputing that the technical or special meaning of the term may often appear from the context, considered that there was a certain utility in laying down a specific rule on the point, if only to emphasise that the burden of proof lies on the party invoking the special meaning of the term.[21]

The interesting thing about this short commentary is that both "technical meaning" and "special meaning" are mentioned. In my judgment, the Commission uses the expression "technical meaning" as a reference to what has also been referred to in this work as technical meaning. "[T]echnical meaning", in the view of the Commission, is a sort of "special meaning" –

this is evident, if nowhere else, in the phrase "a technical or other special meaning". In the terminology used by the International Law Commission, the special meaning would accordingly be the broader concept and the ordinary meaning the more limited one, so that the special meaning of a treaty term would come to include both its neological and technical meanings.

The preparatory work of the Vienna Convention should be contrasted with international judicial opinions. From what I have found there is not one single decision emanating from an international court or arbitration tribunal from 1969 on, indicating that "the ordinary meaning", in the sense of VCLT article 31 § 1, shall not be understood as a reference to technical meaning. On the contrary, I have found a number of decisions indicating the opposite.[22] In my judgment, the practice of international courts and tribunals – because of its overwhelming unanimity and relative recentness – is of a considerably greater weight than the preparatory work of the Vienna Convention. Therefore, all in all, I can only interpret the provisions of the Vienna Convention as follows: it is by reference to both everyday and technical language that "the ordinary meaning" shall be determined. Now, it is my task to present the decisions I adduce to support this opinion. This is the purpose of Section 2.

2 REGARDING THE PROBLEM CAUSED BY SOCIAL VARIATION IN LANGUAGE (CONT'D)

According to the view expressed in judicial opinions from 1969 on, "the ordinary meaning" of a treaty is to be determined not by everyday language alone, but by everyday language and technical language considered as one single whole. I have four illustrative examples of this. My first example is the judgment of the International Court of Justice in the *Case Concerning Kasikili/Sedudu Island.*[23] In 1996, Botswana and Namibia jointly turned to the Court requesting a decision. On the basis of a written agreement from 1890 between the former colonial powers Germany and the United Kingdom, the Court was asked to give its opinion on the boundary to be drawn in the River Chobe between the now independent states Namibia and Botswana.[24] In particular, the parties asked the Court to pronounce on the legal status of an island located in the midst of the river; by Namibia the island was referred to as Kasikili, by Botswana as Sedudu. In article 3, paragraph 2, of the Anglo-German agreement, we find the following provision:

> In Southwest Africa the sphere in which the exercise of influence is reserved to Germany is bounded:

- - -

2. To the east be a line commencing at the above-named point, and following the 20th degree of east longitude to the point of its intersection by the 22nd parallel of south latitude; it runs eastward along that parallel to the point of its intersection by the 21st degree of east longitude; thence it follows that degree northward to the point of its intersection by the 18 parallel of south latitude; it runs eastward along that parallel till it reaches the river Chobe, and descends the centre of the main channel [in the German agreement text: "*im Thalweg des Hauptlaufes*"] of that river to its junction with the Zambesi, where it terminates.[25]

One of the matters over which the parties were in dispute was the meaning of the expression "centre of the main channel", "*Thalweg des Hauptlaufes*". The positions of the parties have been neatly summarised by the court as follows:

Botswana maintains that, in order to establish the line of the boundary around Kasikili/Sedudu Island, it is sufficient to determine the *thalweg* of the Chobe; it is that which identifies the main channel of the river. For Botswana, the words "*des Hauptlaufes*" therefore add nothing to the text.

23. For Namibia, however, the task of the Court is first to identify the main channel of the Chobe around Kasikili/Sedudu Island, and then to determine where the centre of this channel lies:

"The 'main channel' must be found first; the 'centre' can necessarily only be found afterward. This point is equally pertinent to the German translation of the formula '... *im Thalweg des Hauptlaufes ...*' In the same way as with the English text, the search must first be for the '*Hauptlauf*' and for the '*Thalweg*' only after the '*Hauptlauf*' has been found. The '*Hauptlauf*' cannot be identified by first seeking to find the '*Thalweg*'."[26]

As a start, the court declares its adherence to the rules of interpretation expressed in the 1969 Vienna Convention on the Law of Treaties:

The Court will now proceed to interpret the provisions of the 1890 Treaty by applying the rules of interpretation set forth in the 1969 Vienna Convention. It recalls that

"a treaty must be interpreted in good faith, in accordance with the ordinary meaning to be given to its terms in their context and in the light of its object and purpose. Interpretation must be based above all upon the text of the treaty. As a supplementary measure recourse may be had to means of interpretation such as the preparatory work of the treaty."[27]

After this, the reasoning of the Court indicates an act of interpretation described along the following lines:

The Court notes that various definitions of the term "Thalweg" are found in treaties delimiting boundaries and that the concepts of the Thalweg of watercourse and the centre of a watercourse are not equivalent. The word "Thalweg" has variously been taken to mean "the most suitable channel for navigation" on the river, the line "determined by the line of deepest soundings", or "the median line of the main channel followed by boatmen travelling downstream". Treaties or conventions which define boundaries in watercourses nowadays usually refer to the Thalweg as the boundary when the watercourse is navigable and to the median line between the two banks when it is not, although it cannot be said that practice has been fully consistent.

25. The Court further notes that at the time of the conclusion of the 1890 Treaty, it may be that the terms "centre of the [main] channel" and *"Thalweg des Hauptlaufes"* were used interchangeably. In this respect, it is of interest to note that, some three years before the conclusion of the 1890 Treaty, the Institut de droit international stated the following in Article 3, paragraph 2, of the "Draft concerning the international regulation of fluvial navigation", adopted at Heidelberg on 9 September 1887: "The boundary of States separated by a river is indicated by the Thalweg, that is to say, the median line of the channel (*Annuaire de l'Institut de droit international*, 1887–1888, p. 182)", the term "channel" being understood to refer to the passage open to navigation in the bed of the river, as is clear from the title of the draft. Indeed, the parties to the 1890 Treaty themselves used the terms "centre of the channel" and "Thalweg" as synonyms, one being understood as the translation of the other (see paragraph 46 below).

The Court observes, moreover, that in the course of the proceedings, Botswana and Namibia did not themselves express any real difference of opinion on this subject. The Court will accordingly treat the words "centre of the main channel" in Article III, paragraph 2, of the 1890 Treaty as having the same meaning as the words "Thalweg des Hauptlaufes" [...].[28]

Obviously, the means of interpretation used by the Court is the language of international law; more specifically, it is the language of international law as expressed, first, by treaties and conventions delimiting international waterways, and second, by the Institute of International Law (*L'Institut de droit international*) in its draft of 1887. Of course, it is not expressly stated that this is an act of interpretation using conventional language ("the ordinary meaning"). Nevertheless, this is the inevitable inference drawn from the context, particularly from the formulation "[t]reaties or conventions which define boundaries in watercourses nowadays *usually* refer to ...".[29] Accordingly, in the view of the Court it is obviously possible for an applier to interpret a treaty by reference to the language of international law and then justify the operation as an act of interpretation using "the ordinary meaning".

My second example is the international award in the case of *AAPL v. Sri Lanka*.[30] The case involved the application of a treaty concluded by Sri Lanka and the United Kingdom on the promotion and protection of investments.[31] The applicant had invoked article 2 § 2 of the treaty. It reads as follows:

Investments of nationals or companies of either Contracting Party shall at all times be accorded fair and equitable treatment and shall enjoy full protection and security in the territory of the other Contracting Party.[32]

It was argued that by using the expression "shall enjoy full protection and security", Sri Lanka and the United Kingdom had agreed to derogate from the standard of due diligence upheld by customary international law, and to replace it with a standard of strict liability. The arbitration tribunal did not accept this argument:

> [T]he Claimant's construction of Article 2(2) ... cannot be justified under any of the canons of interpretation previously stated [then referred to as "the sound universally accepted rules of treaty interpretation as established in practice, ... and as codified in Article 31 of the Vienna Convention on the Law of Treaties"].[33]

The tribunal added:

> [T]he words "shall enjoy full protection and security" have to be construed according to the "common use which custom has affixed" to them, their *"usus loquendi"*, "natural and obvious sense", and "fair meaning".
>
> In fact, similar expressions, or even stronger wordings like the "most constant protection", were utilized since last century in a number of bilateral treaties concluded to encourage the flow of international economic exchanges and to provide the citizens and national companies established on the territory of the other Contracting Party with adequate treatment for them as well as to their property ("Traité d'Amitié, de Commerce et Navigation", concluded between France and Mexico on 27 November 1886 – *cf.* A. Ch. Kiss, *Répertoire de la Pratique Francaise ..., op. cit.*, Tome III, 1965, para. 1002, p. 637; the Treaty concluded in 1861 between Italy and Venezuela, the interpretation of which became the central issue in the *Sambaggio* case adjudicated in 1903 by the Italy -Venezuela Mixed Claims Commission – *UN Reports of International Arbitral Awards*, vol. X, p. 512 ss.).
>
> 48. The Arbitration Tribunal is not aware of any case in which the obligation assumed by the host State to provide the nationals of the other Contracting State with "full protection and security" was construed as absolute obligation which guarantees that no damages will be suffered, in the sense that any violation thereof creates automatically a "strict liability" on behalf of the host State.[34]

Hence the conclusion:

> Consequently, both the oldest reported arbitral precedent and the latest ICJ ruling confirm that the language imposing on the host State an obligation to provide "protection and security" or "full protection and security as required by international law" ... could not be construed according to the natural and ordinary sense of the words as creating a "strict liability".[35]

Decisive for the meaning of the Anglo-Sri Lankan treaty is quite obviously legal language, and more specifically, the language of international law. Clearly, according to the tribunal, the operation can be justified under the provisions of VCLT article 31, as an act of interpretation using conventional language. Thus, it also seems to be the Court's opinion that an applier can make use of legal language to determine the meaning of a treaty provision, and then justify the operation as an act of interpretation using "the ordinary meaning".

My third example is the international award in the case of *Guinea – Guinea-Bissau Maritime Delimitation*.[36] A court of arbitration had been constituted by the parties to perform various tasks, one of which was to give an opinion on the meaning of certain provisions contained in a treaty concluded in 1886 by the two colonial powers France and Portugal.[37] The issue was whether France and Portugal, by adopting the provisions, could be viewed as having established a general maritime boundary between their respective possessions in West Africa. "The two Parties", the court confirms, ...

> ... unconditionally accept the rule set out in Article 31, paragraph 1, of the Vienna Convention on the Law of Treaties, which is consistent with the practice of international tribunals, by virtue of which the paragraph concerned must be interpreted in good faith, with each word being given its ordinary meaning within the context and in the light of the object and purpose of the Convention.[38]

The court then starts to pin down the meaning of the Franco-Portuguese treaty by studying the terminology used. The dispute between Guinea and Guinea-Bissau, the court observes, mainly originated in the different meanings, which the parties read into the expression "limit".[39]

> Guinea holds that it is synonymous with *boundary* and remarks that it is generally used in this sense in maritime affairs, whereas Guinea-Bissau gives it a less precise meaning in this case. The Tribunal observes that the two expressions must be taken here in their spatial sense, with due regard to their legal connotations. In French as in Portuguese, and according to the definitions provided by linguistic or legal dictionaries, mentioned or not mentioned by the Parties, they are slightly ambiguous.[40]

Again, legal language is resorted to. The fact that this is an act of interpretation using conventional language ("the ordinary meaning") is not expressly stated; but this is an inference clearly to be drawn from the context; for it is clear that the court finds support for its actions in VCLT article 31 § 1. It is equally clear that neither the context, nor the object and purpose of the treaty, is the means of interpretation used by the court. So, all things considered, it appears that according to the court it is possible to make use of legal language, and then to justify the action as an act of interpretation using "the ordinary meaning".

My fourth example is the international award in the *Young Loan Case* – one of the leading cases concerning the interpretation of multilingual treaties.[41] In this case, the Arbitral Tribunal for the Agreement on German External Debts was asked to determine the meaning of certain provisions contained in the 1953 *London Debt Agreement.*[42] The treaty was authenticated in three different language versions – one English, one French, and one German – of which no one version was to be considered more authoritative than the others. Special attention was given to article 2(e) in annex 1 A of the London Agreement, and the following phrase therein: "least depreciated currency" – *"Währung mit der geringsten Abwertung"* – *"devise la moins dépréciée"*. The question arose whether a comparison of the German word ABWERTUNG with the English and French words DEPRECIATION and DÉPRÉCIATION disclosed a difference of meaning, which the application of articles 31–32 of the Vienna Convention did not remove, making it necessary to apply the specific rule of reconciliation laid down in VCLT article 33 § 4. The answer of the tribunal is truly informative. I cite the following excerpt:

Article 31 (1) of the VCT reads as follows:

"A treaty shall be interpreted in good faith in accordance with the ordinary meaning to be given to the terms of the treaty in their context and in the light of its object and purpose."

The decisive terms to be interpreted are the words *Abwertung*, "depreciation", *dépréciation*. The Tribunal has no doubt that if it were to proceed on terminology alone and take the words in their ordinary, everyday sense in the language concerned, it is at least not excluded that the German text would provide one answer to the original query, and the French and English texts a different one. In German, the meaning of the term *Abwertung* is relatively clear. In the proper technical language, it means a reduction in the external value of currency – in relation to a fixed yardstick, *e.g.* gold – by an act of government. (*Cf. e.g.* Gabler's *Banklexikon, Handwörterbuch für das Bank- und Sparkassengewerbe*, 8th edition 1979, p. 15.)

In everyday German usage, however, there is, at least, some uncertainty, inasmuch as the expression "formal" devaluation (*formelle Abwertung*) tends to be used to describe the devaluation of a currency by governmental act, as distinguished from the far more common economic phenomenon of the depreciation of a currency.

In English and French, on the other hand, the terms "depreciation" and *dépréciation*, as they occur in the disputed clause, are normally used to describe the economic phenomenon of depreciation of a currency quite generally, while "formal" devaluation is usually termed "devaluation" or *dévaluation*. (*Cf.* in this context *e.g.* Carreau, *Souveraineté et Coopération Monétaire Internationale*, Paris 1970, p. 208; Nussbaum, *Money in the Law, National and International*, Brooklyn 1950, p. 172.)

However, even if the twin terms "depreciation" – *dépréciation* and "devaluation" – *dévaluation* are distinguishable in the two languages in the way indicated and normally refer to different events, they are also used interchangeably in the two languages to describe the same process, both in practice and in theory and both in everyday and in technical language. (Contemporary writings also contain examples of a continuing terminological uncertainty in these respects. See Carreau, Juillard, Flory, *Droit International Economique*, Paris 1978, p. 232; Hirschberg, *The Impact of Inflation and Devaluation on Obligations*, Jerusalem 1976, p. 40; Horsefield (ed.), *The International Monetary Fund*, 1945/65, Volume II: *Analysis*, Washington 1969, p. 90 *et seq*; *cf.* also Nussbaum, *op. cit.*, p. 172.)

The possibility of the German and English or French texts of the disputed clause having different meanings cannot therefore be ruled out.[43]

Once again we are faced with an example of a treaty interpreted by reference to a technical language – this time the language of banking and finance. As appears from the tribunal's line of reasoning, the treaty is interpreted "in accordance with the ordinary meaning to be given to the terms of the treaty". In an introductory passage the tribunal observes:

[I]f it were to proceed on terminology alone and take the words in their ordinary, everyday sense in the language concerned, it is at least not excluded that the German text would provide one answer to the original query, and the French and English texts a different one.[44]

Based on the wording of this passage, it is tempting to believe that in the tribunal's opinion, conventional language ("the ordinary meaning") is in all respects synonymous with everyday language. Considering the context of the utterance, this conclusion immediately appears a less plausible one. In my opinion, the tribunal's choice of words is merely an act of carelessness. When reasons are given for the first, introductory statement, and the different meanings are presented, it is not only with reference to "everyday language", but also with consideration for the relevant "technical language". Thus, in the opinion of the tribunal it appears an applier, for the purpose of interpretation, can make use of the language of banking and finance, and then justify his action as an act of interpretation using "the ordinary meaning".

3 REGARDING THE PROBLEM CAUSED BY TEMPORAL VARIATION IN LANGUAGE

Earlier in this work, we observed that human language bears a singular characteristic – namely, that it changes. First of all, language changes depending on the social context. Above, we looked into the problem caused by these social variations for the interpretation of treaties. We also established how the problem is to be resolved from the point of view of an interpretation using conventional language ("the ordinary meaning"). Another aspect of the variation of language is the one now to be addressed: it is a fact that language varies over time. Human language conventions are not such that they can ever be said to "stand till". On the contrary, they are under a constant flux. Bit by bit, lexicon, grammar, and pragmatics are created anew: new words and linguistic structures come into use; old ones are abandoned or acquire partly or even completely new meanings.[45] Obviously, changes such as these must also affect the language used in treaties. The following question arises: What language conventions shall an applier employ when he interprets a treaty using conventional language? Shall she employ the conventions adhered to at the time the treaty is interpreted (what we will henceforth be calling CONTEMORARY LANGUAGE)? Or shall she employ the conventions adhered to at the time the treaty was concluded (henceforth: HISTORICAL LANGUAGE)? No answer to this question is given in the Vienna Convention.

Legal literature sheds little additional light on the subject. Some authors categorically dismiss the idea that an applier, for interpretation purposes, should be allowed to consider contemporary language: "the ordinary meaning" of a treaty is determined by historical language, and that language only.[46] "[I]t is a generally accepted principle", Haraszti declares, ...

> ... that by the ordinary meaning of the words the meaning that prevailed at the time when the treaty was concluded has to be understood.[47]

Rousseau considers this principle self-evident:

Il va de soi que l'interprète doit prendre en considération le sens qu'avaient les mots à l'époque de la conclusion du traité, car il y a présomption que ce sens a été adopté par les auteurs de celui-ci [...].[48]

Let me also cite professor Dupuy:

L'interprétation doit prendre appui sur "le texte suivant le sens ordinaire à attribuer à ses termes". C'est ici que la priorité sinon la préférance à accorder au texte lui-même (y compris le préambule et les éventuelles annexes) est marquée par la convention: celui-ci étant l'expression authentique de l'intention des Parties et l'aboutissement de leur négociation, il incarne *prima facie* la manifestation la plus directe de leur volonté. C'est donc lui qu'il convient en premier lieu d'examiner en accordant à ses termes le sens qu'il est ou qu'il était normal, *au moment de la conclusion de l'accord*, de leur attribuer.[49]

Other authors take a more liberal stance.[50] For example, Villiger writes:

This [i.e. the ordinary meaning] is not necessarily the meaning in use at the time of the conclusion of the treaty.[51]

He then adds in a footnote:

This is essentially a matter of good faith, depending on the intentions of the parties [...].[52]

Something similar is expressed in the resolution – that bears the title *"Le problème intertemporel en droit international public"* – adopted by the Institute of International Law in 1975:

Lorsqu'une disposition conventionelle se réfère à une notion juridique ou autre sans la définir, il convient de recourir aux méthodes habituelles d'interprétation pour déterminer si cette notion doit être comprise dans son acception au moment de l'établissement de la disposition ou dans son acception au moment de l'application.[53]

All in all, we are confronted with two different ways of understanding international law. According to the one alternative, the decisive factor for determining "the ordinary meaning" of the terms of a treaty is historical language, and this language only. Let us call this alternative (a). According to the second alternative, the decisive factor for determining "the ordinary meaning" of the terms of a treaty is either historical or contemporary language, depending on the circumstances. We will call this alternative (b). In my judgment, the correct description of the present legal state-of-affairs is that represented by alternative (b), and not alternative (a). Two sets of circumstances support this conclusion.

The first is the object and purpose of the treaty at issue, i.e. the Vienna Convention. When an applier uses conventional language for the interpretation of a treaty provision, it is for the purpose of establishing its legally correct meaning. This, the legally correct meaning of a treaty provision, is a meaning of the kind we call its utterance meaning.[54] Decisive for the utterance meaning of a treaty provision, among other things, is the reference of the expressions used for the provision. REFERENCE – as the term shall here be defined – [55] is the relationship held between an expression and what the expression stands for in the world at the occasion of its utterance.[56] Under such premises alternative (b) appears to be the only possible conclusion. If the object and purpose of using the ordinary meaning is to establish the utterance meaning of the treaty interpreted, and the utterance meaning of a treaty is partly determined by the references of the expressions used for the treaty, then the determining factor for "the ordinary meaning" cannot be historical language, and that language only – so goes the argument. The reason is that if we take the opposite to be true – the assumption represented by alternative (a) – then, for the very same reason, we commit ourselves to a certain assumption. We assume that of pure necessity, the utterer's referring possibilities are limited by the language conventions adhered to at the moment of utterance.[57] The point is that this assumption is not at all tenable. I shall now show why this is so.

As we have already noted, REFERENCE is the relationship that holds between an expression and that for which the expression stands in the world on the occasion of its utterance – what we will call its REFERENT.[58]An expression used by someone to refer to a referent is a REFERRING EXPRESSION.[59] Referring expressions are of different types.[60] First, we have to distinguish between expressions that refer to a single phenomenon and expressions that refer to a group of phenomena. We call the former SINGULAR REFERRING EXPRESSIONS; the latter are called GENERAL REFERRING EXPRESSIONS.[61] Take for example the following passage contained in a special agreement concluded by Guinea and Guinea-Bissau, on 18 February 1983:

> Within 30 days after signature of this Special Agreement, the Parties will each appoint, for purposes of the arbitration, an Agent, and will submit to the Tribunal and the other Party the name and address of said Agent.[62]

We can easily identify the special agreement of 18 February 1983 as the referent of the expression "this Special Agreement". It is equally obvious that the expression "the Parties" refers to Guinea and Guinea-Bissau. Consequently, "this Special Agreement" is a singular referring expression; "the Parties" is a general referring one.

Singular and general referring expressions can be either definite or indefinite referring expressions. A DEFINITE REFERRING EXPRESSION is one that refers to a specific phenomenon or group of phenomena; and, of course, an INDEFINITE REFERRING EXPRESSION is one that refers to a non-specific phenomenon or group of phenomena.[63] In the example above, both "this Special Agreement" and "the Parties" are definite referring expressions. As an example of an indefinite referring expression, let us examine yet another passage taken from the special agreement:

> The Arbitration Tribunal (hereinafter the "Tribunal") will be composed of nationals of third States, which shall be appointed within 30 days after the signature of this Special Agreement, and shall consist of three (3) Members, hereinafter named: M ... appointed by the Republic of Guinea-Bissau; M ... appointed by the People's Revolutionary Republic of Guinea; the third Arbitrator, who will serve as the President of the Tribunal, will be appointed by mutual agreement of the two Parties; in case they cannot reach agreement, the third Arbitrator shall be appointed by the two Arbitrators acting jointly after consultation with the two Parties.[64]

The expression "the two Arbitrators" does not refer to any specific group of individuals; it refers to individuals, any individuals – who are not nationals of Guinea or Guinea-Bissau – appointed by the two parties. Consequently, "the two Arbitrators" can be termed as an indefinite, general referring expression. The expression "the third Arbitrator" does not refer to a specific individual; it refers to an individual, any individual – who is not a national of Guinea or Guinea-Bissau – jointly appointed by the two parties, or by the arbitrators selected by the parties after consultation with the same. Thus, "the third Arbitrator" can be categorised as an indefinite, singular referring expression.

In addition to singular and general referring expressions, a third type of reference must be singled out. Take the following excerpt from the 1967 *Treaty on the Principles Governing the Activities of States in the Exploration and Use of Outer Space, including the Moon and Other Celestial Bodies*:

> States Parties to the Treaty undertake not to place in orbit around the Earth any objects carrying nuclear weapons or any other kinds of weapons of mass destruction, install such weapons on celestial bodies, or station such weapons in outer space in any other manner.[65]

What I would like to draw attention to are the two expressions "nuclear weapons or any other kinds of weapons of mass destruction" and "celestial bodies". The expressions have been articulated in the indefinite plural, but neither is a general referring expression – this much is clear. The expression "nuclear weapons or any other kinds of weapons of mass destruction" does not refer to a specific group of weapons of mass destruction; it refers to the class weapons of mass destruction *as such*. The same applies to the expression "celestial bodies"; it does not refer to a specific collection of celestial bodies, but to celestial bodies considered as a category. Expressions of this type are what we call GENERIC REFERRING EXPRESSIONS.[66]

Among the words and phrases existing in a language, many can usually be used to refer both singularly or generally, as well as generically. Take for example the term CELESTIAL BODIES. First, it can be used to refer to an (indefinite) group of celestial bodies; second, it can be used to refer to the class *celestial bodies* as such. In order for a reader to understand how a specific referring expression is to be categorised, it is clear that in some cases the expression must first be interpreted. It may then be taken as an important piece of information that between singular and general referring expressions on the one hand, and generic referring expressions on the other, there is a significant difference. Singular and general referring expressions are used to express propositions that are time-bound. When a singular or general referring expression is uttered, a (temporal) relationship is established between the occasion of utterance and the point in time or time period at or during which the referent is presumed to exist.[67] Thus, for example, it is not difficult to see that the existence of the referent of the expression "the Parties", in the special agreement cited above between Guinea and Guinea-Bissau, is located at the same point in time as the utterance itself; that is, 18 February 1983. The existence of the referent of the expression "the third Arbitrator" is located at a point in time somewhere between the occasion of utterance and 30 days hence. Generic referring expressions, on the other hand, are used to express propositions that are timeless. When a generic expression is uttered, *no* relationship is established between the time of utterance and the time at which the referent is assumed to exist.[68] For example, in the treaty cited earlier on the installation of weapons of mass destruction in outer space, it appears somewhat irrelevant to ask which day and month, or which year, weapons of mass destruction shall not be installed. The text does not refer to a specific occasion. In a way we can say that the existence of the referent of the expression "nuclear weapons or any other kinds of weapons of mass destruction" is outside time altogether.[69]

When a referring expression is uttered, the referent can be either defined or undefined. If a singular or general referring expression is uttered, and the reference is definite, then the referent is *extensionally* defined.[70] The utterer has in mind a very specific phenomenon or group of phenomena. If the reference is indefinite, then the referent is *intensionally* defined.[71] The utterer does not have in mind a specific phenomenon or group of phenomena, but in principle, the number of possible referents could be listed, since there are specific *properties* a referent must possess. So, for example, in the special agreement between Guinea and Guinea-Bissau, the referent to the expression "the two Arbitrators" is not just any group of individuals; the referent is a group of individuals, of which one is appointed by Guinea and the other by Guinea-Bissau, and neither is a national of Guinea or Guinea-Bissau.

If a generic referring expression is uttered, then immediately things become more complicated: the referent can be either defined or undefined. Consider again the Moon Treaty cited above. The existence of the referent to the expression "nuclear weapons or any other kinds of weapons of mass destruction", as we have already noted, is not located to a specific point in time or time period. There are two possible reasons for this:

(1) It was assumed by the parties that the class *weapons of mass destruction* will remain unaltered for as long as the treaty is in force – those types of weapons that can be said to exist when the treaty is concluded will always exist, and no new ones will ever be produced.
(2) It was assumed by the parties that during the life span of the treaty, the class *weapons of mass destruction* will most likely alter – not every type of weapon that can be said to exist when the treaty is concluded will always exist, and new types will probably be produced.

In the former case, the referent of the expression "nuclear weapons and other weapons of mass destruction" is defined; the referent is the class *weapons of mass destruction*, as that class is known at the time of the treaty's conclusion. In the latter case, the referent is undefined; the referent is the class *weapons of mass destruction*, as that class is known at any given moment.

We can now see why it is wrong to assume that, of pure necessity, an utterer's referring possibilities are limited by the linguistic conventions adhered to when the expression is uttered. As we have seen, one can speak of references of different kinds, such as singular and general references. A singular referring expression is one that refers to a single phenomenon; an expression that refers to a group of phenomena is what we call a general referring expression. Singular and general referring expressions can be either definite or indefinite. The referent of a definite referring expression is something the utterer defines extensionally. The referent of an indefinite referring expression is something the utterer defines intensionally. As long as we use the term reference to mean only singular and general references, there seems to be nothing wrong about the claim that an utterer's referring possibilities are limited by the linguistic conventions adhered to on the occasion of utterance. Taken as a general statement, however, the proposition is clearly incorrect. As we have seen, apart from being singular and general, reference can also be generic. A generic referring expression is one that does not refer to a certain phenomenon or group of phenomena, but to the class of certain phenomena. The referent of a generic referring expression can be something, which is either defined or undefined. If the referent is a class that the utterer assumes will remain unaltered, then the referent is defined.[72] If the referent is a class that the utterer assumes is alterable, then the referent is undefined. Only in the former case are the utterer's referring possibilities limited by the linguistic conventions adhered to on the occasion of utterance. In the latter case, limitations are set by the conventions adhered to at any given moment.

The second set of circumstances that supports alternative (b), making alternative (a) seem even less tenable, are the judicial opinions expressed since 1969 in international courts and tribunals. It is true that cases can be pointed out, where the determining factor for "the ordinary meaning" was clearly historical language.[73] But there are also cases where the determining factor was contemporary language.[74] To illustrate this proposition, I have two particular examples that I would like to present. This is the purpose of Section 4.

4 REGARDING THE PROBLEM CAUSED BY TEMPORAL VARIATION IN LANGUAGE (CONT'D)

My first example is the international award in the case of *La Bretagne Arbitration*.[75] In January of 1985, Canadian authorities had rejected an application for a licence to fish in the St. Lawrence Bay using so-called fish filleting equipment. (A trawler equipped with fish filleting equipment does not need to transport the catch to land to have it cleaned and processed; it can be done at sea. Hence, trawlers that have this kind of equipment greatly increase their fishing capacity.) The application was placed by "La Bretagne", a French trawler registered at St. Pierre et Miquelon, a small group of islands lying just off the Canadian Atlantic coast. France protested. Canada's action, the French government claimed, violated an agreement on fishery matters concluded between the two states in 1972.[76]

One of the provisions to which France called particular attention was article 6 of the Franco-Canadian agreement:

1. Canadian fishery regulations shall be applied without discrimination in fact or in law to the French fishing vessels covered by Articles 3 and 4 [i.e., among others, French trawlers registered in S:t Pierre et Miquelon], including regulations concerning the dimensions of vessels authorized to fish less than 12 miles from the Atlantic coast of Canada.

- - -

3. Before promulgating new regulations applicable to these vessels, the authorities of each of the parties shall give three months prior notice to the authorities of the other party.[77]

The parties held different views as to the meaning of this text. As a reason for their actions in the matter of La Bretagne, Canadian authorities had cited national policy: for several years, no licences for fishing in the St. Lawrence Bay had been granted to trawlers with fish filleting equipment, not even to trawlers registered in Canada. This policy, according to Canada, was a "fishery regulation", in the sense of article 6 § 1. According to France it was not. In the findings of the tribunal, the respective positions of the parties have been summarised as follows:

According to the Canadian Party, this expression in Article 6 constitutes a *renvoi* to all the provisions governing fishery management in Canada, and includes not only the laws and regulations as such but also the administrative practices authorized by the law. As it is the responsibility of the Minister of Fisheries, under Canadian law, to authorize the granting to foreign vessels of licences stipulating the terms and conditions governing their fishing operations, Canada contended that under its domestic law, the fishery licences themselves formed an integral part of the regulation process. Basing itself on the inherent regulatory power it derived from its exclusive jurisdiction over its fishing zone, Canada further argued that its authority extended to all the activities conducted by foreign vessels for the purpose of exploiting the biological resources of the zone and that the regulation of the processing of the catch on board these vessels formed part of its competence as the coastal State.

The French Party, on the contrary, based its position on this point on a restrictive interpretation of the term "fishery regulations" which, in its view, should be taken to mean measures of a general character concerns solely with fishing, i.e. both in the normal acceptance of the term and under Canadian and French legislation, operation designed to catch fish. As the processing of the catch on board fishing vessels does not form part of these operations, France argued that a Canadian regulation on the filleting of fish was not applicable to the French vessels covered by Article 4 of the Agreement.[78]

A first measure taken by the tribunal was to establish the forward-looking character of the expression "fishery regulations". This was done in two steps. First, observes the tribunal, one must not necessarily exclude as part of the extension of "fishery regulations" those norms in Canadian law that were not already in force when the Franco-Canadian fishery agreement was entered into.

[I]n providing for the application of the Canadian fishery regulations to the French vessels allowed to catch fish in Canada's fishing zone, Article 6 clearly does not have the effect of subjecting these vessels only to the regulations in force at the time of the conclusion of the Agreement, especially since paragraph 3 of this article speaks of the promulgation of "new regulations applicable to these vessels".[79]

Secondly, it is necessarily not the case – as France has implicitly argued – that as part of the extension of "fishery regulations", such measures for regulating fishing activities must be excluded that were not already in use on this same occasion.

In stipulating that "Canadian fishery regulations shall be applied without discrimination in fact or in law to the French fishing vessels" and in adding "including the regulations concerning the dimensions of vessels authorized to fish less than 12 miles from the Atlantic coast of Canada", the authors of the 1972 Agreement used the term "fishery regulations" as a generic formula covering all the rules applicable to fishing activities, while the reference to the dimensions of the vessels appears to suggest that a particular purpose was thereby intended, namely the limitation of these vessels' fishing capacity.

However, as this expression was embodied in an agreement concluded for an unlimited duration, it is hardly conceivable that the Parties would have sought to give it an invariable content. Accordingly, in view of the subsequent evolution of international law respecting maritime fisheries, the rules to which the expression refers must not only be taken to be those setting technical standards for the physical conditions in which the fishing is carried on but also those requiring the completion of certain formalities prior to the performance of these activities.

The tribunal observes, for example, that the content of the fishery regulations adopted by a number of coastal States has evolved to some extent since 1972. Whereas at the time of the conclusion of the Agreement, the fishery regulations in force in various States usually confined themselves to specifying forbidden fishing zones or closed seasons, permitted fishing gear and equipment, and the types, age and size of the species that could be caught, the scope of fishery regulations has since been enlarged; this applies to the regulations of both the Parties to the present case. Concern over the more efficient management of fish stocks has led to the introduction of other methods of supervising fishing efforts partly in the form of quotas for individual vessels within the total allowable catch (TAC) and partly in the form of fishing licences or permits for foreign vessels. The system of fishing quotas and licences has in fact become general and was applied by Canada to French fishing vessels through the 1976 Coastal Fisheries Protection Regulations, which formed the first set of regulations applicable to these vessels and laid down the procedures for applying for and issuing the licences. The Tribunal notes, in this connection, that the French Government, by its actions, has accepted the application of this system to the vessels flying its flag and operating in the Canadian fishing zones.

While the Parties' subsequent practice in applying the Agreement has thus enlarged the scope of fishery regulations, this extension has nevertheless occurred without affecting the original meaning of the expression, which must therefore be taken to be that given it in common usage.[80]

The pronouncement speaks for itself. According to the tribunal, the decisive factor for determining "the ordinary meaning" of the expression "fishery regulations" is clearly contemporary language.

My second example is the advisory opinion delivered by the International Court of Justice in the *Namibia Case*.[81] The case originated in the so-called mandate system created by the League of Nations after the First World War. In 1920, the League of Nations had decided to entrust to South Africa the mandate, which the League, up to that point, had itself exercised over the former German colony of South-West Africa. In question was a so-called C-mandate. It meant that South-West Africa was to be administrated under the same laws as those of South Africa itself …

... as integral portions of its territory [...].[82]

Twenty-five years later, the United Nations was founded. As part of the global order that was now to be created, the organisation decided to bring to a close the League of Nations mandate system. Instead, through agreements concluded with the different mandatory states, a trusteeship system was to be established. With South Africa, however, no such agreement was reached, and the legal status of the territory of South-West Africa remained unsettled. In 1950 came the ICJ advisory opinion in the *International Status of South-West Africa Case*. Certainly, the Court observes, there is no obligation on South Africa to relinquish the administration of South-West Africa to the UN trusteeship; but as long as South Africa chooses to retain the mandate, it is still to fulfil all obligations associated with the mandate.[83] In 1966 the UN General Assembly adopted resolution 2145 (XXI). As the resolution plainly declares, since South Africa has failed to fulfil its obligations with regard to the administration of South-West Africa, the mandate is terminated; henceforth, South-West Africa comes under the direct responsibility of the UN.[84] Once again, however, South Africa was to refuse all co-operation. In 1970, after numerous promptings and censure, the UN Security Council turned to the International Court in request for an advisory opinion. The Court was asked to decide on the legal consequences of South Africa's continued presence in South-West Africa, now known as Namibia.[85]

A basic factor in the reasoning of the Security Council was of course that South Africa's presence in Namibia was a breach of the obligations held by that state under international law. Against this assumption several counter-arguments were raised. *Inter alia*, South Africa claimed that a C-mandate was more or less tantamount to an annexation; this appeared clearly from the various statements contained in the preparatory work of the League Covenant.[86] The Court showed no understanding for this line of reasoning. As a mandatory, the Court observed, South Africa had assumed as "a sacred trust" to provide for the "well-being and development" of the South-West African population; this is confirmed in article 22 § 1 of the Covenant:

> To those colonies and territories which as a consequence of the late war has ceased to be under the sovereignty of the States which formerly governed them and which are inhabited by peoples not yet able to stand by themselves under the strenuous conditions of the modern world, there should be applied the principle that the well-being and development of such peoples form a sacred trust of civilisation and that securities for the performance of this trust should be embodied in this Covenant.[87]

In order to live up to this commitment, South Africa must act, not for the annexation of the mandated territory, but rather for its independence and self-determination. Below follows the reasoning adduced by the Court in support of this proposition:

> [T]he subsequent development of international law in regard to non-self governing territories, as enshrined in the Charter of the United Nations, made the principle of self-determination applicable to all of them. The concept of the sacred trust was confirmed and expanded to all "territories whose peoples have not yet attained a full measure of self-government" (Art. 73). Thus it clearly embraced territories under a colonial régime. Obviously, the sacred trust continued to apply to League of Nations mandated territories on which an international status had been conferred earlier. A further important stage in this development was the Declaration on the Granting of Independence to Colonial Countries and Peoples (General Assembly resolution 1514 (XV) of 14 December 1960), which embraced all peoples and territories which "have not yet attained independence". Nor is it possible to leave out of account the political history of mandated territories in general. All those which did not acquire independence, excluding Namibia, were placed under trusteeship. Today, only two out of

fifteen, excluding Namibia, remain under United Nations tutelage. This is but a manifestation of the general development which has led to the birth of so many new States.

53. All these considerations are germane to the Court's evaluation of the present case. Mindful as it is of the primary necessity of interpreting an instrument in accordance with the intentions of the parties at the time of its conclusion, the Court is bound to take into account the fact that the concepts embodied in Article 22 of the Covenant – "the strenuous conditions of the modern world" and "the well-being and development" of the peoples concerned – were not static, but were by definition evolutionary, as also, therefore, was the concept of the "sacred trust". The parties to the Covenant must consequently be deemed to have accepted them as such. That is why, viewing the institutions of 1919, the Court must take into consideration the changes which have occurred in the supervening half-century, and its interpretation cannot remain unaffected by the subsequent development of law, through the Charter of the United Nations and by way of customary law. Moreover, an international instrument has to be interpreted and applied within the framework of the entire legal system prevailing at the time of interpretation. In the domain to which the present proceedings relate, the last fifty years, as indicated above, have brought important developments. These developments leave little doubt that the ultimate objective of the sacred trust was the self-determination and independence of the peoples concerned. In this domain, as elsewhere, the *corpus iuris gentium* has been considerably enriched, and this the Court, if it is faithfully to discharge its functions, may not ignore.[88]

The focus of the whole exercise is the expression "a sacred trust". The Court concludes that, for the understanding of this expression, one must take into consideration the developments in international law since 1919, when the Covenant was concluded. We must note that the Court itself does not expressly pronounce on the means of interpretation exploited. In the literature this has provoked a variety of interpretations. Some authors see a use of the context. Stated more specifically, they see a use of the contextual element described in VCLT article 31 § 3(c); that is, "any relevant rules of international law applicable in the relations between the parties".[89] This is a reading of the decision that does not convince. Based on the wordings used by the Court, the assumption can be made that the means of interpretation referred to at the end of paragraph 53 – in the passage beginning with "Moreover ..." – is not the same as that referred to in the remainder of the paragraph. The means of interpretation referred to in the passage beginning with "Moreover ..." is clearly the contextual element described in VCLT article 31 § 3(c). Therefore, it stands to reason that the means referred to in the remainder of the passage is a different one. In my judgment, this other means of interpretation is conventional language – stated more specifically, conventional language as expressed in article 73 of the UN Charter, and in the *Declaration on the Granting of Independence to Colonial Countries and Peoples*; I cannot see what else it could possibly be.[90] Hence, as I understand the decision, the decisive factor for determining "the ordinary meaning" of "a sacred trust" is contemporary language.

In support of the interpretation of VCLT article 31 earlier referred to as alternative (b), authors have often cited the judgment of the ICJ in the *Aegean Sea Continental Shelf Case.*[91] This practice appears to be based on a misunderstanding – a fact, which I think should be expressly set forth. (Let it be stressed, however, that I remain convinced that alternative (b) is the only correct description of the present legal state-of-affairs – but, of course, I remain so for other reasons than the decision of the ICJ in the *Aegean Sea Continental Shelf Case.*)

So, let us take a closer look at the ICJ judgment in *Aegean Sea Continental Shelf.*[92] During the early 1970s, a dispute had arisen between Greece and Turkey concerning the extent of the two states' continental shelf areas in the Aegean Sea. In August 1976, Greece had turned to the International Court of Justice asking the Court to pronounce on the correct line to be applied for delimiting those areas. As a basis for the jurisdiction of the Court, Greece had cited article 17 of the 1928 *General Act for the Pacific Settlement of International Disputes* – according to which a legal dispute that arises between two parties to the General Act shall be submitted for decision to the Permanent Court of International Justice – together with article 37 of the ICJ Statute – stating that whenever a treaty in force provides for reference of a dispute to the Permanent Court of International Justice, it shall instead be referred to the International Court of Justice. Article 17 of the General Act provides:

> All disputes with regard to which the parties are in conflict as to their respective rights shall, subject to any reservations which may be made under Article 39, be submitted for decision to the Permanent Court of International Justice, unless the parties agree, in the manner hereinafter provided, to have resort to an arbitral tribunal.

Greece had accessed the General Act in 1931, and Turkey in 1934; both states were still bound by their undertakings. However, upon accession, Greece had made this reservation:

> The following disputes are excluded from the procedures described in the General Act ... :
>
> ---
>
> (b) disputes concerning questions which by international law are solely within the domestic jurisdiction of States, and in particular disputes relating to the territorial status of Greece, including disputes relating to its rights of sovereignty over its ports and lines of communication.[93]

The question was whether the reservation made by Greece was to be read as to exclude the jurisdiction of the Court in this particular dispute. Greece naturally denied that this was the case, and did so for several reasons.

One argument put forward by the Greek government was that the Greek reservation was made at a time when the concept of a continental shelf was entirely unknown. Given that a reservation shall be interpreted in accordance with the intentions of its authors, the Greco-Turkish dispute could then not possibly be part of the extension of the expression "disputes relating to the territorial status of Greece". This was an argument the Court refused to accept. What we are confronting here, the Court observed, is a generic term – by "the territorial status of Greece" any matter is referred to, the only condition being that according to international law it can be taken as included in the concept *the territorial status of Greece*.

[T]he presumption necessarily arises that its meaning was intended to follow the evolution of the law and to correspond with the meaning attached to the expression by the law in force at any given time. This presumption, in the view of the Court, is even more compelling when it is recalled that the 1928 Act was a convention for the pacific settlement of disputes designed to be of the most general kind and of continuing duration, for it hardly seems conceivable that in such a convention terms like "domestic jurisdiction" and "territorial status" were intended to have a fixed content regardless of the subsequent evolution of international law.[94]

The fact was that through its actions, Greece itself had already paved the way for this reasoning. The Court explains:

The Greek Government invokes as a basis for the Court's jurisdiction in the present case Article 17 of the General Act under which the parties agreed to submit to judicial settlement all disputes with regard to which they "are in conflict as to their respective rights". Yet the rights that are the subject of the claims upon which Greece requests the Court in the Application to exercise its jurisdiction under Article 17 are the very rights over the continental shelf of which, as Greece insists, the authors of the General Act could have had no idea whatever in 1928. If the Greek Government is correct, as it undoubtedly is, in assuming that the meaning of the generic term "rights" in Article 17 follows the evolution of the law, so as to be capable of embracing rights over the continental shelf, it is not clear why the similar term "territorial status" should not likewise be liable to evolve in meaning in accordance with "the development of international relations" (*P.C.I.J, Series B, No. 4*, p. 24). It may also be observed that the claims which are the subject-matter of the Application relate more particularly to continental shelf rights claimed to appertain to Greece in virtue of its sovereignty over certain islands in the Aegean Sea, including the islands of the "Dodecanese group" (para. 29 of the Application). But the "Dodecanese group" was not in Greece's possession when it acceded to the General Act in 1931; for those islands were ceded to Greece by Italy only in the Peace Treaty of 1947. In consequence, it seems clear that, in the view of the Greek Government, the term "rights" in Article 17 of the General Act has to be interpreted in the light of the geographical extent of the Greek State today, not of its extent in 1931. It would then be a little surprising if the meaning of Greece's reservation of disputes relating to its "*territorial* status" was not also to evolve in the light of the change in the territorial extent of the Greek State brought about by "the development of international relations".[95]

The Court's conclusion is unmistakable: "rights", in the sense of the 1928 General Act, are those rights that can be invoked by reference to the rules and principles of international law applicable whenever the General Act is interpreted. The decisive issue is whether this conclusion is support for alternative (b), according to which, in a situation where contemporary and historical language differ, a treaty shall sometimes be interpreted using the former.[96] The answer must be in the negative. The problem confronted in the *Aegean Sea Continental Shelf Case* is the fact that law has altered. Clearly, the rights of coastal states over the continental shelf are not the same in 1978, when the judgment of the Court is delivered, as they were in 1928, when the General Act was concluded. But this is not necessarily to say that conventional language has changed. On the contrary; if we were to compare the meanings of RIGHTS, according to conventional language in 1978 and 1928 respectively, I would dare to assert that we would find no difference at all. Nevertheless, for the sake of argument, let us follow in the line of some commentators and assume the opposite. Let us assume that the language used by the Court for determining the meaning of "rights" is that of 1978.

The lexical definition of RIGHT is "that which a person [whether legal or not] has a just claim to".[97] The term RIGHTS, according to grammar, denotes an object in the plural. By applying the rules of pragmatics, we can also conclude that the expression "rights" in the 1928 General Act deictically refers back to international law. However, this in itself cannot possibly answer the question why, by the expression "rights", we are to understand those rights that can be invoked by reference to the international laws applicable in 1978. According to conventional language, "rights" can be used in three different ways: (1) as a general referring expression; (2) as a generic referring expression with an unalterable referent; (3) as a generic referring expression with an alterable referent.[98] Thus, even if we were to limit the use of conventional language to that of 1978, the ordinary meaning of "rights" would clearly be ambiguous. To determine which one of the linguistically possible meanings is correct and which one is not, one has to proceed as usual, using other means of interpretation. What the International Court of Justice seems to rely upon for its conclusion is the object and purpose of the treaty. "[I]t is [to be] recalled", the Court observes ...

> ... that the 1928 Act was a convention for the pacific settlement of disputes designed to be of the most general kind and of continuing duration [...].[99]

Hence, what the case involves is not – as some authors seem to have taken for granted – a conflict between two linguistic systems valid at two different points in time. The case involves a collision between language habits internal to one single system. The problem *is not* that the expression "rights" takes on different meanings, depending on whether it is understood in accordance with the language employed in 1928 or that employed in 1978. The problem is that the expression takes on different meanings, even though it is understood in accordance with only one of these languages.

With that, it is time to summarise. As we observed above, there are questions for which we cannot find answers in the text of the Vienna

Convention. One question is whether it is the language employed at the time of a treaty's conclusion (i.e. historical language), or the language employed at the time of interpretation (i.e. contemporary language), that an applier shall employ when he interprets a treaty using the "ordinary meaning". Two views are held in the literature. One is that expressed by authors such as Harazsti, Dupuy and Rousseau – what we have termed as alternative (a) – namely that the determining factor for "the ordinary meaning" is historical language, and this language only. As I have attempted to show, strong arguments can be made against this view. First, it seems to run counter to the object and purpose of the Vienna Convention. Second, it appears to be in conflict with the practice of international courts and tribunals. My conclusion is that alternative (a) should be discarded. A more accurate picture of the current legal state-of-affairs is that expressed by commentators such as Villiger and the Institute for International Law.

That is not to say that I can fully accept what this last group of commentators have to offer. What Villiger and the Institute for International Law imply is that an applier – depending on the circumstances – has the possibility of taking into account both historical and contemporary language. Neither commentator, however, can tell us exactly the circumstances under which the applier shall employ the one language or the other. In my view this position is all too cautious. This is a proposition I will now try to establish.

5 REGARDING THE PROBLEM CAUSED BY TEMPORAL VARIATION IN LANGUAGE (CONT'D)

Quite a few things have already been said about the different types of references and their various uses. We have noted that of pure necessity an utterer's possibilities for singular and general references, but not for generic ones, are limited by the linguistic conventions adhered to on the occasion of utterance. The possibilities for generic reference are limited by the conventions adhered to on the occasion of utterance, on the condition that the referent is one the utterer assumes is unalterable. If the referent is one assumed to be alterable, the referring possibilities are limited by the conventions adhered to at any given moment. Already on this basis it is possible, at least, to assume the content of international law:

> If it can be shown, that the thing interpreted is a generic referring expression with a referent assumed to be alterable, then the decisive factor for determining "the ordinary meaning" of the expression shall be contemporary language. In all other cases, the decisive factor shall be historical language.

The judicial opinions expressed in the *La Bretagne Arbitration* and *Namibia* cases seem to amount to a confirmation of my hypothesis. According to the arbitration tribunal in *La Bretagne*, the expression "fishery regulations" is a generic referring expression.

In stipulating that "Canadian fishery regulations shall be applied without discrimination in fact or in law to the French fishing vessels" ... the authors of the 1972 Agreement used the term "fishery regulations" as a generic formula covering all the rules applicable to fishing activities [...].[100]

And not only that – it is a generic referring expression with a referent assumed by France and Canada to be dynamic.

[A]s this expression was embodied in an agreement concluded for an unlimited duration, it is hardly conceivable that the Parties would have sought to give it an invariable content.[101]

So, the expression must be assumed to refer to rules for the application and granting of fishing licences, irrespective of the fact that when the agreement was concluded, the term FISHERY REGULATIONS, according to conventional language, referred only to those regulations applicable to the enterprise of fishery as such.

Accordingly, in view of the subsequent evolution of international law respecting maritime fisheries, the rules to which the expression refers must not only be taken to be those setting technical standards for the physical conditions in which the fishing is carried on but also those requiring the completion of certain formalities prior to the performance of these activities — [although] at the time of the conclusion of the Agreement, the fishery regulations in force in various States usually confined themselves to specifying forbidden fishing zones or closed seasons, permitted fishing gear and equipment, and the types, age and size of the species that could be caught, the scope of fishery regulations has since been enlarged [...].[102]

Less clear is the opinion delivered by the International Court of Justice in *Namibia*. What the Court says, first of all, is that it is aware that the ultimate purpose of interpreting a treaty is to establish its utterance meaning; second, that the terms contained in the League Covenant, at the conclusion of the Covenant – according to the language employed at that point – stood for something, which is by definition evolutionary; and third, that this is accordingly the manner, in which the parties to the Covenant, too, must be assumed to have used these terms.

Mindful as it is of the primary necessity of interpreting an instrument in accordance with the intentions of the parties at the time of its conclusion, the Court is bound to take into account the fact that the concepts embodied in Article 22 of the Covenant – "the strenuous conditions of the modern world" and "the well-being and development" of the peoples concerned – were not static, but were by definition evolutionary, as also, therefore, was the concept of the "sacred trust". The parties to the Covenant must consequently be deemed to have accepted them as such.[103]

On the whole, however, this seems to amount to the very same thing as saying that the expressions in question are generic referring expressions whose referents the Covenant parties – at the conclusion of the Covenant – assumed would come to alter. After all, only generic referring expressions can be said to stand for something which is "by definition evolutionary". Hence, the following conclusion: for the interpretation of the expression "a sacred trust", the court must take as its starting-point the language of international law, considering the law applicable at the time of interpretation, and not the law applicable in 1919, when the League Covenant was concluded.

That is why, viewing the institutions of 1919, the Court must take into consideration the changes which have occurred in the supervening half-century, and its interpretation cannot remain unaffected by the subsequent development of law, through the Charter of the United Nations and by way of customary law.[104]

Now, the decisive question is whether the judicial opinions expressed in *La Bretagne* and *Namibia* are in themselves sufficient to conclusively substantiate my working hypothesis. On the positive side, at least with regard to the decision in *La Bretagne*, the reasoning expressed is unusually detailed and clear – a fact that makes the decision a particularly weighty argument. On the negative side, two decisions hardly constitute a very persuasive body of evidence. In my opinion, the opinions expressed in the *La Bretagne* and *Namibia cases* do allow for certain conclusions; but the conclusions are not very strong, and it would be beneficial if we could find further evidence to support what we have come up with. The problem is that few international decisions even address the problem caused by temporal variation in language. In the period from 1969 to the present, I have found only five such decisions, of which two have already been cited. The other three are the ICJ judgment in the *Case Concerning Kasikili/Sedudu Island*, and the international awards in the *Young Loan* and *Guinea – Guinea-Bissau Maritime Delimitation* cases, respectively. These latter decisions, however, differ from the former insofar as the language used is historical and not contemporary language. Therefore, these cases could be cited as support for the proposition that the decisive factor for determining "the ordinary meaning" is historical language, and this language only.[105] As I explained earlier, it is my conclusion that this proposition is not tenable. Hence, it appears it is up to me to show that the norm I have adopted can be reconciled with the judgment in the *Case Concerning Kasikili/Sedudu Island*, and the two international awards in the *Young Loan* and *Guinea – Guinea-Bissau Maritime Delimitation* cases.

Let us begin with the judgment of the ICJ in the *Kasikili/Sedudu Island*. This case has already been discussed in this chapter,[106] and I see no need for unnecessary repetition. As we know, the dispute involved the meaning of a written agreement, concluded in the year 1890 by the former colonial powers Germany and the United Kingdom. In article 3, paragraph 2, of the Anglo-German agreement, we find the following provision:

In Southwest Africa the sphere in which the exercise of influence is reserved to Germany is bounded:

2. To the east be a line commencing at the above-named point, and following the 20th degree of east longitude to the point of its intersection by the 22nd parallel of south latitude; it runs eastward along that parallel to the point of its intersection by the 21st degree of east longitude; thence it follows that degree northward to the point of its intersection by the 18 parallel of south latitude; it runs eastward along that parallel till it reaches the river Chobe, and descends the centre of the main channel [in the German agreement text: *"im Thalweg des Hauptlaufes"*] of that river to its junction with the Zambesi, where it terminates.[107]

The question arose whether the two expressions "*Thalweg des Hauptlaufes*" and "centre of the main channel" could be understood to refer to one single referent or not. The first measure taken by the Court was to interpret the provision "in accordance with the ordinary meaning to be given to the terms of the treaty". To this end, the Court brings attention to what appears to be the language of international law employed at the time of interpretation:

The Court notes that various definitions of the term "Thalweg" are found in treaties delimiting boundaries and that the concepts of the Thalweg of watercourse and the centre of a watercourse are not equivalent. The word "Thalweg" has variously been taken to mean "the most suitable channel for navigation" on the river, the line "determined by the line of deepest soundings", or "the median line of the main channel followed by boatmen travelling downstream". Treaties or conventions which define boundaries in watercourses nowadays usually refer to the Thalweg as the boundary when the watercourse is navigable and to the median line between the two banks when it is not, although it cannot be said that practice has been fully consistent.[108]

The Court proceeds with an analysis based on historical language:

The Court further notes that at the time of the conclusion of the 1890 Treaty, it may be that the terms "centre of the [main] channel" and *"Thalweg des Hauptlaufes"* were used interchangeably. In this respect, it is of interest to note that, some three years before the conclusion of the 1890 Treaty, the Institut de droit international stated the following in Article 3, paragraph 2, of the "Draft concerning the international regulation of fluvial navigation", adopted at Heidelberg on 9 September 1887: "The boundary of States separated by a river is indicated by the thalweg, that is to say, the median line of the channel" (*Annuaire de l'Institut de droit international*, 1887–1888, p. 182), the term "channel" being understood to refer to the passage open to navigation in the bed of the river, as is clear from the title of the draft.[109]

After which the Court presents its conclusion:

The Court will accordingly treat the words "centre of the main channel" in Article III, paragraph 2, of the 1890 Treaty as having the same meaning as the words "Thalweg des Hauptlaufes" [...].[110]

Apparently, the factor considered by the Court as decisive for determining "the ordinary meaning" of the expression *"Thalweg des Hauptlaufes"* is historical language. In order for this view to be reconciled with the conclusion I have drawn earlier, certain conditions must be met. More specifically, it must be established that *"Thalweg des Hauptlaufes"* is either a singular or general referring expression, or a generic referring expression with a referent assumed to be unalterable. As it appears, these conditions are indeed fulfilled. *"Thalweg des Hauptlaufes"* in the sense of the Anglo-German treaty seems to be a singular referring expression. The phrase is articulated in the definite singular, and it is used to express a time-bound proposition – the existence of the referent is located to a specific point in time, namely the occasion at which the Anglo-German treaty was concluded. After all, the whole point of entering into a boundary agreement is to establish once and for all the location of a common boundary. Hence, it is all in due order if an applier uses the language of 1890, and not that of 1998, in determining what is to be "the ordinary meaning" of the expression *"Thalweg des Hauptlaufes"*.

Another case already touched upon in this chapter is *the Guinea – Guinea-Bissau Maritime Delimitation.*[111] As we know, the dispute in this case centred on the meaning of a boundary treaty, concluded in 1886 by the two colonial powers France and Portugal. Article 1 of the treaty provides:

> In Guinea, the *boundary* separating the Portuguese possessions from the French possessions will follow, in accordance with the course indicated on Map number 1 attached to the present Convention:
>
> To the north, a line which, starting from Cape Roxo, will remain as much as possible, according to the lay of the land at equal distance from the Cazamance (Casamansa) and San Domingo de Cacheu (Sao Domingos de Cacheu) rivers, up to the intersection of the meridian of 17° 30' longitude west of Paris with parallel of 12° 40' north latitude. Between this point and the meridian of 16° longitude west of Paris, the *boundary* will conform to parallel of 12° 40' north latitude.
>
> To the east, the *boundary* will follow the meridian of 16° west, from parallel 12° 40' north latitude to the parallel of 11° 40' north latitude.
>
> To the south, the *boundary* will follow a line starting from the estuary of the Cajet River, located between Catack Island (which will belong to Portugal) and Tristao Island (which will belong to France), and following the lay of the land, it will remain, as much as possible, at equal distance from the Rio Componi (Tabati) and the Rio Cassini, then from the northern branch of the Rio Componi (Tabati) and the southern branch of the Rio Cassini (Marigot de Kakondo) first and the Rio Grande afterwards. It will end at the intersection of the meridian of 16° west longitude and the parallel of 11° 40' north latitude.
>
> Shall belong to Portugal all islands located between the Cape Roxo meridian, the coast and the southern *limit* represented by a line which will follow the thalweg of the Cajet River, and go in a southwesterly direction through the Pilots' Pass to reach 10° 40' north latitude, which it will follow up to the Cape Roxo meridian.[112]

The question was whether France and Portugal, by adopting this text, could be assumed to have established a general maritime boundary delimiting their respective possessions in West Africa at the time. The Court observes:

The disagreement stems first of all from the meaning to be given to the word *limit*: Guinea holds that it is synonymous with *boundary* and remarks that it is generally used in this sense in maritime affairs, whereas Guinea-Bissau gives it a less precise meaning in this case. The Tribunal observes that the two expressions must be taken here in their spatial sense, with due regard to their legal connotations. In French as in Portuguese, and according to the definitions provided by linguistic or legal dictionaries, mentioned or not mentioned by the Parties, they are slightly ambiguous. First of all, they can mean either a zone, especially in the plural, or a line, which is of course the case here. Secondly, the word *limit* can have two meanings, a general one and a more specific one. This appears in particular in a French dictionary contemporaneous with the signature of the 1886 Convention, the *Dictionnaire général de la langue française du commencement du XVIIe siècle jusqu'à nos jours* (the General Dictionary of the French language from the beginning of the 17th century to today), by Hatzfeld and Darmesteter, which defines *limit* as the "extreme part where a territory, a domain ends", and *boundary* as the "limit which separates the territory of a State from that of a neighboring State".[113]

It is not stated expressly, but the implication is clear enough: the factor considered by the Court as decisive for determining "the ordinary meaning" of the expressions "boundary" and "limit" is the language adhered to in 1886. Neither "boundary" nor "limit" is a generic referring expression with a referent assumed to be alterable. "[B]oundary" and "limit", in the sense of the Franco-Portuguese treaty, both appear to be definite singular referring expressions. The words are articulated in the definite singular; they are used to express time-bound propositions – the existence of the referent is located to a specific point in time, namely the occasion on which the treaty is concluded. Hence, it is all in due order if an applier uses the language of 1886, and not that of 1985, in determining what is to be "the ordinary meaning" of the two expressions "boundary" and "limit".

The *Young Loan Case* was dealt with in Section 2 of this chapter.[114] As we know, an issue of dispute in this case was the meaning of the 1953 *London Debt Agreement* (LDA) and the expression therein: "the least depreciated currency" – *"la devise la moins dépréciée"* – *"der Währung mit der geringsten Abwertung"*. I quote from annex 1(A), article 2(e), of the agreement:

Should the rates of exchange ruling any of the currencies of issue on 1 August 1952, alter thereafter by 5 *per cent.* or more, the instalments due after that date, while still being made in the currency of the country of issue, shall be calculated on the basis of *the least depreciated currency* (in relation to the rate of exchange current on 1 August 1952) reconverted into the currency of issue at the rate of exchange current when the payment in question becomes due.

Au cas où les taux de change en vigueur le 1er août 1952 entre deux ou plusieurs monnaies d'émission subiraient par la suite une modification égale ou supérieure à 5% les versements exigibles après cette date, tout en continuant à être effectués dans la monnaie du pays d'émission, seront calculés sur la base de *la devise la moins dépréciée* par rapport au taux de change en vigeur au 1er août 1952, puis reconvertis dans la monnaie d'émission sur la base du taux de change en vigeur lors de l'échéance du paiement.

Sollte sich der am 1. August 1952 für eine der Emissionswährungen massgebende Wechselkurs später um 5. v. H. oder mehr ändern, so sind die nach diesem Zeitpunkt fälligen Raten zwar nach wie vor in der Währung des Emissionslandes zu leisten; sie sind jedoch auf der Grundlage *der Währung mit der geringsten Abwertung* (im Verhältnis zu dem Wechselkurs vom 1. August 1952) zu berechnen und zu dem im Zeitpunkt der Fälligkeit der betreffenden Zahlung massgebenden Wechselkurs wieder in die Emissionswährung umzurechnen.[115]

The question arose as to whether a comparison of the three authenticated language versions of the treaty revealed a difference in meaning that could not be removed by applying Vienna Convention articles 31–32. The tribunal starts its attempt to pin down the meaning of the treaty by first resorting to conventional language. To establish conventional language, the tribunal takes assistance from a number of texts, including Gabler's *Banklexikon*, published 1979; Carreau's *Souveraineté et Cooperation Monétaire Internationale*, published 1970; Carreau, Juillard and Flory's *Droit International Economique*, published 1978; Hirschberg's *The Impact of Inflation and Devaluation on Obligations*, published 1976; and *The International Monetary Fund*, published in 1969 by Horsefield.[116] The conclusion is that in all three languages the words DEPRECIATION, DÉPRÉCIATION, ABWERTUNG are ambiguous.

The possibility of the German and English or French texts of the disputed clause having different meanings cannot therefore be ruled out.[117]

After this, the tribunal apparently finds it necessary to further reinforce its conclusion:

In the Tribunal's view, the uncertainty arising from a – possible – discrepancy between the texts is not removed if, for interpretation purposes, reference is made to the meaning generally attached to the terms "depreciation" and *dépréciation* at the time the LDA was concluded, *i.e.* in 1952.

Despite the wording of Article 31 (1) of VC[L]T, its intentions might still be met if even today an attempt to determine the "objectified" will of the parties, as expressed in the text of the treaty, were based on the normal significance of the terms used at the time the treaty was concluded. (*Cf. e.g. Case Concerning Rights of U.S. Nationals in Morocco, I.C.J. Reports* 1952, p. 189; McNair, *The Law of Treaties*, Oxford 1961, p. 467; Rousseau, *Droit International Public*, Vol. 1, Paris 1970, p. 281.)

There should not be any doubt that when the LDA was concluded, *i.e.* at a time when the international monetary order was generally characterized by a system of fixed parities agreed with the IMF, and not, as now, by a network of floating, continuously changing exchange rates, the terms "depreciation", "devaluation", *dépréciation* and *dévaluation* usually described the same situation, since any depreciation of a currency in its external relations, in accordance with the system, constitutes a devaluation. How closely these concepts drew together can even be seen from the original wording of the Articles of Agreement of the IMF itself. When Article I (iii) speaks of "'competitive' exchange depreciation", in view of the fixed, the agreed parities, all that could be referred to here is devaluation by act of government.

However, the Tribunal is convinced that the circumstances mentioned are an insufficient reason for having to reduce at the time of the conclusion of the treaty the terms "depreciation" and *dépréciation* to the meaning of the German word *Abwertung*. Even at that time, there was some uncertainty in the use of the terms both in English and in French.[118]

It is not expressly stated, but the implication is clear enough: the factor considered by the tribunal as decisive for determining "the ordinary meaning" of the expressions "the least depreciated currency", *"la devise la moins dé préciée", "der Währung mit der geringsten Abwertung"* is the language used in 1952. None of the expressions are generic referring expressions with a referent assumed to be alterable. The expressions "the least depreciated currency", *"la devise la moins dé préciée"*, and *"der Wä hrung mit der geringsten Abwertung"*, in the sense of the LDA, appear to be indefinite, singular referring expressions. The phrases are articulated in the definite singular, but they do not refer to a particular currency; rather, they refer to any currency from a given set of currencies. The propositions they express are time-bound – the existence of the referent is located to specific occasions, i.e. those occasions on which interest is to be paid.[119] Hence, it would stand to reason if an applier used the language of 1952, and not that of 1980, in determining what is to be "the ordinary meaning" of the expressions "the least depreciated currency", *"la devise la moins dé préciée"*, and "*der Währung mit der geringsten Abwertung*".

These three decisions – *Kasikili/Sedudu Island*, *Young Loan* and *Guinea/Guinea-Bissau Maritime Delimitation* – can of course be read in different ways; this is a fact from which we must not shy away. According to a first reading, "the ordinary meaning", in the opinion held by the tribunals, refers to historical language, since the thing interpreted is a singular referring expression. According to a second reading, "the ordinary meaning", in the opinion of the tribunals, refers to historical language, since other languages can *never* be used for determining that meaning. Taken out of context, therefore, the decisions must be seen as arguments carrying very little weight. Nevertheless is it my judgment that through these three decisions, we find further support for the conclusion I wish to confirm. As I have explained, few international decisions even broach the problem caused by temporal variation in language. From 1969 and onward, I have found only five such decisions: *La Bretagne*, *Namibia*, *Kasikili/Sedudu Island*, *Guinea/Guinea-Bissau Maritime Delimitation* and *Young Loan*. The first two provide us with arguments that clearly support my conclusion. The remaining three are ambiguous. Hence, we can say that from 1969 onward, not a single judicial opinion has been expressed that clearly contradicts our conclusion. Certainly, this is a fact of considerable argumentative value.

6 CONCLUSIONS

According to VCLT article 31 § 1, a treaty shall be interpreted in good faith "in accordance with the ordinary meaning to be given to the terms of the treaty". The purpose of this chapter, as earlier stated, in to describe what this means. Based on the observations made above, the following rule of interpretation can be established:

Rule no. 1

§ 1. If it can be shown that in a treaty provision, there is an expression whose form corresponds to an expression of conventional language, then the provision shall be understood in accordance with the rules of that language.

§ 2. For the purpose of this rule, CONVENTIONAL LANGUAGE means the language employed at the time of the treaty's conclusion, except for those cases where § 3 applies.

§ 3. For the purpose of this rule, CONVENTIONAL LANGUAGE means the language employed at the time of interpretation, on the condition that it can be shown that the thing interpreted is a generic referring expression with a referent assumed by the parties to be alterable.

§ 4. For the purpose of this rule, PARTIES means any and all states for which the treaty is in force at the time of interpretation.

NOTES

1. See e.g. Amerasinghe, p. 191; *Oppenheim's International Law*, pp. 1272–1275; Ost, pp. 288ff.; Sinclair, 1984, pp. 121ff.; Bernhardt, 1984, p. 322; Bos, 1984, p. 147; Yasseen, pp. 19ff.; Rest, p. 144; Lang, pp. 155ff.; Köck, pp. 86ff.; Jacobs, passim; Briggs, p. 708.
2. In older literature, applying principles of etymology is sometimes referred to as a legitimate method of interpretation. (See e.g. Sørensen, 1946, pp. 222–223; Ehrlich, pp. 105–106.)
3. In the language of linguistics, a LEXICON is the total number of words and lexicalised phrases in a language. An important distinction to be made is that between "words" and "word forms". A word often has several different forms of inflection. Among these different inflectional forms of a word, normally one is conventionally used and regarded as its "citation-form", representing the word as a composite whole. In a lexicon the "citation-form" of a word is usually the only inflectional form addressed; LEXEMES is the technical term used for these units. A "lexicalised phrase" is a standard phrase, such as THE UNITED NATIONS.

4. The underlying system of rules for a language is normally divided into morphological, syntactical, pragmatic, and *phonological* rules. Phonological rules describe how sounds in a language are formed and combined. In this work, attention is focused on those rules that apply only to written language. Hence, phonology can be disregarded here.
5. Article 5 § 2.
6. See e.g. *Starke's International Law*, p. 435; Bos, 1984, p. 147; Haraszti, p. 83.
7. Another commonly used term is LITERAL INTERPRETATION. (See Bernhardt, 1984, p. 322; Davidson, p. 135; Ost, p. 288; O'Connell, p. 255.) I am not completely certain how to understand this term. In one sense, LITERAL INTERPRETATION can be taken as synonymous with a reading of a text word-for-word; but this is certainly not an adequate way of characterising the interpretation of a treaty "in accordance with the ordinary meaning to be given to the terms of the treaty". In another sense, LITERAL INTERPRETATION can be taken as synonymous to a reading of a text based on its *literal, and not figurative or symbolic*, meaning; what this might mean in the context of treaty interpretation is beyond me. If a single all-encompassing term shall be used to describe the task performed by an applier when interpreting a treaty provision "in accordance with the ordinary meaning to be given to the terms of the treaty", the most appropriate is LINGUISTIC INTERPRETATION. (Cf. e.g. Voïcu, pp. 41–43; Bernhardt, 1967, p. 497.)
8. Usually, the grammar of a language is defined also to include phonology. In this work, our attention is focused on the written aspects of a language. This allows us to disregard phonology.
9. See, for example, R.A. Hudson, passim; Trudgill, passim.
10. Obviously, it is a simplification to speak of *everyday language* as a unified concept. Even in everyday language, people express themselves in different ways, depending on such factors as region of residence, social status, gender, age, and ethnicity. (See e.g. Hudson, passim; Trudgill, passim.) When used here, the term EVERYDAY LANGUAGE shall be understood as the language normally taught in schools, used in daily newspapers, and applied in similar public contexts. This language, whose character – let it be realised – is rather formal, is what most people consider as some sort of standard. In reality, it is merely one variety among many, though of course it is still of special significance.
11. In the language of sociolinguistics, these varieties are often referred to as REGISTERS. (See e.g. Holmes, pp. 276–283.)
12. See Trudgill, p. 123; Holmes, p. 276.
13. See Trudgill, passim.
14. See e.g. Sinclair, 1984, p. 126; Rest, p. 150. In the early drafts of the current article 31 § 4, this relationship was brought out more clearly. See Draft Articles With Commentaries (1964): "Notwithstanding the provisions of paragraph 1 of article 69, a meaning other than its ordinary meaning may be given to a term if it is established conclusively that the parties intended the term to have that special meaning." (*ILC Yrbk*, 1964, Vol. 2, p. 199, draft article 71.) The fact that the provision eventually came to have a different wording is said to have been the result of nothing else than the authors' desire to simplify earlier versions. (See Yasseen, speaking as Chairman of the ILC Drafting Committee, at the Eighteenth Session, 883rd meeting of the International Law Commission, *ILC Yrbk*, 1966, Vol. 1, Part 2, p. 267, § 94 cf. § 90.) Waldock's drafts from both 1964 and 1966 contain a corresponding clarification. (See Third Report on the Law of Treaties, *ILC Yrbk*, 1964, Vol. 2, p. 52, draft article 70

§ 3; Sixth Report on the Law of Treaties, *ILC Yrbk*, 1966, Vol. 2, pp. 100–101, draft article 69 § 2.)
15. Haraszti, p. 86. (My italics.)
16. Yasseen, pp. 27–28. (Footnotes omitted.)
17. Ruda, at the Sixteenth Session of the International Law Commission, 766th meeting, *ILC Yrbk*, 1964, Vol. 1, p. 283, §§ 9, 11. (My italics.)
18. Rest, p. 144, n. 2.
19. Gottlieb, p. 131.
20. See Ch.10 of this work.
21. Draft Articles with Commentaries (1966), *ILC Yrbk*, 1966, Vol. 2, p. 222, § 17.
22. In addition to the decisions directly cited in the body text, see also *Bosnia Genocide*, § 162; *Bankovic*, §§ 59–62; *La Bretagne Arbitration*, *ILR*, Vol. 82, p. 613; *Lithgow and Others*, *Publ. ECHR*, Ser. A, Vol. 102, pp. 47–48, §§ 113–114; *James and Others*, *Publ. ECHR*, Ser. A, Vol. 98, p. 38, §§ 60–61; *Schiesser*, *Publ. ECHR*, Ser. A, Vol. 34, p. 12, § 28. See also diss. op. Pharand, *La Bretagne Arbitration*, *ILR*, Vol. 82, pp. 659–660, § 70; joint sep. op. Aldrich, Holzmann and Mosk, and joint sep. op. Kashani and Shafeiei, on the Issue of the Disposition of Interest Earned on the Security Account, *Iran-United States*, *A/1*, *ILR*, Vol. 68, pp. 546 resp. 550–552.
23. Case Concerning Kasikili/Sedudu Island (Botswana/Namibia), Judgment of 13 December 1999, ICJ Reports, 1999(II), p. 1045 et seq.
24. In the judgment of the Court, this agreement is referred to simply as "the Anglo-German Agreement of 1 July 1890".
25. The text provided here is that cited by the court. (See § 21 of the judgment.)
26. Ibid., §§ 22–23.
27. Ibid., § 20. (The quoted text originates from the judgment delivered by the ICJ in *Territorial Dispute (Libya/Chad)*, *ICJ Reports*, 1994, pp. 21–22, § 41.)
28. Ibid., §§ 24–25.
29. My emphasis.
30. *Asian Agricultural Products Ltd v. Republic of Sri Lanka* , Award of 27 June 1990, *ILR*, Vol. 106, pp. 417ff.
31. Agreement for the Promotion and Protection of Investments, signed on 13 February 1980.
32. The text cited is that provided by the arbitration tribunal. (See *ILR*, Vol. 106, pp. 478–479.)
33. Ibid., p. 443, § 46 cf. m. § 38.
34. Ibid., p. 443, §§ 47–48.
35. Ibid., p. 444, § 49. (My italics.)
36. Guinea – Guinea-Bissau Maritime Delimitation Case, Award of 14 February 1985, *ILR*, Vol. 77, pp. 636ff.
37. Convention on the Delimitation of French and Portuguese Possessions in West Africa, Signed on 12 May 1886. Note that the text cited is the English translation of the Convention published in *International Law Reports*. The Convention was authenticated in French and Portuguese only. For the authenticated French text, see *Archives Diplomatiques*, Vol. 24 (1887), pp. 5ff.
38. *ILR*, Vol. 77, p. 661, § 46.
39. Ibid., p. 662, § 46.
40. Loc. cit.

41. The Kingdom of Belgium, The French Republic, The Swiss Confederation, The United Kingdom and The United States of America v. The Federal Republic of Germany, Award of 16 May 1980, *ILR*, Vol. 59, pp. 495ff.
42. Agreement on German External Debts, Signed at London, on 27 February 1953.
43. *ILR*, Vol. 59, pp. 530–531, § 18.
44. Ibid., p. 530, § 18.
45. See e.g. Bynon, passim.
46. In addition to the authorities directly cited in the body text, see also Vitányi, p. 52; Bernhardt, 1963, pp. 74–75; Fitzmaurice, 1957, p. 212.
47. Haraszti, p. 89.
48. Rousseau, p. 282.
49. Dupuy, p. 220. (Footnotes omitted.)
50. In addition to the authorities directly cited in the body text, see also Waldock, Sixth Report on the Law of Treaties, *ILC Yrbk*, 1966, Vol. 2, pp. 95–96, § 7, p. 97, §13.
51. Villiger, p. 343.
52. Ibid., n. 169.
53. Résolution adoptée par l'Institut de droit international à la session de Wiesbaden, I. Le problème intertemporel en droit international public, 11 août 1975, § 4, *Annuaire de l'Institut de droit international*, Vol. 56, p. 538.
54. See Ch. 2, Section 1, of this work.
55. Note that in linguistics, the use of this term (REFERENCE) is not always consistent.
56. Cf. Lyons, 1977, p. 174. Note that it is the utterer who invests the expression with reference. Clearly, in terms of explanation and discussion, it makes things easier if we can say that an expression refers to its referent. Hence, this is the terminology I will use in this work. However, it is important that we do not forget what we actually mean when we say that a certain expression refers to a certain phenomenon, namely that a certain speaker or author (or a certain group of speakers or writers) has used the expression to refer to the phenomenon in question.
57. The assumption is implied by Dupuy in the utterance cited above, but it can also be noted in the writings of others. Judge Van Wyk, for example, writes in his dissenting opinion to the judgment delivered by the International Court of Justice in the *South West Africa Cases (Preliminary Objections)*: "As the object of interpretation is to arrive at the intention which existed when the agreement was recorded, it follows that words or phrases must be given that meaning which they bore at the time when the instrument in question was executed." (*ILR*, Vol. 37, p. 190.) This very same way of thinking is expressed by Yasseen in even more detail: "La langue peut évoluer, le sens des mots peut s'élargir, se préciser et, dans un certain mesure, changer. Toutefois, du point de vue linguistique, les mots sont employés dans le sens qu'ils ont eu à l'époque de leur emploi, autrement on fera dire à ceux qui ont parlé ce qu'ils n'ont pas voulu dire et plus encore ce qu'ils n'ont pas pu dire. Il serait artificiel de prêter aux parties l'intention d'avoir, du point de vue linguistique, employé les mots dans un sens évolutif. Il est difficile en effet de présumer que les parties aux traités ont employé, du point de vue linguistique, les mots dans le sens inconnu et peut-être imprévisible que les mots pourraient acquérir dans l'avenir." (Yasseen, pp. 26–27; Footnote omitted.)
58. See Lyons, 1977, p. 177.
59. See ibid., p. 177.
60. See ibid., pp. 177–197.
61. See ibid., p. 178.

62. Special Agreement, signed at Bissau, on 18 February 1983, Article 5 § 1. (The text cited is that provided by the arbitration tribunal. See *ILR*, Vol. 77, p. 643, § 1.)
63. See Lyons, 1977, p. 178.
64. Article 1 § 1. (The text cited is that provided by the Court. See *ILR*, Vol. 77, p. 642, § 1.)
65. Article 4.
66. See Lyons, 1977, pp. 193–197.
67. See ibid., p. 194.
68. Loc. cit.
69. See ibid., p. 680.
70. Cf. ibid., pp. 158–161.
71. Loc. cit.
72. I let it remain unsaid, whether the referent in this case is defined extensionally or intensionally – or possibly extensionally *and* intensionally. (Cf. Lyons, 1977, pp. 207–208.)
73. See Section 5 of this chapter.
74. See Section 4 of this chapter.
75. Dispute Concerning Filleting within the Gulf of St Lawrence (Canada/France), Award of 17 July 1986, *ILR*, Vol. 82, pp. 591ff.
76. Agreement between Canada and France on their Mutual Fishing Relations, signed at Ottawa, on 27 March 1972.
77. The text cited is that provided by the arbitration tribunal. (See *ILR*, Vol. 82, p. 601.)
78. Ibid., pp. 617–618, § 35.
79. Ibid., p. 618, § 36.
80. Ibid., pp. 619–620, § 37. (Footnote omitted.)
81. Legal Consequences for States of the Continued Presence of South Africa in Namibia (South West Africa) Notwithstanding Security Council Resolution 276 (1970), Advisory Opinion of 21 June 1971, *ILR*, Vol. 49, pp. 3ff.
82. Covenant of the League of Nations, article 22 § 6.
83. International Status of South-West Africa, Advisory Opinion of 11 July 1950, ICJ Reports, 1950, pp. 128ff.
84. See UNGA res. 2145 (XXI) of October 1966, §§ 3–4.
85. See UNSC res. 284 (1970).
86. See *ILR*, Vol. 49, p. 18, § 45.
87. The text cited is that provided by the Court (ibid.)
88. Ibid., pp. 21–22, §§ 53–54.
89. See e.g. Sinclair, 1984, p. 140; Jiménez de Aréchaga, pp. 48–50; Elias, 1974, pp. 77–78.
90. Similarly, Waldock, 1981, pp. 540–541.
91. See e.g. *Oppenheim's International Law*, p. 1282, n. 35; Thirlway, 1991, pp. 59–60, Cf. Thirlway, 1989, pp. 139–143; Sinclair, 1984, pp. 125–126; Elias, 1980, pp. 296–302.
92. *Aegean Sea Continental Shelf Case (Greece v. Turkey)*, Jurisdiction, Judgment of 19 December 1978, *ILR*, Vol. 60, pp. 512ff.
93. Note that the text cited is a translated version of the original French text used by the ICJ. Both the original text and the English translation are cited in the judgment. (See *ILR*, Vol. 60, pp. 579–580, § 48.)
94. Ibid., p. 591, § 77.
95. Ibid., p. 592, § 78.

96. The reasoning of the Court gives evidence of the simultaneous interpretation of two separate texts. First, the Court is dealing with the meaning of the Greek government's reservation and the expression "the territorial status of Greece". Second, the Court is dealing with the meaning of the 1928 General Act and the expression "rights". Some authors express themselves as if they were assuming that the Court's reasoning concerning the interpretation of the expression "the territorial status of Greece" could, without further reservation, be cited as support for an interpretation of VCLT article 31. Of course, such a position is open to criticism for reasons separate from those here discussed. Certainly, it must not be taken as evident that the rule applied to interpret treaties is the same one used to interpret reservations; quite the opposite. (Cf. *Fishery Jurisdiction (Spain v. Canada), ICJ Reports*, 1998, p. 453, § 46.) For further discussions of this particular issue, see M. Fitzmaurice, 1999, p. 127 et seq.
97. *Webster's New World Dictionary*, Third College Edition.
98. In the practice of international courts and tribunals, further examples can be found of the type of interpretative situation encountered in *Aegean Sea Continental Shelf*. (See e.g. *Canadian Agricultural Tariffs*, *ILR*, Vol. 110, pp. 579–581, §§ 132–138; *Guinea-Bissau v. Senegal*, *ILR*, Vol. 83, pp. 45–46, §§ 84–85.)
99. See p. 85 of this work.
100. See p. 80 of this work.
101. Loc. cit.
102. Loc. cit.
103. See pp. 82–83 of this work.
104. Loc. cit.
105. See e.g., Villiger, p. 343, n. 169.
106. See Section 2 of this chapter.
107. The text given here is the agreement text as cited in the reasons adduced for judgement, § 21.
108. Ibid., § 24.
109. Ibid., § 25.
110. Loc. cit.
111. See Section 2 of this chapter.
112. Note that the text cited is the English translation of the Convention published in *International Law Reports*. (See *ILR*, Vol. 77, pp. 659–660, § 45. My italics.) The Convention was authenticated in French and Portuguese only. For the authenticated French text, see *Archives Diplomatiques*, Vol. 24 (1887), pp. 5ff.
113. *ILR*, Vol. 77, p. 662, § 49. (Footnote omitted.)
114. See Section 2 of this chapter.
115. The text cited is that provided by the arbitration tribunal. (See *ILR*, Vol. 59, p. 514. My italics.)
116. See ibid., pp. 530–531, § 18 (The passage has been cited earlier in this work, see pp. 80–81.)
117. Ibid., p. 531, § 18.
118. Ibid., § 19.
119. I am assuming, of course, that in the terms of the loan, fixed dates were specified for payment of interest.

CHAPTER 4

USING THE CONTEXT: THE "TEXT" OF A TREATY

The purpose of this chapter – together with Chapters 5 and 6 – is to describe what it means to interpret a treaty using the context. Context is defined in article 31, §§ 2–3 of the Vienna Convention. In paragraph 2, we are told what the context is to comprise:

The context, for the purpose of the interpretation of a treaty, shall comprise, in addition to the text, including its preamble and annexes:
(a) any agreement relating to the treaty which was made between all the parties in connexion with the conclusion of the treaty;
(b) any instrument which was made by one or more parties in connexion with the conclusion of the treaty and accepted by the other parties as an instrument related to the treaty.

Paragraph 3 adds three further elements, which – this is how it reads – shall be taken into account "together with the context", namely …

(a) any subsequent agreement between the parties regarding the interpretation of the treaty or the application of its provisions;
(b) any subsequent practice in the application of the treaty which establishes the agreement of the parties regarding its interpretation;
(c) any relevant rules of international law applicable in the relations between the parties.

These further elements are usually also considered as forming part of the context, in the sense of paragraph 1.[1] I have chosen to follow this practice.[2] It is clear that an investigation into the meaning and use of the context will require considerable discussion. Consequently, I have chosen to divide the concept into three parts. In Chapter 4, I shall first attempt to describe what it means to interpret a treaty using the contextual element described as the "text" of the treaty. In Chapter 5, I shall attempt to describe what it means to interpret a treaty using the elements set out in article 31 § 2, subparagraphs (a) and (b). Finally, in Chapter 6, I shall attempt to describe what it means to interpret a treaty using the elements set out in article 31 § 3.

"A treaty shall be interpreted in good faith in accordance with the ordinary meaning to be given to the terms of the treaty in their context" – this is provided in article 31 § 1.

Un traité doit être interprété de bonne foi suivant le sens ordinaire à attribuer aux termes du traité dans leur contexte [...]

Un tratado deberá interpretarse de buena fe conforme al sentido corriente que haya de atribuirse a los términos del tratado en el contexto de éstos [...].

One thing is immediately evident from reading this text. When an applier uses the context in accordance with the provisions of article 31, the context is not considered independently of other means of interpretation. When the context is used, this is always in relation to conventional language ("the ordinary meaning"). Seen from a different perspective, we could say that when the context is used, it is always a second step in the interpretation process.[3] The question has arisen whether a given complex of facts shall be considered as coming within the scope of application of the norm expressed by a certain treaty provision P; and the provision P has been interpreted using conventional language. However, this (very first) introductory act of interpretation has proved to be insufficient. The ordinary meaning of the treaty provision P is either vague or ambiguous – using conventional language leads to conflicting results. Possibly, conventional language has a role to play in the process to an understanding of the provision, but it must then be supplemented by additional means of interpretation. The idea of using the context is that it will serve as such a supplement. Where the ordinary meaning of a treaty provision is vague, using the context will make the text more precise. Where the ordinary meaning is ambiguous, using the context will help to determine which one of several possible meanings is correct, and which one is not. All this is evident from reading VCLT article 31 § 1.[4] What the provision says is *not* that the terms of a treaty shall be interpreted in their context. What the provision says is that a treaty shall be interpreted "in accordance with the ordinary meaning to be given to the terms of the treaty in their context". Hence, a shorthand description of how the context shall be used could look like this:

> If it can be shown that the interpretation of a treaty provision in accordance with interpretation rule no. 1 leads to conflicting results, and that between the provision and the context there is a relationship governed by the communicative standard S, then the provision shall be understood as if the relationship conformed to this standard.

In this chapter – let me repeat – I shall attempt to describe only what it means to interpret a treaty using the contextual element described as the "text" of that treaty. That being the case, in order for the task to be considered accomplished, the following questions must be answered:

(1) What is meant by "the text" of a treaty?
(2) What communicative standard or standards shall the parties to a treaty be assumed to have followed, when an applier interprets the treaty using "the text" of the treaty?

I shall now give what I consider to be the correct answers to these questions. In Section 1, I shall begin by answering question (1). In Sections 2–4 I shall then answer question (2).

1 "[T]HE TEXT"

What is meant by "the text" of a treaty? According to VCLT article 31 § 1 "[t]he context for the purpose of the interpretation of the treaty shall comprise, in addition to the text, including its preamble and annexes ...".

Aux fins de l'interprétation d'un traité, le contexte comprend, outre le texte, préambule et annexes inclus [...].

Para los efectos de la interpretación de un tratado, el contexto comprenderá, además del texto, incluidos su preámbulo y anexos [...].

What is meant by "the text" of a treaty might appear evident and plain. Nevertheless, as far as my experience goes the following two clarifications are certainly not out of place.

First, let it be established as a fact that, in the sense of the Vienna Convention, a TREATY TEXT is not necessarily the same thing as a set of words and sentences. In addition to a body of text – text *stricto sensu* – treaties also often include a variety of non-textual representations, such as maps, tables, and diagrams.[5] When we read article 31 § 2, it is not clearly understood whether representations of this kind shall be counted as part of the "text" of a treaty. The term TREATY TEXT is ambiguous. It can be used first in the sense of *words and sentences used for an international agreement in written form*, but also in the sense of *document where the authentic and definite expression of an international agreement is to be found, as opposed to preparatory work, unauthenticated translations, and other such documents*. In my view it is in the latter sense, and not the former, that the Vienna Convention uses the term TEXT. The alternative must quite simply be considered unreasonable. If a non-textual representation is contained in a treaty, but it cannot be considered part of the context for interpretation purposes, then only if it comes under the provisions of article 32 will the non-textual representation be of significance for the interpretation process. Such a radical hierarchisation of the various parts of a treaty cannot possibly be what the parties to the Vienna Convention wished to achieve.[6]

Second, let it be realised that a TREATY TEXT, in the sense of the Vienna Convention, is not necessarily tantamount to *one* instrument. A treaty is an agreement; and an agreement can (at least in principle) take the form of any number of instruments, and still be considered as one, single treaty text. "Treaty", as provided in Vienna Convention article 2 § 1(a), "means an international agreement concluded between States in written form and governed by international law, *whether embodied in a single instrument or in two or more related instruments*".[7] One obvious example of this is when states enter into an agreement in order to amend a treaty, concluded at some earlier juncture. Naturally, two instruments, of which one entails an amendment of the other, are always to be considered as integral parts of one single treaty.[8] Another example is when negotiating states, already at the process of drafting a treaty, split up the agreement into several instruments, of which one is drawn up to express the bulk of the agreement, and the others are used for adding detail. As one of the more extreme examples of this practice, mention may be made of an agreement concluded by Yugoslavia and Romania, on 31 November 1963.[9] The agreement contains the following provision:

> This Agreement, the Conventions, the Protocols and all the other instruments concluded in connexion with the construction and operation of the Iron Gates System, which are enumerated in the Final Act signed this day, shall constitute a single unit.[10]

Within the scope of the one single treaty, we would consequently be able to count one "Agreement", five "Conventions", four of which with "Annexes" added, one "Charter", two "Protocols", both with "Annexes" and one with an "Addendum", as well as two "*Échanges des Lettres*".[11]

It is not always easy to determine whether two instruments, both of which have been subject to signature, shall be considered as integral parts of a single treaty, or whether they shall be considered as two separate treaties.[12] Of course, a treaty that consists of multiple instruments may itself point this out in an express provision; take for instance the agreement between Yugoslavia and Romania cited above. In cases like this, the issue is easily settled. Problems arise in cases where the treaty is silent on the matter. Two instruments are not necessarily to be regarded as two separate treaties, just because it is not expressly stated that they are to be considered as an integrated whole. The ultimate determining factors for the relationship between two instruments are the intentions of their parties.[13] To determine whether two or more instruments are to be considered as an integrated whole or as two separate treaties, it is evident that a separate process of interpretation might be needed on occasion.[14]

Intimately linked to this discussion is the question how the applier should conduct himself when faced with two instruments, both of which have been separately signed, where the one has been designated as an annex to the other. It is tempting to believe that two instruments, of which the one has been designated as an annex to the other, shall automatically be considered as integral parts of one single treaty. This is not the case. It is true that in VCLT article 31 § 2 annexes are expressly mentioned. However, on a careful reading no more no less is said than this: for interpretation purposes an annex shall be included in the context *when it is a part of the treaty text.*[15] "The context for the purpose of the interpretation of a treaty shall comprise, in addition to the text, including its preamble and annexes..." – this is how the paragraph reads. Now, of course, this must not lead us to the opposite conclusion, that the fact that an instrument has been designated as an annex is of no importance at all. If an applier is uncertain about the relationship holding between two instruments, and the one is designated as an annex to the other, then clearly this is a circumstance that suggests considering the instruments as parts of a single treaty, and not as two separate treaties. But – and this is the point – it is not a circumstance that conclusively determines the matter. There can be other circumstances suggesting the opposite. Such a circumstance is the content of the annex. In the *Guinea – Guinea-Bissau Maritime Delimitation* case,[16] for example, the court of arbitration had been asked to decide on the effect to be attributed to a series of instruments, designated as "annexes" to an almost 100 year-old convention concluded by France and Portugal. Some of the instruments contained maps expressly referred to in the convention; others contained records and documents deriving from the drafting of the convention.[17] The former were said to belong to the context,[18] whereas the latter, in the view of the court, were to be considered as nothing more than preparatory work.[19]

2 "[T]HE TEXT" PUT TO USE

What communicative standard or standards shall the parties to a treaty be assumed to have followed, when an applier interprets the treaty using "the text" of the treaty? Let us begin by better defining our task. As a label of what an applier does when, in accordance with VCLT article 31, she interprets a treaty using the context, authors have often employed the term SYSTEMATIC INTERPRETATION.[20] When an applier uses the context – this is the assumption – the interpreted treaty provision and the context together form a larger whole, a system.[21] Clearly, however, this assumed system is not a uniform concept. In the literature, SYSTEMATIC INTERPRETATION is used to refer to not one system only but two, depending on whether the authors envision the interpreted treaty provision and its context as the *body of text* constituted by the text and its context, or the set of *norms* expressed. In the former case, SYSTEMATIC INTERPRETATION is based on the existence of a linguistic system;[22] in the latter case it is based on the existence of a system in the logical sense.[23] The use of the context has been described earlier in the following manner:

> If it can be shown that the interpretation of a treaty provision in accordance with interpretation rule no. 1 leads to conflicting results, and that between the provision and the context there is a relationship governed by the communicative standard S, then the provision shall be understood as if the relationship conformed to this standard.[24]

This norm can now be more exactly defined:

> If it can be shown that the interpretation of a treaty provision in accordance with interpretation rule no. 1 leads to conflicting results, and that between the norm content of the provision, and the norms forming the context, there is a relationship governed by the communicative standard S, then the provision shall be understood as if the relationship conformed to this standard.

> If it can be shown that the interpretation of a treaty provision in accordance with interpretation rule no. 1 leads to conflicting results, and that between the expressions used for the provision, and the expressions forming the context, there is a relationship governed by the communicative standard S, then the provision shall be understood as if the relationship conformed to this standard.

Obviously, an applier must take into account not only one but several communicative standards when he interprets a treaty provision using the "text" of the treaty. All in all, I have found that as many as five communicative standards can be established; to simplify reference to these, I will denote them using the letters A to E. The standards are of two different types. The one type is represented by standards A, C, and D, which govern the linguistic relationship that shall be assumed to hold between the expressions used for a an interpreted treaty provision and the expressions forming the context. The other type is represented by standards B and E, which govern the logical relationship that shall be assumed to hold between the norm content of an interpreted treaty provision and the norms forming the context. Let us take a closer look at these different standards. We shall examine them in alphabetical order.

Standard A. It is the general view held in the literature that a word or phrase used on multiple occasions in the text of a treaty shall be assumed to bear a uniform meaning.[25] Thus, it is stated by the authors of *Oppenheim's International Law*:

> The same term used in different places in a treaty may be presumed to bear the same meaning in each [...].[26]

Haraszti writes:

> [I]n conformity with the principle developed in international practice the interpreter has to start from the thesis that the parties to the treaty have intended to use uniform terms in a uniform meaning throughout the treaty.[27]

Professor Bernhardt expresses it in more detail:

> Schließlich ist noch ein mehr technischer Aspekt des vertraglichen Zusammenhangs zu erwähnen. Es dürfte eine Vermutung dafür sprechen, daß bei der abschließenden Redaktion

eines Vertrages die Terminologie regelmäßig in der Weise vereinheitlicht wird, daß gleiche Gegenstände in den verschiedenen Vertragsteilen gleich bezeichnet werden und der Interpret daher davon ausgehen kann, daß wiederkehrende Worte und Formulierungen eine übereinstimmende Bedeutung haben.[28]

So, when an applier interprets a treaty using its "text", then this would be on the basis of the following communicative standard:

> If a state makes an utterance taking the form of a treaty provision, then the provision should be drawn up so that the words and phrases used for the provision are given a consistent meaning, considering the words and phrases forming the context.

Standard B. When an applier interprets a treaty using the context – according to a frequent claim – he shall do so on the basis of the assumption that the different parts of the treaty do not contradict one another.[29] For example, Vitányi writes:

> Modern doctrine regards recourse to the context as a particularly effective means of determining the intention of the parties. It is generally accepted that the meaning of treaty provisions whose words lend themselves to different interpretations cannot be settled without reference to the other clauses, but only in the context of the treaty as a whole. The same applies if the different clauses do not fit happily together, in which event it must be presumed that the parties did not intend contradictions but rather that they meant the clauses to explain each other. International jurisprudence has constantly relied upon this method.[30]

However, exactly what type of contradiction the author is referring to remains unsaid. If a contradiction is said to hold between two provisions of a treaty, it can be of different types: it can be pragmatic, logical, teleological, axiological, and so on. I can only conclude that the contradiction meant in this case is a *logical contradiction*. Two reasons, in particular, substantiate this conclusion.[31] First, one of the most fundamental requirements placed on a logical system is that it be free of logical contradictions. If the context is to be used on the assumption that the different norms of a treaty together form a logical system, such use would then also be on the assumption that the different norms are not logically incompatible. Second, few treaties (if any) are created on such premises that each individual provision can be considered self-sufficient. Normally, a treaty is drawn up as an intricate network, where one of two provisions often functions as a normative complement to the other. Perhaps the one provision contains a definition of the expressions used for the other; perhaps the one provision is to be seen as *lex specialis* in relation to the other, being in this case the *lex generalis*; perhaps the one provision contains an exception to the norm expressed by the other; or perhaps the one provision contains some sort of addendum or supplement to the other. No such complementary provision will have effect if we do not assume the treaty to have been drawn up on the premise that its different parts must be logically compatible. When an applier interprets a treaty using its "text", this would then be on the basis of the following communicative standard:

> If a state produces an utterance taking the form of a treaty provision, then the provision should be drawn up, so that it does not logically contradict the context.

Standard C. A treaty shall be interpreted so that none of the expressions used for the treaty take the form of a pleonasm – this is a view generally accepted by the literature.[32] "[A]ll provisions of the treaty", Thirlway observes, ...

> ... must be supposed to have been intended to have significance and to be necessary to convey the intended meaning; ... an interpretation which reduces some part of the text to the status of a pleonasm, or mere surplussage, [sic!] is prima facie suspect.[33]

Haraszti expresses himself in a similar manner:

> "[A] legal text should be interpreted in such a way that a reason and a meaning can be attributed to every word in the text".[34]

Hogg has termed it "the surplus words rule"; he describes the norm as follows:

> The operation of this rule establishes a presumption that, if possible, every word used in a treaty should be given effect — Its application presupposes that there are two words or groups of words in the text; that one of these words or groups of words is susceptible of two or more reasonable meanings; that the text is ambiguous as to which of the meanings was intended by the parties; and that the choice of one of those meanings would deprive the other word or words of all significance.[35]

All things considered, I have difficulty coming to any other conclusion than this: when an applier interprets a provision using "the text" of the treaty, this is *inter alia* on the basis of the following communicative standard:

> If a state produces an utterance taking the form of a treaty provision, then the provision should be drawn up so that in the context there will be no instance of a pleonasm.

Standard D. According to *Oppenheim's International Law*, when an applier interprets a treaty provision using "the text" of the treaty ...

> ... the use of similar but different terms ... may be presumed to involve dissimilar meanings [...].[36]

This is an assumption generally ignored by authors in the literature; unjustly so, it seems – in international judicial opinions it is quite often expressed.[37]

To my mind, however, the practice of international courts and tribunals allows for more precise conclusions than those formulated in Oppenheim's. Certainly, the way the assumption is expressed by Oppenheim's is better than the way the parallel assumption sometimes has been put in general jurisprudence. For example, Peczenik writes: "If different words and expressions appear in one and the same law, one should assume that their meanings are different, if good reasons do not exist to assume the opposite".[38] The subject of the present discussion is a rule of interpretation earlier described using the following model:

> If it can be shown that the interpretation of a treaty provision in accordance with interpretation rule no. 1 leads to conflicting results, and that between the expressions used for the provision, and the expressions forming the context, there is a relationship governed by the communicative standard S, then the provision shall be understood as if the relationship conformed to this standard.[39]

Note the word relationship. From a purely semantic standpoint, I have difficulty accepting that a relationship could exist between two expressions, simply because they represent the use of different words or lexicalised phrases. What exists between two such expressions or phrases is rather the lack of a relationship. I definitely find it more appealing to say, like in Oppenheim's, that a relationship holds between two expressions if they express words or phrases that are *similar* to one another. Of course, the flaw in this formula it is that we still have only a very faint idea of what "similar" means. Two words or phrases can be SIMILAR to one another, if the two agree from a purely graphical point of view (such as LEG and LEGUME); from the point of view of etymology (such as MEET and MEETING); from the point of view of class (such as MULTIPLICATION and QUALIFICATION); from the point of view of style (such as DELICT and EXONERATE); and so on. My conclusion is that two words or phrases are "similar" to one another, insofar as they belong to the *same lexical field.* So, when an applier interprets a provision using "the text" of the treaty, this would be on the basis of the following communicative standard:

> If a state produces an utterance taking the form of a treaty provision, then the provision should be drawn up so that the words and phrases used for the provision do not take on a meaning equal to the meaning of words and phrases found in the context, in so far as the words or phrases are part of the same lexical field.

In Section 3 of this chapter, this is a proposition I will attempt to further clarify.

Standard E. In the legal literature, writers are of the view that a treaty shall be interpreted so that in no instance can superfluities be found to exist;[40]

let us call this THE RULE OF NON-REDUNDANCY. To name one, Thirlway writes:

> [It is a] rule that the whole of the text must be presumed to have some significance, so that an interpretation which would render part of it redundant is to be rejected [...].[41]

Gordon makes the following observation with regard to the practice of the International Court of Justice:

> A twin-forked rule of interpretation constantly mentioned by the Court is (a) that a treaty must be read as a whole to give effect to all of its terms and avoid inconsistency, and (b) that *no word or provision may be treated as or rendered superfluous.*[42]

A passage often cited is that of Fitzmaurice:

> Treaties are to be interpreted with reference to their declared or apparent objects and purposes; and *particular provisions are to be interpreted* so as to give them their fullest weight and effect consistent with the normal sense of the words and with other parts of the text, and *in such a way that a reason and a meaning can be attributed to every part of the text.*[43]

Evidently, we can consider as a part of this rule – the rule of non-redundancy – what we earlier termed as the *surplus words rule.*[44] Some authors appear to take this idea a step further. They seem to consider *the rule of non-redundancy* and *the surplus words rule* as amounting to the very same thing.[45] This is a position I have difficulty supporting. In my view, *the rule of non-redundancy* is broader. In fact, the idea that a treaty shall be interpreted to steer clear of redundancies stands for two different things, depending on whether "redundant" is defined as *linguistically* or *normatively* redundant.[46] First, a treaty provision shall be understood so that in the context there will be no instance of a pleonasm. (A pleonasm occurs when an expression used for a provision fails to carry more information than is already carried by the context.) Secondly, a treaty provision shall be understood so that in the context there will be no instance of a *logical tautology.* (A logical tautology occurs when a norm expressed by a provision is already spelled out in the context – that is, in the text and the context it is stated in multiple places, each independently of the other, that a specific state of affairs shall, may, or should be realised, or – in the alternative – shall not, may not, or should not be realised.) Therefore, in my view, when *the rule of non-redundancy* is applied, it is not only on the basis of the standard earlier denoted as standard C. It is also on the basis of the following standard:

> If a state produces an utterance taking the form of a treaty provision, then the provision should be drawn up so that in the context there will be no instance of a logical tautology.

Support for this conclusion can be found particularly in the practice of international courts and tribunals.[47] In Section 4 of this chapter, I will attempt to establish this proposition.

3 "[T]HE TEXT" PUT TO USE: DIFFERENT WORDS AND PHRASES SHALL (SOMETIMES) BE GIVEN DIFFERENT MEANINGS

To begin with, let us first establish what is meant by a LEXICAL FIELD. The term has its origins in linguistics. More specifically, it has its origins in structural linguistics – that sub-discipline of linguistics committed to the task of studying and describing the relationships between different words and lexical phrases of a language.[48] According to structural linguistics, human language is organised in such a way that a relationship not only holds between the different units of a lexicon and that which they denote. There is also a relationship holding between the lexical units *themselves*; we can talk about the internal structure of a lexicon.[49] This structure, according to the view held by structural linguistics, is an important factor in explaining why words and lexical phrases mean what they mean. The denotation of a word or phrase in a lexicon – this is the central tenet – is at least partially dependent upon the meaning relationships held between the word or phrase and the remainder of the lexicon.[50] For example, the meaning of the term CHERRY RED depends upon the fact that CHERRY RED can be contrasted with MAROON and BURGUNDY. The meaning of the term HOLIDAY depends upon the fact that HOLIDAY can be contrasted with WORKDAYS. The meaning of the word LION depends upon the fact that LION can be contrasted with FELINE. One way to formalise these meaning relationships held between the different units of a lexicon is to break down the lexicon into smaller lexical fields.[51] If a meaning relationship can be said to hold between two words or phrases in a lexicon, then this is because the different concepts represented by the words and phrases are related; the concepts are parts of a single conceptual field. Each individual set of words and phrases, together covering a conceptual field – thanks to the meaning relationships holding between them – can then be called a lexical field.[52] So, for example, we can talk about a lexical field corresponding to the concept *red*; a lexical field corresponding to the concept *days of the week*; a lexical field corresponding to the concept *predators*; and so on.

The point I am trying to make is this. Assume that an applier is given the task to establish the legally correct meaning of a treaty provision. Naturally, her first step would be to use conventional language. According to the legally recognised rules of interpretation, the applier would then be justified in saying that all words used for the provision bear the meaning given to them in conventional language. In a second stage of the interpretation process, the applier notes that in the treaty there are two words, which – while they are not identical – certainly belong to the same lexical field. On the same basis as before – conventional language – the applier would then also be justified in saying that between these two words, in the sense used for the treaty interpreted, there is a meaning relationship. Of course, this observation can be further exploited. All the applier needs to come up with is a communicative assumption concerning the more precise construction of the relationship holding between the two words. This assumption, according to the view presented here, is the following: when two words belong to the same lexical field, their extensions are not identical. When an applier interprets a treaty provision using "the text" of said treaty, it is namely (among other things) on the basis of the following communicative standard, earlier labeled as standard D:

> If a state produces an utterance taking the form of a treaty provision, then the provision should be drawn up so that the words and phrases used for the provision do not take on a meaning equal to the meaning of words and phrases found in the context, insofar as the words or phrases are part of the same lexical field.[53]

As support for this conclusion I would like to point to the practice of international courts and tribunals.[54] Mention can be made of four decisions in particular.

A first decision is the judgment of the European Court of Human Rights in the case of *Brogan and Others*.[55] In 1984, the applicants – four young men, all residents of Northern Ireland – had been arrested by British police. They were detained, suspected of involvement in terrorist activity, until their subsequent release. The detention for each applicant had been 4 days and 6 hours, 4 days and 11 hours, 5 days and 11 hours, and 6 days and 16 and a half hours, respectively. During this time, however, none of the applicants had been brought before a judge or any other judicial authority. The question arose as to whether the United Kingdom, by these actions, had violated the obligations incumbent upon it according to article 5 § 3 of the *European Convention for the Protection of Human Rights and Fundamental Freedoms*:

> Anyone arrested or detained in accordance with the provisions of paragraph 1.c of this article shall be brought promptly [Fr. "*aussitôt*"] before a judge or other officer authorised by law to exercise judicial power and shall be entitled to trial within a reasonable time or to release pending trial. Release may be conditioned by guarantees to appear for trial.

Attention focused on the expression "promptly". Can the time requirement represented by this expression be considered fulfilled, even though a detention has lasted as long as 4 days and 6 hours, 4 days and 11 hours, 5 days and 11 hours, and six days and 16 and a half hours, respectively? In all four cases, the Court denied that this was so. The reasoning of the Court is extensive; it includes several more or less clearly expressed arguments of interpretation. The following line of reasoning appears particularly interesting:

> The obligation expressed in English by the word "promptly" and in French by the word "*aussitôt*" is clearly distinguishable from the less strict requirement in the second part of paragraph 3 ("reasonable time"/ "*délai raisonnable*") and even from that in paragraph 4 of Article 5 ("speedily"/ "*à bref délai*").[56]

The manner of expression is brief, but the message is clear enough. According to what the Court says, the meaning of the expression "promptly" appears more clearly, when it is compared with the expression "within a reasonable time" in article 5 § 3 and with the expression "speedily" in article 5 § 4. Three reasons support this proposition. The first and second reasons are explicitly stated: (1) the correct meaning of "promptly" is not the same as the meaning of either "within a reasonable time" or "speedily"; (2) the time requirement represented by the expression "promptly" is more demanding than that represented by either the expression "within a reasonable time" or the expression "speedily". The third reason is implied: in an earlier decision – that of *De Jong, Baljet and Van den Brink* –[57] the Court found that three Netherlands servicemen who were placed under military arrest for 7, 11, and 6 days, respectively, but who were never given opportunity to appear before a court during their detainment, could not be considered to have had a "speedily" made decision on the lawfulness of their detainment.[58] For our purposes, the decisive question is this: why does the European Court assume that the correct meaning of "promptly" is not the same as that of the expressions "within a reasonable time" or "speedily"? In terms of conventional language, the differences in meaning are not at all clear-cut. It is incontestable that the expression "promptly" represents the use of a different lexical unit than the expressions "within a reasonable time" and "speedily". It is also plain enough that PROMPTLY, WITHIN A REASONABLE TIME, and SPEEDILY are all parts of a single lexical field. More specifically, they are parts of a field corresponding to the conceptual area *time limit (by which something shall be done)*. Thus – and this is of course the obvious answer to our question – it seems to be the assumption of the European Court, that the parties to the Convention have expressed themselves in accordance with the communicative standard D.

The *Handyside* case –[59] also forming part of the repertoire of the European Court for Human Rights – provides an obvious parallel to the interpretative line of reasoning presented by the Court in *Brogan and Others*. Here, the European Court was asked to decide whether British authorities, by seizing from a publisher all copies of a specific book that he had published, had restricted the publisher's right to freedom of expression in violation of the European Convention, article 10. According to article 10 § 2, the right to freedom of expression is subject only to "such formalities, conditions, restrictions or penalties as are prescribed by law and are necessary [Fr. *'necessaire'*] in a democratic society", among other things, "for the protection of health or morals". It was not disputed that a restriction had indeed taken place, and that the restriction had been made on the basis of "law" and for the protection of "morals". The question was whether the restriction could also be said to have been "necessary". This led the court to make the following observation:

> [W]hilst the adjective "necessary", within the meaning of Article 10 § 2, is not synonymous with "indispensible" (cf., in Articles 2 § 2 and 6 § 1, the words "absolutely necessary" and "strictly necessary" and, in Article 15 § 1, the phrase "to the extent strictly required by the exigencies of the situation"), neither has it the flexibility of such expressions as "admissible", "ordinary" (cf. Article 4 § 3), "useful" (cf. [in] the French text of the first paragraph of Article 1 of Protocol No. 1 [the expression "*utile*"]), "reasonable" (cf. Articles 5 § 3 and 6 § 1) or "desirable".[60]

Clearly, in conventional language, one must consider as relatively fluid the boundaries between the extension of "necessary" on the one hand, and the extension of the expression "absolutely necessary" or the expressions "ordinary", "utile" or "reasonable", on the other. Nevertheless, it is obviously the opinion of the European Court that the meanings of the various expressions are not the same. The question is why. Clearly, the expression "necessary" represents the use of a different lexical unit than the expression "absolutely necessary"; the same applies to the expressions "ordinary", "utile" and "reasonable". It is also clear that NECESSARY and ABSOLUTELY NECESSARY, like the words ORDINARY, UTILE and REASONABLE, all belong to a single lexical field. More specifically, they belong to a field corresponding to the conceptual area *necessity*. Once again, it seems to be the assumption of the European Court, that the parties to the European Convention expressed themselves in accordance with the communicative standard D.

A third decision to be mentioned is the decision of the American Supreme Court in the case of *Air France v. Saks*.[61] On 16 November 1980, the plaintiff, Valerie Saks, had boarded an Air France flight in Paris, bound for Los Angeles. The journey proceeded smoothly until the plane started its approach for landing in California. During landing, the plaintiff had experienced extreme pressure and severe pain in one of her ears, which was later stated to have led to permanent deafness. Nevertheless, the plane's automatic pressure stabilisation system was shown to have functioned normally. The plaintiff brought suit in an American court, claiming that the French airline was responsible for the injuries she had suffered. The basis given for the claim was article 17 of the 1929 Warsaw Convention,[62] according to which a carrier is responsible for personal injuries sustained by passengers ...

... if the accident which caused the damage so sustained took place on board the aircraft.[63]

With respect to the meaning of this provision, however, the views of the defendant clearly differed from that of the plaintiff. According to the plaintiff, the expression "accident" should be understood as *hazard of air travel*. According to the defendant, it was to be understood as *abnormal, unusual or unexpected occurrence aboard the aircraft*. The Supreme Court agreed with the defendant, invoking among other things the following argument:

Article 17 of the Warsaw Convention establishes the liability of international air carriers for harm to passengers. Article 18 contains parallel provisions regarding liability for damage to baggage. The governing text of the Convention is in the French language — The official American translation of this portion of the text, which was before the Senate when it ratified the Convention in 1934, reads as follows:

"Article 17
The carrier shall be liable for damage sustained in the event of the death or wounding of a passenger or any other bodily injury suffered by a passenger, *if the accident which caused the damage* so sustained took place on board the aircraft or in the course of any of the operations of embarking or disembarking."

"Article 18
(1) The carrier shall be liable for damage sustained in the event of the destruction or loss of, or of damage to, any checked baggage or any goods, *if the occurrence which caused the damage* so sustained took place during the transportation by air." 49 Stat 3018–3019.

Two significant features of these provisions stand out in both French and the English texts. First, Article 17 imposes liability for injuries to passengers caused by an "accident", whereas Article 18 imposes liability for destruction or loss of baggage caused by an "occurrence". The difference in the parallel language of Article 17 and 18 implies that the drafters of the Convention understood the word "accident" to mean something different than the word "occurrence", for they otherwise logically would have used the same word in each article.[64]

Despite the fact that in this case, a comparison is made involving only two expressions, the one being compared with the other, while in *Brogan and Others* and *Handyside* one expression was compared with *several* others, in principle the line of reasoning seems to be the same. According to conventional language, the meaning of the expression "accident" overlaps completely with the meaning of the expression "occurrence". The word OCCURRENCE stands for any event. The word ACCIDENT is sometimes used in the sense of an *unintentional, unexpected event, being a cause of personal injury or material loss*, and sometimes in the sense of an *unintentional, unexpected event, regardless of cause*. Nevertheless, in the opinion of the Supreme Court, the correct meaning of the expression "accident" is not the same as that of the expression "occurrence": by "accident" in article

17 of the Warsaw Convention we shall understand ACCIDENT only in the sense of *unintentional, unexpected event, being a cause of personal injury or material loss.* How can this opinion be explained? Clearly, "accident" represents the use of a different lexical unit than "occurrence". It is also a matter of fact that the words ACCIDENT and OCCURRENCE belong to a single lexical field; more specifically, they belong to a field corresponding to the conceptual area of *event*. In my view, the answer to the question is this: it is an assumption of the Court, that the parties to the Warsaw Convention expressed themselves in accordance with the communicative standard D.

A fourth decision to be mentioned is the international award in the case of *Guinea – Guinea-Bissau Maritime Delimitation.*[65] The facts of the case have been described in a previous chapter of this work.[66] To avoid unnecessary repetition, I will restate only the text of the treaty relevant to our present discussion:

In Guinea, the *boundary* separating the Portuguese possessions from the French possessions will follow, in accordance with the course indicated on Map number 1 attached to the present Convention:

To the north, a line which, starting from Cape Roxo, will remain as much as possible, according to the lay of the land at equal distance from the Cazamance (Casamansa) and San Domingo de Cacheu (Sao Domingos de Cacheu) rivers, up to the intersection of the meridian of 17° 30' longitude west of Paris with parallel of 12° 40' north latitude. Between this point and the meridian of 16° longitude west of Paris, the *boundary* will conform to parallel of 12° 40' north latitude.

To the east, the *boundary* will follow the meridian of 16° west, from parallel 12° 40' north latitude to the parallel of 11° 40' north latitude.

To the south, the *boundary* will follow a line starting from the estuary of the Cajet River, located between Catack Island (which will belong to Portugal) and Tristao Island (which will belong to France), and following the lay of the land, it will remain, as much as possible, at equal distance from the Rio Componi (Tabati) and the Rio Cassini, then from the northern branch of the Rio Componi (Tabati) and the southern branch of the Rio Cassini (Marigot de Kakondo) first and the Rio Grande afterwards. It will end at the intersection of the meridian of 16° west longitude and the parallel of 11° 40' north latitude.

Shall belong to Portugal all islands located between the Cape Roxo meridian, the coast and the southern *limit* represented by a line which will follow the thalweg of the Cajet River, and go in a southwesterly direction through the Pilots' Pass to reach 10° 40' north latitude, which it will follow up to the Cape Roxo meridian.[67]

As we know, Guinea and Guinea-Bissau were of different opinions as to the reason why in the last paragraph the expression "the southern *limit*" had been used, while in other paragraphs it was consistently spoken of as "the *boundary*". No disagreement seems to have existed between the disputing parties regarding the meaning of the term BOUNDARY. "*[B]oundary*", according to what is noted, ...

... [is] the "limit which separates the territory of a State from that of a neighboring State".[68]

Even more interesting is that the disputing parties seem to have been of one mind in other respects too. The Court observes:

> [N]either of the two Parties disputes that, in matters pertaining to treaties, the use of different legal terms must be justified by more than the purely literary concern of avoiding repetition.[69]

The implication is clear. There is a rule of interpretation, according to which the expression "limit" shall be assumed to bear a different meaning than that conferred on the expression "boundary"; this assumption shall be held valid, at least as long as other rules of interpretation cannot be adduced suggesting the opposite.

The proposition can be analysed along the lines of the decision in *Air France v. Saks*. According to conventional language, the meaning of "limit" overlaps completely with the meaning of "boundary". The word BOUNDARY is unambiguous: "[it is] the limit which separates the territory of a State from that of a neighbouring State".[70] The word LIMIT is ambiguous; it can be used as synonymous with BOUNDARY, but it can also be used in the more general sense of "[the] extreme part where a territory, or a domain ends".[71] Why, then, are the disputing parties nevertheless of the opinion – apparently shared by the court – that the correct meaning of "limit" is not the same as that of "boundary"? Clearly, "limit" represents the use of a different lexical unit than "boundary". It is also a matter of fact that the words LIMIT and BOUNDARY belong to the same lexical field; more specifically, they belong to a field corresponding to the conceptual area of *the extreme part where a territory, or a domain ends*. Under such premises, I do not see how the answer to the question I have posed can be any other than this: it is an assumption of the Court, that Guinea and Guinea-Bissau expressed themselves in accordance with the communicative standard D.

4 "[T]HE TEXT" PUT TO USE: NO LOGICAL TAUTOLOGIES

As I stated previously, it is my conclusion that when an applier interprets a provision using "the text" of the treaty, one of the communicative standard on which he bases the process is the following, earlier termed as standard E:

> If a state produces an utterance taking the form of a treaty provision, then the provision should be drawn up so that in the context there will be no instance of a logical tautology.[72]

Again, the conclusion is one based mainly on the practice of international courts and tribunals.[73] I would like to provide four examples of this.

My first example is the decision of the International Court of Justice in the *Case Concerning Border and Transborder Armed Actions*.[74] In July 1986, Nicaragua had filed an application with the Hague Court instituting proceedings against the Honduras. According to Nicaragua, Honduran military personnel had been present in Nicaraguan territory, where they had assisted the *"Contras"* in armed raids; in some raids, Honduran personnel had even themselves taken part. Through this action, the Honduras had incurred the responsibility of that state under international law. The opposite party objected, arguing that the Court lacked jurisdiction. As support for its view that the Court had indeed jurisdiction to try the application, Nicaragua had cited the *1948 American Treaty on Pacific Settlement ("the Pact of Bogotá")*, article XXXI of which provides as follows:

In conformity with Article 36, paragraph 2, of the Statute of the International Court of Justice, the High Contracting Parties declare that they recognize, in relation to any other American State, the jurisdiction of the Court as compulsory *ipso facto*, without the necessity of any special agreement so long as the present Treaty is in force, in all disputes of a juridical nature that arise among them concerning:
(a) The interpretation of a treaty;
(b) Any question of international law;
(c) The existence of any fact which, if established, would constitute the breach of an international obligation;
(d) The nature or extent of the reparation to be made for the breach of an international obligation.[75]

This view, claimed the Honduras, was based on a misconception; it assumed an interpretation of the Pact of Bogotá that clearly could not be considered correct.

One of the arguments advanced by the Honduras was that article XXXI of the Bogotá Pact could only be read correctly if placed in relation to the subsequent article XXXII:

When the conciliation procedure previously established in the present Treaty or by agreement of the parties does not lead to a solution, and the said parties have not agreed upon an arbitral procedure, either of them shall be entitled to have recourse to the International Court of Justice in the manner prescribed in Article 40 of the Statute thereof. The Court shall have compulsory jurisdiction in accordance with Article 36, paragraph 1, of the said Statute.[76]

Article XXXII defined the conditions, under which the International Court of Justice could be seized. Article XXXI was relevant only insofar as it defined the extent of the jurisdiction held by the Court, when once it had been seized. Therefore, the Honduras argued, the Court would have no jurisdiction to settle a dispute according to the provisions of article XXXI, in the cases covered by that article, if there had not been previous recourse to conciliation according to article XXXII, which was not the case in the situation at hand. Nicaragua had suggested a different reading of the two articles. According to Nicaragua, articles XXXI and XXXII were autonomous provisions – each conferred jurisdiction upon the Court independently of the other. Hence, the Court would have jurisdiction to settle a dispute according to the provisions of article XXXI, in the cases covered by that article, regardless of whether there had been previous recourse to conciliation according to article XXXII. The Court concurred on this latter interpretation.

In order to establish the flaw in the reading suggested by the Honduras, the Court presented two arguments, the first amounting to an act of interpretation using the ordinary meaning:

> Honduras's interpretation of Article XXXII runs counter to the terms of that Article. Article XXXII makes no reference to Article XXXI; under that text the parties have, in general terms, an entitlement to have recourse to the Court in cases where there has been an unsuccessful conciliation.
>
> It is true that one qualification of this observation is required, with regard to the French text of Article XXXII, which provides that, in the circumstances there contemplated, the party has "le droit de porter *la question* devant la Cour". That expression might be thought to refer back to the question which might have been the subject of the dispute referred to the Court under Article XXXI. It should, however, be observed that the text uses the word "*question*", which leaves room for uncertainty, rather than the word "*différend* (dispute)", used in Article XXXI, which would have been perfectly clear. Moreover, the Spanish, English and Portuguese versions speak, in general terms, of an entitlement to have recourse to the Court and do not justify the conclusion that there is a link between Article XXXI and Article XXXII.[77]

The second argument amounted to an act of interpretation using the context:

> Moreover, Article XXXII, unlike Article XXXI, refers expressly to the jurisdiction which the Court has under Article 36, paragraph 1, of the Statute. That reference would be difficult to understand if, as Honduras contends, the sole purpose of Article XXXII were to specify the procedural conditions for bringing before the Court disputes for which jurisdiction had already been conferred upon it by virtue of the declaration made in Article XXXI, pursuant to Article 36, paragraph 2.[78]

The latter argument is the one on which I would now like to focus attention. It must be admitted the reasoning of the Court can be interpreted in two different ways. According to a first interpretation, the context is used as a supplementary means of interpretation, according to the provisions of VCLT article 32, because the Court considers the ordinary meaning to be unambiguous, but still wishes to have this meaning confirmed.[79] According to a second interpretation, the context is used as a primary means of interpretation, according to the provisions of VCLT article 31, because the Court considers the ordinary meaning to be ambiguous, and hence it must be more precisely defined. Personally, I have difficulty understanding the Court other than according to interpretation no. 2. The Court considers the ordinary meaning to be unambiguous, but nevertheless wishes to be cautious. Even assuming that the ordinary meaning is ambiguous, the interpretation suggested by Nicaragua still remains the only one that agrees with the context – this, as I see it, is the only reasonable way to understand the reasoning of the Court. The question we must then ask ourselves is why the

Court considers such a claim to be justified. The first part of the explanation is given by the Court itself: if articles XXXI and XXXII of the Pact of Bogotá were to be understood according to the reading suggested by the Honduras, then apparently two provisions could be applied – each independently of the other – to confer jurisdiction upon the Court under circumstances, which are (at least) partly identical. The second part of the explanation must then be this: it is an assumption of the Court, that the parties to the Pact of Bogotá expressed themselves in accordance with the communicative standard E.

My second example is the judgment of the European Court for Human Rights in the *Guzzardi* case.[80] In 1973, Michele Guzzardi, an Italian national hailing from Sicily, had been detained and charged by an Italian court for conspiracy and participation in the kidnapping of a well-known Italian businessman. Before the passing of a judgment, a decision was handed down in January 1975 for compulsory residence; suspected of involvement with the Italian Mafia, Guzzardi was placed on Asinara Island for a period of 3 years. The claim made by Guzzardi was that Italy, by making this decision, had acted in violation of its obligations under article 5 of the *European Convention for the Protection of Human Rights and Fundamental Freedoms* . According to the provisions of article 5, everyone has a "right to liberty". A fact relevant to the case was that at that point in time, Italy had still not ratified Additional Protocol No. 4, article 2, which provides for a right to freedom of movement. Naturally, a question was raised concerning the relationship of article 5 of the Convention with article 2 of Additional Protocol No. 4. The Court elaborates on the matter as follows:

> The Court recalls that in proclaiming the "right to liberty", paragraph 1 of Article 5 is contemplating the physical liberty of the person; its aim is to ensure that no one should be dispossessed of this liberty in an arbitrary fashion. As was pointed out by those appearing before the Court, the paragraph is not concerned with mere restrictions on liberty of movement; such restrictions are governed by Article 2 of Protocol No. 4 which has not been ratified by Italy.[81]

Evidently, the Court makes an assumption concerning the relationship held between article 5 § 1 of the European Convention, and article 2 § 1 of Protocol No. 4. According to the literal sense of the term, a right to liberty could very well include a right to freedom of movement; but it does not. The conclusion of the Court is that the different rights have different scopes of application: no restriction of the right to freedom of movement can be considered *ipso facto* a violation of the right to liberty, and vice versa. It is an implicit assumption of the Court that the parties to the European Convention and to Protocol no. 4 have expressed themselves in accordance with the communicative standard E. Consequently, as I read the Court, the European Convention and Protocol No. 4 are seen to be parts of a single treaty text. That Protocol No. 4, for the purpose of interpreting article 5 of the Convention, is to be considered part of "the text" of that treaty, in the sense of VCLT article 31 § 2, is certainly not expressly spelled out in the Protocol. According to the provisions of the Protocol, "[a]s between the High Contracting Parties ... Articles 1–5 of this protocol shall be regarded as additional Articles to the Convention, and all the provisions of the Convention shall apply accordingly". But it remains an unanswered question how the Protocol shall be looked upon from the perspective of the state, which is only a party to the Convention. Instead, as support for the conclusion that the European Convention and Protocol No. 4 are seen by the Court to be parts of a single treaty text, we may turn to the practice of the European Court itself. As the Court has repeatedly stated, the European Convention and its protocols "must be read as a whole".[82] To my mind, this amounts to saying that the European Convention and its protocols are to be considered as together forming the text of one single treaty.

This kind of reasoning used by the European Court in the *Guzzardi* case can also be found in the *dissenting opinion* of Judge Fitzmaurice.[83] I quote:

> Article 2 of this Protocol [Protocol No. 4, that is] states in terms that:
>
> "Everyone lawfully within the territory of a State shall, within that territory, have the right to liberty of movement and freedom to choose his residence."
>
> Put negatively, this prohibits restrictions on movement or place of residence, and from it certain deductions relevant to the present case can be drawn: (a) The existence of this provision [Article 2 of Protocol No. 4, that is] shows either that those who originally framed the Convention on Human Rights did not contemplate that its Article 5 should go beyond preventing actual deprivation of liberty, or extend to mere restrictions on freedom of movement or choice of residence; – or else that the Governments of the Council of Europe did not see Article 5 as covering measures of "deprivation of liberty" where the basic character of those measures consisted primarily of restrictions of movement and place of residence, – or they would not have considered it necessary to draw up a separate Protocol about that. The resulting picture is that Article 5 of the Convention guaranteed the individual against illegitimate imprisonment, or confinement so close as to amount to the same thing – in sum against deprivation of liberty *stricto sensu* – but it afforded no guarantee against restrictions (on movement or place of residence) falling short of that. The latter was effected only by the Protocol, so that in those countries (of which Italy is one) that have not ratified it, such restrictions are not prohibited.
>
> (b) It follows that if Article 5 of the Convention is not to impinge on ground intended to be covered by Article 2 of the Protocol, and is not to do double duty with the latter, it (Article 5) must be interpreted strictly and regarded as limited to cases of actual imprisonment or to detention close enough and strict enough to approximate to a virtually complete derivation of liberty.[84]

Of course, Fitzmaurice does not share the opinion of the Court majority with regard to whether article 5 of the European Convention should be applied to the particular case. According to the majority, article 5 applies.

According to Fitzmaurice it does not – the actions taken by Italy in the case of Guzzardi amount to nothing more than a restriction of the right to freedom of movement, in the sense of article 2 of Additional Protocol No. 4. However, in certain respects Judge Fitzmaurice is still in complete agreement with the majority: when all is said and done, there must be a dividing line between the scope of application covered by the European Convention article 5, and that covered by article 2 in Protocol No. 4.

Article 5 of the Convention is not to impinge on ground intended to be covered by Article 2 of the Protocol ... [it] is not to do double duty with the latter [...].[85]

Obviously, it is not only an assumption of the Court, but also of Fitzmaurice, that the parties to the European Convention and its Protocol No. 4 expressed themselves in accordance with the communicative standard E.

My third example is the international award in the *Beagle Channel Arbitration* case.[86] In 1971, Argentina and Chile had concluded a special agreement to obtain a judicial decision on the territorial claims made by the two parties in the area of *Tierra del Fuego*. The dispute centred mainly on the sovereignty of three islands – Picton, Nueva and Lennox ("the PNL group") – situated in the eastern part of the *Canal Beagle* ("the Beagle Channel"). No territorial rights to the area could be claimed on grounds other than a bilateral Boundary Treaty,[87] signed in 1881 – neither Argentina nor Chile disputed this. However, the parties were of different opinions as to the correct way of reading the agreement. Among other things, different opinions were held on the meaning of articles II and III:

Article II
In the southern part of the Continent, and to the north of the Straits of Magellan, the boundary between the two countries shall be a line, which, starting from Point Dungeness, shall be prolonged by land as far as Monte Dinero; from this point it shall continue to the west, following the greatest altitudes of the range of hillocks existing there, until it touches the hill-top of Mount Aymond. From this point the line shall be prolonged up to the intersection of the 70th meridian with the 52nd parallel of latitude, and thence it shall continue to the west coinciding with this latter parallel, as far as the divortia aquarum of the Andes. The territories to the north of such a line shall belong to the Argentine Republic, and to Chile those extending to the south of it, without prejudice to what is provided in Article III, respecting Tierra del Fuego and adjacent islands.

Article III
In Tierra del Fuego a line shall be drawn, which starting from the point called Cape Espiritu Santo, in parallel 52° 40', shall be prolonged to the south along the meridian 68° 34' west of Greenwich until it touches Beagle Channel. Tierra del Fuego, divided in this manner, shall be Chilean on the western side and Argentine on the eastern. As for the islands, to the Argentine Republic shall belong Staten Island, the small islands next to it, and the other islands there may be on the Atlantic to the east of Tierra del Fuego and of the eastern coast of Patagonia; and to Chile shall belong all the islands to the south of Beagle Channel up to Cape Horn, and those there may be to the west of Tierra del Fuego.[88]

According to Chile, article II attributed to her all the territory and islands south of the line between Point Dungeness and the Andes as far as Cape Horn, subject only to the provisions of article III. According to Argentina, article II confined the allocations of Chile to the territory and islands south of the Point Dungeness-Andes Line, only to the extent of the area lying north of the Straits of Magellan. When a decision is eventually made by the Court on the matter, it is exceptionally well-reasoned. To bring out the flaw in the reading suggested by Chile, the Court ventured a series of arguments. One argument is the following:

> The objection that can be made ... is that Article III proceeds to make allocations of territorities [sic!] and islands south of the Straits of Magellan, not only to Argentina, but also to Chile. If it confined itself to doing the former alone – allocating territorities [sic!] and islands to Argentina – there would be no difficulty. Such allocations would thereby be taken out of Chile's global allocation under Article II and would go to Argentina, while all areas not specifically so allocated would automatically remain Chilean by virtue of Article II. The moment, however, that Article III proceeds (as is the fact) to make allocations to Chile, as well as to Argentina, of localities south of the Straits, it merely does all over again what (according to the Chilean contention) is supposed already to have been done globally under Article II. In other words, if Chile's view of Article II is correct, the attributions made to her under Article III would appear to be redundant and unnecessary.[89]

The text speaks for itself. Quite obviously, it is an assumption of the Court that the parties to the 1881 Boundary Treaty have expressed themselves in accordance with the communicative standard E.

My fourth example is the advisory opinion given by the International Court of Justice in *Namibia*.[90] The facts of the case have already been described in part in earlier chapters,[91] and I will not repeat myself. As we know, South Africa, acting in the capacity of a mandatory state, had administered the former German colony of Southwest Africa. In October 1966, the UN General Assembly had adopted resolution 2145 (XXI).[92] In the resolution, the General Assembly noted that for years, "South Africa has failed to fulfil its obligations in respect of the administration of the Mandated Territory"; it decided that the administration "is therefore [to be considered as] terminated" – "henceforth Southwest Africa comes under the direct responsibility of the United Nations"; and it called the attention of the Security Council to the resolution.[93] Upon this request, the Security Council had adopted resolution 276, declaring illegal the continued presence of the South African authorities in Namibia, and calling upon states to refrain from any dealings with the Government of South Africa that were inconsistent with the resolution.[94] Therefore, in August 1970 the Security Council decided to submit to the International Court of Justice a request for an advisory opinion.[95] The issue to be clarified was the legal consequences of South Africa's continued presence in Namibia, notwithstanding Security Council resolution 276.

One of the questions the Court had to answer in order to accomplish this task concerned the request directed by the Security Council to the international community in resolution 276. As a basis for adopting the resolution, the Security Council had cited article 24 § 1 of the UN Charter:

> In order to ensure prompt and effective action by the United Nations, its Members confer on the Security Council primary responsibility for the maintenance of international peace and security, and agree that in carrying out its duties under this responsibility the Security Council acts on their behalf.

The question was whether the decision of the Council should be seen as imposing a legal obligation upon the member states. According to what was alleged by the South African Government, the answer had to be in the negative. It is true that in article 25 of the UN Charter, the following is provided:

> The Members of the United Nations agree to accept and carry out the decisions of the Security Council in accordance with the present Charter.

But – according to the contention – article 25 pertained only to enforcement measures adopted under Chapter 7 of the Charter, and therefore it did not apply to decisions adopted by the Security Council under the provisions of article 24. The Court was of a different opinion:

> Article 25 is not confined to decisions in regard to enforcement action but applies to "the decisions of the Security Council" adopted in accordance with the Charter.[96]

It is interesting to examine the reasons given to justify this reading:

> If Article 25 had reference solely to decisions of the Security Council concerning enforcement action under Articles 41 and 42 of the Charter, that is to say, if it were only such decisions which had binding effect, then Article 25 would be superfluous, since this effect is secured by Articles 48 and 49 of the Charter.[97]

Clearly, it is an assumption of the Court that the parties to the UN Charter have expressed themselves in accordance with the communicative standard E.

5 CONCLUSIONS

According to VCLT article 31 § 1, a treaty shall be interpreted in good faith "in accordance with the ordinary meaning given to the terms of the treaty in their context". As a means of interpretation, the context comprises an exceptionally wide range of data. Therefore, to facilitate presentation, I have chosen to divide the concept into three parts, each part comprising a separate chapter of this work. The purpose of the current chapter is to describe what it means to interpret a treaty using "the text" of said treaty. Based on the observations made above, the following five rules of interpretation can be established:

Rule no. 2

§ 1. If it can be shown that the interpretation of a treaty provision in accordance with interpretation rule no. 1 leads to conflicting results, and that not only in the provision interpreted, but also in some other part of the text of said treaty, a word or phrase is included, the usage of which in one of the two possible ordinary meanings can be considered consistent, while in the other it cannot, then the former meaning shall be adopted.
§ 2. For the purpose of this rule, the TEXT of a treaty means any and all instruments, of which – considered from the point of view of the parties – the treaty can be considered comprised.
§ 3. For the purpose of this rule, PARTIES means any and all states for which the treaty is in force at the time of interpretation.

Rule no. 3

§ 1. If it can be shown that the interpretation of a treaty provision in accordance with interpretation rule no. 1 leads to conflicting results, and that somewhere in the text of said treaty a norm is expressed, which – in light of the provision interpreted – in one of the two possible ordinary meanings can be considered to involve a logical contradiction, while in the other it cannot, then the latter meaning shall be adopted.
§ 2. For the purpose of this rule, the TEXT of a treaty means any and all instruments, of which – considered from the point of view of the parties – the treaty can be considered comprised.
§ 3. For the purpose of this rule, the TEXT of a treaty means not only textual representations but also non-textual ones.
§ 4. For the purpose of this rule, PARTIES means any and all states for which the treaty is in force at the time of interpretation.

Rule no. 4

§ 1. If it can be shown that the interpretation of a treaty provision in accordance with interpretation rule no. 1 leads to conflicting results, and that somewhere in the text of said treaty there is an expression, which – in light of the provision interpreted – in one of the two possible ordinary meanings can be considered a pleonasm, while in the other it cannot, then the latter meaning shall be adopted.
§ 2. For the purpose of this rule, the TEXT of a treaty means any and all instruments, of which – considered from the point of view of the parties – the treaty can be considered comprised.
§ 3. For the purpose of this rule, PARTIES means any and all states for which the treaty is in force at the time of interpretation.

Rule no. 5
§ 1. If it can be shown that the interpretation of a treaty provision in accordance with interpretation rule no. 1 leads to conflicting results, and that in the provision interpreted, as well as in some other part of the text of said treaty, words or phrases are included, the usage of which in one of the two possible ordinary meanings can be considered to differ, while in the other meaning the usage does not, then the latter meaning shall be adopted, provided that the words or phrases, if not identical, can nevertheless be considered to be parts of the same lexical field.
§ 2. For the purpose of this rule, the TEXT of a treaty means any and all instruments, of which – considered from the point of view of the parties – the treaty can be considered comprised.
§ 3. For the purpose of this rule, PARTIES means any and all states for which the treaty is in force at the time of interpretation.

Rule no. 6
§ 1. If it can be shown that the interpretation of a treaty provision in accordance with interpretation rule no. 1 leads to conflicting results, and that somewhere in the text of said treaty a norm is expressed, which – in light of the provision interpreted – in one of the two possible ordinary meanings can be considered to involve a logical tautology, while in the other it cannot, then the latter meaning shall be adopted.
§ 2. For the purpose of this rule, the TEXT of a treaty means any and all instruments, of which – considered from the point of view of the parties – the treaty can be considered comprised.
§ 3. For the purpose of this rule, PARTIES means any and all states for which the treaty is in force at the time of interpretation.

NOTES

1. See e.g. *Oppenheim's International Law*, p. 1274, n. 17; Villiger, p. 344; Bos, 1984, p. 184; Köck, p. 90; Lang, p. 157; Elias, 1974, p. 75; Degan, 1968, p. 17. See Draft Articles With Commentaries (1966): "[T]he word 'context' in the opening phrase of paragraph 2 is designed to link all the elements of interpretation mentioned in this paragraph to the word 'context' in the first paragraph and thereby incorporate them in the provision contained in that paragraph. Equally, the opening phrase of paragraph 3 'There shall be taken into account *together with the context*' is designed to incorporate in paragraph 1 the elements of interpretation set out in paragraph 3." (*ILC Yrbk*, 1966, Vol. 2, p. 220, § 8.)
2. By so doing – and I want to emphasise this – I do not assume a reading of the Vienna Convention incompatible with conventional language. VCLT article 31 § 2 provides: "The context for the purpose of the interpretation of a treaty shall comprise ... ('Aux fins de l'interprétation d'un traité, le contexte comprend ...' – 'Para los efectos de la interpretación de un tratado, el contexto comprenderá ...'.)" The word COMPRISE,

COMPREND, COMPRENDER is ambiguous. It can be used in the sense of *contain; include; embrace*; but it can also be used in the sense of *consist of; composed of or constituted by*. In my opinion, the one sense used for the provisions of article 31 § 2 is the former. I consider the description given in § 2 to be an exemplification of what is meant by "the context" used in article 31 § 1. Only in combination with the provisions of § 3 can the description given in § 2 be considered an exhaustive definition of *the context*. What I am therefore forced to accept is that "the context" used in § 2 stands for something different than "the context" used in § 3. "[T]he context" used in § 2 is co-referent with "the context" used in § 1. According to conventional language, "the context" used in § 3 can be understood in two ways. It can be understood as co-referent with "The context" in § 1; and it can be understood as a reference to *the context, as described in § 2*. In my opinion, the expression shall be understood in the latter sense.

3. Cf. Ch. 1, Section 3, of this work.
4. It is also evident from reading the preparatory work of the Vienna Convention. From the Commentary adopted by the International Law Commission in 1966, I quote the following passage: "*Paragraph 1* [of draft article 27, later to be adopted as VCLT article 31] contains three separate principles. The first – interpretation in good faith – flows directly from the rule *pacta sunt servanda*. The second principle is the very essence of the textual approach: the parties are to be presumed to have that intention which appears from the ordinary meaning of the terms used by them. The third principle is one both of common sense and good faith; the ordinary meaning of a term is not to be determined in the abstract but in the context of the treaty and in the light of its object and purpose." (Draft Articles With Commentaries (1966), *ILC Yrbk*, 1966, Vol. 2, p. 221, § 12.)
5. For an excellent introduction to this topic, see Weissberg, pp. 781–803.
6. Several circumstances support this conclusion. One such circumstance is the definition provided by the Vienna Convention itself. TREATY, in the sense of the Convention, means an international agreement "in written form" (article 2 § 1); that is, in practice, a TREATY is an agreement, which is neither oral nor tacit. (See Draft Articles With Commentaries (1966), *ILC Yrbk*, 1966, Vol. 2, p. 190, § 3.) Another circumstance involves the judicial opinions expressed. That a non-textual representation contained in a treaty shall be considered part of that treaty's text is an inference seemingly to be made based on the practice of international courts and tribunals. See e.g. *Guinea – Guinea-Bissau Maritime Delimitation*, where two maps attached as annexes to a convention were considered parts of the context "in keeping with the views of the Parties themselves, and Article 31, paragraph 2, of the Vienna Convention on the Law of Treaties" (*ILR*, Vol. 77, p. 670, § 70).
7. My italics.
8. Cf. VCLT art. 39: "*A treaty* may be amended by agreement between the parties." (My italics.) See also *U.S.-France Air Services Award*, *ILR*, Vol. 54, p. 329, § 50, cf. p. 304; *Air Transport Services Agreement Arbitration*, *ILR*, Vol. 38, pp. 230–231. For a seemingly different view, see Seidl-Hohenveldern, 1998, p. 13.
9. *Final Act, Agreement and other Acts relating to the establishment and operation of the Iron Gates Water Power and Navigation System on the River Danube* . All signed at Belgrade, on 30 November 1963. The text cited is the official English translation of the agreement, which was authenticated only in Romanian and Serbo-Croatian.
10. *Agreement concerning the construction and operation of the Iron Gates Water Power and Navigation System on the River Danube* , Article 22, excerpt. The text cited is the

official English translation of the agreement, which was authenticated only in Romanian and Serbo-Croatian.

11. Cf. Final Act, Article I.
12. See, further, Voïcu, pp. 165–172.
13. See *Oppenheim's International Law*, pp. 1211, 1274, n. 15; Yasseen, p. 38; Elias, 1974, p. 75. See also Draft Articles With Commentaries (1966), *ILC Yrbk*, 1966, Vol. 2, p. 221, § 13, cit. *Ambatielos (Preliminary Objection), ICJ Reports*, 1952, pp. 43, 75.
14. See e.g. *Ambatielos (Preliminary Objection), ICJ Reports*, 1952, pp. 41–44.
15. This means that for the purpose of interpreting an annex to a treaty, the context shall include the "main instrument" as well as any other annexes possibly drawn up. (See e.g. *Young Loan, ILR*, Vol. 59, pp. 533–540.)
16. Guinea – Guinea-Bissau Maritime Delimitation Case, Award of 14 February 1985, *ILR*, Vol. 77, pp. 636ff.
17. Ibid., p. 636 et passim.
18. Ibid., p. 664, §§ 54–55, pp. 669–670, §§ 69–70.
19. Ibid., pp. 669–670, §§ 69–70, cf. p. 657, § 39.
20. See e.g. Ress, pp. 30, 43; Ost, pp. 290–291; Bernhardt, 1984, p. 322; Bos, 1984, p. 147; Matscher, 1983, pp. 562–563; Lang, pp. 157–158; Schwarzenberger, 1957, pp. 505–508.
21. See e.g. Matscher, 1983, p. 562; Vitányi, p. 53; Yasseen, p. 33; Haraszti, pp. 104–105; Lang, p. 157; Rousseau, pp. 285–286; Bernhardt, 1963, p. 69, n. 338, cit. De Visscher, 1959, p. 384; Fitzmaurice, 1963, pp. 150–152.
22. Cf. e.g. *Oppenheim's International Law*, p. 1273, n. 12; Seidl-Hohenveldern, 1992, p. 92; Haraszti, pp. 89–90; Matscher, 1983, p. 562; Müller, pp. 129–130; Bernhardt, 1963, pp. 85–86.
23. Cf. e.g. Merrills, p. 75, cit. *Johnston and Others, Publ. ECHR*, Ser. A, Vol. 112, § 57; Ost, p. 291, cit. *Guzzardi*, diss. op. Fitzmaurice, *Publ. ECHR*, Ser. A, Vol. 39, p. 52; von Glahn, p. 504; Yasseen, pp. 33–34; Haraszti, pp. 104–105; Müller, pp. 129–130; De Visscher, 1963, pp. 59–61; Degan, 1963, p. 98, cit. *Corfu Channel (Merits), ICJ Reports*, 1949, p. 26; Schwarzenberger, 1957, p. 508.
24. See p. 102 of this work.
25. In addition to the authorities directly cited in the text below, see Akehurst, 1987, p. 203; Matscher, 1983, p. 562. See also the judicial opinions expressed by international courts and tribunals, e.g. *Canadian Agricultural Tariffs, ILR*, Vol. 110, p. 579, § 134; *La Bretagne Arbitration, ILR*, Vol. 82, pp. 620–621, §§ 38–39; *Guinea – Guinea-Bissau Maritime Delimitation, ILR*, Vol. 77, pp. 663–664, § 52.
26. *Oppenheim's International Law*, p. 1273, n. 12, cit. *Ministry of Defence v Ergialli, ILR*, Vol. 26, p. 732.
27. Haraszti, p. 108.
28. Bernhardt, 1963, pp. 85–86, cit. *Diversion of Water from the Meuse, PCIJ*, Ser. A/B, No. 70, p. 24, and Judge Hudson's *individual opinion* appended to that same case, ibid., p. 75.
29. In addition to Vitányi, see Akehurst, 1987, p. 203; Matscher, 1983, pp. 562–563; Yasseen, pp. 33–34.
30. Vitányi, p. 54. (Footnotes omitted.)
31. See also the judicial opinions expressed by international courts and tribunals, e.g. *Maritime Delimitation: Jan Mayen, ILR*, Vol. 100, p. 418, § 26; *Soering, Publ. ECHR*, Ser. A, Vol. 161, p. 40, § 103; *Border and Transborder Armed Actions, ILR*, Vol. 84, pp. 239–240, §§ 35–36; *Johnston and Others, Publ. ECHR*, Ser. A, Vol. 112,

p. 26, § 57; *Guinea – Guinea-Bissau Maritime Delimitation*, *ILR*, Vol. 77, p. 664, §§ 53–54.

32. In addition to the authorities directly cited in the text, see Hummer, p. 115; Gordon, pp. 814–815; Bernhardt, 1963, p. 80; Fitzmaurice, 1957, pp. 211, 223; Schwarzenberger, 1957, p. 503; Grossen, pp. 109–111. See also the judicial opinions expressed by international courts and tribunals, e.g. *Canadian Agricultural Tariffs*, *ILR*, Vol. 110, pp. 581–582, § 140; *AAPL v. Sri Lanka*, *ILR*, Vol. 106, pp. 445–446, § 52; *Quatar v. Bahrain*, *ILR*, Vol. 102, p. 60, § 35; *Namibia*, *ILR*, Vol. 49, p. 25, §§ 66–67.
33. Thirlway, 1991, p. 44.
34. Haraszti, p. 89. The quotation derives from *Anglo-Iranian Oil*, *ICJ Reports*, 1952, p. 105.
35. Hogg (II), p. 11.
36. *Oppenheim's International Law*, p. 1273, n. 12, cit. *Certain Expenses of the United Nations*, *ICJ Reports*, 1962, p. 159.
37. See e.g. La Grand Case, *ICJ Reports*, 2001, pp. 501–502, § 100; *El Salvador/Honduras*, *ILR*, Vol. 97, p. 499, § 374; *E. v. Norway*, *Publ. ECHR*, Ser. A, Vol. 181-A, p. 27, § 64; *Brogan and Others*, *Publ. ECHR*, Ser. A, Vol. 145-B, p. 32, § 59; *Guinea – Guinea-Bissau Maritime Delimitation*, *ILR*, Vol. 77, pp. 663–664, § 52; *Air France v. Saks*, *ILR*, Vol. 96, p. 118; *Sunday Times (No. 1)*, *Publ. ECHR*, Ser. A, Vol. 30, pp. 35–36, § 59; *Handyside*, *Publ. ECHR*, Ser. A, Vol. 24, p. 22, § 48; *Certain Expenses of the United Nations*, *ICJ Reports*, 1962, p. 159.
38. Peczenik, 1995, p. 332; author's translation. In a similar manner, see Wróblewski, 1992, p. 99.
39. See above, in the introduction to this chapter.
40. In addition to the authorities directly cited in the text, see Amerasinghe, pp. 194, 195–196; Akehurst, 1987, p. 203; Bernhardt, 1963, p. 80; De Visscher, 1963, pp. 84–86; Hogg (II), pp. 6–13; Schwarzenberger, 1957, p. 507; Grossen, pp. 109–111.
41. Thirlway, 1991, p. 25, cit. *IMCO*, *ICJ Reports*, 1960, p. 160.
42. Gordon, p. 814. (Footnote omitted; my italics.)
43. Fitzmaurice, 1957, p. 211. (My italics.) As the passage makes clear, a connection exists between *the rule of non-redundancy* on the one hand, and on the other hand what legal authors term as THE PRINCIPLE OF EFFECTIVENESS. We will have reason to return to this fact in subsequent chapters of this work. (See Ch. 7, Sections 4–5, of this work.)
44. See, p. 108 of this work.
45. See e.g. Hogg (II), pp. 6–13 – why else is it called *the surplus* ***words*** *rule* ? – Amerasinghe, pp. 195–196; Berlia, pp. 306–308. Some authors seem aware of the distinction but make no attempt to explain it. (See e.g. Gordon, pp. 814–815; Bernhardt, 1963, p. 80; Fitzmaurice, 1957, pp. 211, 223, and Fitzmaurice, 1951, pp. 19–20; Schwarzenberger, 1957, pp. 503, 507; Grossen, pp. 109–111.)
46. See Thirlway, 1991, pp. 44–48; De Visscher, 1963, pp. 84–85.
47. See e.g. *Raimondo v. Italy*, Publ. ECHR, Ser. A, Vol. 281-A, p. 19, § 39; *Border and Transborder Armed Actions*, *ILR*, Vol. 84, p. 245, § 45; *Guzzardi*, *Publ. ECHR*, Series A, Vol. 39, p. 33, § 92, and diss. op. Fitzmaurice, ibid., pp. 51–52, § 6; *Beagle Channel Arbitration*, *ILR*, Vol. 52, p. 140, § 35; *Namibia*, *ILR*, Vol. 49, p. 43, § 113.
48. See e.g. Lyons, 1977, pp. 230–269.
49. Ibid., pp. 230–238.
50. Loc. cit.
51. Ibid., pp. 250–269.

52. Ibid., p. 254.
53. See Section 2 of this chapter.
54. See p. 108, n. 37 of this work.
55. Case of Brogan and Others, Judgment of 29 November 1988, *Publ. ECHR*, Ser. A, Vol. 145-B.
56. *Publ. ECHR* , Ser. A, Vol. 145-B, p. 32, § 59.
57. Case of De Jong, Baljet and Van den Brink, Judgment of 22 May 1984, *Publ. ECHR*, Ser. A, Vol. 77.
58. Ibid., pp. 325–27, §§ 55–59.
59. Handyside Case, Judgment of 7 December 1976, *Publ. ECHR*, Ser. A, Vol. 24.
60. *Publ. ECHR* , Ser. A, Vol. 24, p. 22, § 48.
61. *Air France v. Saks* , Opinion of 4 March 1985, *ILR*, Vol. 96, pp. 113ff.
62. Convention for the Unification of Certain Rules Relating to International Transportation by Air, Signed at Warsaw, on 12 October 1929.
63. The text cited is that provided by the Court. (See *ILR*, Vol. 96, p. 117.)
64. Ibid., pp. 117–118.
65. Guinea – Guinea-Bissau Maritime Delimitation Case, Award of 14 February 1985, *ILR*, Vol. 77, pp. 636ff.
66. See Ch. 3, Sections 2 and 5, of this work.
67. Note that the text cited is the English translation of the Convention published in *International Law Reports*. The Convention was authenticated in French and Portuguese only. For the authenticated French text, see *Archives Diplomatiques*, Vol. 24 (1887), pp. 5ff.
68. *ILR* , Vol. 77, p. 662, § 49.
69. Ibid., p. 663, § 52.
70. Ibid., p. 662, § 49.
71. Loc. cit.
72. See Section 2 of this chapter.
73. See p. 110, n. 47 of this work.
74. *Case Concerning Border and Transborder Armed Actions (Nicaragua v. Honduras)* , Judgment of 20 December 1988, *ILR*, Vol. 84, pp. 219ff.
75. The text cited is that provided by the Court. (See *ILR*, Vol. 84, p. 233, § 20.)
76. Ibid., p. 243, § 42.
77. Ibid., p. 245, § 45.
78. Loc. cit.
79. On the interpretation of treaties using the context as a supplementary means of interpretation, see Ch. 8, Section 6, of this work.
80. *Guzzardi Case* , Judgment of 6 November 1980, *Publ. ECHR*, Ser. A, Vol. 39.
81. *Publ. ECHR* , Ser. A, Vol. 39, p. 33, § 92.
82. See e.g. *Abdulaziz, Cabales and Balkandali, Publ. ECHR*, Ser. A, Vol. 94, p. 31, § 60; *Kjeldsen, Busk Madsen and Pedersen, Publ. ECHR*, Ser. A, Vol. 23, p. 26, § 52; *Belgian Linguistics (Merits), Publ. ECHR*, Ser. A, Vol. 6, p. 30, § 1.
83. Dissenting opinion of Judge Sir Gerald Fitzmaurice, Guzzardi Case, *Publ. ECHR*, Ser. A, Vol. 39, pp. 49–55.
84. Ibid., pp. 51–52, § 6. (Footnote omitted.)
85. See p. 121 of this work.
86. *Beagle Channel Arbitration (Argentina v. Chile)* , Award of 18 February 1977, *ILR*, Vol. 52, pp. 93ff.

87. Tratado de Limítes, Signed at Buenos Aires, on 23 July 1881.
88. The agreement was authenticated in Spanish. The text cited above is the English translation used by the Court (ibid., pp. 8–9).
89. Ibid., p. 140, § 35.
90. Legal Consequences for States of the Continued Presence of South Africa in Namibia (South West Africa) Notwithstanding Security Council Resolution 276 (1970), Advisory Opinion of 21 June 1971, *ILR*, Vol. 49, pp. 3ff.
91. See Ch. 3, Section 4 of this work.
92. See GA res. 2145 (XXI) of October 1966, §§ 3–4.
93. Ibid., operative paragraphs 3, 4, and 9, respectively.
94. See SC res. 276 (1970), operative paragraphs 2 and 5, respectively.
95. See SC res. 284 (1970).
96. *ILR* , Vol. 49, p. 43, § 113.
97. Loc. cit.

CHAPTER 5

USING THE CONTEXT: THE ELEMENTS SET OUT IN VCLT ARTICLE 31 § 2(A) AND (B)

The purpose of this chapter to describe what it means to interpret a treaty, using the two contextual elements set out in article 31 § 2, subparagraphs (a) and (b). Article 31 § 2 provides as follows:

> The context for the purpose of the interpretation of a treaty shall comprise, in addition to the text, its preamble and annexes:
> (a) any agreement relating to the treaty which was made between all the parties in connexion with the conclusion of the treaty;
> (b) any instrument which was made by one or more parties in connexion with the conclusion of the treaty and accepted by the other parties as an instrument related to the treaty.

Earlier, we established the following shorthand description of how the context is to be used:

> If it can be shown that the interpretation of a treaty provision in accordance with interpretation rule no. 1 leads to conflicting results, and that between the provision and the context there is a relationship governed by the communicative standard S, then the provision shall be understood as if the relationship conformed to this standard.[1]

Two questions remain to be answered, in order for the task set for this chapter to be considered completed:

(1) What is meant by "any agreement relating to the treaty which was made between all the parties in connexion with the conclusion of the treaty", and "any instrument which was made by one or more parties in connexion with the conclusion of the treaty and accepted by the other parties as an instrument related to the treaty"?

(2) What communicative standard or standards shall the parties to a treaty be assumed to have followed, when an applier interprets the treaty using said "agreements" and "instruments"?

I shall now give what I consider to be the correct answers to these questions. In Sections 1–3, I shall begin by answering question (1). In Sections 2–4, I shall then answer question (2).

1 THE MEANING OF SUBPARAGRAPH (A): INTRODUCTION

In addition to "the text" of a treaty, two classes of phenomena shall be counted as part of the context, according to the provisions of VCLT article 31 § 2. The first of these classes is the one described in subparagraph (a), namely "any agreement relating to the treaty which was made between all the parties in connexion with the conclusion of the treaty".

> [T]out accord ayant rapport au traité et qui est intervenu entre toutes les parties à l'occasion de la conclusion du traité ...

> Todo acuerdo que se refiera al tratado y haya sido concertado entre todas las partes con motivo de la celebración del tratado ...

Four conditions must be met in order for a phenomenon to fit this description: (1) the phenomenon must be included in the extension of the expression "agreement"; (2) it must be a question of an agreement "relating to the treaty"; (3) the agreement must have been made "between all the parties"; and (4) it must have been made "in connexion with the conclusion of the treaty". Let us examine each of these points one by one. We shall begin with the last three.

In order for an agreement to fit the description set forth in subparagraph (a), it must be a question of an agreement "relating to the treaty" (Fr. *"ayant rapport au traité"*; Sp. *"que se refiera al tratado")*. It is not entirely clear from the wording of the Vienna Convention what is meant by "relating to". However, all things considered, I find it hard to believe that the qualifications used for subparagraph (a) differ very much from those inserted in subparagraph (b). The word used for subparagraph (a) is the same used for subparagraph (b), namely the verb RELATE (TO), AVOIR RAPPORT (À), REFERIRSE (A). Subparagraph (b) speaks of "any instrument which was made by one or more parties in connexion with the conclusion of the treaty and accepted by the other parties as an instrument related to the treaty" (Fr. "*en tant qu'instrument ayant rapport au traité*"; Sp. "*como instrumento referente al tratado*"). If a party has accepted an instrument as "relating to" a treaty, clearly she has accepted that the instrument and the treaty – even though they are not parts of a single treaty text – nevertheless are exceptionally closely connected. By the same token, the fact that an agreement can be characterised as "relating to" a treaty, in the sense of subparagraph (a), would imply that the parties have accepted that some close affinity exists between the two.[2] Hence, the following comment made by Yasseen must be viewed as misleading:

> L'accord ou l'instrument doit avoir un rapport avec le traité; il doit concerner la matière sur laquelle porte le traité, clarifier certaines notions prévues ou limiter le champ d'application du traité.[3]

Naturally, if a relationship can be shown to bear between the words and phrases used for an agreement and the text of a treaty, this is a circumstance indicating that we are dealing with an agreement "relating to" the treaty.[4] But it is not an absolute requirement. What ultimately determines the relationship between an agreement and a treaty are the intentions of their parties. To determine these intentions a variety of means may be used, of which the text of the agreement is surely not the only one (even though, of course, it remains a means of very high significance).

In order for an agreement to fit the description set forth in subparagraph (a), it must have been made "between all the parties" (Fr. *"entre toutes les parties"*; Sp. *"entre todas las partes"*). PARTY, according to the definition given in VCLT article 2 § 1(g), means "a state which has consented to be bound by the treaty and for which the treaty is in force". What determines whether an agreement shall be considered "made between all the parties" is the state-of-affairs, which prevails when a treaty is interpreted – and not that, which prevailed when the agreement was made.[5] Apparently, in order for an agreement to fit the description set forth in subparagraph (a), each and every one of those states that are bound by the treaty at the time of interpretation must be bound by the agreement.

In order for an agreement to fit the description set forth in subparagraph (a), it must have been made "in connexion with the conclusion of the treaty" (Fr. *"à l'occasion de la conclusion du traité"*; Sp. *"con motivo de la celebraciòn del tratado")*. Considering the language of international law, the "conclusion" of a treaty is an expression that can cause confusion. In one sense, THE CONCLUSION OF THE TREATY (Fr. LA CONCLUSION DU TRAITÉ; Sp. LA CELEBRACIÓN DEL TRATADO) can be used as equivalent to *the point in time when a treaty is established as definite*. In another sense, it can be used to stand for *the time interval from when negotiations on a treaty are started to when a treaty finally enters into force*.[6] This ambiguity is evidenced already by a quick glance at the Vienna Convention,[7] where the term CONCLUSION OF THE TREATY frequently appears.[8] As an instance where CONCLUSION occurs in the sense of *the point in time when a treaty is established as definite*,[9] article 49 may clearly be singled out:

> If a State has been induced to conclude a treaty by the fraudulent conduct of another negotiating State, the State may invoke the fraud as invalidating its consent to be bound by the treaty.

NEGOTIATING STATE, in the terminology used for the Vienna Convention, means "a State which took part in the drawing up and adoption of the text of the treaty".[10] As an instance where CONCLUSION occurs in the sense of *the time interval from when negotiations on a treaty is started to when a treaty finally enters into force*,[11] we may point to article 7 § 2:

In virtue of their functions and without having to produce full powers, the following are considered as representing their State:
(a) Heads of State, Heads of Government and Ministers for Foreign Affairs, for the purpose of performing all acts relating to the conclusion of a treaty;
(b) heads of diplomatic missions, for the purpose of adopting the text of a treaty between the accrediting State and the State to which they are accredited;
(c) representatives accredited by States to an international conference or one of its organs, for the purpose of adopting the text of a treaty in that conference, organization or organ.

Apparently, the authority assigned to heads of state, heads of government, and ministers for foreign affairs, for "all acts relating to the conclusion of a treaty", is to be distinguished from the authority given to heads of diplomatic missions "for the purpose of adopting the text of a treaty". In principle, I see no obvious reason why in VCLT article 31 § 2(a) the word CONCLUSION could not be understood in the one sense just as well as the other. According to the opinion generally held in the literature, an agreement fits the description set forth in subparagraph (a) only on the condition that the agreement has been made in connection with the establishing of the interpreted treaty as definite.[12] Thus, I shall consider the matter settled.

In order for an agreement to fit the description set forth in subparagraph (a), it must be comprised in extension of the expression "any agreement" (Fr. *"tout accord"*; Sp. *"[t]odo acuerdo"*). The expression "agreement" causes us problems. In subparagraph (a), AGREEMENT means an agreement in the legal-technical sense – this much is clear. Many international transactions come about without the parties involved having an intention to commit themselves other than in a moral or political sense. Such agreements – in the literature denoted as "gentlemen's agreements", "non-binding agreements", "agreements de facto", "non-juridical agreements", and so forth –[13] are not included in the extension of the expression "agreement". In order for an international transaction to be categorised as an agreement in the sense of subparagraph (a), the states involved must have had a law-creating intention – the transaction must have created an agreement with a legal effect.[14] The difficult question is whether "agreement" shall be understood to require a certain form. In conventional language, the word AGREEMENT (Fr. ACCORD; Sp. ACUERDO) is ambiguous. In one sense, AGREEMENT can be used as equivalent to a (written) contract. In another sense, it can be used as synonymous to a mutual understanding; an intention mutually held among two or more legal subjects to create law.[15] Assuming the expression "agreement" to have been used in the former sense, it clearly refers to agreements in written form only. Let us term this interpretation alternative A. Assuming the expression "agreement" to have been used in the latter sense, it refers to any agreement, regardless of form. Let us call this interpretation alternative B.

Both interpretation alternatives A and B find supporters in the literature. According to some authors, it seems the form of an agreement is decisive for its classification under VCLT article 31 § 2(a).[16] Elias, for example, refers to "agreement" as a synonym of "document":

The meaning and scope of the term "context" as used in the several paragraphs of this Article [i.e. VCLT article 31] are defined in paragraph 2 as including the preamble as well as those documents that form annexes to the treaty in question. The other *documents* that should be regarded as comprised in the "context" are of two types: (i) any agreement relating to the treaty which was made in connection with the conclusion of the treaty, and (ii) any instrument which was made in connection with the conclusion of the treaty and accepted by the other parties as an instrument related to the treaty. In other words, for a *document* to be regarded as forming part of the context of a treaty for the purpose of its interpretation, it must be the result of an agreement by all the parties to the treaty, must have been made in connection with the conclusion of the treaty and must be understood as such by all of them.[17]

Sinclair speaks of agreements, which must "be drawn up" in connection with the conclusion of the treaty:

It is of course essential that the agreement or instrument should be related to the treaty. It must be concerned with the substance of the treaty and clarify certain concepts in the treaty or limit its field of application. It must equally *be drawn up* on the occasion of the conclusion of the treaty.[18]

According to the opinion of other authors, the form of an agreement is irrelevant.[19] "Ce qui importe ici", writes Yasseen, for example, ...

... c'est l'accord en tant que tel; peu importe sa forme. Cet accord peut être écrit, faire objet d'un instrument, mais peut également être oral.[20]

Müller is equally explicit:

d) Vertragsergänzende Nebenabreden bei oder nach Vetragsabschluß (Art. 31 Ziff. 2(a) und Ziff. 3(a) VRK)

In der allgemeinen Interpretationsregel von Art. 27 ILC-Entwurf (Art. 31 VRK) sind als Mittel authentischer Vertragsinterpretation Vereinbarungen *(agreements, accords)* genannt, die unter den Parteien in Zusammenhang mit oder nach dem Vertragsabschluß zustande kamen. Es ist auffallend, daß hier von *agreements (accords)* und nicht von *treaties (traités)* die Rede ist. Dies deutet darauf hin, daß auch mündliche und stillschweigende Vereinbarungen zwischen Vertragsparteien eingeschlossen sind, die in Zusammenhang mit einem förmlichen Vertrag *(treaty, traité)* entstanden.[21]

All things considered, legal doctrine cannot be considered a very helpful means for the determination of law.

In my opinion, the latter group of authors – not the former – is the one that correctly describes the prevailing legal state-of-affairs. Hence, I now need to present the arguments that support this opinion. This is the task in Section 2.

2 THE MEANING OF SUBPARAGRAPH (A): "ANY AGREEMENT"

A first argument at odds with the view that "any agreement" refers to agreements in written form only – what we have termed as interpretation alternative A – is that this view appears to be not so easily reconciled with the legally recognised rules for the interpretation of treaties. Rather, these rules seem to support the proposition that by "agreement" we shall understand an agreement, whatever form it assumes – what we have termed as interpretation alternative B.

First of all, consider the context. AGREEMENT (Fr. ACCORD; Sp. ACUERDO) is a word much used in the provisions of the Vienna Convention. Beyond article 31 § 2(a), it can be found in article 2 § 1(a), article 3, article 24 § 2, article 31 § 3(a) and (b), article 39, article 40 §§ 2, 4 and 5, article 41 §§ 1 and 2, article 58 §§ 1 and 2, and in article 60 § 2(a). According to article 2 § 1(a), a treaty means "an international agreement concluded between States in written form". Article 3 speaks of international agreements to which the Convention does not apply, *inter alia* "international agreements not in written form". In article 24 § 2 we are told at what point in time a treaty shall enter into force, where this has not been agreed upon by the negotiating states: "Failing any such provision or agreement, a treaty enters into force as soon as consent to be bound by the treaty has been established for all the negotiating States". According to article 31 § 3, when an applier interprets a treaty he shall include in the context "any subsequent agreement between the parties regarding the interpretation of the treaty or the application of its provisions" [subparagraph (a)], as well as "any subsequent practice in the application of the treaty which establishes the agreement of the parties regarding its interpretation" [subparagraph (b)]. Articles 39–41 tell us when, and under what conditions, a treaty may be amended or modified: an amendment, like a modification, is effected by "agreement". Article 58 provides when, and under what conditions, the parties to a multilateral treaty "may conclude an agreement to suspend the operation of provisions of the treaty, temporarily and as between themselves alone". And, finally, according to article 60 § 2, any material breach of a multilateral treaty by one of the parties entitles "the other parties by unanimous agreement to suspend the operation of the treaty in whole or in part or to terminate it either (i) in the relations between themselves and the defaulting State, or (ii) as between all the parties".

In all these instances, the word AGREEMENT refers to agreements irrespective of form. I articles 24 and 31 § 3(b), this appears already in the wording of the Convention. The same applies to articles 2 and 3: if AGREEMENT were to refer only to written agreements, then it would be a tautology to speak of an "agreement in written form"; to speak of "agreements in non-written form" would be pure nonsense. Of course, the meaning of article 31 § 3(a) is not equally apparent; but, according to a view generally held in the literature, AGREEMENT shall be read in this case in the broader sense.[22] As for articles 39–41, 58 and 60, strong reasons provoke a similar reading. In the Draft Articles adopted by the ILC in 1966, the following short Commentary is appended to the provisions on the termination and suspension of treaties:

> The Commission considered that, whatever may be the provisions of a treaty regarding its own termination, it is always possible for all the parties to agree together to put an end to the treaty. It is also considered that the particular form which such an agreement may take is a matter for the parties themselves to decide in each case. The theory has sometimes been advanced that an agreement terminating a treaty must be cast in the same form as the treaty which is to be terminated or at least constitute a treaty form of equal weight. The Commission, however, concluded that this theory reflects the constitutional practice of particular States and not a rule of international law. In its opinion, international law does not accept the theory of the "*acte contraire*". The States concerned are always free to choose the form in which they arrive at their agreement to terminate the treaty.[23]

The provisions concerning the amendment and modification of treaties are explained in a similar manner:

> [T]he Commission did not consider that the theory of the "*acte contraire*" has any place in international law. An amending agreement may take whatever form the parties to the original treaty may choose.[24]

When it comes to the parties to the Vienna Convention, I see no reason to assume that they have taken a position other than that of the International Law Commission. Considering interpretation rule no. 2 – according to which a treaty shall be interpreted based on the assumption that words and phrases are consistently used – then in article 31 § 2(a), too, AGREEMENT would be used in the sense of a legally binding agreement, regardless of form.[25]

A second circumstance that can be adduced to support interpretation alternative B is the object and purpose of the interpreted treaty. Nothing says that an international agreement between states must assume some certain form. According to international law, the legal effect of a non-written agreement is equal to that of a written one. Clearly, this principle would be contravened if the expression "agreement" in subparagraph (a) were to be interpreted as synonymous with "written agreement". Two states (A and B) may each have concluded a treaty with a third state (C), and the contracting parties may in each case have agreed – states A and C putting down the agreement in writing, states B and C having satisfied themselves with an oral agreement – that a specific expression used for the treaty shall be given a specific meaning. Both agreements are binding under international law; but, according to the provisions of VCLT article 31 § 2(a), only one can be included in the context, when the two treaties are subsequently interpreted. Such a radical hierarchisation of written and non-written agreements can hardly be what the parties to the Vienna Convention wished to achieve. Certainly, written agreements are normally more easily dealt with than non-written ones, from the point of view of proving the agreement.[26] When two or more states conclude an agreement concerning the interpretation of a treaty, without later confirming it by means of a written contract, then sometimes the agreement can be difficult to establish. However, I cannot see that this alone would be sufficient reason to exclude non-written agreements from the scope of VCLT article 31 § 2(a). After all, non-written agreements come within the scope of article 31 § 3(a).[27] Given that article 31 § 2(a) shall be understood so that by applying the article a result is not achieved, which is not among the objects and purposes of the treaty, the expression "agreement" would then have to be interpreted in accordance with interpretation alternative B – it would have to refer to agreements irrespective of form.[28]

If any circumstance could be seen to support interpretation alternative A, then that would be the strict division applied in the Vienna Convention of primary and supplementary means of interpretation. In order for a non-written agreement to be used as a means of interpretation, it must be established. The problem is that, often, little proof is available other than the documents produced during the drafting of the interpreted treaty – what we would otherwise classify as its preparatory work *(travaux préparatoires)*.[29] Considering this, the argument can be made that the provisions of article 31 § 2(a) should be applied with some caution. If non-written agreements are accepted as part of the context – this is how the argument goes – then we open up for a very far-reaching use of preparatory work, already at one of the earlier stages of the interpretation process.[30] This can hardly be what the parties to the Vienna Convention intended. In VCLT article 32, preparatory work has been listed a supplementary means of interpretation, which an applier may resort to for two purposes only: (i) when the use of primary means of interpretation leads to a meaning in need of confirmation; (ii) when the use of primary means of interpretation "[l]eaves the meaning ambiguous or obscure", or "[l]eads to a result which is manifestly absurd or unreasonable".[31] Given that article 31 § 2(a) shall be understood so that by applying the article a result is not achieved, which is not among the objects and purposes of the treaty, the expression "agreement" would then have to be interpreted in accordance with interpretation alternative A – it would have to refer to agreements in the written form only.[32]

In my opinion, this argument should be met with suspicion. Assuming that the expression "agreement" refers to agreements irrespective of form, a non-written agreement – simply because it happens to be made in connection with the conclusion of a treaty – would not necessarily fit the description set forth in article 31 § 2(a). In order for an agreement to come within the scope of article 31 § 2(a), certain conditions must be met.[33] First, there is the condition that the agreement be binding under international law. In order for a transaction to be categorised as an agreement in the sense of subparagraph (a), it must be the intention of the states involved to create law. This in itself disqualifies most of the agreements that can possibly be established by means of *travaux préparatoires*. Second, there is the condition that the agreement be "relating to the treaty". In order for an agreement to come within the scope of subparagraph (a), the agreement and the treaty, according to their parties, must be exceptionally closely connected. Note that in this case, "treaty" means the treaty adopted as final, and nothing else. Surely, we might study *travaux préparatoires* and find that, at a certain point during the drafting process, the negotiating states reached an agreement regarding the interpretation or application of the treaty text *then at hand*. This does not necessarily mean that the agreement bears a relation to the text of the treaty finally adopted at a later point. Subsequent negotiations may have resulted in the "treaty content" to which the agreement relates being abandoned. In general terms, it can probably be said that the earlier an agreement is made during the drafting process, the greater the risk that the agreement does not bear the relationship to the treaty required by article 31 § 2(a). Third, there is the condition that the agreement be made "in connexion with the conclusion of the treaty" – i.e. at the point in time when the treaty was established as definite. It is not entirely clear what is meant by the requirement that an agreement be made "in connexion with" a treaty's conclusion. Apparently, there is room for some flexibility.[34] However, the following may safely be established: not all agreements made "in connexion with the conclusion" of a treaty can be classified as "relating to the treaty". All things considered, the proposition discussed – the one suggesting that, in the application of article 31 § 2(a), non-written agreements cannot possibly be accepted, without also forcing us to accept a *very far-reaching* use of *travaux préparatoires* – is one, which I personally find difficult to endorse. I can agree that non-written agreements cannot be accepted without also forcing us to accept a certain use of *travaux préparatoires*. Yet, I cannot see how this use of *travaux préparatoires* could be anything but limited.

Further support for interpretation alternative B can be found in the fact that interpretation alternative A is not in accord with international judicial opinions. International courts and tribunals appear to view "agreement" as a reference to agreements, irrespective of form. I have two examples of this.[35]

My first example is the international award of the NAFTA Panel of Arbitration in the case of *Canadian Agricultural Tariffs*.[36] On 1 January 1995, Canada had begun applying a new customs tariff, the result being that imports of American agricultural products above a certain quota were now charged with increased duty. The United States Government objected, claiming that the tariff was in excess of those that had earlier been decided upon in the North American Free Trade Agreement (NAFTA). Canada defended its actions, citing article 4 § 2 of the 1994 *WTO Agreement on Agriculture*. Under this agreement, Canada argued, she was under the obligation to convert into tariff form all existing non-tariff barriers applicable to American agricultural products. The question arose as to whether this claim was justified, or whether the only obligation incumbent on Canada was to eliminate non-tariff barriers – the conversion of non-tariff barriers into tariff form being merely an option.

According to the Panel, no answer to this question could be given merely by consulting the wording of the 1994 Agreement:

> [I]t becomes necessary to look beyond the text of the provision to its context, to any subsequent agreement or practice of the parties and, if necessary, to supplementary means of interpretation such as the *travaux préparatoires* of the WTO *Agreement on Agriculture* and the circumstances of its conclusion more generally. This approach is expressly contemplated by Vienna Convention Articles 31 and 32.
>
> 173. The starting point of this analysis must be the negotiations constituting the Uruguay Round [ending with the adoption and signature of, among other instruments, the WTO Agreement on Agriculture].[37]

This gave the Panel cause for the following historical survey:

> The objective of the negotiations in relation to agricultural trade as set out in the *Punta del Este Declaration* was to:
>
> "... achieve greater liberalization of trade in agriculture ... by
> (i) improving market access through, *inter alia*, the reduction of import barriers; ..."
>
> 174. The mechanisms for achieving this, as first proposed by the United States in 1988, was the conversion of non-tariff barriers to "tariff equivalents", a process known as "tariffication". The essence of tariffication was that States were required to eliminate their agricultural non-tariff barriers and were permitted to establish tariff-rate quotas in their place.
>
> 175. The United States tariffication proposal formed the basis of subsequent discussion in the Negotiating Group on Agriculture. Thus, the Chairman of this Group circulated a draft text of a *Framework Agreement on Agricultural Reform Programme* on 11 July 1990 which provided, *inter alia*, for the "conversion of all border measures other than normal customs duties into tariff equivalents".
>
> 176. This formulation was later reflected in the Dunkel Draft submitted to the Uruguay Round participants on 20 December 1991. This contained, in Part B of the draft "Text on

Agriculture", a section entitled "Agreement on Modalities for the Establishment of Specific Binding Commitments under the Reform Programme" which set out the modalities to be adopted for tariffication. Annex 3 of this draft, in paragraph 3, provided that "[t]ariff equivalents *shall* be established for all agricultural products subject to border measures other than ordinary customs duties ..." (emphasis added).

177. These tariffication modalities were subsequently issued separately by the Chairman of the Market Access Group on 20 December 1993 – under the heading "Modalities for the Establishment of Specific Binding Commitments under the Reform Programme" – as a guide to States in the preparation of their tariff schedules. Annex 3 of the Modalities Document reproduced, in paragraph 3, the provision first set out in the Dunkel Draft, *viz.* "[t]ariff equivalents *shall* be established for all agricultural products subject to border measures other than ordinary customs duties ..." (emphasis added).[38]

Clearly, the Modalities Document provided clues to the interpretation of the 1994 Agreement. In the oral pleadings before the panel, Canada had noted:

[T]he Modalities Document was the foundation for the final conclusion of the *Agreement on Agriculture* --- [While the] Modalities Document may not itself have treaty status, ... it is an essential part of the context and background without which Article 4.2 [*of the Agreement on Agriculture*] cannot be understood.[39]

The Panel could do nothing but agree:

In the Panel's view, the Dunkel Draft, the Modalities Document, and the documents on which they were based, may properly be taken into account when interpreting the WTO *Agreement on Agriculture*. They form part of the *travaux préparatoires* and circumstances of the conclusion of the WTO *Agreement on Agriculture* to which reference may be made according to the Vienna Convention Article 32. In this regard, the Panel observes that the obscurity of meaning of Article 4.2 of the WTO *Agreement on Agriculture* justifies recourse to such supplementary material for purposes of interpretation. The Panel also considers that the Modalities Document may be regarded as part of the context of the WTO *Agreement on Agriculture* for the purposes of interpretation pursuant to Vienna Convention Article 31(2) [...].[40]

According to the Panel, the Modalities Document should be seen to come within the scope of VCLT article 31 § 2. Of course, is not clearly said that the Document should be seen to come specifically within the scope of subparagraph (a); but this actually seems to be the only possibility. The Panel also seems eager to show that the view held by Canada is indeed a correct description of history: the 1994 Agreement *was* concluded against the background of the Modalities Document. The Modalities Document is not a treaty. If, nevertheless, it is to be considered the expression of a legally binding agreement, then this agreement can only be non-written.

My second example is the judgment of the International Court of Justice in the case concerning *Border and Transborder Armed Actions*.[41] The facts of the case have already been touched upon in earlier chapters,[42] and I will not unnecessarily repeat myself. As we know, Nicaragua and the Honduras were of different opinions as to the interpretation of article XXXI in the 1948 American Treaty on Pacific Settlement ("the Pact of Bogotá"):

> In conformity with Article 36, paragraph 2, of the Statute of the International Court of Justice, the High Contracting Parties declare that they recognize, in relation to any other American State, the jurisdiction of the Court as compulsory *ipso facto*, without the necessity of any special agreement so long as the present Treaty is in force, in all disputes of a juridical nature that arise among them concerning:
> (a) The interpretation of a treaty;
> (b) Any question of international law;
> (c) The existence of any fact which, if established, would constitute the breach of an international obligation;
> (d) The nature or extent of the reparation to be made for the breach of an international obligation.[43]

The Honduras had advanced the argument that article XXXI of the Pact of Bogotá could only be read correctly if placed in relation to the subsequent article XXXII. However, this was not the only argument the Honduras had presented to support its position. In May 1986, the Honduras had deposited a document with the General Secretary of the UN, declaring its wish to modify the effect of an earlier declaration made according to the provisions of article 36 § 2 of the ICJ Statute. This reservation, the Honduras contended, had a double effect. First, the dispute between Nicaragua and the Honduras was excluded from the jurisdiction that would otherwise be had by the Hague Court according to article 36 § 2 of the ICJ Statute. Secondly, the dispute was excluded from the jurisdiction that would otherwise be had by the Court according to article XXXI of the Pact of Bogotá. Like the first argument advanced by the Honduras, which – as we know – the Court considered unfounded,[44] this argument was rejected as well:

> The Honduran argument as to the effect of the reservation to its 1986 Declaration on its commitment under Article XXXI of the Pact ... cannot be accepted.[45]

Let us put to scrutiny the various arguments set forth by the Court to justify its conclusion.

The first is a reference to the wording of the interpreted treaty provision:

> Article XXXI nowhere envisages that the undertaking entered into by the parties to the Pact might be amended by means of a unilateral declaration made subsequently under the Statute, and the reference to Article 36, paragraph 2, of the Statute is insufficient in itself to have that effect.[46]

After this, the Court turns its attention to the other provisions of the Pact:

> The fact that the Pact defines with precision the obligations of the parties lends particular significance to the absence of any indication of that kind. The commitment in Article XXXI applies *ratione materiae* to the disputes enumerated in that text; it relates *ratione personae* to the American States parties to the Pact; it remains valid *ratione temporis* for as long as that instrument itself remains in force between those States.

35. Moreover, some provisions of the Treaty restrict the scope of the parties' commitment. Article V specifies that procedures under the Pact "may not be applied to matters which, by their nature, are within the domestic jurisdiction of the State". Article VI provides that they will likewise not apply

"to matters already settled by arrangement between the parties, or by arbitral award or by decision of an international court, or which are governed by agreements or treaties in force on the date of the conclusion of the present Treaty".

Similarly, Article VII lays down specific rules relating to diplomatic protection.

Finally, Article LV of the Pact of Bogotá enables the parties to make reservations to that instrument which "shall, with respect to the State that makes them, apply to all signatory States on the basis of reciprocity". In the absence of special procedural provisions those reservations may, in accordance with the rules of general international law on the point as codified by the 1969 Vienna Convention on the Law of Treaties, be made only at the time of signature or ratification of the Pact or at the time of adhesion to that instrument.[47]

The Court uses what it calls the "*travaux préparatoires*":

Further confirmation of the Court's reading of Article XXXI is to be found in the *travaux préparatoires*. In this case these must of course be resorted to only with caution, as not all the stages of the drafting of the texts at the Bogotá Conference were the subject of detailed records. The proceedings of the Conference were however published, in accordance with Article 47 of the Regulations of the Conference, in Spanish, and certain recorded discussions of Committee III of the Conference throw light particularly upon the contemporary conception of the relationship between Article XXXI and declarations under Article 36 of the Statute.

The text which was to become Article XXXI was discussed at the meeting of Committee III held on 27 April 1948. The representative of the United States reminded the meeting that his country had previously, under Article 36, paragraph 2, of the Statute, made a declaration of acceptance of compulsory jurisdiction that included reservations; he made it clear that the United States intended to maintain those reservations in relation to the Pact of Bogotá. The representative of Mexico replied that States which wished to maintain such reservations in their relations with the other parties to the Pact would have to reformulate them as reservations to the Pact, under Article LV. The representatives of Columbia and Ecuador, members of the drafting group, confirmed that interpretation. The representative of Peru asked whether an additional Article should not be added to the draft in order to specify that adhesion to the treaty would imply, as between the parties to it, the automatic removal of any reservations to declarations of acceptance of compulsory jurisdiction. The majority of Committee III considered, however, that such an Article was not necessary and the representative of Peru went on to say, after the vote, that "we should place on record what has been said here, to the effect that it is understood that adhesion is unconditional and that reservations are automatically removed" *(translation by the Registry)*.

38. This solution was not contested in the plenary session, and Article XXXI was adopted by the Conference without any amendments on that point.

As a consequence the United States, when signing the Pact, made a reservation to the effect that:

"The acceptance by the United States of the jurisdiction of the International Court of Justice as compulsory *ipso facto* and without special agreement, as provided in this Treaty, is limited by any jurisdictional or other limitations contained in any Declaration deposited by the

United States under Article 36, paragraph 4, of the Statute of the Court, and in force at the time of the submission of any case."

It is common ground between the Parties that if the Honduran interpretation of Article XXXI of the Pact be correct, this reservation would not modify the legal situation created by that Article, and therefore would not be necessary [...].[48]

After which the Court concludes by noting the practice of the treaty parties since 1948:

They [the Parties to the Pact, that is] have not, at any time, linked together Article XXXI and the declarations of acceptance of compulsory jurisdiction made under Article 36, paragraphs 2 and 4, of the Statute. Thus, no State, when adhering to or ratifying the Pact, has deposited with the United Nations Secretary-General a declaration of acceptance of compulsory jurisdiction under the conditions laid down by the Statute. Moreover, no State party to the Pact (other than Honduras in 1986) saw any need, when renewing or amending its declaration of acceptance of compulsory jurisdiction, to notify the text to the Secretary-General of the OAS, the depository of the Pact, for transmission to the other parties.

Also, in November 1973 El Salvador denounced the Pact of Bogotá and modified its declaration of acceptance of compulsory jurisdiction with a view to restricting its scope. If the new declaration would have been applicable as between the parties to the Pact, no such denunciation would have been required to limit similarly the jurisdiction of the Court under Article XXXI.[49]

The interesting thing about this line of reasoning is the way the Court uses "*travaux préparatoires*". The question arises: What means of interpretation is the Court resorting to here? Two readings can be considered plausible. According to a first reading, the Court resorts to the preparatory work of the Pact of Bogotá as a supplementary means of interpretation, in the sense of VCLT article 32. According to a second reading, the Court resorts to the preparatory work of the Pact of Bogotá, not as a means of interpretation in the sense of the VCLT, but as a way of establishing an agreement of the kind described in VCLT article 31 § 2(a) – the agreement then, naturally, not being a written but a non-written one. Personally, I opt for the second of the two readings. Two sets of circumstances prove me right. The first is the way the United States' reservation is used by the Court. That reservation is not part of the PREPARATORY WORK of the Pact of Bogotá, in the sense of the Vienna Convention. Assuming that the Court's argument does not exceed the framework represented by the rules of interpretation laid down in international law, the more likely conclusion is that when the reservation is turned to, it is only a way of confirming an agreement already indicated in the proceedings.

The second set of circumstances that show I am right is the order in which the preparatory work of the Pact of Bogotá appears in the findings. It cannot be doubted that the correct meaning of the interpreted provision is determined already, by the use of conventional language. The means subsequently used – the other provisions of the Pact, "*travaux préparatoires*", and the subsequent practice of the parties – serve only as confirmation. There is nothing strange about this. According to international law, the context may be used not only as a primary means of interpretation in the sense of VCLT article 31. It can also be used as a supplementary means in the sense of VCLT article 32.[50] If an applier interprets a treaty – whether in order to determine a meaning, or to confirm a meaning already determined – and she has already made use of "the text" of said treaty, then it is hardly a natural progression if, in a second step, she proceeds to use *travaux préparatoires*, and then subsequent practice. A natural progression would be one where the applier has instead used the context – more specifically, the contextual elements set out in VCLT article 31 § 2. All things considered, I arrive at the following conclusion: according to a view held by the International Court of Justice, the expression "agreement" refers to agreements irrespective of form.

3 THE MEANING OF SUBPARAGRAPH (B)

The second class of phenomena that shall be counted as part of the context, according to VCLT article 31 § 2, in addition to "the text" of a treaty, is the one described in subparagraph (b), namely "any instrument which was made by one or more parties in connexion with the conclusion of the treaty and accepted by the other parties as an instrument related to the treaty."

[T]out instrument établi par une ou plusieurs parties à l'occasion de la conclusion du traité et accepté par les autres parties en tant qu'instrument ayant rapport au traité.

Todo instrumento formulado por una o más partes con motivo de la celebración del tratado y aceptado por las demás como instrumento referente al tratado.

Three conditions must be met for a phenomenon to fit this description: (1) the phenomenon must be included in the extension of the expression "instrument"; (2) it must be a question of an instrument "which was made by one or more parties ... and accepted by the other parties as an instrument related to the treaty"; and (3) the instrument must have been made "in connexion with the conclusion of the treaty". Let us examine each of these points one by one. We shall take them in the order in which they have been listed.

In order for a phenomenon to fit the description in subparagraph (b), it must be included in the extension of the expression "instrument" (Fr. *"instrument"*; Sp. *"instrumento"*). According to the terminology used for the Vienna Convention, INSTRUMENT, INSTRUMENT, INSTRUMENTO means a legally relevant document of some sort.[51] In contrast to the provisions of subparagraph (a), where – as we observed in Section 2 – it does not matter whether an agreement is written or non-written, the requirements of subparagraph (b) would accordingly be more exacting. In order for a phenomenon to fit the description in subparagraph (b), it must bear the form of a written document.

In order for an instrument to fit the description in subparagraph (b), it must be a question of a document "which was made by one or more parties ... and accepted by the other parties as an instrument related to the treaty" (Fr. *"établi par une ou plusieurs parties ... et accepté par les autres parties en tant qu'instrument ayant rapport au traité"*; Sp. *"formulado por una o más partes ... y aceptado por las demás como instrumento referente al tratado")*. According to the definition given in VCLT article 2 § 1(g), PARTY means "a State which has consented to be bound by the treaty and for which the treaty is in force".[52] What determines whether a document shall be considered "made by one or more of the parties...and accepted by the other parties" is the state-of-affairs prevailing when a treaty is interpreted – and not that which prevailed when the document was drawn up.[53] Apparently, in order for a document to be considered part of the context, according to subparagraph (b), each and every one of those states that are bound by the treaty at the time of interpretation shall either themselves be authors of the instrument, or they shall subsequently have accepted it as being "an instrument related to the treaty".[54] If a party has accepted an instrument to be "an instrument related to" a treaty, clearly he has accepted that the instrument and the treaty, even if they are not parts of a single treaty text, nevertheless are exceptionally closely connected. Such an acceptance – and this is the view generally held – can be either express or implicit.[55] Clearly, to establish whether the connection between a treaty and an instrument has been accepted or not, a separate process of interpretation might be needed on occasion.

In order for an instrument to fit the description in subparagraph (b), the instrument must have been made "in connexion with the conclusion of the treaty" (Fr. *"à l'occasion de la conclusion du traité"*; Sp. *"con motivo de la celebración del tratado")*. This requirement, in contrast to the other two given above, causes certain problems. In the language of international law, CONCLUSION (Fr. CONCLUSION; Sp. CELEBRACIÓN) remains an ambiguous term;[56] the same applies, even if we were to restrict ourselves to the terminology used for the Vienna Convention.[57] CONCLUSION, in one sense of the word, can be used as equivalent to the point in time when a treaty is established as definite.[58] In another sense it can be used to stand for the time interval from when negotiations on a treaty are started to when a treaty finally enters into force.[59] Further complexity is added by the fact that the entry into force of a treaty is in turn not a unanimous concept. THE ENTRY INTO FORCE OF A TREATY, in one sense of the term, stands for the entry into force of a treaty as such. In another sense, it stands for the entry into force of the treaty for a state.[60] All in all, this provides us with the following interpretation alternatives:

(1) The "conclusion of the treaty" means the point in time when the interpreted treaty was established as definite.
(2) The "conclusion of the treaty" means the time interval from when negotiations on the interpreted treaty started to when the treaty entered into force for the very first time.
(3) The "conclusion of the treaty" means the time interval from when negotiations on the interpreted treaty started to when the treaty entered into force for its parties.

Interpretation alternative (3) – let it be clear – is in turn open for two different interpretations. According to the one alternative, an instrument made "in connexion with the conclusion of a treaty" is something mutually shared by all parties to the treaty: an instrument will, *for all parties*, fit the description in subparagraph (b), as long as it was made in connection with the entry into force of the interpreted treaty for the state that last became a party. According to the other alternative, whether an instrument is made "in connexion with the conclusion of a treaty" is a relative matter: an instrument may, for different parties, both fit and not fit the description of subparagraph (b), depending on whether the instrument was made or not made in connection with the entry into force of the interpreted treaty for the respective parties. The latter of these two alternatives is clearly absurd, and hence may be immediately dismissed. For it was indeed one of the most clearly expressed purposes of the interpretation regime created by the Vienna Convention to reach an agreement on a set of *generally applicable* rules.[61] Accordingly, interpretation alternative (3), as hitherto stated, could then be given a more precise definition:

(3) The "conclusion of the treaty" means the time interval from when negotiations on the interpreted treaty started to when the treaty entered into force for the state that last became a party.

The decisive question, then, is whether the meaning of subparagraph (b) is that represented by alternative (1), (2) or (3). In support of interpretation alternative (3) we may cite the object and purpose of the interpreted treaty. Generally held to be among the phenomena typically falling within the provisions of article 31 § 2(b),[62] are the reservations and *interpretative declarations* made to a treaty.[63] If we take this view to be correct, but still opt for interpretation alternative (1) or (2), the application of VCLT article 31 § 2(b) will have clearly discriminatory effects. Two states may have expressed their consent to be bound by a treaty – the one prior to the "conclusion of the treaty", the other after – and both would be parties to the treaty, the one not more so than the other. However, assuming both states to have formulated, concomitantly with their consent, either reservations to the treaty or interpretative declarations, only the one state's reservation or declaration will come under the provisions of VCLT article 31 § 2(b). This can hardly be what the parties to the Vienna Convention intended. Given that the provisions of article 31 § 2(b) shall be understood so that by applying the article a result is not achieved, which is not among the objects and purposes of the treaty, the "conclusion of the treaty" would then have to be synonymous with the time interval from when negotiations on the interpreted treaty started to when the treaty entered into force for the state that last became a party.[64]

On the other hand, the object and purpose of the interpreted treaty can also be seen to support interpretation alternative (1). As we observed earlier, in article 31 § 2(a), the "conclusion of the treaty" means the point in time when the treaty was established as definite.[65] If, in article 31 § 2(b), the "conclusion of the treaty" would be interpreted along the lines of interpretation alternative (2) or (3), then the undoubted effect would be that the "conclusion of the treaty" in subparagraph (a) referred to one thing, while in subparagraph (b) it referred to quite another. This can hardly be what the parties to the Vienna Convention intended. It is true that in the terminology of the Vienna Convention, the word CONCLUSION is not an unambiguous one – the word is not consistently used throughout the Convention. However, in none of the 27 instances where the word CONCLUSION is used can it be said to bear an inconsistent meaning *within a single article*.[66] That the word would bear an inconsistent meaning *within a single paragraph* appears even less likely. For further confirmation of this view, I would like to draw the reader's attention to the pragmatic relationship that holds between paragraphs 2 and 3 of VCLT article 31. In article 31 § 3(a) and (b) mention is made of "any *subsequent* agreement between the parties regarding the interpretation of the treaty or the application of its provisions", and "any *subsequent* practice in the application of the treaty which establishes the agreement of the parties regarding its interpretation".[67] Clearly, in both cases "subsequent" refers back to the expression used for article 31 § 2: "the conclusion of the treaty".[68] If indeed it is our position that in subparagraph (a), the "conclusion of the treaty" refers to one thing, while in subparagraph (b) the expression refers to quite another, then this fine picture would be seriously flawed. It strikes me as reasonable that the parties to the Vienna Convention under such premises would have indicated, in some way or another, which one "conclusion" "subsequent" refers to – that of subparagraph (a) or that of subparagraph (b). This has not been done. Given that the text of article 31 § 2(b) shall be understood so that by applying the article a result is not achieved, which is not among the objects and purposes of the treaty, the "conclusion of the treaty" would then have to be synonymous with the point in time when the interpreted treaty was established as definite.[69]

Based on this survey, what should be our conclusions? It seems we can immediately dismiss interpretation alternative (2). As noted, interpretation alternatives (1), (2) and (3) are all in harmony with the text of VCLT article 31 § 2(b) interpreted "in accordance with the ordinary meaning to be given to the terms of the treaty". But only interpretation alternatives (1) and (3) can be considered to agree with that text, considering also the context and the object and purpose of the interpreted treaty. The more difficult task is to exclude, in the same manner, any one of interpretation alternatives (1) and (3). To my knowledge, no support for either alternative can be drawn from the preparatory work of the Convention. Nor does it appear that the expression at issue has yet been seriously brought into focus by international courts and tribunals. My conclusion is that at this moment, the prevailing legal state-of-affairs cannot be convincingly determined. There are reasons for adopting interpretation alternative (1), but there are also reasons for adopting interpretation alternative (3); and, to my mind, none of these reasons so obviously outweigh the others that only one of the alternatives can possibly be considered correct.

4 THE "AGREEMENT" AND THE "INSTRUMENT" PUT TO USE

What communicative standard or standards shall the parties to a treaty be assumed to have followed, when an applier interprets the treaty using the two classes of phenomena described in VCLT article 31 § 2(a) and (b)? With regard to using the context, there is reason to repeat part of what we have already noted. In Chapter 4, we observed that in the legal literature, the act of interpretation using context is often termed as SYSTEMATIC INTERPRETATION.[70] When an applier uses the context – this is the assumption – the interpreted treaty provision and the context together form a larger whole, a system. I also noted that the system assumed in the legal literature is not a uniform concept.[71] The term SYSTEMATIC INTERPRETATION is used to refer to not one type of system but two, depending on whether authors envision the interpreted treaty provision and its context authors as the body of text constituted by the text and its context, or the set of norms expressed. In the former case, SYSTEMATIC INTERPRETATION is based on the existence of a system of a linguistic character; in the latter case it is based on the existence of a system in the logical sense. On the basis of these observations, I then put into words the five communicative standards assumed by an applier when he interprets a provision using "the text" of the treaty interpreted; these standards have been designated by the letters A to E. They are of two types. Standards A, C, and D govern the linguistic relationship that shall be assumed to hold between the expressions used for an interpreted treaty provision and the expressions forming the context. Standards B and E govern the logical relationship that shall be assumed to hold between the norm content of an interpreted treaty provision and the norms forming the context.

Now, the decisive question is whether these same communicative standards shall be applied when, instead of using "the text" of a treaty, the applier uses the two contextual elements set out in VCLT article 31 § 2(a) and (b). For me, the answer is clearly in the negative. When an applier interprets a treaty using the contextual elements described in article 31 § 2(a) and (b), this is on the assumption that the interpreted treaty provision and the context form a system *only in the logical sense.* Several reasons can be adduced to support this conclusion. First, very high expectations are placed on a treaty provision when it is considered as part of a linguistic system, compared to when it is considered as part of a system in the logical sense. The provision is expected to be drawn up in such a way that the usage of those words and phrases included in the provision, viewed in the light of the words and phrases included in the context, can be considered consistent; the provision is expected to be drawn up in such a way that nowhere in the context does it give rise to a pleonasm; and the provision is expected to be drawn up in such a way that those words and phrases included in the provision do not take on a meaning equal to the meaning of words and phrases included in other parts of the context, insofar as these words and phrases can be considered to be parts of the same lexical field.[72] If a treaty is to be considered part of two systems, of which one is linguistic and the other logical, then it seems only reasonable that the extension of the former be limited to include only part of that of the latter. An inherent line of limitation would then seem to be formed by the text of the interpreted treaty.[73] Even if we admit that, for interpretation purposes, there is an exceptionally close connection between the text of a treaty and the contextual elements described in VCLT article 31 § 2(a) and (b), common sense tells us that they should still be seen as separate linguistic units. Second, article 31 § 2(a) defines as part of the context "any agreement relating to the treaty which was made between all the parties in connexion with the conclusion of the treaty". "Agreement" – as we earlier observed – refers to any legally binding agreement to be applied within the framework of international law, whether it is written or not.[74] If a communicative standard governs the relationship between an interpreted treaty provision and an agreement relating to the treaty, whatever form it assumes, then obviously this relationship cannot be the one that holds between the various *expressions* used for those two accords.

Among the five communicative standards I have found to be applicable, when an applier interprets a treaty provision using "the text" of said treaty, only standards B and E govern the logical relationship that shall be assumed to hold between the norm content of an interpreted treaty provision and the norms forming the context. These standards have been stated earlier along the following lines:

Standard B
If a state produces an utterance taking the form of a treaty provision, then the provision should be drawn up so that it does not logically contradict the context.

Standard E
If a state produces an utterance taking the form of a treaty provision, then the provision should be drawn up so that in the context there will be no instance of a logical tautology.[75]

Of course, we should not take for granted that both standards B and E are applicable for an interpretation of a treaty using the contextual elements set out in VCLT article 31 § 2(a) and (b), simply because they are both applicable for an interpretation using "the text". That standard B is applicable is plain enough. One of the most basic requirements placed on a logical system is that it be free of logical contradictions. However, strong reasons demonstrate that standard E, too, shall apply. According to several commentators, we shall count as an "agreement relating to the treaty which was made between all the parties in connexion with the conclusion of the treaty", among other things, certain legally binding agreements of interpretation.[76] When such an agreement is used for the interpretation of a treaty, and this is done based on the communicative assumption that the treaty and the agreement do not logically contradict one another, the interpretation arrived at is an AUTHENTIC INTERPRETATION (Fr. INTERPRÉTATION AUTHENTIQUE).[77] An authentic interpretation does not compete on equal terms with an interpretation arrived at through an application of the rules laid down in the Vienna Convention (or the identically similar rules of customary international law); the authentic interpretation always takes precedence. After all, the rules laid down in the Vienna Convention remain *jus dispositivum* – they apply only on the condition, and to the extent, that the parties to a treaty have not come to agree between themselves on something else.[78] Accepting the suggestion that a legally binding interpretation agreement can be used according to the provisions of VCLT article 31 § 2(a), then, as a result, this must be on the basis of some other communicative standard than B.

Further confirmation for this view is provided, if we consider the obvious relationship that holds (at least on paper) between the contextual element described in VCLT article 31 § 2(a) and that described in article 31 § 3(a).

Article 31 § 3(a) speaks of "any subsequent agreement between the parties regarding the interpretation of the treaty or the application of its provisions". As it appears, the phrase "any agreement relating to the treaty" used for § 2(a) is a shortened form of "any … agreement between the parties regarding the interpretation of the treaty or the application of its provisions" used for § 3(a).[79] Two communicative standards are assumed when an applier interprets a treaty using a "subsequent agreement" according to § 3(a): standard B and standard E.[80] Arguably, given the obvious relationship that holds between the contextual element described in § 2(a) and that described in article § 3(a), those two standards should also be assumed when the applier interprets a treaty using an "agreement relating to the treaty" according to § 2(a). All things considered, the conclusion I draw is the following: when an applier interprets a treaty using the contextual elements described in VCLT article 31 § 2(a) and (b), it is on the basis of not only standard B but also standard E.

5 CONCLUSIONS

According to VCLT article 31 § 1, a treaty shall be interpreted in good faith "in agreement with the ordinary meaning given to the terms of the treaty in their context and in the light of its object and purpose". For a means of interpretation, the context comprises an exceptionally wide range of data. Therefore, to facilitate presentation, I have chosen to divide the concept into three parts, each part made the subject of a separate chapter of this work. The purpose of this current chapter is to describe what it means to interpret a treaty using the contextual elements set out in VCLT article 31 § 2(a) and (b). Based on the observations made in this chapter, the following four rules of interpretation can be established:

Rule no. 7

§ **1**. If it can be shown that the interpretation of a treaty provision in accordance with interpretation rule no. 1 leads to conflicting results, and that in connection with the conclusion of said treaty, the parties made an agreement, which relates to the treaty, and – in light of the provision interpreted – in one of two possible ordinary meanings can be considered to involve a logical contradiction, while in the other it cannot, then the latter meaning shall be adopted.

§ **2**. For the purpose of this rule, AGREEMENT means any agreement governed by international law, whether written or not.

§ **3**. For the purpose of this rule, the CONCLUSION of a treaty means the point in time when the treaty was established as definite.

§ **4**. For the purpose of this rule, PARTIES means any and all states for which the treaty is in force at the time of interpretation.
§ **5**. For the purpose of this rule, saying that an agreement RELATES TO a treaty is tantamount to saying that in the view of the parties, the agreement and the treaty are exceptionally closely connected.

Rule no. 8
§ **1**. If it can be shown that the interpretation of a treaty provision in accordance with interpretation rule no. 1 leads to conflicting results, and that in connection with the conclusion of said treaty, the parties made an agreement, which relates to the treaty, and – in light of the provision interpreted – in one of two possible ordinary meanings can be considered to involve a logical tautology, while the other cannot, then the latter meaning shall be adopted.
§ **2**. For the purpose of this rule, AGREEMENT means any agreement governed by international law, whether written or not.
§ **3**. For the purpose of this rule, the CONCLUSION of a treaty means the point in time when the treaty was established as definite.
§ **4**. For the purpose of this rule, PARTIES means any and all states for which the treaty is in force at the time of interpretation.
§ **5**. For the purpose of this rule, saying that an agreement RELATES TO a treaty is tantamount to saying that in the view of the parties, the agreement and the treaty are exceptionally closely connected.

Rule no. 9
§ **1**. If it can be shown that the interpretation of a treaty provision in accordance with interpretation rule no. 1 leads to conflicting results, and that in connection with the conclusion of said treaty, one or more parties made an instrument, which was later accepted by the other parties as related to the treaty, and – viewed in the light of the provision interpreted – in one of two possible ordinary meanings can be considered to involve a logical contradiction, while the other cannot, then the latter meaning shall be adopted.
§ **2**. For the purpose of this rule, PARTIES means any and all states for which the treaty is in force at the time of interpretation.

Rule no. 10
§ **1**. If it can be shown that the interpretation of a treaty provision in accordance with interpretation rule no. 1 leads to conflicting results, and that in connection with the conclusion of said treaty, one or more parties made an instrument, which was later accepted by the other parties as related to the treaty, and – viewed in the light of the provision interpreted – in one

of two possible ordinary meanings can be considered to involve a logical tautology, while the other cannot, then the latter meaning shall be adopted. **§ 2.** For the purpose of this rule, PARTIES means any and all states for which the treaty is in force at the time of interpretation.

NOTES

1. See p. 102 of this work.
2. See e.g. Elias, 1974, p. 75; Castrén, at the eighteenth session, 870th meeting, of the ILC, *ILC Yrbk*, 1966, Vol. 1, Part 2, p. 189, § 54. Differently Jiménez de Aréchaga, at the same meeting, ibid., pp. 190–191, § 73.
3. Yasseen, p. 37.
4. Cf. *S.D. Myers*, sep. op. judge Schwartz, *ILR*, Vol. 121, p. 148.
5. Note that in order for an agreement to be counted as part of the context, in the sense of VCLT article 31 § 2(a), it must have been made in connection with the conclusion of the interpreted treaty. According to the terminology used for the Vienna Convention, no state can be a party to a treaty before it enters into force.
6. See Vierdag, 1988, pp. 76–82.
7. Ibid., pp. 82ff.
8. To be exact, 27 times: in articles 2 § 1(a), 3, 4, 6, 7 § 2(a), 30 § 5, 31 § 2(a), 31 § 2(b), 32, 40 § 2(b), 41 § 1, 41 § 2, 46 – in its heading and in § 1 – 48 § 1, 49, 52, 53, 58 § 1, 59 – in its heading and in § 1 – 62 § 1, 74 – in its heading and twice in the text of the article – and in the headings of VCLT Part II and of Section 1.
9. Other obvious examples include articles 2 § 1(a), 3, 4, 40 § 2 and 49.
10. See VCLT article 2 § 1(e).
11. Other obvious examples include articles 6, 46, 52, 59, and the heading of VCLT Part II and of Section 1.
12. See Reuter, 1987, pp. 404–405; Sinclair, 1984, pp. 129–130; Jiménez de Aréchaga, p. 45; Yasseen, pp. 37–38; E. Lauterpacht, p. 444; Haraszti, p. 89; Rest, p. 146, n. 1; Jennings, p. 549; Bernhardt, 1967, p. 498. See also Australia, at the first session of the Vienna Conference, 31st meeting of the Committee of the Whole, *Official Records*, p. 169, § 59; and Yasseen, speaking as Chairman of the Drafting Committee, at the same session, 74th meeting of the Committee of the Whole, ibid., p. 442, § 31.
13. See Aust, p. 787.
14. See Villiger, p. 344; Yasseen, p. 37; E. Lauterpacht, p. 444; Haraszti, p. 146, n. 181, cf. pp. 145–147; Elias, 1974, p. 75; Favre, 1974, p. 253; Müller, p. 13, cf. pp. 104–105; Schwarzenberger, 1969, p. 220; Degan, 1968, p. 17. See also The Federal Republic of Germany, at the Vienna Conference, Second session, 13th plenary meeting, *Official Records*, p. 57, § 64; Romania, at the Vienna Conference, First session, 31st meeting of the Committee of the Whole, ibid., p. 169, §§ 55–57; and Draft Articles With Commentaries (1966), *ILC Yrbk*, 1966, Vol. 2, p. 221, § 14.
15. Note that nothing in international law says that an agreement drawn up by two states must assume a certain form – from a legal point of view, written agreements are no more binding than non-written ones.
16. In addition to the authorities cited in the text, see Bernhardt, 1999, p. 14; Jiménez de Aréchaga, p. 44; Haraszti, p. 89; Rest, pp. 145–146; Jennings, p. 549.
17. Elias, 1974, pp. 74–75. (My italics.)

18. Sinclair, 1984, p. 129 (My italics; footnote omitted.)
19. In addition to the authorities cited in the text, see Villiger, p. 344; Favre, 1974, p. 253.
20. Yasseen, p. 37.
21. Müller, pp. 131–132. (Footnote omitted.)
22. See Ch. 6, Section 1 of this work.
23. Draft Articles With Commentaries (1966), *ILC Yrbk*, 1966, Vol. 2, p. 249, § 3. (Footnote omitted.)
24. Ibid., pp. 232–233, § 4.
25. See Ch. 4 of this work.
26. Cf. the Federal Republic of Germany, at the Vienna Conference, Second session, 13th plenary meeting, *Official Records*, p. 57, § 64.
27. See Ch. 6, Section 1, of this work.
28. Cf. interpretation rule no. 15. (See Ch. 7 of this work.)
29. When two states disagree about the meaning of a treaty, and the one claims that when the treaty was concluded the two parties had already orally agreed to a specific interpretation of the treaty, then normally the other state has no interest in confirming this claim.
30. Cf. The Federal Republic of Germany, at the Vienna Conference Second session, 13th plenary meeting, *Official Records*, p. 57, § 64.
31. See further Ch. 10 of this work.
32. Cf. interpretation rule no. 15 (See Ch.7 of this work.)
33. See Section 2 of this chapter.
34. Cf. *Oppenheim's International Law*: "The phrase 'in connection [sic!] with the conclusion of the treaty' is not the same as 'at the time of the conclusion of the treaty': but, on the other hand, too long a lapse of time between the treaty and the additional agreement might prevent it from being regarded as made in connection with 'the conclusion of the treaty" (p. 1274) .Cf. also Yasseen: "L'accord ou l'instrument doit être établi à l'occasion de la conclusion du traité. Il y a ici une certaine notion de contemporanéité, l'un ou l'autre peut être concomitant à cette conclusion, mais il peut la précéder ou la suivre sans s'en éloigner trop" (p. 38).
35. Possibly, see also *Yaung Chi Oo Trading*, *ILR*, Vol. 127, p. 83, § 74.
36. In the Matter of Tariffs Applied by Canada to Certain US-origin Agricultural Products (CDA-95–2008–01), Award of 2 December 1996, *ILR*, Vol. 110, pp. 543ff.
37. *ILR*, Vol. 110, p. 590, §§ 172–173.
38. Ibid., pp. 590–591, §§ 173–177. (Footnote omitted.)
39. The text cited is that provided by the Panel. (See ibid., p. 110, p. 562, § 60. Footnote omitted.)
40. Ibid., p. 591, § 179.
41. *Case Concerning Border and Transborder Armed Actions (Nicaragua v. Honduras)*, Judgment of 20 December 1988, *ILR*, Vol. 84, pp. 219ff.
42. See Ch. 4, Section 4, of this work.
43. The text cited is that provided by the Court. (See *ILR*, Vol. 84, p. 233, § 20.)
44. See pp. 117–120 of this work.
45. Ibid., p. 243, § 41.
46. Ibid., p. 239, § 34.
47. Ibid., pp. 239–240, §§ 34–35.
48. Ibid., pp. 240–241, §§ 37–38.
49. Ibid., p. 242, § 40.

50. See Ch. 8, Section 6, of this work.
51. Cf. e.g. articles 2 § 1(a), 13, 16, 67, 68 and 77 § 1.
52. VCLT article 2 § 1(g).
53. Note that in order for a document to be counted as part of the context, in the sense of VCLT article 31 § 2(b), it must have been made in connection with the conclusion of the interpreted treaty. According to the terminology used for the Vienna Convention, no state can be a party to a treaty before it enters into force.
54. Judging by the opinions expressed in the literature, the fact that a document is accepted "as an instrument related to the treaty" seems to also imply that the content of the document is to some degree accepted. See Villiger, p. 344; McRae, pp. 169–170; Elias, 1974, p. 75; Bernhardt, 1967, p. 498. See also Jiménez de Aréchaga, at the ILC's 18th session, 870:e meeting, *ILC Yrbk*, 1966, Vol. 1, Part 2, pp. 190–191, § 73; Castrén, on the same occasion, ibid., p. 189, § 54); Rosenne, at the ILC's 16th session, 769:e meeting, *ILC Yrbk*, 1964, Vol. 1, p. 313, § 54.
55. See Villiger, p. 344; McRae, pp. 189–170. See also Waldock, Sixth Report on the Law of Treaties, *ILC Yrbk*, 1966, Vol. 2, p. 98, § 16; and possibly also *Pulau Ligitan and Pulau Sipadan*, § 48. This view is further supported by the fact that, according to most experts, we shall include among the various phenomena typically coming within the scope of subparagraph (b) instruments of ratification, insofar as they contain reservations or *interpretative declarations* (Fr. *déclarations interprétatives*). (See e.g. Villiger, p. 344; Voïcu, p. 189, Waldock, Fourth Report on the Law of Treaties, *ILC Yrbk*, 1965, Vol. 2, p. 49, § 2; El-Erian, at the ILC's Seventeenth session, 797:e meeting, *ILC Yrbk*, 1965, Vol. 1, p. 153, § 60; Bartoš at the ILC's sixteenth session, 769:e meeting, *ILC Yrbk*, 1964, Vol. 1, p. 313, § 50; Ago, speaking as Chairman, on the same occasion, ibid., p. 313, § 51.) As is well known, the acceptance of a reservation does not need to be explicit. (See VCLT article 20 § 5.)
56. See Vierdag, 1988, pp. 76–82.
57. See ibid., pp. 82ff.
58. This is the sense seemingly assumed for the word CONCLUSION, CONCLUSION, and CELEBRACIÓN in VCLT articles 2 § 1(a), 3, 4, 31 § 2(a), 32, 40 § 2 and 49.
59. This is the sense seemingly assumed for the word CONCLUSION, CONCLUSION, and CELEBRACIÓN in VCLT articles 6, 7 § 2(a), 46, 52 and 59, as well as in the headings of VCLT Part II and Section 1.
60. See VCLT article 24.
61. See e.g. Draft Articles With Commentaries (1966): "Most cases submitted to international adjudication involve the interpretation of treaties, and the jurisprudence of international tribunals is rich in reference to principles and maxims of interpretation — Any attempt to codify the conditions of the application of those principles of interpretation whose appropriateness in any given case depends on the particular context and on a subjective appreciation of varying circumstances would clearly be inadvisable. Accordingly the Commission confines itself to trying to isolate and codify the comparatively few general principles which appear to constitute general rules for the interpretation of treaties." (*ILC Yrbk*, 1966, Vol. 2, pp. 218–219, § 5.)
62. See p. 148, n. 55 of this work.
63. By an INTERPRETATIVE DECLARATION we shall understand a unilateral statement made by a state, at the conclusion of a treaty, with the purpose of clarifying its position vis-à-vis the meaning of some part of the treaty, in contrast to a reservation, which is

made with the purpose of excluding or modifying the legal effects of the treaty. (Cf. Horn, pp. 236–237; Voïcu, pp. 182–189.)

64. Cf. interpretation rule no. 15. (See Ch. 7 of this work.)
65. See Section 2 of this chapter.
66. One article that more than once mentions the CONCLUSION of a treaty is article 41:
    1. "Two or more of the parties to a multilateral treaty may conclude an agreement to modify the treaty as between themselves alone if...
    2. Unless in a case falling under paragraph 1 (a) the treaty otherwise provides, the parties in question shall notify the other parties of their intention to conclude the agreement and of the modification to the treaty for which it provides."

    According to Vierdag, in this article the word CONCLUDE is used inconsistently. In paragraph 1, the word refers to the time interval from when negotiations on the agreement started to when the agreement entered into force; in paragraph 2, it refers to the point in time when the agreement is established as definite. (See Vierdag, 1988, p. 86.) I am not convinced. I can accept the interpretation that in paragraph 2 the word CONCLUDE refers to the point in time when the agreement is established as definite. However, I think there are persuasive arguments against accepting the interpretation suggested by Vierdag as regards paragraph 1. According to the reading I would like to suggest, the expression "conclude the agreement" used for paragraph 2 refers back to the expression "conclude an agreement" used for paragraph 1. If such is the case, in paragraph 1, too, the word CONCLUDE must refer to the point in time when the agreement is established as definite.
67. My italics.
68. See Ch. 6, Sections 1 and 2, of this work.
69. Cf. interpretation rule no. 15. (See Ch. 7 of this work.)
70. See Ch. 4, Section 2, of this work.
71. Loc. cit.
72. See above, in Ch. 4, of this work.
73. Symptomatic of this is the fact that a number of authors speak of CONTEXT IN THE STRICT SENSE and CONTEXT IN THE BROAD SENSE, where CONTEXT IN THE STRICT SENSE refers to "the text" of the interpreted treaty, and CONTEXT IN THE BROAD SENSE refers to the two contextual elements described in VCLT article 31 § 2(a) and (b). (See e.g. Köck, p. 90; Haraszti, p. 88.)
74. See Section 1 of this chapter.
75. See p. 107 and p. 110 of this work, respectively.
76. See e.g. Villiger, p. 344; Yasseen, p. 37; Schwarzenberger, 1969, p. 220; Voïcu, p. 103. See also Australia, at the Vienna Conference First session, 31st meeting of the Committee of the Whole, *Official Records*, p. 169, § 59; and Romania, on the same occasion, ibid., p. 169, § 55.
77. On authentic interpretation in general, see e.g. *Oppenheim's International Law*, pp. 1268–1269; Skubiszewski, 1983, pp. 898–902; Karl, 1983, pp. 40–45, 204–211; Haraszti, pp. 43–51; Voïcu, pp. 73–110, 137–217; Bernhardt, 1963, pp. 44–46.
78. See Ch. 1, Section 1, of this work.
79. A more detailed description of the contextual element set out in article 31 § 3(a) is provided in Ch. 6, Section 1, of this work.
80. See Ch. 6, Section 6 of this work.

CHAPTER 6

USING THE CONTEXT: THE ELEMENTS SET OUT IN VCLT ARTICLE 31 § 3

The purpose of this chapter is to describe what it means to interpret a treaty, using the contextual elements set down in article 31 § 3. Article 31 § 3 provides as follows:

> [When appliers use the context according to the provisions of VCLT article 31 § 1, they shall take] into account together with the context [described in § 2]:
> (a) any subsequent agreement between the parties regarding the interpretation of the treaty or the application of its provisions;
> (b) any subsequent practice in the application of the treaty which establishes the agreement of the parties regarding its interpretation;
> (c) any relevant rules of international law applicable in the relations between the parties.

Earlier, we established the following shorthand description of how the context is to be used:

> If it can be shown that the interpretation of a treaty provision in accordance with interpretation rule no. 1 leads to conflicting results, and that between the provision and the context there is a relationship governed by the communicative standard S, then the provision shall be understood as if the relationship conformed to this standard.[1]

Two questions remain to be answered, in order for the task set for this chapter to be considered completed:

(1) What is meant by "any subsequent agreement between the parties regarding the interpretation of the treaty or the application of its provisions"; "any subsequent practice in the application of the treaty which establishes the agreement of the parties regarding its interpretation"; and "any relevant rules of international law applicable in the relations between the parties"?
(2) What communicative standard or standards shall the parties to a treaty be assumed to have followed, when an applier interprets the treaty making use of said "agreement[s]", "practice[s]" and "rules of international law"?

I shall now give what I consider to be the correct answers to these questions. In Sections 1–5, I shall begin by answering question (1). In Section 6, I shall then proceed to answering question (2).

1 SUBPARAGRAPH (A)

According to Vienna Convention article 31 § 3, three different classes of phenomena shall be seen to come within the scope of this paragraph. One such class is the one described in subparagraph (a), namely "any subsequent agreement between the parties regarding the interpretation of the treaty or the application of its provisions".

[T]out accord ultérieur intervenu entre les parties au sujet de l'interprétation du traité ou de l'application de ses dispositions ...

Todo acuerdo ulterior entre las partes acerca de la interpretación del tratado o de la aplicación de sus disposiciones ...

Four conditions must be met in order for a phenomenon to fit this description: (1) the phenomenon must be included in the extension of the expression "agreement"; (2) the agreement must be one made "between the parties"; (3) the agreement must be "subsequent"; and (4) it must be "regarding the interpretation of the treaty or the application of its provisions". Let us examine each of these points one by one.

In order for a phenomenon to fit the description in subparagraph (a), it must fall within the extension of the expression "agreement" (Fr. *"accord"*; Sp. *"acuerdo")*. In subparagraph (a), AGREEMENT means an agreement in the legal-technical sense; that is to say, an act performed with the purpose of establishing a legal relationship.[2] Many international transactions occur without the parties involved having an intention to commit themselves other than politically or morally. Such agreements – denoted in the literature as gentlemen's agreements, non-binding agreements, agreements *de facto*, non-legal agreements, and so on[3] – are not included in the extension of the expression "agreement". In order for an international transaction to be categorised as an agreement in the sense of subparagraph (a), the states involved must have had the intention to create law – the intention must have been to conclude a legally binding agreement governed by international law. On the other hand, there seems to be no requirement with regard to the form of the agreement. It is a generally held view among legal authorities that the expression "agreement" refers to any international agreement, whether written or not.[4]

In order for an agreement to fit the description in subparagraph (a), it must be one made "between the parties" (Fr. *"entre les parties"*; Sp. *"entre las partes")*. PARTY, according to the definition given in VCLT article 2 § 1(g), means "a State which has consented to be bound by the treaty and for which the treaty is in force". By "the parties" all parties are meant.[5] In the legal regime established by articles 31–33 of the Vienna Convention, a recurring theme is that normally, a phenomenon cannot be included in the context for the interpretation of a treaty, if all parties have not accepted it. Whether or not a state shall be considered a party in the sense of subparagraph (a) is determined based on the state-of-affairs that prevails when a treaty is interpreted, not on the state-of-affairs that once prevailed when the agreement was made.[6] Apparently, in order for an agreement to fit the description set forth in article 31 § 3(a), each and every one of those states bound by the treaty at the time of interpretation, must be bound by the agreement.

In order for an agreement to fit the description in subparagraph (a), it must be "subsequent" (Fr. *"ultérieur"*; Sp. *"ulterior")*. The expression "subsequent" refers back to the content of article 31 § 2: both subparagraph (a) and subparagraph (b) use the expression "the conclusion of the treaty".[7] "[T]he conclusion of the treaty", in the sense of article 31 § 2(a), means the point in time when the interpreted treaty was established as definite.[8] The meaning of the identical expression used for article 31 § 2(b) is (as yet) not entirely clear. Arguably, it refers either to the point in time when the interpreted treaty was established as definite, or to the time interval from when negotiations on the interpreted treaty started to when the treaty finally entered into force for the state that last became a party.[9] Given that the provisions of article 31 § 3(a) shall be understood so that the content of article 31 § 2 is not pragmatically contradicted, we arrive at the following conclusion: a "subsequent agreement" means an agreement made either after the point in time when the interpreted treaty was established as definite, or after the point when the treaty finally entered into force for the state that last became a party. Of these two alternatives, the latter must at once be dismissed; it is simply unreasonable. Assuming that a "subsequent agreement" is one concluded after the point when the interpreted treaty finally entered into force for the state that last became a party, then for many agreements the quality of being subsequent would be temporary indeed. An agreement concluded between two states, both of which have been parties to the interpreted treaty since it first entered into force, would only be subsequent as long as no other state expresses its consent to be bound – and this regardless of whether the new party also becomes a party to the agreement – since the agreement is no longer subsequent for all parties. A state-of-affairs such as this cannot possibly be what the parties to the Vienna Convention wished to achieve. Consequently, a "subsequent" agreement shall be understood as one whose earliest existence cannot be traced further back than to the point in time when the interpreted treaty was established as definite.

Another question is at what point, at the very earliest, an agreement can be said to exist, in the sense of subparagraph (a). Obviously, if it is a requirement that in each particular case it must be established whether an agreement is "subsequent" or not, then it is not sufficient if the conclusion of the treaty can be determined, but not that of the agreement. In order for an agreement to be considered "subsequent", to my mind, the contents of said agreement must have been accepted at a point later than that which marks the interpreted treaty's conclusion. If a "subsequent agreement" means a transaction, which occurs after the point in time which marks the conclusion of the interpreted treaty, and the conclusion of the treaty is determined to be the point when the treaty was established as definite, then arguably the existence of the agreement must be tied to that same point. Further support for this understanding can be found in the provisions of Vienna Convention article 30. Article 30 brings into focus the situation where two treaties are found to be in conflict, and the one treaty is "earlier" while the other is "later"; in the heading of article 30 it is spoken of as "successive treaties relating to the same subject-matter". In the legal literature, different opinions have been expressed as to the implications of a treaty being termed as "earlier" or "later" than another. According to some authors, the decisive criterion is the point in time when a treaty was established as definite.[10] According to others, the determining factor is the point in time when a treaty entered into force.[11] Differences aside, no one author seems to have doubts that the criterion applied to the one treaty shall also be applied to the other. Two treaties (A and B) are "successive" with regard to each other, either because A was authenticated at a point later than B, or because A entered into force at a point later than B. Similarly, it seems a reasonable assumption that an agreement can be considered "subsequent" to a treaty, in the sense of VCLT article 31 § 3(a), either because it was authenticated at a point later than the authentication of the treaty, or because the agreement entered into force for the parties at a point later than the entry into force of the treaty.

In order for an agreement to fit the description in subparagraph (a), it must be "regarding the interpretation of the treaty or the application of its provisions" (Fr. *"au sujet de l'interpré tation du traité ou de l'application de ses dispositions"*; Sp. *"acerca de la interpretación del tratado o de la aplicación de sus disposiciones")*. Of course, an agreement "regarding" the interpretation of a treaty or the application of its provisions means an agreement, *the purpose of which* is to clarify the meaning of a treaty or to serve in some other manner as a guide for application.[12] An agreement cannot be said to be REGARDING the interpretation of a treaty or the application of its provisions, in the sense of subparagraph (a), merely because it includes a passage that could be of use for the interpretation or the application of the treaty. Less clear is the meaning of the expression "application". In article 31 § 3(b), the APPLICATION of a treaty refers to any action taken by an applier on the basis of the interpreted treaty.[13] It seems a reasonable assumption that in subparagraph (a), the word APPLICATION should be given this meaning too. Consequently, an agreement regarding the "application" of a treaty does not necessarily need to amount to a set of rules for the APPLICATION of the treaty in the legal-technical sense of the word. It can also be equivalent to an instruction concerning the use of the treaty in the more general sense. A typical example is when arrangements are made for the implementation of the treaty. Even if we concur in the opinion of some authors,[14] that it is not completely practicable to distinguish between the *interpretation* and the *application* of a rule of law,[15] it is nevertheless clear that in the particular context examined, the concepts only partially overlap with each other. It might be that an agreement regarding the "interpretation of the treaty" also has regard to "the application of its provisions", and vice versa. However, it need not necessarily be the case. It seems as if the parties to the Vienna Convention have anticipated the possibility that an agreement, even if it has not been made to clarify the meaning of a treaty, can nevertheless be of use when the treaty is interpreted.

2 SUBPARAGRAPH (B): INTRODUCTION

The second class of phenomena that shall be counted as part of the context, according to VCLT article 31 § 3, is the one described in subparagraph (b), namely "any subsequent practice in the application of the treaty which establishes the agreement of the parties regarding its interpretation".

[T]oute pratique ultérieurement suivie dans l'application du traité par laquelle est établi l'accord des parties à l'égard de l'interprétation du traité ...

Toda práctica ulteriormente seguida en la aplicación del tratado por la cual conste el acuerdo de las partes acerca de la interpretación del tratado ...

In order for a phenomenon to fit the description set out in subparagraph (b), four conditions must be met: (1) the phenomenon must be such, that it can be considered a "practice"; (2) it must be a question of a practice "in the application of the treaty"; (3) the practice must be "subsequent"; and (4) it must be a practice "which establishes the agreement of the parties regarding its interpretation". Let us examine these points one by one, in numerical order.

In order for a phenomenon to fit the description in subparagraph (b), it must be such that it can be considered a "practice" (Fr. *"pratique"*; Sp. *"práctica")*. By "practice" we mean the output of a treaty – admittedly, not a very potent definition, but a better description hardly seems possible. In the text of VCLT article 31 § 3(b), the emphasis is not on the word practice; instead, it lies on the qualifications attached to this word.[16] "[P]ractice" is simply the sum total of a number of applications – any applications – as long as they "establish the agreement of the parties regarding its interpretation". According to this definition, "practice" does not necessarily emanate only from the parties themselves. All appliers of a treaty are potential creators of "practice", whether it be the state parties themselves, or the non-state organ – possibly an international organisation – with which the application might have been entrusted.[17] Nor can "practice" be limited to the positive aspects of a treaty's use. "[P]ractice" can be the sum total of a number of (positive) actions; but it can also be the result of omissions, manifesting itself in the absence of (positive) actions arguably expected.[18]

A question that has garnered attention in the literature is whether a single, one-time application of a treaty in itself can be considered sufficient for us to speak of a "practice", or whether additional applications are required.[19] In my view there is something laboured about this discussion. Of course, considering the realities of life, it is often required that "practice" takes the form of a series of applications. A single application is normally not capable of establishing an agreement held among the parties to an interpreted treaty. However, from a principle point of view, I find it difficult to see why *one* application cannot constitute a "practice" if *two* can. The emphasis in the Vienna Convention – I repeat – is not on the word PRACTICE. Considering this, it seems to be the only reasonable interpretation that a "practice" can consist of any number of applications, one or two or many – just as long as they "establish the agreement of the parties regarding its interpretation".

In order for a practice to fit the description in subparagraph (b), it must be a practice "in the application of the treaty" (Fr. *"suivie dans l'application du traité"*; Sp. *"seguida en la aplicación del tratado")*. Generally speaking, THE APPLICATION of a treaty is defined as action taken in accordance with the provisions of that treaty. "L'application", Yasseen writes, ...

> ... est l'opération qui assure le passage de l'abstrait au concret, elle détermine les conséquences de la règle dont le sens est dégagé par l'interprétation dans une situation concrète.[20]

In subparagraph (b), "application" stands for a broader concept.[21] Accordingly, it can be considered an "application" when the provisions of a treaty are invoked to support a decision or an action of a state in a specific situation;[22] when the provisions of a treaty are invoked to support the pleadings of a state in a legal dispute;[23] when the provisions of a treaty are invoked to support the position of a state at a diplomatic conference;[24] when the provisions of a treaty are invoked to support the position of a state at a meeting of an international organisation;[25] when the provisions of a treaty are the cause for an official communication, for example a protest or an expression of appreciation;[26] when the provisions of a treaty, for a parliament, are the cause for introducing new law;[27] when the provisions of a treaty are the cause for concluding a new international agreement or the cause for the way the new agreement is drafted;[28] and so forth. Just as with the expression "practice", it seems that we should not read too much into the expression "in the application of the treaty". By "the application of the treaty" paragraph (b) quite simply refers to each and every measure taken *on the basis of the interpreted treaty.*[29]

In order for a practice to fit the description in subparagraph (b), it must be "subsequent" (Fr. *"ulté rieurement suivie"*; Sp. *"ulteriormente seguida")*. The expression "subsequent" refers back to expression "the conclusion of the treaty" used in VCLT article 31 § 2.[30] I see no reason to doubt that the *conclusion* assumed in the text of subparagraph (b) is also the one assumed in the text of subparagraph (a).[31] Hence, "subsequent practice" should be understood to mean a practice, only if originated after the point in time when the interpreted treaty was established as definite.

In order for a practice to fit the description in subparagraph (b), it must be a practice "which establishes the agreement of the parties regarding its interpretation" (Fr. *"par laquelle est é tabli l'accord des parties à l'égard de l'interprétation du traité"*; Sp. *"por la cual conste el acuerdo de las partes acerca de la interpretación del tratado")*. In the terminology of the Vienna Convention, PARTY means "a State which has consented to be bound by the treaty and for which the treaty is in force".[32] By "the parties" all parties are meant.[33] In the legal regime established by articles 31–33 of the Vienna Convention, it is a recurring theme that, normally, a phenomenon cannot be included in the context for the interpretation of a treaty, if all parties have not accepted it. Whether or not a state shall be considered a party, in the sense of subparagraph (b), is determined based on the state-of-affairs that prevails when a treaty is interpreted.[34] It seems that in order for a practice to fit the description set forth in subparagraph (b), the agreement established by the practice must be all-inclusive: each and every one of those states, which are bound by the interpreted treaty at the time of interpretation, must embrace the agreement. A practice "which establishes the agreement" means a practice, on the basis of which the assumption can arguably be made that an agreement exists.[35] Thus, a practice "which establishes the agreement of the parties regarding its [i.e. the treaty's] interpretation" will not necessarily be a practice, to which all parties themselves have contributed. All parties must have acquiesced in the interpretation. However, if the circumstances allow for the assumption that a party has consented, even though the party itself did not contribute to the practice, then this shall be sufficient.[36]

A distinction must be made between a practice "which establishes the agreement between the parties regarding its [i.e. the treaty's] interpretation", and a practice which establishes an agreement of the parties concerning a *modification* of the treaty. If two or more states enter into a treaty, but then decide that for one reason or another, the content of the treaty is no longer satisfactory, then, of course, they are free to agree on a modification of the treaty. Such an agreement can be realised in different ways. First of all, it can be realised in the way perceived by the Vienna Convention – through negotiation and adoption of yet another treaty.[37] However, a modification of a treaty can also be effected in more informal ways – by a subsequent practice in the application of the treaty, which establishes an agreement of the parties to a modification of said treaty.[38] Clearly, there is a very close kinship between a subsequent practice in the application of a treaty, which establishes an agreement of the parties to a modification of the treaty on the one hand, and on the other a "subsequent practice which establishes agreement between the parties regarding its interpretation". Formally, however, we are talking about two completely different things. When a practice establishes an agreement to a modification of a treaty, then the agreement is considered an integral part of the treaty (or, rather, the agreement which the treaty expresses). The agreement *shall* have legal effect; and that effect extends to all cases, to which the treaty could conceivably be applied. When a practice establishes an agreement concerning the interpretation of a treaty, then the agreement is merely a means of interpretation. The agreement *may* have a legal effect, depending upon the possible conflicts with other means of interpretation; but when the agreement has a legal effect, the effect is limited to the particular case at hand.[39]

Now, the question naturally arises how we are to distinguish between a subsequent practice which establishes an agreement of the parties to a modification of a treaty, and a practice "which establishes the agreement between the parties regarding its interpretation". Some authors seem to have resigned to the problem altogether. For example, Sinclair writes:

> It will be apparent that the subsequent practice of the parties may operate as a tacit or implicit modification of the terms of the treaty. It is inevitably difficult, if not impossible, to fix the dividing line between interpretation properly so called and modification effected under the pretext of interpretation. There is therefore a close link between the concept that subsequent practice is an element to be taken into account in the interpretation of a treaty and the concept that a treaty may be modified by subsequent practice of the parties.[40]

In my view, this is a position grounded in some degree of confusion. Generally speaking, it is of course true that in the terminology of the Vienna Convention, the word INTERPRETATION cannot be defined in more precise terms than the following: INTERPRETATION of a treaty means the application of a legally accepted rule of interpretation.[41] According to this definition, as long as a practice can be justified by reference to a legally accepted rule of interpretation, irrespective of the rule referred to, it would be considered a practice which establishes an agreement regarding the "interpretation" of a treaty – without a doubt a very daunting criterion. However, the issue at hand is not a usage of the word INTERPRETATION in general, but rather the specific usage of that word in the context of VCLT article 31 § 3(b). In this provision, the word INTERPRETATION bears a very specific meaning. As we observed earlier, when appliers use a subsequent practice to interpret a treaty, this is always in relation to conventional language.[42] A subsequent practice is used, either – in the case where the ordinary meaning of a treaty provision is vague – to make the ordinary meaning appear more precise, or – in the case where the ordinary meaning of a treaty provision remains ambiguous – to determine which one of the two possible ordinary meanings is correct and which one is not. In order to serve in this capacity, a subsequent practice needs no further justification apart from the obvious – that it is consistent with conventional language. Hence, a subsequent practice in the application of a treaty can be said to establish an agreement between the parties regarding the treaty's "interpretation" insofar as practice is consistent with "the ordinary meaning to be given to the terms of the treaty".[43]

In the text of VCLT article 31 § 3(b), a problematic choice of words is the expression "agreement" (Fr. "*accord*"; Sp. "*acuerdo*"). Clearly, "agreement" means a concordance held among the parties to the interpreted treaty with regard to its meaning. Less clear is the *type of concordance* assumed. In the older literature, practice is described as an aid for the determination of THE HISTORICAL INTENTION – the concordance upon which the interpreted treaty was originally concluded.[44] In the contemporary literature, authors are less categorical: the historical intention is still considered to be an "agreement"; but so are certain SUBSEQUENT CONCORDANCES, that is to say concordances arrived at after the conclusion of the interpreted treaty.[45] By THE HISTORICAL INTENTION, authors refer to a concordance held with the intention to create law. THE HISTORICAL INTENTION is a concordance among the parties to the interpreted treaty with regard to what meaning the treaty *shall* be given. Less clear is what authors refer to when they speak of a SUBSEQUENT CONCORDANCE. According to the meaning ascribed to the term in conventional language, SUBSEQUENT CONCORDANCE can be used to stand for different things. It can be used to stand for a concordance among the parties to the interpreted treaty with regard to what meaning the treaty *shall* be given; and it be used to stand for a concordance among the parties to the interpreted treaty with regard to what meaning the treaty *may* be given. Just like the historical intention, a SUBSEQUENT CONCORDANCE can be held with the intention to create law; but not necessarily so.[46]

According to some authors, a subsequent concordance is to be considered an "agreement" solely in those cases where it is the intention of the parties to create law.[47] For other authors, a subsequent concordance is to be considered an "agreement", regardless of whether or not it is the intention of the parties to create law.[48] Few authors consider a subsequent concordance to be an "agreement" solely in those cases where it is *not* the intention of the parties to create law.[49] In my judgment, a subsequent concordance is *in any event not* an "agreement" when it is held with the intention to create law. When a subsequent practice establishes an agreement between the parties to a treaty regarding its interpretation, and the agreement is a subsequent concordance held with a law-creating intention, then we are faced with a legally binding interpretative agreement (Fr. UN ACCORD INTERPRÉTATIF). When such an agreement is used for the interpretation of a treaty, it can be done on the basis of two different communicative assumptions.[50] In the first of these two assumptions, the parties have expressed themselves in such a way that, considering the context, the interpreted provision does not give rise to a logical tautology. On the second assumption, the parties have expressed themselves so that, considering the context, the interpreted provision does not give rise to a logical contradiction. In the former case, the act performed amounts to an interpretation in the sense of the Vienna Convention. In the latter case, the act performed amounts to something else – it amounts to what is commonly called an authentic interpretation (Fr. UN INTERPRÉTATION AUTHENTIQUE).[51] An authentic interpretation does not compete on equal terms with an interpretation arrived at through an application of the rules laid down in the Vienna Convention (or the identical rules of customary international law); it always takes precedence. After all, the rules laid down in the Vienna Convention are *jus dispositivum* – they apply only on the condition, and to the extent, that the parties to a treaty have not agreed among themselves on something else.[52] When an applier uses a "subsequent practice" for the interpretation of a treaty, it is only on the basis of the assumption that the treaty and the practice – or, rather the agreement that practice establishes – do not logically contradict one another.[53] Considering this, a subsequent concordance cannot possibly be seen an "agreement", in the sense of VCLT article 31 § 3(b), when it is held with the intention to create law.

Now, the difficult question is what all this says about the credibility of the international law literature. Contemporary authors agree that in the extension of the expression "agreement" we shall include not only the meaning originally intended, but also certain SUBSEQUENT CONCORDANCES. However, authors do little to help us understand what, according to them, a SUBSEQUENT CONCORDANCE actually is. Taken *en masse*, authors can be said to be of the opinion, either that a subsequent concordance is to be considered an "agreement" only in those cases where it is held with a law-creating intention. Or, they contend that a subsequent concordance is to be considered an "agreement", in those cases where it is held with a law-creating intention, as well as in those cases where such an intention is absent. The correct position, according to how I perceive things, is that a subsequent concordance *in any event* is *not* to be considered an "agreement", in those cases where it is held with a law-creating intention. This would imply that a majority of authors have misjudged the issue completely. Assuming this to be the case, the decisive question is whether we should give the literature the benefit of the doubt and assume that authors are right, at least regarding the claim that a subsequent concordance would be considered an "agreement" where it is *not* held with a law-creating intention. Or should we assume that authors have erred completely, and that subsequent practice – as claimed in the earlier literature – is merely an aid for the determination of the historical intention? This is a delicate question. In my opinion, the extension of the expression "agreement" includes subsequent concordances. However, I am also of the firm opinion that the literature alone does not adequately support this conclusion. Sufficient support can be found in international judicial opinions. The practice of international courts and tribunals convincingly shows that a subsequent concordance is to be considered an "agreement", in those cases where it is not held with a law-creating intention.[54] This is a proposition I will now try to establish.

3 SUBPARAGRAPH (B): THE EXPRESSION "AGREEMENT"

Three examples can be used to illustrate the proposition that, according to the opinion of international courts and tribunals, a subsequent concordance is to be considered an "agreement" in those cases where it is not held with a law-creating intention. A first example is the international award in the case of *Heathrow Airport User Charges*.[55] In 1977, the USA and the United Kingdom had concluded an air services agreement, commonly referred to as Bermuda 2. In this agreement, provisions had been included regarding airport charges. In 1979 and 1980, on two occasions, the United Kingdom had decided to increase charges for the use of state-owned Heathrow Airport. For the American airlines TWA and Pan-American this resulted in a combined increase in charges of 70 to 80 percent. The airlines found this to be unacceptable, and a civil process was initiated. A settlement was reached in February 1983. As a result of this settlement, on 6 April 1983 the governments of the United States and the United Kingdom signed a *Memorandum of Understanding ("MoU")*. In this document, the two states acknowledge that the earlier dispute between them has been set aside, and that no future legal action will be taken with respect to the period up to and including 31 March 1983. In addition, they express their viewpoints regarding future pricing policies. In paragraph 5 we find the following passage:

The [US Government] USG has expressed a number of concerns about the [British Airports Authority] BAA's peak pricing practices. In particular, the USG believes that (1) all traffic should bear at least some capital costs; (2) all traffic should bear its share of operating costs; (3) peak periods, where established at any airport, should encompass all periods of comparable activity at that airport; and (4) no peak charge should be assessed with respect to any service or facility unless a charge is also assessed for such service or facility during off-peak periods. [Her Majesty's Government] HMG sees force in the last three of these views and will commend them to the BAA, as well as drawing all the USG concerns to the attention of the BAA so that they may be taken into account in their collaborative review of peak pricing.[56]

One would believe the issue to be settled; but it was not. In April 1984, the US Deputy Assistant Secretary for Transportation and Telecommunications sent a letter to the UK Department of Transport, observing that the obligations assumed by the United Kingdom through the conclusion of Bermuda 2 and the MoU of 1983 had not yet been fulfilled. Four years later, in December 1988, the states agreed to initiate international arbitration proceedings. No sooner had the arbitration tribunal been constituted than the first problem arose. The parties disagreed on how to put the question, which the tribunal would then be requested to answer. In particular, there was disagreement concerning the importance that the arbitration tribunal should assign to the 1983 MoU. The American government maintained that the instrument was legally binding, arguing that it be given the same kind of respect as the provisions of Bermuda 2. The United Kingdom declared a contrary opinion:

[T]he MoU is not the source of independent obligations --- [It] no more deserves specific mention in the Terms of Reference than anything else relevant to the interpretation of Bermuda 2, such as, for example, subsequent practice.[57]

In this situation, the task of the tribunal was to formulate its own mandate, and the tribunal did so in the following manner:

1. The Tribunal is requested to decide whether, in relation to the charges imposed for the use of Heathrow Airport upon airlines designated by the Government of the United States of America under Article 3 of the Air Services Agreement, done at Bermuda on 23 July 1977, the Government of the United Kingdom have failed to fulfil their obligations under Article 10 of the said Air Services Agreement, interpreted having regard to *inter alia* the Memorandum of Understanding between the two Governments on Airport User Charges of April 6, 1983, in any of the charging periods beginning on or after 1 April 1983.

2. If the answer to the foregoing question is in the affirmative, the Tribunal is further requested to decide what, if any, remedy or relief should be awarded.[58]

However, the last word regarding the importance of the MoU had not been uttered. As one might expect the question was raised again in connection with the interpretation of Bermuda 2. According to the USA, the MoU was to be considered a subsequent agreement, to be used for the interpretation of Bermuda 2 under the provisions of Vienna Convention article 31 § 3(a). According to the United Kingdom, the instrument was to be considered a subsequent practice to be used under the provisions of Vienna Convention article 31 § 3(b). The tribunal concurred in the latter opinion:

In the judgment of the Tribunal, the MoU constitutes consensual subsequent practice of the Parties and, certainly as such, is available to the Tribunal as an aid to the interpretation of Bermuda 2 and, in particular, to clarify the meaning to be attributed to expressions used in the Treaty and to resolve any ambiguities.

6.8 The Tribunal notes that, even in respect of the second, third and fourth of the views of USG as recorded in paragraph 5 of the MoU, although HMG said that it saw force in those views, it clearly stopped short of accepting any duty to use its best efforts to ensure that the views were respected. However even if, contrary to the Tribunal's impression, the MoU were intended in the respects here under consideration to create independent legally enforceable obligations as opposed to merely recording the understandings of the Parties, the Tribunal would lack jurisdiction in respect of those obligations, as such, since its jurisdiction is derived from Article 17 of the Treaty which refers only to disputes "arising under this Treaty". The MoU is therefore available to the Tribunal as a potentially important aid to interpretation but is not a source of independent legal rights and duties capable of enforcement in the present Arbitration.[59]

The statement speaks for itself. Obviously, according to the tribunal, a subsequent concordance is to be considered an "agreement", in the sense of VCLT article 31 § 3(b), even though it is not held with a law-creating intention.

My second example is the international award in the *Young Loan* case.[60] The facts of this case have already been brought into discussion,[61] and I will not unnecessarily repeat myself. As we observed earlier, the parties were in dispute as to the meaning of the 1953 London Debt Agreement (LDA) and the following expression: "least depreciated currency" (Ger. *"Währung mit der geringsten Abwärtung"*; Fr. *"devise la moins dépréciée")*. The arbitration tribunal begins by declaring itself true to the rules of interpretation laid down in VCLT articles 31–33. Hence, in order to determine the meaning of the expression "least depreciated currency" (Ger. *"Währung mit der geringsten Abwärtung"*; Fr. *"devise la moins dépréciée")*, the tribunal first resorts to conventional language,[62] then to the contextual elements set out in VCLT article 31 § 2,[63] and to the object and purpose of the treaty.[64] Then the tribunal proceeds to examine the contextual elements set out in VCLT article 31 § 3(a) and (b).[65] The reasoning of the tribunal opens as follows:

According to Article 31 (3) (a) and (b) of the VC[L]T, interpretation of a treaty must take account both of subsequent agreements between the contracting parties on interpreting the treaty and of subsequent practice in the application of the treaty from which a consensus between the parties regarding the interpretation of specific parts of the treaty might be deduced.

First, it is undisputed that the parties to the LDA were unable to agree on a particular interpretation of the clause in question after the LDA had been concluded. An attempt to do so in October 1953 in Basel proved fruitless. The continuing differences of opinion are most clearly evidenced by the fact that after a few further vain attempts, the dispute was eventually brought before the Arbitral Tribunal.

An indication of at least a tacit subsequent understanding between the contracting parties on a particular rendering of the term "depreciated" in the clause in dispute might, therefore, at best be found in the relevant practice of the parties concerned.[66]

Already this passage indicates that in the view of the tribunal, a subsequent concordance can indeed be considered an "agreement", in the sense of VCLT article 31 § 3(b), even though it is not a legally binding agreement governed by international law. First of all, the tribunal notes the non-existence of a subsequent agreement in the sense of § 3(a). However, according to how things are obviously viewed by the tribunal, this does not rule out the existence of an agreement in the sense of § 3(b). Second, the word used in the reasoning of the tribunal to denote a concordance in the sense of § 3(a) is not the same as that used to denote a concordance in the sense of § 3(b). In § 3(a) the concordance referred to is denoted by the word AGREEMENT; in § 3(b) the concordance referred to is denoted first by the word CONSENSUS, and then by the word UNDERSTANDING. This same opinion is manifested in the manner in which the tribunal describes the relevant official documents, *inter alia* a communication from the President of the United States to the American Senate, and a letter from the Bank of England to the German *Federal Debt Administration* (FDA):

The communication from the President of the United States to the Senate of 10 April 1953 points out that the gold clause should no longer be applied in cases of "further depreciation" and that, instead of the gold clause, the clause in dispute *should* now be applied in those cases where one of the currencies concerned "has depreciated by 5 *per cent.* or more" - - - [T]he letter from the Bank of England to the Federal Debt Administration [sic!] of 2 April 1953 stated, in connection with the calculation method under the disputed clause, that such calculations *should* be based on "the currency most favourable to bondholders".[67]

When the tribunal says that a treaty provision *should* be applied in a certain way – "the clause in dispute should now be applied", "under the disputed clause ... calculation should be based on" – it obviously carries a meaning different from when it says that a provision *shall* be applied. All in all, I have difficulty coming to a conclusion other than this: in the view of the tribunal, a subsequent concordance is to be considered an "agreement", in the sense of VCLT article 31 § 3(b), even though it is not held with an intention to create law.

My third example is the international award in the *Beagle Channel Arbitration*.[68] The facts of the case have already been introduced,[69] and I see no reason for unnecessary repetition. As we know, the parties were in dispute as to the meaning of articles II and III of the 1881 Argentine-Chilean Boundary Treaty. To support its interpretation of the two articles, Chile had cited the behaviour of the parties in the period immediately following the conclusion of the 1881 agreement:

Thus in 1892 a decree fostering colonization was published in the Official Gazette of the Republic, and a sub-delegation was established on Lennox Island; in 1894 a system of land leases through public auction was inaugurated as a consequence of a law of 1893, also published in the Official Gazette; in 1896 a concession on Picton was granted to a British settler of distinction, Thomas Bridges; in 1905 a postal service was established. Indeed, in the period extending from 1892 through 1905, numerous official documents dealt with acts of jurisdiction in the three islands and many of them described the islands as lying south of the Beagle Channel - - -

(c) Chile contends, and the evidence appears to support the contention, that most of these activities (which were openly carried out) were well known to the Argentine authorities. Thus in the period between 1892–1898 the Argentine Governor at Ushuaia specifically and on several occasions drew the attention of the authorities in Buenos Aires to various Chilean acts on the islands, but without eliciting any positive reaction. According to Chile, at no time did Argentina register any reservation of rights, or initiate any protest, until 1915, and even this protest was limited to two of the three islands.[70]

"The subsequent conduct of the two Governments", claimed Chile, ...

... confirms the Chilean interpretation of the Treaty, if it be the case that the textual approach is not considered to be conclusive.[71]

Argentina protested, contending that practice could not be assigned the importance that Chile would want it to have. These opinions of the parties soon proved to differ not so much as to the content of practice, but as to the content of the rules of interpretation as such.

Argentina and Chile were in agreement insofar as they both considered a subsequent practice to be a means of interpretation open to use, even though the agreement established is not the historical intention, but rather a subsequent concordance. The differences concerned the more precise nature of such a subsequent concordance. According to Argentina, a subsequent concordance was not to be considered an "agreement", in the sense of VCLT article 31 § 3(b), if it was not held by the parties with the intention to create law. According to Chile, the case was the opposite. The arguments are cited by the court as follows:

First and foremost Argentina invokes the express terms of the Vienna Convention, Article 31, paragraph 3(b), which specifies that in interpreting a treaty

"There shall be taken into account, together with the context:

(b) Any subsequent practice in the application of the Treaty [sic!] which establishes the agreement of the Parties [sic!] regarding its interpretation."

The key word in this article, according to Argentina, is "agreement", and the Protocol of 1893 (see *supra*, paragraphs 73–78) is cited as a typical illustration of what was intended. She interprets the Convention as requiring a manifestation of the "common will" of the Parties and denies that the "unilateral acts" of Chile can be said to manifest any kind of agreed interpretation or common will. This being so, she asserts that the entire Chilean argument lacks relevance. Chile's answer to this line of reasoning takes the form of a simple denial of the meaning of the Vienna Convention advanced by Argentina. The concept of "agreement" in the clause cited does not require a formal "synallagmatic" transaction. It means consensus, and can be satisfied if "evidenced by the subsequent practice of the Parties which can only involve the acts, the conduct, of the Parties duly evaluated" (Oral Proceedings, VR/19, p. 184). The agreement, so Chile maintains, stems *from conduct* – in this instance from the open, persistent and undisturbed exercise of sovereignty by Chile over the islands, coupled with knowledge by Argentina and the latter's silence.[72]

After this, the reasoning of the court makes an interesting reading:

[T]he Court cannot accept the contention that no subsequent conduct, including acts of jurisdiction, can have probative value as a subsidiary method of interpretation unless representing a formally stated or acknowledged "agreement" between the Parties. The terms of the Vienna Convention do not specify the ways in which "agreement" may be manifested. In the context of the present case the acts of jurisdiction were not intended to establish a source of title independent of the terms of the Treaty; nor could they be considered as being in contradiction of those terms as understood by Chile. The evidence supports the view that they were public and well-known to Argentina, and that they could only derive from the Treaty. Under these circumstances the silence of Argentina permits the inference that the acts tended to confirm an interpretation of the meaning of the Treaty independent of the acts of jurisdiction themselves.[73]

It seems reasonably clear that the court agrees with Chile, not just with respect to the interpretation of the 1881 Boundary Treaty, but also with respect to the interpretation of VCLT article 31 § 3(b).[74] However, it must be admitted that nowhere in the court's statement is this expressly stated. According to what the court says, subsequent practice may be a valuable means of interpretation, although it does not amount to an agreement in the formal sense of the word; that is, it does not amount to an agreement that two or more parties bring into being by declaring their intentions expressly. A tacit agreement may amount to a legally binding agreement, just as it may amount to a concordance not held with a law-creating intention. However, considering that the court concurs with the interpretation of Chile of the 1881 Boundary Treaty, it is hard to believe that in the opinion of the court, a subsequent practice would be a valuable means of interpretation, only when it amounts to a legally binding agreement, whether tacit or express; for this was exactly the interpretation that Argentina had supported. If the court agrees with Chile with respect to the interpretation of the 1881 Boundary Treaty, but does so based upon what Argentina, and not Chile, claims to be the correct interpretation of the Vienna Convention, then an explanation of this rather odd way of reasoning would have been expected. No such explanation is given. On the whole, then, the only reasonable assumption is that in the view of the court, a subsequent concordance would have to be considered an "agreement", in the sense of VCLT article 31 § 3(b), even though it is not held with the intention to create law.

4 SUBPARAGRAPH (C): INTRODUCTION

The third and final class of phenomena coming within the scope of VCLT article 31 § 3, is the one described in subparagraph (c), namely "any relevant rules of international law applicable in the relations between the parties".

[T]oute règle pertinente de droit international applicable dans les relations entre les parties.

Toda norma pertinente de derecho internacional aplicable en las relaciones entre las partes.

Two conditions must be met in order for a phenomenon to fit this description: (1) the phenomenon must be included in the extension of the expression "relevant rules of international law"; and (2) it must be a question of a rule that is "applicable in the relations between the parties". Let us examine these points one by one.

In order for a phenomenon to fit the description in subparagraph (c), it must be included in the extension of the expression "any relevant rules of international law" (Fr. *"toute rè gle pertinente de droit international"*; Sp. *"[t]oda norma pertinente de derecho internacional")*. "[R]ules of international law", according to most authors, include all rules which spring from any of the formal sources of international law, that is to say, from international agreements, from customary international law, or from "the general principles of law recognized by civilized nations".[75] Some authors wish to give the expression a more limited meaning. According to Schwarzenberger, the extension of the "rules of international law" is limited to those rules deriving from customary international law and from the general principles of law, and it does not include those which derive from international agreements.[76] According to Sinclair, the extension is limited to those rules deriving from international agreements and from customary international law, and it does not include those which derive from the general principles of law.[77] Neither of these views, however, appears to be well founded. The reason given by Schwarzenberger for the proposition that rules deriving from international agreements should not be included in the extension of the expression "rules of international law" is that relevant international agreements are already covered by the provisions of subparagraph (a), which of course is an erroneous conclusion. All international agreements that are "relevant" when a treaty is interpreted do not necessarily come along as "subsequent"; nor do they necessarily "[regard] the interpretation of the treaty or the application of its provisions".[78] The reason Sinclair might have had for the suggestion that the general principles of law should be excluded is not openly expressed; but in any case the suggestion seems difficult to reconcile with the text of the Vienna Convention. The text speaks of "*any* relevant rules of international law" (Fr. "*toute* règle pertinente de droit international"; Sp. "*[t]oda* norma pertinente de derecho internacional").[79] Arguably, this can only be understood as a reference to any rule of international law, whatever the source.

The use of the expression "relevant" strikes me as a bit odd. It is commented on by Uibopuu:

> [T]he reference to "relevant rules" in Art. 31 para 3(c) in the Convention can be taken as an indication that analogy to rules of International Law other than directly applicable to the subject-matter of the case were to be excluded.[80]

I am inclined to concur. When appliers use the "relevant rules of international law", they always base their action on a very specific communicative assumption. According to this assumption, the parties to the interpreted treaty have expressed themselves in such a way that the treaty does not logically contradict any of the "relevant rules of international law applicable in the relations between the parties".[81] The point is that appliers, faced with two conflicting conventional meanings, shall be able to dismiss the one as logically incompatible with "relevant rules of international law". So, the only sensible interpretation of subparagraph (c) must be this: a rule of international law is to be considered "relevant", if (and only if) it governs the state of affairs, in relation to which the interpreted treaty is examined. How else would it be possible to dismiss an interpretation alternative as logically incompatible with "relevant rules of international law"?

In order for a rule of law to fit the description in subparagraph (c), the rule must be "applicable in the relations between the parties" (Fr. *"applicable dans les relations entre les parties"*; Sp. *"aplicable en las relaciones entre las partes")*. The expression "applicable in the relations between the parties" appears to be problematic. The meaning of "the parties" can easily be established. PARTY, in the terminology of the Vienna Convention, means "a State which has consented to be bound by the treaty and for which the treaty is in force".[82] By "the parties" all parties are meant.[83] Whether a rule of international law shall be considered "applicable in the relations between the parties" is determined based on the state-of-affairs, which prevails when a treaty is interpreted, and not on the state-of-affairs, which prevailed when the relevant rule of law entered into force.[84] In order for a rule of law to fit the description in subparagraph (c), each and every one of those states, which are bound by the interpreted treaty at the time of interpretation, must also be bound by the relevant rule of law. More difficult to understand is the expression "applicable". An "applicable" rule is one that can be applied to the relationship held between the parties to the interpreted treaty on a certain assumed occasion. This occasion can either be the point in time when the treaty was concluded; or it can be the very moment of interpretation. The former alternative is the one that best conforms to the earlier legal doctrine. In his influential article of 1953, Fitzmaurice states as follows:

In a considerable number of cases, the rights of States (and more particularly of parties to an international dispute) depend or derive from rights, or a legal situation, existing at some time in the past, or on a treaty concluded at some comparatively remote date ... It can now be regarded as an established principle of international law that in such cases the situation in question must be appraised, and the treaty interpreted, in the light of the rules of international law as they existed at the time, and not as they exist today.[85]

In the contemporary literature authors are less categorical. Today, the general opinion is that an applier – depending on the circumstances – has the possibility of using not only those rules which were applicable at the time when the interpreted treaty was concluded, but also those applicable at the time of interpretation.[86] The decisive question then appears to be the following: Under what particular circumstances shall the two respective categories of rules be used? When, exactly, shall the expression "relevant international rules of law" be considered a reference to those rules, which were applicable at the time when the interpreted treaty was concluded? And when shall it be considered a reference to those rules, which are applicable at the time of interpretation?

In my judgment, this issue of variations in law over time is to be resolved in the very same manner we used previously to resolve the issue of temporal variation in language.[87]

> If it can be shown, that the thing interpreted is a generic referring expression with a referent assumed by the parties to be alterable, then the decisive factor for determining the meaning of the "relevant rules of international law" shall be the law applicable at the time of interpretation. In all other cases, the decisive factor shall be the law applicable at the time when the interpreted treaty was concluded.

Some support for this conclusion can be found in the literature. Sinclair writes for example:

The International Court of Justice has lent its support to this concept that certain provisions of a treaty may be interpreted and applied in the light of international law as it has evolved and developed since the time when the treaty was concluded. It has however done so within carefully circumscribed limits. In its advisory opinion on the *Legal Consequences for States of the continued presence of South Africa in Namibia*, the Court stated:

"Mindful as it is of the primary necessity of interpreting an instrument in accordance with the intentions of the parties at the time of its conclusion, the Court is bound to take into account the fact that the concepts embodied in Article 22 of the Covenant – 'the strenuous conditions of the modern world' and 'the well-being and development' of the peoples concerned – were not static, but were by definition evolutionary, as also, therefore, was the concept of the 'sacred trust'. The parties to the Covenant must consequently be deemed to have accepted them as such. That is why, viewing the institutions of 1919, the Court must take into consideration the changes which have occurred in the supervening half-century, and its interpretation cannot remain unaffected by the subsequent development of law, through the Charter of the United Nations and by way of customary law. Moreover, an international instrument has to be interpreted and applied within the framework of the entire legal system prevailing at the time of the interpretation."

--- [T]here is scope for the narrow and limited proposition that the evolution and development of the law can be taken into account in interpreting certain terms in a treaty which are by their very nature expressed in such general terms as to lend themselves to an evolutionary interpretation. But this must always be on condition that such an evolutionary interpretation does not conflict with the intentions and expectations of the parties as they may have been expressed during the negotiations preceding the conclusion of the treaty.[88]

Elias expresses something similar:

While it may be useful to refer to the state of the law at the time of conclusion of the treaty as governing its interpretation, it is necessary to take into account as well the so-called intertemporal law in its application to the interpretation of treaties; that is to say, to have regard to the problem of the effect of the evolution of the law on the interpretation of the legal terms used in a treaty. Of course, the intention of the parties is a relevant consideration in the application of international law to the interpretation of the treaty. In the *Namibia Case*, the International Court has summarised the legal position as follows: [here follows the passage from the ICJ advisory opinion already found in the quotation of Sinclair].[89]

Yasseen observes in more detail:

C'est le traité lui-même qui indique si ses dispositions pourraient subir l'effet du l'évolution du droit international.

Tout ici est affaire d'espèce, tout dépend de ce que le traité prévoit, de ce que les parties veulent. Certaines catégories de traités dont le but est d'établir une solution stable sont réfractaires à tout changement. Même si les parties à ces traités ne le disent pas expressément, il est raissonable de présumer que leur intention est en harmonie avec le but qu'elles poursuivent et, par conséquent, inconciliable avec la remise en question d'un règlement qu'elles veulent définitif. Nous citerons l'example des traités établissant des frontières. Mais d'autres catégories peuvent de par leur nature se prêter à une interprétation évolutive, notamment les traités normatifs qui énoncent des règles de droit et surtout les traités de codification et de développement progressif de droit international. Même écrites, les règles de droit ne sont pas à l'abri de l'èvolution subsèquente de l'ordre juridique dont elles font partie. Il est donc aisé de présumer que les parties à ces traités ne s'opposent pas à ce que ces traités ou certaines de leurs dispositions soient interprétés à la lumière du droit international en vigueur à l'époque de cette interprétation.[90]

The most precise commentary is perhaps the one given by Jiménez de Aréchaga:

During the discussion of [VCLT article 31] paragraph 3 (c) in the International Law Commission, it was proposed to insert the qualifying words "in force at the time of conclusion of the treaty". A contrary suggestion was made at Vienna by the delegation of Czechoslovakia: "in force at the time of application of the treaty". The article as adopted has put aside both these opposing time-references. The reason is that this is a question which must remain open and depends on whether the parties intended to incorporate in the treaty some legal concepts with a meaning that would remain unchanged, or intended to leave certain terms as elastic and open-ended, subject to change and susceptible of receiving the meaning they might acquire in the subsequent development of the law. There are terms which must be understood according to the legal concepts prevailing at the time of conclusion of the treaty: for instance, a treaty conferring on another State rights in the territorial sea must be interpreted in the light of the concept of the territorial sea in force at the time of concluding the treaty and not as incorporating the wider notion this term has subsequently acquired. On the other hand, and perhaps more exceptionally, there are terms in a treaty obviously inviting an interpretation in harmony with the conditions and opinions prevailing from time to time.

The International Court of Justice found in its Advisory Opinion on the question of *Namibia* that this had occurred with the terms "sacred trust", "strenuous conditions of the modern world" and "well-being and development" of dependent peoples. The Court stated in this respect: [here follows the passage from the ICJ advisory opinion already found in the quotation of Sinclair].[91]

Nevertheless, considering the way authors express themselves, I cannot see how the literature alone could possibly be advanced as sufficient support for the conclusion here suggested. The literature simply lacks the precision that such support would require. First, it is my judgment that the decisive criterion for using the "relevant rules of international law" is the type of referring expression interpreted. The question is whether or not the thing interpreted is a generic referring expression with a referent assumed by the parties to the treaty to be alterable. According to several authors, the only decisive criterion is THE INTENTIONS OF THE PARTIES, which indeed remains a very vague criterion.[92] Second, it is my judgment that appliers can interpret a treaty using "relevant international rules of law" without having to distinguish between the different varieties of a language.[93] If someone asks whether the meaning of the expression "applicable" shall be determined based on the law applicable at the time of interpretation, or whether it shall be determined based on the law applicable at the time when the treaty was concluded, then the answer will not differ merely because the word interpreted belongs to a certain linguistic variety (e.g. everyday language, the language of ecology, the language of shipping, banking and finance language, the language of law, etcetera). It seems that according to some authors the temporal variation of law is simply a problem that arises in connection with the interpretation of terms belonging to the language of law.[94] Hence, all things considered, I cannot conclude my argument at this early stage and expect the reader to accept my assertions as credible. I must present the additional reasons I believe can be used to support my conclusion. This is the purpose of Section 5.

5 THE MEANING OF SUBPARAGRAPH (C): "APPLICABLE"

Based on what I have asserted, the issue of variations in law over time is to be resolved in the very same manner as that we used earlier to resolve the issue of temporal variation in language.

> If it can be shown, that the thing interpreted is a generic referring expression with a referent assumed by the parties to be alterable, then the decisive factor for determining the meaning of the "relevant rules of international law" shall be the law applicable at the time of interpretation. In all other cases, the decisive factor shall be the law applicable at the time when the interpreted treaty was concluded.[95]

Several arguments support this conclusion.

A first argument is the object and purpose of the interpreted treaty. Clearly, a certain level of agreement exists between the object and purpose conferred on the provisions of VCLT article 31 § 1 that governs the use of conventional language, and the object and purpose conferred on the provisions of article 31 § 3(c). One of the intentions underlying article 31 § 1 is that appliers should be able to take into consideration the language of international law. By "the ordinary meaning" of the terms of a treaty we must understand the meaning ascribed to these terms not only in everyday language, but also in the language of law.[96] The easy way to determine the language of international law is to consult some sort of lexicon or dictionary. However, things are not always that simple – in some cases, lexicons and dictionaries are simply not of help. To determine the conventions of language in such cases, actual utterances must be examined.[97] Of course, particularly important utterances are those that can be found in international treaties. It seems a fair assumption that all this was common knowledge for the parties to the Vienna Convention. Accordingly, just like VCLT article 31 § 3(c), the provision that governs the use of conventional language would seem to rely on the existence of written agreements. On such premises, it stands to reason that both provisions apply according to the same principles.

My second argument amounts to an interpretation of the literature. In the literature, the different issues of how language and law vary over time are often addressed conjointly.[98] On occasion, the issues are treated without any real indication given that they are actually two separate issues, and not just one.[99] However, even if authors tend to cause confusion about the issue of temporal variation of international law, it nevertheless seems they give us clear information on one point: the issue of variation in law should be addressed using an approach similar to that used in addressing the issue of variation in language. This position appears particularly in the writings of Elias, Sinclair and Jiménez de Aréchaga. In the texts of all three authors, we find a short excerpt from the ICJ advisory opinion in the *Namibia* case.[100] However, if we examine the excerpt more closely, we see that the primary issue dealt with by the court is not the use of "relevant international rules of law", but rather the use of conventional language.[101] Thus, it seems we have two options. Either we assert about the authors that they are guilty of a pure misunderstanding, which is not a very appealing option considering the fact that Elias, Sinclair and Jiménez de Aréchaga are such recognised authorities. Or, we assume that when the three authors cite the opinion of the Hague Court, this is not in order to provide direct support for the conclusion they draw, but merely as part of a reasoning *ex analogia*. Clearly, the latter option seems the most acceptable.

My third argument is the practice of international courts and tribunals after 1969. As an answer to the question addressed in Section 4 of this chapter, a norm was articulated. This norm appears to be the one generally applied in international courts and tribunals. I have particularly two examples of this.[102]

My first example is the judgment of the International Court of Justice in the case of *Gabčíkovo -Nagymaros Project.*[103] In September 1977, Hungary and the former Czechoslovakia had concluded a treaty regarding the construction and operation of a joint investment project in the Danube River.[104] Two important purposes of the project were to produce hydro-electric power and improve conditions for navigation on the river. The costs would be divided equally between the parties, who would also – once the project came to completion – benefit in equal measure from the power produced. The treaty addressed many issues, including the construction of two series of locks: one upstream at Gabčíkovo, in Czechoslovakian territory; and one downstream at Nagymaros, in Hungarian territory. In addition to guidelines for the construction project as such, the agreement contained provisions concerning the preservation of water quality and the protection of fishery and natural resources. I cite from articles 15, 19 and 20:

Article 15. Protection of Water Quality

1. The Contracting Parties shall ensure, by the means specified in the joint contractual plan, that the quality of the water in the Danube is not impaired as a result of the construction and operation of the System of Locks.

Article 19. Protection of Nature

The Contracting Parties shall, through the means specified in the joint contractual plan, ensure compliance with the obligations for the protection of nature arising in connection with the construction and operation of the System of Locks.

Article 20. Fishing Interests

The Contracting Parties, within the framework of national investment, shall take appropriate measures for the protection of fishing interests in conformity with the Danube Fishing Agreement, concluded at Bucharest on 29 January 1958.

According to the agreement, all the technical details of the project would be specified in a separate instrument – designated by the parties as "the Joint Contractual Plan" – which could later be updated as the parties saw fit.[105]

By 1989, construction in Czechoslovakian Gabčíkovo had advanced well, while in Hungarian Nagymaros construction was still in a preliminary phase. On the heels of political upheaval and a drastically changed economic situation, public opinion in Hungary had turned to scepticism toward the project, based partly on ecological reasons. In October 1989, the Hungarian Government decided to permanently abandon the works at Nagymaros. Czechoslovakia protested, and the parties began negotiations towards an agreed modification of the project. However, no agreement was ever reached. In November 1991, Czechoslovakia unilaterally commenced construction of what it called the provisional solution. In May 1992 the Hungarian government sent a *Note Verbale* to its Czechoslovakian counterpart, allegedly terminating the 1977 treaty. One year later, in April 1993, Hungary and Slovakia – the latter as acknowledged successor to the rights and obligations of Czechoslovakia – mutually decided to file an application with the International Court of Justice for a final decision on the matter.

One of the issues to be dealt with by the ICJ was the effect of Hungary's 1992 *note*. In its pleadings, Hungary had presented five arguments, which she asserted gave her cause for terminating the 1977 treaty. According to one argument, application of the treaty was precluded because of new requirements in international environmental law. This argument did not convince the Court. In the law of treaties, only two rules would make the more recent requirements of international environmental law grounds for termination, given the circumstances of the case: the ones expressed in articles 62 and 64 of the VCLT, concerning the effect of a fundamental change of circumstances, and the development of new *jus cogens*, respectively. The former rule, the Court observes, is quite obviously inapplicable. In order for a fundamental change of circumstances to give a state legitimate cause to withdraw from a treaty, the change must have been completely unforeseen by Hungary and Czechoslovakia, when in 1977 they concluded the treaty. Such was not the case with regard to the developments in international environmental law.

> What is more, the formulation of Articles 15, 19 and 20, designed to accommodate change, made it possible for the parties to take account of such developments and to apply them when implementing those treaty provisions.[106]

The second rule assumes the existence of a new peremptory norm of international law.

Neither of the Parties [has however] contended that new peremptory norms of environmental law had emerged since the conclusion of the 1977 Treaty, and the Court will consequently not be required to examine the scope of Article 64 of the Vienna Convention on the Law of Treaties.[107]

This observation, the court concludes – obviously intent on developing to some degree the issue touched upon in the passage above – must not be taken to mean that the new norms of international environmental law have no relevance at all.

[T]he Court wishes to point out that newly developed norms of environmental law are relevant for the implementation of the Treaty and that the Parties could, by agreement, incorporate them through the application of Articles 15, 19 and 20 of the Treaty. These articles do not contain specific obligations of performance but require the parties, in carrying out their obligations to ensure that the quality of water in the Danube is not impaired and that nature is protected, to take new environmental norms into consideration when agreeing upon the means to be specified in the Joint Contractual Plan.

By inserting these evolving provisions in the Treaty, the parties recognized the potential necessity to adapt the Project. Consequently, the Treaty in not static, and is open to adapt to emerging norms of international law. By means of Articles 15 and 19, new environmental norms can be incorporated in the Joint Contractual Plan.[108]

What the court says is clearly topical for the interpretation of treaties as well: article 15 requires that the parties, in drafting the Joint Contractual Plan, consider the rules of international environmental law originating after 1977. The reason to pay this statement specific attention is that the requirement noticed by the Court is not something, which can be drawn expressly from the treaty as such. In article 15, the only thing stated is that the parties shall ensure that the water quality in the Danube River does not deteriorate. If the Court reaches the conclusion that international environmental laws must be taken into consideration, then this is on the basis of reasons other than the mere text of the article. The true reason lies in the rules of interpretation applied by the Court. Apparently, the Court takes for granted that the 1977 treaty can be interpreted using "relevant rules of international law". In my judgment, the use of "relevant rules of international law" can be described along the lines of the following rule of interpretation:

> If it can be shown that the interpretation of a treaty provision in accordance with interpretation rule no. 1 leads to conflicting results, and that a relevant rule of international law exists, which is applicable in the relations between the parties, and – considered in light of the provision interpreted – in one of two possible ordinary meanings involves a logical contradiction, while in the other it does not, then the latter meaning shall be adopted.[109]

Hence, for the interpretation of article 15, the "relevant rules of international law" would – according to the Court – be considered a reference to the law applicable at the time of interpretation. The question remains how the Court can justify such an opinion.

The thing interpreted is the expression "[t]he Contracting Parties ensure ... that the quality of the water in the Danube is not impaired". According to conventional language, this is either a singular referring or a generic referring expression.[110] It can be used to refer either to a single occasion, on which the parties ensure the water quality in the Danube River. Or it may be used to refer to a more extended state-of-affairs, whose existence in time has not been determined. Clearly, the thing interpreted is a generic referring expression. A generic referring expression, in turn, can be used in two different ways. It can be used to refer to a referent – in this case a specific state-of-affairs – assumed by the utterer to be unalterable. It can also be used to refer to a referent, which the utterer assumes will alter. The observation made by the Court is that article 15 has been designed to accommodate change; that the provisions expressed are evolving; that the parties recognised the necessity of adapting the project (to better correspond to changing circumstances); and that, therefore, the content of the treaty is not static. Arguably, this is tantamount to saying that the expression interpreted is a generic referring expression with a referent assumed by the parties to be alterable.

My second example is the ICJ advisory opinion in the *Namibia* case.[111] The facts of this case have already been stated,[112] and I will not engage in unnecessary repetition. As we know, the dispute involved the purpose of the so-called C-mandates. According to South Africa, a C-mandate was more or less tantamount to an annexation, and it maintained that this was evident in the various statements reported in the preparatory work to the Covenant of the League of Nations. For the International Court of Justice, a C-mandate was something else. Under article 22 § 1 of the League Covenant, South Africa, as a mandatory over South-West Africa, had assumed as "a sacred trust" to provide for the "well-being and development" of the South-West African population. Article 22 § 1 provides:

> To those colonies and territories which as a consequence of the late war has ceased to be under the sovereignty of the States which formerly governed them and which are inhabited by peoples not yet able to stand by themselves under the strenuous conditions of the modern world, there should be applied the principle that the well-being and development of such peoples form a sacred trust of civilisation and that securities for the performance of this trust should be embodied in this Covenant.[113]

In order to live up to this commitment, the court observed, South Africa must act, not for the annexation of the mandate territory, but instead for its independence and self-determination:

[T]he subsequent development of international law in regard to non-self governing territories, as enshrined in the Charter of the United Nations, made the principle of self-determination applicable to all of them. The concept of the sacred trust was confirmed and expanded to all "territories whose peoples have not yet attained a full measure of self-government" (Art. 73). Thus it clearly embraced territories under a colonial régime. Obviously, the sacred trust continued to apply to League of Nations mandated territories on which an international status had been conferred earlier. A further important stage in this development was the Declaration on the Granting of Independence to Colonial Countries and Peoples (General Assembly resolution 1514 (XV) of 14 December 1960), which embraced all peoples and territories which "have not yet attained independence". Nor is it possible to leave out of account the political history of mandated territories in general. All those which did not acquire independence, excluding Namibia, were placed under trusteeship. Today, only two out of fifteen, excluding Namibia, remain under United Nations tutelage. This is but a manifestation of the general development which has led to the birth of so many new States.

53. All these considerations are germane to the Court's evaluation of the present case. Mindful as it is of the primary necessity of interpreting an instrument in accordance with the intentions of the parties at the time of its conclusion, the Court is bound to take into account the fact that the concepts embodied in Article 22 of the Covenant – "the strenuous conditions of the modern world" and "the well-being and development" of the peoples concerned – were not static, but were by definition evolutionary, as also, therefore, was the concept of the "sacred trust". The parties to the Covenant must consequently be deemed to have accepted them as such. That is why, viewing the institutions of 1919, the Court must take into consideration the changes which have occurred in the supervening half-century, and its interpretation cannot remain unaffected by the subsequent development of law, through the Charter of the United Nations and by way of customary law. Moreover, an international instrument has to be interpreted and applied within the framework of the entire legal system prevailing at the time of interpretation. In the domain to which the present proceedings relate, the last fifty years, as indicated above, have brought important developments. These developments leave little doubt that the ultimate objective of the sacred trust was the self-determination and independence of the peoples concerned. In this domain, as elsewhere, the *corpus iuris gentium* has been considerably enriched, and this the Court, if it is faithfully to discharge its functions, may not ignore.[114]

The thing interpreted by the Court is the expression "a sacred trust". The conclusion is that, in reading this expression, particular regard must be paid to the development brought about in international law since 1919, the year the Covenant was concluded. We shall note that the Court itself does not expressly mention the means of interpretation it exploits. As I stated earlier, my understanding of the Court is as follows: the means of interpretation used are first conventional language – more specifically, the language expressed in article 73 of the Charter of the United Nations, and in the "Declaration on the Granting of Independence to Colonial Countries and Peoples" – and then, at the end of § 53 (in the passage beginning with

"Moreover"), the "relevant rules of international law". Consequently, for the interpretation of the expression "a sacred trust", the "relevant rules of international law" would, according to the Court, be considered a reference to the law applicable at the time of interpretation. The decisive question is what the Court thinks might justify such a finding.

Let me remind the reader how the Court explained its finding that the ordinary meaning of "a sacred trust" should be determined based on the language conventions adhered to at the time of interpretation.[115] The Court says, first of all, that it is aware that the ultimate purpose of all treaty interpretation is to determine the utterance meaning of the interpreted treaty; second, that the terms used in the League Covenant, according to the language adhered to in 1919, represented something evolutionary; and third, that therefore it must be assumed that the parties to the Covenant, too, used the terms in this manner.

> Mindful as it is of the primary necessity of interpreting an instrument in accordance with the intentions of the parties at the time of its conclusion, the Court is bound to take into account the fact that the concepts embodied in Article 22 of the Covenant – "the strenuous conditions of the modern world" and "the well-being and development" of the peoples concerned – were not static, but were by definition evolutionary, as also, therefore, was the concept of the "sacred trust". The parties to the Covenant must consequently be deemed to have accepted them as such.[116]

As we observed earlier, this is tantamount to saying that the expressions in question are generic referring expressions with referents assumed to be alterable.[117] It is my understanding of the Court that, in fact, this explanation pertains not only to the use of conventional language, but also to the use of "relevant rules of international law".

As a consequence of this understanding, what I need to explain is the following passage:

> Moreover, an international instrument has to be interpreted and applied within the framework of the entire legal system prevailing at the time of interpretation.[118]

Treaties shall be interpreted with consideration only for those rules of law that are applicable at the time of interpretation – this is what the court literally says, which cannot possibly be what it intended to say. First of all, the utterance would be clearly incompatible with international law as it currently stands. The dominant opinion in the modern literature is that an applier – depending upon the circumstances – has the possibility of taking into consideration not only the law applicable at the time when the interpreted treaty was concluded, but also the law applicable at the time of interpretation.[119] Second, the expression would be clearly incompatible with the overall point made by the Court. If the Court were of the opinion that treaties should be interpreted with consideration only for those rules of law that are applicable at the moment of interpretation, then there is no reasonable explanation why the Court so strongly emphasises the development of law as such.

> In the domain to which the present proceedings relate, the last fifty years ... have brought important developments --- [T]his the Court, if it is faithfully to discharge its functions, may not ignore.[120]

Considering the context, the more probable interpretation is that the Court merely wants to call our attention to the prevailing legal state-of-affairs. The Court wishes to remind us that in contrast with the earlier doctrine, according to current international law, appliers have the possibility of not only using those rules of law that were once applicable at the conclusion of the interpreted treaty, but also those rules that are applicable at the time of interpretation.

6 THE CONTEXTUAL ELEMENTS PUT TO USE

What communicative standard or standards shall the parties to a treaty be assumed to have followed, when an applier interprets the treaty using the three classes of phenomena provided in VCLT article 31 § 3? With regard to the use of context, there is reason to repeat part of what we have already noted. In Chapter 4, we observed that in the legal literature, the act of interpretation using context is often termed as SYSTEMATIC INTERPRETATION.[121] When an applier uses the context – this is the assumption – the interpreted treaty provision and the context together form some kind of larger whole, a system. I also noted about the system assumed in the legal literature that it is not a uniform concept.[122] The term SYSTEMATIC INTERPRETATION is used to refer to not one type of system but two, depending on whether authors envision the interpreted treaty provision and its context as the *body of text* constituted by the text and its context, or the set of *norms* expressed. In the former case, SYSTEMATIC INTERPRETATION is based on the existence a system of a linguistic character; in the latter case it is based on the existence of a system in the logical sense. Based on these observations, I then put into words the five communicative standards assumed by appliers when they interpret a provision using "the text" of the treaty interpreted; these standards have been designated with the letters A to E.[123] The standards are of two types. Standards A, C and D govern the linguistic relationship assumed to hold between the expressions used for an interpreted treaty provision and the expressions used for the context. Standards B and E govern the logical relationship that shall be assumed to hold between the norm content of an interpreted treaty provision and the norms comprised by the context.

As we observed in Chapter 5, partly different communicative standards are to be assumed by appliers, when they use the contextual elements described in VCLT article 31 § 2(a) and (b), compared to when they use "the text" of a treaty. When using the contextual elements of article 31 § 2(a) and (b), appliers shall base their operations solely on the assumption that the interpreted treaty provision and the context form a system in the logical sense.[124] Among the different arguments I advanced to support this conclusion, one was the fact that the expectations placed on a treaty provision are considerably higher when it is considered part of a linguistic system, compared to when it is considered part of a system in the logical sense.[125] If a treaty is to be considered part of two systems, of which the one is linguistic and the other logical, then it stands to reason that the extension of the former should be limited to include only part of the latter. As we noted, the inherent line of limitation is formed by the text of the interpreted treaty.[126] This same argument should be valid also when appliers use the contextual elements described in VCLT article 31 § 3. If, when they use the contextual elements set out in article 31 § 2(a) and (b), appliers are not to assume that the interpreted treaty provision and the context form a system in the linguistic sense, nor should they assume so when they use the elements described in article 31 § 3.

Further confirmation of this proposition is provided if we consider the nature of the three classes of phenomena set out in article 31 § 3. Subparagraph (a) speaks of "any subsequent agreement between the parties regarding the interpretation of the treaty or the application of its provisions". As observed, "agreement" refers to any legally binding agreement regardless of form, including not only written agreements but also non-written ones.[127] If a communicative standard governs the relationship held between an interpreted treaty provision and a subsequent non-written agreement, then obviously this relationship cannot be the one that holds between the expressions used for these two accords. Subparagraph (b) speaks of "any subsequent practice in the application of the treaty which establishes agreement between the parties regarding its interpretation". A practice does not take the form of a text. If a communicative standard governs the relationship held between an interpreted treaty provision and a subsequent practice, then obviously this relationship cannot be the one that holds between expressions used for the treaty and those that appear in the practice. Subparagraph (c) speaks of "relevant rules of international law applicable in the relations between the parties". "[R]ules of international law" means each and every rule that springs from international agreements, from customary international law, or from "the general principles of law recognized by civilized nations".[128] Customary international law does not take the form of a text; nor do the general principles of law recognized by civilized nations. If a communicative standard governs the relationship held between an interpreted treaty provision and a rule of international law, whatever its source, then clearly this relationship cannot be the one that holds between the expressions used for the interpreted treaty provision and the rule.[129] All things considered, I have difficulty arriving at any other conclusion than this: when an applier interprets a treaty using a "subsequent agreement", a "subsequent practice", or any one of the "relevant rules of international law", it is solely on the assumption that the interpreted treaty provision and the context form a system in the logical sense.

The communicative standard assumed when an applier uses the "relevant rules of international law" is easily established. According to an opinion generally held in the literature, a treaty shall always be assumed compatible with those other rules of international law that apply in the relation between the parties, as long as the opposite has not been shown to be the case.[130] See for example O'Connell, who notes with regard to the provisions of VCLT article 31 § 3(c):

> The process of interpretation supposes that the parties contemplate a result not incompatible with customary international law.[131]

Oppenheim's International Law declares:

> "[I]t is a rule of interpretation that a text emanating from a Government must, in principle, be interpreted as producing and as intended to produce effects in accordance with existing law and not in violation of it".[132]

Let us also cite a passage from the records of the 770th meeting of the ILC:

> Mr. de **LUNA** said that the text of a treaty was never drawn up *in vacuo* — In cases where a treaty did not expressly say whether its provisions should be interpreted in a manner derogating from or consistent with a rule of international law in force, the interpretation should be in conformity with the rule in question, for States were presumed to be under a duty to conform with international law, even were it was a case of *jus dispositivum*.[133]

Hence, when appliers interpret a treaty using "relevant rules of international law", they do so on the basis of the communicative standard B:

> If a state produces an utterance taking the form of a treaty provision, then the provision should be drawn up so that it does not logically contradict the context.[134]

It seems obvious that this standard B should also be assumed when appliers use a "subsequent agreement" or a "subsequent practice"; for the most fundamental requirement placed on a logical system is that it be free of logical contradiction. However, concentrating on the use of a "subsequent agreement", I wish to go one step further. Using a "subsequent agreement", appliers also assume that the parties to the interpreted treaty have abided by the communicative standard E:

> If a state produces an utterance taking the form of a treaty provision, then the provision should be drawn up in such a way that in the context there will be no instance of a logical tautology.[135]

To support this proposition, I will offer one argument only, and that is the opinion expressed in the legal literature. According to a view generally held in the literature, we shall count as a "subsequent agreement between the parties regarding the interpretation of the treaty or the application of its provisions" certain legally binding interpretation agreements.[136] When such an agreement is used for the interpretation of a treaty, and this is done based on the communicative assumption that the treaty and the agreement do not logically contradict one another, the interpretation arrived at is an AUTHENTIC INTERPRETATION (Fr. UN INTERPRÉTATION AUTHENTIQUE).[137] An authentic interpretation does not compete on equal terms with an interpretation arrived at through an application of the rules laid down in the Vienna Convention (or the identical rules of customary international law); the authentic interpretation always takes precedence. After all, the rules of interpretation laid down in the Vienna Convention are *jus dispositivum* – they apply only on the condition, and to the extent, that the parties to a treaty have not come to agree between themselves on something else.[138] If we accept the suggestion that a legally binding interpretation agreement can be used according to the provisions of VCLT article 31 § 3(a), then, as a result, this usage must be based on some other communicative standard than B. All things considered, the conclusion I draw is the following: when appliers interpret a treaty using the contextual element described in article 31 § 3(a), they do so on the basis of not only standard B but also standard E.

7 CONCLUSIONS

According to VCLT article 31 § 1, a treaty shall be interpreted in good faith "in agreement with the ordinary meaning given to the terms of the treaty in their context and in the light of its object and purpose". As a means of interpretation, the context comprises an exceptionally wide range of data. Therefore, to facilitate presentation, I have chosen to divide the concept into three parts, each part being the subject of a separate chapter of this work. The purpose of this chapter is to describe what it means to interpret a treaty using the contextual elements described in VCLT article 31 § 3. Based on the observations made in this chapter, the following four rules of interpretation can be established:

Rule no. 11

§ 1. If it can be shown that the interpretation of a treaty provision in accordance with interpretation rule no. 1 leads to conflicting results, and that subsequent to the conclusion of the treaty the parties made an agreement regarding the interpretation of the treaty or the application of its provisions, and the agreement – in light of the provision interpreted – in one of the two possible ordinary meanings can be considered to involve a logical contradiction, while in the other it cannot, then the latter meaning shall be adopted.

§ 2. For the purpose of this rule, AGREEMENT means any agreement governed by international law, whether written or not.

§ 3. For the purpose of this rule, an agreement was made SUBSEQUENT to the conclusion of a treaty, if (and only if) it was made after the point in time when the interpreted treaty was established as definite.

§ 4. For the purpose of this rule, PARTIES means any and all states for which the treaty is in force at the time of interpretation.

§ 5. For the purpose of this rule, an agreement is one REGARDING the interpretation of a treaty or the application of its provisions, if (and only if) the agreement was made with the purpose of either clarifying the meaning of said treaty, or of serving in some other manner as a guide for its application.

Rule no. 12

§ 1. If it can be shown that the interpretation of a treaty provision in accordance with interpretation rule no. 1 leads to conflicting results, and that subsequent to the conclusion of the treaty the parties made an agreement regarding the interpretation of the treaty or the application of its provisions, and the agreement – in light of the provision interpreted – in one of the two possible ordinary meanings can be considered to involve a logical tautology, while in the other it cannot, then the latter meaning shall be adopted.

§ 2. For the purpose of this rule, AGREEMENT means any agreement governed by international law, whether written or not.

§ 3. For the purpose of this rule, an agreement was made SUBSEQUENT to the conclusion of a treaty, if (and only if) it was made after the point in time when the interpreted treaty was established as definite.

§ 4. For the purpose of this rule, PARTIES means any and all states for which the treaty is in force at the time of interpretation.

§ 5. For the purpose of this rule, an agreement is one REGARDING the interpretation of a treaty or the application of its provisions, if (and only if) the agreement was made with the purpose of either clarifying the meaning of said treaty, or of serving in some other manner as a guide for its application.

Rule no. 13

§ **1**. If it can be shown that the interpretation of a treaty provision in accordance with interpretation rule no. 1 leads to conflicting results, and that subsequent to the conclusion of the treaty a practice has developed, which can be said to establish the agreement of the parties regarding the interpretation of said treaty, so that the practice – in light of the provision interpreted – in one of the two possible ordinary meanings can be considered to involve a logical contradiction, while in the other it cannot, then the latter meaning shall be adopted.

§ **2**. For the purpose of this rule, PRACTICE means any number of applications, one or many.

§ **3**. For the purpose of this rule, the APPLICATION of a treaty means any and all measures based on the treaty.

§ **4**. For the purpose of this rule, a practice is considered SUBSEQUENT to the conclusion of a treaty, if (and only if) it developed after the point in time when the interpreted treaty was established as definite.

§ **5**. For the purpose of this rule, PARTIES means any and all states for which the treaty is in force at the time of interpretation.

§ **6**. For the purpose of this rule, AGREEMENT means not only the concordance upon which the treaty was originally concluded, but also any possible concordance arrived at after the conclusion of the treaty, excluding, however, interpretative agreements governed by international law.

§ **7**. For the purpose of this rule, a practice establishes agreement with regard to the INTERPRETATION of a treaty, only on the condition that practice agrees with the treaty, when interpreted in accordance with rule no. 1.

Rule no. 14

§ **1**. If it can be shown that the interpretation of a treaty provision in accordance with interpretation rule no. 1 leads to conflicting results, and that a relevant rule of international law is applicable in the relationship between the parties, and the rule – considered in light of the provision interpreted – in one of the two possible ordinary meanings can be considered to involve a logical contradiction, while in the other it cannot, then the latter meaning shall be adopted.

§ **2**. For the purpose of this rule, RULE OF INTERNATIONAL LAW means any and all rules whose origin can be traced to a formal source of international law.

§ **3**. For the purpose of this rule, PARTIES means any and all states for which the treaty is in force at the time of interpretation.

§ **4**. For the purpose of this rule, whether a rule of law is APPLICABLE or not is determined based upon the legal state-of-affairs that prevailed at the time when the treaty was concluded, unless otherwise applies according to § 5.

§ 5. For the purpose of this rule, whether a rule of law is APPLICABLE or not is determined based upon the legal state-of-affairs prevailing at the time of interpretation, provided that it can be shown that what is being interpreted is a generic referring expression with a referent assumed by the parties to be alterable.

NOTES

1. See p. 102 of this work.
2. See Yasseen, pp. 44–45; Schwarzenberger, 1969, p. 220; Bartoš, at the ILC's eighteenth session, 870:th meeting, *ILC Yrbk*, 1966, Vol. 1, Part 2, p. 192, § 91. See also, implicitly, Villiger, p. 344; Rest, p. 146; Bernhardt, 1967, p. 499; Draft Articles With Commentaries (1966), *ILC Yrbk*, 1966, Vol. 2, p. 221, § 14, who all speak of "subsequent agreements" as a form of authentic interpretation. AUTHENTIC INTERPRETATION usually means a legally binding interpretation agreement to be applied within the framework of international law. (See e.g. *Oppenheim's International Law*, p. 1268; Skubiszewski, 1983, p. 898; Karl, 1983, pp. 40–41.)
3. See Aust, p. 787.
4. See, expressly, Yasseen, p. 45; Müller, pp. 131–132; Bernhardt, 1967, p. 499. See, implicitly, Villiger, p. 344, cf. p. 343 and in particular n. 181, in which the author refers to (among other things) the following statement by Yasseen: "Ce qui importe ici, c'est l'accord en tant que tel; peu importe sa forme". A different opinion seems to be the one that Bartoš expressed, at the ILC's eighteenth session, 870th meeting, *ILC Yrbk*, 1966, Vol. 1, Part 2, p. 192, § 91.
5. See, implicitly, Sinclair, 1984, p. 136; Yasseen, p. 44. See also Voïcu, pp. 176–177. Several authors refer to "successive agreements" as a form of authentic interpretation. (See n. 2 on this page). AUTHENTIC INTERPRETATION usually means an interpretation agreement, which is to be considered legally binding for all the original parties (See e.g. *Oppenheim's International Law*, p. 1268; Skubiszewski, 1983, p. 898; Haraszti, p. 43).
6. Cf. Ch. 5 of this work, concerning the meaning of the word PARTY in the context of VCLT article 31 § 2(a) and (b).
7. I cannot see what else "subsequent" might refer to. (See, in a similar vein, Villiger, p. 344; Elias, 1974, p. 75; Müller, p. 131; Bernhardt, 1967, p. 499.)
8. See Ch. 5, Section 1, of this work.
9. See Ch. 5, Section 3, of this work.
10. See e.g. Mus, pp. 220–222; Sinclair, 1984, p. 98; Zuleeg, p. 256.
11. See e.g. Czaplinski and Danilenko, p. 19; Dahl, p. 282; Sørensen, 1973, p. 54.
12. See, implicitly, Villiger, p. 344; Sinclair, 1984, p. 136; Yasseen, pp. 44–47; Rest, p. 146; Bernhardt, 1967, p. 499; Draft Articles With Commentaries (1966), *ILC Yrbk* , 1966, Vol. 2, p. 222, § 14; Waldock, Sixth report on the Law of Treaties, ibid., p. 98, § 18, which all speak of "subsequent agreements" either as a form of authentic interpretation (Fr. INTERPRÉTATION AUTHENTIQUE), or as synonymous with interpretative agreements (Fr. ACCORDS INTERPRÉTATIFS). Naturally, an authentic interpretation, like

an interpretative agreement, is an agreement whose *express purpose* is to clarify the meaning of a treaty.

13. See Section 2, of this chapter.
14. See e.g. Bos, 1984, p. 112; Maluwa, p. 343; Haraszti, p. 16.
15. Of course, the proposition is valid only insofar as it concerns the *operative interpretation* of treaties. The meaning of this concept has been explained in Ch. 1, Section 3, of this work.
16. Strictly speaking, what an applier uses for the interpretation of a treaty is not practice as such, but rather the agreement established by practice. Compare the way an applier uses the preparatory work of a treaty. We may say that appliers use the *travaux préparatoires*, but actually they use the concordance established by the *travaux*.
17. See Ress, pp. 38–42; Amerasinghe, pp. 198–200; Thirlway, 1991, pp. 49–50; *Oppenheim's International Law*, pp. 1274–1275, n. 20; McGinley, pp. 212–213, Elias, 1974, pp. 76–77; Bernhardt, 1984, p. 323; Sinclair, 1984, pp. 137–138; Karl, 1983, pp. 115–117. For a different opinion, see O'Connell, p. 262.
18. See Thirlway, 1991, pp. 50–51, cit. *Border and Transborder Armed Actions, ICJ Reports*, 1988, p. 87, § 36, and *Nicaragua v. United States, ICJ Reports*, 1984, p. 410, § 40; Merrills, pp. 81–82, cit. *Soering*; *Publ. ECHR*, Ser. A, Vol. 161, § 103; McGinley, pp. 212, 214; Karl, 1983, pp. 114–115.
19. For authorities supporting the broader interpretation, see Amerasinghe, p. 199, cit. *IMCO, ICJ Reports*, 1960, pp. 167–168, and *European Commission of the Danube, PCIJ*, Ser. B, No. 14, pp. 57–58; E. Lauterpacht, p. 457. For authorities supporting the more narrow interpretation, see Sinclair, 1984, p. 137; Yasseen, p. 48; Capotorti, p. 208, as he is cited by Thirlway, 1991, p. 53, n. 254.
20. Yasseen, p. 10.
21. It is symptomatic that authors sometimes refer to "subsequent practice" ("*pratique ultérieur")* by means of terms such as SUBSEQUENT CONDUCT (Haraszti, pp. 138, 140; Jacobs, p. 329), CONDUITE SUBSÉQUENTE (Cot, p. 632 et passim), and CONDUITE ULTÉRIEUR (Lang, p. 162).
22. See e.g. Wolfke, pp. 34–35; Sinclair, 1984, p. 137, cit. *Chamizal*, AJIL, Vol. 5 (1911), p. 805; Yasseen, p. 48.
23. See e.g. McGinley, pp. 218–219, cit. *Certain Expenses of the United Nations.*
24. See e.g. McGinley, p. 212, cit. *Rights of US Nationals in Morocco, ICJ Reports*, 1952, p. 211.
25. See e.g. Amerasinghe, p. 199; Thirlway, 1991, p. 57; Elias, 1974, pp. 76–77 – all citing *Namibia, ICJ Reports*, 1971, p. 22, § 22.
26. Cf. e.g. Thirlway, 1991, p. 51, cit. *Nicaragua v. United States, ICJ Reports*, 1984, p. 410, § 40; McGinley, pp. 212, 214; Karl, 1983, p. 115.
27. See e.g. McGinley, p. 212; Jacobs, p. 328, cit. *Anglo-Iranian Oil, ICJ Reports*, 1952, p. 107; McNair, 1961, p. 426.
28. See e.g. Merrill, pp. 81–82, cit. *Soering, Publ. ECHR*, Ser. A, Vol. 161, § 103; Matscher, 1983, p. 564.
29. Similarly, see Di Stefano, p. 42; Karl, 1983, p. 114.
30. Cf. Di Stefano, p. 42; Thirlway, 1991, pp. 48, 55; Haraszti, p. 138; Jacobs, p. 328; Bernhardt, 1967, p. 499. See also Yasseen, who maintains that a "subsequent practice" cannot be anything but a practice that chronologically follows the conclusion of the interpreted treaty, since it is a question of a practice "in the application of the treaty" (p. 47). This argument is not tenable. A treaty does not necessarily need to enter into

force in order to be *applied*. According to VCLT article 25, a treaty shall be provisionally applied *pending its entry into force*, if the parties to the treaty so agree (whether in writing or not). On provisional application in general, see Lefeber, pp. 81–95.

31. Cf. Section 1 of this chapter.
32. VCLT article 2 § 1(g).
33. See Thirlway, 1991, p. 52; Villiger, p. 344; McGinley, p. 217; Sinclair, 1984, p. 138; Karl, 1983, pp. 188–194; Yasseen, pp. 48, 52; Elias, 1974, p. 76; Haraszti, p. 141; Jennings, p. 549.
34. Cf. the meaning of the word PARTY in VCLT article 31 § 2(a) and (b). (See Ch. 5, Sections 1 and 3, of this work.)
35. The exact amount of practice required to establish an agreement between the parties to the interpreted treaty remains a question of judgment that can only be decided on a case-by-case basis.
36. Cf. Thirlway, 1991, p. 56, n. 262; Villiger, p. 344; McGinley, p. 225; Yasseen, pp. 48–49; Elias, 1974, p. 76; Haraszti, p. 141.
37. See articles 39–40.
38. See e.g. Wolfke, pp. 34–35; Di Stefano, pp. 54–67; Ress, p. 41; Thirlway, 1991, pp. 48, 52; Sinclair, 1984, p. 138; Verdross och Simma, pp. 505–506; Yasseen, p. 51; Akehurst, 1974/1975, pp. 277–278; Haraszti, pp. 143–145.
39. An entirely different matter is that a judicial interpretation based on a subsequent practice often has an influence on the continued application of the treaty.
40. Sinclair, 1984, p. 138.
41. Cf. Hexner, p. 124.
42. See the introduction to this chapter, and the introduction to Ch. 4.
43. Similarly, see Wolfke, p. 34; Thirlway, 1991, p. 52; Akehurst, 1987, p. 204; Bernhardt, 1967, p. 499. For a different opinion, see Karl, 1983, pp. 36–39, who nevertheless appears to have founded his opinion on the same misconception as Sinclair.
44. See e.g. Bernhardt, 1963, p. 131; De Visscher, 1963, p. 124; McNair, 1961, p. 424; Schwarzenberger, 1957, p. 532.
45. See Ress, pp. 38–42; Di Stefano, pp. 44–54; Amerasinghe, p. 199; Thirlway, 1991, pp. 52–56; *Oppenheim's International Law*, p. 1275, n. 20; Akehurst, 1987, p. 204; Villiger, p. 344; McGinley, p. 227; Sinclair, 1984, pp. 135–137; Karl, 1983, p. 190; Yasseen, p. 49; Müller, p. 132; Jacobs, pp. 327–331. For a different opinion, see Haraszti, pp. 142–143.
46. See Karl, 1983, pp. 144–147.
47. See e.g. Sinclair, 1984, p. 137; Yasseen, pp. 48, 52; Elias, 1974, p. 76; Schwarzenberger, 1969, p. 220; Bernhardt, 1967, p. 499.
48. See e.g. Amerasinghe, p. 199; McGinley, pp. 218, 227; Karl, 1983, pp. 190–194; Jacobs, p. 331.
49. For an example of such an author, see, implicitly, Rest, pp. 39–42, especially p. 41, n. 151.
50. Cf. Ch. 5, Section 4, of this work.
51. On authentic interpretation in general, see e.g. Pan, pp. 503–535; *Oppenheim's International Law*, pp. 1268–1269; Skubiszewski, 1983, pp. 898–902; Karl, 1983, pp. 40–45, 204–211; Haraszti, pp. 43–51; Voïcu, pp. 73–110, 137–217; Bernhardt, 1963, pp. 44–46.
52. See Ch. 1, Section 1, of this work.
53. See Section 6 of this chapter.

54. In addition to the authorities cited in the text, see *Hagerman v. United States and Others*, *ILR*, Vol. 92, pp. 724–725; *Riley and Butler v. The Commonwealth*, *ILR*, Vol. 87, p. 154; and possibly also *Bankovic*, § 62.
55. United States-United Kingdom Arbitration Concerning Heathrow Airport User Charges, Award of 30 November 1993, *ILR*, Vol. 102, pp. 216ff.
56. The text cited here is that provided by the arbitration tribunal. (See *ILR*, Vol. 102, pp. 563–564, Appendix IV.)
57. Ibid., p. 549.
58. Ibid., p. 551.
59. Ibid., p. 353, §§ 6.7–6.8.
60. The Kingdom of Belgium, The French Republic, The Swiss Confederation, The United Kingdom and the United States of America v. The Federal Republic of Germany, Award of 16 May 1980, *ILR*, Vol. 59, pp. 495ff.
61. See Ch. 3, Sections 2 and 5, of this work.
62. See *ILR*, Vol. 59, pp. 530–531, §§ 18–19.
63. Ibid., pp. 531–540, §§ 20–29.
64. Ibid., pp. 540–541, § 30.
65. Ibid., pp. 541–543, § 31.
66. Ibid., pp. 541–542, § 31.
67. Ibid., p. 542, § 31. (The italics used for the word *should* are mine.)
68. *Beagle Channel Arbitration (Argentina v. Chile)*, Court of Arbitration, Award of 18 February 1977, *ILR*, Vol. 52, pp. 93ff.
69. See Ch. 4, Section 4, of this work.
70. *ILR*, Vol. 52, pp. 221–222, § 166. (Footnote omitted.)
71. Ibid., p. 223, § 167. (Footnote omitted.)
72. Ibid., p. 223, § 168.
73. Ibid., p. 224, § 169.
74. In the reasoning of the Court, one expression calls for comments. The court speaks of the probative value of conduct "as a subsidiary method of interpretation". One could easily get the impression that the court uses subsequent practice according to the provisions of VCLT article 32. (For more on the context considered as a supplementary means of interpretation, see Ch. 8 of this work). Another meaning emerges when the expression is seen in the light of its broader textual context. According to a more plausible reading, the court uses subsequent practice in the same way as Chile and Argentina have done earlier – as a way of making more precise the conventional meaning of the 1881 treaty, applying the provisions of Vienna Convention article 31. [See, especially, Chile's observation: "The subsequent conduct of the two Governments confirms the Chilean interpretation of the Treaty, if it be the case that the textual approach is not considered to be conclusive". (See p. 199 of this work.)] On the other hand, this ambiguity in the reasoning of the court hardly makes a difference for our discussion. The context used according to the provisions of VCLT article 32 is the exact same context described in article 31 §§ 2 and 3. (See Ch. 8 of this work.) If a subsequent concordance is to be considered an "agreement" for the application of VCLT article 32, even though it is not held with a law-creating intention, then it can be considered so for the application of VCLT article 31as well.
75. See Pauwelyn, p. 254; ILC, Report of the ILC Study Group on the Fragmentation of International Law, 2006, § 426; McLachlan, p. 290; Marceau, p. 1087; Villiger, p. 268; Matscher, 1983, p. 561; Yasseen, p. 63; Haraszti, p. 146, n. 181; Waldock, at the ILC's

sixteenth session, 769th meeting, *ILC Yrbk*, 1964, Vol. 1, p. 310, § 10, cf. p. 316, §§ 13, 17. See also, implicitly, *Oppenheim's International Law*, p. 1275, n. 21.

76. Schwarzenberger, 1969, p. 220.
77. Sinclair, 1984, p. 139.
78. Further on the meaning of the expressions "subsequent" and "regarding the interpretation of the treaty or the application of its provisions ", see Section 1 of this chapter.
79. My emphasis.
80. Uibopuu, p. 4. Cf. Villiger: "[T]he rules must be 'relevant', i.e. concern the subject-matter in question" (p. 268).
81. See Section 6 of this chapter.
82. VCLT, article 2 § 1(g).
83. See, expressly, Pauwelyn, pp. 257–259; Matscher, 1983, p. 561; Yasseen, p. 63; Haraszti, p. 148; Bernhardt, 1967, p. 500. See also EC–Biotechnical Products, pp. 299–300. For a different opinion, see Marceau, according to whom "the parties" appears to refer to the states parties of a dispute. (Marceau, p. 1087.)
84. Cf. Sections 1 and 3 of this chapter, on the meaning of the word PARTY in the context of VCLT article 31 § 3(a) and (b), respectively. Cf. Ch. 5, on the meaning of the word PARTY in the context of article 31 § 2.
85. Fitzmaurice, 1953, p. 5.
86. See Higgins, 1996, pp. 173–181; Dupuy, p. 221; *Oppenheim's International Law*, p. 1275, n. 21, 1281–1282; Sinclair, 1984, pp. 139–140; Verdross and Simma, pp. 496–499; Elias, 1980, pp. 285–307; Jiménez de Aréchaga, pp. 48–50; Yasseen, pp. 64–67; Rest, p. 150; Jacobs, pp. 330–331. Cf. also Ress, pp. 35–37; Thirlway, 1991, pp. 57–60, cf. Thirlway, 1989, pp. 135–143; and Sørensen, 1973, pp. 90–91 – all of whom refuse to clearly specify whether the problem they confront is one of variation in language only, or one of variation in language as well as in law.
87. See Ch. 3 of this work.
88. Sinclair, 1984, pp. 139–140. (Footnote omitted.)
89. Elias, 1974, p. 77. (Footnote omitted.)
90. Yasseen, pp. 66–67. (A footnote and the number of a paragraph have been omitted.)
91. Jiménez de Aréchaga, pp. 48–49. (Footnotes omitted.)
92. See e.g. Elias and Sinclair, as earlier cited. For a discussion on the various meanings that could be associated with the term INTENTIONS OF THE PARTIES, see Ch. 2, Section 1, of this work.
93. See Ch. 2, Section 2, of this work.
94. See e.g. Elias och Jiménez de Aréchaga, as earlier cited.
95. See p. 87 of this work.
96. See Ch. 3, Sections 1 and 2, of this work.
97. Another way to determine the language of international law (if not technical language in general) is by asking for an expert opinion. (Cf. for example sep. op. Aldrich, Holtzmann and Mosk, on the Issue of the Disposition of Interest Earned on the Security Account, *ILR*, Vol. 68, pp. 546–547.)
98. See e.g. Higgins, 1996, pp. 173–181; Ress, pp. 35–37; Thirlway, 1991, pp. 57–60, cf. Thirlway, 1989, pp. 135–143; *Oppenheim's International Law*, pp. 1281–1282; McWhinney, pp. 179–199; Waldock, 1981, pp. 535–547; Elias, 1980, pp. 285–307; Sørensen, 1973, pp. 89–94.

99. See e.g. Higgins, 1996, pp. 173–181; McWhinney, pp. 179–199; Elias, 1980, pp. 285–307.
100. Legal Consequences for States of the Continued Presence of South Africa in Namibia (South West Africa) Notwithstanding Security Council Resolution 276 (1970), Advisory Opinion of 21 June 1971, *ILR*, Vol. 49, pp. 3ff.
101. See Ch. 3, Section 4, of this work.
102. In addition to the examples provided in the body text, see possibly *OSPAR*, § 103; *Ijzeren Rijn*, § 79; *US–Shrimp*, § 130.
103. Case Concerning the Gab Gabcíkovo-Nagymaros Project, Judgment of 25 September 1997, *ILR*, Vol. 116, pp. 2ff.
104. Treaty between the Hungarian People's Republic and the Czechoslovak Socialist Republic Concerning the Construction and Operation of the Gabcíkovo-Nagymaros System of Locks, Signed at Budapest, on 16 September 1977.
105. Several such updates were later made.
106. *ILR*, Vol. 116, p. 74, § 104.
107. Ibidem, p. 76, § 112.
108. Ibidem, pp. 76–77, § 112.
109. See Section 7 of this chapter.
110. For a more detailed description of these concepts, see Ch. 3 of this work.
111. Legal Consequences for States of the Continued Presence of South Africa in Namibia (South West Africa) Notwithstanding Security Council Resolution 276 (1970), Advisory Opinion of 21 June 1971, *ILR*, Vol. 49, pp. 3ff.
112. See Ch. 3 of this work.
113. The text cited is that provided by the court. (See *ILR*, Vol. 49, p. 18, § 45.)
114. Ibid., pp. 21–22, §§ 53–54.
115. See Ch. 3, Section 4, of this work.
116. *ILR*, Vol. 49, p. 21, § 53.
117. See Ch. 3, Section 4, of this work.
118. *ILR*, Vol. 49, p. 21, § 53.
119. See Section 4 of this chapter.
120. *ILR*, Vol. 49, pp. 21–22, § 53.
121. See Ch. 4, Section 2, of this work.
122. Loc. cit.
123. See Ch. 4, Sections 2–4, of this work.
124. See Ch. 5, Section 5, of this work.
125. Loc. cit.
126. Loc. cit.
127. See Section 1 of this chapter.
128. See Section 4 of this chapter.
129. Some authors, such as Yasseen and Haraszti, can be read (at least implicitly) to mean that there is a standard that governs the relationship between the expressions used for an interpreted treaty on the one hand, and on the other, the expressions used for a rule of international law, where "a rule of international law" can be nothing but a rule laid down in another treaty. (See Yasseen, p. 63; Haraszti, p. 148.) This is an opinion clearly at odds with a basic assumption – that which precludes the existence of a communicative standard governing the relationship held between an interpreted treaty provision and a relevant rule of international law *of a specific kind*, for example a rule laid down in a written agreement.

130. In addition to the authorities cited in the text, see Amerasinghe, p. 203, cit. *Namibia*, *ICJ Reports*, 1971, pp. 31, 41; Czaplinski and Danilenko, p. 13; Yasseen, p. 63, cit. *Georges Pinson*, *Recueil des sentences arbitrales*, Vol. 5, p. 422; Haraszti, pp. 146, 149–150; Bernhardt, 1967, p. 500; De Visscher, 1963, p. 92; see also, implicitly, Villiger, p. 268. Cf. *Al Adsani v. United Kingdom*, ILR, Vol. 123, p. 40, § 55; *Fogarty v. United Kingdom*, ibid., Vol. 123, p. 65, § 35.
131. O'Connell, p. 261, cit. *Reparation for Injuries*, *ICJ Reports*, 1949, p. 182. In a footnote to the cited passage, the following explanation has been added: "Article 27(3)(c) states that relevant rules of international law may be resorted to in treaty interpretation". This is a clear reference to VCLT article 31 § 3(c).
132. *Oppenheim's International Law*, p. 1275. The authority cited by Oppenheim's is the ICJ in *Rights of Passage (Preliminary Objections)*, *ICJ Reports*, 1957, p. 142.
133. De Luna, at the ILC's sixteenth session, 770th meeting, *ILC Yrbk*, 1964, Vol. 1, pp. 316–317, §§ 29–30.
134. See Ch. 4, Section 2, of this work.
135. Loc. cit.
136. See e.g. Skubiszewski, 1983, p. 899; Sinclair, 1984, p. 136; Karl, 1983, pp. 186, 190, 192, 194; Yasseen, pp. 44–47; Bernhardt, 1967, p. 499; Voïcu, pp. 104–105; implicitly, *Oppenheim's International Law*, p. 1274, n. 19, cf. p. 1268. See also Draft Articles With Commentaries (1966), *ILC Yrbk*, 1966, Vol. 2, p. 222, § 15; Waldock, Sixth Report on the Law of Treaties, ibid., p. 98, § 18.
137. On authentic interpretation in general, see e.g. *Oppenheim's International Law*, pp. 1268–1269; Skubiszewski, 1983, pp. 898–902; Karl, 1983, pp. 40–45, 204–211; Haraszti, pp. 43–51; Voïcu, pp. 73–110, 137–217; Bernhardt, 1963, pp. 44–46.
138. See Ch. 1, Section 1, of this work.

CHAPTER 7

USING THE OBJECT AND PURPOSE

It is the purpose of this chapter to describe what it means to interpret a treaty using its object and purpose. "A treaty shall be interpreted in good faith in accordance with the ordinary meaning to be given to the terms of the treaty... in the light of its object and purpose" – this is provided in article 31 § 1.

Un traité doit être interprété de bonne foi suivant le sens ordinaire à attribuer aux termes du traité ... à la lumière de son objet et de son but.

Un tratado deberá interpretarse de buena fe conforme al sentido corriente que haya de atribuirse a los términos del tratado ... teniendo en cuenta su objeto y fin.

One thing is immediately evident from reading this text. When an applier uses the object and purpose of a treaty in accordance with the provisions of VCLT article 31, the object and purpose is not considered independently of other means of interpretation. The object and purpose is always used in relation to conventional language ("the ordinary meaning"). Seen from a different perspective, we could say that when appliers use the object and purpose of a treaty, it is always a second step in the interpretation process.[1] The question has arisen whether or not a given complex of facts shall be considered to come within the scope of application of the norm expressed by a certain treaty provision P, and the provision P has been interpreted using conventional language. However, this (very first) introductory act of interpretation has been found insufficient. The ordinary meaning of the treaty provision P is either vague or ambiguous – the use of conventional language leads to conflicting results. Possibly, conventional language has a role to play in the process of gaining understanding of the treaty, but then it must be supplemented by additional means of interpretation. The idea of using the object and purpose is that it will serve as such a supplement. Where the ordinary meaning of a treaty provision is vague, using the object and purpose will make the meaning of the provision more precise. Where the ordinary meaning is ambiguous, using the object and purpose will help to determine which one of two possible meanings is correct, and which one is not. All this is evident from VCLT article 31 § 1.[2] What the provision says is *not* that the terms of a treaty shall be interpreted in the light of its object and purpose. What the provision says is that a treaty shall be interpreted "in accordance with the ordinary meaning to be given to the terms of the treaty ... in the light of its object and purpose". Hence, if we wish to give a shorthand description of how the object and purpose of a treaty shall be used, the description could look like this:

> If it can be shown that the interpretation of a treaty provision in accordance with interpretation rule no. 1 leads to conflicting results, and that between the provision and the object and purpose of the treaty there is a relationship governed by the communicative standard S, then the provision shall be understood as if the relationship conformed to this standard.

Two questions must be answered, in order for my task to be considered completed:

(1) What is meant by "the object and purpose" of a treaty?
(2) What communicative standard or standards shall the parties to a treaty be assumed to have followed, when an applier interprets the treaty using its "object and purpose"?

I shall now give what I consider to be the correct answers to these questions. In Sections 1–3, I shall begin by answering question (1). In Sections 4–5, I shall then answer question (2).

1 ON THE MEANING OF "OBJECT AND PURPOSE" IN GENERAL

In VCLT article 31 § 1, "the object and purpose" of a treaty means those reasons for which the treaty exists – sometimes termed as the *ratio legis* or the treaty's *raison d'être.*[3] As with all things, the object and purpose of a treaty is in essence subjective. If we say of a thing that it has a certain object or a certain purpose, then it is only because someone, according to what we assume, confers on the thing this very object or purpose. Of course, different people may confer different objects and purposes on a thing. For some, a bottle of wine can be a means of intoxication; others may consider the wine an accompanying drink to a meal; still others may view it as a collector's item and an investment. The question is what concept or human idea we assume, when in Vienna Convention article 31 we speak of "the object and purpose" of a treaty.

At this juncture it may be useful to consider international law from the perspective of national legal doctrine. Sometimes, the interpretation of a treaty using its object and purpose is referred to by the term TELEOLOGICAL INTERPRETATION.[4] In certain national legal systems, jurisprudence distinguishes between two types of teleological interpretation, termed as subjective and objective.[5] According to this terminology, interpretation is SUBJECTIVE TELEOLOGICAL when a law is interpreted based on the objects and purposes presumedly conferred on the law by the original "lawmaker". If, on the other hand, the law is dissociated from its authors, and instead the applier ventures to interpret it based on the objects and purposes presumedly assigned to the law by the legal community – given the laws of the nation at large – or by people in general, then interpretation is OBJECTIVE TELEOLOGICAL.[6] This division into subjective and objective teleological interpretation has no counterpart in international law. Here, teleological interpretation is merely subjective. It is a view generally held in the literature that when appliers interpret a treaty using its object and purpose, it is *always* based on those objects and purposes assumedly conferred on the treaty by the treaty parties.[7] Considering the ultimate goal of all treaty interpretation, I really have difficulty seeing how an act of objective teleological interpretation would at all be possible. When an applier interprets a treaty using its object and purpose, it is to determine the legally correct meaning of that treaty.[8] The legally correct meaning of a treaty has been defined earlier as follows: those pieces of information conveyed by the treaty with regard to its norm content, according to the intentions of the treaty parties – all those states, for which the treaty is in force – insofar as these intentions can be considered mutually held.[9] Given this, "the object and purpose" of a treaty can hardly be anything other than the object and purpose, which the parties to the treaty intended it to have – or rather, more specifically, *mutually* intended it to have.

So, the ultimately determining factor for what shall be considered the content of *the object and purpose* of a treaty would, as things stand, be the intentions of the treaty parties. To determine the object and purpose of a treaty it is evident that a separate process of interpretation might sometimes be needed.[10] In some cases, the intentions of the parties to a treaty with regard to its object and purpose are bound to be considered unclear. Some authors, however, wish to go a step further. For instance, according to professors Bos and Sur, the object and purpose of a treaty is something that *always* must be determined through an interpretation process – before the object and purpose of a treaty has been determined through interpretation, the treaty cannot possibly be subjected to an act of interpretation using its object and purpose.[11] By making this assertion, the authors (quite understandably) slip up in their thinking. The flaw of their argument is that they do not distinguish between the object and purpose of a treaty in relation to a specific interpretation alternative (that is to say, a specific norm) on the one hand, and on the other hand the object and purpose of a treaty in relation to that treaty's norm content *in extenso*.

When appliers determine the object and purpose of a treaty, it is only in relation to a specific interpretation alternative. What the applier wants to know is whether she can arguably assert about two specific interpretation alternatives – of which neither, from the point of view of conventional language, and that language only, can be considered more correct than the other – that only one is correct from the point of view of the object and purpose of the interpreted treaty. Of course, professors Bos and Sur are right in the sense that *sometimes*, a relatively high degree of clarity must be obtained with regard to the object and purpose of a treaty vis-à-vis that treaty's norm content *in extenso*, before the object and purpose of the treaty can be determined vis-à-vis the given interpretation alternatives; and, of course, they are right in the sense that achieving this clarity *often* requires a separate process of interpretation. This typically ought to be the case when the applier has to choose between two interpretation alternatives, both of which lead to a realisation of the object and purpose, but one of them does so to a greater degree than the other. But the two professors are clearly wrong, when they assert that determining the object and purpose of a treaty vis-à-vis two given interpretation alternatives *always* requires a separate process of interpretation. An applier may be somewhat unclear about the object and purpose of a treaty vis-à-vis its norm content *in extenso*. But at the same time, she can be completely clear about the object and purpose of the treaty vis-à-vis the two interpretation alternatives she is to consider. For example, often one does not need to know much about the object and purpose of a treaty vis-à-vis its norm content *in extenso*, to observe that a specific interpretation alternative leads to a result that does *not* agree with the object and purpose.

An important distinction to be made is that between "the object and purpose" of a treaty on the one hand, and on the other hand those reasons that are the CAUSE (Fr. MOTIF) for the treaty.[12] By the "object and purpose" of a treaty – as stated earlier – we understand the reasons for which the interpreted treaty exists. Of course, this definition is ambiguous in the sense that we cannot directly determine from its wording whether by "reasons" we mean the state-of-affairs, which the parties expect either shall or should be the consequence of their agreement, or the state-of-affairs of which, assumedly, the agreement itself is a consequence. The former state-of-affairs is non-factual; it belongs to the time subsequent to the establishing of the treaty as definite.[13] With the terminology of the Vienna Convention this is what we would usually call the "object and purpose" of a treaty. As an example, we could say that the object and purpose of the *European Convention for the Protection of Human Rights and Fundamental Freedoms* is to defend and uphold the ideal of a democratic society.[14] The latter state-of-affairs is factual; it belongs to the time prior to the establishing of the treaty as definite.[15] This is what we call the CAUSE for a treaty. Accordingly, we could say that the experiences of World War II and Nazi Germany were the cause, when in 1949 the Council of Europe decided to draft a European Convention for the protection of human rights.[16] The cause for a treaty is not included in the extension of the "object and purpose" of a treaty, in the sense of VCLT article 31. All means of interpretation listed in article 31 relate to the interpreted treaty – or rather the agreement expressed by the treaty – as it stands either at the point in time when the treaty is established as definite, or subsequent to that point.[17] Clearly, the cause for a treaty does not fit this description. If the cause for a treaty can be determined, then it shall be used according to the provisions of VCLT article 32, as part of "the circumstances of its [i.e. the treaty's] conclusion".[18]

2 "OBJECT AND PURPOSE" – ONE CONCEPT OR TWO? MOREOVER, REGARDING THE VARIATION OF AN OBJECT AND PURPOSE OVER TIME

It is a conspicuous fact that VCLT article 31 speaks both of a treaty's "object" (Fr. *"objet"*; Sp. *"objeto"*) and a treaty's "purpose" (Fr. *"but"*; Sp. *"fin")*. In everyday language, the words OBJECT (Fr. OBJET; Sp. OBJETO) and PURPOSE (Fr. BUT; Sp. FIN) are quite clearly synonymous. Hence, as long as we stay within the bounds of everyday language, and everyday language only, it is an utter tautology to speak of a treaty's "object and purpose".[19] Of course, the parties to the Vienna Convention might have used the expressions "object" *("objet", "objeto")* and "purpose" *("but", "fin")* in a special or some sort of technical meaning. In French (public) law, the distinction is sometimes made between the OBJET and BUT of a legal transaction.[20] L'OBJET D'UN ACTE is then understood to be the direct and immediate consequence of the performance of a legal transaction.

> [L]'objet d'un acte réside dans les droits et les obligations auxquels il donne naissance. L'objet d'un acte, c'est donc la norme qu'il crée.[21]

LE BUT D'UN ACTE, on the other hand, is the result achieved through L'OBJET.

> [L]es droits et les obligations crées par l'acte ne constituent pas une fin en eux-mêmes. Il ne sont que le moyen d'atteindre un résultat donné. Et c'est ce résultat qui forme, pour le ou les auteurs de l'acte, le but recherché.[22]

There are authors in the French international law literature who maintain that a parallel distinction should be valid for international law as well, and especially so for the application of VCLT article 31.[23] The problem is that no matter how elucidative the terminology of the French legal doctrine might seem, this assertion does not agree with the way the words OBJECT (OBJET, OBJETO) and PURPOSE (BUT, FIN) are generally used by actors of international law.[24] English authors can at one point speak of a treaty's OBJECT, then jump to the treaty's PURPOSE, and in the next breath speak of the treaty's OBJECT AND PURPOSE, without any evidence of a consistent semantic pattern.[25] The same applies to German authors who interchangeably speak of the ZIEL of a treaty, the ZWECK of a treaty, and the ZIEL UND ZWECK of a treaty.[26] Symptomatic are the abundance of variants used. In addition to the phrases OBJECT AND PURPOSE and ZIEL UND ZWECK, respectively, the literature offers a number of similar words and word combinations: in the English literature, AIM, PURPOSE AND OBJECTIVE, PURPOSE AND AIM, FUNCTION, PURPOSES AND FUNCTIONS, TARGET, END ... [27] in the German, GEGENSTAND, SINN UND ZWECK, ... [28] I fail to see that by using these terms, actors in international law intend something new.

Equally indeterminate is the language that comes forth in the Vienna Convention itself. Several provisions mention the OBJECT AND PURPOSE (OBJET ET BUT, OBJETO Y FIN) of a treaty, one such provision being article 18.[29] Up to the conclusion of the Vienna Conference's first session in 1968, the text of article 18 – then discussed as (draft) article 15 – read as follows: "acts tending to frustrate the object of a treaty". The Drafting Committee, however, later changed it to read: "acts which would defeat the object and purpose of a treaty". The Committee explains the revision in the following manner:

> The Drafting Committee had replaced the words "acts tending to frustrate the object of a treaty" by the words "acts which would defeat the object and purpose of a treaty". It wished to emphasize that that was a purely drafting change, made in the interests of clarity. It had added the word "purpose" to the word "object" because the expression "[the treaty's] object and purpose" was frequently used in the convention. The absence of the word "purpose" in the introductory phrase of article 15 might lead to difficulties in interpretation. The change in no way affected the substance of the provision and did not widen the obligation imposed on States by article 15.[30]

Article 60 § 3(b) speaks disjunctively about a treaty's "object or purpose" *("objet ou but", "objeto o fin")*:

> A material breach of a treaty, for the purpose of this article, consists in... (b) the violation of a provision essential to the accomplishment of the object or purpose of the treaty.

It is true that this could be understood to mean that, according to Vienna terminology, OBJECT and PURPOSE are two different things. The more reasonable reading, however, is to regard article 60 as yet another indication of the fact, that in drafting the text of the Vienna Convention – regardless of what the text itself might suggest – the authors were acting under the belief that there would be no difference at all between the meaning of a treaty's OBJECT (OBJET, OBJETO) and the meaning of its PURPOSE (BUT, FIN). For how can we possibly say that a breach of a treaty is material, simply because it consists of a violation of a provision essential to the accomplishment of the treaty's object, and the treaty's object alone, if we simultaneously claim that a treaty's OBJECT is those rights and obligations expressed by the treaty? Are not all breaches of a treaty *by definition* such that they thwart the accomplishment of the treaty's OBJECT in this sense?

All things considered, there are convincing reasons to believe, what even many French authors have been compelled to admit: the distinctions made in the French legal doctrine between OBJET and BUT cannot explain the way these words are used in VCLT article 31.[31] This result might seem to discourage. However, the question is if we really need to expend more energy on trying to establish the meaning of the words OBJECT and PURPOSE, in the sense of VCLT article 31, given the assumption that each of the two words OBJECT and PURPOSE could be dealt with separately from the other. My answer to this question is in the negative. The reason is that we can quite easily establish the meaning of the expression "object and purpose", as long as we regard it as a single lexical unit – in the terminology of linguistics, it would be called an idiomatic phrasal lexeme. As we noted, when the two words OBJECT and PURPOSE are considered independently of each other, they cannot be said to stand for what the French legal doctrine denotes with the two terms OBJET and BUT, respectively. However, when THE OBJECT AND PURPOSE is considered as a phrasal lexeme, then the meaning of that lexeme plainly corresponds to the *computed meanings* ascribed to those terms in the French legal doctrine. When an applier interprets a provision of a treaty using the treaty's "object and purpose", he can understand the provision in two different ways – this is evident from the literature.[32] First, the applier can understand the provision in light of the rights and obligations expressed in the treaty. Second, he can understand the provision in light of the state-of-affairs (or states-of-affairs) which the parties to the treaty expect to attain through applying said rights and obligations.

Hence, it seems we are left with two alternatives. Either we understand the expression "object and purpose" in such a way that the two words OBJECT andPURPOSE each come off as synonymous with the sum total of OBJET and BUT in the sense of the French legal doctrine. Or, we draw the conclusion that the two words OBJECT and PURPOSE, considered independently from each other, carry no intelligent meaning at all – the expression "object and purpose" is synonymous with OBJET and BUT in the sense of the French legal doctrine, not because this comes off as the result when the individual meanings of the two words OBJECT and PURPOSE are computed in a grammatically correct manner, but because this is the meaning of the expression when considered as a single lexical unit.[33] Of course, the first alternative does not agree with interpretation rule no. 4:

> If it can be shown that the interpretation of a treaty provision in accordance with interpretation rule no. 1 leads to conflicting results, and that somewhere in the text of said treaty an expression is included, which – in light of the provision interpreted – in one of the two possible ordinary meanings of the interpreted treaty provision can be considered a pleonasm, while in the other it cannot, then the latter meaning shall be adopted.[34]

However, from a purely practical standpoint, I cannot see how the choice of interpretation alternative would really make a difference. If we know the meaning of the expression "object and purpose", then there are no reasons other than purely semantic ones for determining the merits of each respective alternative. Hence, whatever the individual meanings of the two words OBJECT andPURPOSE might be (if such meanings even exist), I have chosen to leave the issue as it stands.

Earlier, we observed how the conventions of human language change over time, and how this predicament shall be approached by appliers when they interpret a treaty using conventional language. Similarly, we observed how appliers shall approach temporal variations in the context, more particularly in the contextual element set out in VCLT article 31 § 3(c). Conventional language and the context are not, however, the only means of interpretation whose contents may vary. Another means prone to variation is the object and purpose of a treaty – more specifically, the state-of-affairs (or states-of-affairs), which the parties to the treaty expect to attain through applying the treaty. For the sake of clarity, this state-of-affairs will henceforth be termed in Greek as the *telos*, or – if the plural is intended – the *teloi*, of the treaty. Of course, the parties to a treaty may *ab initio* already have stated its *telos* to permit an alteration – using a generic referring expression with a referent assumed to be alterable.[35] This is, however, not the situation I am referring to. What I wish to address – let it be clear – is the situation where the parties to a treaty, despite the fact that at the time of concluding the treaty they might have had a completely clear picture of what the treaty's *telos* was to be,[36] later changed their minds. There are several reasons for why such a considerable change of heart may occur. Assume for example that the *telos* of a treaty is something the parties expect to attain, not only through the means represented by the treaty itself, but through the combined effect of the treaty and some other means, and that these other means undergo change, so that the treaty's original *telos* can no longer be attained.[37] Or assume that the instrumental relationship that holds between the treaty and its *telos* was not completely defined at the start, but in part is created, so to speak, by the later use of the treaty, and that the norm contents of the treaty gradually undergo changes.[38]

Obviously, the concept represented by the "object and purpose" of a treaty is not such that it must necessarily exist at a specific point in time. It is the general view held among authors that an applier – depending on the circumstances – shall have the possibility of taking into consideration, not only the *telos* that the treaty assumedly may have had at its conclusion, but also the *telos* that the treaty assumedly has at the time of interpretation.[39] As noted earlier, the decisive factors for determining the "object and purpose" of a treaty are the intentions held by its parties.[40] The crux of the matter is that these intentions – depending on the circumstances – might not only be the intentions held at the time when the treaty was concluded, but also the intentions held at the time of interpretation. Evidently, the literature is cause for further questions. When shall the *telos* of a treaty be determined based on the intentions held at the time of its conclusion? And when shall it be determined based on the intentions held at the time of interpretation? The literature does not provide us with a definitive answer.

Personally, I see no other possible solution to this issue than to use the criteria that we have earlier defined for resolving the issue of temporal variations in language and law.[41]

> If it can be shown that the thing interpreted is a generic referring expression with a referent assumed by the parties to be alterable, then the *telos* of a treaty shall be determined based on the intentions held by the parties at the time when the treaty is interpreted. In all other cases, the *telos* shall be determined based on the intentions held at the time when the treaty was concluded.

Of course, the principle source of support for this proposition is the context. The parallel between these different groups of issues – the issues concerning variations in the *telos* of a treaty, and those concerning variations in language and law, respectively – is simply so obvious that any other solution appears unthinkable. In addition, functional links exist between the different means of interpretation, provoking the need for a comprehensive solution. For how do appliers go about determining the *telos* of a treaty? I would argue that in one way or another, the *telos* of a treaty is always determined based on the text of said treaty understood in accordance with the ordinary meaning to be given to its terms. Considering this, it would surely cause difficulties if some other criterion determined the *telos* of a treaty, than that which determines the contents of "the ordinary meaning". All things considered, I will regard the issue as settled.

3 TREATIES WITH SEVERAL OBJECTS AND PURPOSES

It is a well-known fact that normally, not only one *telos* is conferred on a treaty by its parties. When a treaty is concluded, it is often with the intention that several *teloi* be attained, all at the same time. First of all, it is generally the case that a specific *telos* is conferred on each and every provision. These *teloi* are typically relatively concrete. Normally, however – assuming that the scope of the treaty is not exceptionally small – one can count on also finding a number of *teloi*, which relate to several provisions in combination or to the treaty as a whole. These *teloi* are typically relatively abstract. To illustrate, it seems that in the *European Convention for the Protection of Human Rights and Fundamental Freedoms*, the *telos* of article 6 paragraph 3(d) is to ensure the accused criminal of a full equality of arms throughout the criminal process,[42] while the combined *telos* of article 6 paragraphs 1, 2 and 3 is to ensure that the accused is given a fair trial[43] and the *telos* conferred on the convention as a whole is to promote and defend the ideal of a democratic society.[44]

Considering this background, the text of the Vienna Convention indeed looks peculiar. Article 31 § 1 does not speak of the objects and purposes of a treaty in the plural, but of its "object and purpose" in the singular. All things considered, however, I find it difficult to see how we could possibly treat as correct an interpretation of the text in accordance with its wording. It is the general view held among authors, that when appliers interpret a treaty using its object and purpose, they really cannot leave out any of the *teloi* that the parties assumedly intended to attain.[45] Among the range of authors having addressed this issue, either in connection with the adoption of the Vienna Convention or subsequent to it, I have found only one who hints at anything else – namely, professor Jacobs. He writes:

> The change from "objects and purposes" to "object and purpose" in the final draft may have been intended to give greater certainty, on the ground that there was less likely to be controversy on what was the principal object and purpose of a treaty than on which of several possibly conflicting objects and purposes should determine the meaning of a disputed term.[46]

What the author appears to be saying is that when appliers interpret a treaty using its object and purpose, they would have only one single *telos* to consider; and this, in the terminology of Jacobs, is "the principal object and purpose of the treaty". In my judgment, this is a reading that does not agree with the rules of interpretation laid down in international law.

According to international law, two first-order rules of interpretation are applicable *prima facie* , when appliers set out to determine whether they shall understand the expression "object and purpose" as a reference to the *telos* of a treaty in the singular, or as a reference to the *teloi* of the treaty in the plural. Let us call these rules numbers 1 and 18. Interpretation rule no. 1 states:

> If it can be shown that in a treaty provision, there is an expression whose form corresponds to an expression of conventional language, then the provision shall be understood in accordance with the rules of that language.[47]

Interpretation rule no. 18 provides as follows:

> If, by using the preparatory work of a treaty, a concordance can be shown to exist, as between the parties to said treaty, and with regard to the norm content of an interpreted treaty provision, then the provision shall be understood in such a way that it logically agrees with the concordance.[48]

These two rules are in conflict with one another.

As observed earlier, applying interpretation rule no. 1 leads us to the conclusion that we shall understand the "object and purpose" of a treaty to refer to the *telos* of the treaty in the singular. Applying interpretation rule no. 18 leads us to the conclusion that we shall understand the "object and purpose" of a treaty to refer to the *teloi* of the treaty in the plural. As noted by professor Jacobs, up to the point in 1966, when the International Law Commission finally presented its proposed text to the ILC Drafting Committee, it carried the wording "objects and purposes"; this was subsequently changed by the committee to "object and purpose".[49] The implication is that this fact alone would be sufficient reason for us to believe that when appliers interpret a treaty, they would only have one single *telos* to consider. (The assumption is that when modifications are made in the draft of a treaty this typically involves a modification of the treaty as well, from the perspective of its meaning.) Personally, I would like to suggest that as a matter of fact, the preparatory work of the Vienna Convention is uncommonly strong support for the exact opposite. During the eighteenth session of the ILC, members repeatedly and consistently spoke of "objects and purposes" – in accordance with the draft then existing – and no opposition to this language seems to have been voiced.[50] However, when the Drafting Committee presented its revised text at the close of the session, no reason was given for why the expression "objects and purposes" had been changed to "object and purpose".[51] It is not the Drafting Committee's place to introduce, on its own volition, anything of substance in those texts discussed earlier among the members of the ILC in plenary session.[52] As a consequence, it is difficult to believe that the expression "object and purpose", in the revised draft presented by the ILC Drafting Committee, should mean anything other than the "objects and purposes" is was meant to replace. If the expression "objects and purposes" shall be read as a reference to the *teloi* of a treaty in the plural, then the expression "object and purpose" must be read in the same way.

Under international law, two second-order rules of interpretation govern the conflict between interpretation rules nos. 1 and 18.[53] Let us call them numbers 40 and 41. Interpretation rule no. 40 states:

If it can be shown that the interpretation of a treaty provision in accordance with any one of interpretation rules nos. 1–16 leads to a result, which is different from that obtained by interpreting the provision in accordance with any one of interpretation rules no. 17–39, and that the application of the former rule either leaves the meaning of the interpreted treaty provision ambiguous or obscure, or amounts to a result which is manifestly absurd or unreasonable, then the provision shall not be understood in accordance with this former rule.

Interpretation rule no. 41 provides as follows:

If it can be shown that the interpretation of a treaty provision in accordance with any one of interpretation rules nos. 1–16 leads to a result, which is different from that obtained by interpreting the provision in accordance with any one of interpretation rules nos. 17–39, then, rather than with the latter of the two rules, the provision shall be understood in accordance with the former, except for those cases where interpretation rule no. 40 applies.

In my judgment, the latter of these two rules is the one that determines the relationship between interpretation rules nos. 1 and 18, in the situation where an applier sets out to determine whether he shall understand the expression "object and purpose" in article 31 as a reference to the *telos* of a treaty in the singular, or as a reference to the *teloi* of the treaty in the plural: if it can be shown that the interpretation of the expression "object and purpose" in accordance with interpretation rule no. 1 leads to a result, which is different from that obtained by interpreting the expression in accordance with rule no. 18, then the expression shall not be understood in accordance with interpretation rule no. 1. It would then be up to me to establish that the application of interpretation rule no. 1 either leaves the meaning of the interpreted provision ambiguous or obscure, or that it leads to a result which is manifestly absurd or unreasonable. Evidently, the application of interpretation rule no. 1 does not leave the meaning of the interpreted treaty provision ambiguous or obscure. Now, the question is whether I can establish that the application leads to a result which is manifestly absurd or unreasonable.

In the situation at hand, saying that the application of interpretation rule no. 1 leads to a result which is manifestly absurd or unreasonable is tantamount to saying that interpretation rules nos. 1 and 18 are based on communicative assumptions, arguably of which the assumption underlying an application of the former rule is significantly weaker than the assumption underlying an application of the latter.[54] Interpretation rule no. 1 is based on the assumption, that parties to a treaty express themselves in such a way that every expression in the treaty, with a form corresponding to an expression of conventional language, bears a meaning that agrees with the rules of that language.[55] Translated to the interpretation of the expression "object and purpose", the idea could be expressed as follows:

> The parties to the Vienna Convention have expressed themselves in such a way that the meaning of the expression "object and purpose" agrees with the rules of conventional language.

For the sake of simplicity, let us term this as the assumption underlying the application of rule no. 1. Interpretation rule no. 18 is based on the assumption that parties to a treaty express themselves in such a way that the treaty and its preparatory work are logically compatible, insofar and to the extent that, by using the preparatory work, good reasons can be provided showing a concordance to exist, as between the parties to the treaty, with regard to its norm content.[56] Translated to the interpretation of the expression "object and purpose", the idea could be expressed in the following manner:

> The parties to the Vienna Convention have expressed themselves in such a way, that the meaning of VCLT article 31 § 1 logically agrees with the preparatory work of VCLT, insofar and to the extent that by using the preparatory work, good reasons can be provided showing a concordance to exist, as between the parties to the Vienna Convention, and with regard to the norm content of article 31 § 1.

Let us term this as the assumption underlying an application of rule no. 18.

As far as I can see, there are only two ways of showing that an assumption A is substantially weaker than an assumption B. First, arguments may be presented undermining the assumption A. Second, arguments may be presented reinforcing the assumption B. I will now present two arguments, which undermine the assumption underlying the application of rule no. 1.

First, it is evident that reading the Vienna Convention in the way suggested by professor Jacobs would lead to severe practical problems. In making his suggestion, Jacobs assumes that treaties always have a single, principal, and all-embracing *telos*, to which every other *telos* of the treaty can be said to be subordinate. They do not. Many treaties have several principal *teloi*;[57] I dare say most have.[58] When appliers interpret a treaty "in light of its object and purpose", and they find that the treaty has more than one principal *telos*, then appliers – having embraced Jacobs's reading – are faced with two alternatives. Either appliers conclude that for the interpretation of the treaty in question the object and purpose cannot be used at all, since it is apparent that the interpreted treaty bears more than one single, principal, and all-embracing *telos*. Or, appliers postulate that a treaty – even though in general terms it cannot be said to have a single, principal, and all-embracing *telos* – always bears a single, principal, and all-embracing *telos* in each specific case; and they then proceed to determine which of the treaty's several principal *teloi* is the weightiest. Both alternatives seem equally dubious. The first alternative raises serious doubts, since it greatly reduces the significance of the object and purpose in the process of interpretation. If only those treaties that bear a single, principal *telos* were to be interpreted using the object and purpose, then the use of this means would be more the exception than the rule. This is counter to the idea of the object and purpose as a "principal means of interpretation".[59] The second alternative raises doubts since it makes interpretation excessively labour-intensive. If a treaty has more than one principal *telos*, and by the "object and purpose" of a treaty we mean all those *teloi* that the treaty assumedly has, then clearly there is the possibility that using the object and purpose will lead to different results, depending upon which of the treaty's principal *teloi* is actually used. Then, but only then, must the relative weight of the *teloi* be established. If, however, by the "object and purpose" of a treaty we were to understand its single, principal, and all-embracing *telos*, then the relative weight of the *teloi* must always be established. The question whether appliers, by using different *teloi* will be faced with conflicting results, appears entirely irrelevant; for it is only after the point when the relative weights of the *teloi* have been established, that we can say whether the use of object and purpose leads to an intelligible result at all.

Second, I can see no good reason why, for the purpose of interpretation, appliers should be free to use the single, principal *telos* of a treaty, but have to completely ignore all *teloi* of a lower degree of abstraction. The reason Jacobs gives is that typically, a single, principal *telos* is easier to determine than the relative weight of the less abstract *teloi*.[60] The basis for this claim is somewhat unclear. As far as I can see, it must be based on one of the following three assumptions:

(1) A treaty never has more than one principal *telos*, but it always has different *teloi* of a lower degree of abstraction, and when the latter are used to interpret a treaty, it typically leads to conflicting results.

(2) A treaty may have more than one principal *telos*, but the relative weight of these different principal *teloi* is typically easier to determine than the relative weight of the less abstract *teloi*.

(3) A treaty may have more than one principal *telos*, but it is more frequently the case that by using the less abstract *teloi* of a treaty, appliers will be faced with conflicting results.

The first assumption is obviously wrong. As observed, many treaties have two or more principal *teloi*, out of which we cannot comfortably consider one to be weightier than the others. Hence, the assumption that treaties never have more than one principal *telos* does simply not stand up to reality. The second assumption is certainly dubious. I can see no support whatsoever for the idea that the relative weight of the principal *teloi* of a treaty typically would be easier to determine than the relative weight of its less abstract *teloi*. As a matter of fact, there is considerable reason to believe the situation to be quite the opposite. The more concrete a *telos*, the easier it should be to determine; and the easier a *telos* is to determine, the easier it should be to determine its relative weight. The third assumption must also be seriously called into question. It is true that a treaty may have more than one *telos*, but this is not at all rare; on the contrary. I dare say it is very rare indeed that a treaty does *not* have more than one *telos*.[61] It does not seem a plausible suggestion that the less abstract *teloi* of a treaty would lead to conflicting results with such a great frequency. All things considered, it seems we have little reason to embrace what Jacobs argues, namely that the principal *telos* of a treaty is typically easier to determine than the relative weight of the less abstract *teloi*. Along with these two arguments we may note the absence of counter-arguments. I can see no single argument that either supports the assumption underlying the application of rule no. 1, or that undermines the assumption underlying the application of rule no. 18. Of course, it is a matter of judgment whether this means that the assumption underlying the application of rule no. 1 is *significantly* weaker than the assumption underlying the application of rule no. 18. Personally, I find it difficult to arrive at any other conclusion. In my judgment, for the interpretation of the expression "object and purpose", the application of interpretation rule no. 1 can indeed be shown to lead to a result, "which is manifestly absurd or unreasonable", in the sense of interpretation rule no. 40. If the interpretation of the expression "object and purpose" in accordance with interpretation rule no. 1 leads to a result, which is different from that obtained by interpreting the expression in accordance with interpretation rule no. 18, then in my judgment, the expression shall not be understood in accordance with rule no. 1. The expression shall be understood in accordance with rule no. 18 – it shall be considered a reference to the *teloi* of a treaty in the plural.

4 THE "OBJECT AND PURPOSE" PUT TO USE

What communicative standard or standards shall the parties to a treaty be assumed to have followed, when an applier interprets the treaty using its "object and purpose"? When appliers interpret a treaty using its object and purpose, the following communicative standard must be taken for granted:

> If a state produces an utterance taking the form of a treaty provision, then this provision should be drawn up so that, by applying the provision, the *teloi* of the treaty are attained to the greatest possible extent.[62]

According to what some authors imply, this is the only standard that should be taken into account.[63] Personally, I assert the opposite. Support for this position can be found in the literature taken at large. According to the great majority of authors, appliers have two ways to proceed when they interpret a provision of a treaty using its "object and purpose". First, they can understand the provision in light of the rights and obligations expressed in the treaty; second, they can understand the provision in light of its *teloi*.[64] However, with the standard established above, appliers will be limited to interpreting a treaty in light of its *teloi*. Hence, if we take the majority of authors to be right, then obviously further communicative standards need to be taken into consideration. The question is what standard or standards we are talking about. On this point, the literature can no longer provide us with a clear answer.

One way of answering the question is to consult the preparatory work of the Vienna Convention. It is indeed remarkable that in the provisions of the Convention we find no reference whatsoever to the PRINCIPLE OF EFFECTIVENESS, in the literature interchangeably referred to as THE PRINCIPLE UT RES MAGIS VALEAT QUAM PEREAT or LA RÈGLE D'EFFET UTILE.[65] The fact is that an express inclusion of the principle of effectiveness was the subject of serious discussion in the ILC already at a first round of drafting, provoked by a proposal of the Special Rapporteur, Sir Humphrey Waldock. Waldock had proposed an article along the following lines:

> *Article 72. – Effective interpretation of the terms* (ut res magis valeat quam pereat)
> In the application of articles 70 and 71 a term of a treaty shall be so interpreted as to give it the fullest weight and effect consistent –
> (a) with its natural and ordinary meaning and that of the other terms of the treaty; and
> (b) with the objects and purposes of the treaty.[66]

The proposal never garnered any significant support, however,[67] and it was later unanimously rejected.[68] A particularly interesting observation is the grounds given for the rejection.

First of all, it was thought that Waldock had formulated the principle of effectiveness in excessively broad terms, so that his text ran the risk of being misused to support a so-called extensive interpretation.[69] Waldock himself had warned about giving the principle of effectiveness too much significance. There is a tendency, Waldock had stated in his report, to equate effective with extensive or liberal interpretation, by which the principle of effectiveness is stretched to its extreme.[70] The importance given to the principle of effectiveness in international law is considerably less.

> Properly limited, it does not call for "extensive" or "liberal" interpretation in the sense of an interpretation going beyond what is expressed or necessarily implied in the terms.[71]

These reservations, the ILC marked, should have been more clearly set forward in the draft article that Waldock had proposed. Second – and more importantly – there were reasons to question whether draft article 72 was not in effect actually redundant.[72] If it is indeed the case, the Commission explained, that the principle of effectiveness does not carry more import than Waldock had suggested, then the principle was merely a repetition of what the Rapporteur had already put to words in other draft articles. All things considered, then, draft article 72 had little to contribute.[73]

[I]n so far as the maxim *Ut res magis valeat quam pereat* reflects a true general rule of interpretation, it is embodied in article 69, paragraph 1 [later to be adopted as VCLT article 31 § 1], which requires that a treaty shall be interpreted in good faith in accordance with the ordinary meaning to be given to its terms in the context of the treaty and in the light of its objects and purposes.[74]

What the ILC says is of course highly interesting: some aspects of the principle of effectiveness are already included by the ILC Draft Articles adopted in 1964 – more specifically, in the provisions recognising the context and the object and purpose of a treaty as acceptable means of interpretation. There is reason to believe the same link exists between the principle of effectiveness and the provisions drawn up on the use of these same means in the 1969 Vienna Convention.[75]

Evidently, we have reason to examine the principle of effectiveness more closely. Two things need to be observed with regard to the meaning of the principle of effectiveness. The first is the import of the principle. Taken to the extreme, the principle of effectiveness stands for the concept of a treaty being an instrument of greatest possible effectiveness.[76] Applied within the limits of international law, however, the principle must be balanced against a number of other ideals – this was observed by Waldock in 1964,[77] and it still applies today. Therefore, seen in its proper context, what the principle of effectiveness is really all about is not that appliers shall attempt to interpret a treaty to make it as effective as possible, but that appliers shall attempt to make sure that the treaty is not *ineffective*.[78]

[W]here a text is ambiguous or defective, but a possible, though uncertain, interpretation of it would give the agreement some effect, whereas otherwise it would have none, a court is entitled to adopt that interpretation, on the legitimate assumption that the parties must have intended their agreement to have some effect, not none.[79]

The second thing that must be observed is the meaning of the word effectiveness. The effectiveness of a phenomenon is not something that can be said to exist *in abstracto*. It is pure nonsense to state, concerning the interpretation of a treaty, that it shall be performed avoiding results that make the treaty ineffective, if we cannot at the same time identify the measure used to determine the effectiveness of the treaty. To better clarify matters, let us seek the assistance of international legal doctrine. It is a view generally held in the literature that if the principle of effectiveness can be applied to interpret a treaty, then this is because the treaty is assumed to be effective (1) from the point of view of its meaning, (2) from the point of view of its norm content, or (3) from the point of view of its *teloi*; the treaty is assumed to be linguistically, normatively and teleologically effective, respectively.[80]

In other words, if appliers interpret a treaty in accordance with the principle of effectiveness, the communicative standards assumed would be the following:

- If a state produces an utterance taking the form of a treaty provision, then the provision should be drawn up so that in the context there will be no instance of a pleonasm.
- If a state produces an utterance taking the form of a treaty provision, then the provision should be drawn up, so that by applying the provision a result is not obtained, which is not among the *teloi* conferred on the treaty.
- If a state produces an utterance taking the form of a treaty provision, then the provision should be drawn up so that in applying the provision, no other part of the treaty becomes normatively useless.

The first standard on the list may be identified with an act of interpretation using the context; it is comprised by the communicative standard designated by the letter C.[81] The second standard may be identified with an act of interpretation using the object and purpose of a treaty; it is comprised by the following standard – henceforth to be termed as communicative standard F – outlined at the beginning of this section:

> If a state produces an utterance taking the form of a treaty provision, then this provision should be drawn up so that, by applying the provision, the *teloi* of the treaty is attained to the greatest possible extent.[82]

Only the last of the three standards included in the list above – henceforth to be termed as communicative standard G – can be said to imply something new. It may not be identified with an act of interpretation using the context, and it cannot be considered included in the communicative standard F. With this observation in mind, it seems we can arrive at conclusions.

We have ventured earlier the assumption that aspects of the principle of effectiveness are comprised in the interpretation of treaties using the context and the object and purpose in accordance with VCLT article 31 § 1. We have shown standard G to be one of the communicative standards assumed by an applier, when he interprets a treaty in accordance with the principle of effectiveness. And we noted about the communicative standard G that it cannot be identified with an act of interpretation using the context. Given these premises, it is obvious that the communicative standard G must be identified with an act of interpretation using the object and purpose. When appliers interpret a treaty using the object and purpose of that treaty, this shall be done not only on the basis of the communicative standard F, but also on the basis of standard G. As further support for this proposition, I would like to cite the practice of international courts and tribunals.[83] This is what I will do in Section 5.

5 THE "OBJECT AND PURPOSE" PUT TO USE (CONT'D)

Among the tier of opinions included in the practice of international courts and tribunals, three cases in particular may be noticed. A first case is the judgment of the International Court of Justice in the case concerning *Border and Transborder Armed Actions*.[84] The facts of this case have already been reported earlier in this work,[85] and I see no reason for unnecessary repetition. As we know, Nicaragua and the Honduras were of different opinions as to the meaning of the following articles XXXI and XXXII in the *1948 American Treaty on Pacific Settlement ("the Pact of Bogotá")*.

Article XXXI
In conformity with Article 36, paragraph 2, of the Statute of the International Court of Justice, the High Contracting Parties declare that they recognize, in relation to any other American State, the jurisdiction of the Court as compulsory *ipso facto*, without the necessity of any special agreement so long as the present Treaty is in force, in all disputes of a juridical nature that arise among them concerning:
(a) The interpretation of a treaty;
(b) Any question of international law;
(c) The existence of any fact which, if established, would constitute the breach of an international obligation;
(d) The nature or extent of the reparation to be made for the breach of an international obligation.

Article XXXII
When the conciliation procedure previously established in the present Treaty or by agreement of the parties does not lead to a solution, and the said parties have not agreed upon an arbitral procedure, either of them shall be entitled to have recourse to the International Court of Justice in the manner prescribed in Article 40 of the Statute thereof. The Court shall have compulsory jurisdiction in accordance with Article 36, paragraph 1, of the said Statute.[86]

The Honduras had advanced the argument that article XXXI could only be read correctly if placed in relation to the article XXXII. According to the Honduras, the International Court of Justice would have no jurisdiction to settle a dispute under the provisions of article XXXI, in the cases covered by that article, if there had not previously been recourse to conciliation, according to the provisions of article XXXII. According to Nicaragua, each article should be read independently. The Hague Court would have jurisdiction to settle a dispute under the provisions of article XXXI, in the cases covered by that article, regardless of whether there had previously been recourse to conciliation, according to the provisions of article XXXII. As stated earlier, the Court concurred with the latter interpretation, invoking among other things the following argument:

It is, moreover, quite clear from the Pact that the purpose of the American States in drafting it [i.e. Article XXXI] was to reinforce their mutual commitments with regard to judicial settlement. This is also confirmed by the *travaux préparatoires*: the discussion at the meeting of Committee III of the Conference held on 27 April 1948 has already been referred to in paragraph 37 above. At that meeting, furthermore, the delegate of Colombia explained to the Committee the general lines of the system proposed by the Sub-Committee which had prepared the draft; the Sub-Committee took the position "that the principal procedure for the peaceful settlement of conflicts between the American States had to be judicial procedure before the International Court of Justice" *(translation by the Registry)*. Honduras's interpretation would however imply that the commitment, at first sight firm and unconditional, set forth in Article XXXI would, in fact, be emptied of all content if, for any reason, the dispute were not subjected to prior conciliation. Such a solution would be clearly contrary to both the object and the purpose of the Pact.[87]

Clearly, two different acts of interpretation are described by the Court. First, reference is made to an act of interpretation using the *telos* of the interpreted treaty. The *telos* conferred on article XXXI by the American States ...

...[is] to reinforce their mutual commitments with regard to judicial settlement.

In the case at hand, this *telos* would never be attained by applying article XXXI, if the treaty were to be given the interpretation suggested by the Honduras. Hence, this interpretation cannot be considered correct. Second, reference is made to an act of interpretation using the norm content of the interpreted treaty. If a reading like the Honduras's were to be accepted – if it had indeed been the case, that the Court had no jurisdiction, according to the provisions of article XXXI, until conciliation had first been attempted, according to the provisions of article XXXII – then article XXXI would clearly have no practical meaning at all. Indeed, in a case where conciliation *has* been attempted (without however succeeding), then the remedies to be applied are those of article XXXII. The disputing parties shall first make attempts to conclude a special agreement; if they do not succeed, then each party shall be entitled to bring the dispute before the International Court of Justice, which of course they already have, given the provisions of article XXXI. Consequently, the interpretation suggested by the Honduras cannot be considered correct. The two acts of interpretation may be plainly stated as follows. In the former line of reasoning, it is the assumption of the Court that the American States have expressed themselves in accordance with the communicative standard F. In the latter line of reasoning, it is the assumption that the American States have expressed themselves in accordance with the communicative standard G.

A second case to be noted is the judgment of the European Court of Human Rights in the *Colozza* case.[88] In November 1974, an Italian investigating judge had issued a warrant for the arrest of Italian citizen Giacinto Colozza; in addition to this, two warrants were later issued, in May and June 1975, respectively. However, since Colloza was not easily located, on no occasion had it been possible to arrest him. Quite obviously, Colozza no longer lived at the address he had last given, and his new address remained unknown. Therefore, in accordance with Italian law, he was declared *latitante*, that is to say he was declared a person wilfully evading the execution of a court warrant. Colozza was charged, and in May 1976, in his absence and after a trial about which he evidently had had no knowledge at all, an Italian court sentenced him to six years in prison. There was no possibility for appeal. The question arose as to whether Italy, through these decisions, had acted in violation of article 6 of the *European Convention for the Protection of Human Rights and Fundamental Freedoms*. This gave the Court occasion to comment on the meaning of this article:

> Although this is not expressly mentioned in paragraph 1 of Article 6, the object and purpose of the Article taken as a whole show that a person "charged with a criminal offence" is entitled to take part in the hearing. Moreover, subparagraphs (c), (d) and (e) of paragraph 3 guarantee to "everyone charged with a criminal offence" the right "to defend himself in person", "to examine or have examined witnesses" and "to have the free assistance of an interpreter if he cannot understand or speak the language used in court", and it is difficult to see how he could exercise these rights without being present.[89]

The cited reasoning bears parallels to that presented by the ICJ in the case concerning *Border and Transborder Armed Actions*. The thing examined by the European Court is the content of 6 § 1 and § 3(c), (d) and (e). I cite:

> 1. In the determination of his civil rights and obligations or of any criminal charge against him, everyone is entitled to a fair and public hearing within a reasonable time by an independent and impartial tribunal established by law.
>
> ...
>
> 3. Everyone charged with a criminal offence has the following minimum rights: ...
>   (c) to defend himself in person or through legal assistance of his own choosing or, if he has not sufficient means to pay for legal assistance, to be given it free when the interests of justice so require;
>   (d) to examine or have examined witnesses against him and to obtain the attendance and examination of witnesses on his behalf under the same conditions as witnesses against him;
>   (e) to have the free assistance of an interpreter if he cannot understand or speak the language used in court.

Two different acts of interpretation are described. The first is an act of interpretation using the *telos* of the interpreted treaty. The *telos* conferred on article 6 § 1 is to ensure the person charged with a criminal offence of a fair trial.[90] For a person charged with a criminal offence, this *telos* would never be attained if the person were not given the right as well to take part in the court hearings. Consequently, such a right must be considered included in the scope of article 6 § 1. The second act of interpretation described by the court is one using the norm content of the interpreted treaty. If a person charged with a criminal offence would not have the right to take part in the court hearings, nor would he be able to exercise the rights provided in article 6 § 3(c), (d), and (e). Again, a right to take part in the court hearings must be considered to follow from the provisions of article 6 § 1. In the former line of reasoning, it is an assumption of the Court that the parties to the European Convention have expressed themselves in accordance with the communicative standard F. In the latter line of reasoning, it is the assumption that the parties have expressed themselves in accordance with the communicative standard G.

My third example of the practice established by international courts and tribunals is once again a case chosen from the repertoire of the European Court for Human Rights; it is the *Belgian Linguistic* case.[91] The decision bears a significant difference from the two already cited. In the case concerning *Border and Transborder Armed Actions*, as well as the *Colozza* case, a treaty provision is interpreted using the norms contained in other provisions of the treaty. However, nothing prevents an applier from also using the norm contents of the very provision interpreted. When an applier interprets a treaty provision, it is because she is uncertain about the meaning of the provision vis-à-vis a specific case. The issue is whether, on the basis of the text of the provision, the applier may be justified in asserting the existence of a specific norm that can then be applied for solving the case. This does not necessarily mean that the applier is uncertain about the meaning of the provision vis-à-vis its entire extension. In fact, the case is usually the opposite. Even if an applier happens to be uncertain whether, on the basis of the text of a treaty provision, he may be justified in asserting the existence of a certain concrete norm, the applier is often completely certain about the existence of a number of other concrete norms assertable on the exact same basis. Of course, these other norms can be used for interpreting the treaty provision, in quite the same way as the applier would normally use the norm content expressed in other parts of the treaty. This is exactly the strategy practiced by the European Court in *Belgian Linguistic*.

The case originated from the education policy practiced in Belgium during the 1960's. Between June 1962 and January 1964, a total of six complaints of alleged human rights violations were lodged with the European Commission. The applicants – all Belgian nationals – were all residents of a region that Belgian language laws categorised as exclusively Flemish-speaking. They, for their part, had French as their first language, and they wanted their children to attend schools where they would be taught in French. However, according to Belgian language laws, all compulsory education in exclusively Flemish-speaking areas was to be performed in Flemish. Certain exceptions were permitted. Special education in French could be provided during an interim period, if local authorities decided that there was a need for it. In the areas where the applicants lived, however, no such decision had been taken. As a result, no government-financed education in French was provided; and this was exactly the subject matter of the complaints. In addition, complaints were made about the sanctions entailed by Belgian language laws. For example, school-leaving certificates would not be given official recognition, if it was established that language law regulations had not been followed at the issuing school. The question arose whether this Belgian policy should be seen to amount to a violation of article 2 of the European Convention, Protocol No. 1. The article reads:

No person shall be denied the right to education. In the exercise of any functions which it assumes in relation to education and to teaching, the State shall respect the right of parents to ensure such education and teaching in conformity with their own religious and philosophical convictions.

Since the European Court had never before been given opportunity to address the contents of this article, it apparently felt it an appropriate occasion for uttering a few general comments. First, the Court noted that the text of article 2 was indeed formulated in a negative manner. However, this was not cause to reject the fact that the right to education could also entail certain "positive" obligations:

The negative formulation indicates ... that the Contracting Parties do not recognise such a right to education as would require them to establish at their own expense, or to subsidise, education of any particular type or at any particular level. However, it cannot be concluded from this that the State has no positive obligation to ensure respect for such a right as is protected by Article 2 of the Protocol.[92]

It remained to be seen whether the right could be defined more precisely:

To determine the scope of the "right to education", within the meaning of the first sentence of Article 2 of the Protocol, the Court must bear in mind the aim of this provision. It notes in this context that all member States of the Council of Europe possessed, at the time of the opening of the Protocol to their signature, and still do possess, a general and official educational system. There neither was, nor is now, therefore, any question of requiring each State to establish such a system, but merely of guaranteeing to persons subject to the jurisdiction of the Contracting Parties the right, in principle, to avail themselves of the means of instruction existing at a given time.

The Convention lays down no specific obligations concerning the extent of these means and the manner of their organisation or subsidisation. In particular the first sentence of Article 2 does not specify the language in which education must be conducted in order that the right to education should be respected. It does not contain precise provisions similar to those which appear in Articles 5 (2) and 6 (3) (a) and (e). However the right to education would be meaningless if it did not imply in favour of its beneficiaries, the right to be educated in the national language or in one of the national languages, as the case may be.

4. The first sentence of Article 2 of the Protocol consequently guarantees, in the first place, a right of access to educational institutions existing at a given time, but such access constitutes only a part of the right to education. For the "right to education" to be effective, it is further necessary that, inter alia, the individual who is the beneficiary should have the possibility of drawing profit from the education received, that is to say, the right to obtain, in conformity with the rules in force in each State, and in one form or another, official recognition of the studies which he has completed.[93]

Clearly, the means of interpretation used by the Court is the object and purpose of the treaty. This is indicated at the very beginning of the Court's line of reason:

To determine the scope of the "right to education", within the meaning of the first sentence of Article 2 of the Protocol, the Court must bear in mind the aim of this provision.

Even clearer on this point is the authentic French version of the Court's findings:

Pour dégager la portée du "droit à l'instruction", au sens de la première phrase se l'article 2 du Protocole, la Cour doit tenir compte de l'objet de cette disposition.

To be more exact, what the reasoning of the Court indicates is an act of interpretation using the norm content of article 2, Protocol No. 1. Article 2, the Court observes, provides a right for any individual residing in the territory of a state party to avail herself of the existing educational system. Using this observation as a basis, further conclusions can be made. A first conclusion is that a person residing in the territory of a state party, according to article 2 of Protocol No. 1, has the right to require that education is provided in at least one of the national languages. This line of reason can be described in the following manner:

> Article 2 provides a right for each and every individual residing in the territory of a state party to avail himself of the existing educational system. If it were the case, that a person residing in the territory of a state party could not require that education be provided in at least one of the national languages, then that person would not be able to exercise the right to avail himself of the existing educational system.

> Therefore, a person residing in the territory of a state party, according to article 2 of Protocol No. 1, has the right to require that education be provided in at least one of the national languages.

A second conclusion drawn by the court is that a person residing in the territory of a state party, according to article 2 of Protocol No. 1, has the right to require that studies completed receive official recognition. The reasoning can be described in the following way:

> Article 2 provides a right for each and every individual residing in the territory of a state party to avail herself of the existing educational system. If it were the case, that a person residing in the territory of a state party could not require that studies completed receive official recognition, then that person would not be able to exercise the right to avail herself of the existing educational system. Therefore, a person residing in the territory of a state party, according to article 2 of Protocol no. 1, has the right to require that studies completed receive official recognition.

In both cases, it is clearly the assumption of the court that the parties to the European Convention have expressed themselves in accordance with the communicative standard G.

6 CONCLUSIONS

According to VCLT article 31 § 1, a treaty shall be interpreted in good faith "in accordance with the ordinary meaning to be given to the terms of the treaty ... in the light of its object and purpose". It is the purpose of this chapter to describe what this means. Based on the observations above, the following two rules of interpretation can be established:

Rule no. 15

§ 1. If it can be shown that the interpretation of a treaty provision in accordance with interpretation rule no. 1 leads to conflicting results, and that the treaty has a certain *telos*, which in one of the two possible ordinary meanings, by applying the provision, will be realised to a greater extent than in the other, then the former meaning shall be adopted.

§ 2. For the purpose of this rule, TELOS means any state-of-affairs, which according to the parties should be attained by applying the interpreted provision.

§ 3. For the purpose of this rule, the TELOS of a treaty is determined based upon the intentions held by the parties at the time of the treaty's conclusion, except for those cases where § 4 applies.

§ **4**. For the purpose of this rule, the TELOS of a treaty is determined based upon the intentions held by the parties at the time of interpretation, provided it can be shown that the thing interpreted is a generic referring expression with a referent assumed by the parties to be alterable.
§ **5**. For the purpose of this rule, PARTIES means any and all states for which the treaty is in force at the time of interpretation.

Rule no. 16
If it can be shown that the interpretation of a treaty provision in accordance with interpretation rule no. 1 leads to conflicting results, and that somewhere in the text of that treaty a norm is expressed, which – in light of the provision interpreted – in one of the two possible ordinary meanings can be considered in practice normatively useless, while in the other it cannot, then the latter meaning shall be adopted.

NOTES

1. Cf. Ch. 1, Section 3, of this work.
2. This is also evident from the preparatory work of the Vienna Convention. In the ILC Commentary of 1966, we read the following passage: "*Paragraph 1* [of draft article 27, later to be adopted as VCLT article 31] contains three separate principles. The first – interpretation in good faith – flows directly from the rule *pacta sunt servanda*. The second principle is the very essence of the textual approach: the parties are to be presumed to have that intention which appears from the ordinary meaning of the terms used by them. The third principle is one of both common sense and good faith; the ordinary meaning of a term is not to be determined in the abstract but in the context of the treaty and in the light of its object and purpose." (Draft Articles With Commentaries (1966), *ILC Yrbk*, 1966, Vol. 2, p. 221, § 12.)
3. See e.g. Villiger, p. 321; Vitányi, p. 56; Yasseen, p. 55; Rousseau, p. 272; Pessou, at the ILC's sixteenth session, 765th meeting, *ILC Yrbk*, 1964, Vol. 1, p. 278, § 45.
4. See e.g. McRae, p. 221; Amerasinghe, p. 195; Seidl-Hohenveldern, 1992, p. 93; Ost, pp. 292–293; Villiger, pp. 343–344; Bernhardt, 1984, p. 322; Bos, 1984, p. 147; Verdross and Simma, p. 492; Briggs, p. 708. Note, however, that some authors use the phrase TELEOLOGICAL INTERPRETATION in a more restricted sense, to denote what I will later be calling OBJECTIVE TELEOLOGICAL INTERPRETATION. (See e.g. Thirlway, 1991, p. 38; Brownlie, p. 631; Sinclair, 1984, p. 131; Jacobs, p. 336; Fitzmaurice, 1957, pp. 207–209.)
5. See e.g. Peczenik, 1995, pp. 364–365; Larenz, pp. 328–339; Bydlinski, pp. 449–463.
6. It should be noted that the terminology is not entirely consistent. Sometimes an interpretation is called objective teleological because the law interpreted is completely dissociated from the original lawmaker. Sometimes an interpretation is called objective teleological because the object and purpose put to use is not the one conferred on the law by the original lawmaker, but only a rational construction of that object and purpose. In my opinion, the latter usage of language must be considered somewhat peculiar. Just as with the utterance meaning of a treaty, the object and purpose of a law can never be determined with complete certainty; it can only be assumed. (The object and purpose conferred on a law by the

original lawmaker can only be determined through the assumption that the lawmaker drew up the law expressing "himself" in a rational manner (that is, in accordance with certain communicative standards). Even in the simple case where the object and purpose of a law is expressly stated in the text of the law itself, the object and purpose can be determined only on the assumption that the lawmaker uses conventional language to convey this piece of information.) If the interpretation of a law is defined as OBJECTIVE TELEOLOGICAL, merely because the object and purpose used is not the one conferred on the law by the original lawmaker, but rather is a rational construction of that object and purpose, and yet we know that a law cannot – under any circumstances – be interpreted using the object and purpose *with full certainty* conferred on the law by the original lawmaker, then I fail to see what a subjective teleological interpretation could possibly denote. Hence, if the distinction between objective and subjective teleological interpretation is to be at all meaningful, the term OBJECTIVE TELEOLOGICAL INTERPRETATION can be used only in the sense stated here.

7. Ost, p. 292; Sinclair, 1984, p. 131; Bos, 1984, p. 153; Vitányi, p. 57; Yasseen, pp. 55, 57; Köck, p. 88; Haraszti, pp. 112–113; Cot, pp. 648–649; De Visscher, 1963, p. 64; Favre, 1974, pp. 82–83.
8. See Ch. 2, Section 1, of this work.
9. Loc. cit.
10. A commonly debated topic in the literature is the method to be used for determining the object and purpose of a treaty. (See e.g. Farer, p. 25; Haraszti, p. 112; Jacobs, p. 337; Sinclair, 1984, p. 135; Villiger, pp. 343–344; Jiménez de Aréchaga, pp. 43–44; Yasseen, p. 57; Köck, p. 39; Müller, pp. 130–131; Gottlieb, pp. 124, 126; Bernhardt, 1963, p. 89; Hogg (II), pp. 49–50.) As far as I can see, however, we must leave this debate without comment. In the rules of interpretation laid down in the Vienna Convention we are told only how to determine the meaning of a treaty with regard to its norm content. Therefore, the issue of how to determine the object and purpose of a treaty would seem to fall outside the framework established for this work.
11. See Bos, 1984, p. 153; Sur, p. 228.
12. Cf. e.g. Sur, pp. 223, 231–232; Jacqué, 1972, p. 169, n. 190. Cf. also Anscombe, pp. 144–152.
13. Cf. Sur, p. 223, cit. Bonnard, pp. 369, 371, and Vedel, p. 530, and Sur, pp. 227–231; Jacqué, 1972, p. 141, cit. Dehaussy, § 81; Rousseau, p. 272.
14. See e.g. *Kjeldsen, Busk Madsen and Pedersen, Publ. ECHR*, Ser. A, Vol. 23, p. 27, § 53.
15. Cf. Sur, p. 223, cit. Bonnard, pp. 369, 371, and Vedel, p. 530, and Sur, pp. 227–231; Jacqué, 1972, p. 141, cit. Dehaussy, § 81, and Jacqué, p. 169, n. 190, cit. Laubadère, p. 479; Rousseau, p. 272.
16. See Robertson and Merrills, pp. 1ff.
17. Cf. Draft Articles With Commentaries (1966), *ILC Yrbk*, 1966, Vol. 2, p. 220, § 10; Elias, 1974, p. 79; Jennings, p. 550; Reuter, 1989, pp. 75–76.
18. See Ch. 8, Section 3, of this work.
19. My emphasis.
20. See e.g. Vedel, pp. 517–538; Duguit, pp. 316–325; Bonnard, pp. 363–393. See also *Vocabulaire Juridique*, 1987, under the entry **But**, "Objectif; fin poursuivie. Ex. but d'une loi, d'un acte juridique, d'un groupement", and under the entry **Objet** – du contrat, "(b) En un sens technique, l'ensemble des droits et obligations que le contrat est destiné à faire naître".
21. Jacqué, 1972, p. 142.

22. Loc. cit.
23. See e.g. Tchivounda, p. 634; Vitányi, pp. 56–57; Favre, 1960, p. 83.
24. This is not to say that exceptions do not exist. One oft-cited decision is *Minority Schools in Albania*, PCIJ, Ser. A/B, No. 64, p. 17. From more recent times, an authority to be noted is *Border and Transborder Armed Actions*: "Such a solution would be clearly contrary to both the object and the purpose of the Pact" (*ILR*, Vol. 84, p. 244, § 46).
25. See e.g. Davidson, p. 131; Thirlway, 1991, pp. 38–42; Merrills, pp. 76–77; Bernhardt, 1984, p. 322; Haraszti, p. 112, n. 98; O'Connell, p. 255.
26. See e.g. Verdross and Simma, p. 492; Hilf, pp. 101–102; Köck, pp. 88–89. The official German translation of the VCLT – BGBl. 1985 II 925 – article 31 § 1 reads as follows: "Ein Vertrag ist nach Treu und Glauben in Übereinstimmung mit der gewöhnlichen, seinen Bestimmungen in ihrem Zusammenhang zukommenden Bedeutung und im Lichte seines Zieles und Zweckes auszulegen."
27. See e.g. Ost, pp. 292–295; von Glahn, pp. 504–505; Bernhardt, 1984, p. 322; Vitányi, p. 56; Haraszti, pp. 112–113; O'Connell, p. 255.
28. See e.g. Verdross and Simma, p. 492; Hilf, pp. 101–102; Müller, pp. 130–131.
29. The OBJECT AND PURPOSE (OBJET ET BUT, OBJETO Y FIN) of a treaty is mentioned also in articles 18, 19, 20 § 2, 33 § 4, 41 § 1 and 58 § 1. However, in none of these instances is the meaning of the phrase clearer than in article 31. (With regard to articles 19 and 20, cf. Lijnzaad, pp. 39–40; Teboul, pp. 695–696; Coccia, p. 23.)
30. Yasseen, Speaking as Chairman of the Drafting Committee, at the Vienna Conference's first session, 61st meeting of the Committee of the Whole, *Official Records*, p. 361, § 101.
31. See e.g. Jacqué, 1991, p. 381; Sur, p. 228; Rousseau, p. 272; Voïcu, p. 33; Dehaussy, § 81; Berlia, p. 308; De Visscher, 1963, p. 62, n. 1.
32. It seems we have reason to recall the observation made earlier: according to some authors, the two words OBJECT and PURPOSE, in the sense of the expression "the object and purpose", are synonymous with the meanings ascribed to OBJET and BUT in the French legal doctrine; according to others, they are not. However, no one author seems to question the fact that the extension of "the object and purpose" comprises the meaning of the word OBJET as well as that of the word BUT.
33. This alternative has indeed been suggested by others. See e.g. Reuter, 1989, p. 628; Villiger, pp. 343–344, n. 176; Bos, 1984, pp. 153–154; Yasseen, p. 57.
34. See Ch. 4 of this work.
35. Cf. e.g. *Canadian Agricultural Tariffs*, *ILR*, Vol. 110, pp. 579–583, §§ 134–145; *Loizidou v. Turkey*, *Publ. ECHR*, Ser. A, Vol. 310, pp. 25–28, §§ 67–77; *Namibia*, *ILR*, Vol. 49, pp. 20–22, §§ 49–54.
36. Note: it need not necessarily be the case that the drafters of a treaty, at the time of conclusion, have a completely clear vision of what shall be considered the *telos* of that treaty. Such a clear vision may develop later, for example in connection with the application of the treaty. (Cf. Cot, pp. 648–649.)
37. For an excellent article on the different relationships that can exist between a law and its *telos*, see Summers, 1982, pp. 60–80.
38. Concerning this phenomenon of a law, so to speak, defining its own *telos*, see ibid., pp. 69–70.
39. See e.g. Thirlway, 1991, p. 41, cit. *Namibia*, *ICJ Reports*, 1971, p. 31, § 53, and Thirlway, 1989, pp. 135–143; Villiger, pp. 343–344, § 513, n. 176; Karl, 1983, p. 185;

Ganshof van der Meersch, pp. 114–116; Yasseen, p. 59; Jacobs, pp. 337–338; Cot, p. 649. See also, although in the context of another provision, Lijnzaad, pp. 39–40; Teboul, p. 697.

40. See Section 1 of this chapter.
41. See Chapters 3 and 5 of this work, respectively.
42. See e.g. *Vidal, Publ. ECHR*, Ser. A, Vol. 235-B, p. 32, § 33.
43. See e.g. *Campbell and Fell, Publ. ECHR*, Ser. A, Vol. 80, p. 43, § 91.
44. See e.g. *Kjeldsen, Busk Madsen and Pedersen, Publ. ECHR*, Ser. A, Vol. 23, p. 27, § 53.
45. See, more or less expressly, Villiger, pp. 321–322; Yasseen, p. 58; Rest, p. 144, n. 6; Gottlieb, pp. 124, 126. See also, implicitly, Merrills, p. 76; Ost, pp. 292–293; Amerasinghe, p. 195; Brownlie, pp. 631–632; von Glahn, pp. 504–505; Bernhardt, 1984, p. 322; Sinclair, 1984, p. 134, cit. diss. op. Fitzmaurice, *National Union of Belgian Police, ILR*, Vol. 57, pp. 293–294; Verdross and Simma, p. 492; Haraszti, p. 112, n. 99.
46. Jacobs, p. 337. (Footnote omitted.)
47. See Ch. 3 of this work.
48. See Ch. 8 of this work.
49. See p. 212 of this work.
50. See various members at the ILC's eighteenth session, 869th meeting (§§ 52–70), 870, 871 and 872 (§§ 1–24), *ILC Yrbk*, 1966, Vol. 1. Part 2, pp. 183–200.
51. See Yasseen, speaking as Chairman of the Drafting Committee, at the ILC's eighteenth session, 883rd meeting, *ILC Yrbk* , 1966, Vol. 1. Part 2, p. 267, §§ 90–91. The statement reads as follows: "The words 'in the context of the treaty and in the light of its object and purpose' had been taken from paragraph 1(a) of the new text proposed by the Special rapporteur in his report (A/CN.4/186/Add.6)." However, strangely enough, the specified report still mentioned "objects and purposes" in the plural.
52. Cf. Report of the International Law Commission covering the work of its tenth session, 28 April-4 July 1958, *ILC Yrbk*, 1958, Vol. 2, p. 108, § 65.
53. See Ch. 10 of this work.
54. For a more detailed treatment of the expression "leads to a result that is manifestly absurd or unreasonable", see Ch. 10 of this work.
55. See the introduction to Ch. 3 of this work.
56. See Ch. 8 of this work.
57. I have assumed it to be clear what is meant by "the principal object and purpose of a treaty". It is not. (Cf. Summers, 1977, pp. 129–130.)
58. Cf. ibid., with regard to the *teloi* of laws: "Legal goal structures are inherently complex in the following way: it is always possible to differentiate several levels of goals along an ascending means-end continuum in which the realization of lower-level goals (often explicitly formulated in the law) serves higher-level goals (often not so formulated). Thus, for any law we can identify one or more 'immediate'-level goals, one or more 'intermediate'-level goals, and one or more 'higher or ultimate'-level goals — [A]t each of the three (there might be more) 'goal levels' so far identified, we will usually find more than one intended goal". (p. 128). See also Summers, 1982: "An effective legal rule is like a scarce economic resource: it cannot be had without giving up other things, in part or in whole. Thus, a legal rule reflects some effort to accommodate conflicting goals in an optimal way. Rarely does a single goal rank so far ahead of others that the others can be considered simply dispensable in event of conflict. Instead, the overall aim will be to maximize the realization of conflicting goals in accord with some implicit or explicit scheme of priorities. A full description of the constellation of

goals that lies behind and figures in a rule therefore takes into account the conflicting nature of the goals and the network of priority relations between them. Goals conflict in different ways, and priority relations may themselves be complex." (pp. 65–66).

59. If the means of interpretation listed in VCLT article 32 can be termed as "supplementary", then naturally for the means listed in article 31 we must be able to use the term PRINCIPAL MEANS. (By the way, even Jacobs has adopted this terminology; see Jacobs, p. 326.) Apart from the fact that the alternative has consequences running counter to the idea of the object and purpose of a treaty as a principal means of interpretation, the alternative is also incompatible with the practice of international courts and tribunals. Judicial bodies often use the object and purpose of a treaty in order to determine its meaning.
60. See p. 212 of this work.
61. Cf. p. 215, n. 58 of this work.
62. Note that when applier uses the object and purpose, it is because the ordinary meaning of the interpreted treaty is either vague or ambiguous – in the former case, the object and purpose is used to make the ordinary meaning more precise; in the latter, the object and purpose is used to determine which of several meanings is to be considered correct and which one is not. In the case of an extreme teleological interpretation, the ordinary meaning is not a limitation. The teleological interpretation reflected in the provisions of VCLT article 31 is a moderated version.
63. I fail to see how the consequence of Bos's and Sur's line of reasoning could be anything else. (See Bos, 1984, p. 153; Sur, p. 228.)
64. See Section 2 of this chapter.
65. I have taken for granted that in international law the three terms – THE PRINCIPLE OF EFFECTIVENESS, UT RES MAGIS VALEAT QUAM PEREAT, andLA RÈGLE D'EFFET UTILE – are all used to stand for the same thing. Thirlway and Amerasinghe use the terms in a slightly different manner. According to Thirlway and Amerasinghe, the principle of effectiveness comprises two rules – by them termed as LA RÈGLE DE EFFET UTILE and LA RÈGLE DE L'EFFICACITÉ. "The first is the rule that all provisions of the treaty or other instrument must be supposed to have been intended to have significance and to be necessary to convey the intended meaning; that an interpretation which reduces some part of the text to the status of a pleonasm, or mere surplussage, is prima facie suspect. The second is the rule that the instrument as a whole, and each of its provisions, must be taken to have been intended to achieve some end, and that an interpretation which would make the text ineffective to achieve the object [and purpose] in view is, again, prima facie suspect." (Thirlway, 1991, p. 44; cf. Amerasinghe, pp. 195–196.) This terminology does not agree with the literature at large, where the terms THE PRINCIPLE OF EFFECTIVENESS, UT RES MAGIS VALEAT QUAM PEREAT, andLA RÈGLE D'EFFET UTILE are used interchangeably, without any noticeable difference in meaning. (See e.g. Pauwelyn, p. 247; White, pp. 332–333; Golsong, p. 154; Sinclair, 1984, p. 118; Verdross and Simma, p. 494; Vitányi, p. 59; Yasseen, pp. 71–74; Haraszti, pp. 166–170; Rest, p. 49; Rousseau, p. 270; Jennings, p. 549; Draft Articles With Commentaries (1966), *ILC Yrbk*, 1966, Vol. 2, p. 219, § 6, see especially the reference to *Interpretation of Peace Treaties*, *ICJ Reports*, 1950, p. 229; Berlia, pp. 306–308; Waldock, Third Report on the Law of Treaties, *ILC Yrbk*, 1964, Vol. 2, pp. 60–61, §§ 27–30; Bernhardt, 1963, p. 96; Degan, 1963, p. 102; McNair, 1961, pp. 383–384; Fitzmaurice, 1957, p. 211.) What makes the terminology of Thirlway and Amerasinghe even more peculiar is that they both draw support from an article by Berlia. (See Thirlway, 1991, p. 44, n. 207; Amerasinghe,

p. 195, n. 62.) According to Berlia, however, THE PRINCIPLE OF EFFECTIVENESS and LA RÈGLE D'EFFET UTILE are synonymous. (See Berlia, pp. 306–308.)

66. Third Report on the Law of Treaties, *ILC Yrbk*, 1964, Vol. 2, p. 53.
67. In the name of fairness, it must be added that even Waldock admitted he was very doubtful about his proposal. (See ibid., p. 60, § 27.)
68. See the decision at the ILC's sixteenth session, 766th meeting, *ILC Yrbk*, 1964, Vol. 1, p. 291, § 120.
69. See various members, at the ILC's sixteenth session, 766th meeting, ibid., pp. 288–291, §§69–120. (See especially statements by de Luna, § 73; Chairman (Ago), speaking as member, § 91; Rosenne, § 92; Ruda, §§ 95–96.) Cf. Draft Articles With Commentaries (1964), *ILC Yrbk*, 1964, Vol. 2, p. 201, § 8.
70. See Third Report on the Law of Treaties, ibid., p. 60, § 27.
71. Loc. cit.
72. See various members, at the ILC's sixteenth session, 766th meeting, *ILC Yrbk*, 1964, Vol. 1, pp. 288–291, §§ 69–120. (See especially statements by Verdross, §§ 71, 109; Castrén, § 73; Ruda, § 95; Chairman (Ago), speaking as member, § 102; Lachs, § 110.) Cf. Draft Articles With Commentaries (1964), *ILC Yrbk*, 1964, Vol. 2, p. 201, § 8.
73. See the Chairman's conclusions, at the ILC's sixteenth session, 766th meeting, *ILC Yrbk*, 1964, Vol. 1, p. 291, §§ 119–120. Cf. Draft Articles With Commentaries (1964), *ILC Yrbk*, 1964, Vol. 2, p. 201, § 8.
74. Draft Articles With Commentaries (1964), loc. cit.
75. This is a conclusion apparently shared by other authors. (See e.g. Golsong, p. 153; *Oppenheim's International Law*, p. 1280, n. 25; Villiger, p. 344; Sinclair, 1984, p. 118; Vitányi, p. 60; Yasseen, p. 74; Haraszti, p. 167, n. 39; Elias, 1974, p. 74.)
76. See e.g. Haraszti, p. 170; Rest, p. 47; Fitzmaurice and Vallat, pp. 312–313; Bernhardt, 1963, p. 96; Fitzmaurice, 1957, pp. 222–223; Schwarzenberger, 1957, p. 520; Lauterpacht, 1949, pp. 69–70.
77. See p. 218 of this work.
78. See e.g. Amerasinghe, pp. 195–196; Golsong, p. 154; Thirlway, 1991, p. 47, *Oppenheim's International Law*, pp. 1280–1281; Vitányi, pp. 58–60; Haraszti, pp. 166–170; Elias, 1974, p. 74; Gutiérrez Posse, pp. 229–254; Fitzmaurice, 1971, p. 373; Draft Articles With Commentaries (1966), *ILC Yrbk*, 1966, Vol. 2, p. 219, § 6.
79. Fitzmaurice, 1971, p. 373.
80. See e.g. Amerasinghe, pp. 195–198; Thirlway, 1991, pp. 44–48; *Oppenheim's International Law*, pp. 1280–1281; Haraszti, pp. 166–170; Gutiérrez Posse, pp. 229–254; Rest, pp. 47–53; O'Connell, p. 255; Waldock, Third Report on the Law of Treaties, *ILC Yrbk*, 1964, Vol. 2, pp. 60–61, §§ 27–30; Berlia, pp. 306–308; Degan, 1963, pp. 102–106; Fitzmaurice, 1957, pp. 220–223; Fitzmaurice, 1951, pp. 18–20.
81. See Ch. 4, Section 2, of this work.
82. See p. 217 of this work.
83. In addition to the decisions cited in the text, see *AAPL v. Sri Lanka*, *ILR*, Vol. 106, pp. 445–446, § 52; *Artico*, *Publ. ECHR*, Ser. A, Vol. 37, pp. 15–16, §§ 32–33; *Luedicke, Belkacem and Koç*, *Publ. ECHR*, Ser. A, Vol. 29, pp. 17–18, § 42; *Namibia*, *ILR*, Vol. 49, p. 25, §§ 66–67; possibly also *Pope & Talbot v. Canada*, *ILR*, Vol. 122, p. 384, §§ 117–118; *US-Shrimp*, § 121; *Bosnia Genocide*, §§ 167–169.
84. *Case Concerning Border and Transborder Armed Actions (Nicaragua v. Honduras)*, Judgment of 20 December 1988, *ILR*, Vol. 84, pp. 219ff.
85. See Ch. 4, Section 4, of this work.

86. The text cited is that provided by the court. (See *ILR*, Vol. 84, p. 233, § 20 and p. 243, § 42.)
87. Ibid., p. 244, § 46. (Footnote omitted.)
88. Colozza Case, Judgment of 12 February 1985, *Publ. ECHR*, Ser. A, Vol. 89.
89. Ibid., p. 14, § 27.
90. See p. 238 of this work.
91. Case "Relating to Certain Aspects of the Laws on the Use of Languages in Education in Belgium" (Merits), Judgment of 23 July 1968, *Publ. ECHR*, Ser. A, Vol. 6.
92. Ibid., p. 31, § 3.
93. Ibid., p. 31, §§ 3–4.

CHAPTER 8

USING THE SUPPLEMENTARY MEANS OF INTERPRETATION

The purpose of this chapter is to describe what it means to interpret a treaty using the supplementary means of interpretation, according to the provisions of Vienna Convention article 32. As we know, describing what it means to interpret a treaty using some certain means of interpretation is tantamount to clarifying and putting to words the rule or rules of interpretation, through which the use of this means has to be effectuated.[1] In the literature, and in the practice of international courts and tribunals, as well as in the practice of states, actors refer to the use of supplementary means of interpretation in two fundamentally different ways. First, actors refer to a set of elements, which they allege can be used to supplement the means of interpretation listed in VCLT article 31. Examples include the preparatory work of the interpreted treaty, the circumstances of its conclusion, and treaties *in pari material*. Second, actors refer to a number of rules – referred to interchangeably as norms, principles or maxims – all held to be applicable according to the provisions of VCLT article 32. Examples include the principle of *contra proferentem*, the principle of *ejusdem generis*, and the rule of necessary implication. Given the organisation chosen for this work, these inconsistencies in the usage of language present some genuine challenges.

As I have stated earlier, the starting point for my inquiry into the rules of interpretation laid down in international law is the means of interpretation recognised as acceptable by the Vienna Convention. The reason why I have chosen this mode of organisation is partly definitional. Every single rule of interpretation applicable according to the provisions of VCLT articles 31–32 can also be described as the use of some specific means of interpretation. There is also a practical reason for my choice. Articles 31–32 have been drafted in such a way that normally, we could not possibly clarify and put to words a rule of interpretation before first having established the means of interpretation presupposed by that rule. However, defining the means of interpretation presupposed by a rule of interpretation is never an end in itself. If it so happens that the sources used for this work allow me to determine *immediately* the contents of a series of rules, which are all held to be applicable according to the provisions of VCLT article 32, then I cannot see the point of also identifying the presupposed means of interpretation. The problem is that an inquiry into the use of supplementary means of interpretation will differ considerably depending upon whether, in the sources exploited for that inquiry, authorities refer to the use of supplementary means simply by pointing out the elements that can be used according to VCLT article 32, or whether they proceed to outline directly the rules of interpretation that can be applied according to that article. To simplify presentation, I have therefore chosen to divide my investigation into two separate chapters. In Chapter 8, I shall describe what it means to interpret a treaty using supplementary means of interpretation, in the sense of the set of elements that can be used to supplement the means of interpretation listed in VCLT article 31. In Chapter 9, I shall describe what it means to interpret a treaty using supplementary means of interpretation, in the sense of the rules of interpretation that can be applied according to VCLT article 32.

"Recourse may be had to supplementary means of interpretation ... in order to confirm the meaning resulting from the application of article 31, or to determine the meaning when the interpretation according to article 31: (a) leaves the meaning ambiguous or obscure; or (b) leads to a result which is manifestly absurd or unreasonable" – this is provided in VCLT article 32.

Il peut être fait appel à des moyens complémentaires d'interprétation ... en vue, soit de confirmer le sens résultant de l'application de l'article 31, soit de déterminer le sens lorsque l'interprétation donnée conformément à l'article 31: (a) laisse le sens ambigu ou obscur; ou (b) conduit à un résultat qui est manifestement absurde ou déraisonnable.

Se podrá acudir a medios de interpretación complementarios ... para confirmar el sentido resultante de la aplicación del artículo 31, o para determinar el sentido cuando la interpretación dada de conformidad con el artículo 31: (a) Deje ambiguo o oscuro el sentido; o (b) Conduzca a un resultado manifiestamente absurdo o irrazonable.

One thing is immediately evident from this text. When appliers use the supplementary means of interpretation, the task may be approached in two fundamentally different ways. Supplementary means of interpretation can be used independently of other means of interpretation, or they can be used relative to conventional language, subject to the bounds set by the "ordinary meaning". According to VCLT article 32, the supplementary means of interpretation can be used for the interpretation of a treaty provision only in the following three situations:

(1) Appliers wish to confirm a meaning obtained through the application of article 31.
(2) Appliers wish to determine the meaning of a treaty provision, because interpreting the treaty according to article 31 leaves the meaning ambiguous or obscure.

(3) Appliers wish to determine the meaning of a treaty provision, because interpreting the treaty according to article 31 leads to a result which is manifestly absurd or unreasonable.

In a situation where appliers wish to determine the meaning of a treaty provision, because interpreting the treaty according to article 31 leads to a result which is manifestly absurd or unreasonable, the supplementary means of interpretation are used independently of other means. In a situation where appliers wish to determine the meaning of a treaty provision, because interpreting the treaty according to article 31 leaves the meaning ambiguous or obscure,[2] the supplementary means of interpretation are used either independently of other means or relative to conventional language. The use of supplementary means is independent of other means, when the interpreted treaty provision contains an expression that does not exist in conventional language, making the three primary means of interpretation – conventional language, the context, and the object and purpose of the treaty – altogether useless. The use of supplementary means is relative to conventional language, when one or more of the three primary means can be used, but lead to conflicting results. In a situation where appliers wish to confirm a meaning of a treaty provision obtained through the application of article 31, then once again supplementary means of interpretation are used either independently of other means or relative to conventional language. The use of supplementary means is independent of other means when confirmation concerns the use of conventional language. The use is relative to conventional language when confirmation concerns a use of the context or of the object and purpose.

Hence, if we wish to give a shorthand description of how the supplementary means of interpretation shall be used, it could look like this:

> If it can be shown that the interpretation of a treaty provision in accordance with interpretation rule no. 1 leads to conflicting results, and that between the provision and any given supplementary means of interpretation there is a relationship governed by the communicative standard S, then the provision shall be understood as if the relationship conformed to this standard.
>
> If it can be shown that between an interpreted treaty provision and any given supplementary means of interpretation, there is a relationship governed by the communicative standard S, then the provision shall be understood as if the relationship conformed to this standard.

Two questions remain to be answered, in order for the task in this chapter to be considered accomplished:

(1) What is meant by "supplementary means of interpretation"?

(2) What communicative standard or standards shall the parties to a treaty be assumed to have followed when an applier interprets the treaty using "supplementary means of interpretation"?

I shall now give what I consider to be the correct answers to these questions. The chapter is organised so that in Sections 1–6 I begin by answering question (1). In Section 7, I shall then answer question (2).

1 THE MEANING OF "SUPPLEMENTARY MEANS OF INTERPRETATION"

What is meant by "supplementary means of interpretation"? According to the provisions of Vienna Convention article 32, an applier may have recourse to "supplementary means of interpretation, including the preparatory work of the treaty and the circumstances of its conclusion". The expression "supplementary means of interpretation" is somewhat perplexing. Obviously, we need to consider as part of the "supplementary means of interpretation" "the preparatory work of the treaty" (Fr. *"[les] travaux préparatoires";* Sp. *"los trabajos preparatorios del tratado")* and "the circumstances of its conclusion" (Fr. *"[les] circonstances dans lesquelles le traité a été conclu";* Sp. *"las circunstancias de su celebración").* However, it is evident that "the preparatory work of the treaty" and "the circumstances of its conclusion" are not necessarily the only elements that can be used by appliers according to that article. Further elements may be included in the extension of the "supplementary means of interpretation" – this is implied by the expression "including" (Fr. *"et notamment";* Sp. *"en particular").*[3] Naturally, the expression "supplementary means of interpretation" must be seen to refer back to the contents of customary international law.[4] The problem is to determine exactly the type of reference intended.

There are three possible alternatives. In one sense, "supplementary means of interpretation" can be viewed as a general (and definite) referring expression.[5] Hence, according to a first interpretation alternative, "supplementary means of interpretation" would refer to *a limited number* of those means of interpretation that can be used by appliers, according to the laws of international custom, in a situation where the primary means have proved insufficient. In another sense, "supplementary means of interpretation" can be read as a generic referring expression that refers to the class *supplementary means of interpretation* as such.[6] As we know, when an utterer produces a generic referring expression, in some cases the expression refers to a defined referent, while in other it refers to a referent that remains undefined. Hence, according to a second interpretation alternative, "supplementary means of interpretation" would refer to all those means of interpretation that can be used by appliers, according to customary international law, in a situation where the primary means have proved insufficient, *given the contents of customary international law at the point in time when the Vienna Convention was established as definite*. According to a third interpretation alternative, "supplementary means of interpretation" would refer to all those means of interpretation that can be used by appliers, according to customary international law, in a situation where the primary means have proved insufficient, *given the contents of customary international law at any given moment*.

The first of the three alternatives may immediately be dismissed. As we have established, the rules of interpretation laid down in VCLT articles 31–33 have a content identical to that of the rules laid down in customary international law.[7] As far as interpretation alternatives 2 and 3 are concerned, the former hardly seems plausible. If we assume that the expression "supplementary means of interpretation" has a defined referent, we must also assume the parties to the Vienna Convention to have operated under the following expectation: during the lifetime of the Vienna Convention, the contents of the class *supplementary means of interpretation* – as defined in customary international law – will not ever change.[8] This assumption is clearly not tenable. In 1969, when the Vienna Convention was established as definite, it was expected that the Convention would remain in force for rather a long time. Considering this, the parties to the Convention must have acted under the assumption that the contents of the then-current class *supplementary means of interpretation* would probably be altered. Moreover, interpretation alternative no. 3 is the one generally embraced in the legal literature.[9] All things considered, I find it difficult to come to a conclusion other than this: "supplementary means of interpretation" refers to all those means of interpretation that can be used by appliers, according to customary international law, in a situation where the primary means have proved insufficient, *given the contents of customary law at any given moment*.

I have chosen to divide my inquiry into the meaning of the "supplementary means of interpretation" as follows. In Section 2, I shall begin by explaining the expression "the preparatory work of the treaty". In Section 3, I shall then explain the expression "the circumstances of its [i.e. the treaty's] conclusion". Lastly, in Sections 4–6, I shall attempt to identify what other supplementary means of interpretation are available to appliers, according to the provisions of VCLT article 32, apart from "the preparatory work of the treaty" and "the circumstances of [the treaty's] conclusion".

2 "THE PREPARATORY WORK OF THE TREATY"

"[T]he preparatory work of the treaty" is an expression not very easily grasped. The main reason for this is the vagueness of the term PREPARATORY WORK (Fr. TRAVAUX PRÉPARATOIRES; Sp. TRABAJOS PREPARATORIOS). The meaning of THE PREPARATORY WORK of a treaty is easy to *exemplify* . Typical examples include the correspondence (letters, notes, memoranda) between two or more negotiating states during the drafting of a treaty; preliminary drafts or proposals for a treaty together with suggested modifications; records of the negotiations held (minutes, summary records, *comptes rendus*); records of international conferences; reports, declarations, statements, and other similar documents used at such conferences; and so forth.[10] The difficult task is to *define* in an all-inclusive manner the concept represented by that term.

Clearly, the meaning of THE PREPARATORY WORK of a treaty is ultimately a result of the particular treaty-making process followed by negotiating states. The problem is that in international law, no general rule can be found stating in more detail the procedure for making a treaty. In principle, negotiating states are free to choose the mode that they consider best suited for their particular task. As a consequence, practice varies considerably.[11] In part, practice varies depending on the number of negotiating states, and on the particular type of issue to be addressed by a treaty. For instance, a bilateral interpretation agreement may be concluded after little more than an exchange of notes,[12] while for the adoption of a multilateral treaty a much more complex procedure is required – especially so when the number of negotiating states is large, and the issue addressed is one of universal importance. Partly, practice varies depending on *when* the treaty is drafted. Today, treaties are often concluded following other treaty-making processes than those typically employed, let us say, a hundred years ago.

With these facts in mind we will more easily grasp the expression "the preparatory work of the treaty". Two conclusions can be drawn. A first conclusion is that the expression "the preparatory work of the treaty" has a referent, which is generically defined. As we know, the rules of interpretation laid down in the Vienna Convention shall be generally applicable – they shall apply regardless of the number of states that are parties to a treaty, and regardless of the subject matter covered. Therefore, if there are variations in practice with regard to the choice of treaty making processes, depending on the number of negotiating states, and on the particular type of issue addressed, I find it hard to believe that the parties to the Vienna Convention acknowledged practice only in part. The more natural conclusion is that practice was acknowledged as a whole. A second conclusion that can be drawn is that the referent of the expression "the preparatory work of the treaty" does not exist at any one defined point in time. When the Vienna Convention was adopted, the assumption was that it would remain in force for rather a long period of time. If there are variations in practice with regard to the choice of treaty making processes, depending on when the treaty is drafted, I am not willing to believe that "the preparatory work of the treaty" refers only to those treaty-making processes, which were followed when the Convention was adopted. The reasonable conclusion is that the parties to the Convention simply wished to allow negotiating states, by freely choosing the particular treaty making process, to determine themselves what the meaning of "the preparatory work" would be *for their specific treaty.*[13]

All things considered, it seems we have good reason to concur with the following frank observation:

> [P]reparatory work is of an extremely heterogeneous character.[14]

If we would venture to define what is meant by "the preparatory work of the treaty", the definition can only be expressed in the broadest of terms. Tentatively, drawing heavily on the literature, I would like to propose something along the following lines:

> By "the preparatory work of the treaty" we should understand any representation, whether textual or non-textual, produced during the drafting of a treaty.[15]

To make the picture complete, there are indeed authors who express opinions, which in one or more aspects seem to deviate from the definition stated above. Some of these opinions are such that they may be ignored straight away;[16] some are such that I would like to bring into the open and expressly refute them. These latter opinions can be summarised by the following three propositions:

(1) The meaning of "the preparatory work" of a treaty shall be limited to include only such representations that emanate directly from the negotiating states themselves.

(2) In order for a representation to be considered part of "the preparatory work" of a treaty, each and every party which was not itself a negotiating state must have had at least an opportunity to acquaint itself with the contents of the representation; that opportunity must have existed prior to the moment when the party in question expressed its consent to be bound.

(3) The meaning of "the preparatory work" of a treaty shall not be limited to include only such representations that are produced during the drafting of a treaty.

Let us scrutinise each of these propositions. We shall take them in the order they occur.

(1) The meaning of "the preparatory work" of a treaty shall be limited to include only such representations that emanate directly from the negotiating states themselves. Contemporary treaty-making processes often involve individuals or groups of individuals – referred to as *special rapporteurs*, *expert-consultants*, *committees of experts*, and so forth – that do not act in the capacity of states.[17] The task with which these persons are assigned is to provide some kind of expert opinion, possibly in the form of a first draft proposal of a treaty, or – if a draft proposal already exists – in the form of proposed modifications. According to some authors, such expert opinions – although they are undoubtedly produced during the drafting of a treaty – cannot be considered included in the extension of "the preparatory work".[18] I find this interpretation unreasonably restrictive.

To support my opinion, I would like to adduce the object and purpose of the treaty. It is the idea underlying the provisions of VCLT article 32 that by using the preparatory work of a treaty, appliers will have the possibility of coming to a conclusion concerning the legally correct meaning of the provision interpreted. When appliers wish to establish the legally correct meaning of a treaty provision, and for that purpose use the preparatory work of the treaty, they always do so on the basis of a specific communicative assumption. This assumption may be stated as follows: the parties to the treaty expressed themselves in such a way that the provision interpreted logically coheres with the preparatory work of the treaty, insofar and to the extent that, by using the preparatory work of the treaty, good reasons can be provided showing a concordance to exist, between the parties to the treaty, with regard to its norm content.[19] Considering this, "the preparatory work of the treaty" cannot be confined to only those representations, which emanate directly from the negotiating states. Of course, if a representation emanates from an individual acting in the capacity of an expert, and not of a state representative, that representation cannot unreservedly be said to establish a concordance of the treaty parties. Whether or not a representation can be said to establish a concordance depends on the circumstances of each particular case. Take for example the preparatory work of VCLT articles 31–33. Generally speaking, it seems more probable that the 1966 ILC Draft articles establish a concordance, showing what the parties to the Vienna Convention consider to be the norm content of articles 31–33, than the report of that same year submitted by the ILC's special rapporteur, Sir Humphrey Waldock – while the 1966 ILC Draft Articles were referred to the Vienna Diplomatic Conference as "the basic proposal for consideration",[20] the principal purpose of Waldock's report was to serve as a basis for the commission's own internal work. But such an assessment *in casu* must also be made by appliers when they deal with a representation emanating from the negotiating states themselves. Of the great mass of representations produced by negotiating states while drafting a treaty, not many may subsequently be said to establish a concordance showing what the parties to the treaty consider to be the treaty's norm content. All things considered, strong reasons suggest we should not accept the proposition that a representation produced during the drafting of a treaty shall not be considered part of "the preparatory work", merely because the representation is not an act of a state.

(2) In order for a representation to be considered part of "the preparatory work" of a treaty, each and every party which was not itself a negotiating state must have had at least an opportunity to acquaint itself with the content of the representation; that opportunity must have existed prior to the moment when the party in question expressed its consent to be bound. When a state expresses its consent to be bound by a multilateral treaty, normally that state has not itself participated in all phases of the treaty-making process – take for instance the case of the state, which becomes a party to a treaty by accession.[21] This typically means that there will certainly be representations dating from the drafting process, to which not all of the parties may later be said to have contributed. According to the oft-cited statement of the Permanent Court of International Justice in the *International Commission of the River Oder*, such representations cannot be seen to form part of the preparatory work of the treaty.[22] This statement of the Court has been subsequently criticised,[23] *inter alia* by the International Law Commission. In practical terms, the Commission states in its 1966 Commentary, it does not stand to reason that we should treat a representation as not forming part of the preparatory work of a treaty, just because all treaty parties were not involved in its production – especially so if we consider the many important multilateral treaties that are open to general accession.[24] In addition, it is the opinion of contemporary legal doctrine that the principle expressed by the PCIJ is not reflective of actual state practice, if it ever was.[25] Some authors, however, seem reluctant to follow this idea through to its logical consequence. They claim that if a representation produced during the drafting of a treaty is not to be considered outside the extension of "the preparatory work" of the treaty, although one of the treaty parties was not itself involved in its production, then at least this state, prior to the point in time when it expresses its consent to be bound, must have had a genuine opportunity to acquaint itself with the contents of that representation.[26] This is a position that I personally consider far too restrictive, the main reason being once again the object and purpose of the Vienna Convention.

As observed, when appliers use "the preparatory work" of a treaty to establish the correct meaning of a treaty provision, they do so on the basis of a specific communicative assumption. This assumption may be stated as follows: the parties to the treaty expressed themselves in such a way that the provision interpreted logically coheres with the preparatory work of the treaty, insofar and to the extent that, by using the preparatory work of the treaty, good reasons can be provided showing a concordance to exist, between the parties to the treaty, with regard to its norm content. "[P]arties" means those states, and all those states, which are bound by the treaty at the time of interpretation.[27] In a context like this, it cannot be considered decisive if a representation, which was produced during the drafting of a treaty, was not known to a state at the time it expressed its consent to be bound by that treaty. From a practical point of view, it is certainly not guaranteed that the representation is of use for the process of interpretation, in the sense that on the basis of the representation a conclusion can be drawn with regard to the meaning of the interpreted treaty provision; quite the opposite. If a representation was not available to a state prior to when it expressed its consent to be bound, then clearly this gives us good reason to assume that that state does not concur with the concordance that the representation might otherwise be claimed to establish. But – and this is the point – there might be other circumstance that give reason to assume the opposite. Of course, all possible circumstances with a bearing on the issue must be taken into account, if we are to determine correctly whether the representation in question can really be said to establish a concordance between all treaty parties. All things considered, I find it difficult to accept that a representation produced during the drafting of a treaty should not be considered part of its "preparatory work", for the simple reason that not every party, before it expressed its consent to be bound, had a chance to acquaint itself with the content of said representation.

(3) The meaning of "the preparatory work" of a treaty shall not be limited to include only such representations that are produced during the drafting of a treaty. In addition to the representations produced by negotiating states during the drafting of a treaty, up to the point when the treaty is established as definite, a varying quantity of representations is often produced after that point by states acting unilaterally. Typical examples include reports used by national decision-making bodies when determining whether to ratify a treaty, together with the records and documents generated by the national decision-making process. According to some authors, these representations shall also be considered included in the extension of "the preparatory work" of the ratified treaty, in the sense of VCLT article 32.[28] Several reasons controvert this idea, one being the doctrine at large.[29] What is more, the

idea appears to be in direct conflict with the text of the Vienna Convention, as understood in accordance with conventional language and in light of its object and purpose.

PREPARATORY WORK, TRAVAUX PRÉPARATOIRES, TRABAJOS PREPARATORIOS, according to the everyday meaning of the adjective PREPARATORY, PRÉPARATOIRE, PREPARATORIO, is work performed to make something prepared for a specific purpose. Naturally, in our case *the thing* prepared is the interpreted treaty. It is less clear what the treaty is being prepared *for*. However, if we wish to speak about the preparatory work of a treaty, and by treaty mean *any* treaty, then I can see only two possible interpretation alternatives. According to a first alternative, the treaty is prepared so that it can be established as definite. According to a second alternative, it is prepared so that the negotiating states can express their consent to be bound by the treaty. The latter alternative is in turn open for two different interpretations. Either we consider "the preparatory work" of a treaty to stand for a fully uniform concept: *for each and every party* to a treaty a representation is part of "the preparatory work" of that treaty, if the representation was produced before the point in time when the last party expressed its consent to be bound. Or, we consider "the preparatory work" of a treaty to stand for a relative concept: from the point of view of the parties to a treaty, a representation can at one and the same time be part and not be part of "the preparatory work" of that treaty, depending upon whether the representation was produced before or after the point in time when each respective party expressed its consent to be bound. According to both interpretations, the expression "the preparatory work of the treaty" is seen to have an extension, which is not necessarily constant over time. If, on two different occasions, an international court is given the task of interpreting a multilateral treaty open for general accession, and for that purpose the court uses "the preparatory work" of the treaty, then there is nothing to stop the interpretation process from leading to different results, depending upon the constitution of the preparatory work at each particular moment of interpretation. This can hardly be what the parties to the Vienna Convention wished to achieve. When the International Law Commission criticised the decision of the PCIJ in the *International Commission of the River Oder*, it was precisely with the argument that from a practical point of view, it would be rather peculiar if a representation could be used as part of "the preparatory work" of a treaty during its introductory years of existence, but was then suddenly considered unusable because one of the states that later became a party to the treaty had not itself been engaged in its drafting.[30] All things considered, I cannot arrive at any other conclusion than this: "the preparatory work" of a treaty, in the sense of VCLT article 32, means all those representations produced in the preparation for the establishing of the treaty as definite.[31]

3 "THE CIRCUMSTANCES OF [THE TREATY'S] CONCLUSION"

If earlier "the preparatory work of the treaty" has been called an expression, which is not easily grasped, then quite possibly it is even more difficult to fully grasp "the circumstances of [the treaty's] conclusion". Several things tend to puzzle appliers. First of all, there is the ambiguity inherent in the grammatical construction THE CIRCUMSTANCES OF (Fr. LES CIRCONSTANCES DANS LESQUELLES; Sp. LA CIRCUNSTANCIAS DE). "[T]he circumstances of [the treaty's] conclusion", according to the ordinary meaning of the construction THE CIRCUMSTANCES OF, we shall understand to be *the general conditions under which a treaty was concluded; the states-of-affairs by which the conclusion of a treaty was affected or influenced.* Apparently, in order for a state-of-affairs to be considered part of "the circumstances of [the treaty's] conclusion", that state-of-affairs must be related to the treaty's conclusion in some way or another. However, the nature of this relationship remains to be established. From a purely linguistic point of view, I can think of three alternatives:

(1) It must be the case, that the existence of the state-of-affairs can be dated to a point in time, which at least partially coincides with the existence of the treaty's conclusion.
(2) It must be the case, (i) that the existence of the state-of-affairs can be dated to a point in time, which at least partially coincides with the existence of the treaty's conclusion, and (ii) that the existence of the state-of-affairs at least partly caused the treaty's conclusion.
(3) It must be the case, that the existence of the state-of-affairs at least partly caused the treaty's conclusion.

The first interpretation alternative conflicts with common sense. When appliers use "the circumstances of [the treaty's] conclusion", it is because they wish to establish the legally correct meaning of a treaty provision. But of all those states-of-affairs that exist at the time of a treaty's conclusion, not more than a tiny fraction can ever provide guidance as to what that meaning is. Therefore, categorising a state-of-affairs as part of "the circumstances of [the treaty's] conclusion", merely because that state-of-affairs and the treaty's conclusion wholly or partially co-existed, must be considered an unreasonably broad interpretation. The second interpretation alternative disagrees with the view generally held in the literature. Several authors refer to "the circumstances of [the treaty's] conclusion", both as "the circumstances of the parties at the time the treaty was entered into", "*les circonstances des parties au moment de la conclusion du traité*" – which comprises, among other things, the cause for a treaty –,[32] and as "the historical background of the treaty", "*les origines historiques du traité*".[33]

Seen from the perspective of interpretation alternative (2), this language is clearly incorrect. THE HISTORICAL BACKGROUND OF THE TREATY, LES ORIGINES HISTORIQUES DU TRAITÉ is a term, which does not primarily denote a state-of-affairs whose existence coincides with the conclusion of the interpreted treaty, but one whose existence precedes this conclusion. All things considered, the only plausible interpretation alternative seems to be the one termed as alternative (3). In other words, in order for a state-of-affairs to be considered part of "the circumstances of [the treaty's] conclusion", the only requirement would be that the existence of the state-of-affairs at least partly was the cause for the conclusion.[34]

Another difficulty appliers are bound to encounter when using "the circumstances of [the treaty's] conclusion" is the expression "conclusion" (Fr. *"conclu"*; Sp. *"celebración")*. In the language of international law, THE CONCLUSION OF THE TREATY (Fr. LA CONCLUSION DU TRAITÉ; Sp. LA CELEBRACIÓN DEL TRATADO) is an ambiguous term;[35] and it makes no difference if we limit ourselves to the terminology of the Vienna Convention.[36] In one sense of the term, THE CONCLUSION OF A TREATY can be usedto refer to the point in time when the treaty is established as definite.[37] In another sense it can be used as synonymous with the time interval from when negotiations on a treaty are begun to when the treaty finally enters into force.[38] Further complexity is added by the fact that THE ENTRY INTO FORCE OF A TREATY is in turn a term for which the usage is not consistent. THE ENTRY INTO FORCE OF A TREATY can in some instances be used to stand for *the entry into force of the treaty as such*; in some, it can be used to stand for *the entry into force of the treaty for a state*.[39] All in all, this gives us the following interpretation alternatives:

(1) The "conclusion" of a treaty means the point in time when the treaty was established as definite.
(2) The "conclusion" of a treaty means the time interval from when negotiations on a treaty began to when the treaty finally entered into force for the very first time.
(3) The "conclusion" of a treaty means the time interval from when negotiations on a treaty began to when the treaty finally entered into force for the treaty parties.

Interpretation alternative (3) seems to run counter to the object and purpose of the Vienna Convention. According to this interpretation, the circumstances of a treaty's conclusion is a relative concept – from the point of view of the parties, a state-of-affairs can at one and the same time be part of and not be part of "the circumstances ", depending upon whether that state-of-affairs for each individual party was a cause for the conclusion of the treaty or not. This can hardly be what the parties to the VCLT intended.

Interpretation alternative (2) is a poor match with the context. In VCLT article 32, two examples are provided of what shall be considered included in the "supplementary means of interpretation", namely "the preparatory work of the treaty" and "the circumstances of its conclusion". By "the preparatory work of the treaty" – this was one of the observations made in the Section 2 of this chapter – we understand a set of representations produced before the point in time when the treaty was established as definite.[40] Considering the close pragmatic relationship that holds between "the preparatory work of the treaty" and "the circumstances of its conclusion", it stands to reason that this point in time should also be decisive for the meaning of "the circumstances".[41] Furthermore, this is the interpretation that best agrees with the literature. Authors speak at times of "the circumstances of [a treaty's] conclusion", and at other times of "the historical background against which the treaty has been negotiated",[42] "the political situation prevailing at the time the treaty was negotiated",[43] *"[les] circonstances dans lesquelles l'accord a été negocié",*[44] *"[les] circonstances dans lesquelles ont eu lieu les négociations diplomatiques ayant précédé la conclusion du traité",*[45] without any noticeable semantic distinction. Let me also cite Ambassador Yasseen, who – as we noted earlier – had an uncommonly active role in the formation of the Vienna Convention, first as member of the International Law Commission, and then as chairman of the Vienna Conference's Drafting Committee:

> Il est logique que les circonstances dans lesquelles le traité a été conclu influencent la rédaction du traité.[46]

All things considered, I fail to see how any other interpretation alternative could be considered well-founded than the one termed as alternative (1).

A third problem encountered is the relationship held between "the circumstances of [the treaty's] conclusion" and the system of rules laid down in VCLT articles 31 and 32 considered as a whole. Clearly, *the circumstances of the treaty's conclusion* has an extension, which in some cases borders on the extension of other means of interpretation. Many of the phenomena that are merely close to being defined as the context or the object and purpose of the treaty, and thus cannot be taken into account by appliers using these means of interpretation, can instead be considered at the stage when appliers use "the circumstances of [the treaty's] conclusion". Examples of such phenomena include the cause for the treaty;[47] agreements relating to the treaty, made in connection with the treaty's conclusion, but which are not governed by international law, or which were not made between all treaty parties;[48] and international agreements entered into either before or in connection with the conclusion of the treaty, but which are not governed by international law, or which are not applicable in the relationship between all treaty parties.[49] The problem is that when "the circumstances of [the treaty's] conclusion" are used for the interpretation of a treaty, together with other means of interpretation, the different means will not only border on each other, but – considering the criteria hitherto established, and these criteria only – will also partially overlap. Much of what we consider to be part of "the context" or "the preparatory work of the treaty" will also be considered part of "the circumstances of [the treaty's] conclusion".[50] If the contents of VCLT articles 31–32 are to be described as a coherent system of rules, then obviously the extension of "the circumstances of [the treaty's] conclusion" must be further delimited. Such a delimitation could be made using the following terms:

> By "the circumstances of [the treaty's] conclusion" we mean any state-of-affairs, whose existence at least partly caused the conclusion of the treaty, unless this state-of-affairs can be considered comprised by "the context" or "the preparatory work" of the treaty.

4 OTHER SUPPLEMENTARY MEANS OF INTERPRETATION: RATIFICATION WORK

In my judgment, three means of interpretation can be used by appliers according to the provisions of VCLT article 32, apart from "the preparatory work of the treaty" and "the circumstances of its conclusion". The first of these means are the representations unilaterally produced by a state when it decides whether to ratify a treaty or not –[51] what we will be terming here as RATIFICATION WORK. Several authors consider ratification work to be an accepted means of interpretation.[52] Clearly, however, ratification work cannot be considered part of any means of interpretation *expressly* recognised as accepted by the Vienna Convention. It does not fit the description set forth in article 31 § 3(b), and hence cannot be considered part of a "subsequent practice", as asserted by professor Haraszti.[53] In order for an act of a state to be considered part of a "subsequent practice", it must be performed "in the application of the treaty".[54] Nor can ratification work be considered part of the preparatory work of a treaty, in the sense of VCLT article 32, as some authors imply.[55] For a representation to be included in the extension of the expression "the preparatory work" of a treaty, it must have been produced during the drafting of said treaty – that is, not after the point in time when the treaty was established as definite.[56] Nevertheless, it is a fact that ratification work often contains information, based on which the applier more fully than otherwise will be able to form an opinion on how the ratified treaty was perceived when adopted. It appears less likely that this information should not be considered at all in the interpretation process. The question arises: Could ratification work – still under the provisions of VCLT article 32 – possibly be used as a means of interpretation in and of itself? In my judgment, the answer to this question should be in the affirmative. Support for this opinion can be drawn from the practice of international courts and tribunals.[57] To illustrate, I will provide three examples.

My first example is the judgment of the International Court in the *Case Concerning Oil Platforms (Preliminary Objections)*.[58] In October 1987, as well as in April 1988, the USA had attacked and destroyed three oil platforms situated on the Iranian continental shelf of the Persian Gulf, and belonging to a state-owned Iranian oil company. By taking these actions, the Iranian government claimed, the USA had violated the obligations incumbent upon her under international law. Consequently, Iran filed an application with the International Court of Justice requesting a decision to this effect. The question arose as to whether the Court was empowered to hear the case. As a basis for the jurisdiction of the Court, Iran had invoked article XX1, paragraph 2 of the 1955 *Treaty of Amity, Economic Relations and Consular Rights*:

> Any dispute between the High Contracting Parties as to the interpretation or application of the present Treaty, not satisfactorily adjusted by diplomacy, shall be submitted to the International Court of Justice, unless the High Contracting Parties agree to settlement by some other pacific means.[59]

According to what was alleged, several articles of the 1955 Treaty had been breached by the USA. The US government, for its part, refused to concede that even a single violation of the treaty had taken place.

Among the many provisions that had been violated, according to the allegations of Iran, one was the following, laid down in article I:

> There shall be firm and enduring peace and sincere friendship between the United States ... and Iran.[60]

Article I, maintained the Iranian government, does not merely express a recommendation or desire of the parties; it imposes actual legal obligations, committing the parties to sustaining peaceful and friendly relations. Thus, under the provisions of article I, the parties would have to comply with the minimum requirement of conducting themselves in accordance with the rules of international custom established in the field of peaceful and friendly relations. "This interpretation", the Court summarised, "is said to be required by the context, and to be reinforced by the circumstances in which the Treaty was concluded".[61] In the view of the defendant, the Iranian government read far too much into article I. Article I, the USA contended, did not impose a standard in any legal sense of the word; all it contained was a statement of aspiration.

That interpretation is called for in the context and on account of the "purely commercial and consular" character of the Treaty. It is said to correspond to the common intention of the Parties, and to be confirmed by the circumstances in which the Treaty was concluded and by the practice of the Parties.[62]

The latter interpretation is the one with which the Court concurred:

Article I ... cannot, taken in isolation, be a basis for the jurisdiction of the Court.[63]

Let us reflect upon the reasons provided by the Court to justify its position. The Court starts out by referring to the object and purpose of the 1955 Treaty:

[T]he object and purpose of the Treaty of 1955 was not to regulate peaceful and friendly relations between the two States in a general sense. Consequently, Article I cannot be interpreted as incorporating into the Treaty all of the provisions of international law concerning such relations.[64]

After this, it proceeds by turning its attention to the documents produced by the parties themselves in an attempt to strengthen their respective positions:

[I]t may be thought that, if that Article [Article I that is] had the scope that Iran gives it, the Parties would have been led to point out its importance during the negotiations or the process of ratification. However, the Court does not have before it any Iranian document in support of this argument. As for the United States documents introduced by the two Parties, they show that at no time did the United States regard Article I as having the meaning now given to it by the Applicant.

A clause of this type was inserted after the end of the Second World War into four of the Treaties of Friendship and Commerce or Economic Relations concluded by the United States, i.e., those concluded with China, Ethiopia and Iran as well as with Oman and Muscat. Indeed, during the negotiation of the Treaty with China, the United States Department of State had indicated, in a memorandum addressed to its embassy in Chongqing, that if such a clause was not customary in treaties of this kind concluded by the United States, its inclusion was nonetheless justified in that case "in view of the close political relations between China and the United States". But, during the discussions in the United States Senate that preceded the ratification of the four Treaties, the clause does not, according to the material submitted to the Court, appear to have been given any particular attention. Only in the message from the Secretary of State whereby he transmitted the Treaty with Ethiopia to the Senate, after referring to the provisions in question, was it pointed out that:

"Such provisions, though not included in recent treaties of friendship, commerce and navigation, are in keeping with the character of such instruments and serve to emphasize the essentially friendly character of the treaty."[65]

Finally, the Court concludes by referring to subsequent practice:

The practice followed by the Parties in regard to the application of the Treaty does not lead to any different conclusions. The United States has never relied upon that Article in proceedings involving Iran and, more particularly, did not invoke that text in the case concerning *United States Diplomatic and Consular Staff in Teheran*. Neither did Iran rely on that Article, for example in the proceedings before this Court in the case concerning the *Aerial Incident of 3 July 1988*.[66]

To my mind, this is a clear example of ratification work being used as a means of interpretation. We shall note that two sets of ratification work are used, for two separate interpretation processes. In a first instance, the documents used are those emanating from the ratification of the American-Iranian treaty of 1955; the treaty interpreted is the one between the USA and Iran. In a second instance, the documents used are those emanating from the ratification of a treaty between the USA and Ethiopia; the treaty interpreted is the one between the USA and Ethiopia, which is then in turn used for the interpretation of the 1955 Treaty between the USA and Iran. Of course, nowhere in the reasoning of the Court is it expressly stated, that ratification work is used as an independent means of interpretation; however, this is the clear implication. The means used is not subsequent practice – this is made clear by the context. Nor is it the preparatory work of the 1955 Treaty – the Court expressly distinguishes between what has occurred "during the negotiations" and what has taken place "during ... the process of ratification".[67] This squares well with what we have stated earlier with regard to the contents of VCLT article 32: none of the means of interpretation expressly recognised as acceptable in article 32 pertain to the time subsequent to the establishing of the treaty as definite.[68] For the very same reason, it can hardly be a purport of the Court that the documents in question shall be considered part of the circumstances of the interpreted treaty's conclusion. It seems that the parties thought they should be considered as such. As a confirmation of their respective interpretations, both parties expressly cite "the circumstances in which the Treaty was concluded".[69] We should note, however, that this is not a terminology used by the Court itself. The conclusion to be drawn is the following: in the view of the Court, ratification work can be considered a means of interpretation in and of itself.

My second example is the judgment of the ICJ in the *ELSI* case – one of the few cases so far decided in Chamber – and the dissenting opinion of Judge Schwebel.[70] In 1987, the United States Government had filed an application with the ICJ requesting it to declare that the USA had an outstanding claim to compensation against Italy. The claim allegedly arose out of Italy's treatment of two American corporations in relation to their ownership of an Italian-registered limited company, *Elettronica Sicula SpA ("ELSI")*. As a basis for her claim, the USA had invoked the 1948 Italian-American *Treaty of Friendship, Commerce and Navigation*, including a *Supplementary Agreement* of 1951. The American effort was fruitless. The Court found that no breach of the Italian-American agreement had occurred. Thus, the American claim to compensation had to be rejected.

Two judges have chosen to append individual opinions to the decision of the Court, one of them being Judge Oda.[71] In his *separate opinion*, Oda presents a series of propositions that differ from those of the Court in several important aspects. One such proposition is that the Italian-American agreement did not protect the interests of American stockholders in a company conducting business in Italy, when the company had been incorporated according to Italian law.[72] The other judge who chose to deliver an individual opinion is Judge Schwebel. In an elaborate dissenting opinion, Schwebel argues a position completely contrary to that supported by Judge Oda. Schwebel's first move is to attempt to categorise his position as one justified by article 32 of the Vienna Convention:

> In the current case, the Parties attached radically different interpretations to the provisions of the Treaty and its Supplementary Agreement which were at issue between them. It is undeniable that, when their conflicting arguments are matched together, the meaning of some of the Treaty's provisions are ambiguous or obscure; indeed, each of the Parties maintained that the opposing interpretation led to results which, if not manifestly absurd, were unreasonable. Thus, according to the Vienna Convention, this is a case in which recourse to the preparatory work and circumstances of the Treaty's conclusion was eminently in order.
>
> What were the circumstances of the conclusion of the Supplementary Agreement which forms an integral part of the Treaty itself? And what does the Treaty's preparatory work and processes of ratification demonstrate its purpose, or a paramount purpose of the Treaty, to be and what light do these processes shed on the interpretation to be attached to its provisions?[73]

He then cites excerpts from both Italian and American ratification work: "the debate in the [Italian] Chamber of Deputies on ratification of the Supplementary Agreement";[74] "[t]he Report to the Senate of Italy";[75] "[t]he Report of the Secretary of State of the United States which was transmitted to the United States Senate in connection with its advice and consent to ratification of the Supplementary Agreement";[76] "the Report of the Committee on Foreign Affairs and Colonies of the Senate of Italy of 28 May 1949".[77] By the way Judge Schwebel expresses himself, it is evident that in his view, the documents in question can be used according to the provisions of VCLT article 32, as a means of interpretation in and of itself.

My third example is the international award in the *Beagle Channel Arbitration* case.[78] The facts of this case have been stated in this work,[79] and I will not indulge in unnecessary repetition. As we know, Argentina and Chile had expressed different opinions about the meaning to be given to articles II and III of the 1881 *Tratado de Límites*. To support their respective positions, both parties had cited occurrences taking place between the signing of the 1881 treaty and its ratification. Argentina had invoked a speech made by the Argentinean chief negotiator in the National Chamber of Deputies. Chile had invoked a speech made by the Chilean chief negotiator to his Chamber of Deputies. Both speeches were made partly to present and explain the treaty concluded, and partly to defend certain aspects of the treaty. It is to be noted how these different events are described by the court. The court starts by categorising the speeches as "[c]onfirmatory or corroborative incidents and material";[80] in other words, as supplementary means of interpretation. Furthermore, they have been termed as belonging to "[t]he immediate post-Treaty period".[81] By using this language, it is evident that the court distinguishes between the speeches on the one hand, and on the other hand the occurrences taking place during "the period of the negotiations" – the preparatory work of the treaty is addressed using other terms.[82] For the very same reason, it is equally obvious that, according to the court, the speeches made in the Argentinean and Chilean Chambers of Deputies cannot be considered part of the "subsequent conduct".[83]

This picture must be considered reinforced by the individual opinion delivered by Judge Gros.[84] Gros presents arguments that in some aspects differ from those of the court. His first move is to examine the preparatory work and the circumstances of the interpreted treaty's conclusion:

> The present territorial dispute between the two Parties must be viewed from within the complex of its development at the time – from 1810–1881 – and in particular from that of the very special relations existing between two States that every factor tends to bring together by reason of their common origins, ethical, political and social outlook and habits of thought in the widest sense. What is in question is not an issue of sovereignty *in abstracto* but – after seventy years of effort – of defining a frontier between Argentina and Chile extending over 5,000 kms. On the specific matter of the disputed islands, information concerning the negotiations of 1881 is still inadequate, but those of 1876 are well documented; and in that context there exists a firm proposal, put forward by the Government of the Argentine Republic, described as non-negotiable, and understood as such by the Chilean negotiator (Barros Arana Telegram of 5 July 1876 and Despatch of 10 July 1876, Chilean Annexes 21 and 22). This is of great importance, since Basis 3 of 1876 was carried over to become the text of Article III of 1881. The responsibility for this text, in 1876, was the Argentine Government's; and it is this same text, as also the accompanying circumstances, explanatory incidents of the negotiations, and the way in which the latter developed, together with the official commentaries which were to follow in 1876 and 1881, that constitute the sources for the interpretation of the clause that attributes the disputed islands.[85]

As further confirmation, he then brings into the picture the speeches made in the Argentinean and Chilean Chambers of Deputies:

> It is by taking into account all the aspects of those negotiations in 1876–1881, and the special social context of the international relations between the two States, that the intention of the Parties may be rediscovered in the text of Article III – an intention confirmed by the declarations of the political personalities responsible in the matter of the frontier. It is this whole complex comprising the text, its historical origins, the general political circumstances of the negotiation, and the explanation given by the negotiators and statesmen, which decided me to vote for the Decision of the Court.[86]

All things considered, it seems that, in the opinion of the court, ratification work can be used according to the provisions of VCLT article 32, as a means of interpretation in and of itself.

5 OTHER SUPPLEMENTARY MEANS OF INTERPRETATION: TREATIES *IN PARI MATERIA*

A second means of interpretation that can be used by an applier according to the provisions of VCLT article 32, apart from "the preparatory work of the treaty" and "the circumstances of its conclusion", is treaties *in pari materia.*[87] By a TREATY IN PARI MATERIA we are to understand an instrument, the subject matter of which is identical – at least partly – with the subject matter covered by the treaty interpreted. Of course, such an instrument may sometimes be considered a part of "the context". According to VCLT article 31 § 3(c), when appliers use the context, they shall take into consideration "relevant rules of international law applicable in the relations between the parties". Other times the instrument may be considered a part of "the circumstances of [the interpreted treaty's] conclusion". This is the case, for example, when the interpreted treaty was drafted or designed based on another treaty already in existence.[88] However, many cases remain where an instrument can be categorised as a treaty *in pari materia*, but where it *cannot* be used as already included in one of the means expressly recognised as acceptable by the Vienna Convention. The question is whether in these cases, treaties *in pari materia* may be considered a means of interpretation in and of itself. In my judgment, the answer to this question should be in the affirmative. As support for this opinion, I would like to cite the practice of international courts and tribunals.[89] I will do so with the following three examples.

My first example is once again the judgment of the International Court of Justice in the *Case Concerning Oil Platforms (Preliminary Objections).*[90] Since the facts of the case have already been reviewed in an earlier section of this chapter,[91] I will not engage in unnecessary repetition. As we know, the USA and Iran were in dispute as to the meaning the 1955 American-Iranian *Treaty of Amity, Economic Relations and Consular Rights*, article I:

> There shall be firm and enduring peace and sincere friendship between the United States ... and Iran.[92]

According to Iran, article I imposes actual legal obligations, committing the parties to sustaining peaceful and friendly relations. According to the USA, the article was to be regarded merely as a statement of aspiration. This latter, American interpretation was the one later confirmed by the Court.

In the findings of the Court, the principal ground presented for its understanding of the 1955 Treaty is its object and purpose. However, as additional confirmation, the Court has also invoked the three "Treaties of Friendship and Commerce or Economic Relations", which – on the same occasion as the 1955 Treaty between the USA and Iran – were concluded between the USA and China, Ethiopia, and Oman and Muscat, respectively:

A clause of this type was inserted after the end of the Second World War into four of the Treaties of Friendship and Commerce or Economic Relations concluded by the United States, i.e., those concluded with China, Ethiopia and Iran as well as with Oman and Muscat. Indeed, during the negotiation of the Treaty with China, the United States Department of State had indicated, in a memorandum addressed to its embassy in Chongqing, that if such a clause was not customary in treaties of this kind concluded by the United States, its inclusion was nonetheless justified in that case "in view of the close political relations between China and the United States". But, during the discussions in the United States Senate that preceded the ratification of the four Treaties, the clause does not, according to the material submitted to the Court, appear to have been given any particular attention. Only in the message from the Secretary of State whereby he transmitted the Treaty with Ethiopia to the Senate, after referring to the provisions in question, was it pointed out that:

"Such provisions, though not included in recent treaties of friendship, commerce and navigation, are in keeping with the character of such instruments and serve to emphasize the essentially friendly character of the treaty."[93]

For the purpose of an interpretation of the 1955 *Treaty of Amity, Economic Relations and Consular Rights* between the USA and Iran, these three agreements can without a doubt be considered treaties *in pari materia*. No explanation is given by the Court to indicate that the invoked treaties between the USA and China, Ethiopia, and Oman and Muscat, respectively, are considered part of the preparatory work of the 1955 Treaty or the circumstances of its conclusion. It is apparent that, in the view of the Court, treaties *in pari materia* can be used as a means of interpretation in and of itself.

My second example is the judgment of the ICJ in the *Case Concerning the Arbitral Award of 31 July 1989*.[94] In 1985, Senegal and Guinea-Bissau had concluded a special agreement to resolve certain disagreements concerning the delimitation of their respective maritime boundaries. The origin of the dispute was a boundary agreement concluded in 1960 between Senegal as an autonomous state within the French *Communauté*, and the then-Portuguese province of Guinea.[95] The task of the tribunal was to deliver a decision on the following issues:

Article 2

The Tribunal is requested to decide in accordance with the norms of international law on the following questions:

1. Does the Agreement concluded by an exchange of letters on 26 April 1960, and which relates to the maritime boundary, have the force of law in the relations between the Republic of Guinea-Bissau and the Republic of Senegal?
2. In the event of a negative answer to the first question, what is the course of the line delimiting the maritime territories appertaining to the Republic of Guinea-Bissau and the Republic of Senegal respectively?[96]

The award was pronounced on 31 July 1989.[97] The arbitration tribunal found that the 1960 agreement had indeed the force of law, and that it could be invoked in the relations between Senegal and Guinea-Bissau. Having answered question 1 in the affirmative, the tribunal did not consider it necessary to proceed to answering also question 2. In August 1989, Guinea-Bissau had filed an application with the International Court of Justice, requesting the Court to give its opinion on the validity of the 1989 award. According to the argument of Guinea-Bissau, the award was to be considered null and void, since the tribunal had exceeded its powers by (among other things) not providing sufficient justification for answering only question 1 and not question 2.

The Court begins by defining its task:

It [i.e. the Court] has simply to ascertain whether by rendering the disputed Award the Tribunal acted in manifest breach of the competence conferred on it by the Arbitration Agreement, either by deciding in excess of, or by failing to exercise, its jurisdiction.

48. Such manifest breach might result from, for example, the failure of the Tribunal properly to apply the relevant rules of interpretation to the provisions of the Arbitration Agreement which govern its competence.[98]

The Court declares it will take "the relevant rules of interpretation" to be those reflected in articles 31 and 32 of the Vienna Convention.[99] Then it takes a first step in the interpretation process by reminding us of the ordinary meaning:

In the present case, Article 2 of the Arbitration Agreement presented a first question concerning the 1960 Agreement, and then a second question relating to delimitation. A reply had to be given to the second question "in the event of a negative answer to the first question". The Court notes that those last words, which were originally proposed by Guinea-Bissau itself, are categorical.[100]

Obviously, it is the opinion of the Court that in order to clarify the provision at issue, nothing more is needed than conventional language. Nevertheless, the Court seems anxious to confirm its position. For this very purpose it invokes a special agreement concluded between Guinea and Guinea-Bissau in 1983:

In fact in the present case the Parties could have used some such expression as that the Tribunal should answer the second question "taking into account" the reply given to the first, but they did not; they directed that the second question should be answered only "in the event of a negative answer" to that first question. In that respect, the wording was very different from that to be found in another Arbitration Agreement to which Guinea-Bissau is a party, that concluded on 18 February 1983 with the Republic of Guinea. By that Agreement, those two States asked another tribunal to decide on the legal value and scope of another Franco-Portuguese delimitation convention and annexed documents, and then "according to the answers given" to those initial questions, to determine the "course of the boundary between the maritime territories" of the two countries.[101]

For the interpretation of the 1985 special agreement between Senegal and Guinea-Bissau, this second agreement can without doubt be considered a treaty *in pari materia*. No explanation is given to indicate that the 1983 special agreement is considered part of either the preparatory work of that treaty, or of the circumstances of its conclusion. It appears that in the view of the Court, treaties *in pari materia* may be used as a means of interpretation in and of itself.

My third example is the judgment of the European Court of Human Rights in the *Müller and Others* case.[102] In 1981, Josef Felix Müller, a young Swiss artist, had been invited to show some of his pictures in an exhibition of modern art in Fribourg. His works depicted a number of explicit sexual acts, both heterosexual and homosexual in nature. The pictures offended the authorities. Müller's works were seized, and together with the exhibition organisers Müller was sentenced for breaking Swiss laws banning obscene publications. The question arose whether Switzerland, by taking these measures, had acted in violation of its obligations under article 10 of the *European Convention for the Protection of Human Rights and Fundamental Freedoms*. This gave the European Court occasion to make the following general comment on the contents of this article:

Admittedly, Article 10 does not specify that freedom of artistic expression, in issue here, comes within its ambit; but neither, on the other hand, does it distinguish between the various forms of expression. As those appearing before the Court all acknowledged, it includes freedom of artistic expression – notably within freedom to receive and impart information and ideas – which affords the opportunity to take part in the public exchange of cultural, political and social information and ideas of all kinds. Confirmation, if any were needed, that this interpretation is correct, is provided by the second [sic!] sentence of paragraph 1 of Article 10, which refers to "broadcasting, television or cinema enterprises", media whose activities extend to the field of art. Confirmation that the concept of freedom of expression is such as to include artistic expression is also to be found in Article 19 § 2 of the International Covenant on Civil and Political Rights, which specifically includes within the right of freedom of expression information and ideas "in the form of art".[103]

Clearly, when the European Court interprets the European Convention for the Protection of Human Rights, the *International Covenant on Civil and Political Rights* can be considered a treaty *in pari materia*. There can be no doubt that the European Court uses the International Covenant to confirm an interpretation already performed according to the provisions of

VCLT article 31. For the interpretation of the European Convention, the International Covenant cannot be considered a relevant rule of international law, in the sense of VCLT article 31 § 3(c). The states that are parties to the International Covenant are not identical to those that are parties to the European Convention. It is apparent that, in the view of the European Court, treaties *in pari materia* may be used as a means of interpretation in and of itself.

6 OTHER SUPPLEMENTARY MEANS OF INTERPRETATION: THE CONTEXT

A third means of interpretation that can be used by appliers according to the provisions of VCLT article 32, apart from "the preparatory work of the treaty" and "the circumstances of its conclusion", is the context. The point is that some uses of the context are not allowed under the provisions of article 31, but it would still make sense to exploit them under the provisions of article 32. When appliers use the supplementary means of interpretation according to VCLT article 32, the task to be performed is partly different from the task for which they use the context or the object and purpose of the treaty according to the provisions of article 31. When appliers use the context or the object and purpose of a treaty, according to the provisions of article 31, they have already used conventional language, but they have discovered that it leads to conflicting results.[104] Supplementary means of interpretation, on the other hand, can be used for three different purposes: (1) appliers wish to confirm a meaning obtained through the application of article 31; (2) appliers wish to determine the meaning of a treaty provision, because interpreting the treaty according to article 31 leaves the meaning ambiguous or obscure; (3) appliers wish to determine the meaning of a treaty provision, because interpreting the treaty according to article 31 leads to a result which is manifestly absurd or unreasonable.[105]

Considering these different tasks, it is obviously the case that appliers, by using the context or the object and purpose according to the provisions of article 32, would in many cases obtain a result more far-reaching than that which they are capable of obtaining when they use these same means according to the provisions of article 31. When the context or the object and purpose are used by appliers according to the provisions of article 31, the ensuing interpretation result must be partially or completely reconciled with the interpreted treaty provision when read in accordance with conventional language. This is a limitation appliers do not have to observe when they use supplementary means of interpretation, according to the provisions of article 32. When appliers use supplementary means of interpretation, the purpose being the one earlier referred to as (3), the ensuing interpretation result may well go beyond the limits set by the ordinary meaning.

From a practical point of view, I see no reason why the context and the object and purpose could not be used as supplementary means of interpretation. The question is whether such usage may be considered correct as a matter of principle. When it comes to using the object and purpose, the answer must be considered a given. Evidently, VCLT article 32 indirectly approves of a certain use of the object and purpose by allowing for an application of the rule of necessary implication.[106] Considering the very limited conditions under which the rule of necessary implication applies, it does not seem likely that the object and purpose – parallel to this – could also be used as a "full" supplementary means of interpretation, in the same way as the preparatory work of the treaty and the circumstances of its conclusion. When it comes to using the context, however, the issue is somewhat more complicated. Prima facie there are reasons for using the context as a supplementary means of interpretation according to the provisions of article 32, but there are also prima facie reasons for *not* using the context as such a means of interpretation. All things considered, however, I would like to argue that only the former conclusion can be considered well-founded. In my opinion, there are *conclusive* reasons for using the context as a supplementary means of interpretation, but there are not conclusive reasons for the opposite. To support this position, I would like to cite the rules of interpretation laid down in international law.

According to international law, two first order rules of interpretation are *prima facie* applicable, when an applier sets out to determine whether or not the context shall be considered a "supplementary means of interpretation". Let us call them by the numbers 1 and 18. Interpretation rule no. 1 provides:

> If it can be shown that in a treaty provision, there is an expression whose form corresponds to an expression of conventional language, then the provision shall be understood in accordance with the rules of that language.[107]

Interpretation rule no. 34 may be stated as follows:

> If it can be shown that a treaty provision permits an act or a state-of-affairs, which – from the point of view of the parties – can be considered less tolerable than another generically identical act or state-of-affairs, then the provision shall be understood to permit this second act or state-of-affairs, too.[108]

Unfortunately, the application of interpretation rules nos. 1 and 34 leads to conflicting results.

Applying interpretation rule no. 34, we come to the result that the context *shall* be considered a "supplementary means of interpretation". According to interpretation rule no. 34, the context shall be considered a "supplementary means of interpretation", if good reasons can be provided showing that, as part of the extension of this expression, another means is included, the usage of which can be considered less tolerable to the parties to the Vienna Convention than a usage of the context. In the Vienna Convention, the legally acceptable means of interpretation have been arranged in the form of two separate articles. Article 31 lists the means of interpretation, which appliers primarily shall use for the interpretation of a treaty – they have earlier been termed as PRIMARY MEANS OF INTERPRETATION. Article 32 lists the means of interpretation, which appliers shall use in case the primary means of interpretation prove insufficient for determining the legally correct meaning of an interpreted treaty provision. Of course, the basic idea underlying this arrangement is that, typically, the means of interpretation listed in article 31 are better indicators of the legally correct meaning of a treaty provision than the means listed in article 32.[109] One of the means listed in article 31 is the context; one of the means listed in article 32 is the preparatory work of the treaty. Seen in this light, when appliers use the preparatory work of a treaty for the interpretation of a treaty, arguably, this act of interpretation can be considered less tolerable to the parties to the Vienna Convention than an act of interpretation using the context. Given the contents of interpretation rule no. 34, the context shall then be considered a "supplementary means of interpretation".

Applying interpretation rule no. 1, we come to the result that the context *shall not* be considered a "supplementary means of interpretation". According to interpretation rule no. 1, the context shall not be considered a "supplementary means of interpretation" if it can be shown that, when applying the rules of conventional language, the context cannot be denoted as a SUPPLEMENTARY MEANS OF INTERPRETATION. In conventional language, for a given phenomenon to be denoted as SUPPLEMENTARY, there must be a second phenomenon, to which the first may be considered a supplement. It is the implicit meaning conveyed by the expression "supplementary means of interpretation" that the means listed in article 32 are a supplement to those listed in article 31. In other words, the expression "supplementary means of interpretation" (deictically) refers back to the primary means of interpretation. It follows that the means of interpretation listed in article 32 have an identity completely different from those listed by article 31: no single element can be used as a supplementary means of interpretation according to the provisions of article 32, if, according to the provisions of article 31, it can already be used as a primary means of interpretation. The context can be used as a primary means of interpretation according to the provisions of article 31. Given interpretation rule no. 1, then, the context shall not be considered a "supplementary means of interpretation".

Thus, interpretation rules nos. 1 and 34 are in clear conflict. This conflict can be resolved according to a rule of international law – this much is clear. Complexity is added by the fact that under the regime established by the Vienna Convention, the conflict between interpretation rules nos. 1 and 34 is governed by two second-order rules of interpretation. Let us call them by the numbers 40 and 41. Interpretation rule no. 40 states:

> If it can be shown that the interpretation of a treaty provision in accordance with any one of interpretation rules nos. 1–16 leads to a result, which is different from that obtained by interpreting the provision in accordance with any one of interpretation rules no. 17–39, and that the application of the former rule either leaves the meaning of the interpreted treaty provision ambiguous or obscure, or amounts to a result which is manifestly absurd or unreasonable, then the provision shall not be understood in accordance with this former rule.[110]

Interpretation rule no. 41 provides as follows:

> If it can be shown that the interpretation of a treaty provision in accordance with any one of interpretation rules nos. 1–16 leads to a result, which is different from that obtained by interpreting the provision in accordance with any one of interpretation rules nos. 17–39, then, rather than with the latter of the two rules, the provision shall be understood in accordance with the former, except for those cases where interpretation rule no. 40 applies.[111]

In my judgment, in the situation where an applier sets out to determine whether the context shall be considered a "supplementary means of interpretation", the rule that determines the relationship between interpretation rules nos. 1 and 34 is the latter: if it can be shown that the interpretation of the expression "supplementary means of interpretation" in accordance with interpretation rule no. 1 leads to a result, which is different from that obtained by interpreting the expression in accordance with interpretation rule no. 34, then the expression shall not be understood in accordance with interpretation rule no. 1. It would then be my task to establish that the application of interpretation rule no. 1 either leaves the meaning of the interpreted treaty provision ambiguous or obscure, or leads to a result which is manifestly absurd or unreasonable. Quite clearly, the application of interpretation rule no. 1 does not leave the meaning of the interpreted treaty provision ambiguous or obscure. The decisive question is whether I can establish that the application leads to a result which is manifestly absurd or unreasonable.

In the situation at hand, saying that the application of interpretation rule no. 1 leads to a result which is manifestly absurd or unreasonable is tantamount to saying that interpretation rules nos. 1 and 34 are based on communicative assumptions, of which the assumption underlying an application of the former is arguably substantially weaker than the assumption underlying an application of the latter.[112] Interpretation rule no. 1 is based on the assumption that parties to a treaty express themselves in such a way that every expression included in the treaty, whose form corresponds to an expression of conventional language, bears a meaning that agrees with the rules of that language.[113] Translated to the interpretation of the expression "supplementary means of interpretation", the idea could be expressed as follows:

> The parties to the Vienna Convention have expressed themselves in such a way that that the meaning of the expression "supplementary means of interpretation" agrees with the rules of conventional language.

For the sake of simplicity, let us term this as the assumption underlying the application of rule no. 1. Interpretation rule no. 34 is based on the assumption, that parties to a treaty express themselves in such a way that, arguably, from the point of view of the parties, every act or state-of-affairs permitted by the treaty can be considered more tolerable than those generically identical acts or state-of-affairs that are not permitted.[114] Translated to the interpretation of the expression "supplementary means of interpretation", the idea could be expressed in the following manner:

> The parties to the Vienna Convention have expressed themselves in such a way that every act or state-of-affairs permitted by article 32 can be considered more tolerable to the parties than those generically identical acts or state-of-affairs that the article does not permit.

Let us term this as the assumption underlying application of rule no. 34.

As far as I can see, there are only two ways of showing that an assumption A is substantially weaker than an assumption B. First, arguments can be presented undermining the assumption A. Second, arguments can be presented reinforcing the assumption B. I will now present three arguments, which either reinforce the assumption underlying the application of interpretation rule no. 34, or undermine the assumption underlying the application of rule no. 1.

For my first argument, I would like to begin by directing attention to Vienna article 31 § 2. According to article 31 § 2, the context includes – in addition to the text of the interpreted treaty – "any agreement relating to the treaty which was made between all the parties in connexion with the conclusion of the treaty", and "any instrument which was made by one or more parties in connexion with the conclusion of the treaty and accepted by the other parties as an instrument related to the treaty". However, in principle, such agreements and documents – had it not been the case that, according to the provisions of VCLT article 32, the context should be considered a means of interpretation in and of itself – could also have been taken into account, forming part of "the preparatory work of the treaty" or "the circumstances of its conclusion".[115] They would then be included in the extension of the "supplementary means of interpretation". Thus, the contents of article 31 § 2 would appear to undermine the assumption underlying application of rule no. 1.

For my second and third arguments, I take as a starting-point the so-called rule of necessary implication. According to the general opinion expressed in the literature, the rule of necessary implication is a norm, which can be applied on the basis of VCLT article 32.[116] The contents of the norm may be described in terms of the following two rules of interpretation:

Rule no. 30
If it can be shown that according to linguistics a meaning can be read into a treaty provision by implication, and that such an implication is necessary to avoid that, by applying the provision, a result is attained which is not among the *teloi* conferred on the treaty, then this meaning shall be adopted.

Rule no. 31
If it can be shown that according to linguistics, a meaning can be implicitly read into a treaty provision, and that such an implication is necessary to avoid that, by applying the provision, another part of the treaty will in practice be normatively useless, then this meaning shall be adopted.[117]

Obviously, the means of interpretation, on which these two rules are being based, is the object and purpose of the treaty.[118] Consequently, at least partly, the object and purpose would seem to be a "supplementary means of interpretation". This is certainly a very interesting observation, for two reasons. First, the object and purpose is an element, which cannot be denoted as a SUPPLEMENTARY MEANS OF INTERPRETATION, at least not as long as we abide by the rules of conventional language. Second, arguably, an act of interpretation using the object and purpose of a treaty can be considered more tolerable for the states parties to the Vienna Convention than an act of interpretation using the preparatory work of the treaty, the circumstances of its conclusion, ratification work, or treaties *in pari materia* – all elements comprised in the extension of the expression "supplementary means of interpretation". Thus, the rule of necessary implication would seem to undermine the assumption underlying the application of interpretation rule no. 1.

In addition to the three arguments outlined above, we may note the absence of counter-arguments. I fail to find a single argument that either reinforces the assumption underlying the application of interpretation rule no. 1 or that undermines the assumption underlying the application of interpretation rule no. 34. Naturally, it is matter of judgment whether this means that the assumption underlying the application of interpretation rule no. 1 is *substantially* weaker than the assumption underlying the application of interpretation rule no. 34. Personally, I find it difficult to arrive at any other conclusion. For the determination whether the context shall be considered a "supplementary means of interpretation" or not, it can indeed be shown that the application of interpretation rule no. 1 "leads to a result which is manifestly absurd or unreasonable", in the sense of rule no. 40. In other words, if interpreting the expression "supplementary means of interpretation" in accordance with interpretation rule no. 1 leads to a result, which is different from that obtained by interpreting the expression in accordance with interpretation rule no. 34, then in my judgment the expression "supplementary means of interpretation" shall not be understood in accordance with rule interpretation no. 1. Instead, it shall be understood in accordance with interpretation rule no. 34: the context shall be considered a "supplementary means of interpretation".

7 THE "SUPPLEMENTARY MEANS OF INTERPRETATION" PUT TO USE

What communicative standard or standards shall the parties to a treaty be assumed to have followed, when an applier interprets the treaty using "supplementary means of interpretation"? There is a significant difference between a usage of the primary means of interpretation and a usage of the supplementary means. As we know, in order for a rule of interpretation to apply, the applier must be able to show that a state-of-affairs exists that comes within the scope of application of that rule. Generally speaking, this task may be described by a single sentence: by using a given means of interpretation, good reasons must be provided showing a concordance to exist between the parties to the interpreted treaty with regard to its norm content. Seeking better precision, we will of course have more difficulty describing the task. If we say that good reasons are provided showing a concordance to exist between the parties to a treaty with regard to its norm content, then the precise import of this undertaking will differ considerably depending on the means of interpretation we have assumed. These differences are particularly marked if we compare the way appliers use supplementary means of interpretation according to VCLT article 32, with the way they use primary means according to article 31.

When appliers use a primary means of interpretation, they are told specifically under what circumstances they may successfully argue, on the basis of that means, that a concordance exists between the parties to the interpreted treaty with regard to its norm content.[119] Conventional language, for example, cannot be used for the interpretation of a treaty provision, unless it can be shown that the provision contains an expression whose form corresponds to that of an expression used in conventional language.[120] And a rule of international law cannot be used as part of "the context" for the interpretation of a given treaty provision, unless it can be shown to govern the act or state-of-affairs, in relation to which the provision is interpreted.[121] When appliers use a "supplementary means of interpretation", they are not acting under similar constraints. The appliers are not specifically told under what circumstances they may successfully argue, on the basis of each and every means of interpretation, that a concordance exists between the parties to the interpreted treaty with regard to its norm content. If an applier argues that by using a certain supplementary means of interpretation a concordance can be shown to exist between the parties to a certain treaty with regard to its norm content, then this should be sufficient, as long as the applier can show the proposition in question to be supported by good reasons.[122] In other words, when appliers interpret a treaty using a "supplementary means of interpretation", the communicative standard assumed is the following:

> If a state produces an utterance taking the form of a treaty provision, then the provision should be drawn up so that what is comprised by each and every supplementary means of interpretation is not logically contradicted, insofar, and to the extent, that by using the means in question good reasons can be provided showing a concordance to exist between the parties to the treaty with regard to its norm content.

I wish to immediately add a point of clarification to this statement. As we well know, when appliers interpret a treaty according to the provisions of VCLT article 32, they may use the preparatory work of that treaty. According to some authors, when appliers use the preparatory work of a treaty, it is because they wish to establish the intentions assumed to be held by the treaty parties at the point in time when the treaty was established as definite.[123] Consider for instance the following statement of professor Amerasinghe, concerning the way to interpret the statute of an international organisation:

> *Intention of the parties – travaux préparatoires.* The actual intention of the parties at the time the constitution of an organization was formulated, as evidenced in the *travaux pré paratoires*, has sometimes been sought in attempts to interpret constitutional texts.[124]

The message cannot be missed. When appliers use the preparatory work of a treaty, primary attention should be focused on the state-of-affairs that existed at the time of its conclusion. What appliers wish to establish by using the preparatory work is the concordance possibly arrived at by the negotiating states, at the point in time when the treaty was established as definite. In my view, this proposition is acceptable only on the condition that certain qualifications are added.

When appliers interpret a treaty provision, in accordance with the provisions of VCLT articles 31–32, it is to determine the legally correct meaning of the provision in question. This legally correct meaning of a treaty provision has earlier been defined as follows:

> The correct meaning of a treaty should be identified with the pieces of information conveyed by that treaty with regard to its norm content, according to the intentions of the treaty parties – all those states, for which the treaty is in force – insofar as these intentions can be considered mutually held.[125]

It might be that on one point this definition deserves to be clarified. The legally correct meaning of a treaty provision is an utterance meaning.[126] By the utterance meaning of a text we mean the content of the utterance or utterances expressed by that text.[127] An utterance, in turn, can be described as the use by a specific subject of a specific piece of written or spoken language on a specific occasion.[128] Now, it is an important characteristic of a treaty provision that in each and every case it expresses several utterances, all at the same time. There are always two or more parties to a treaty. If two or more states – by whatever means – have consented to be bound by a treaty, then we can also say about the text of that treaty that it embodies an equal number of separate utterances. These utterances will not necessarily be made on the exact same occasion. If we take a treaty with two parties only, it is usually the case that the treaty was consented to by both parties simultaneously. If we take instead a multilateral treaty, the case is often the opposite. Consider any wide-reaching international, multilateral treaty open for general accession: naturally, different parties will have given their consent on different occasions. Obviously, given our ambition to properly clarify the concept of the legally correct meaning of a treaty, the definition given above is in need of adjustment:

> The correct meaning of a treaty should be identified with the pieces of information conveyed by that treaty with regard to its norm content, according to the intentions of the treaty parties – all those states, for which the treaty is in force – at the moment in time when each respective utterance is made, insofar as these intentions can be considered mutually held.

As anyone might expect, the point I want to make is the following. In one sense, professor Amerasinghe is outright correct when he argues that what appliers wish to establish by using the preparatory work of a treaty is the concordance that possibly existed among the negotiating states at the point in time when the treaty was established as definite. If the purpose of using the preparatory work of a treaty is to establish the utterance meaning of that treaty, then clearly the only relevant question is whether by using the preparatory work a concordance can be established *between those states that are parties to the treaty at the time of interpretation.* Of course, such a concordance may have existed already at the point in time when the treaty was established as definite. But it may also have come into existence on some later occasion; it all depends on when the parties to the treaty expressed their consent to be bound. However, let it be realised that by using the preparatory work of a treaty, and the preparatory work only, appliers cannot possibly establish a concordance arrived at subsequent to the establishing of the treaty as definite. The meaning of the expression "the preparatory work of the treaty", in the sense of VCLT article 32, is limited to include only such representations that were produced *during the drafting of the treaty in question.* The best that can accomplished by an applier using the preparatory work of a treaty, and the preparatory work only, is if he can show a concordance to have existed among the negotiating states at the point in time when the drafting of the treaty came to a conclusion, i.e. when the treaty was established as definite.

In another sense professor Amerasinghe is simply wrong. As a general proposition, it cannot be considered correct that what appliers wish to establish by using the preparatory work of a treaty is the concordance that possibly existed among the negotiating states at the point in time when the treaty was established as definite. In principle, when appliers set out to interpret a treaty, the situation confronted must be one of the following two: (1) among the states that are parties to the treaty at the time of interpretation, each participated in the capacity of a negotiating state during the process of its drafting; (2) at the time of interpretation other states are parties to the treaty than those who once participated in its drafting. In the first of the two situations, it is obvious that the legally correct meaning of the interpreted treaty can be identified with the concordance possibly arrived at by the negotiating states, at the point in time when the treaty is established as definite. In the second situation, it may be the case, but not necessarily so. The utterance meaning of the interpreted treaty can be identified with the concordance possibly arrived at by the negotiating states at the point in time when the treaty is established as definite, but only on the condition that there are good reasons for assuming the concordance to be espoused by the other parties to the treaty.[129] Only in the first situation can it correctly be asserted, that what appliers wish to establish by using the preparatory work is the concordance that possibly existed among the negotiating states at the time when the treaty was established as definite.

8 CONCLUSIONS

"Recourse may be had to supplementary means of interpretation ... in order to confirm the meaning resulting from the application of article 31, or to determine the meaning when the interpretation according to article 31: (a) leaves the meaning ambiguous or obscure; or (b) leads to a result which is manifestly absurd or unreasonable" – this is provided in VCLT article 32. It is the purpose set for this chapter to describe what this means. Based on the observations made in this chapter, the following ten rules of interpretation can be established:

Rule no. 17
§ 1. If it can be shown that the interpretation of a treaty provision in accordance with interpretation rule no. 1 leads to conflicting results, and by using the preparatory work of the treaty a concordance can be shown to exist, as between the parties to the treaty, and with regard to the norm content of the interpreted treaty provision, so that the provision – in light of the preparatory work – in one of the two possible ordinary meanings can be considered to involve a logical contradiction, while in the other it cannot, then the latter meaning shall be adopted.
§ 2. For the purpose if this rule, THE PREPARATORY WORK of a treaty means any representation produced in the process of drafting the treaty, whether textual or not.
§ 3. For the purpose of this rule, PARTIES means any and all states for which the treaty is in force at the time of interpretation.

Rule no. 18
§ 1. If, by using the preparatory work of a treaty, a concordance can be shown to exist, as between the parties to said treaty, and with regard to the norm content of an interpreted treaty provision, then the provision shall be understood in such a way that it logically agrees with the concordance.
§ 2. For the purpose if this rule, THE PREPARATORY WORK of a treaty means any representation produced in the process of drafting the treaty, whether textual or not.
§ 3. For the purpose of this rule, PARTIES means any and all states for which the treaty is in force at the time of interpretation.

Rule no. 19
§ **1**. If it can be shown that the interpretation of a treaty provision in accordance with interpretation rule no. 1 leads to conflicting results, and by using the circumstances of the treaty's conclusion a concordance can be shown to exist, as between the parties to the treaty, and with regard to the norm content of the interpreted treaty provision, so that the provision – in light of the circumstances of the treaty's conclusion – in one of the two possible ordinary meanings can be considered to involve a logical contradiction, while in the other it cannot, then the latter meaning shall be adopted.
§ **2**. For the purpose of this rule, a CIRCUMSTANCE OF THE TREATY'S CONCLUSION means any state-of-affairs, whose existence at least partially can be said to have caused the conclusion, except for those cases where this state-of-affairs can be taken into account already for the application of the interpretation rules nos. 7–14 or 17–18.
§ **3**. For the purpose of this rule, the CONCLUSION of a treaty means the point in time when the treaty was established as definite.
§ **4**. For the purpose of this rule, PARTIES means any and all states for which the treaty is in force at the time of interpretation.

Rule no. 20
§ **1**. If, by using the circumstances of a treaty's conclusion, a concordance can be shown to exist, as between the parties to said treaty, and with regard to the norm content of an interpreted treaty provision, then the provision shall be understood in such a way that it logically agrees with the concordance.
§ **2**. For the purpose of this rule, a CIRCUMSTANCE OF THE TREATY'S CONCLUSION means any state-of-affairs, whose existence at least partially can be said to have caused the conclusion, except for those cases where this state-of-affairs can be taken into account already for the application of the interpretation rules nos. 7–14 or 17–18.
§ **3**. For the purpose of this rule, the CONCLUSION of a treaty means the point in time when the treaty was established as definite.
§ **4**. For the purpose of this rule, PARTIES means any and all states for which the treaty is in force at the time of interpretation.

Rule no. 21
§ **1**. If it can be shown that the interpretation of a treaty provision in accordance with interpretation rule no. 1 leads to conflicting results, and by using any ratification work of the treaty, a concordance can be shown to exist, as between the parties to the treaty, and with regard to the norm content of the interpreted treaty provision, so that the provision – in light of the ratification work used – in one of the two possible ordinary meanings

can be considered to involve a logical contradiction, while in the other it cannot, then the latter meaning shall be adopted.
§ 2. For the purpose of this rule, RATIFICATION WORK means any representation unilaterally produced by a state in the process of deciding whether to ratify the treaty.
§ 3. For the purpose of this rule, PARTIES means any and all states for which the treaty is in force at the time of interpretation.

Rule no. 22
§ 1. If, by using any ratification work of a treaty, a concordance can be shown to exist, as between the parties to said treaty, and with regard to the norm content of an interpreted treaty provision, then the provision shall be understood in such a way that it logically agrees with the concordance.
§ 2. For the purpose of this rule, RATIFICATION WORK means any representation unilaterally produced by a state in the process of deciding whether to ratify the treaty or not.
§ 3. For the purpose of this rule, PARTIES means any and all states for which the treaty is in force at the time of interpretation.

Rule no. 23
§ 1. If it can be shown that the interpretation of a treaty provision in accordance with interpretation rule no. 1 leads to conflicting results, and by using a treaty *in pari materia* a concordance can be shown to exist, as between the parties to the treaty, and with regard to the norm content of the interpreted treaty provision, so that the provision – in light of the treaty *in pari materia* – in one of the two possible ordinary meanings can be considered to involve a logical contradiction, while in the other it cannot, then the latter meaning shall be adopted.
§ 2. For the purpose of this rule, a TREATY IN PARI MATERIA means a treaty whose subject matter is identical – at least partly – with the subject matter covered by the treaty interpreted.
§ 3. For the purpose of this rule, PARTIES means any and all states for which the treaty is in force at the time of interpretation.

Rule no. 24
§ 1. If, by using a treaty *in pari materia*, a concordance can be shown to exist, as between the parties to the interpreted treaty, and with regard to the norm content of the interpreted treaty provision, then the provision shall be understood in such a way that it logically agrees with the concordance.
§ 2. For the purpose of this rule, PARTIES means any and all states for which the treaty is in force at the time of interpretation.

Rule no. 25

§ 1. If it can be shown that the interpretation of a treaty provision in accordance with interpretation rule no. 1 leads to conflicting results, and by using the context of the provision a concordance can be shown to exist, as between the parties to the treaty, and with regard to the norm content of the interpreted treaty provision, so that the provision – in light of the context – in one of the two possible ordinary meanings can be considered to involve a logical contradiction, while in the other it cannot, then the latter meaning shall be adopted.

§ 2. For the purpose of this rule, the CONTEXT of an interpreted treaty provision means any element that fits the description provided in article 31 §§ 2 and 3 of the 1969 Vienna Convention on the Law of Treaties.

§ 3. For the purpose of this rule, PARTIES means any and all states for which the treaty is in force at the time of interpretation.

Rule no. 26

§ 1. If, by using the context of an interpreted treaty provision, a concordance can be shown to exist, as between the parties to said treaty, and with regard to the norm content of the interpreted provision, then the provision shall be understood in such a way that it logically agrees with the concordance.

§ 2. For the purpose of this rule, the CONTEXT of an interpreted treaty provision means any element that fits the description provided in article 31 §§ 2 and 3 of the 1969 Vienna Convention on the Law of Treaties.

§ 3. For the purpose of this rule, PARTIES means any and all states for which the treaty is in force at the time of interpretation.

NOTES

1. See Ch. 1, Section 5, of this work.
2. For a more detailed discussion of the expression "ambiguous or obscure", see Ch. 10, Section 3, of this work.
3. Similarly, *Oppenheim's International Law*, p. 1276; Villiger, p. 345; Yasseen, pp. 79–80; Greig, pp. 480–481; Rest, p. 155; Hilf, p. 88; Gross, p. 117; Schröder, p. 130; Degan, 1968, p. 18; Bernhardt, 1967, p. 502; see also, implicitly, Karl, 1983, p. 194; Sinclair, 1984, p. 140. For a different opinion, see Dupuy, p. 221.
4. In linguistics it would be termed as deictic reference.
5. Regarding the concept *general referring expression* in general, see Ch. 3, Section 3, of this work.
6. Regarding the concept *generic referring expression* in general, see loc. cit.
7. See Ch. 1, Section 2, of this work.
8. Cf. Ch. 3, Section 3, of this work.
9. See e.g. Karl, 1983, p. 187; Hilf, p. 88; Bernhardt, 1967, p. 502; Sinclair, 1984, pp. 117–118. Cf. also *Oppenheim's International Law*, p. 1276; Villiger, p. 345; Yasseen, pp. 79–80; Rest, p. 155; Gross, p. 117.

10. See e.g. *Starke's International Law*, p. 437; *Oppenheim's International Law*, p. 1277; Seidl-Hohenveldern, 1992, p. 95; Brownlie, p. 630; Yasseen, p. 83; Haraszti, pp. 120–121; Verzijl, pp. 317–318; Rest, pp. 54–55; O'Connell, p. 263; Sharma, p. 372.
11. The following texts provide an excellent overview: *Review of the Multilateral Treaty-Making Process* (1985), in extenso; Verzijl, p. 122 et seq.; Hamzeh, pp. 178–189.
12. See e.g. Exchange of Notes between the United States of America and the Federal People's Republic of Yugoslavia, on 28 November 1962.
13. Cf. Elias, 1974, pp. 81–82; Yasseen, p. 83. Cf. also Rosenne, at the ILC's eighteenth session, 872nd meeting, *ILC Yrbk*, 1966, Vol. 1, Part 2, p. 201, § 35; and, implicitly, Draft Articles With Commentaries (1966), *ILC Yrbk*, 1966, Vol. 2, p. 223, § 20.
14. Haraszti, p. 120.
15. Cf. *Starke's International Law*, pp. 437–438; *Oppenheim's International Law*, pp. 1277–1278; Seidl-Hohenveldern, 1992, p. 95; Brownlie, p. 630; Villiger, p. 345; Sinclair, 1984, pp. 141–147; Verdross and Simma, pp. 492–494; Yasseen, pp. 83–90; Elias, 1974, pp. 80–82; Haraszti, pp. 117–138; Lang, pp. 164–168; Briggs, pp. 705–712; Verzijl, pp. 317–318; Rest, pp. 54–60; O'Connell, pp. 262–264; Sharma, p. 372; Jennings, pp. 550–552; Voïcu, pp. 48–52; Rosenne, 1963, pp. 1378–1388; Bernhardt, 1963, pp. 109–120; De Visscher, 1963, pp. 115–121.
16. On the whole, most of these opinions seem to be such that they can be summarised by one the following five statements (or by variations of these). (1) The meaning of "the preparatory work" of a treaty shall be limited to include only *written* representations. (*Oppenheim's International Law*, p. 1277, n. 9.) (2) The meaning of "the preparatory work" of a treaty shall be limited to include only representations *mutually* produced by the negotiating states. (De Visscher, 1963, p. 115.) (3) The meaning of "the preparatory work" of a treaty shall be limited to include only such representations that can be said to have *made their mark* on the text of the final agreement. (O'Connell, p. 262; Haraszti, p. 125.) (4) The meaning of "the preparatory work" of a treaty shall be limited to include only such representations *that establish a concordance* of the parties with regard to the interpretation of the treaty. (O'Connell, p. 262; Haraszti, p. 122.) (5) The meaning of "the preparatory work of the treaty" includes a representation produced during the drafting of a treaty, but only on the condition either that all parties were involved in its production, or that the representation had been made public before the parties expressed their consent to be bound by the treaty. (*Starke's International Law*, pp. 437–438.)
17. See e.g. *Review of the Multilateral Treaty-Making Process* (1985), passim.
18. See Voïcu, p. 50; De Visscher, 1963, p. 115.
19. See Section 7 of this chapter.
20. GA res. 2278 (XXII), § 7. (My italics.)
21. Another (if somewhat unusual) case is when a state has indeed been involved in the drafting of a treaty, but for one or another reason was excluded from specific discussions during the process. (See for example *Young Loan*, *ILR*, Vol. 59, pp. 495ff., especially pp. 544–545.)
22. Case Relating to the Territorial Jurisdiction of the International Commission of the River Oder, Judgment of 10 September 1929, *PCIJ*, Ser. A, No. 23, p. 42.
23. The author who first made clear his rejection of this idea was Hersch Lauterpacht. (See Lauterpacht, 1934, pp. 805–808, or Lauterpacht, 1935, pp. 584–586.)
24. See Draft Articles With Commentaries (1966), *ILC Yrbk*, 1966, Vol. 2, p. 223, § 20.

25. See, expressly, *Starke's International Law*, pp. 437–438; Seidl-Hohenveldern, 1992, p. 95; *Oppenheim's International Law*, p. 1278; Sinclair, 1984, pp. 142–144; Verdross and Simma, pp. 492–493, n. 8; Yasseen, pp. 89–90; Elias, 1974, p. 82; Haraszti, pp. 122–123; Lang, p. 165; Rest, pp. 58–59; Rosenne, 1963, pp. 1378–1383. See also, implicitly, Brownlie, p. 630; Villiger, p. 345.
26. See Seidl-Hohenveldern, p. 95; *Oppenheim's International Law*, p. 1278; Verdross and Simma, pp. 492–493, n. 8; Rest, p. 59.
27. See Section 7 of this chapter.
28. See Bernhardt, 1963, p. 112; Ruegger, at the Institute of International Law and its session in Grenada, 1956, *Annuaire de l'Institut de droit international*, Vol. 46 (1956), pp. 342–343. For the somewhat older literature, see Spencer, p. 124; Lauterpacht, 1934, p. 719.
29. See Ris, p. 112; Yasseen, p. 83; Haraszti, pp. 120–121; Verzijl, p. 317; Rest, p. 54; O'Connell, p. 262; Voïcu, p. 163, n. 73.
30. See Draft Articles with Commentaries (1966), *ILC Yrbk*, 1966, p. 223, § 20.
31. Professor Vierdag has come to the same conclusion. (See Vierdag, 1988, p. 86.) The fact is that it agrees exceptionally well with the preparatory work of the Vienna Convention. The ILC states in its 1966 Commentary, with regard to the then existing draft and the relationship held between the means of interpretation listed in articles 27 and 28, later to be adopted as VCLT articles 31 and 32, respectively: "The elements of interpretation in article 27 all relate to the agreement between the parties at *the time when or after it received authentic expression in the text. Ex hypothesis* this is not the case with preparatory work". (Draft Articles With Commentaries (1966), *ILC Yrbk*, 1966, Vol. 2, p. 220, § 10.) Nothing in the records from the Vienna Conference can be seen to indicate a departure from this idea.
32. See Sinclair, 1984, p. 141; Yasseen, p. 90; Haraszti, p. 119; Voïcu, p. 53.
33. See Sinclair, 1984, p. 141; Vitányi, p. 67; Yasseen, p. 91; Haraszti, pp. 118–120; Voïcu, pp. 52–54, cf. n. 178. See also Waldock, Third Report on the Law of Treaties, *ILC Yrbk*, 1964, Vol. 2, p. 59, § 22.
34. Cf. *EC-Poultry*, § 83. It is quite another thing that this requirement sets up limitations for the existence of the state-of-affairs in time. In order for a state-of-affairs to be categorised as the cause of a treaty's conclusion, this state-of-affairs must have existed at a point in time not later than the end of the treaty's conclusion – this goes without saying.
35. See Vierdag, 1988, pp. 76–82.
36. See ibid, pp. 82ff.
37. This is the sense in which the word CONCLUSION, CONCLUSION, CELEBRACIÓN seems to have been used, for example, in VCLT articles 2 § 1(a), 3, 4, 31 § 2(a), 49.
38. This is the sense in which the word CONCLUSION, CONCLUSION, CELEBRACIÓN seems to have been used, for example, in VCLT articles 6, 7 § 2(a), 31 § 2(b), 46, 52.
39. See VCLT article 24.
40. See Section 2 of this chapter.
41. Cf. the ILC Commentary of 1966: "The elements of interpretation in article 27 all relate to the agreement between the parties at *the time when or after it received authentic expression in the text. Ex hypothesis* this is not the case with preparatory work". (Draft Articles With Commentaries (1966), *ILC Yrbk*, 1966, Vol. 2, p. 220, § 10.)
42. Sinclair, 1984, p. 141.
43. Haraszti, p. 119.

44. Dupuy, p. 222.
45. Voïcu, p. 52.
46. Yasseen, p. 90.
47. See Ch. 7, Section 1, of this work.
48. See Ch. 5, Section 1, of this work, cf. VCLT article 31 § 2(a).
49. See Ch. 6, Section 4, of this work, cf. VCLT article 31 § 3(c).
50. Concerning the use of "the context" as a supplementary means of interpretation, see Section 6 of this chapter.
51. With regard to these, see Section 2 of this chapter.
52. See Torres Bernárdez, p. 743, n. 46; Yasseen, p. 83; Haraszti, pp. 121–122; Verzijl, pp. 320–321, cit. *Anglo-Iranian Oil*, *ICJ Reports*, 1952, p. 93, and *Howard Claim*, *ILR*, Vol. 18, pp. 410–411; Bernhardt, 1963, p. 112; Ruegger, at the Institute of International Law and its session in Grenada, 1956, *Annuaire de l'Institut de droit international*, Vol. 46 (1956), pp. 342–343. For the somewhat older literature, see e.g. Spencer, p. 124; Lauterpacht, 1934, p. 719.
53. Haraszti, p. 122.
54. See Ch. 6, Section 2, of this work.
55. See e.g. Bernhardt, 1963, p. 112; Ruegger, at the Institute of International Law and its session in Grenada, 1956, *Annuaire de l'Institut de droit International*, Vol. 46 (1956), pp. 342–343.
56. See Section 2 of this chapter.
57. In addition to the authorities cited in the text, see diss. op. Ajibola, *Territorial Dispute (Libya/Chad)*, *ILR*, Vol. 100, pp. 66–67, §§ 66–70; *S.D. Myers*, *ILR*, Vol. 121, p. 140, § 62; *Mondev*, *ILR*, Vol. 125, pp. 145–146, § 111; *Maritime Delimitation: Jan Mayen*, *ILR*, Vol. 99, p. 419, § 22; *Guinea – Guinea-Bissau Maritime Delimitation*, *ILR*, Vol. 77, p. 669, § 70; *Rainbow Navigation v. Department of the Navy*, *ILR*, Vol. 96, p. 103.
58. *Case Concerning Oil Platforms (Islamic Republic of Iran v. United States of America)*, Preliminary Objection, Judgement of 12 December 1996, *ICJ Reports*, 1996 (II), pp. 803ff.
59. The text cited is the one provided by the court. (See *ICJ Reports*, 1996 (II), p. 809, § 15.)
60. Ibid., p. 812, § 24.
61. Ibid., p. 812, § 25.
62. Ibid., p. 813, § 26.
63. Ibid., p. 815, § 31.
64. Ibid., p. 814, § 28.
65. Ibid., pp. 814–815, § 29.
66. Ibid., p. 815, § 30.
67. Ibid., p. 814, § 29.
68. See Sections 2 and 3 of this chapter.
69. See p. 251 of this work.
70. Dissenting Opinion of Judge Schwebel, Case Concerning *Elettronica Sicula SpA (ELSI) (United States v. Italy)*, *ILR*, Vol. 84, pp. 400ff.
71. Separate opinion of Judge Oda, Case Concerning *Elettronica Sicula SpA (ELSI) (United States v. Italy)*, ibid., pp. 389ff.
72. Ibid., p. 395.
73. Ibid., p. 403.

74. Ibid., p. 404.
75. Loc. cit.
76. Ibid., p. 405.
77. Loc. cit.
78. *Beagle Channel Arbitration (Chile v. Argentina)*, Award of 18 February 1977, *ILR*, Vol. 52, pp. 93ff.
79. See Ch. 4, Section 4, of this work.
80. *ILR*, Vol. 52, p. 186.
81. Loc. cit.
82. See ibid., pp. 220–226, §§ 164–175.
83. See ibid., for example p. 144, § 47, p. 145, § 48, p. 163, § 67, p. 178, § 97, pp. 187–188, § 114.
84. Declaration of Judge Gros, *Beagle Channel Arbitration*, ibid., pp. 228ff.
85. Ibid., pp. 228–229, § 2.
86. Ibid., p. 229, § 2.
87. See Berman, p. 317; Thirlway, 1991, pp. 66–71; *Starke's International Law*, p. 438; Villiger, p. 345; Verdross and Simma, p. 494; Verzijl, p. 324; Haraszti, p. 148; Bernhardt, 1967, p. 500. See also, implicitly, Merrills, pp. 224–225.
88. Cf. e.g. *Guinea – Guinea-Bissau Maritime Delimitation*, *ILR*, Vol. 77, pp. 673–674, § 81; Van der Mussele, *Publ. ECHR*, Ser. A, Vol. 70, p. 16, § 32; *US-France Air Services Award*, *ILR*, Vol. 54, p. 334, §§ 67–68; *Italy-United States Air Transport Arbitration*, *ILR*, Vol. 45, p. 414.
89. In addition to the authorities cited in the text, see diss. op. Ajibola, *Territorial Dispute (Libya/Chad)*, *ILR*, Vol. 100, pp. 66–67, §§ 66–70; *Maritime Delimitation: Jan Mayen*, *ILR*, Vol. 99, p. 419, § 22; *Guinea – Guinea-Bissau Maritime Delimitation*, *ILR*, Vol. 77, p. 669, § 70; *Rainbow Navigation v. Department of the Navy*, *ILR*, Vol. 96, p. 103.
90. *Case Concerning Oil Platforms (Islamic Republic of Iran v. United States of America)*, Preliminary Objection, Judgment of 12 December 1996, *ICJ Reports*, 1996 (II), pp. 803ff.
91. See Section 4 of this chapter.
92. The text cited is the one provided by the court. (See *ICJ Reports*, 1996 (II), p. 812, § 24.)
93. Ibid., pp. 814–815, § 29.
94. *Case Concerning The Arbitral Award of 31 July 1989 (Guinea-Bissau v. Senegal)*, Judgment of 2 March 1990, *ILR*, Vol. 92, pp. 1ff.
95. Exchange of letters between France and Portugal, on 26 April 1960, for the purpose of defining the maritime boundary between the Republic of Senegal and the Portuguese territory of Guinea.
96. Note that the original agreement exists only in French and Portuguese. The text cited is the English translation used by the court. (See *ILR*, Vol. 92, p. 34, § 14.)
97. *Guinea-Bissau v. Senegal*, Award of 31 July 1989, *ILR*, Vol. 83, pp. 1ff.
98. *ILR*, Vol. 92, p. 45, §§ 47–48.
99. Ibid., pp. 45–46, § 48.
100. Ibid., p. 46, § 50.
101. Ibid., pp. 46–47, § 51.
102. Case of Müller and Others, Judgment of 24 May 1988, *Publ. ECHR*, Ser. A, Vol. 133.
103. Ibid., p. 19, § 27.

104. See Ch. 4–7 of this work, especially the introductions to till Ch. 4 and Ch. 7.
105. See the introduction to this chapter.
106. See Ch. 9, Section 4, of this work.
107. See Ch. 3 of this work.
108. See Ch. 9, Section 6, of this work.
109. Cf. Draft Articles with Commentaries (1966): "Although a few Governments indicated a preference for allowing a larger role to preparatory work and even for including it in the present article [what is now VCLT art. 31], the majority appeared to be in agreement with the Commission's treatment of the matter. Certain members of the Commission also favoured a system which would give a more automatic role to preparatory work and other supplementary means in the process of interpretation. But the Commission considered that the relationship established between the 'supplementary' elements in interpretation in present article 28 [what is now VCLT art. 32] – which accords with the jurisprudence of the International Court on the matter – should be retained. The elements of interpretation in article 27 [what is now VCLT art. 31] all relate to the agreement between the parties *at the time when or after it received authentic expression in the text. Ex hypothesis* this is not the case with preparatory work which does not, in consequence, have the same authentic character as an element of interpretation, however valuable it may sometimes be in throwing light on the expression of the agreement in the text — Accordingly, the Commission was of the opinion that the distinction made in articles 27 and 28 [what is now VCLT arts. 31 and 32] between authentic and supplementary means of interpretation is both justified and desirable." (*ILC Yrbk*, 1966, Vol. 2, p. 220, § 10.)
110. See Ch. 10 of this work.
111. Loc. cit.
112. For a more detailed treatment of the expression "leads to a result that is manifestly absurd or unreasonable", see Ch. 10 of this work.
113. See the introduction to Ch. 3 of this work.
114. See Ch. 9, Section 6, of this work.
115. Cf. Thirlway, 1991, pp. 36–37; Amerasinghe, pp. 201–202; Bernhardt, 1984, p. 323; Yasseen, p. 84; Elias, 1974, p. 75; Rest, p. 145; Jennings, p. 549; Schwarzenberger, 1957, pp. 516, 531; Fitzmaurice, 1951, pp. 12–13. See also Draft Articles with Commentaries (1966), *ILC Yrbk*, 1966, Vol. 2, p. 221, § 13 *in fine*.
116. See Ch. 9, Section 4, of this work.
117. Loc. cit.
118. Loc. cit.
119. There is one, and only one, exception to this; and that is when a treaty is interpreted using a "subsequent practice in the application of the treaty which establishes the agreement of the parties regarding its interpretation".
120. See the introduction to Ch. 3 of this work.
121. See Ch. 6, Section 4, of this work.
122. See Thirlway, 1991, p. 36; Amerasinghe, p. 200; *Oppenheim's International Law*, p. 1277; Villiger, p. 345; Bos, 1984, p. 152; Yasseen, p. 90; Lang, p. 164; O'Connell, p. 262; Draft Articles With Commentaries (1966), *ILC Yrbk*, 1966, Vol. 2, p. 223, § 18; Waldock, Third Report on the Law of Treaties, ibid., p. 58, § 21; Jennings, p. 552; Bernhardt, 1963, p. 112. See also, implicitly, Merrills, p. 90; Sinclair, 1984, p. 141; Haraszti, pp. 122, 123, 131; Sharma, p. 286.
123. See also Haraszti, p. 138.

124. Amerasinghe, p. 200.
125. See p. 33 of this work.
126. See Ch. 2, Section 1, of this work.
127. Loc. cit.
128. Loc. cit.
129. Here, there is an obvious parallel to the provisions of VCLT article 31 § 3(b): all parties to a treaty need not necessarily contribute to a practice, for it to be considered one that "establishes agreement between the parties regarding [the treaty's] interpretation". (Cf. Ch. 6, Section 2, of this work.)

CHAPTER 9

USING SUPPLEMENTARY MEANS OF INTERPRETATION (CONT'D)

"[S]upplementary means of interpretation", according to the provisions of VCLT article 32, "[may be used] in order to confirm the meaning resulting from the application of article 31, or to determine the meaning when the interpretation according to article 31: (a) Leaves the meaning ambiguous or obscure; or (b) Leads to a result which is manifestly absurd or unreasonable". In Chapter 8, I began investigating the contents of this article 32. The task I took on was to establish what it means to interpret a treaty using "supplementary means of interpretation", in the sense of the set of elements that can be used to supplement the means of interpretation listed in VCLT article 31. In this chapter, I shall attempt to conclude this investigation. The task assumed is to establish what it means to interpret a treaty using "supplementary means of interpretation", in the sense of the rules of interpretation that can be applied according to VCLT article 32.[1]

In the literature, several rules are mentioned as candidates for the list of rules applicable when the primary means of interpretation have been found to be insufficient. In my opinion, eight of these rules may be considered a use of the "supplementary means of interpretation". They are as follows: the rule of restrictive interpretation; the principle of *contra proferentem*; exceptions shall be narrowly interpreted; the rule of necessary implication; interpretation *per analogiam*; interpretation *per argumentum a fortiori*; interpretation *per argumentum e contrario*; and the principle of *ejusdem generis*. I have chosen to organise this chapter so that in Sections 1 through 8, I shall begin by arguing this position in "positive" terms. The purpose is to establish the status of these eight rules, and to define their norm content. In Section 9, I shall then argue my position in "negative" terms. I shall introduce a series of rules, which according to some authors should be considered a use of the "supplementary means of interpretation", and I shall attempt to explain why I believe they *cannot* be regarded as such.

1 THE RULE OF RESTRICTIVE INTERPRETATION

The rule of restrictive interpretation – sometimes referred to as the *principle* of restrictive interpretation, or in Latin termed as the maxim *in dubio mitius* –[2] is probably among the most rarely applied rules of interpretation in twentieth century international case law. Nevertheless, it is a view generally held in the literature that it should still be considered part of international law.[3] Based on this fact, it is my conclusion that the rule of restrictive interpretation is a valid rule of international law.

As examples of cases where the rule of restrictive interpretation has been applied, authors note three cases in particular; they will be cited here only in brief. A first example is the international award in the case concerning *Kronprins Gustaf Adolf*:

> [I]t must be observed that, considering the natural state of liberty and independence which is inherent in sovereign states, they are not to be presumed to have abandoned any part thereof, the consequence being that the high contracting parties to a treaty are to be considered as bound only within the limits of what can be clearly and unequivocally found in the provisions agreed to and that those provisions, in case of doubt, are to be interpreted in favour of the natural liberty and independence of the party concerned.[4]

A second case is the judgment of the Permanent Court of International Justice in the *International Commission of the River Oder*:

> [T]he Court ... [cannot] accept the Polish Government's contention that, the text being doubtful, the solution should be adopted which imposes the least restriction on the freedom of States. This argument, though sound in itself, must be employed only with the greatest caution. To rely upon it, it is not sufficient that the purely grammatical analysis of a text should not lead to definite results; there are many other methods of interpretation, in particular, reference is properly had to the principles underlying the matter to which the text refers; it will be only when, in spite of all pertinent considerations, the intention of the Parties still remains doubtful, that the interpretation should be adopted which is most favourable to the freedom of States.[5]

A third case is the advisory opinion delivered by the PCIJ in the *Frontier between Turkey and Iraq*:

> In its telegram to the Court of October 8th, the Turkish Government adduced as an argument in favour of the correctness of its contentions, the fact that the Council itself had felt constrained to ask the Court for an advisory opinion as to the nature of the powers derived by it from Article 3 of the Treaty of Lausanne. This argument appears to rest on the following principle: if the wording of a treaty provision is not clear, in choosing between several admissible interpretations, the one which involves the minimum of obligations for the Parties should be adopted. This principle may be admitted to be sound. In the present case, however, the argument is valueless, because, in the Court's opinion, the wording of Article 3 is clear.[6]

Together, these three decisions tell us all we want to know about the contents of the rule of restrictive interpretation.

First of all, we can tell what should be understood when we talk about restrictive interpretation.[7] When a treaty is interpreted and the rule of restrictive interpretation is applied, the means of interpretation assumed is the principle of state sovereignty. Restrictive interpretation is what we speak about when a treaty is interpreted in favour of the freedom of action inherent in all states as sovereign subjects – a fact that may be observed especially in the rulings in the *International Commission of the River Oder* and the *Kronprins Gustaf Adolf*. Given that a treaty always implies that, for every state bound by that treaty sovereign freedom of action is partly relinquished, restrictive interpretation – just as it is described in the *Frontier Between Turkey and Iraq* – would then be tantamount to an act of interpretation, the purpose of which is to limit those obligations of states laid down in the interpreted treaty.

Secondly, we are allowed to define how the rule of restrictive interpretation operates in the context of the other rules laid down in VCLT articles 31–32. As observed in Chapter 8 of this work, when appliers interpret a treaty using a "supplementary means of interpretation", the task may be approached in two fundamentally different ways. "[S]upplementary means of interpretation" can be used independently of other means of interpretation, or they can be used relative to conventional language, subject to the limits set by "the ordinary meaning".[8] Judging from the way the rule of restrictive interpretation is expressed in the three examples cited, it seems that the principle of state sovereignty is a means of interpretation that may only be used relative to conventional language. When the rule of restrictive interpretation is applied it is not to limit as far as possible the obligations of the parties to the interpreted treaty.[9] The purpose of the exercise, rather, may be described as the making of a choice: among the two possible ordinary meanings, appliers are to adopt the one by which the obligations of the parties will be most fully limited.

Hence, if the rule of restrictive interpretation shall be put to words, it may be stated as follows:

Rule no. 27
If it can be shown that the interpretation of a treaty provision in accordance with interpretation rule no. 1 leads to conflicting results, and that the provision contains an obligation, whose extension in one of the two possible ordinary meanings is comparably greater than it is in the other, then the latter meaning shall be adopted.

With this choice of words, I have claimed to be reproducing what was earlier termed as the view "generally held in the literature". To make the picture complete, there are indeed authors who express opinions which do not agree with the one generally held. Two of these opinions are especially worthy of mention.

A first dissenting opinion concerns the means of interpretation, on which the rule of restrictive interpretation is allegedly based. As observed earlier, the means of interpretation used by appliers for the interpretation of a treaty in accordance with the rule of restrictive interpretation is the principle of state sovereignty. According to some authors the means used is another, namely relative sovereignty.[10] Consider for example the following statement by Rest:

> Die neuere Völkerrechtslitteratur geht im Anschluß an die Klassiker des modernen Völkerrechts von dem Bestehen einer Auslegungsregel aus, wonach nach geltendem Völkerrecht grundsätzlich Einschränkungen der relativen Souveränität nich vermutet werden dürfen, mit der Folge, daß vertragliche Bestimmungen, die eine Einschränkung der staatlichen Freiheit enthalten, restriktiv auszulegen seien.[11]

I have to admit that I am not completely certain what Rest really has in mind when he writes "*der relativen Souveränität*". Principles demand optimisation; there is always some certain state of affairs that should be attained to the highest possible (legal or factual) degree.[12] According to the principle of state sovereignty, a state – within the realm of competence inherent in statehood – should have an *unlimited power* to act according to its liking.[13] Hence, if "*Souveränität*" is short for the principle of state sovereignty, RELATIVE SOUVERÄNITÄT would be a complete contradiction in terms.

Given that Rest expresses himself within the bounds set by conventional language, only one interpretation remains. What Rest has in mind when speaking of "*der relativen Souveränität*" is the freedom of action that remains for a state, when all obligations incumbent upon that state according to international law have been excluded – given, once again, that with every obligation entered into by a state, its freedom of action is partly relinquished. According to the rule of restrictive interpretation, a treaty provision would then have to be interpreted in such a way that logically, it cannot be considered inconsistent with any other obligation held by the parties to said treaty under international law. This reading in turn lends itself to two different interpretations. Either we take "*die relative Souveränität*" to stand for a relative concept, dependent upon the party specifically addressed: according to the rule of restrictive interpretation, a treaty provision shall be interpreted in such a way, that for each individual party it cannot be considered logically inconsistent with any other obligation *held by that party* under international law. Or, we take "*die relative Souveränität*" to stand for a fully uniform concept: according to the rule of restrictive interpretation, a treaty provision shall be interpreted in such a way that logically, it cannot be considered inconsistent with any other obligation *mutually held* by the parties under international law. The first interpretation alternative must be dismissed, since it is clearly unreasonable. It meets with the same problem as a relative interpretation of the two expressions "the preparatory work of the treaty" (VCLT article 32) and "the conclusion of the treaty" (article 31 § 2).[14] The second interpretation alternative is at variance with a rule of interpretation laid down in international law (earlier termed as rule no. 6), according to which a treaty provision shall be interpreted so that nowhere in the text of that treaty there will be no instance of a logical tautology.[15] For if it is the meaning conveyed by the rule of restrictive interpretation that a treaty provision shall be interpreted so that it cannot be considered logically inconsistent with any other obligation *mutually held* by the parties to said treaty under international law, then the rule only repeats what is already stated in VCLT article 31 § 3(c), together with article 32 concerning a use of the context as a supplementary means of interpretation. All things considered, it is my conclusion that the position of Rest is unfounded.

A second dissenting opinion that I consider especially worthy of mention concerns the *applicability* of the rule of restrictive interpretation. According to what I have suggested, the rule of restrictive interpretation shall apply regardless of what kind of treaty is interpreted. Some authors wish to limit the applicability of the rule, arguing that it does not apply for the interpretation of treaties covering certain kinds of subject matter.[16] This view appears difficult to reconcile with the considerations underlying the rule of restrictive interpretation. When appliers interpret a treaty in accordance with the rules laid down in the Vienna Convention – the rule of restrictive interpretation excepted – there is no absolute guarantee that this will lead to a legally acceptable interpretation result. There is always a slight possibility that by using the primary means of interpretation, appliers arrive at a result which is either ambiguous or obscure, or manifestly absurd or unreasonable, and despite a use of the supplementary means of interpretation the appliers are incapable of producing something better. To avoid situations of this kind, we need a rule that establishes who in the last instance has the burden of proof. If two states are in dispute as to the norm content of a given treaty provision, we must be able to say which of these parties shall bear the risk, should it prove impossible to establish the contents of the provision with any sufficient clarity. Shall it be the entitled or the obligated party? In view of the way international law is fundamentally structured, the answer must be a given. The idea of states as sovereign subjects is one of the most basic principles known in international law. When a state enters a treaty, thereby assuming obligations in relation to another state vis-à-vis a certain kind of behaviour, then this shall be considered an *exception* to the freedom of action held by that state according to the principle of state sovereignty.[17] Therefore, if appliers who interpret a treaty are faced with a situation where they are forced to presume that the parties have either retained or relinquished sovereign freedom of action, the alternative of choice must naturally be the former.[18] I can see no reason why this choice should lead to different results depending upon the kind of subject matter covered by the treaty interpreted.

2 THE PRINCIPLE OF *CONTRA PROFERENTEM*

Another norm finding widespread support in the literature is the one denoted as the principle (or rule) of *contra proferentem.*[19] Clearly, therefore, the principle of *contra proferentem* must be considered a valid norm of international law.[20] Less clear is the meaning of the principle. Two definitions can be found in the literature. According to a first definition, if an expression contained in a treaty provision can be shown to be unclear, then the provision shall be interpreted to the disadvantage of the party who once suggested the expression *(der sie vorgeschlagen hat).*[21] Let us call this definition A. According to a second definition, if a treaty provision can be interpreted in two different ways, then it shall be interpreted to the disadvantage of the party who once unilaterally proffered the treaty for acceptance.[22] We shall call this definition B. Definition A appears unreasonably broad.[23] It is the fundamental idea underlying the principle of *contra proferentem*, that the party who once had the sole responsibility of drafting a treaty is also the one that ought to be penalised, should the meaning of the provision later be shown to be unclear. A state who accepts a treaty without having taken part in its drafting typically has more difficulty predicting the consequences of its acceptance, compared to the difficulty had by the state who unilaterally proffered the treaty, in predicting the consequences of its offer. Considering this, it can be seen as a reasonable solution that it is the latter state and not the former who shall bear the risk, should it prove impossible to clearly establish the content of the treaty.[24] It *cannot* be considered a reasonable solution that the risk is borne by a state, simply because in normal, mutual negotiations this state proposed a treaty to be worded in a specific way, and this wording endures up to and into the treaty's final adoption. All in all, I can arrive at no other conclusion than this: definition B is the only correct description of the *contra proferentem* principle.

Considering the contents of the *contra proferentem* principle, it seems to be the natural conclusion that the principle is applicable only for the interpretation of a very specific kind of treaty. According to some authors, the principle is applicable without any such limitations.[25] Hence, the principle of *contra proferentem* would be applicable for the interpretation of a treaty, regardless of whether its content is of a "two-sided" or a "many-sided" nature. (The content of a treaty has a two-sided nature, if the treaty has two parties only, or – should there be more than two parties – if the treaty has been drawn up in such a way, that one of the parties has rights and obligations toward each and every one of the others, and vice versa, but these other parties do not have corresponding rights and obligations toward each other.[26] The content of a treaty has a many-sided nature, if it does not have a two-sided nature.) First, it is probably a rare occurrence that a state unilaterally proffers a treaty for acceptance, when the content of the treaty has a many-sided nature.[27] Second, severe problems of principle would arise if the *contra proferentem* principle were considered applicable for the interpretation also of those treaties with a content of a many-sided nature. If two states are of different opinions as to the interpretation of a treaty provision, and the dispute is submitted for settlement by an international court or tribunal, then the provision might very well come to be understood in two different ways, depending upon whether the state which unilaterally proffered the treaty for acceptance is a party to the dispute or not. Such a double standard cannot be accepted. Like cases are to be judged alike – this is a fundamental principle upheld in every legal system. All things considered, I arrive at the following conclusion: the principle of *contra proferentem* is applicable only for the interpretation of treaties with a content of a two-sided nature.[28]

Hence, if the principle of *contra proferentem* shall be put to words, it may be stated along the following lines:

Rule no. 28

§ **1**. If it can be shown (i) that the interpretation of a treaty provision in accordance with interpretation rule no. 1 leads to conflicting results, (ii) that the content of the treaty has a two-sided nature, (iii) that the treaty was concluded through one of the negotiating parties unilaterally proffering the treaty for acceptance by the other(s), and (iv) that the provision, in one of the two possible ordinary meanings, is of greater disadvantage for this active party than it is in the other, then the former meaning shall be adopted.

§ **2**. For the purpose of this rule, saying that the content of a treaty has a TWO-SIDED NATURE is tantamount to saying that the treaty has two parties only, or – should there be more than two parties – that the treaty has been constructed in such a way, that one of the parties has rights and obligations toward each and every one of the others, and vice versa, but these other parties do not have corresponding rights and obligations toward each other.

§ **3**. For the purpose of this rule, PARTIES means any and all states for which the treaty is in force at the time of interpretation.

3 EXCEPTIONS SHALL BE NARROWLY INTERPRETED

That exceptions shall be narrowly interpreted is a proposition emphasised by several authors in the literature.[29] Taken on its own, the suggestion is far from unambiguous. If a treaty provision can be interpreted in two different ways, and the provision contains an *exception* whose extension in one of the two possible meanings is less than it is in the other, then the former meaning shall be adopted – this much is apparent.[30] Not so apparent, however, is the meaning of "exception".

The noun EXCEPTION requires an object – it makes no sense to say that a provision contains an exception, if it cannot also be said from *what* there is an exception. In this case, it seems that we have two alternatives. "Exception" either refers to a deviation from the rights and obligations held by the parties under the interpreted treaty, or to a deviation from the rights and obligations held by the parties under international law in general.[31] Professor Bernhardt endorses the former alternative:

> Das Gebot *der restriktiven Auslegung von Ausnahmevorschriften* scheint einen verhältnismäßig festen Platz in der völkerrechtlichen Auslegungslehre einzunehmen --- In diesem Zusammenhang ist eine Präzisierung erforderlich: Das Problem, ob vom allgemeinen Völkerrecht abweichende – allgemeine oder spezielle – Vertragsbestimmungen restriktiv, d.h. under weitestmöglicher Beachtung der gewohnheitsrechtlichen Regeln zu interpretieren sind, ist schon an anderer Stelle erörtet worden, es interessiert hier nicht. Zu behandeln ist nur noch die Frage, ob vertragliche Ausnahme- und Spezialbestimmungen, die eine Durchbrechung allgemeiner Vorschriften und Prinzipien derselben vetraglichen Vereinbarung enthalten – und diesen grundsätzlich als *lex specialis* vorgehen – im Zweifel einschränkend zu interpretieren sind.[32]

It must be admitted that of all authors who comment on the issue, no one expresses an opinion in such plain words as Bernhardt. However, in the final analysis it is my judgment that the opinion held by professor Bernhardt well agrees with current doctrine.[33]

All things considered, this allows for the following rule to be stated:

Rule no. 29

If it can be shown (i) that the interpretation of a treaty provision in accordance with interpretation rule no. 1 leads to conflicting results, (ii) that the provision contains an exception to a right or an obligation laid down in said treaty, and (iii) that the extension of the exception in one of the two possible ordinary meanings is comparably greater than it is in the other, then the latter meaning shall be adopted.

4 THE RULE OF NECESSARY IMPLICATION

Before we start to seriously examine the rule of necessary implication, a terminological issue needs to be settled. NECESSARY IMPLICATION, in the terminology I have adopted, means an act of interpretation based on the assumption that the parties to the interpreted treaty have expressed themselves through implication. In the literature, such an act of interpretation is denoted using two different terms. A first term, IMPLIED POWERS, is used when the content of the interpreted treaty provision is a norm that confers a power on an international organisation (or an organ of such an organisation).[34] (For example, state A may have made an agreement with state B to the effect that the international organisation O is permitted to act towards A in a certain manner M.) A second term, NECESSARY IMPLICATION, is used when the content of the interpreted provision is not a norm that confers a power on an international organisation, or when the subject onto whom the power is conferred is not an international organisation (nor an organ of such an organisation).[35] This language can be explained by the etymology of the two terms. IMPLIED POWERS has its origins in constitutional law,[36] while NECESSARY IMPLICATION appears to have been taken from the law of civil contract.[37] However, from a practical point of view, I see no real need for the distinction. In the final analysis it is quite clear that IMPLIED POWERS and NECESSARY IMPLICATION stand for one single idea, the only difference being that it is applied to treaties of different contents.[38] Therefore, since the rules of interpretation laid down in the Vienna Convention do not distinguish between treaties of different contents, and since the meaning of IMPLIED POWERS is less neutral than that of NECESSARY IMPLICATION, I have chosen to use only the latter term. Nevertheless, to avoid confusion I would like to expressly point out that the term NECESSARY IMPLICATION, in the sense of this work, has a meaning broader than that sometimes ascribed to it by other authors. In this work, NECESSARY IMPLICATION means an act of interpretation based on the assumption that the parties to the interpreted treaty have expressed themselves through implication, *regardless of what that treaty contains.*[39]

Authors seem to have no doubt that the rule of necessary implication is a norm that belongs to the realm of international law.[40] The doubts that do exist concern the content of the rule. According to the terminology of linguistics, when a person implies something, communication occurs without the help of conventional language.[41] This is also the meaning given to the word IMPLICATION when actors in international law refer to the rule of necessary implication.[42] Hence, the rule of necessary implication can be applied only under very specific conditions. Once the limits set by conventional language have been exceeded, no natural restrictions exist for the very far-reaching interpretations that may very well be the consequence. If we cannot exactly define the circumstances, under which a meaning may implicitly be read into a treaty, then there is a considerable risk that in the end the significance of conventional language for the interpretation process will be very small. The dividing line between the interpretation and modification of a treaty would once and for all be erased. (The fact that the rule of necessary implication is applicable only on the condition that the primary means of interpretation can be shown to result in a meaning which is manifestly absurd or unreasonable,[43] makes very little difference.) Hence, if we make it our task to establish the content of the rule of necessary implication, the decisive question to be answered seems to be the following: from the point of view of international law, under what conditions may parties to a treaty, with good reason, be assumed to have expressed themselves through implication? If it can be shown that some certain meaning may implicitly be read into a treaty provision, and that an implication is necessary, then this implied meaning shall be adopted – this much is clear. But what exactly do we mean by "necessary"? On this point the literature is of no avail.

One way of better handling the literature is to have the rule of necessary implication examined as the usage of a supplementary means of interpretation – in the same manner as we earlier examined "the preparatory work of the treaty" and "the circumstances of its conclusion". As observed in Chapter 8, when a treaty is interpreted using a supplementary means of interpretation, the task may be approached in two fundamentally different ways. "[S]upplementary means of interpretation" can be used independently of other means of interpretation, or they can be used relative to conventional language.[44] As previously established, if a person expresses herself through implication, this occurs without the help of conventional language. Hence, the contents of the rule of necessary implication should fit the following schematic description:

> If it can be shown that between an interpreted treaty provision and some certain means of interpretation M there is a relationship governed by the communicative standard S, then the provision shall be understood as if the relationship conformed to this standard.

Two questions must be answered before a conclusion can be drawn about the content of the rule of necessary implication:

(1) What means of interpretation are used for the application of the rule of necessary implication?

(2) What communicative standard or standards shall the parties to a treaty be assumed to have followed when appliers interpret the treaty in accordance with the rule of necessary implication?

The answer to the first question may easily be given. The means of interpretation used is "the object and purpose" of the interpreted treaty – this much is evident from the literature.[45] Consider Professor Gordon, for instance, who describes implied powers as a type of teleological interpretation.[46] For his treatment of the two phenomena implied powers and necessary implication, Professor Schwarzenberger uses as a heading the term FUNCTIONAL INTERPRETATION.[47] "[S]uch a construction", it is observed, ...

> ... pays little attention to the letter of a treaty, but concentrates on the effective realisation of its objects and purposes or, in other words, its spirit.[48]

The very same two phenomena are examined by Professor Amerasinghe under the heading "The object and purpose – teleology".[49] Maybe the proposition is even more clearly expressed by Professor Merrills; in his book, *The Development of International Law by the European Court of Human Rights*, he states the following about the Court's mode of interpreting the European Convention through implication:

> The contrast between the cases in which the Court has acceded to the argument that an unstated right should be implied and those in which it has not, demonstrates the extent to which the Court is prepared to use a broad conception of the object and purpose of the Convention as a guiding principle in its interpretation.[50]

Question (2) is a more difficult one. A fair guess is that the rule of necessary implication is less a matter of determining how the parties to the interpreted treaty have expressed themselves than a matter of determining how they have *not* expressed themselves. We need to remember that when appliers use the rule of necessary implication, the result will always be a meaning that exceeds the limits set by conventional language. The supplementary means of interpretation can be used to bring about such a result only in situations where the interpretation of a treaty according to VCLT article 31 can be shown to lead to a meaning which is manifestly absurd or unreasonable.[51] Professor Skubiszewski seems to share to this line of thought (even though I think he goes too far when he asserts that in most cases, an implication will not lead to an interpretation that agrees with the intentions of the parties):

> The process of implication should not be identified with the discovery of the intention of the parties. The link of necessity unites the purpose, the function or the power already granted to the power which is now implied. Quite often, what results from necessity was not and could not have been foreseen and, therefore, cannot be regarded as intended by the parties. Hence establishing a nexus between intention and implication would in most instances amount to a useless fiction. Intention referred to in the context of implication will in most cases indicate

a purpose or a task that Member States wish to be fulfilled. The International Court of Justice appears to have used this term in that specific meaning when it said that the United Nations "could not carry out the intentions of its founders if it was devoid of international personality".

When the Court speaks of "necessity", it appears that it thinks that a contrary solution, i.e., the rejection of what is implied, cannot be imputed to the Members of the organization. They cannot be supposed to object to it. But that is something else than reading into the text the intention of the parties.[52]

Taken on their own merit, however, these considerations can hardly be considered sufficient.

One way for us to answering question (2) is to return to our earlier observation regarding the use of a treaty's "object and purpose" and the principle of effectiveness. According to what is commonly expressed in the literature, a close relationship exists between the rule of necessary implication and the principle of effectiveness.[53] More specifically, it seems as if the rule of necessary implication would be an application of the principle of effectiveness.[54] This appears particularly in the Third Report on the Law of Treaties, which Waldock submitted to the International Law Commission in 1964. As we recall from Chapter 7, Waldock suggested that the principle of effectiveness be expressly included among a series of so-called "general rules" of interpretation.[55] According to Waldock, two reasons would justify such an approach.

The first is that the principle has a special significance as the basis upon which it is justifiable to imply terms in a treaty for the purpose of giving efficacy to an intention necessarily to be inferred from the express provisions of the treaty. The second is that in this sphere – the sphere of implied terms – there is a particular need to indicate the proper limits of the application of the principle if too wide a door is not to be opened to purely teleological interpretations.[56]

As observed in Chapter 7, the following three communicative standards form the basis for an application of the principle of effectiveness:

- If a state produces an utterance taking the form of a treaty provision, then the provision should be drawn up so that in the context there will be no instance of a pleonasm.
- If a state produces an utterance taking the form of a treaty provision, then the provision should be drawn up so that by applying the provision a result is not obtained, which is not among the *teloi* conferred on the treaty.
- If a state produces an utterance taking the form of a treaty provision, then the provision should be drawn up so that by applying the provision no other part of the treaty will be normatively useless.[57]

The first standard on the list may be identified with an act of interpretation using the context; here it can be ignored. Only the second and third standard can be said to involve a use of "the object and purpose". Given that the rule of necessary implication is an application of the principle of effectiveness, and that the means of interpretation assumed is the object and purpose of the treaty, then either of these two standards would form the basis for an application of the rule of necessary implication. It matters little that these same standards have already been said to form a basis for a use of the object and purpose, according to the provisions of Vienna Convention article 31. The effect we achieve by applying the rule of necessary implication is not identical to the one achieved by using the object and purpose according to the provisions of VCLT article 31. According to the provisions of VCLT article 31, the object and purpose shall be used relative to conventional language.[58] Such an interpretation inevitably leads to a result that can be reconciled with conventional language. This is not the case with the result that ensues from an application of the rule of necessary implication.

All things considered, if we wish to put to words the rule of necessary implication, it seems it could be stated as follows:

Rule no. 30

§ 1. If it can be shown that according to linguistics a meaning can be read into a treaty provision by implication, and that such an implication is necessary to avoid a situation where, by applying the provision a result is attained which is not among the *teloi* conferred on the treaty, then this meaning shall be adopted.

§ 2. For the purpose of this rule, TELOI means the state or states of affairs, which according to the parties should be attained by applying the interpreted provision.

§ 3. For the purpose of this rule, the TELOI of a treaty are determined based upon the intentions held by the parties at the time of the treaty's conclusion, except for those cases where § 4 applies.

§ 4. For the purpose of this rule, the TELOI of a treaty are determined based upon the intentions held by the parties at the time of interpretation, granted it can be shown that the thing interpreted is a generic referring expression with a referent assumed by the parties to be alterable.

§ 5. For the purpose of this rule, PARTIES means any and all states for which the treaty is in force at the time of interpretation.

Rule no. 31

If it can be shown that according to linguistics a meaning can be implicitly read into a treaty provision, and that such an implication is necessary to avoid a situation where, by applying the provision, another part of the treaty will be normatively useless, then this meaning shall be adopted.

It is my judgment that with these two rules, I have given an account of what I earlier termed as "the general view held in the literature". Of course – as is almost always the case – some authors are inclined to disagree; they have other opinions about the content and meaning of the rule of necessary implication. Among these opinions, two in particular are worthy of mention.

The first concerns the qualifier *necessary*. According to conventional language, NECESSARY can be used both in the stronger sense of *indispensable; absolutely imperative*, and in the weaker sense of *essential* or *vital*. According to Professors Skubiszewski and Elihu Lauterpacht, when we speak of "the rule of necessary implication" NECESSARY is used in the latter, weaker sense of the word.[59] This is a view that seems to be based on a misconception of the thing, *for which* an implication is supposed to be necessary. In the rule of necessary implication, an implication is necessary in order to avoid a result, which is not among the *teloi* of the treaty.[60] In order for the rule to be applicable, we must be able to show, first, that the interpreted treaty provision can be understood not only in a way that can be reconciled with conventional language, but also in a way that completely ignores the rules of conventional language; and secondly, that the rules of conventional language need to be set aside, lest an application of the treaty is to result in a state of affairs, which is not among the treaty's *teloi*. Given this fact, it cannot possibly be in the weaker sense of *essential* that we speak about a rule of NECESSARY implication. When we apply the rule of necessary implication, we have no more than two alternatives. We choose between understanding a treaty in a way that can be reconciled with conventional language, and understanding it with complete disregard for that language (through implication, that is). If it is established that only through the latter interpretation will an application of the treaty lead to a state of affairs, which is among the treaty's *teloi*, then naturally – given the alternative – an implication is imperative for ensuring that an application of the treaty does not result in something, which is not the treaty's *teloi*.

What professors Lauterpacht and Skubiszewski seem to believe is that when an implication is categorised as necessary, it is for the simple reason that is necessary for attaining a treaty's *teloi*. For if this is assumed, the rule of NECESSARY implicationcannot possibly be read in the stronger sense of *indispensable*. Showing that an implication is indispensable for ensuring that the application of a treaty provision does not result in a state of affairs which is not among the treaty's *teloi* is tantamount to showing that the *teloi* of the treaty cannot be attained as long as we abide by the rules of conventional language. Obviously, this can be done only on the condition that a description is given of the instrumental relationship that holds between the *teloi* of the treaty and the specific application at hand. Such a description is not easily achieved. We have to remember that when a treaty provision is applied, this specific application does not operate in a vacuum. If the *teloi* of the treaty are attained, this is often the combined effect of many factors, including not only the possible further application of the interpreted provision, but also other parts of the treaty, public international law in general, and if nothing else the world at large. It goes without saying that the condition set forth cannot possibly be fulfilled.

A second opinion I would like to address concerns the meaning of the term IMPLICATION. In THE RULE OF NECESSARY IMPLICATION, an implication is necessary if (and only if) it can be considered indispensable either to ensure that the application of the interpreted treaty provision does not result in a state of affairs which is not among the *teloi* of the treaty, or to prevent another part of the treaty from becoming normatively useless The basis for making the implication is always an assumption about the interpreted treaty's *teloi* or norm content. Some authors, including Professors Haraszti and Elihu Lauterpacht, use a considerably more limited basis. According to them, in order for a *telos* of a treaty to be used as a basis for implication it must be *explicit*; the same is said about the treaty's norm content.[61] For two reasons this assumption does not carry great weight.

First, the assumption does not agree with what linguistics is telling us about implication in general. One of the premises that a reader uses to determine the meaning of a text – whether this is done by implication or not – is a contextual assumption, that is to say, an assumption derived from a context.[62] A context is an aggregate of assumptions about the world at large, to which a reader has access when she is confronted with a text that she wishes to understand.[63] According to linguistics, contextual assumptions – for instance, the assumptions made by a reader about a treaty's *teloi* or norm content – are in no way limited to those that can be accessed through decoding of the interpreted treaty text or by inferring messages communicated explicitly.[64]

Secondly, the assumptions expressed by Haraszti and Lauterpacht are contrary to how we are supposed to otherwise address the determination of a treaty's "object and purpose". The fact is that in international law, there are no rules to which an applier in doubt can defer to establish the *teloi* of a treaty.[65] In the Vienna Convention articles 31–33, the applier is instructed how to proceed when uncertain about the *norm content* of a treaty provision. However, there is nothing in these articles to suggest that the contents of a treaty provision can only be determined by inferences about what the parties to said treaty may have communicated *explicitly*; quite the opposite. According to what we have already established, by applying the provisions of VCLT article 32 we are allowed to determine the norm content of a treaty through implication, if only under very specific conditions.[66] All things considered, I find it difficult to see how the views of Haraszti and Lauterpacht could be considered anything but groundless.

5 INTERPRETATION *PER ANALOGIAM*

First of all, it is necessary that we establish some sort of definition. As we know, ANALOGY means *partial resemblance*. Two phenomena are said to be ANALOGOUS to one another, if in some significant respect they can be thought of as similar or comparable, although all things considered they are still different. In general, interpretation *per analogiam* occurs where appliers draw a conclusion about the meaning of a treaty provision based on the observation that an analogy holds between two distinct phenomena.[67] The first of these phenomena is the specific case or state of affairs, in regard to which the meaning of the interpreted treaty provision is to be determined. This state-of-affairs is one, which we *cannot* clearly say whether or not it shall be considered as coming within the scope of application of the treaty provision in question. The second phenomenon is yet another case, be it hypothetical or factual. This is a state-of-affairs, which we *can* clearly say that it shall be considered as coming within the scope of application of either the interpreted treaty provision,[68] or of some other provision *in pari materia*.[69] In the former case we may say that the analogy is *internal*, in the latter that it is *external*.[70] Interpretation *per analogiam*, to the extent that it can be considered a mode of reasoning based on the assumption about the existence of external analogy, will not be examined in this section. Such an act of interpretation can be performed already on the basis of either interpretation rule no. 25 – corresponding to a use of the context – or on the basis of rule no. 23 – corresponding to a use of a treaty *in pari materia*. Consequently, in this work, interpretation *per analogiam* will refer only to the mode of reasoning based on the assumption about the existence of internal analogy.

Authors seem generally positive to the idea of interpreting treaties *per analogiam*.[71] In my judgment, this is sufficient basis to say that an interpretation *per analogiam* is one supported by international law. Admittedly, in the earlier literature, several authors express the opinion that an interpretation *per analogiam* does not have the support of international law.[72] The reasons they cite are two. First, some authors maintain that from a purely semantic standpoint, legal interpretation and legal argumentation *per analogiam* are two different things. According to conventional language – this is what they allege – there is no place for a legal argument *per analogiam* until all avenues provided in VCLT articles 31–33 have been tried.[73] Second, interpretation *per analogiam* is said to be "constructive" – an act of interpretation *per analogiam* will more likely lead to a modification of a treaty than to a mere determination of its norm content.[74]

If we examine these two assertions from a critical stance we must surely consider the former as groundless. There are simply too many users of language talking about interpretation *per analogiam* for one to say that from a purely semantic standpoint, legal interpretation and legal argumentation *per analogiam* are two different things. The second assertion is the weightier one. Clearly, when an act of interpretation *per analogiam* is performed there is a risk that it will lead to an expansion of the interpreted treaty's norm content. Still, the assertion is too categorical. Considering the way the Vienna Convention has been designed, the risk that an act of interpretation *per analogiam* will lead to a modification of the interpreted treaty should not be greater than the risk that lies in applying any other rule of interpretation. As we must remember, supplementary means of interpretation are only used to determine the meaning of an interpreted treaty provision when the rules laid down in VCLT article 31 lead to a meaning which is either ambiguous or obscure, or manifestly absurd or unreasonable. All things considered, I see no reason to be overly concerned about the scepticism expressed in the earlier literature regarding the legal status of interpretation *per analogiam.*

As we established earlier, when a treaty is interpreted using "supplementary means of interpretation", it can be done in two fundamentally different ways. "[S]upplementary means of interpretation" can be used independently of other means of interpretation, or they can be used relative to conventional language.[75] Some means of interpretation can only be used independently of other means of interpretation; such is the case with the object and purpose of the treaty when used in connection with an application of the rule of necessary implication.[76] Others can only be used relative to conventional language; such is the case with the principle of state sovereignty when used in connection with an application of the rule of restrictive interpretation.[77] Still others can be used both independently and relative to conventional language, for instance the preparatory work of the treaty.[78] It is not entirely clear to which group interpretation *per analogiam* belongs. According to some authors, an interpretation *per analogiam* can sometimes be performed on the basis of a previous use of conventional language; sometimes it can occur *ab initio* – needing no basis at all.[79] According to other authors, it seems interpretation *per analogiam* can only occur *ab initio.*[80]

My judgment is that we should take a liberal stance, adopting the view of the former group of authors. As support for this position I would like to advance an interpretation *per argumentum a fortiori*. When a supplementary means of interpretation is used relative to conventional language, the interpretation result is always a meaning permitted by the rules of conventional language.[81] When a supplementary means of interpretation is used *ab initio*, the result *may* be a meaning permitted by conventional language; but it may also be a meaning not permitted by that language.[82] Thus, from the point of view of the parties, an interpretation *per analogiam* should be considered less tolerable when it occurs on the basis of a previous use of conventional language, than when it occurs *ab initio*. One of the rules that can be invoked to justify an act of interpretation *per argumentum a fortiori* is the following:

> If it can be shown that a treaty provision permits an act or a state-of-affairs, which – from the point of view of the parties – can be considered less tolerable than another generically identical act or state-of-affairs, then the provision shall be understood to permit this second act or state-of-affairs, too.[83]

Given that an act of interpretation *per analogiam* can be considered permitted by international law when performed independently of conventional language, an act of that kind would also seem to be permitted when performed relative to conventional language.

Consequently, all things considered, it appears that interpretation of treaties *per analogiam* can be described by the following two rules of interpretation:

Rule no. 32
§ 1. If it can be shown (i) that the interpretation of a treaty provision in accordance with interpretation rule no. 1 leads to conflicting results, (ii) that two states-of-affairs are analogous to one another, (iii) that the one state-of-affairs is governed by the interpreted treaty provision, and (iv) that in one of the two possible ordinary meanings the other state-of-affairs comes within the scope of application of the provision, whereas in the other meaning it does not, then the former meaning shall be adopted.
§ 2. For the purpose of this rule, saying that two states-of-affairs are ANALOGOUS to one another is tantamount to saying that in some significant respect they can be thought of as similar or comparable.

Rule no. 33
§ 1. If it can be shown that of two states-of-affairs, which are analogous to one another, the one comes within the scope of application of an interpreted treaty provision, then the provision shall be understood in such a way that the other comes within that scope of application, too.

§ 2. For the purpose of this rule, saying that two states-of-affairs are ANALOGOUS to one another is tantamount to saying that in some significant respect they can be thought of as similar or comparable.

6 INTERPRETATION *PER ARGUMENTUM A FORTIORI*

It is a view generally held in the literature that treaties shall be interpreted *per argumentum a fortiori*.[84] In my judgment, this is sufficient basis to say that such acts of interpretation have the support of international law. Interpretation *per argumentum a fortiori* may be divided into two types of arguments. The first pertains to the interpretation of such treaty provisions where an action or a state-of-affairs is governed in negative terms,[85] the provision expressing a prohibition.[86] Arguments of this kind are often stated by the Latin phrase *a minori ad majus*: if a treaty provision prohibits an action or a state-of-affairs that is more tolerable than another, then the provision shall be understood to forbid this second action or state-of-affairs, too. The second type of argument pertains to the interpretation of such treaty provisions where an action or a state-of-affairs is governed in positive terms,[87] the provision expressing permission.[88] Arguments of this kind are often stated by the Latin phrase *a majori ad minus*: if a treaty provision allows an action or a state-of-affairs that is less tolerable than another, then the provision shall be understood to permit this second action or state-of-affairs, too.

Four remarks need to be made with regard to the interpretation of treaties *per argumentum a fortiori*. A first remark concerns the word *tolerable*. In order to say whether an action or a state-of-affairs is more or less tolerable than another, one must be able to state the viewpoint from which the tolerability of the different actions or states-of-affairs shall be judged. One must be able to say for whom the actions or states-of-affairs are more or less tolerable. To my mind, it is obvious that this viewpoint is that of the parties to the interpreted treaty.

A second remark concerns *the object of the tolerability assessment* – the different actions or states-of-affairs. In order to say whether an action or a state-of-affairs is more or less tolerable than another, we must be able to compare the different actions or states-of-affairs in some way. Some kind of class commonality – a generic kinship – must be established.[89]

A third remark concerns the *tolerability assessment as such*. In order to say whether an action or a state-of-affairs is more or less tolerable than another, we often need to make a value judgment.[90] Assume, for instance, that Norway has promised not to contest the territorial sovereignty possessed by Denmark with regard to all of Greenland. Obviously more than a simple logical deduction is required to allow the conclusion that Norway, by this same promise, has committed itself not to occupy Eastern Greenland.[91] Any statement to the effect that Norway's occupation of Eastern Greenland is a less tolerable action than that of Norway contesting the territorial sovereignty possessed by Denmark with regard all of Greenland, requires a value judgment.[92] This judgment is not free of limitation. One must not accept as correct each and every claim that a person makes regarding the relative tolerability of two actions or states-of-affairs. Whoever claims that a certain action or state-of-affairs is less tolerable than another, this is not sufficient to consider the claim justified, if that person cannot show that the claim is supported by good reasons.

A fourth remark addresses the relationship between the interpretation of treaties *per argumentum a fortiori* and the use of conventional language. As we have observed numerous times, when appliers use the supplementary means of interpretation, the task may be approached in two fundamentally different ways. "[S]upplementary means of interpretation" can be used independently of other means of interpretation, and they can be used relative to conventional language. The literature is not entirely clear as to whether an act of interpretation *per argumentum a fortiori* can only be performed *ab initio* – independently of conventional language – or if it can also be performed based on a previous use of conventional language. Still, it is apparent that several authors consider the interpretation of treaties *per argumentum a fortiori* to be a form of argumentation closely related to the interpretation of treaties *per analogiam.*[93] Given that an act of interpretation *per analogiam* can be performed both *ab initio* and on the basis of a previous use of conventional language, I am inclined to think it unlikely that interpretation *per argumentum a fortiori* should not be approached in a similar manner.

All things considered, it appears that the interpretation of treaties *per argumentum a fortiori* can be described by the following four rules of interpretation:

Rule no. 34

§ **1**. If it can be shown that a treaty provision permits an act or a state-of-affairs, which – from the point of view of the parties – can be considered less tolerable than another generically identical act or state-of-affairs, then the provision shall be understood to permit this second act or state-of-affairs, too.

§ **2**. For the purpose of this rule, PARTIES means any and all states for which the treaty is in force at the time of interpretation.

Rule no. 35

§ 1. If it can be shown (i) that the interpretation of a treaty provision in accordance with interpretation rule no. 1 leads to conflicting results, (ii) that the provision permits an action or a state-of-affairs, which – from the point of view of the parties – can be considered less tolerable than another generically identical action or state-of-affairs, and (iii) that in one of the two possible ordinary meanings, this other action or state-of-affairs comes within the scope of application of the interpreted provision, whereas in the other meaning it does not, then the former meaning shall be adopted.

§ 2. For the purpose of this rule, PARTIES means any and all states for which the treaty is in force at the time of interpretation.

Rule no. 36

§ 1. If it can be shown that a treaty provision prohibits an act or a state-of-affairs, which – from the point of view of the parties – can be considered more tolerable than another generically identical act or state-of-affairs, then the provision shall be understood to prohibit this second act or state-of-affairs, too.

§ 2. For the purpose of this rule, PARTIES means any and all states for which the treaty is in force at the time of interpretation.

Rule no. 37

§ 1. If it can be shown (i) that the interpretation of a treaty provision in accordance with interpretation rule no. 1 leads to conflicting results, (ii) that the provision prohibits an action or a state-of-affairs, which – from the point of view of the parties – can be considered more tolerable than another generically identical action or state-of-affairs, and (iii) that in one of the two possible ordinary meanings, this other action or state-of-affairs comes within the scope of application of the interpreted provision, whereas in the other meaning it does not, then the former meaning shall be adopted.

§ 2. For the purpose of this rule, PARTIES means any and all states for which the treaty is in force at the time of interpretation.

7 INTERPRETATION *PER ARGUMENTUM E CONTRARIO*

Interpretation of treaties *per argumentum e contrario* – sometimes also referred to using the Latin maxim *expressio unius est exclusio alterius* – is a form of argumentation that receives extensive support in the literature.[94] Clearly, an act of interpretation *per argumentum e contrario* conforms to the standards of international law. Less clear is what such an act interpretation should be seen to imply. Some guidance is provided by the Latin expression *expressio unius est exclusio alterius*: to explicitly make mention of one is to exclude another.[95] EXPLICITLY MAKING MENTION OF a referent is tantamount to *referring to that referent using conventional language*. But what should be understood by the two expressions "one" and "another"? The word ANOTHER requires an object. In the expression "to explicitly make mention of one is to exclude another", it seems logical that this object would be the same as that of "one". In all reason, the expression "another" should be read to mean *another of the same type as "one thing"*. Hence: if, according to conventional language, an expression is used to refer to a referent of a particular type (such as a group of people, objects, or states-of-affairs), then this expression shall not be seen to refer to any additional referent of that same type (assuming that such additional referents do exist). Considered on its own, this analysis is of course meagre support for any satisfying conclusions. Therefore, let us see if further confirmation can be found in the practice of international courts and tribunals.

As examples of the interpretation of treaties *per argumentum e contrario*, two decisions are mentioned most often in the literature. One is the judgment of the Permanent Court of International Justice in the case of *The S.S. Wimbledon*.[96] McNair neatly summarises the decision in the following manner:

In the *Wimbledon* case Germany claimed the right to close the Kiel Canal against a British ship, chartered to a French company and carrying a cargo of munitions for Poland then at war with Russia, in spite of Article 380 of the Treaty of Versailles of 1919, which provided that

"The Kiel Canal and its approaches shall be maintained free and open to the vessels of commerce and of war of all nations at peace with Germany on terms of entire equality."

The second paragraph of Article 381 contained the following provision

"No impediment shall be placed on the movement of persons or vessels other than those arising out of police, customs, sanitary, emigration or immigration regulations and those relating to the import or export of prohibited goods. ..."

Germany argued for a restrictive interpretation of the Treaty. M. Basdevant, in presenting the French argument, said (translation):

"In Article 381, therefore, there are no provisions which could be held to justify the measures taken in regard to the ss. 'Wimbledon'. The provisions of this Article are restrictive; they refer to 'no impediment other than'.... It is therefore impossible to add any other impediments to those therein expressly mentioned."

The Permanent Court accepted and applied these arguments; it said

"The right of the [German] Empire to defend herself against her enemies by refusing to allow their vessels to pass though the canal is therefore proclaimed and recognized. In making this reservation in the event of Germany not being at peace with the nation whose vessels of war or of commerce claim access to the canal, the Peace Treaty clearly contemplated the possibility of a future war in which Germany was involved. If the conditions of access to the canal were also to be modified in the event of a conflict between two Powers remaining at peace with the German Empire, the Treaty would not have failed to say so. It has not said so and this omission was no doubt intentional."

Again, the Court said

"The idea [*la pensée*] which underlies Article 380 and the following articles of the Treaty is not to be sought by drawing an analogy from these provisions but rather by arguing *a contrario*, a method of argument which excludes them."[97]

The other decision often mentioned is the advisory opinion of the PCIJ in *Railway Traffic between Lithuania and Poland.*[98] In 1931, the League of Nations had brought a request to the PCIJ:

Do the international engagements in force oblige Lithuania in the present circumstances, and if so in what manner, to take the necessary measures to open for traffic or for certain categories of traffic the Landwarów-Kaisiadorys railway sector?[99]

In meeting the request of the League, the Court came to occupy itself with (among many other agreements) the so-called Memel Convention, concluded between the British Empire, France, Italy and Japan on the one side, and Lithuania on the other. Article 3 of the Memel Convention's third annex contains the following provision:

[T]he Lithuanian Government shall ensure the freedom of transit by sea, by water *or by rail*, of traffic coming from or destined for the Memel territory or in transit through the said territory, and shall conform in this respect with the rules laid down by the Statute and Convention on the Freedom of Transit adopted by the Barcelona Conference [...].[100]

The Barcelona Statute expresses for Lithuania the following obligation:

... [to] facilitate free transit, by rail or waterway, on routes *in use convenient for international transit.*[101]

The Court considered it clear that the railway sector Landwarów-Kaisiadorys could not be considered "in use", in the sense of the Barcelona Statute. Nevertheless, the Court obviously found this simple observation to be in need of reinforcement:

Furthermore, it must be remembered that, under the last paragraph of Article 3 of Annex III to the Memel Convention, to which reference has been made above, the Lithuanian Government undertakes "to permit and to grant all facilities for the traffic *on the river* to or from or in the port of Memel, and not to apply, in respect of such traffic, on the ground of the present political relations between Lithuania and Poland, the stipulations of Articles 7 and 8 of the Barcelona Statute on the Freedom of Transit and Article 13 of the Barcelona Recommendations relative to Ports placed under an International Régime".

These are obviously circumstances calculated to promote freedom of transit *via* the port of Memel, for the provisions which Lithuania abandons her right to apply are designed to place certain restrictions on this freedom. But it is to be observed that this clause in the Memel Convention applies solely to waterways and not to railways.

Seeing that the Memel Convention expressly forbids Lithuania to invoke Article 7 of the Barcelona Statute, with reference to freedom of transit by waterway, it is clear, on the other hand, that she might avail herself of it with regard to railways of importance to the Memel territory. And accordingly, even if the Landwarów-Kaisiadorys railway sector were in use and could serve Memel traffic, Lithuania would be entitled to invoke Article 7, as a ground for refusing to open this sector for traffic or for certain categories of traffic, in case of an emergency affecting *her safety* or *vital interests*.[102]

These two excerpts comfortably help us to a better understanding of the interpretation *per argumentum e contrario*. In summary, I would like to propose a rule saying something along the following lines:

Rule no. 38
If it can be shown that in a treaty provision there is an expression, which according to conventional language is used to refer to a smaller part of a larger, generically defined class, then the provision shall be understood in such a way that the extension of the expression comprises this smaller part only, and not any other part of the class.

"The provisions of this Article", observes the applicant in the *Wimbledon* case, regarding the interpretation of article 381 of the Treaty of Versailles, ...

... refer to 'no impediment other than'. It is therefore impossible to add any other impediments to those therein expressly mentioned.[103]

"[I]mpediment[s] placed on the movement of persons or vessels ... arising out of police, customs, sanitary, emigration or immigration regulations and those relating to the import or export of prohibited goods" is an expression which, according to conventional language, is used to refer to a smaller part of a larger, generically defined class, namely *impediments placed on the movement of persons and vessels. Impediment placed on the movement of S.S. Wimbledon* is another part of this larger class. Similar arguments are presented in the *Railway Traffic between Lithuania and Poland* case.

Seeing that the Memel Convention expressly forbids Lithuania to invoke Article 7 of the Barcelona Statute, with reference to freedom of transit by waterway, it is clear, on the other hand, that she might avail herself of it with regard to railways of importance to the Memel territory.[104]

"Traffic on the river to or from or in the port of Memel" is an expression, which according to conventional language is used to refer to a smaller part of a larger, generically defined class, namely *traffic to or from or in the port of Memel. Railway to the Memel territory* is another part of this larger class. Therefore, in both *Wimbledon* and *Railway Traffic between Lithuania and Poland*, the cited interpretation arguments could be described as an application of treaty interpretation rule no. 38. It seems the content of this rule has been correctly described.[105]

Not all authors seem prepared to support this conclusion: that an act of interpretation *per argumentum e contrario* should be described as the application of a rule of interpretation, independent of those other rules of interpretation laid down in international law. The implication is that an act of interpretation *per argumentum e contrario* could be considered a use of conventional language, already supported by the provisions of Vienna Convention article 31.[106] The assumption is that an act of interpretation *per argumentum e contrario* has nothing to contribute besides that which is already the result of an act of interpretation using conventional language. This assumption is clearly incorrect. It is true that an act of interpretation per *argumentum e contrario* must always lead to the exact same interpretation result as earlier achieved by appliers using conventional language. If it can be shown that in a treaty provision, there is an expression, which according to conventional language is used to refer to a smaller part of a larger, generically defined class, then – when using conventional language – the provision shall be understood in such a way that the extension of the expression comprises this smaller part only, and not any other part of the class. However, it is not true that in a process of interpretation, an act of interpretation *per argumentum e contrario* plays a role identical to that already played by conventional language. An act of interpretation *per argumentum e contrario* has a role that conventional language cannot possibly play: it can be employed to confirm the use of conventional language. Indeed, conventional language cannot be used to confirm its own use. This seems to be ignored by certain authors.

8 THE PRINCIPLE OF *EJUSDEM GENERIS*

According to many authors in the literature, a treaty shall be interpreted through application of the principle of *ejusdem generis*.[107] In my judgment, this is sufficient reason for us to conclude that the principle is a valid rule of international law. However, the question is still what the principle stands for –in the literature, authors seem to think this obvious. The only real explanation offered by the literature is the following:

> The *ejusdem generis* doctrine is to the effect that general words when following (or sometimes preceding) special words are limited to the *genus*, if any, indicated by the special words.[108]

The purposes and goals of this work demand better explanations. If we wish to reach the level of understanding where the principle of *ejusdem generis* can be described in terms of a proper rule of interpretation, we must clarify the views expressed in the literature. We can do so by drawing on the judicial opinions expressed by courts and tribunals. Three cases in particular could then be examined.[109]

A first case is the advisory opinion delivered by the PCIJ in *Competence of the ILO for Agriculture.*[110] In 1922, the League of Nations had turned to the PCIJ, requesting that the court issue an advisory opinion to clarify certain issues about the competence of the International Labour Organization (ILO). The ILO's competence had been established by the member states of the League in the preamble of the ILO Statute (*Treaty of Versailles*, Part XIII). The preamble reads as follows:

Whereas universal and lasting peace can be established only if it is based upon social justice;
And whereas conditions of labour exist involving such injustice, hardship and privation to large numbers of people as to produce unrest so great that peace and harmony of the world are imperilled; and an improvement of those conditions is urgently required; as, for example, by the regulation of the hours of work, including the establishment of a maximum working day and week, the regulation of the labour supply, the prevention of unemployment, the provision of an adequate living wage, the protection of the worker against sickness, disease and injury arising out of his employment, the protection of children, young persons and women, provision for old age and injury, protection of the interests of workers when employed in countries other than their own, recognition of the principle of equal remuneration for equal value, recognition of the principle of freedom of association, the organisation of vocational and technical education and other *measures*;
Whereas also the failure of any nation to adopt humane conditions of labour is an obstacle in the way of other nations which desire to improve the conditions in their own countries;
The High Contracting Parties, moved by sentiments of justice and humanity as well as by the desire to secure the permanent peace on the world, and with a view to attaining the objectives set forth in this Preamble, agree to the following Constitution of the International Labour Organisation [...].[111]

The Court's response to the League of Nations request is divided into two separate decisions. Both decisions contain abundant information, with several important points. Particularly interesting in this context is the Court's observation with regard to the meaning of the expression "measures", used in the preamble cited above. In its first decision, the Court had commented upon the contents of paragraph 2 in the following manner:

The comprehensive character of Part XIII is clearly shown in the Preamble, which declares that "conditions of labour", (*"conditions de travail")*, exist "involving such injustice, hardship and privation to large numbers of persons [sic!] as to produce unrest so great that the peace and harmony of the world are imperilled". An improvement of these conditions the Preamble declares to be urgently required in various particulars, the examples given being (1) "the regulation of the hours of work, including the establishment of a maximum working day and week"; (2) "the regulation of the labour supply"; [...].[112]

In its second decision, the Court found that there were things to be added to this commentary:

In the opinion this day rendered on the question of competence as regards the regulation of the conditions of agricultural labour, the Court has given a full and detailed exposition of the powers of the International Labour Organisation under Part XIII of the Treaty of Versailles;

and it is unnecessary to repeat what was there so amply set forth. The object for which the International Labour Organisation was founded was the amelioration of the lot of the workers and the adoption of humane conditions in matters such as the hours of labour, the labour supply, prevention of unemployment, an adequate living wage, protection against sickness, disease and injury arising out of employment, the protection of children, young persons and women, provision for old age and injury, the protection of workmen employed in countries other than their own, freedom of association, vocational and technical education, and, as the Treaty says, "other measures", which must mean measures to improve the conditions of labour and to do away with injustice, hardship and privation.[113]

A second case to be examined in this context is the decision of the Iran-United States Claims Tribunal in *Grimm v. Iran.*[114] In 1982, the plaintiff, Mrs. Grimm – an American citizen – had turned to the *Iran-United States Claims Tribunal* claiming she had a right to compensation for damages. According to the claim, Mrs. Grimm had suffered damages because of the murder of her husband, Mr. Grimm – an American citizen active in the management of a multinational, Iran-based oil company – at the time the Islamic regime took power in 1978. Mrs. Grimm demanded both compensation for her financial loss owing to the death of her husband, and compensation for the mental anguish she had suffered. As a basis for her claim, the plaintiff argued that the Islamic government had neglected to (sufficiently) protect her husband; in so doing, the government had failed to live up to international standards of due diligence. To the plaintiff, it was not to be doubted that the tribunal had the jurisdiction needed for trying the case. Mrs. Grimm was an American citizen; her claim could be seen to relate to "measures affecting property rights", as required by article II, paragraph 1 of *the Claims Settlement Declaration*:[115]

An international arbitral tribunal (the Iran-United States Claims Tribunal) is hereby established for the purpose of deciding claims of nationals of the United States against Iran and claims of nationals of Iran against the United States, and any counterclaim which arises out of the same contract, transaction or occurrence that constitutes the subject matter of that national's claim, if such claims and counterclaims ... arise out of debts, contracts (including transactions which are the subject of letters of credit or bank guarantees), expropriations or other *measures affecting property rights* [...].[116]

The tribunal itself came to the conclusion that it *did not* have the necessary jurisdiction for trying the claim of Mrs. Grimm. In the opinion of the tribunal, there were two arguments of interpretation in particular that should be seen to contradict the suggestions made by the plaintiff with regard to the meaning of the above quoted paragraph 1. The first argument can be described as a use of conventional language:

It would perhaps be possible to accept that the words "other measures" may cover both acts and failures to act and that for Mrs. Grimm "property rights" have arisen or are involved in this case. However, to hold in the context of Article II, paragraph 1, that such "property rights" were affected by the alleged failure to protect Mr. Grimm is far from the natural understanding of the circumstances that this failure just affected the life and safety of Mr. Grimm. Furthermore, compensation for mental anguish, grief and suffering can obviously not be a property right that was affected by the alleged failure to provide adequate protection for Mr. Grimm. The right to such compensation, if any, arose out of the assassination; it did not even exist prior to the assassination and could not be affected by the failure to provide protection.[117]

The second argument is an application of the *ejusdem generis* principle:

[U]nder the well-known principle of *ejusdem generis* the words "other measures" in Article II, paragraph 1, ought to be, especially in the context of "debts and contracts", construed as generically similar to "expropriations" and the alleged failure to provide protection is in no way similar to expropriations.[118]

My third case derives from a Canadian court, *the Alberta Court of Queens Bench*; it is the *Alberta Provincial Employees* case.[119] In 1977, the parliament of the Canadian province of Alberta had passed a law, according to which a large majority of public sector employees were forbidden to strike. The state workers' labour organisation protested, arguing that that the law was in conflict with the obligations incumbent upon Canada according to several international agreements, one such agreement being the *1966 International Covenant on Economic, Social and Cultural Rights*; therefore, the law should be considered invalid. The right to strike is plainly stated in article 8 § 1(d) of the 1966 Covenant. This right is relative in the sense that according to article 8 § 2, the parties retain the right to take certain kinds of restrictive actions. Paragraph 2 reads:

This article shall not prevent the imposition of lawful restrictions on the exercise of these rights by members of the armed forces or of the police or of *the administration of the State*.[120]

Chief Justice Sinclair makes the following remark about the meaning of this treaty provision:

Counsel for the union argues that the words "administration of the State" ought to be equated to the armed forces or to the police under a rule of documentary construction known as *ejusdem generis*. With respect, I cannot accept this suggestion because I believe the three functions to be essentially distinct.[121]

These three excerpts from international case law help us to better understand the meaning of the *ejusdem generis* principle. Let us begin with the first quoted excerpt. In its first advisory opinion in the *Competence of the ILO for Agriculture* case, the PCIJ cites from the Statute of the International Labour Organization:

[T]he Preamble ... declares that "conditions of labour", (*"conditions de travail")*, exist "involving such injustice, hardship and privation to large numbers of persons [sic!] as to produce unrest so great that peace and harmony of the world are imperilled".[122]

The examples provided in the preamble, observes the Court, are particular aspects in which an improvement of "conditions of labour" are seen to be "urgently required". In its second opinion, the Court makes the following statement with regard to the meaning of the expression "measures":

> "other measures" ... must mean measures to improve the conditions of labour and to do away with injustice, hardship and privation.[123]

Together, these two observations assume the form of an interpretation argument.

The argument can be analysed as being comprised of five propositions, of which one is the conclusion: no referents of the expression " measures" belong to any other class than *measures to improve the conditions of labour and to do away with injustice, hardship and privation.* The remaining four propositions form the premises of the argument. Proposition no. 1 addresses the relationship between the expression "measures" and the preamble's long list of examples – the expression "the regulation of the hours of work, including the establishment of a maximum working day and week, the regulation of the labour supply, the prevention of unemployment, ...". It is the suggestion of the Court that, according to conventional language, the expression "measures" should be considered related to the expression "the regulation of the hours of work, including the establishment of a maximum working day and week, the regulation of the labour supply, the prevention of unemployment, ...". According to conventional language, the expression "other" acquires part of its meaning through the presence of another expression in the text or discourse, to which the expression "other" can be said to (deictically) refer. In the Statute of the International Labour Organization this can be only one expression: "the regulation of the hours of work, including the establishment of a maximum working day and week, the regulation of the labour supply, the prevention of unemployment, ...". Proposition no. 2 addresses the reference of the expression "the regulation of the hours of work, including the establishment of a maximum working day and week, the regulation of the labour supply, the prevention of unemployment, ...". It is the suggestion of the Court that the referents of the expression are members of a certain, generically defined class, namely *measures to improve the conditions of labour and to do away with injustice, hardship and privation.* Note that proposition no. 2 cannot be evaluated in terms of being true or false. The reference of an expression in a treaty is determined by the intentions of the utterers; these intentions can only be assumed.[124] Therefore, proposition no. 2 can only be evaluated in terms of it being well-founded.[125] Proposition no. 3 addresses the extension of the expression "measures", when interpreted in accordance with conventional language. It is the suggestion of the Court that, according to conventional language, "measures" has an extension, which includes members of the class *measures to improve the conditions of labour and to do away with injustice, hardship and privation.* Lastly, proposition no. 4 addresses the contents of the principle of *ejusdem generis.* The suggestion of the Court can be expressed as follows: given that propositions no. 1 and no. 3 can be regarded as true, and that proposition no. 2 can be considered well-founded, then the preamble to the Statute of the International Labour Organization shall be understood under the assumption that no referents of the expression "measures" belong to any other class than *measures to improve the conditions of labour and to do away with injustice, hardship and privation.*

This analysis of the PCIJ opinion delivered in *Competence of the ILO for Agriculture* makes it possible already at this juncture to say something about the meaning of the principle of *ejusdem generis.* As a first, tentative hypothesis I would like to propose a rule of interpretation along the following lines:

Rule no. 39
If it can be shown (i) that in a treaty provision two expressions are included, of which the one (expression A), according to conventional language, can be considered related to the other (expression B), (ii) that all the referents of the former expression (A) can be considered to be members of a certain, generically defined class, and (iii) that, according to conventional language, all the members of this class are referents of the latter expression (B), then the provision shall be understood under the assumption that no referents to this second expression (B) belong to any other class.

Now, let us take a closer look at *Grimm v. Iran* and *Alberta Provincial Employees.*

The principle of *ejusdem generis*, observes *the Iran-United States Claims Tribunal* in *Grimm v. Iran*, can be applied for the interpretation of the expression "measures affecting property rights", used in article II, paragraph 1 of the Claims Settlement Declaration:

> [U]nder the well-known principle of *ejusdem generis* the words "other measures" in Article II, paragraph 1, ought to be, especially in the context of "debts and contracts", construed as generically similar to "expropriations" [...].[126]

Three conditions must be met in order for us to consider this application to be fully in accordance with interpretation rule no. 39. First, we must be able to show that according to conventional language, the expression "measures affecting property rights" bears a relation to the expression "expropriation". Second, we must be able to show that for good reasons, all the referents of the expression "expropriation" can be considered to be members of a certain, generically defined class. Third, we must be able to show that according to conventional language, the expression "measures affecting property rights" has an extension that comprises said members of this class. All these conditions seem to be fulfilled. The first condition is met, since the expression "measures" in article II, paragraph 1 of the Claims Settlement Declaration is preceded by the expression "other", whose meaning – as already observed – is partially acquired through the presence of another expression in the text, to which "other" can be said to (deictically) refer. In paragraph 1, this expression can only be "expropriations". The second condition is met, since the verb EXPROPRIATE is defined in dictionaries *inter alia* as *to deprive of ownership*. The extension of the term DEPRIVATION OF OWNERSHIP is obviously broader than that of EXPROPRIATION. The third condition is met, since according to the lexicon and grammar of the English language, the expression "measures affecting property rights" clearly has an extension that includes (among others) the members of the class *deprivation of ownership*. All in all, it seems the case of *Grimm v. Iran* could be considered a confirmation of interpretation rule no. 39.

The principle of *ejusdem generis*, observes Chief Justice Sinclair in the case of *Alberta Provincial Employees*, is not applicable for the interpretation of the expression "administration of the State", used in article 8 § 2 of the International Covenant on Economic, Social and Cultural Rights. Three conditions must be met in order for us to be able to interpret the expression "administration of the State" in accordance with interpretation rule no. 39. First, we must be able to show that the expression "administration of the State", according to conventional language, bears a relation to the expression "members of the armed forces or ... the police". Second, we must be able to show that, for good reasons, all the referents to the expression "members of the armed forces or ... the police" can be considered members of a certain, generically defined class. Third, we must be able to show that according to conventional language, the expression "administration of the State" has an extension that includes (among others) the members of this specific class. It is the suggestion of Chief Justice Sinclair that this last condition has not been met. Possibly, there is a certain, generically defined class that includes all the referents of the expression "members of the armed forces or ... the police"; but according to conventional language, this class cannot be included in the extension of the expression "administration of the State":

> I cannot accept this suggestion [that the words "administration of the State" ought to be equated to the armed forces or to the police] because I believe the three functions to be essentially distinct.[127]

Again, it seems as if *Alberta Provincial Employees* could be considered a confirmation of interpretation rule no. 39. Hence, I will take this to be a correct description of the *ejusdem generis* principle.[128]

Not all authors seem prepared to support the conclusion that the principle of *ejusdem generis* should be described as a rule of interpretation in and of itself, separate from those other rules of interpretation that can be applied according to international law. Some authors seem to think that an application of the principle of *ejusdem generis* could be considered a use of conventional language, justified already under the provisions of Vienna Convention article 31.[129] The assumption is that a use of conventional language, under conditions identical to those that exist when the principle of *ejusdem generis* is applied, always leads to the exact same interpretation result. This assumption is not tenable. Take for example the text of the aforementioned Claims Settlement Declaration, article II, paragraph 1. Through an application of the *ejusdem generis* principle, we can obtain the result that none of referents of the expression "measures affecting property rights" belong to any other class than *deprivation of ownership*. This same result cannot be achieved by a mere use of conventional language. By using conventional language, we may possibly be able to show that the expression "measures affecting property rights" bears a relation to the expression "expropriations", and that the expression "measures affecting property rights" has an extension that includes members of the class *deprivation of ownership*. But this is not enough. To draw the conclusion that no referents to the expression "measures affecting property rights" belong to any other class than *deprivation of ownership*, we must also be able to show that all referents of the expression " expropriations" are members of the class *deprivation of ownership*. This requires a value judgment; and this value judgment cannot be produced on the basis of conventional language alone. Obviously, if the principle of *ejusdem generis* shall be taken into consideration for the interpretation of treaties, it must be described as a rule of interpretation in and of itself.

9 OTHER CLAIMED INTERPRETATION RULES

According to some authors, treaties shall be interpreted *in favorem debitoris*.[130] The principle *in favorem debitoris* can be expressed in the following way:

> If it can be shown (i) that the interpretation of a treaty provision in accordance with interpretation rule no. 1 leads to conflicting results, (ii) that the interpreted provision expresses an obligation placed upon the parties to the treaty in different ways, and (iii) that the extension of

the obligation in one of the two possible ordinary meanings is greater than in the other, then the latter meaning shall be adopted.[131]

Looking at the way some authors argue the point, it seems they take for granted that the principle *in favorem debitoris* could be considered a rule of interpretation in and of itself, independent of those otherwise applicable according to international law.[132] In my judgment, this is an assumption we should view with some scepticism.

One rule of interpretation laid down in international law is the one earlier termed as the rule of restrictive interpretation (rule no. 27):

If it can be shown that the interpretation of a treaty provision in accordance with interpretation rule no. 1 leads to conflicting results, and that the provision contains an obligation, whose extension in one of the two possible ordinary meanings is comparably greater than it is in the other, then the latter meaning shall be adopted.[133]

Clearly, a similarity exists between the principle *in favorem debitoris* and the rule of restrictive interpretation, and their respective scopes of application. Each and very case that comes within the scope of the principle *in favorem debitoris* comes within the scope of the rule of restrictive interpretation as well. Given interpretation rule no. 6 – according to which a treaty provision shall be understood so that in the text of that treaty there will be no instance of a logical tautology – I find it difficult to arrive at any other conclusion than this: the principle *in favorem debitoris* should not be considered a rule of interpretation in and of itself.

Another form of argumentation that some authors suggest we should include among the rules of interpretation laid down in international law is the maxim *lex specialis*,[134] sometimes denoted by authors using the more comprehensive expression *lex specialis derogat generali*,[135] or the corresponding negative expression *generalia specialibus non derogat*.[136] The meaning of this maxim remains rather unclear. According to some authors, it appears as if *lex specialis* would stand (at least in part) for a rule identical to the one that we have earlier termed as the principle of *ejusdem generis* (rule no. 39).[137] According to other authors, it seem as if *lex specialis* would stand (at least in part) for a rule identical to the one that we have earlier termed as interpretation rule no. 6.[138] Still others seem to consider *lex specialis* a rule to be applied for the resolution of norm conflicts:

If it can be shown that two legal rules are in conflict with one another, and that the one (norm A) bears a relation to the other (norm B), that for good reasons can be described as that between *lex specialis* and *lex generalis*, respectively, then only the former norm (A) shall be applied.[139]

I cannot feel convinced by any of these arguments.

In the first and second of the three senses above, the maxim *lex specialis* would be found to be at variance with interpretation rule no. 6, according to which a treaty provision shall be understood so that in the text of that treaty there will be no instance of a logical tautology. If the maxim *lex specialis* were to be considered a rule of interpretation in and of itself, then in the former sense of the maxim, the principle of *ejusdem generis* (rule no. 39) would appear to be superfluous. In the second sense of the maxim, interpretation rule no. 6 would appear to be superfluous. In the third sense, the maxim *lex specialis* would appear to be at odds with interpretation rule no. 2, according to which the words and phrases used for a treaty shall be given a consistent meaning. The purpose of *lex specialis*, in the third sense of the maxim, is to resolve conflicts between legal norms. No conflict can be said to exist between two norms laid down in a treaty until the provisions where those two norms are expressed have been clarified. However, VCLT article 32 talks of "supplementary means of interpretation"; and INTERPRETATION, in the terminology used for other parts of the Vienna Convention, means the *clarification of an unclear text of a treaty*.[140] If the maxim *lex specialis* were to be considered a rule of interpretation, then upon the application of this rule the word INTERPRETATION would stand for something which it does not stand for upon the application of the other rules of interpretation. All things considered, the conclusion I draw is that *lex specialis* should not be considered a rule of interpretation in and of itself.

NOTES

1. For further explanations, see the introduction to Chapter 8 of this work.
2. See *Oppenheim's International Law*, pp. 1278–1279; Seidl-Hohenveldern, 1992, p. 93; Verdross and Simma, p. 493; Bernhardt, 1963, p. 143; and implicitly, Orakhelashvili, p. 534. See also *R (Marchiori) v. Environment Agency*, *ILR*, Vol. 127, p. 601; *EC-Beef Hormones*, § 165. Note, however, that the maxim *in dubio mitius* is at times also used as a synonym of what I – like many others and for the sake of clarity – have referred to as comprised by the principle of *in favorum debitoris*. (See e.g. McNair, 1961, p. 462; Lauterpacht, 1950, pp. 402–403.) About the principle *in favorem debitoris*, see Section 9 of this chapter.
3. See *Oppenheim's International Law*, pp. 1278–1279; Seidl-Hohenveldern, 1992, p. 93; *Starke's International Law*, pp. 436–437; Brownlie, p. 631; Akehurst, 1987, p. 205; Vitányi, p. 65; Verdross and Simma, pp. 493–494; Bos, 1984, pp. 156–157, 145–146; Haraszti, pp. 154–163; Rest, pp. 70–71; O'Connell, p. 256; Degan, 1963, pp. 106–111; Berlia, pp. 312–320; Hogg (II), pp. 19–28; De Visscher, 1957, p. 249; Grossen, pp. 119–120. See also, more or less implicitly, Verzijl, pp. 316–317; Bernhardt, 1967, p. 502. In contrast, Lauterpacht, 1950, pp. 406–407.
4. The Kronprins Gustaf Adolf; The Pacific (United States and Sweden), Award of 18 July 1932, *ILR*, Vol. 6, p. 375. Among the authorities who cite this decision, see

e.g. Verdross and Simma, p. 493, n. 11; Verzijl, pp. 316–317; O'Connell, p. 256, n. 69; Degan, 1963, p. 109; Lauterpacht, 1950, p. 406.

5. Case Relating to the Territorial Jurisdiction of the International Commission of the River Oder, Judgment of 10 September 1929, *PCIJ*, Ser. A, No. 23, p. 26. Among the authorities who cite this decision, see e.g. Brownlie, p. 631, n. 48; Vitányi, p. 65, n. 131; Haraszti, p. 160; O'Connell, p. 256, n. 69; Bernhardt, 1963, p. 148; Grossen, p. 120; Lauterpacht, 1950, p. 405.
6. *Article 3, Paragraph 2, of the Treaty of Lausanne (Frontier Between Turkey and Iraq)*, Advisory Opinion of 21 November 1925, *PCIJ*, Ser. B, No. 12, p. 25. Among the authorities who cite this decision, see e.g. *Oppenheim's International Law*, pp. 1278–1279, n. 16; Verdross and Simma, p. 493, n. 11; Vitányi, p. 65, n. 131; Bos, 1984, pp. 156–157, 145–146; O'Connell, p. 256, n. 69; Berlia, p. 316; Grossen, p. 120.
7. The adjective RESTRICTIVE requires an object: according to conventional language, one cannot speak of *restrictive interpretation*, if it cannot be specified *which interpretation is meant to be restrictive*.
8. See the introduction to Chapter 8 of this work.
9. Hence, when Grossen observes "Les etats sont présumés avoir limité au minimum leur souverainité", it must be considered a bit misleading. (Grossen, p. 119.)
10. See Rest, pp. 71–72; Seidl-Hohenveldern, 1992, p. 93.
11. Rest, p. 70. (Footnotes omitted.)
12. See Alexy, 1994, pp. 75–77.
13. See e.g. Schwarzenberger, 1955, pp. 214–227, especially pp. 214–216.
14. See Ch. 8, Section 2, and Ch. 5, Sections 1 and 3, respectively, in this work.
15. See Ch. 4 of this work.
16. See Morrisson, pp. 361–375. See also, more or less explicitly, Brownlie, p. 631.
17. Cf. Schwarzenberger, 1955: "[S]ubjects of international law are bound by rules of an international legal order *if this can be shown to exist*" (p. 216). (My italics.)
18. Similarly, Vitányi, p. 65; Haraszti, p. 155; Hogg (II), pp. 27–28. Cf. also *Kronprins Gustaf Adolf*, see the quotation on p. 311 of this work.
19. Note, however, that at times the principle of *contra proferentem* has also been used to denote an interpretation *in favorem debitoris*. (See e.g. Rousseau, pp. 297–298; Degan, 1963, p. 114.) Such a usage of language cannot be considered correct. An interpretation of a treaty *in favorem debitoris*, in this context, amounts to much the same as (or rather amounts to a special case of) an application of *the rule of restrictive interpretation*. See more on this in Section 9 of this chapter.
20. See e.g. Aust, p. 201; Seidl-Hohenveldern, 1992, pp. 92–93; *Oppenheim's International Law*, p. 1279; Verdross and Simma, p. 493; Haraszti, pp. 188–191; Rest, p. 80; O'Connell, p. 257; Rousseau, p. 298; Berlia, pp. 321–327; Bernhardt, 1963, pp. 184–185; De Visscher, 1963, pp. 110–111; Degan, 1963, pp. 114–116; McNair, 1961, p. 464; Lauterpacht, 1949, pp. 63–64.
21. See Seidl-Hohenveldern, 1992, pp. 92–93; Verdross and Simma, p. 493; Rest, p. 80. See also McNair: "[I]n case of ambiguity a provision must be construed against the party which drafted *or* proposed that provision" (McNair, 1961, p. 464). (My italics.)
22. See *Oppenheim's International Law*, p. 1279; Haraszti, p. 188; Rousseau, p. 298; O'Connell, p. 257; Berlia, pp. 324–327; Degan, 1963, p. 115; Bernhardt, 1963, pp. 184–185; De Visscher, 1963, p. 111; Lauterpacht, 1949, pp. 63–64.

23. Definition B can be read as a more precise version of definition A. A party may have suggested that an expression be used for a treaty provision, without having unilaterally proffered the treaty for acceptance; but a party who has unilaterally proffered a treaty for acceptance is always *ipso facto* also the party who suggested the expression to be used for the provision interpreted.
24. Cf. Haraszti, p. 188; Köck, p. 53; Rest, p. 80; O'Connell, p. 257; Rousseau, p. 298; Bernhardt, 1963, p. 185; Lauterpacht, 1949, p. 64.
25. See, explicitly, Lauterpacht, 1949, p. 64. See also, more or less explicitly, Seidl-Hohenveldern, 1992, pp. 92–93; Verdross and Simma, p. 493; Haraszti, pp. 188–189; Köck, pp. 53–54.
26. Cf. for example Treaty of Peace with Italy, Signed at Paris, on 10 February 1947.
27. In general, it is rather unusual that a state unilaterally proffers a treaty for acceptance.
28. Several other authors seem to have arrived at this same conclusion. (See, implicitly, *Oppenheim's International Law*, pp. 1276, 1279; O'Connell, p. 257; Bernhardt, 1963, p. 185; McNair, 1961, p. 464.) There are also authors who claim that the principle of *contra proferentem* is applicable only for the interpretation of *traités-contrats*. (See e.g. Rest, p. 80; Rousseau, p. 298; Berlia, pp. 321–327; De Visscher, 1963, p. 110.)
29. See *Oppenheim's International Law*, p. 1279; Nowak, p. xxiv; Merrills, pp. 77, 114, 116; Ganshof van der Meersch, pp. 116–117; Bleckmann, p. 179; Verzijl, p. 317; O'Connell, p. 257; Bernhardt, 1963, pp. 182–184; Dahm, p. 56; Soubeyrol, p. 693. The opinion seems not shared by Pauwelyn. (Pauwelyn, p. 250.)
30. When a treaty is interpreted using "supplementary means of interpretation" – as we observed in Chapter 8 of this work – the process can be performed in two fundamentally different ways. "Supplementary means of interpretation can be used alone, and they can be used cumulatively, in combination with the means of interpretation known as conventional language". It is clear that the rule regarding restrictive interpretation of exceptions – just like *the rule of restrictive interpretation* – must always be based on a use of the means of interpretation conventional language.
31. Cf. e.g. Dahm, p. 56.
32. Bernhardt, 1963, p. 182. (Footnotes omitted.)
33. See, implicitly, *Oppenheim's International Law*, p. 1279; Nowak, p. xxiv; Merrills, pp. 77, 114, 116; Ganshof van der Meersch, pp. 116–117; Bleckmann, p. 179; O'Connell, p. 257; Soubeyrol, p. 693.
34. See e.g. Amerasinghe, pp. 196–198; Skubiszewski, 1989, pp. 855–868; Akehurst, 1987, p. 205; Verdross and Simma, pp. 494–495; E. Lauterpacht, pp. 423–432; Tunkin, pp. 185–188; Rest, p. 52; Chaumont, pp. 472–479; Gordon, pp. 816–821; Bernhardt, 1963, pp. 97–107; Schwarzenberger, 1957, pp. 522–525; Fitzmaurice, 1952, pp. 5–6.
35. See e.g. Rest, p. 52; Bernhardt, 1963, pp. 97–107; Schwarzenberger, 1957, pp. 525–526.
36. See e.g. Skubiszewski, 1989, pp. 855–856; Bernhardt, 1963, p. 98.
37. Cf. Hogg (I), pp. 428–429.
38. Similarly, Rest, p. 52; Bernhardt, 1963, p. 98.
39. Similarly, Hogg (I), pp. 409–441.
40. See e.g. Amerasinghe, pp. 196–198; Skubiszewski, 1989, pp. 855–868; Akehurst, 1987, p. 205; Verdross and Simma, pp. 494–495; E. Lauterpacht, pp. 423–432; Tunkin, pp. 185–188; Haraszti, pp. 171–173; Rest, p. 52; Chaumont, pp. 472–479; O'Connell, p. 257; Gordon, pp. 816–821; Bernhardt, 1963, pp. 97–107; Hogg (I), pp. 409–441; Schwarzenberger, 1957, pp. 522–525; Fitzmaurice, 1952, pp. 5–6.

41. See e.g. Blakemore, pp. 57–63.
42. See e.g. *Reparation for Injuries*: "Under international law, the Organization [i.e. United Nations] must be deemed to have those powers which, *though not expressly provided in the Charter*, are conferred upon it by necessary implication as being essential to the performance of its duties." (*ICJ Reports*, 1949, p. 182. My italics.) The case is cited by Amerasinghe, p. 196; Akehurst, 1987, p. 205; Verdross and Simma, p. 495; E. Lauterpacht, p. 424; Tunkin, pp. 185–186; Haraszti, p. 172; Rest, p. 52, n. 5; Chaumont, p. 473; Gordon, p. 817; Hogg (I), pp. 409–410; Schwarzenberger, 1957, p. 522; Fitzmaurice, 1952, p. 5.
43. See pp. 290–291 of this work.
44. See the introduction to Ch. 8 of this work.
45. In addition to the authorities cited in the text, see e.g. Skubiszewski, 1989, pp. 857–859; Akehurst, 1987, p. 205; Verdross and Simma, pp. 494–495; Tunkin, pp. 185–188, especially p. 188; Haraszti, pp. 171–172; Rest, p. 51; Chaumont, pp. 470–483; Hogg (I), pp. 427–441, especially p. 441; Fitzmaurice, 1952, p. 6.
46. See Gordon, p. 816.
47. See Schwarzenberger, 1957, pp. 521–526.
48. Ibid., p. 517.
49. See Amerasinghe, pp. 196–198.
50. Merrills, p. 87.
51. See the introduction to Ch. 8 of this work.
52. Skubiszewski, 1989, pp. 860–861.
53. See Skubiszewski, 1989, p. 860; Amerasinghe, pp. 196–198; Akehurst, 1987, p. 205; E. Lauterpacht, p. 423; Tunkin, p. 185; Haraszti, p. 171; Rest, pp. 51–52; Chaumont, p. 472; O'Connell, p. 257; Gordon, p. 820; Schwarzenberger, 1957, p. 523.
54. See E. Lauterpacht, p. 423 and pp. 423–432 cf. p. 420; Amerasinghe, pp. 196–198; Haraszti, p. 171; Rest, pp. 51–52, cf. p. 47; Chaumont, p. 472; Waldock, Third Report on the Law of Treaties, *ILC Yrbk*, 1964, Vol. 2, p. 61, § 29. See also Draft Articles With Commentaries (1966): "Properly limited and applied, the maxim [*ut res magis valeat quam pereat*] does not call for an 'extensive' or 'liberal' interpretation in the sense of an interpretation going beyond what is expressed or necessarily to be implied in the terms of the treaty." (*ILC Yrbk*, 1966, Vol. 2, p. 219, § 6.)
55. See Section 4 of Ch. 7 in this work.
56. Third Report on the Law of Treaties, *ILC Yrbk*, 1964, Vol. 2, p. 61, § 29.
57. See p. 220 of this work.
58. See the introduction to Ch. 7 of this work.
59. See Skubiszewski, 1989, pp. 861–862; E. Lauterpacht, pp. 430–432.
60. For the sake of simplicity, I concentrate on the application of interpretation rule no. 30 concerning the use of the *teloi* of a treaty. The same line of reasoning can be brought to bear on the application of interpretation rule no. 31 concerning the use of a treaty's norm content.
61. See E. Lauterpacht, 423; Haraszti, p. 171. A commonly cited opinion containing similar views is Judge Hackworth's dissenting opinion in *Reparations for Injuries* (*ICJ Reports*, 1949, p. 198).
62. See Ch. 2 of this work.
63. Loc. cit.
64. Loc. cit.
65. See Ch. 7, Section 1 of this work.

66. See interpretation rules nos. 18, 20, 22, 24 and 26.
67. Bleckmann distinguishes between two types of analogies: *Gesetzesanalgie* and *Rechtsanalogie*. "Gesetzesanalogie soll vorliegen, wenn von einem besonderen Rechtssatz auf einen anderen besonderen Rechtssatz geschlossen wird, Rechtsanalogie, wenn aus mehreren besonderen Rechtssätzen auf einer höheren gemeinsammen Rechtssatz, der als Ausdruck eines allgemeineren Prinzips angesehen wird." (Bleckmann, p. 176.) Obviously, when we deal exclusively with interpretation, only the former type of analogy may be in question.
68. See Bos, 1984, pp. 143–144; Rest, p. 78; Rousseau, p. 275; Bernhardt, 1963, p. 181; De Visscher, 1963, p. 38; Jokl, p. 106.
69. See Vitányi, pp. 54–55; Rousseau, p. 275; Degan, 1963, pp. 100–102; Spencer, pp. 71ff.
70. Similarly, Rousseau, p. 275.
71. See Bos, 1984, pp. 143–144; Karl, 1979, pp. 19–20; Bleckmann, pp. 177–178; Verzijl, p. 316; Rest, pp. 78–79; Rousseau, pp. 275–278; Voïcu, p. 48; De Visscher, 1963, pp. 38–44; Dahm, p. 53; Guggenheim, pp. 128–129; Sørensen, 1946, pp. 225–226. For a different opinion, see: Bernhardt, 1963, pp. 181–182; cf. however Bernhardt, 1967, p. 502; Jokl, pp. 104–109.
72. See e.g. Bernhardt, 1963, pp. 181–182; Jokl, pp. 104–109.
73. See e.g. Bernhardt, 1963, pp. 181–182.
74. See Vitányi, pp. 54–55; Degan, 1963, pp. 100–102; Spencer, pp. 71ff. Cf. also Rousseau, p. 275.
75. See the introduction to Ch. 8 of this work.
76. See Section 4 in this chapter.
77. See Section 1 in this chapter.
78. See Section 2 in Chapter 8 of this work.
79. See, expressly, Rousseau, pp. 275–278; De Visscher, 1963, pp. 40–41.
80. See Rest, p. 78; Guggenheim, p. 128. *Interpretation per analogiam* appears to be defined in this same manner in certain national legal systems. See e.g. Peczenik, 1995, with regard to Swedish law: "*Gesetzsanalogie* means that (1) the case in question lies outside the natural area of linguistic application for the particular law being applied; in other words, outside both its essence and its periphery, but (2) the case is nevertheless judged using this law, since (3) this law regulates other cases bearing considerable similarity to the case at hand." (p. 341; authors translation).
81. See the introduction to Ch. 8 of this work.
82. Loc. cit.
83. See Section 6 of this chapter (interpretation rule no. 34).
84. See Simon, pp. 105–106; Bleckmann, p. 162; Verzijl, p. 316; Haraszti, p. 110; Rest, p. 79; Voïcu, p. 47; De Visscher, 1963, p. 113; Schwarzenberger, 1957, pp. 513–514; Sørensen, 1946, p. 225.
85. See Simon, p. 106, n. 374.
86. Cf. Peczenik, 1987: "*Regulative norms* qualify (1) actions or (2) conditions as directed, permitted or prohibited." (p. 15; authors translation.)
87. See Simon, p. 106, n. 374.
88. See n. 85 in this chapter.
89. I assume this is why some authors classify interpretation *per argumentum a fortiori* as a type of interpretation *per analogiam*. (See e.g. Bleckmann, p. 162. See also Peczenik, 1995, p. 361.) I am reluctant to make this classification. The authors seem

to assume that we can equate the requirement of generic kinship – that must be met when we interpret a treaty *per argumentum a fortiori* – and the requirement of significant similarity – that must be met when we interpret a treaty *per analogiam*. If this assumption were correct, then an argument that comes within the scope of an interpretation *per argumentum a fortiori* will also always come within the scope of an interpretation *per analogiam*. Would this not make interpretation *per argumentum a fortiori* semantically superfluous?

90. This is not to say that it is impossible. With regard to interpretation *per argumentum a fortiori* under Swedish law, professor Peczenik observes: "In a few isolated cases, the relationship more-less can be established without value judgment through logical deduction or empirical observations. To cause that no tax be levied on the taxpayer is clearly more than to cause that an insufficient tax be levied. The latter act is a crime according to 2 § 2 of the Swedish Law on the Crime of Tax Evasion; hence, the former act is as well." (Peczenik, 1995, p. 361; authors translation.)
91. Cf. *Legal Status of Eastern Greenland*, *PCIJ*, Ser. A/B, No. 53, p. 73.
92. In actuality, two value judgments are necessary. In order to justify the claim that a Norwegian occupation of eastern Greenland is a less tolerable act than that of Norway contesting the territorial sovereignty possessed by Denmark with regard to all of Greenland, an applier must be able to defend the proposition that a Norwegian occupation of eastern Greenland is an act generically identical to that of Norway contesting the territorial sovereignty possessed by Denmark with regard to all of Greenland. She must also be able to defend the proposition that a Norwegian occupation of eastern Greenland is a less tolerable act than that of Norway contesting the territorial sovereignty possessed by Denmark with regard to all of Greenland. Neither of these propositions can be justified by an applier in a value-free way. Justification of the latter proposition naturally requires that the former can be justified. Therefore, I have chosen to simplify the issue somewhat and say that only *one* value judgment is required.
93. See, explicitly, Bleckmann, p. 162; Ehrlich, pp. 112–113; in addition, implicitly, Verzijl, p. 316; Sørensen, 1946, pp. 225–226. See also Peczenik, 1995, p. 361.
94. See e.g. Aust, p. 201; *Oppenheim's International Law*, pp. 1279–1280; Brownlie, p. 629; Bos, 1984, p. 141; Haraszti, pp. 110–111; Verzijl, p. 316; Rest, pp. 79–80; Bernhardt, 1963, pp. 180–181; De Visscher, 1963, p. 113; Degan, 1963, pp. 113–114; McNair, 1961, pp. 399–410; Schwarzenberger, 1957, pp. 511–512; Fitzmaurice, 1951, p. 25. See also *Plama*, § 191.
95. Cf. *The Law Dictionary: A Dictionary of Legal Words and Phrases with Latin and French Maxims of the Law Translated and Explained*, Gilmer's Revision, sixth edition.
96. The S.S. "Wimbledon", Judgment of 17 August 1923, *PCIJ*, Ser. A, No. 1. Among the authorities who cite this decision, see e.g. Haraszti, pp. 110–111; Degan, 1963, pp. 113–114; De Visscher, 1963, p. 113; McNair, 1961, pp. 400–401; Schwarzenberger, 1957, p. 513.
97. McNair, 1961, pp. 400–401. (Footnotes omitted.)
98. Railway Traffic between Lithuania and Poland (Railway Sector Landwarów-Kaisiadorys), Advisory Opinion of 15 October 1931, *PCIJ*, Ser. A/B, No. 42. Among the authorities who cite this decision, see e.g. Verzijl, p. 316; Rest, pp. 79–80; Bernhardt, 1963, p. 180; Schwarzenberger, 1957, p. 512.
99. *PCIJ*, Ser. A/B, No. 42, p. 5.
100. The text cited is that provided by the court. (See *PCIJ*, Ser. A/B, No. 42, p. 16.)

101. The text cited is that provided by the court. (See loc. cit.)
102. Ibid., p. 17–18.
103. See p. 300 of this work.
104. See pp. 301–302 of this work.
105. Additional support for this conclusion can be found in the national law literature. In interpretation rule no. 38, the maxim *expressio unius est exclusio alterius* is expressed in the same way as it appears to be used in common-law countries. (See e.g. Bennion, pp. 823, 844–850.)
106. See primarily Brownlie, pp. 628–629. See also *Oppenheim's International Law*, pp. 1279–1280, cf. however p. 1275 and the title of § 633.
107. See e.g. Aust, p. 201; *Oppenheim's International Law*, pp. 1279–1280; Brownlie, p. 629; Köck, p. 49; Haraszti, p. 192; Bernhardt, 1963, p. 176, n. 809; McNair, 1961, pp. 393–399; Schwarzenberger, 1957, p. 510. Note that certain authors denote the principle using other terms than *ejusdem generis*. (See e.g. Köck, p. 49; Haraszti, p. 192; Schwarzenberger, 1957, p. 510.)
108. *Oppenheim's International Law*, p. 1280, n. 20. For an almost identical definition, see Brownlie, p. 629; and McNair, 1961, p. 393.
109. International case law does not offer an abundance of examples that can be used to establish the application (and applicability) of the principle of *ejusdem generis*. However, in addition to the cases cited in the main text, the following may be mentioned: *Buchanan and Co. Ltd v. Babco Ltd.*, Opinion of Lord Edmund-Davies, *ILR*, Vol. 74, p. 610; *Quazi v. Quazi*, Opinion of Lord Scarman, *ILR*, Vol. 74, p. 552; *Social Insurance (Alsace-Lorraine)*, *American Journal of International Law*, Vol. 20 (1926), p. 570; *Administrative Decision No. II*, *American Journal of International Law*, Vol. 18 (1924), p. 184.
110. Competence of the ILO for Agriculture, Advisory Opinion of 12 August 1922, *PCIJ*, Ser. B, No. 2–3.
111. My italics.
112. *PCIJ*, Ser. B, No. 2–3, p. 25.
113. Ibid., p. 55, continued on p. 57.
114. Grimm v. The Government of the Islamic Republic of Iran (Case No. 71), Award of 18 February 1983, *ILR*, Vol. 71, pp. 650ff.
115. Declaration of the Government of the Democratic and Popular Republic of Algeria Concerning the Settlement of Claims by the Government of the United States of America and the Government of the Islamic Republic of Iran, 19 January 1981.
116. My italics.
117. *ILR*, Vol. 71, p. 652.
118. Loc. cit.
119. Re Alberta Union of Provincial Employees et al and the Crown in Right of Alberta, Judgment of 25 July 1980, *ILR*, Vol. 90, pp. 181ff.
120. My italics.
121. *ILR*, Vol. 90, p. 188.
122. See p. 304 of this work.
123. See p. 305 of this work.
124. See Ch. 3, Section 3 of this work.
125. Of course, proposition no. 2 must be considered well-founded. From a grammatical point of view, the expression "the regulation of the hours of work, including the establishment of a maximum working day and week, the regulation of the labour

supply, the prevention of unemployment, ..." bears a clear relation to the second sentence of the second paragraph: "an improvement of those conditions is urgently required". The expression "conditions" in the second sentence of the second paragraph refers anaphorically to the first sentence of the second paragraph, and the expression "conditions of labour ... involving such injustice, hardship and privation to large numbers of people as to produce unrest so great that peace and harmony of the world are imperilled". This conclusion can be made, since the expression "conditions" is preceded by the expression "those", which according to the rules established for the English language, acquires part of its meaning through the presence, earlier in the same text, of another expression, to which "those" can be said to refer. In the preamble to the Statute of the International Labour Organization, this expression can only be one, namely, "conditions of labour ... involving such injustice, hardship and privation to large numbers of people as to produce unrest so great that peace and harmony of the world are imperilled".

126. See p. 306 of this work.
127. See p. 306 of this work.
128. Additional support for this conclusion can be found in the national law literature. In interpretation rule no. 39, the principle of *ejusdem* is expressed in the same way as it appears to be used in common-law countries. (See e.g. Bennion, pp. 823, 828–840; Williams, 1943, pp. 119–128.)
129. See Brownlie, pp. 628–629; Bernhardt, 1963, p. 176, n. 809, as well as *Oppenheim's International Law*, pp. 1279–1280; however, cf. p. 1275 and the title of § 633.
130. See e.g. Seidl-Hohenveldern, 1992, p. 93; *Oppenheim's International Law*, p. 1279; O'Connell, pp. 256–257; Rousseau, pp. 297–298; Degan, 1963, p. 114; McNair, 1961, pp. 462, 765–766; Fitzmaurice, 1957, p. 238; Lauterpacht, 1950, pp. 402–403. It should be noted that sometimes an act of interpretation *in favorem debitoris* is denoted using different terms. For example, Lauterpacht and McNair refer to the act of interpretation *in favorem debitoris*, denoting it by the maxim *in dubio mitius*. Degan and Rousseau refer to the act, denoting it by the principle of *contra proferentem*.
131. Cf. Seidl-Hohenveldern, 1992, p. 93; *Oppenheim's International Law*, p. 1279; O'Connell, pp. 256–257; Rousseau, pp. 297–298; Degan, 1963, p. 114; McNair, 1961, pp. 462, 765–766; Fitzmaurice, 1957, p. 238; Lauterpacht, 1950, pp. 402–403.
132. See e.g. Seidl-Hohenveldern, 1992, p. 93; McNair, 1961, pp. 462, 765–766; Fitzmaurice, 1957, p. 238; Lauterpacht, 1950, pp. 402–403.
133. See p. 281 of this work.
134. See e.g. McLachlan, p. 291; Aust, p. 201; Mus, p. 218; De Visscher, 1963, pp. 104–105; Schwarzenberger, 1957, pp. 510–511.
135. See e.g. *Starke's International Law*, p. 437; Schwarzenberger, 1957, pp. 510–511.
136. See e.g. *Oppenheim's International Law*, p. 1280; Haraszti, pp. 191–192; Voïcu, p. 47; Fitzmaurice, 1957, pp. 236–238.
137. See e.g. Haraszti, pp. 191–192; Schwarzenberger, 1957, pp. 510–511.
138. See e.g. Haraszti, pp. 191–192; Fitzmaurice, 1957, pp. 236–238; Schwarzenberger, 1957, pp. 510–511. With regard to interpretation rule no. 6, see Ch. 4 of this work.
139. See e.g. Mus, p. 218; *Starke's International Law*, p. 437; *Oppenheim's International Law*, p. 1280; De Visscher, 1963, pp. 104–105.
140. See Ch. 1, Section 3, of this work.

CHAPTER 10

THE RELATIONSHIPS BETWEEN DIFFERENT MEANS OF INTERPRETATION

The purpose of this work to clarify and put to words those rules of interpretation that can be invoked by appliers on the basis of international law. According to general jurisprudence, rules of interpretation classify as of two different types, often termed as first-order and second-order rules of interpretation, respectively.[1] A first-order rule of interpretation tells appliers how a treaty provision shall be understood in cases where it has been shown to be unclear. A first-order rule of interpretation informs appliers of the relationship that shall be assumed to hold between an interpreted treaty provision and a given means of interpretation.[2] A second-order rule of interpretation tells appliers how a treaty provision shall be understood in cases where two first-order rules of interpretation have been shown to be in conflict with one another. A second-order rule of interpretation informs appliers of the relationship that shall be assumed to hold between two given first-order rules of interpretation.[3] As a result of the investigations conducted in Chapters 3–9 of this work, we have obtained quite an extensive set of rules, which – for the sake of simplicity – we have termed using the numbers 1 through 39. These are all first-order rules of interpretation. In this chapter, I shall proceed to investigate the various second-order rules of interpretation laid down in international law.

Of all the provisions comprised by VCLT articles 31–33, two are of principal interest. The first is the one included in article 32: "Recourse may be had to supplementary means of interpretation ... in order to confirm the meaning resulting from the application of article 31, or to determine the meaning when the interpretation according to article 31: (a) Leaves the meaning ambiguous or obscure; or (b) Leads to a result which is manifestly absurd or unreasonable."

Il peut être fait appel à des moyens complémentaires d'interprétation ... en vue, soit de confirmer le sens résultant de l'application de l'article 31, soit de déterminer le sens lorsque l'interprétation donnée conformément à l'article 31: (a) laisse le sens ambigu ou obscur; ou (b) conduit à un résultat qui est manifestement absurde ou déraisonnable.

Se podrá acudir a medios de interpretación complementarios ... para confirmar el sentido resultante de la aplicación del artículo 31, o para determinar el sentido cuando la interpretación dada de conformidad con el artículo 31: (a) Deje ambiguo o oscuro el sentido; o (b) Conduzca a un resultado manifiestamente absurdo o irrazonable.

The second provision referred to is the one set forth in article 31 § 1: "A treaty shall be interpreted in good faith in accordance with the ordinary meaning to be given to the terms of the treaty in their context and in the light of its object and purpose."

Un traité doit être interprété de bonne foi suivant le sens ordinaire à attribuer aux termes du traité dans leur contexte et à la lumière de son objet et de son but.

Un tratado deberá interpretarse de buena fe conforme al sentido corriente que haya de atribuirse a los términos del tratado en el contexto de éstos y teniendo en cuenta su objeto y fin.

What do these two provisions imply? This is what we shall now try to establish.

The organisation of this chapter is similar to that of previous chapters in this work. As in Chapters 3–9, I will divide Chapter 10 according to the different means of interpretation that can be used by appliers for the interpretation of treaties. A first task will be to determine the relationship that shall be assumed to hold among primary and supplementary means of interpretation. This is the subject of Sections 1–6. A second task will be to determine the relationship that shall be assumed to hold among the primary and supplementary means of interpretation, respectively. This is the subject of Section 7.

1 THE RELATIONSHIP BETWEEN PRIMARY AND SUPPLEMENTARY MEANS OF INTERPRETATION: AN INTRODUCTION

According to VCLT article 32, appliers may have recourse "to supplementary means of interpretation ... in order to confirm the meaning resulting from the application of article 31, or to determine the meaning when the interpretation according to article 31: (a) Leaves the meaning ambiguous or obscure; or (b) Leads to a result which is manifestly absurd or unreasonable". A key feature in this passage is the expression "determine" (Fr. "*déterminer*"; Sp. "*determinar*"). Determining the meaning of a treaty using some certain means of interpretation is tantamount to understanding the text in accordance with the rule or rules of interpretation, through which the usage has to be effectuated.[4] If a treaty can be interpreted using both supplementary and primary means of interpretation, and the use of different means of interpretation leads to conflicting results, then the supplementary and primary means of interpretation cannot possibly *both* be used to "determine" the meaning of the treaty. Earlier, we described the use of supplementary means of interpretation as the application of interpretation rules nos. 17–39.[5] The use of primary means of interpretation has been described as the application of interpretation rules nos. 1–16.[6] Consequently, as a preliminary rendering of VCLT article 32, we may establish the following sentence:

> If it can be shown that the interpretation of a treaty provision in accordance with any one of the interpretation rules nos. 1–16 leads to a result, which is different from that obtained by interpreting the provision in accordance with any one of the interpretation rules nos. 17–39, and that the application of the former rule either leaves the meaning of the provision "ambiguous or obscure", or "leads to a result which is manifestly absurd or unreasonable", then the provision shall be understood in accordance with the latter of the two rules.

This sentence will henceforth be termed as norm sentence NS_1.

Of course, in and of itself, norm sentence NS_1 amounts to a very cautious reading – too cautious, according to many. In purely grammatical terms – this much is clear – article 32 expresses permission. According to its wording, supplementary means of interpretation is something, to which recourse "*may* be had" (auxquelles "[i]l *peut* être fait appel", a cuales "[s]e *podrá* acudir").[7] The majority of authors, however, seem to agree that the provision shall also be applied *e contrario*.[8] Not only does article 32 give permission; it shall also be understood to express a prohibition. The prohibition goes as follows: appliers may *not* have recourse to the supplementary means of interpretation to determine the meaning of a treaty provision, when interpreting the provision according to article 31 *neither* leaves the meaning of the text "ambiguous or obscure", *nor* "leads to a result which is manifestly absurd or unreasonable". More neatly put, it can also be expressed in the following manner:

> If it can be shown that the interpretation of a treaty provision in accordance with any one of the interpretation rules nos. 1–16 leads to a result, which is different from that obtained by interpreting the provision in accordance with any one of the interpretation rules nos. 17–39, then the provision shall be understood in accordance with the former of the two rules, except for those cases where it can be shown that the application of this former rule leaves the meaning of the provision "ambiguous or obscure", or "leads to a result which is manifestly absurd or unreasonable".

This sentence will henceforth be termed as norm sentence NS_2.

Now we have made some headway in our inquiry. As a preliminary rendering of article 32, we have established two norm sentences, and to facilitate reference we have denoted them as NS_1 and NS_2. However, there is still some work to be done before the contents of article 32 can be put to words in the form of a true rule of interpretation. First, we must define more precisely the relationship between our two classes of rules: rules nos. 1–16 and rules nos. 17–39. As observed earlier, there are several possible avenues that may be taken by states if they wish to establish a rule of law to govern the relationship between two first-order rules of interpretation. [9] Assume that states have established two rules of interpretation (A and B) that, in practice, they suspect will often lead to different results. Assume also that states decide to establish a rule of interpretation D, according to which all future conflicts between rules A and B will be resolved so that, whatever treaty provision is interpreted, it shall be read only in application of interpretation rule A. In principle, this can be done in two ways. Either states decide that treaty provisions shall *not* be read in accordance with interpretation rule B; or states decide that *rather than* with rule B, treaty provisions shall be read in accordance with interpretation rule A – which is not really the same thing. In both cases, interpretation rule D is a reason not to understand treaty provisions in accordance with interpretation rule B; thus far, the contents of the two rules are identical. The difference is that in the former case, interpretation rule D is a *conclusive reason* to not understand a treaty provision in accordance with interpretation rule B, while in the second case, interpretation rule D is only a *reason pro tanto*. In practice, this difference can be of greatest significance.

Imagine the following scenario. We interpret a treaty provision (T) and discover that there are three first-order rules of interpretation (A, B and C), which all can be applied *prima facie* . The problem is that they do not all lead to identical results. While the result obtained by applying rule A compares to that obtained by applying rule C, the result that ensues from an application of B differs. In other words, rules A and B are in conflict with one another, as are rules B and C; but no conflict exists in the relationship between rules C and A. Now, assume the following second-order rule of interpretation (D) can be established:

> If it can be shown that the interpretation of a treaty provision in accordance with interpretation rule A leads to a result, which is different from that obtained by interpreting the provision in accordance with interpretation rule B, then the provision shall not be understood in accordance with interpretation rule B.

Interpretation rule D resolves the conflict that exists between rules A and B. But it also resolves the conflict that exists between rules B and C; for interpretation rule D is a conclusive reason to not understand treaty provision T in accordance with interpretation rule B. Hence, when rule D is applied, the effect is that rule B loses its normative power, not only with respect to rule A, but quite generally, with respect to each and every other first-order rule of interpretation, with which it might possibly collide. The situation would be different if, instead, the imaginary rule D had been described in the following manner:

> If it can be shown that the interpretation of a treaty provision in accordance with interpretation rule A leads to a result, which is different from that obtained by interpreting the provision in accordance with interpretation rule B, then rather than being understood in accordance with rule B, the provision shall be understood in accordance with interpretation rule A.

Interpretation rule D resolves the conflict that exists between rules A and B. However, the conflict that exists between interpretation rules B and C remains; for interpretation rule D is merely a reason *pro tanto* to not understand treaty provision T in accordance with rule B. When rule D is applied, the effect is that interpretation rule B loses its normative power, but only with respect to interpretation rule A. The conflict that holds between interpretation rules B and C still remains.

The problem with the norm sentences NS_1 and NS_2 would then be that they allow for different readings. Naturally, the question is how the passage concluding the two sentences should be understood: "then the provision shall be understood in accordance with the latter [in NS_2: 'the former'] of the two rules". Should we take this as an instruction to the effect that appliers shall not understand the interpreted treaty provision in accordance with the "losing" rules of interpretation nos. 1–16 and 17–39, respectively? If that is the case, the norm expressed will form a conclusive reason to not understand the interpreted treaty provision in accordance with the "losing" rules of interpretation nos. 1–16 and 17–39, respectively. Or should we understand the passage as an instruction to the effect that prior to the "losing" rules of interpretation nos. 1–16 and 17–39, respectively, we shall understand the provision in accordance with the "winning" rules? Then instead, the norm expressed will form only a reason *pro tanto* to not understand the interpreted treaty provision in accordance with the "losing" interpretation rules nos. 1–16 and 17–39, respectively. Choosing between these two alternatives, my conclusion is that norm sentences NS_1 and NS_2 must be given different interpretations. This is a proposition that I will now try to establish.

2 THE RELATIONSHIP BETWEEN PRIMARY AND SUPPLEMENTARY MEANS OF INTERPRETATION: THE SECOND-ORDER RULE AS A CONCLUSIVE REASON OR AS A REASON *PRO TANTO*

To repeat: the question to be answered is whether the norms expressed by norm sentences NS_1 and NS_2 should be considered as conclusive reasons to not understand an interpreted treaty provision in accordance with the "losing" rules nos. 1–16 and 17–39, respectively, or whether they should be considered merely as reasons *pro tanto*. Let us begin with addressing norm sentence NS_1. It is my opinion that norm sentence NS_1 should be regarded in the former manner – the norm that the sentence expresses is a conclusive reason to not understand an interpreted treaty provision in accordance with the "losing" interpretation rules nos. 1–16 and 17–39, respectively. The main argument, which I believe supports my conclusion, is the concept of interpretation assumed in the Vienna Convention. As observed earlier, interpreting a treaty, according to the terminology of the Vienna Convention, is tantamount to clarifying the text of a treaty that has been shown to be unclear.[10] From this definition two norms of interpretation can be derived – in the aggregate often referred to as THE DOCTRINE OF PLAIN MEANING (LA RÈGLE DU SENS CLAIR),[11] OF THE PRINCIPLE OF NATURAL AND ORDINARY MEANING.[12] According to the first of the two norms, a process of interpretation shall be concluded when one arrives at a point where the interpreted treaty provision can be regarded as clear.[13] According to the second norm, a process of interpretation shall *not* be concluded, as long as the interpreted treaty provision *cannot* be regarded as clear.[14] Of course, neither of these norms are something that governs the result of the interpretation process,[15] which after all is the subject to be dealt with in this work.[16] They are both norms that govern the interpretation process as such. However, at least the second of the two norms is of major relevance, when – given that the use of primary and supplementary means of interpretation lead to conflicting results – we need to determine which of the results shall be considered legally correct. Perhaps this will come out more clearly if instead the norm is expressed in the following manner:

> Whatever first-order rule of interpretation is applied for the understanding of a treaty provision, if the ensuing meaning cannot be considered clear, it shall not be regarded as normative.

Right away, the crucial point of the problem turns out to be this: what do we mean when we say that the meaning of a treaty cannot be considered clear? What is the criterion, by which appliers are to judge the clarity of a treaty provision? The general view held among authors is that the relevant criterion is the one that can be discerned from VCLT article 32. In order for a treaty provision to be considered clear – this is how the text is to be read – the meaning given to the provision must not be "ambiguous or obscure"; nor must the meaning be "manifestly absurd or unreasonable".[17] The essence of this analysis would then seem to be the following:

> Whatever first-order rule of interpretation is applied for the understanding of a treaty provision, if the ensuing meaning is either "ambiguous or obscure", or amounts to a result which is "manifestly absurd or unreasonable", that meaning shall not be regarded as normative.[18]

If we accept this conclusion, then the norm expressed by norm sentence NS_1 can be understood in only one way, namely as a conclusive reason to not understand a treaty provision in accordance with any of the interpretation rules nos. 1–16. Norm sentence NS_1 could accordingly be given a more precise wording:

> If it can be shown that the interpretation of a treaty provision in accordance with any one of the interpretation rules nos. 1–16 leads to a result, which is different from that obtained by interpreting the provision in accordance with any one of the interpretation rules nos. 17–39, and that the application of the former rule either leaves the meaning of the provision "ambiguous or obscure", or "leads to a result which is manifestly absurd or unreasonable", then the provision shall not be understood in accordance with this former rule.

Now, let us see if this same approach can be used to more precisely define the meaning of norm sentence NS_2. Earlier, norm sentence NS_2 was articulated as follows:

> If it can be shown that the interpretation of a treaty provision in accordance with any one of the interpretation rules nos. 1–16 leads to a result, which is different from that obtained by interpreting the provision in accordance with any one of the interpretation rules nos. 17–39, then the provision shall be understood in accordance with the former of the two rules, except for those cases where it can be shown that the application of this former rule leaves the meaning of the provision "ambiguous or obscure", or "leads to a result which is manifestly absurd or unreasonable".

In my judgment, the passage "then the treaty provision shall be understood in accordance with the former of the two rules" shall be understood as an instruction to the effect that rather than being understood in accordance with rules nos. 17–39, the interpreted treaty provision shall be understood in accordance with rules nos. 1–16. This conclusion does not immediately follow from the wording of the Vienna Convention.[19] As a heading for article 32, the drafters have chosen the expression "Supplementary means of interpretation" *("Moyens complémentaire d'interprétation", "Medios de interpretación complementarios").* However, in and of itself, the word SUPPLEMENTARY (Fr. COMPLÉMENTAIRE; Sp. COMPLEMENTARIOS) only informs us that the means of interpretation set forth in article 32 are something to be used (should the need arise) as an addition or as a supplement to those set forth in article 31.[20] If a treaty provision has been shown to be unclear, the initial step for the applier shall not be to interpret the provision using the means of interpretation set forth in article 32. Instead, according to the wording of article 32, the initial step shall be to interpret the provision using the means of interpretation set forth in article 31. Only in those cases where the initial step of the interpretation process proves insufficient – when applying the rules of article 31 either leaves the meaning of the interpreted treaty provision "ambiguous or obscure", or "leads to a result that is manifestly absurd or unreasonable" – only then shall the provision be interpreted using the means recognised as acceptable in article 32.

Thus, on the face of it, article 32 would seem designed mainly to govern the process of interpretation as such. In this work, article 32 is of interest only because it can be considered as governing the results of the interpretation process.[21] The task before us is not to determine how appliers shall proceed, from the purely methodological perspective, when they interpret a treaty using the primary and supplementary means of interpretation. The situation that poses the problem in this work can be described as follows: a treaty provision has be shown to be unclear, and we have to choose between two different interpretation alternatives; the one alternative can be described as the result of an act using a primary means of interpretation, the other as the result of an act using a supplementary means of interpretation; in neither case do we face a result "which is manifestly absurd or unreasonable", or one that leaves the meaning of the interpreted provision "ambiguous or obscure"; we are now keen on determining which of the two interpretation alternatives we shall consider correct. This problem is not one that can be solved by simply referring to the wording of VCLT article 32, and the wording of article 32 only. A solution must be sought elsewhere.

Some assistance can indeed be found in the literature. Among the several authors that may readily be cited is Professor Villiger:

> A result arrived at by the use of primary means of Art. 31 prevails over solutions suggested by the *travaux*.[22]

With regard to the draft finally adopted by the ILC in 1966, Jennings makes the following remarks:

> Article 28 on the other hand is said to be wholly subordinate to Article 27, for it relates to "supplementary means of interpretation, including the preparatory work of the treaty and the circumstances of its conclusion ...".[23]

Schröder comments on the very same draft:

> Der Vergleich der Art 27 und 28 ergibt, daß die Interpretation an Hand des Vetragstextes den Vorrang vor den travaux préparatoires und den Umständen bei Vetragsschluß haben soll.[24]

The three authors all have different ways of expressing themselves, yet the substance is the same: when appliers have to choose between using a primary and a supplementary means of interpretation to determine the meaning of a treaty provision, greater attention should be paid to the former.

In addition to this, several authors have commented upon the relationship assumed to be held between primary and supplementary means of interpretation, noting that the former are *hierarchically superior* to the latter.[25] Jacobs, to name one, reports with reference to the ILC draft of 1966:

> In its distinction between Article 27, "General rule of interpretation" and Article 28, "Supplementary means of interpretation", the draft appears to establish a clear hierarchy in favour of the ordinary meaning of the words which suggests a textual approach.[26]

I cannot perceive this to be anything but synonymous with what we have already observed, along with authorities such as Villiger, Jennings and Schröder: in a situation where we are forced to choose between a primary and a supplementary means of interpretation, greater attention should be paid to the former. HIERARCHY involves rank and precedence. The word HIERARCHY stands for a system, in which different persons or objects bear a relation to each other based on their different importance or authority, *not implying*, however, that one or several of these people or objects should be considered as lacking in importance or authority completely. A relationship held between two people is hierarchical, if (and only if) the will of the one can be generally considered more important, but the will of the other, at least in some situations, can be considered more important than the will of a third person. If we have a discussion about the relationship held between primary and supplementary means of interpretation, and I make the remark that the former are hierarchically superior to the latter, but by saying so I mean that a supplementary means of interpretation – just because it happens to be in conflict with a primary means of interpretation, and just because of its lower hierarchical rank – loses the normative power normally conferred upon it, then, indeed, this would not be the ordinary way of using the word HIERARCHY.

This same discussion of hierarchies can be found in the preparatory work of the Vienna Convention. As a starting point for the Vienna Conference of 1968 and 1969, the International Law Commission had prepared a draft. In this draft – as in the Convention that was finally adopted – different means of interpretation had been separated and arranged as two separate articles (articles 27 and 28), the latter of which bore the heading "Supplementary means of interpretation".[27] This draft was heavily criticised by the USA,[28] who later during the conference pressed for changes.[29] The American proposal was that articles 27 and 28 of the ILC draft should be combined and replaced by a single article, in which largely the same elements (or means) of interpretation were listed, but with no details regarding the conditions under which each element should be used.[30] The reaction of the other participating states was unusually harsh. A few delegations declared a willingness to support the proposal,[31] but the great majority expressed strong dissent.[32] The argument made – for as well as against – was that, by accepting the American proposal, all means of interpretation would be given the exact same level of authority; the hierarchy that the ILC had tried to establish between primary and supplementary means of interpretation would be undermined completely. All things considered, it seems that strong reasons support the proposition that in norm sentence NS_2, the norm expressed should be regarded as a reason *pro tanto*. Hence, norm sentence NS_2 can be revised to read:

> If it can be shown that the interpretation of a treaty provision in accordance with any one of the interpretation rules nos. 1–16 leads to a result, which is different from that obtained by interpreting the provision in accordance with any one of the interpretation rules nos. 17–39, then, rather than being understood in accordance with the latter of the two rules, the provision shall be understood in accordance with the former, except for those cases where it can be shown that the application of this rule leaves the meaning of the provision "ambiguous or obscure", or "leads to a result which is manifestly absurd or unreasonable".

One task remains before the content of VCLT article 32 can be set forth conclusively: we must define more precisely the conditions, on which the relationship between the two classes of means is dependent. If the need arises to interpret a treaty provision, and the use of primary and supplementary means of interpretation leads to conflicting results, there are two possible solutions to the problem. According to the first of the solutions, appliers shall *not understand* the provision using the primary means of interpretation. This solution is practised in cases where it can be shown that the use of primary means of interpretation either leaves the meaning of the interpreted provision "ambiguous or obscure", or "leads to a result which is manifestly absurd or unreasonable". According to the second solution, *rather than* understanding the provision using the supplementary means of interpretation, appliers shall understand the provision using the primary means of interpretation. This solution is practised in cases where it *cannot* be shown that the use of primary means of interpretation leaves the meaning of the interpreted provision "ambiguous or obscure", or that it "leads to a result which is manifestly absurd or unreasonable". Two questions arise:

(1) What do we mean when we say that the use of primary means of interpretation leaves the meaning of an interpreted treaty provision "ambiguous or obscure"?

(2) What do we mean when we say that the use of primary means of interpretation "leads to a result which is manifestly absurd or unreasonable"?

In Sections 3 through 6 of this chapter, I will make an attempt to answer these questions. The first question will be addressed in Section 3; the second question will be addressed in Sections 4–6.

3 THE EXPRESSION "AMBIGUOUS OR OBSCURE"

What do we mean when we say that the use of primary means of interpretation leaves the meaning of an interpreted treaty provision "ambiguous or obscure"? I can see four different types of situations that might create problems for the applier who interprets a treaty provision using primary means of interpretation:

(1) Drawing up the provision, the parties used an expression whose form corresponds to an expression of conventional language; the expression has already been interpreted in accordance with interpretation rule no. 1; but the conventional meaning of the expression is ambiguous; and none of the interpretation rules nos. 2–16 can be applied to the effect that only one of the two possible meanings can be considered correct.

(2) Drawing up the provision, the parties used an expression whose form corresponds to an expression of conventional language; the expression has already been interpreted in accordance with interpretation rule no. 1; but the conventional meaning of the expression is vague; and none of the interpretation rules nos. 2–16 can be applied to the effect that the conventional meaning can be sufficiently defined.

(3) Drawing up the provision, the parties used an expression whose form corresponds to an expression of conventional language; the expression has already been interpreted in accordance with interpretation rule no. 1; but the conventional meaning of the expression is either vague or

ambiguous; and though several of the interpretation rules nos. 2–16 can be applied, the application of different rules leads to different results.

(4) Drawing up the provision, the parties used an expression whose form *does not* correspond to an expression of conventional language; hence, none of the interpretation rules nos. 1–16 can be applied.[33]

For me, it is clear that all four scenarios were in mind for those who drafted the text of article 32. In situations (1) and (2), as well as in situations (3) and (4), the use of the primary means of interpretation leads to a result that leaves the meaning of the interpreted provision "ambiguous or obscure". However, considering the way article 32 has been worded, we should be aware that this is a reading that meets with certain problems.

The root of these problems is the expression "the meaning" (Fr. "*le sens*"; Sp. "*el sentido*"). In VCLT article 32, the word MEANING (Fr. SENS; Sp. SENTIDO) appears three times. This is how the article reads: "Recourse may be had to supplementary means of interpretation ... in order to confirm *the meaning* resulting from the application of article 31, or to determine *the meaning* when an interpretation according to article 31: (a) Leaves *the meaning* ambiguous or obscure; or (b) Leads to a result which is manifestly absurd or unreasonable".[34] In each instance, "the meaning" refers to *the meaning of the interpreted treaty* – I have taken this for granted.[35] However, it is clear that the meaning of the expression "the meaning" cannot be the same throughout the text of article 32. The first occurring expression refers to *the meaning of a treaty that ensues from the application of VCLT article 31*. The second occurring expression stands for something else; clearly, in this case "the meaning" shall be understood to refer to *the correct meaning of the treaty*. Less clear is the purport of the third occurring expression.

On a first immediate reading – especially considering the expression "leaves" (cf. the text of article 32: "*leaves the meaning ambiguous or obscure*", "*laisse le sens ambigu ou obcure*", "*[d]eje ambiguo o oscuro el sentido*") – one might easily draw the conclusion that "the meaning" refers to *the correct meaning of the treaty*. However, interpretation rule no. 15 argues against such an interpretation:

> If it can be shown that the interpretation of a treaty provision in accordance with interpretation rule no. 1 leads to conflicting results, and that the treaty has a certain *telos*, which in one of the two possible ordinary meanings, by applying the provision, will be realised to a greater extent than in the other, then the former meaning shall be adopted.[36]

It is a *telos* conferred on the regime of interpretation laid down in VCLT articles 31 through 33 – and indeed a very important one – that it shall govern the operative interpretation of treaties.[37] However, in an operative situation of interpretation, it is pure anomaly to speak of the correct meaning of a treaty as something ambiguous. For an operative interpretation, it must be considered axiomatic that for each and every particular case, and for each and every treaty provision, there is a meaning, which cannot only be considered correct, but will also allow a final decision to be made in the case.[38] Thus, by definition, the correct meaning of a treaty cannot be anything other than unambiguous. Given that the text of article 32 shall be understood in accordance with interpretation rule no. 15, then we cannot unconditionally say of the third "the meaning" in the article that it stands for *the correct meaning of the treaty.*

The alternative is that the third "the meaning" in article 32 stands for *the meaning of a treaty that ensues from the application of VCLT article 31.* This is hardly a more attractive alternative. As I stated earlier, it is clear for me that when the drafters drew up the text of article 32 – including the passage "when an interpretation according to article 31: (a) Leaves the meaning ambiguous or obscure" – they had four scenarios in mind.[39] One of these has earlier been described as follows:

(4) Drawing up the provision, the parties used an expression whose form *does not* correspond to an expression of conventional language; hence, none of the interpretation rules nos. 1–16 can be applied.[40]

In order for situation (4) to be counted as part of the extension of the text in question, the situation must occur because the use of primary means of interpretation, according to Vienna Convention terminology, has left the meaning "obscure" (Fr. *"obscure"*; Sp. *"oscuro")*, not "ambiguous" (Fr. *"ambigu"*; Sp. *"ambiguo")*. However, interpretation rule no. 1 argues against such an interpretation:

If it can be shown that in a treaty provision, there is an expression whose form corresponds to an expression of conventional language, then the provision shall be understood in accordance with the rules of that language.[41]

In dictionaries, the word OBSCURE is defined as *unknown; concealed, hidden.* Semantically, however, it is pure nonsense to speak of the meaning of a treaty obtained through an application of VCLT article 31 as unknown, concealed or hidden. Given that the text of VCLT article 32 shall be understood in accordance with interpretation rule no. 1, then we cannot unconditionally say of the third "the meaning" in the article that it refers to *the meaning of a treaty that ensues from the application of VCLT article 31.* All things considered – given that we maintain the position that all the situations (1) through (4) fall under the extension of the text here put to scrutiny – it seems that we would be forced to accept the rather odd conclusion that the expression "the meaning" stands for two completely different things, depending on whether we read it in connection with the expression "ambiguous" or the expression "obscure". In the former case it refers to the meaning of a treaty that ensues from the application of VCLT article 31. In the latter case, it refers to the correct meaning of the treaty.

4 THE EXPRESSION "LEADS TO A RESULT WHICH IS MANIFESTLY ABSURD OR UNREASONABLE"

What do we mean when we say that the use of primary means of interpretation "leads to a result which is manifestly absurd or unreasonable"? As I see it, there are two important issues we need to resolve concerning the meaning of the expression "leads to a result which is manifestly absurd or unreasonable" ("*conduit à un résultat qui est manifestement absurde ou déraisonnable", "[c]onduzca a un resultado manifiestamente absurdo o irrazonable").* First, we must ask ourselves how the qualifier "manifestly absurd or unreasonable" is to be read in relation to the main word "result". Grammatically, we have only one interpretation alternative; henceforth, we will be terming this alternative by the letter (a):

> Supplementary means of interpretation may be used to determine the meaning of a treaty, when an interpretation according to VCLT article 31 leads to a result, which is manifestly *either* absurd *or* unreasonable.[42]

The reading that I will profess is a completely different one. In my judgment, the meaning of the expression "absurd or unreasonable" cannot be determined by a mere combining of the individual meanings of the words ABSURD, OR and UNREASONABLE in a syntactically correct manner. Rather, the expression "absurd or unreasonable" is used as an idiomatic phrasal lexeme – in the expression "absurd or unreasonable", the constituent units "absurd", "or" and "unreasonable" simply have no independent meaning at all. In other words, the interpretation I would like to propose is the following:

> Supplementary means of interpretation may be used to determine the meaning of a treaty, when an interpretation according to VCLT article 31 leads to a result, which is manifestly "absurd or unreasonable", where the expression "absurd or unreasonable" is to be considered an idiomatic phrasal lexeme.

This second interpretation alternative – henceforth to be termed by the letter (b) – is also the one that first presents itself when we look to the literature to see what authors generally say about the expression "absurd or unreasonable" ("*absurde ou déraisonnable").* It is a striking fact that when authors comment upon the use of supplementary means of interpretation, almost never do they distinguish between an interpretation result which is "absurd" (Fr. *"absurde")* and one which is "unreasonable" (Fr. *"déraissonable").*[43] It remains to be seen whether this reading of VCLT article 32 can also be justified by reference to the rules of interpretation laid down in international law.

Interpretation rule no. 1 argues *against* alternative (b):

> If it can be shown that in a treaty provision, there is an expression whose form corresponds to an expression of conventional language, then the provision shall be understood in accordance with the rules of that language.[44]

As far as I can tell, neither in everyday nor in any technical language is there a convention, which associates the phrase ABSURD OR UNREASONABLE with any other meaning than that obtained in combining ABSURD, OR and UNREASONABLE in accordance with current syntax. Consequently, given that the text of VCLT article 32 shall be understood in accordance with interpretation rule no. 1, interpretation alternative (a) – not (b) – would then be the one we should advocate.

In favour of alternative (b), interpretation rule no. 18 can be adduced:

> If, by using the preparatory work of a treaty, a concordance can be shown to exist, as between the parties to said treaty, and with regard to the norm content of an interpreted treaty provision, then the provision shall be understood in such a way that it logically agrees with the concordance.[45]

In the preparatory work of the Vienna Convention there is not the slightest suggestion of a discussion that sheds light on or compares the content of the conceptual pair: *a result which is absurd* and *a result which is unreasonable.* To a great extent, "absurd or unreasonable" is used as an idiomatic phrasal lexeme.[46] And when it is not used as an idiomatic phrasal lexeme, this seems merely to be a means to simplify expression or to avoid repetition. One and the same person can speak of a result which is absurd or unreasonable, and then about a result which is absurd, or a result which is unreasonable, without anything in the protocols to suggest that these different expressions are not wholly co-referent.[47] Whether taken together or seen on their own, these facts all give the impression that the parties to the Vienna Convention regard the expression "absurd or unreasonable" *("absurde ou déraisonnable", "absurdo o irrazonable")* as a single, indivisible idiom. Hence, given that the text of VCLT article 32 shall be understood in accordance with interpretation rule no. 18, alternative (b), and not (a), would then be the one we should advocate.

Hence, in the given situation, it is apparent that there is a conflict between interpretation rules nos. 1 and 18. In the Vienna Convention there are rules for resolving such conflicts. Earlier in this work, the content of these rules have provisionally been described in the form of two norm sentences, termed as NS_1 and NS_2. Norm sentence NS_1 states:

> If it can be shown that the interpretation of a treaty provision in accordance with any one of the interpretation rules nos. 1–16 leads to a result, which is different from that obtained by interpreting the provision in accordance with any one of the interpretation rules nos. 17–39, and that the application of the former rule either leaves the meaning of the provision "ambiguous or obscure", or "leads to a result which is manifestly absurd or unreasonable", then the provision shall not be understood in accordance with this rule.

Norm sentence NS_2 reads as follows:

> If it can be shown that the interpretation of a treaty provision in accordance with any one of the interpretation rules nos. 1–16 leads to a result, which is different from that obtained by interpreting the provision in accordance with any one of the interpretation rules nos. 17–39, then, rather than being understood in accordance with the latter of the two rules, the provision shall be understood in accordance with the former, except for those cases where it can be shown that the application of this rule leaves the meaning of the provision "ambiguous or obscure", or "leads to a result which is manifestly absurd or unreasonable".

It is my judgment that the text of Vienna Convention article 32 shall not be understood in accordance with interpretation rule no. 1. Accordingly, it is my task to show that an interpretation according to rule no. 1 leaves the meaning of article 32 "ambiguous or obscure", or that it "leads to a result which is manifestly absurd or unreasonable". Clearly, an interpretation according to rule no. 1 does not leave the meaning of article 32 "ambiguous or obscure". The decisive question is whether I can show that an interpretation according to interpretation rule no. 1 "leads to a result which is manifestly absurd or unreasonable".

With this question, we move unavoidably onward to the next issue that I stated would be dealt with in Sections 4–6 of this chapter. As I understand the matter, there are two issues that we need to resolve concerning the meaning of the expression "leads to a result which is manifestly absurd or unreasonable" [48] First, we must ask ourselves how the qualifier "manifestly absurd or unreasonable" is to be read in relation to the headword "result". Second, we must ask ourselves this: how shall an applier go about justifying a claim that an interpretation according to VCLT article 31 "leads to a result which is manifestly absurd or unreasonable"? The first question is something that we have already begun to examine. However, wishing to answer the question conclusively, it is apparent that we are faced with some serious difficulties. The answer to our first question obviously presupposes the answer to our second. In order to establish interpretation alternative (b) as correct, I must be able to show that an interpretation of VCLT article 32 in accordance with rule no. 18 "leads to a result which is manifestly absurd or unreasonable". The problem is that the answer to our second question presupposes an answer to the first. In order for us to determine how appliers should go about justifying the proposition that an interpretation according to VCLT article 31 "leads to a result which is manifestly absurd or unreasonable", we need to know how the qualifier "manifestly absurd or unreasonable" shall be read in relation to the main word "result". I shall now turn my attention to answering question number two. To do so, I will assume interpretation alternative (b) – not (a) – to be the correct reading of VCLT article 32. When our second question has been answered I will return once again to answering question number one.

5 THE EXPRESSION "LEADS TO A RESULT WHICH IS MANIFESTLY ABSURD OR UNREASONABLE" (CONT'D)

How should the applier proceed to justify the proposition that an interpretation according to VCLT article 31 "leads to a result which is manifestly absurd or unreasonable"? As stated earlier, the expression "absurd or unreasonable" (*"absurde ou déraisonnable", "absurdo o irrazonable")* shall not be understood in accordance with conventional language. The question is how we should then read the expression. It is apparent that the words ABSURD, ABSURDE, ABSURDO and UNREASONABLE, DÉRAISONNABLE, IRRAZONABLE share a certain degree of kinship. UNREASONABLE, DÉRAISONNABLE, IRRAZONABLE, according to conventional language, represents *the quality of not being justifiable*; the same holds true for the word ABSURD, ABSURDE, ABSURDO. Consequently, saying that interpreting a certain treaty provision T through the application of a certain first-order rule of interpretation A leads to a result, which is ABSURD, ABSURDE, ABSURDO or UNREASONABLE, DÉRAISONNABLE, IRRAZONABLE, would in both cases be tantamount to saying:

> The reasons for not understanding treaty provision T in accordance with rule A are stronger than those for the opposite.

Of course, some distinction of meaning exists between the words ABSURD, ABSURDE, ABSURDO and UNREASONABLE, DÉRAISONNABLE, IRRAZONABLE. If the interpretation of a treaty through application of a certain interpretation rule A leads to a result which is ABSURD, ABSURDE, ABSURDO, then in relative terms, the reasons to not understand the text in accordance with interpretation rule A are stronger than those that would have prevailed, had the application of rule A instead led to a result which is UNREASONABLE, DÉRAISONNABLE, IRRAZONABLE. I believe it is against this background that we must view the meaning of "absurd or unreasonable" (*"absurde ou déraisonnable", "absurdo o irrazonable"*). If the interpretation of a treaty through the application of a certain rule of interpretation leads to a result, which is "absurd or unreasonable" (*"absurde ou déraisonnable", "absurdo o irrazonable"*), then this is because there are reasons to not understand the text in accordance with the rule in question. In relative terms, these reasons are stronger than those that would have prevailed, had the interpretation instead led to a result which is UNREASONABLE, DÉRAISONNABLE, IRRAZONABLE, but they are not fully as strong as in the situation where the interpretation produces a result which is ABSURD, ABSURDE, ABSURDO.[49]

To this we shall add the meaning of the expression "manifestly". If the interpretation of a treaty provision in accordance with any of the interpretation rules nos. 1–16 leads to a result, which is different from that obtained by interpreting the provision in accordance with any of the interpretation rules nos. 17–39, and the applier is of the opinion that in the prevailing situation the provision shall not be understood in accordance with the former rule, but rather with the latter, then he must not only show that the application of the former rule leads to a result which is "absurd or unreasonable". He must also show this fact to be manifest – the result must be shown to be "manifestly" (Fr. *"manifestement"*; Sp. *"manifiestamente")* absurd or unreasonable. The expression "manifestly" embodies a requirement of significance. Hence, saying that the interpretation of a certain treaty provision T through the application of a certain first-order rule of interpretation A "leads to a result which is manifestly absurd or unreasonable" would be tantamount to saying:

> The reasons for not understanding treaty provision T in accordance with rule A are *significantly stronger* than those for the opposite.

Seeking to determine the contents of VCLT article 32, there is one further thing that we need to clarify. Assume that we interpret a treaty provision (T) by applying two different rules of interpretation: those rules being, first, any one out of rules nos. 1–16, for example rule no. 1; secondly, any one out of rules nos. 17–39, for example interpretation rule no. 18. In addition, suppose that the two rules are in conflict with one another: depending upon whether treaty provision T is interpreted in accordance with rule no. 1 or rule no. 18, different results will ensue. And last of all, suppose that we want to defend the proposition that treaty provision T shall not be understood in accordance with rule no. 1, since by applying that rule we will end up with a result "which is manifestly absurd or unreasonable". In order for us to justify the proposition, we must be in the position to show the reasons for *not* understanding treaty provision T in accordance with rule no. 1 to be significantly stronger than the reasons that can be adduced for the opposite proposition – that provision T *shall* be understood in accordance with interpretation rule no. 1. The question is what kind of reasons we are talking about. Obviously, we are talking about something other than the reasons represented by interpretation rules nos. 1 and 18. If we interpret treaty provision T by applying rules nos. 1 and 18, and we discover that those two rules are in conflict, then certainly, rule no. 18 is a reason for the proposition that provision T *shall* not be understood in accordance with interpretation rule no. 1, whereas rule no. 1 is a reason for the proposition that provision T *shall not* be understood in accordance with rule no. 18. However, faced with a conflict between interpretation rules nos. 1 and 18, we cannot ever say that the one is significantly stronger than the other. Both are part of international law, and as such they are equally strong.

It seems that in fact the reasons we are discussing are a matter of the reasons *underlying* the rules of interpretation. When a rule of interpretation is applied, it is always on the basis of some specific communicative assumption. This issue was brought up in detail in Chapter 2 of this work. Take for example interpretation rule no. 1:

If it can be shown that in a treaty provision, there is an expression whose form corresponds to an expression of conventional language, then the provision shall be understood in accordance with the rules of that language.[50]

Why should we interpret a treaty provision, for example the one in VCLT article 32, through application of interpretation rule no. 1? The answer is twofold. In part, it is because (in international law) there is a meta-norm to the effect that if a need to interpret a treaty provision arises, then the provision shall be understood in accordance with the utterances produced by the parties to the treaty by means of the provision. In part, it is because we assume that the parties to the treaty expressed themselves in accordance with the following standard:

If a state makes an utterance taking the form of a treaty provision, then the provision should be drawn up so that every expression in the provision, whose form corresponds to an expression of conventional language, bears a meaning that agrees with that language.[51]

It can also be expressed as follows:

The parties to the Vienna Convention have expressed themselves in such a way that the meaning of the expression "leads to a result which is manifestly absurd or unreasonable" agrees with conventional language.

This latter assumption is what I have earlier called a communicative assumption.

As we know, a communicative assumption carries more or less weight, depending upon the reasons that can be shown either in support or in rebuttal of the assumption. In the particular situation confronted – we interpret treaty provision T, and we have shown that interpretation rules nos. 1 and 18 are in conflict with one another. Now, we wish to show that there are significantly stronger reasons for not understanding treaty provision T in accordance with rule no. 1 than there are reasons for the opposite – it might therefore seem a sound suggestion that we direct our attention not to interpretation rules nos. 1 and 18 as such, but to the communicative assumptions underlying those rules. What we need to show is that the application of interpretation rules nos. 1 and 18 is based on assumptions, of which the assumption underlying the application of rule no. 1 is significantly weaker than the assumption underlying the application of rule no. 18. Given the basic assumptions of this work, the fact is that I cannot see any other reasonable reading of VCLT article 32. All things considered, I would like to describe the meaning of the expression "leads to a result which is manifestly absurd or unreasonable" as follows:

> If it can be shown that the interpretation of a treaty provision in accordance with any one of the interpretation rules nos. 1–16 leads to a result, which is different from that obtained by interpreting the provision in accordance with any one of the interpretation rules nos. 17–39, and that the application of the two rules is based on communicative assumptions, of which, for good reasons, the assumption underlying the application of the former can be considered significantly weaker than the assumption underlying the application of the latter, then the provision shall not be understood in accordance with this former rule.

6 THE EXPRESSION "LEADS TO A RESULT WHICH IS MANIFESTLY ABSURD OR UNREASONABLE" (CONT'D)

It seems we can now return to our introductory question: how is the qualifier "manifestly absurd or unreasonable" to be read in relation to the main word "result"? Two alternative readings have been discussed. According to a first alternative – earlier termed as alternative (a) – supplementary means of interpretation may be used to determine the meaning of a treaty, when an interpretation according to VCLT article 31 leads to a result, which is manifestly *either* absurd *or* unreasonable.[52] According to a second alternative – alternative (b) – supplementary means of interpretation may be used to determine the meaning of a treaty, when an interpretation according to VCLT article 31 leads to a result, which is manifestly "absurd or unreasonable", where the expression "absurd or unreasonable" is to be considered an idiomatic phrasal lexeme.[53] As support for alternative (b), we have cited interpretation rule no. 18:

> If, by using the preparatory work of a treaty, a concordance can be shown to exist, as between the parties to said treaty, and with regard to the norm content of an interpreted treaty provision, then the provision shall be understood in such a way that it logically agrees with the concordance. [54]

As support for alternative (b), we have cited have interpretation rule no. 1:

> If it can be shown that in a treaty provision, there is an expression whose form corresponds to an expression of conventional language, then the provision shall be understood in accordance with the rules of that language.[55]

The interpretation alternative that I have suggested to be correct is alternative (b). Thus, I must now show that an interpretation of article 32 in accordance with interpretation rule no. 1 "leads to a result which is manifestly absurd or unreasonable". I must show that the application of interpretation rules no. 1 and no. 18 are based on communicative assumptions, of which, for good reasons, the assumption underlying the application of the former can be considered significantly weaker than the assumption underlying the application of the latter.

Interpretation rule no. 1 is based on the assumption that when a state produces an utterance taking the form of a treaty, it always does so in such a way that every expression used in the treaty, whose form corresponds to an expression of conventional language, agrees with the rules of that language.[56] Translated to the interpretation of VCLT article 32, and the expression "leads to a result which is manifestly absurd or unreasonable", this can be stated as follows:

> The parties to the Vienna Convention have expressed themselves in such a way that the meaning of the expression "leads to a result which is manifestly absurd or unreasonable" agrees with conventional language.

For the sake of simplicity, let us term this as the assumption underlying the application of interpretation rule no. 1.

Interpretation rule no. 18 is based on the assumption, that parties to a treaty express themselves in such a way that the treaty and its preparatory work are logically compatible, insofar and to the extent that, by using the preparatory work, good reasons can be provided showing a concordance to exist, between the parties to the treaty, with regard to its norm content.[57]

Translated to the interpretation of VCLT article 32, and the expression "leads to a result which is manifestly absurd or unreasonable", this can be stated as follows:

> The parties to the Vienna Convention have expressed themselves in such a way, that the meaning of VCLT article 32 logically agrees with the preparatory work of VCLT, insofar and to the extent that by using the preparatory work, good reasons can be provided showing a concordance to exist, between the parties to the Vienna Convention, and with regard to the norm content of article 32.

For simplicity's sake, we will term this as the assumption underlying the application of interpretation rule no. 18.

As far as I can see, there are only two ways of showing that an assumption A is significantly weaker than an assumption B. First, arguments can be presented undermining assumption A. Second, arguments can be presented reinforcing assumption B. I will now present two arguments, which undermine the assumption underlying the application of rule no. 1.

The first argument focuses on the wording of the expression "absurd or unreasonable". According to the conventional meaning of this expression, one may use supplementary means of interpretation to determine the meaning of a treaty, when an interpretation according to VCLT article 31 leads to a result which is manifestly "absurd" or "unreasonable". According to conventional language, the result of an act of interpretation is termed as ABSURD ...

> ... [when it is] so clearly untrue or unreasonable as to be laughable or ridiculous.[58]

Hence, according to the wording of VCLT article 32, the extensions of the two expressions "a result which is manifestly absurd" and "a result which is manifestly ... unreasonable" would be such that the former is entirely included in the latter – "a result which is manifestly absurd" is also, by the very same reason, "a result which is manifestly ... unreasonable". Given that the parties to the Vienna Convention have expressed themselves in such a way that the meaning of the expression "leads to a result which is manifestly absurd or unreasonable" agrees with the rules of conventional language, then the expression "absurd" (Fr. *"absurde"*; Sp. *"absurdo")* would be utterly superfluous, at least in the practical sense. Thus, the wording of the expression "absurd or unreasonable" must be said to undermine the assumption underlying the application of interpretation rule no. 1.

The second argument focuses on the wording of the expression "manifestly absurd". According to conventional language, the result of an act of interpretation is referred to as MANIFESTLY ABSURD when the absurdity of the result is manifest. The word MANIFEST, in turns, is defined in dictionaries as *evident; obvious; easily noticed.* Hence, according to the conventional meaning of the expression "manifestly absurd", it seems it would be an unmitigated tautology. If the result of interpretation is ABSURD, then this is exactly because absurdity is manifest; it cannot be made more manifest than it already is. Thus, the wording of the expression "manifestly absurd" must be said to undermine the assumption underlying the application of interpretation rule no. 1.

These two arguments can be augmented with the absence of arguments to the contrary. I am unable to find an argument that either reinforces the assumption underlying the application of interpretation rule no. 1 or undermines the assumption underlying the application of interpretation rule no. 18. Naturally, it is a matter of judgment as to whether this means that the assumption underlying the application of interpretation rule no. 1 could be considered significantly weaker than the assumption underlying the application of interpretation rule no. 18. For my part, I find it difficult to draw any other conclusion. In my judgment, it can indeed be shown that in the given interpretation situation, the application of interpretation rule no. 1 "leads to a result which is manifestly absurd or unreasonable". If it can be shown that, according to interpretation rule no. 1, the expression "leads to a result which is manifestly absurd or unreasonable" shall be interpreted in a way different than according to interpretation rule no. 18, then, as a result, the expression shall not be understood in accordance with interpretation rule no. 1. This is precisely the position I maintain.

7 THE RELATIONSHIP BETWEEN PRIMARY MEANS OF INTERPRETATION AND SUPPLEMENTARY MEANS OF INTERPRETATION, RESPECTIVELY

As I stated earlier, it is the purpose of this chapter to investigate the content of the set of second-order rules of interpretation laid down in international law. I have chosen to organise the chapter according to the different means of interpretation that can be used in the interpretation of treaties. As my first task, I have undertaken to determine the relationship that shall be assumed to hold between primary and supplementary means of interpretation. This has been the subject of Sections 1–6. As a second task, I have decided to determine the relationship that shall be assumed to hold among primary means of interpretation and supplementary means of interpretation, respectively. This is the subject of Section 7. Two questions shall be answered:

(1) What is the relationship that shall be assumed to hold among the different *primary* means of interpretation?
(2) What is the relationship that shall be assumed to hold among the different *supplementary* means of interpretation?

Let us start with the first of the two questions.

What is the relationship that shall be assumed to hold as among the different primary means of interpretation? When appliers interpret a treaty using primary means of interpretation, they need to be observant of the strong interdependency that exists between conventional language on the one hand, and the context and the object and purpose of the treaty on the other. When appliers apply the provisions of Vienna Convention article 31, the context and the object and purpose of the treaty may only be used relative to conventional language ("the ordinary meaning").[59] Article 31 § 1 does *not* instruct appliers to interpret the terms of a treaty with regard to their context and in the light of the treaty's object and purpose. It instructs appliers to interpret the treaty "in accordance with the ordinary meaning to be given to the terms of the treaty in their context" and "in accordance with the ordinary meaning to be given to the terms of the treaty … in the light of its object and purpose". Given this observation, it is not unjustified to argue that an ordinary meaning independent of the context and the object and purpose simply does not exist: if an applier interprets a treaty provision using first conventional language, and second, the context or the object and purpose, and it turns out that the use of different means leads to conflicting results, then the provision shall not be understood using conventional language.

Above anything else – apart from the text in article 31 § 1 – one thing can be adduced in support of this proposition; and this is the concept of interpretation assumed in the Vienna Convention. When the rules of interpretation laid down in VCLT articles 31–33 are applied, it is to clarify a text shown to be unclear.[60] From this concept two very important norms can be derived; they both govern the process of interpretation as such.[61] According to the one norm, a process of interpretation shall *not* be concluded, as long as the interpreted treaty provision *cannot* be regarded as clear.[62] If appliers interpret a treaty provision using some certain means of interpretation, only to conclude that the provision acquires a meaning which still cannot be regarded as clear, then this meaning shall not be considered normative. As we have noted, it is the general view held in the literature that a treaty provision cannot be considered clear as long as the meaning of that provision remains ambiguous.[63] If appliers interpret a treaty provision using some certain means of interpretation, only to conclude that the meaning of the provision still remains ambiguous, then, according to the literature, this meaning should not be considered normative. The use of conventional language ("the ordinary meaning") has been described earlier as the application of interpretation rule no. 1.[64] The use of the context and the object and purpose of the treaty has been described as the application of interpretation rules nos. 2–16.[65]

A condition for applying any of interpretation rules nos. 2–16 is that the application of interpretation rule no. 1 leaves the meaning of the interpreted treaty provision ambiguous.[66] If the application of interpretation rule no. 1 *does not* leave the meaning of the interpreted treaty provision ambiguous, then interpretation rule no. 1 cannot ever be in conflict with any of the interpretation rules nos. 2–16. The sum and substance of this can be described as follows:

> If it can be shown that the interpretation of a treaty provision in accordance with interpretation rule no. 1 leads to a result, which is different than that obtained by interpreting the provision in accordance with any of the interpretation rules nos. 2–16, then it shall not be understood in accordance with interpretation rule no. 1.

Hence, according to international law, the relationship between the primary means of interpretation would be such that the context and the object and purpose must be considered as of generally greater authority than conventional language. Now the question is whether, in a similar fashion, the internal relationship between the context and the object and purpose has been settled once and for all in a rule of a general content. Nothing of this sort can be derived from the text of the Vienna Convention – a fact that agrees with what originally seems to have been the intention, judging by comments made in the literature.[67] This view is further confirmed by a quick look at the preparatory work of the Vienna Convention. In the final draft adopted by the International Law Commission in 1966 there is a rule titled "*Article 27. General rule of interpretation*".[68] This rule – the text of which, with one minor exception,[69] corresponds entirely with that of final article 31 – is commented upon by the Commission as follows:

> The Commission re-examined the structure of article 27 in the light of the comments of Governments and considered other possible alternatives ... It considered that the article, when read as a whole, cannot properly be regarded as laying down a legal hierarchy of norms for the interpretation of treaties. The elements of interpretation in the article have in the nature of things to be arranged in some order. But it was considerations of logic, not any obligatory legal hierarchy, which guided the Commission in arriving at the arrangement proposed in the article. Once it is established – and on this point the Commission was unanimous – that the starting point of interpretation is the meaning of the text, logic indicates that "the ordinary meaning to be given to the terms of the treaty in their context and in the light of its object and purpose" should be the first element to be mentioned. Similarly, logic suggests that the elements comprised in the "context" should be the next to be mentioned since they form

part of or are intimately related to the text. Again, it is only logic which suggests that the elements in paragraph 3 – a subsequent agreement regarding the interpretation, a subsequent practice establishing the understanding of the parties regarding the interpretation and relevant rules of international law applicable in the relations between the parties – should follow and not precede the elements in the previous paragraphs. The logical consideration which suggests this is that these elements are extrinsic to the text. But these three elements are all of an obligatory character and by their very nature could not be considered to be norms of interpretation in any way inferior to those which precede them.[70]

All things considered, I find it difficult to arrive at any other conclusion than this: according to international law, the authority of the context shall not be regarded as greater than that of the object and purpose, and the authority of the object and purpose shall not be regarded as greater than that of the context. From a legal point of view, the authorities of the two means of interpretation are perfectly equivalent. If it can be shown that the interpretation of a treaty provision in accordance with any of interpretation rules nos. 2–16 leads to a result, which is different from that obtained by interpreting the provision in accordance with any other of the rules nos. 2–16, then this is a conflict that must be resolved in some other manner than by the application of a rule of law.

What is the relationship that shall be assumed to hold among the different supplementary means of interpretation of interpretation? Let us once again turn our attention to the text of article 32. As an explanation of the expression "supplementary means of interpretation" we are given only two examples, namely "the preparatory work of the treaty" and "the circumstances of its conclusion". Based on this, some authors draw the conclusion that according to the Vienna Convention, "the preparatory work of the treaty" and "the circumstances of its conclusion" shall be considered more important than other supplementary means of interpretation. One such author is Alfred Rest:

Ausdrücklich werden als "supplementary means" lediglich die Vorarbeiten und die Begleitumstände des Vetragsschlusses genannt. Diese Aufzählung sollte wohl weniger enumerativen Charakter haben, als vielmehr lediglich der Hervorhebung der beiden wichtigsten Auslegungsmittel dienen.[71]

Saying that a means of interpretation (A) is generally more important than another means of interpretation (B) is tantamount to saying that the means of interpretation A possesses an authority that, regardless of the circumstances, must be considered greater than the authority of the means of interpretation B. If appliers interpret a treaty using "the preparatory work of the treaty" or "the circumstances of its conclusion", as well as some other supplementary means of interpretation, and they discover that a conflict exists between the different means of interpretation, then the conflict would always be resolved with "the preparatory work of the treaty" and "the circumstances of its conclusion", respectively, coming out as final "victors" – all according to Rest. Personally, I find it difficult to see how such a reading of VCLT article 32 could be considered correct.

Obviously, the reading that Rest seems to advocate is diametrically opposite to the text of the Vienna Convention as interpreted using conventional language. This is how the text of article 32 reads:

Recourse may be had to supplementary means of interpretation, including the preparatory work of the treaty and the circumstances of its conclusion ...

Il peut être fait appel à des moyens complémentaires d'interprétation, et notamment aux travaux préparatoires et aux circonstances dans lesquelles le traité a été conclu ...

Se podrá acudir a medios complementarios, en particular a los trabajos preparatorios del tratado y a las circunstancias de su celebración ...

Nothing in the term INCLUDING, ET NOTAMMENT, EN PARTICULAR indicates that, according to the Vienna Convention, "the preparatory work of the treaty" and "the circumstances of its conclusion" would have an authority that is somehow greater than that possessed by other supplementary means of interpretation. In any event, the reading that Rest seems to advocate is another than that imparted through the application of interpretation rules nos. 1–16. Such an interpretation is certainly not beyond the bounds of possibility. There are elements in the rules of interpretation laid down in international law that open up for the possibility of understanding a treaty provision by setting aside the rules of conventional language. The possibility is, however, strictly limited. First, the applier must be able to show that understanding the provision according to a non-conventional meaning has the support of one or more of the interpretation rules nos. 17–39. Second, the applier must be able to show that understanding the provision in accordance with conventional language amounts to a result "which is manifestly absurd or unreasonable".

Nothing in the description of article 32 given by Rest gives the slightest indication that these two conditions are met. In fact, I think strong reasons suggest the opposite to be the case. As we know, the ultimate purpose of an act of interpretation is to determine the legally correct meaning of a treaty.[72] If we agree with the proposition that "the preparatory work of the treaty" and "the circumstances of its conclusion", according to the Vienna Convention, possess an authority greater than that possessed by other supplementary means of interpretation, then as part of the "bargain" we would also need to accept the following proposition: "the preparatory work of the treaty" and "the circumstances of its conclusion", according to what is assumed by the parties to the Vienna Convention, are typically better indicators of the correct meaning of a treaty provision than for example an act of interpretation *per analogiam* or an application of *the rule of necessary implication*. Is this proposition really acceptable? I think not – not when we know that "the preparatory work of the treaty" and "the circumstances of its conclusion" are means of interpretation whose origins relate to the time prior to when a treaty is adopted as definite; and not when we know that in many instances, a treaty continues to be in force for a very long time, in some cases up to hundreds of years. All things considered, the reading suggested by Rest seems to be entirely without merit. My conclusion is that the legal authority possessed by "the preparatory work of the treaty" and "the circumstances of its conclusion" is exactly that very same authority possessed by other supplementary means of interpretation.[73] If it can be shown that the interpretation of a treaty provision in accordance with any one of interpretation rules nos. 17–39 leads to a result, which is different than that obtained by interpreting the provision in accordance with any one of interpretation rules nos. 17–39, then this is a conflict that must be resolved in some other manner than by the application of a rule of law.

8 CONCLUSIONS

It is the purpose of this chapter to describe the relationship that shall be assumed to hold between, and among, the various means of interpretation recognised as acceptable by the Vienna Convention. According to international law, what is the relationship that shall be assumed to hold between primary and supplementary means of interpretation? And what is the relationship that shall be assumed to hold among the primary and the supplementary means of interpretation, respectively? These are the two questions I have undertaken to answer. Based on the observations made in this chapter, the following three rules of interpretation can be established:

Rule no. 40

§ **1**. If it can be shown that the interpretation of a treaty provision in accordance with any one of interpretation rules nos. 1–16 leads to a result, which is different from that obtained by interpreting the provision in accordance with any one of interpretation rules nos. 17–39, and that the application of the former rule either leaves the meaning of the interpreted treaty provision ambiguous or obscure, or amounts to a result which is manifestly absurd or unreasonable, then the provision shall not be understood in accordance with this former rule.

§ **2**. For the purpose of this rule, the meaning of a treaty provision shall be considered AMBIGUOUS OR OBSCURE, if interpreting the provision in accordance with any one of interpretation rules nos. 2–16 leads to a result, which is different than that obtained by interpreting the provision in accordance with any other of those fifteen rules.

§ 3. For the purpose of this rule, saying that the application of a rule of interpretation LEADS TO A RESULT WHICH IS MANIFESTLY ABSURD OR UNREASONABLE is tantamount to saying that the application of the two conflicting rules – the first being one among rules numbered 1 to 16, the other being one among the rules numbered 17 to 39 – is based on communicative assumptions, of which the assumption underlying the application of the former rule can be considered significantly weaker than the assumption underlying the application of the latter.

Rule no. 41

If it can be shown that the interpretation of a treaty provision in accordance with any one of interpretation rules nos. 1–16 leads to a result, which is different from that obtained by interpreting the provision in accordance with any one of interpretation rules nos. 17–39, then, rather than being understood in accordance with the latter of the two rules, the provision shall be understood in accordance with the former, except for those cases where interpretation rule no. 40 applies.

Rule no. 42

If it can be shown that the interpretation of a treaty provision in accordance with interpretation rule no. 1 leads to a result, which is different from that obtained by interpreting the provision in accordance with any one of interpretation rules nos. 2–16, then the provision shall not be understood in accordance with interpretation rule no. 1.

NOTES

1. See Ch. 1, Section 1, of this work.
2. See Ch. 2, Section 5, of this work.
3. Ibid., Section 6, of this work.
4. See Ch. 1, Section 5, and Ch. 2, Section 5, of this work.
5. See Chapters 8–9 of this work.
6. See Chapters 3–7 of this work.
7. My emphasis.
8. See, explicitly, Thirlway, 1991, pp. 33–36; *Oppenheim's International Law*, pp. 1275–1276; Greig, pp. 478, 481; Yasseen, pp. 80–82; Haraszti, pp. 102–103; Hummer, pp. 98–99; Lang, pp. 164–165; Köck, p. 93; Jacobs, pp. 325–326; Degan, 1968, p. 19. See also, more or less implicitly, Ress, p. 37; Merrills, p. 92; Reuter, 1989, pp. 75–76; Amerasinghe, pp. 191–192; E. Lauterpacht, p. 439; Dupuy, pp. 219, 221; Brownlie, p. 630; Sinclair, 1984, p. 141; Bernhardt, 1984, p. 323; Tabory, pp. 202–205; Jiménez de Aréchaga, p. 47; Elias, 1974, pp. 79–80; Favre, 1974, p. 254; Jennings, p. 550; Gross, p. 117; Schröder, p. 124; Bernhardt, 1967, p. 495, n. 12.
9. See Ch. 2, Section 6, of this work.

10. See Ch. 1, Section 3, of this work.
11. See e.g. Bernhardt, 1984, p. 322; Yasseen, p. 81; Elihu Lauterpacht, pp. 417–419; Voïcu, p. 27; Berlia, pp. 297–305; McNair, 1961, p. 367. According to some authors, the doctrine of plain meaning is inadequate. (See e.g. Schwebel, 1996, pp. 541–547; Schwebel, 1997, pp. 797–804; Hummer, pp. 87–163; Klabbers, 2003, pp. 267–288; McNair, 1961, p. 372; McDougal, pp. 992–1000; McDogal, Laswell and Miller, pp. 78–82.) For a rebuttal of this argument, see Linderfalk, 2007(a), pp. 140–144.
12. See e.g. Thirlway, 1991, p. 21; Brownlie, pp. 628–629; Greig, pp. 477–484; Favre, 1974, p. 253; Fitzmaurice, 1957, p. 211. According to some authors, the principle of natural and ordinary meaning – the doctrine of plain meaning – is inadequate. (See e.g. Schwebel, 1996, pp. 541–547; Schwebel, 1997, pp. 797–804; Hummer, pp. 87–163; Klabbers, 2003, pp. 267–288; McNair, 1961, p. 372; McDougal, pp. 992–1000; McDogal, Laswell and Miller, pp. 78–82.) For a rebuttal of this argument, see Linderfalk, 2007(a), pp. 140–144.
13. Cf. Linderfalk, 2007(a), p. 141; Ress, p. 37; Thirlway, 1991, p. 33; Ris, pp. 119–120; Brownlie, p. 630; Bernhardt, 1984, p. 322; Yasseen, p. 81; Haraszti, pp. 91–104; Favre, 1974, p. 254; O'Connell, p. 253; Degan, 1968, p. 13.
14. Cf. Linderfalk, 2007(a), p. 141; Yasseen, p. 81; Bernhardt, 1967, p. 503.
15. We should recall the observations made in Chapter 1, Section 3, namely that the provisions of VCLT articles 31–33 can be seen to govern both the result of the interpretation process and the interpretation process as such.
16. See the limitations in Ch. 1, Section 3, of this work.
17. See, explicitly, Ress, p. 37; Thirlway, 1991, pp. 24–25; *Oppenheim's International Law*, pp. 1275–1276; Brownlie, p. 630; Bernhardt, 1984, p. 322; Yasseen, pp. 81–82; Haraszti, pp. 91–102; Favre, 1974, p. 254. See also, more or less implicitly, Amerasinghe, pp. 200–201; Sinclair, 1984, p. 127; Jiménez de Aréchaga, pp. 46–47; Elihu Lauterpacht, p. 417; Köck, p. 86; Hummer, pp. 98–99; Greig, pp. 477–481; Bernhardt, 1967, p. 503.
18. Similarly, Ress, p. 37; Amerasinghe, pp. 200–201; *Oppenheim's International Law*, pp. 1272–1273; Bernhardt, 1984, p. 322; Jiménez de Aréchaga, pp. 46–47; Hummer, p. 99, n. 44; Haraszti, pp. 91–102; Greig, pp. 477–481. According to several authors, this should also be considered a result of the provision in VCLT article 31 § 1, according to which a treaty shall be interpreted *in good faith ("de bonne foi", "de buena fe").* (See e.g. *Oppenheim's International Law*, p. 1272; Sinclair, 1984, p. 120; Yasseen, pp. 22–23.)
19. Some commentators express themselves as if this were indeed the case. (See e.g. Jennings, p. 550; Sharma, p. 388.)
20. Cf. Draft Articles with Commentaries (1966): "The word 'supplementary' emphasizes that article 28 does not provide for alternative, autonomous, means of interpretation but only for means to aid an interpretation governed by the principles contained in article 27." (*ILC Yrbk*, 1966, Vol. 2, p. 223, § 19.)
21. See limitations in Ch. 1, Section 3, of this work.
22. Villiger, p. 346, n. 212. (My italics.)
23. Jennings, p. 550.
24. Schröder, p. 124.
25. See e.g. Verdross and Simma, p. 493, n. 9; Yasseen, p. 87; Tabory, p. 205; Sharma, p. 389; Gross, p. 117; Jacobs, p. 326; Jennings, p. 550; Bernhardt, 1967, p. 495.

26. Jacobs, p. 326. (Footnote omitted.)
27. See Draft Articles with Commentaries (1966), *ILC Yrbk*, 1966, Vol. 2, pp. 217–218.
28. See Comments on the final draft articles on the law of treaties prepared by the International Law Commission at its eighteenth session, Report of the Secretary-General (UN Doc. A/6827 and Add. 1 and 2), *UN General Assembly, Official Records*, Annexes to the 22nd session, Agenda item 86, p. 26.
29. See *Documents of the Conference*, p. 149, § 269.
30. Cf. USA, at the first session of the Vienna Conference, 31st meeting of the Committee of the Whole, *Official Records*, pp. 167–168, §§ 38–50.
31. See Vietnam, at the first session of the Vienna Conference, 31st meeting of the Committee of the Whole, *Official Records*, p. 168, § 51; Switzerland, at the same meeting, ibid., p. 180, § 27.
32. See, at the first session of the Vienna Conference, 32nd meeting of the Committee of the Whole, Tanzania, *Official Records*, p. 173, §§ 14–15, 17; and at the first session of the Vienna Conference, 33rd meeting of the Committee of the Whole, United Kingdom, ibid., p. 178, §§ 8–9; Argentina, ibid., p. 180, § 24; Nigeria, ibid., p. 181, §§ 35–37; Mexico, ibid., p. 181, § 40; Cuba, ibid., p. 182, §§ 44–45; Portugal, ibid., pp. 182–183, § 56; Madagascar, ibid., p. 183, §§ 61–63.
33. A point of clarification might be appropriate. As observed, the rules of interpretation laid down in the Vienna Convention must be seen to govern both the result of the interpretation process and the interpretation process as such. (See Ch. 1, Section 3 of this work.) What I am interested in establishing are the rules that govern the result of the interpretation process. The task is to explain the concept of a correct interpretation result considered from the point of view of international law. According to what I have just stated, there are four different types of situations that might create problems for the applier who interprets a treaty provision using primary means of interpretation. This statement must be adjusted somewhat, depending upon whether we are talking about the result of the interpretation process or the process of interpretation as such. Of course, all situations of type (1)–(4) can be seen to pose problems if we make it our task to explain the concept of a correct process of interpretation, considered from the point of view of international law. However, the same does not apply if we instead imagine the situation of an applier, who wishes to know whether, from the point of view of international law, a given interpretation proposition can be considered correct. In such a case, only situations (1)–(3) will cause problems. If none of the rules nos. 1–16 is applicable, then naturally no conflict can arise between our two categories of rules – nos. 1–16 and nos. 17–39.
34. My italics.
35. I have taken for granted that the text in article 32 refers back to the text in article 31 § 1: "A *treaty* shall be interpreted in good faith in accordance with the ordinary meaning to be given to the terms of the treaty in their context ...". Another possible interpretation is that the text in article 32 instead refers back to the text in 31 § 4: "A special meaning shall be given to a *term*...". (All italics mine.)
36. See pp. 227–228 of this work.
37. With regard to the concept of *operative interpretation*, more details are provided in Ch. 1, Section 3 of this work.
38. Loc. cit.
39. See pp. 331–332 of this work.
40. Loc. cit.
41. See p. 95 of this work.

42. Strictly speaking, there are *two* grammatically correct interpretations of the expression "leads to a result which is manifestly absurd or unreasonable". The problem is the syntax of the expression "manifestly absurd or unreasonable". The expression "manifestly" can be understood to qualify both "absurd" and "unreasonable", and it can be understood to qualify only "absurd" and not "unreasonable". In this discussion, I have disregarded this grammatical ambiguity.
43. See, however, Schwebel, 1997: "[I]t is not infrequent that the 'ordinary meaning' of the terms of a treaty, even if found to be unambiguously such, leads to a result which, if not 'manifestly absurd' is 'unreasonable' " (p. 799).
44. See p. 95 of this work.
45. See p. 269 of this work.
46. See e.g. Poland, at the second session of the Vienna Conference, 13th plenary meeting, *Official Records,* p. 58, § 68; Waldock, Sixth Report on the Law of Treaties, *ILC Yrbk*, 1966, Vol. 2, p. 99, § 20; Reuter, at the ILC's eighteenth session, 871st meeting, *ILC Yrbk*, 1966, Vol. 1, Part 2, p. 195, § 22; Ago, at the ILC's eighteenth session, 872nd meeting, ibid., p. 202, § 51; Yasseen (speaking as member), at the ILC's eighteenth session, 873rd meeting, ibid., pp. 203–204, § 13; Rosenne, at the same meeting, ibid., p. 205, § 30; Waldock, at the same meeting, ibid., p. 206, § 39; Waldock, Third Report on the Law of Treaties, *ILC Yrbk*, 1964, Vol. 2, p. 57, § 16, p. 58, § 20; Draft Articles With Commentaries (1964), ibid., p. 205, § 16; Ago (speaking as chairman), at the ILC's sixteenth session, 765th meeting, *ILC Yrbk*, 1964, Vol. 1, p. 281, §§ 86, 92; Ruda, at the ILC's sixteenth session, 766th meeting, ibid., p. 283, § 12; Yasseen, at the same meeting, ibid., p. 286, § 49.
47. See e.g. Bulgaria, at the first session of the Vienna Conference, 32nd meeting of the Committee of the Whole, *Official Records,* p. 176, § 56; Yasseen (speaking as member), at the ILC's eighteenth session, 873rd meeting, *ILC Yrbk*, 1966, Vol. 1, Part. 2, pp. 203–204, § 13; Rosenne, at the same meeting, ibid., p. 205, § 30; Draft Articles With Commentaries (1964), *ILC Yrbk*, 1964, Vol. 2, p. 204, § 15.
48. See pp. 333–334 of this work.
49. Cf. Fitzmaurice – on page 10 of his 1951 article – quotes the following passage from the ICJ decision in the *(Second) Admissions* case: "If, on the other hand, the words in their natural and ordinary meaning are ambiguous or lead to an unreasonable result [sont équivoques ou conduisent à des résultats déraisonnables], then and only then, must the Court, by resort to other methods of interpretation, seek to ascertain what the parties really did mean [avaient en réalité dans l'ésprit] when they used these words. As the Permanent Court said in the case concerning the *Polish Postal Service in Danzig* (P.C.I.J., Series B, No. 1, p. 39):
'It is a cardinal principle of interpretation that words must be interpreted in the sense which they would normally have in their context, unless such interpretation would lead to something unreasonable or absurd.'
When the Court can give effect to a provision of a treaty by giving to the words used in it their natural and ordinary meaning, it may not interpret the words by seeking to give them some other meaning." An interesting point in this context is the footnote that Fitzmaurice has added to the French expression "*déraisonnable*" in the quotation: "The French term *déraisonnable* is somewhat stronger than the English 'unreasonable' and means something more like 'contrary to reason'."
50. See p. 95 of this work.
51. See p. 61 of this work.

52. See p. 334 of this work.
53. See p. 335 of this work.
54. See p. 335 of this work.
55. See p. 335 of this work.
56. See the introduction to Ch. 3 in this work.
57. See Ch. 8, Section 7, of this work.
58. *Webster's New World Dictionary*, Third College Edition.
59. See Chapters 4–7 of this work, especially the introductions to Chapters 4 and 7.
60. See Ch. 1, Section 3, of this work.
61. See Ch. 10, Section 2, of this work.
62. Loc. cit.
63. Loc. cit.
64. See Ch. 3 of this work.
65. See Chapters 4–7 of this work.
66. Loc. cit.
67. See e.g. Ris, p. 118; *Oppenheim's International Law*, p. 1272, n. 6; Villiger, p. 345; Tabory, pp. 202–205; Haraszti, p. 102; Mehrish, p. 62; Gross, p. 119; Schröder, p. 124; Bernhardt, 1967, p. 495, n. 12; Jennings, p. 550.
68. Draft Articles with Commentaries (1966), *ILC Yrbk*, 1966, Vol. 2, p. 217.
69. The exception being the text in § 3(a). In the 1966 draft, article 27 § 3(a) reads: "Any subsequent agreement between the parties regarding the interpretation of the treaty". The Vienna Convention text contains the following addition: "... or the application of its provisions".
70. Draft Articles with Commentaries (1966), *ILC Yrbk*, 1966, Vol. 2, p. 220, § 9.
71. Rest, p. 151. (Footnote omitted.)
72. See Ch. 2, especially Section 1, of this work.
73. Similarly, *Oppenheim's International Law* , pp. 1276–1277; Yasseen, p. 79; Tabory, pp. 202–205; Schröder, p. 124.

CHAPTER 11

THE SPECIAL RULE REGARDING THE INTERPRETATION OF TREATIES AUTHENTICATED IN TWO OR MORE LANGUAGES

When states initiate negotiations on the conclusion of a treaty, and negotiations are successful, the negotiating states will reach a point at which the drafting stage can be brought to a close. They will then proceed to confirm that a final and definite text of treaty is in hand. After this point when confirmation is provided, we say the treaty *has been authenticated.*[1] In international law, there is no generally applicable norm stating in what language or languages a treaty shall be authenticated. In principle, the negotiating states are free to choose the language or languages they find suitable for the purpose. Considering this, the abundance of strategies illustrated by the practice of states is perhaps not surprising.[2] A simple situation arises when there are only two states concluding a treaty. In drafting a bilateral treaty, states usually authenticate the text of that treaty in two language versions, one in each party's respective language, with the possible addition of a third version written in one of the so-called "international languages". Other solutions are applied when the parties number three or more. It does happen that in the drafting of multilateral treaties, the negotiating states authenticate enough texts so that each of the parties receives the treaty in its native language – this is especially so when drafting involves a small number of states, or when the negotiating states represent a limited number of languages. When negotiating states represent a larger number of languages, they almost always agree to limit the number of authenticated texts. Here, the most common solution is to authenticate the treaty in one or more "international languages"; or, if the treaty is drafted under the auspices of an international organisation, in the official language of that organisation. Today, for example, all treaties adopted by the UN General Assembly are authenticated in six languages: Arabic, Chinese, English, French, Russian and Spanish.[3]

Drafting a treaty in several languages is a difficult task that requires particular attention to detail and great care.[4] Not only must the negotiating states arrive at an agreement that can be accepted by all; they must also ensure that texts authenticated later are equivalent in meaning. The result is not always the desired one. Actually, it seems to be more the rule than the exception that a comparison of the authenticated texts of a treaty discloses a difference in meaning. Often, this is brought about more by the inherent characteristics of human languages than by anything else; many words are simply impossible to translate from one language to another without at least some change in meaning.[5] Nevertheless, at times one finds discrepancies so glaring that they cannot be anything but the product of oversight. An excellent example is article 6 §§ 2 and 3(c) of the *European Convention for the Protection of Human Rights and Fundamental Freedoms*.[6]

2. *Everyone charged with a criminal offence* shall be presumed innocent until proved guilty according to law.
3. *Everyone charged with a criminal offence* has the following minimum rights: ... (c) to defend himself in person or through legal assistance of his own choosing **or**, if he has not sufficient means to pay for legal assistance, to be given it free when the interests of justice so require; [...].

2. *Toute personne accusée d'une infraction* est présumée innocente jusqu'à ce que sa culpabilité ait été légalement établie.
3. *Tout accusé* a droit notamment à: ... (c) se défendre lui-même ou avoir l'assistence d'un défenseur de son choix **et**, s'il n'a pas les moyens de rémunérer un défenseur, pouvoir être assisté gratuitement par un avocat d'office, lorsque les intérêts de la justice l'exigent; [...].[7]

If a comparison of the different authenticated texts of a treaty discloses a difference in meaning, special interpretation problems arise. According to VCLT article 33 § 3, the terms of a treaty shall be presumed to have the same meaning in each authenticated text. The idea is that when we apply a multi-language treaty, normally there should be no need to scrutinise and compare all of the authenticated texts, considering all the time and effort inherent in such an examination. On the contrary, we should be able to select one of the texts – in principle, any one of them – and rely upon it.[8]However, the situation will be entirely changed once a difference in meaning has been discovered. A treaty is and always will be a single agreement, comprised of a single set of provisions, even if the treaty happens to be expressed in several different languages. If the treaty is applied, and the parties do not heed the difference in meaning detected, then of course this is at odds with the idea of the treaty as a single, integrated unit. The only correct thing to do is to ensure that the authenticated texts all convey the same meaning. The texts must be reconciled. It is the purpose of this chapter to describe how such reconciliation shall be achieved.

Our starting point is the rule in article 33 of the Vienna Convention, the heading of which is "Interpretation of treaties authenticated in two or more languages". I cite from § 4:

Except where a particular text prevails in accordance with paragraph 1, when a comparison of the authentic texts discloses a difference of meaning which the application of articles 31 and 32 does not remove, the meaning which best reconciles the texts, having regard to the object and purpose of the treaty, shall be adopted.

Sauf le cas où un texte déterminé l'emporte conformément au paragraph 1, lorsque la comparaison des textes authentiques fait apparaître une différence de sens que l'application des articles 31 et 32 ne permet pas d'éliminer, on adoptera le sens qui, compte tenu de l'objet et du but du traité, concilie le mieux ces textes.

Salvo en el caso en que prevalezca en texto determinado conforme a lo previsto en el párrafo 1, cuando la comparación de los textos auténticos revele una diferencia de sentido que no pueda resolverse con la aplicación de los artículos 31 y 32, se adoptará el sentido que mejor concilie esos textos, habida cuenta del objeto y del fin del tratado.

Considering the purpose of this chapter, § 1 also seems relevant:

When a treaty has been authenticated in two or more languages, the text is equally authoritative in each language, unless the treaty provides or the parties agree that, in case of divergence, a particular text shall prevail.

Lorsqu'un traité a été authentifié en deux ou plusieurs langues, son texte fait foi dans chacune de ces langues, à moins que le traité ne dispose ou que les parties ne conviennent qu'en cas de divergence un texte déterminé l'emportera.

Cuando un tratado haya sido autenticado en dos o más idiomas, el texto hará igualmente fe en cada idioma, a menos que el tratado disponga o las partes convengan que en caso de discrepancia prevalecerá uno de los textos.

One thing is clear upon reading the text of the Vienna Convention. If a multi-language treaty must be applied, and two authenticated texts cannot be compared without a difference in meaning revealing itself, several methods of reconciliation are available; all attempts at harmonisation must be performed in a predetermined order. First, the applier shall investigate whether the difference in meaning cannot be removed through the application of VCLT articles 31 and 32. Second – should the first method be insufficient – the applier shall establish whether the treaty provides, or the parties agree, that in case of divergence, a particular text shall prevail. Third – should this second method, too, be insufficient – "the meaning which best reconciles the texts, having regard to the object and purpose of the treaty, shall be adopted". I have organised this chapter so that in Section 1, I begin by trying to clarify the various modes of reconciliation provided in VCLT article 33. In Sections 2 and 3, I will then pay particular attention to the method that, for authors in the literature, seems to have presented the most problems, namely the third of the above-mentioned methods.

1 GENERAL OBSERVATIONS ON THE METHODS OF RECONCILIATION

Assume that an applier sets out to interpret a multi-language treaty, but that he soon discovers that the authenticated texts cannot be compared without the comparison disclosing a difference in meaning. According to the provisions of VCLT article 33 § 4, the applier shall then first ensure that the difference is one "which the application of article 31 and 32 does not remove" (Fr. *"que l'application des articles 31 et 32 ne permet pas d'éliminer"*; Sp. *"que no pueda resolverse con la aplicación de los artículos 31 y 32")*. The applier shall determine by an application of the usual rules of interpretation what should be considered the correct meaning of the treaty. In fact, most differences in meaning can be eliminated using this first method of reconciliation.[9] An example of this is the judgment of the European Court of Human Rights in the *Van der Mussele* case.[10]

In 1976, Eric Van der Mussele, a young Belgian, completed his law degree and began working as a trainee *("avocat stagiaire")* at a Belgian law firm. His purpose was to obtain the practical experience needed to seek membership in the Belgian bar *("l'Ordre des avocats")*. During his trainee period, Van der Mussele was required to defend several clients without receiving any compensation for his work. The question arose whether these duties fell within the bounds set out in the *European Convention for the Protection of Human Rights and Fundamental Freedoms* . Van der Mussele maintained this was not the case and lodged a complaint with the European Commission, citing among other things European Convention, article 4 § 2:

> No one shall be required to perform forced or compulsory labour.

Belgium took the opposing view, and in time the case was turned over to the European Court. The issue gave the court an occasion to explore the meaning of the expression "labour" (Fr. *"travail")*:

> It is true that the English word "labour" is often used in the narrow sense of manual work, but it also bears the broad meaning of the French word *"travail"* and it is the latter that should be adopted in the present context. The Court finds corroboration of this in the definition included ... in Article 4 § 3(d) of the European Convention ("any work or service", *"tout travail ou service"*) [...].[11]

Let us examine this statement more closely.

First, it is clear that upon comparing the English text of article 4 § 2 with the French text, the court discovered a difference in meaning. The French word TRAVAIL is unambiguous. It is used in the widest sense to mean *work in general*, that is, both blue-collar and white-collar work. The English word LABOUR is ambiguous. It can be used in the narrow sense of *blue-collar work*, but – like TRAVAIL – it can also be used in the wider sense of *work in general.* The case can be illustrated by the following Venn diagram. (The meaning of LABOUR corresponds to both areas M_1 and area M_2, while the meaning of TRAVAIL corresponds only to area M_2.)

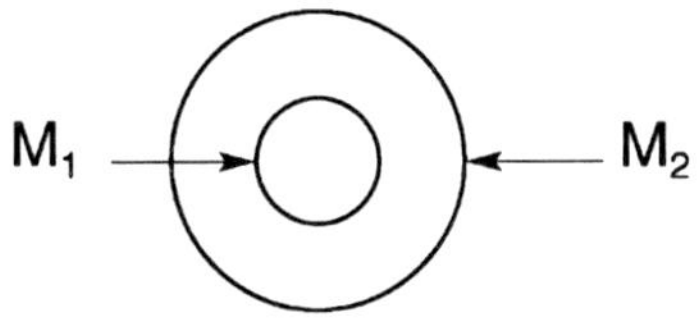

Secondly, the court has gone further and asked whether the difference in meaning between the English and French texts might possibly be removed through an application of VCLT articles 31 and 32. Apparently, this is indeed the case. Using the context, the court has been able to eliminate one of the two possible ordinary meanings of the expression "labour"; hence, area M_1 can be disregarded. The argument might be summarised in the following manner:

> The text of European Convention article 4 § 2 contains the expression "labour". The ordinary meaning of the word LABOUR is ambiguous: in one sense, it can be used to refer to blue-collar work only, in another sense it can be used to refer to *work in general.* According to article 4 § 3 of the European Convention, the extension of the expression "forced or compulsory labour" shall not be understood to include "work or service which forms part of normal civic obligations". The expression "any work or service" shall be understood to mean not only blue-collar work but *work in general, white collar-work included.* Hence, given interpretation rule no. 3 – according to which a treaty provision shall be understood in such a way that it does not logically contradict those other provisions contained in said treaty – the expression "labour" in article 4 § 2 shall also be understood to mean *work in general.*

If it is often the case, that by applying VCLT articles 31 and 32 appliers will be able to reconcile the different authenticated texts of a treaty, then there are also situations where the usual rules of interpretation do not suffice. It is a simple fact, that application of articles 31 and 32 will not always result in all authenticated texts being understood to have the same meaning. According to the provisions of Vienna article 33 § 4, two additional methods of reconciliation remain. The choice depends on the situation at hand.

A first situation arises when "the treaty provides or the parties agree that, in case of divergence, a particular text shall prevail" (Fr. *"le traité ... dispose ou ... les parties ... conviennent qu'en cas de divergence un texte déterminé l'emportera"*; Sp. *"el tratado disponga o las partes convengan que en caso de discrepancia prevalecerá uno de los textos")*. In practice, we can envision two cases: (1) the parties have agreed that one of the authenticated texts shall prevail;[12] or (2) the parties have agreed that another, unauthenticated text shall prevail.[13] In legal terms, the effect is the same. If the parties to a treaty have not only authenticated the treaty in two or more different language versions, but have also had the foresight to provide a solution for any eventual differences found in the authenticated texts, then naturally we must respect such agreements. After all, the rules of interpretation laid down in international law are *jus dispositivum* – they apply only on the condition, and to the extent, that the parties to a treaty have not come to agree among themselves on something else.

A second situation arises when the parties have left open the issue of priority among the various texts, or have expressly agreed that all texts shall be equally valid.[14] As a last resort, "the meaning which best reconciles the texts, having regard to the object and purpose of the treaty", shall then be adopted (Fr. *"on adoptera le sens qui, compte tenu de l'objet et du but du traité, concilie le mieux ces textes"*; Sp. *"se adoptará el sentido que mejor concilie esos textos, habida cuenta del objeto y del fin del tratado")*. With that, we arrive at a provision which, judging from the literature, seems to have been the cause of great uncertainty.[15] Through the years, several questions have been discussed:

- In the terminology of the Vienna Convention, what do we mean when we say that two texts shall be *reconciled*?
- What does the Vienna Convention mean by instructing appliers to adopt the meaning which "best" reconciles the authenticated texts?
- What role is intended for "the object and purpose of the treaty" in process of reconciliation?

No great elucidation in these issues has been achieved. On the whole, the opinions expressed in the literature appear to confuse more than clarify. My judgment is that to a large part, the whole discourse is built on a misunderstanding and on a lack of familiarity with the rules laid down in VCLT articles 31–32 in general. Perhaps the wording of article 33 § 4 is not entirely fortunate. However, it is hardly as problematic as some authors would like us to think. The task for Sections 2 and 3 of this chapter is to see if some greater clarity can be achieved.

2 REGARDING THE METHOD DESCRIBED IN VCLT ARTICLE 33 § 4

What does the Vienna Convention mean by instructing appliers to adopt the meaning "which best reconciles the [authenticated] texts, having regard to the object and purpose of the treaty"? Let us begin by simplifying the analysis; we disregard the clause "having regard to the object and purpose of the treaty". The task of appliers would then be to adopt "the meaning which best reconciles the [authenticated] texts". Much of the confusion around VCLT article 33 § 4 seems to have originated in a misconception of what it actually means, when appliers are told to *reconcile* two or more authenticated texts of a treaty. Assume that a text of a treaty imposes upon each party P the obligation to take a certain type of action A within a specified period of time T, given that some kind of state-of-affairs S can be shown to exist. Now assume that the treaty has been authenticated in two different languages, English and French:

Everyone arrested or detained ... shall be brought *promptly* before a judge [...].
Toute personne arrêtée ou détenue ... doit être *aussitôt* traduite devant un juge [...].[16]

Lastly, assume that an applier has compared the two authenticated texts, and that he has found a difference in meaning that cannot possibly be removed through the application of VCLT articles 31 and 32: the French expression *"aussitôt"* appears to place the parties under greater time pressure than the English "promptly".[17] The difference can be illustrated by the following Venn diagram. (M_1 corresponds to the extension of the expression "[e]veryone arrested or detained is brought promptly before a judge"; M_2 corresponds to the extension of the expression *"[t]oute personne arrêtée ou détenue ... est aussitôt traduite devant un juge".*)

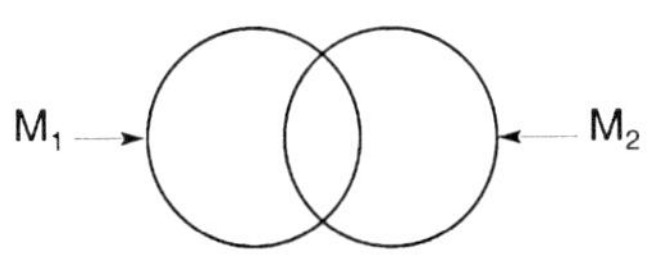

How should an applier approach the task of reconciling the *meanings* M_1 and M_2? Obviously, the applier cannot just adopt either M_1 or M_2. To reconcile two meanings is to make them compatible in terms of their content. The applier cannot make M_1 and M_2 compatible content-wise by simply adopting M_1, since M_1 does not include all the referents of M_2. Nor can the applier simply adopt M_2, since M_2 does not include all the referents of M_1. It appears the applier must seek some other solution. One possibility would be for the applier to adopt the meaning (M_1+M_2), which corresponds to the combined areas of M_1 and M_2. Another possibility would be to adopt the meaning (M_1.M_2), which corresponds to the area shared by M_1 and M_2. A third possibility would be for the applier to find some other meaning, for example M_3, which relates to M_1 and M_2 in some other way.

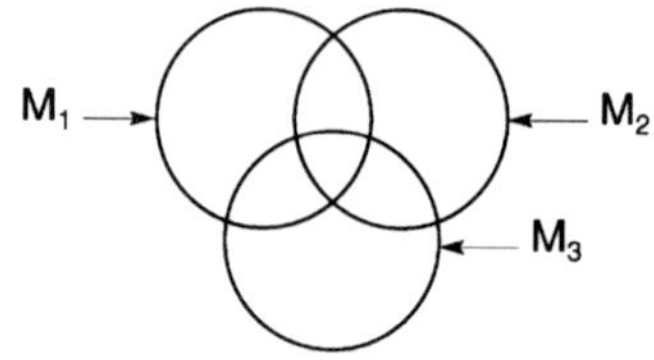

After this little experiment, we can turn our attention once again to the provisions of Vienna Convention article 33 § 4. Let me repeat: "When a comparison of the authentic texts discloses a difference of meaning which the application of articles 31 and 32 does not remove, the meaning which best reconciles the *texts*, having regard to the object and purpose of the treaty, shall be adopted".[18] Clearly, it is not the *meanings* M_1 and M_2, which the Vienna Convention directs the applier to reconcile. The task of the applier is to reconcile the *texts* in which the meanings M_1 and M_2 are expressed. The difference may seem trivial. The consequences are of undoubtable significance.

Suppose once again the scenario I just described. In what way can an applier reconcile the English and French texts? To reconcile two texts is to make their respective contents compatible; it is to arrange in some way so that both texts convey the same meaning. Of course, one way to make the English and French treaty texts compatible in terms of their content is to assume meaning M_1 or M_2. Another way is to assume M_3; a third is to assume M_1+M_2; yet another way is to assume M_1.M_2 – indeed, it seems the applier can assume any meaning. The English and French treaty texts appear equally compatible in terms of their content regardless of the meaning chosen. In such a situation, it is naturally pertinent to enquire about the specific options available to the applier. According to the provisions of VCLT article 33 § 4, the applier must make some kind of comparison. The applier's task is to set side by side a number of alternative meanings, and then choose the one "which best reconciles the [authenticated] texts". The exact scope of this comparison, however, remains unclear. Shall the applier be compelled to limit her comparison to the meanings already given, that is, meanings M_1 and M_2? Or – as some commentators seem to suggest – shall the applier be free to seek other solutions beyond M_1 and M_2, if for any reason she finds a meaning that better reconciles the authenticated texts?[19]

Let us assume the latter alternative. Suppose an applier who is faced with the task of identifying the meaning that best reconciles the authenticated texts of a multi-language treaty; and suppose that applier can choose not only among the meanings already given, but also among other meanings. A question immediately comes to mind: How shall these other meanings be "found"? The Vienna Convention contains nothing to enlighten us. Nevertheless, it is difficult to believe the parties to the Convention truly wished to leave this task of identification completely to the applier. Anyone who can influence the content of the selection available to the applier – that group of meanings from which the applier shall choose the one that best reconciles the authenticated texts – is clearly also provided with an opportunity to influence the result of the entire reconciliation process. As noted earlier, an applier can reconcile the texts of a multi-language treaty by adopting any meaning; no meaning is such that it cannot be included in the applier's selection. Hence, if we assume that an applier can himself determine the selection of meanings, then we must also accept that the applier is fully capable of deciding the outcome of the entire reconciliation process. Judicial application becomes just as arbitrary and difficult to predict as if VCLT article 33 § 4 had not existed. Such an interpretation is clearly at odds with interpretation rule no. 16:

> If it can be shown that the interpretation of a treaty provision in accordance with interpretation rule no. 1 leads to conflicting results, and that somewhere in the text of that treaty a norm is expressed, which – in light of the provision interpreted – in one of the two possible ordinary meanings can be considered in practice to be normatively useless, while in the other it cannot, then the latter meaning shall be adopted.[20]

All things considered, there seems to be good reason to greet the assumption described with a large dose of scepticism. One cannot reasonably assume the parties to the Vienna Convention to have envisioned the meaning of VCLT article 33 § 4 in such a way, that an applier – seeking to identify the meaning that best reconciles the authenticated texts – can choose not only a meaning already given, but also other possible meanings. Comparison must be limited to the meanings already given.

Accordingly, the applier's problem would be reduced considerably. The only question remaining to be answered is this: The applier wishes to find the meaning that best reconciles the authenticated texts – which of those meanings already given shall he adopt? Suppose an applier finds himself in a situation similar to that described in the example above – the applier must choose between meaning M_1 and meaning M_2. Suppose also that the applier (for whatever reason) selects M_1. By so doing, it is obvious that the applier makes the English and French texts compatible in terms of content; but they would be just as compatible had the applier chosen to adopt M_2. As long as it is the applier's task to reconcile the authenticated texts, and nothing else, both meanings are equally good. One cannot be said to be better than the other.

With that, it is time to insert once again the clause "having regard to the object and purpose of the treaty". If the applier is compelled to choose either M_1 or M_2 as the meaning "which best reconciles [the authenticated] texts", but both meanings reconcile the authenticated texts equally well, there must be some additional aspect in which M_1 and M_2 can be compared. The applier requires some criterion that can help him determine whether to choose M_1 or M_2. Of course, the idea is that "the object and purpose of the treaty" shall be this criterion. When the Vienna Convention directs an applier to adopt the meaning "which best reconciles the [authenticated] texts, having regard to the object and purpose of the treaty", then it is quite simply the applier's task to choose the meaning that, better than any other, leads to a realisation of the treaty's object and purpose. The Convention can hardly be read in any other way.

3 REGARDING THE METHOD DESCRIBED IN VCLT ARTICLE 33 § 4 (CONT'D)

Let us step back a bit from VCLT article 33 § 4 and consider the provision from a broader perspective. Let us consider the provisions contained in article 33 § 4 in light of the "normal" rules of interpretation laid down in articles 31 and 32. It is a notable fact that the rules of interpretation laid down in the Vienna Convention contain two references to "the object and purpose" of an interpreted treaty. Anyone assuming the task of interpreting a multi-language treaty obviously runs the risk of having to use this means of interpretation more than once: first, when according to VCLT article 31 § 1, the applier interprets the treaty using "the object and purpose" of the treaty; and second, when according to article 33 § 4, the applier adopts the meaning "which, having regard to the object and purpose of the treaty, best reconciles the [authenticated] texts".

From a practical point of view, one may question whether it can indeed be considered warranted to interpret a treaty twice using the same means of interpretation. A number of authors are absolutely sceptical to this idea.[21] "Es ist nicht recht einleuchtend", writes Meinhard Hilf, for example, ...

> ... warum trotz einer Ausrichtung am Vertragsgegenstand und -zweck in einem Fall sich eine Textdivergenz als unauflösbar darstellen kann, während im anderen Fall die erneute Berücksichtigung des Vertragszweckes offensichtlich eine Auflösung soll herbeiführen können.[22]

Waldemar Hummer is more explicit:

> The repeated introduction of the "object" and "purpose" of a treaty as "points of reference" seems to be at first glimpse a redundant formulation since the reconciliation of the texts has

to be hammered out, "having regard to the object and purpose of the treaty", a formulation which seems to be most similar to the operation under Art. 31 para. 1 of the Vienna Convention; but how can it be carried out since the difference of meaning which has to be removed by reconciling the texts is one "which the application of Articles 31 and 32 does not remove" (!) ?[23]

My judgment is that Hilf and Hummer – the authors must excuse my using them as representatives for a larger group of authors – have somewhat misinterpreted the rules of the Vienna Convention, and that the scepticism uttered is therefore unfounded. Both authors seem to have built their statements on two assumptions. First, they appear to assume that it is the exact same act of interpretation the applier performs, when first – according to the provisions of article 31 § 1 – interpreting a multi-language treaty using the treaty's object and purpose, and then – according to the provisions of article 33 § 4 – when adopting the meaning "which, having regard to the object and purpose of the treaty, best reconciles the [authenticated] texts". Secondly, the authors seem to take for granted that an application of article 33 § 4 can never lead to a result different from that obtained through an application of article 31 § 1; all texts that can be reconciled through an application of the former provision can also be reconciled through an application of the latter. Neither assumption can be said to hold true. The fact is that article 33 § 4 has a unique role to play in the reconciliation of multi-language treaties. This role differs from that played by article 31 § 1; it is a role of which article 31 § 1 is not even capable – this is my assertion. I shall now elaborate.

Consider first the Hilf-Hummer assumption that appliers perform two identical acts of interpretation when first – according to the provisions of article 31 § 1 – interpreting a multi-language treaty using the object and purpose of the interpreted treaty, and second – according to the provisions of article 33 § 4 – when adopting the meaning "which, having regard to the object and purpose of the treaty, best reconciles the [authenticated] texts". Clearly, the authors have a picture of the different acts of interpretation that does not correspond to the one presented in this work. When appliers interpret a treaty according to the provisions of VCLT article 31 § 1, the object and purpose can be used only relative to conventional language ("the ordinary meaning").[24] Seen from a different perspective, we could say that when appliers use the object and purpose of a treaty, it is always a second step in the broader interpretation process. The question has arisen whether a given complex of facts shall be considered to fall within the scope of application of the norm expressed by a certain treaty provision P; and the provision P has been interpreted using conventional language. However, this (very first) introductory act of interpretation has proved insufficient. The ordinary meaning of the treaty provision P is either vague or ambiguous – the use of conventional language leads to conflicting results. The act in question has quite simply resulted in multiple ordinary meanings. According to VCLT article 31 § 1, in such a case the applier shall also interpret P using the object and purpose of the treaty. In so doing the applier first determines the object and purpose of P; then the applier compares the alternative ordinary meanings relative to the object and purpose of P; and finally, the applier adopts the meaning through which the object and purpose are best realised.

When appliers interpret a treaty provision P, according to VCLT article 33 § 4, and they adopt the meaning "which, having regard to the object and purpose of the treaty, best reconciles the [authenticated] texts", appliers proceed in much the same way as when they interpret the provision, according to VCLT article 31 § 1, using the treaty's object and purpose, as long as nothing but the intellectual process is considered. The applier first determines the object and purpose of P; then the applier compares a number of given interpretation alternatives relative to the object and purpose of P; and finally, the applier chooses the alternative through which the object and purpose of P is best realised. The difference lies in the respective starting points for the two acts of interpretation. When appliers interpret a treaty provision P – according to VCLT article 31 § 1 – using the object and purpose of said treaty, they never have more than one language version (at a time) to examine. The appliers' basis for work is the alternative meanings found to exist, when interpreting P "in accordance with the ordinary meaning of the terms of the treaty". When appliers – according to VCLT article 33 § 4 – adopt the meaning "which, having regard to the object and purpose of the treaty, best reconciles the [authenticated] texts", they always have multiple texts to consider. The basis is the alternative meanings found by appliers when they interpreted the treaty in accordance with VCLT articles 31 and 32. At the application of article 31 § 1, appliers always work with a material consisting of several meanings ascribed to one text; at the application of article 33 § 4, appliers have several meanings to examine, but also several texts, and more than one meaning is never ascribed to a text. Clearly, the two acts of interpretation are not identical, when an applier first – according to the provisions of article 31 § 1 – interprets a multi-language treaty using the object and purpose of the treaty, and then – according to the provisions of article 33 § 4 – adopts the meaning "which, having regard to the object and purpose of the treaty, best reconciles the [authenticated] texts".

If it is now clear that Hilf and Hummer have little support for their first assumption, the same can be said about the second assumption as well. All texts that can be reconciled by applying VCLT article 33 § 4 cannot be reconciled by applying article 31 § 1, as Hilf and Hummer seem to believe. Suppose that a multi-language treaty has been authenticated in two languages – English and French. Suppose also that an applier has compared the two texts and discovered that they bear a difference in meaning, which cannot be removed using conventional language. Finally, for the sake of simplicity, let us suppose the ordinary meaning of both the English and French texts to be unambiguous.[25] The following four situations are possible.

(1) No one referent of the English text is a referent of the French text, and no one referent of the French text is a referent of the English text. (For example, the English expression "cow" can never be used to refer to a referent of the French "cheval", and vice versa.) Let area M_e correspond to the ordinary meaning of the English text, and area M_f correspond to the ordinary meaning of the French text, and the situation may be illustrated as follows:

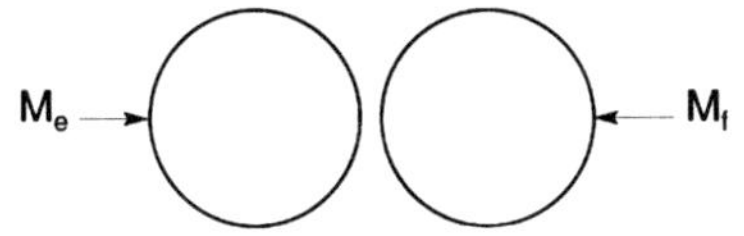

(2) Some (but not all) referents of the English text are referents of the French text, and some (but not all) referents of the French are referents of the English text. (For example, the English expression "[e]veryone arrested or detained is brought promptly before a judge" can in some (but not all) cases be used to refer to the referents of the French expression *"[t]oute personne arrêtée ou détenue ... est aussitôt traduite devant un juge"*, and vice versa.[26])

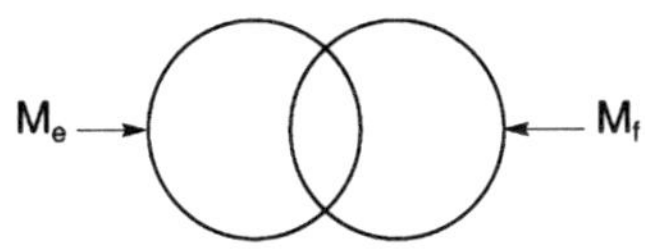

(3) All referents of the French text are referents of the English text, but only some referents of the English text are referents of the French text. (For example, the English expression "industrial conditions" can in all cases be used to refer to the referents of the French *"conditions industrielle"*, but only in some cases can the French *"conditions industrielle"* be used to refer to the referents of the English "industrial conditions".[27])

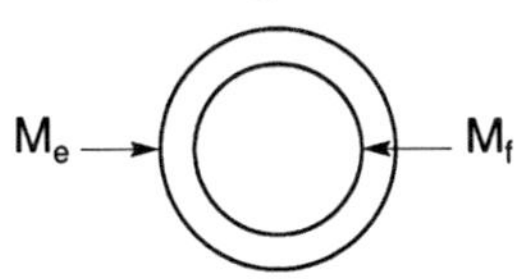

(4) All referents of the English text are referents of the French text, but only some referents of the French text are referents of the English text. (For example, the French *"tout accusé"* can in all cases be used to

refer to the referents of the English "everyone charged with a criminal offence", but only in some cases can the French *"tout accusé"* be used to refer to the referents of the English "everyone charged with a criminal offence".[28])

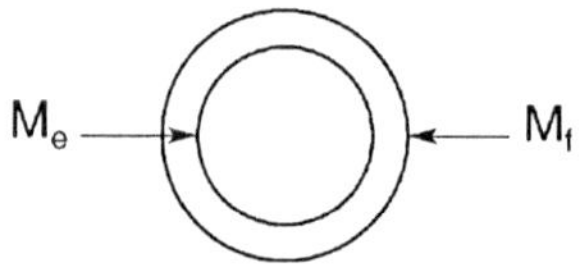

All in all, it seems the ordinary meanings of the English and French texts could relate to one another in four different ways. Hence, the cases we confront are of four types only. Let us examine these four cases more closely to see whether in each case the English and French texts can be reconciled – first, through an application of VCLT article 33 § 4, and then through an application of article 31 § 1.

From the start it is clear that the English and French texts can always be reconciled through an application of VCLT article 33 § 4; this is true regardless of whether M_e and M_f are related to one another as in cases (1), (2), (3) or (4). All the applier has to do is identify the meaning, M_e or M_f, which best leads to a realisation of the treaty's object and purpose, and then discard the other. The question is whether the two texts can be reconciled just as easily through an application of article 31 § 1. The answer must be in the negative. When appliers interpret a treaty – according to VCLT article 31 § 1 – using its object and purpose, a result cannot ever be obtained that cannot in any way be reconciled with the ordinary meaning of the interpreted treaty. The appliers' task is to compare the alternative ordinary meanings that resulted upon interpretation of the treaty using conventional language; they shall then adopt the one through which the treaty's object and purpose are best realised. In order for appliers to be at all able to reconcile two authenticated texts of a treaty using its object and purpose, at least one of the alternative ordinary meanings must be common for both texts. This is not so in the first of the four cases above. The ordinary meaning of the English text does not refer to a single one of the referents of the French text, and the ordinary meaning of the French text does not refer to a single one of the referents of the English text. In the second case, it might be that the English and French texts can be reconciled; this is so if the ordinary meaning of at least one of the texts can be considered vague. If the ordinary meanings of both the English and the French texts are completely precise, reconciliation cannot be achieved.[29] In the third case, it might be that the English and French texts can be reconciled; this is so if the ordinary meaning of the *English* text can be considered vague. Lastly, in the fourth case, it might be that the two texts can be reconciled; this is if the ordinary meaning of the *French* text can be considered vague.

In contrast to what other authors have argued, we can therefore maintain that appliers will not always be able to reconcile the authenticated texts of multi-language treaty using that treaty's object and purpose, in accordance with the provisions of article 31 § 1. Given that authenticated texts of a multi-language treaty can always be reconciled through an application of VCLT article 33 § 4, the application of VCLT article 33 § 4 *can* indeed lead to results different from those obtained through an application of article 31 § 1. This is precisely the proposition I wished to establish.

4 CONCLUSIONS

When appliers compare two authenticated texts of a multi-lingual treaty and the comparison discloses a difference in meaning, the texts must be reconciled. It is the purpose of this chapter to describe the various methods through which such reconciliation shall be obtained, according to the provisions of VCLT article 33. Based on the observations made in this chapter, the following two rules of interpretation can be established:

Rule no. 43
If it can be shown (i) that a treaty has been authenticated in two or more languages, (ii) that two of the authenticated texts, by applying interpretation rules nos. 1–42, will still have to be understood in two different meanings, and (iii) that by applying the treaty in the one meaning, the object and purpose of the treaty will be realised to a greater extent than in the other, then the former meaning shall be adopted, except for those cases where interpretation rule no. 44 applies.

Rule no. 44
If it can be shown (i) that a treaty has been authenticated in two or more languages, (ii) that two of the authenticated texts, by applying interpretation rules nos. 1–42, will still have to be understood in two different meanings, and (iii) that the parties have agreed that in such cases a particular text shall prevail, then the treaty shall be understood in accordance with the meaning conveyed by that text.

NOTES

1. It is important to distinguish between an authenticated text of treaty and official translations of that treaty. In the relationship between the parties to a treaty, only the authenticated text can be considered valid. For more on the concept of *authentication*

(Fr. *athentification*; Sp. *autentificación*), see VCLT article 10. See also *Oppenheim's International Law*, pp. 1223–1224; Verdross and Simma, pp. 452–454; Rosenne, 1983, pp. 759–784; FitzGerald, pp. 364–371.

2. Cf. Shelton, pp. 613–618; Hilf, pp. 27–34; Tabory, pp. 36–39; Verzijl, pp. 181–201.
3. See *Review of the Multilateral Treaty-Making Process* (1985), passim.
4. Cf. e.g. Aceves, pp. 187ff.; Shelton, pp. 623–627; Rosenne, 1987, pp. 417–431.
5. Cf. Hilf, pp. 20–26.
6. In at least two cases, these differences in meaning have been formally handled by the European Court of Human Rights. (See *Pakelli, Publ. ECHR*, Ser. A, Vol. 64, p. 15, § 31; *Öztürk, Publ. ECHR*, Ser. A, Vol. 73, p. 17, §§ 46–47.)
7. My italics and emphasis.
8. See Kuner, pp. 953–964; Germer, pp. 412–414; Tabory, pp. 196–200.
9. See e.g. *La Grand Case, ICJ Reports*, 2001, pp. 502–506, §§ 101–109; *Niemetz v. Germany, Publ. ECHR*, Ser. A, Vol. 251-B, §§ 30–31; *Border and Transborder Armed Actions, ILR*, Vol. 84, p. 244, § 45; *ELSI*, ibid., pp. 373–377, §§ 113–119; *Nicaragua v. USA (Jurisdiction), ILR*, Vol. 76, pp. 117ff., §§ 30ff.; *Öztürk, Publ. ECHR*, Ser. A, Vol. 73, § 47; *Van der Mussele, Publ. ECHR*, Ser. A, Vol. 70, § 33; *De Wilde, Ooms and Versyp* , *Publ. ECHR*, Ser. A, Vol. 12, § 76; *Delcourt, Publ. ECHR*, Ser. A, Vol. 11, § 25. Cf. however, *Prosecutor v. Blaskic, ILR*, Vol. 109–110, § 326.
10. Van der Mussele Case, Judgment of 23 November 1983, *Publ. ECHR*, Vol. 70.
11. Ibid., p. 17, § 33.
12. See e.g. *International Telecommunication Convention* and its final clause: "IN WITNESS WHEREOF the respective plenipotentiaries have signed the Convention in each of the Chinese, English, French, Russian and Spanish languages, in a single copy in which, in case of dispute, the French text shall prevail".
13. Cf. VCLT article 33 § 2.
14. Cf. e.g. *the European Convention for the Protection of Human Rights and Fundamental Freedoms* and final clause: "Done at Rome this 4th day of November 1950, in English and in French, both texts being equally authentic".
15. See e.g. Urueña, pp. 217–220; Sinclair, 1984, pp. 147–152; Tabory, pp. 176–178, 195–208; Yasseen, pp. 104–110; Hummer, pp. 114–123; Mössner, pp. 273–302; Hilf, in particular pp. 48–103; Germer, pp. 400–427.
16. *The European Convention for the Protection of Human Rights and Fundamental Freedoms*, article 5 § 3. (My italics.)
17. Cf. the European Court of Human Rights in the *Brogan and Others* case: "'[P]romptly' in paragraph 3 may be understood as having a broader significance than '*aussitôt*', which literally means immediately". (*Publ. ECHR*, Ser. A, Vol. 145-B, p. 32, § 59.)
18. My italics.
19. See Sinclair, 1984, p. 152; Mössner, pp. 301–302; Tabory, p. 202. See also joint diss. op. Robinson, Bathurst and Monguilan, *Young Loan, ILR*, Vol. 59, p. 578.
20. See p. 228 of this work.
21. In addition to the authorities cited in the main text, see Urueña, p. 219; Germer, pp. 425–427; Yasseen, p. 107.
22. Hilf, pp. 101–102.
23. Hummer, p. 122. (Footnote omitted.)
24. See the introduction to Ch. 7 of this work.
25. Of course, when the ordinary meanings of the texts are both ambiguous and vague, additional results are possible.

26. Cf. *Brogan and Others*, *Publ. ECHR*, Ser. A, Vol. 145-B, p. 32, § 59.
27. Cf. *Competence of the ILO for Agriculture*, *PCIJ*, Ser. B, No. 2–3, pp. 33–37.
28. Cf. *Öztürk*, *Publ. ECHR*, Ser. A, Vol. 73, p. 17, § 47.
29. A point of clarification might be warranted. In each of the four diagrams, the reader finds two circular areas, which are intended to correspond to the ordinary meanings of the English and French texts. These areas shall be understood so that in a situation where the ordinary meaning ascribed to a text remains vague, then all the alternative ordinary meanings fall *inside* the circle. In my experience, a reader will always be able to say how the ordinary meanings of two texts relate to one another, even though one or both meanings happen to be vague. For example, if the ordinary meanings of two texts relate to one another as in case 3 above, then the reader would be able to say that the meaning of the one text is more restrictive than the other.

CHAPTER 12

REFLECTING ON THE OUTCOME: INTERNATIONAL LAW ON A SCALE BETWEEN RADICAL LEGAL SKEPTICISM AND THE ONE-RIGHT-ANSWER THESIS

Throughout the many pages of this work, a constant purpose has been to investigate the currently existing regime established in international law for the interpretation of treaties, as expressed in Articles 31–33 of the 1969 Vienna Convention the Law of Treaties. As stated in the introductory Chapter 1, despite the adoption of the Vienna Convention and the existence of the three articles just mentioned, it is still far from clear to what contents the international law on treaty interpretation shall be applied.[1] The design of Articles 31–33 has invited a host of different opinions.[2] As a simple way of illustrating the problem, the various views expressed by international law scholars and other commentators were placed on a scale, whose two opposing ends were said to represent either one of the two most radical positions. To facilitate reference, I have referred to them as radical legal skepticism and the one-right-answer thesis, respectively.[3]

According to radical legal skepticism, legal norms are not capable of constraining political judgment. Hence, whenever some certain understanding is advanced as the correct interpretation of some certain treaty provision, the only question to be asked in assessing the interpretation is that whether it is legitimate or not.[4] Already at an early stage of this work I recommended against accepting the ideas of radical legal skepticism. I would like to think that by the completion of this work, my recommendations stand reinforced. As shown in the above Chapters 2–11, the regime laid down in Vienna Convention Articles 31–33 is best described as a system of rules. Not only does international law provide information on the interpretation data (or means of interpretation) to be used by appliers when interpreting a treaty provision. It also instructs the appliers how, by using each datum, they shall argue to arrive at a conclusion about the meaning of the interpreted provision. Furthermore, international law to some extent also determines what weight the different data of interpretation shall be afforded when appliers discover that, depending on the specific datum they bring to bear on the interpretation process, the conclusion arrived at will be different. Hence, it would be my assessment that in any process of interpretation, Articles 31–33 indeed constrain the scope for political judgement. As I have come to conclude, radical legal scepticism should not be accepted as a sound description of the current legal state of affairs.

On the other hand, neither would I be prepared to accept the description provided by the one-right-answer thesis. According to the one-right-answer thesis, interpretation of treaties is a field of activity leaving no room for political judgment. From this point of view, the legal regime created in international law for the interpretation of treaties is considered absolute, in the sense that appliers can interpret a treaty according to the standards of international law and be perfectly certain of always arriving at a determinate result in a completely value-free way. Whenever some certain understanding is advanced as the correct interpretation of some certain treaty provision, the only question to be asked in assessing the interpretation is that concerning its legal correctness.[5] As indicated in the above Chapters 3–11, this description is also far from reality. I my assessment, the regime laid down in Vienna Convention Articles 31–33 amounts to a system of rules, but the system would still have to be described as to some extent open-textured. The rules provide a framework for the interpretation process; but within this framework, the political judgment of each individual applier is still allowed to play a part (although, of course, not the leading part suggested by radical legal skepticism).

As I would like to think, in any process of interpretation, appliers operate under a twofold ambition. First, having adopted a certain understanding of some certain treaty, they want to be able to show the understanding to conform to what is provided in international law. They wish others to regard the understanding as legally correct. Secondly, they want to be able to present the understanding as legitimate. They wish others to regard the understanding as warranted by reasons separate from international law. Given that this idea is accepted, and given my conclusion about the system of rules laid down in VCLT Article 31–33 as being to some extent open-textured, a constructive debate on interpretation matters obviously would have to be concerned with two questions:

(1) What first- and second-order rules of interpretation can be invoked by an applier, citing the prevailing legal regime laid down in VCLT Articles 31–33?
(2) How should the open-texturedness of said rules of interpretation be used by appliers, in order to optimize legitimacy of the interpretation result?

Arguably, if ever there is going to be a rational discussion on the latter of the above two questions, it is essential that appliers realize to which factors the open-texturedness of the rules is actually owed. In the following

Sections 1–3 of the present Chapter, drawing on the earlier Chapters 3–11, I will try to identify these factors in more detail. As I will suggest, factors can be described as being of three different kinds. They concern the identification of the various means of interpretation relative to the specific treaty provision interpreted; they concern the establishment of the various relationships assumed in the rules of interpretation; and they concern the resolution of conflicts occurring in the application of the first-order rules of interpretation. The organisation of Chapter 12 will follow this categorisation.

1 DETERMINING THE CONTENTS OF THE MEANS OF INTERPRETATION

Of the several elements that contribute to the open-texturedness of the system of rules laid down in Articles 31–33 of the Vienna Convention a first factor concerns the determination of the different means of interpretation exploited in the interpretation process. According to the model established in the above Chapter 2, a first-order rule of interpretation applies on the showing of some specific kind of relationship to exist between the treaty provision interpreted and some certain means of interpretation.[6] Hence, using a first-order rule of interpretation, appliers always draw on the existence of some specific means of interpretation. Obviously, in order to apply a first-order rule of interpretation, the contents of the various means of interpretation (or set of interpretation data) relative to the specific treaty provision interpreted will have to be determined. Sometimes, such a task insists upon value judgment. To some extent, this was indicated already in the course of my investigations contained in the above Chapters 3–9. However, recapitulating the contents of the various first-order rules of interpretation, I will now try to bring out the point more clearly.

Invoking Rule no. 1, appliers draw on the existence of a conventional language. For the purpose of Rule no. 1, conventional language means all varieties used within the larger language community, including those referred to as technical languages. As experience has repeatedly shown, when interpretation concerns the meaning of a term belonging to a technical language, that term may not always be listed in a dictionary. Sometimes, the contents of the technical language will have to be determined by the applier herself, on the basis of the various uses of the term interpreted, relying on inductive reasoning. Such reasoning entails value judgment. Moreover, in choosing between a language employed at the time of the interpreted treaty's conclusion and a language employed at the time of interpretation, the applier will sometimes have to determine whether or not the thing interpreted is a generic referring expression with a referent assumed by the treaty parties to be alterable.[7] This requires a separate process of interpretation – one that cannot be justified invoking VCLT Articles 31–33.

Invoking any one of Rules nos. 2–6, appliers would have to be prepared to define the extension of the larger treaty text, a provision of which is interpreted.[8] As already noted in the above Chapter 4, the question sometimes arises whether two instruments shall be considered as integral parts of a single treaty, or whether they shall be considered as two separate treaties.[9] Once again, the applier will then have to fall back on the parties' intentions. For the purpose of Rules nos. 2–6, the text of a treaty refers to whatever the parties to the treaty consider the treaty to be comprised of. Obviously, in order to determine the contents of this means of interpretation relative to the specific provision interpreted, a separate process of interpretation might on occasion be needed.[10] For the justification of this process, the rules laid down in VCLT Articles 31–33 are of no help.

Invoking Rules nos. 7 and 8, appliers draw on the existence of an agreement relating to the treaty interpreted, made between its parties in connection with the treaty's conclusion.[11] For the purpose of these two rules, an agreement relates to a treaty if (and only if) the parties consider the agreement and the treaty exceedingly closely connected.[12] As stated in the above Chapter 5, the agreement has to be binding under international law.[13] However, the form of the agreement is not important, and consequently, for the purpose of Rules no. 7 and 8, an agreement can be written or non-written.[14] Quite clearly, in the application of said rules, value judgments may sometimes be needed to determine whether an agreement exist between the parties to the treaty interpreted, and whether it is binding or not; especially so in the case of non-written agreements. Furthermore, value judgments may be needed to determine whether an agreement established to exist *relates* to the interpreted treaty or not.

Invoking Rules nos. 9 and 10, appliers draw on the existence of an instrument made by one or more parties to the interpreted treaty in connection with its conclusion, and accepted by the other parties as an instrument related to said treaty.[15] Arguably, the existence of an instrument can be objectively determined. But in order for Rules nos. 9 and 10 to be brought into play, appliers will also need to determine whether the instrument has been accepted by all as related to the treaty or not. As indicated in the above Chapter 5, the phenomena typically falling within the scope of application of Rules nos. 9 and 10 are the reservations and interpretative declarations made by states, either at the time of signature, or contained in their instruments of ratification or accession.[16] In those cases, the relationship between treaty and instrument will never be a point of dispute. However, Rules no. 9 and 10 clearly allow for the use of other kinds of instruments as well, as long as they are made in connection with the interpreted treaty's conclusion (whatever that is).[17] Hence, and given that the meaning of "instrument" can only be defined generically, the possibility that in some instances at least, value judgment may be called for in the determination of whether or not an instrument has been accepted as related to the treaty seems difficult to rule out altogether.

Invoking Rule no. 11 or Rule no. 12, appliers draw on the existence of an agreement entered into by the parties to the treaty interpreted, regarding the interpretation of said treaty or the application of its provisions.[18] For the purpose of these rules, an agreement has to be binding under international law.[19] The form of the agreement is not important, and consequently, like in case of Rules no. 7 and 8, an agreement can be written or non-written.[20] Arguably, in order to determine whether in the sense of Rules nos. 11 and 12 an agreement exists or not, appliers will sometimes have to be bring value judgments to bear on the interpretation process; especially so in the case of non-written agreements.

Invoking Rule no. 13, appliers draw on the fact that in the application of the interpreted treaty, a practice has developed, establishing an agreement between the parties regarding its interpretation.[21] In the course of the above Chapter 6, I suggested that for the purpose of Rule no. 13, a practice can be formed by any number of applications, one as well as many.[22] Accepting this suggestion, determining the existence of an agreement would still have to be seen as a matter leaving scope for subjectivities. By share necessity, an applier who wishes to establish an agreement on the basis of a practice will have to rely on inductive reasoning. As noted before, such reasoning entails value judgment.

Invoking Rule no. 14, appliers draw on the existence of a rule of international law applicable in the relations between the parties to the interpreted treaty.[23] For the purpose of Rule no. 14, "a rule of international law" refers to any and all rules whose origin can be traced to a formal source of international law.[24] Not only other international agreements can come within the scope of application of Rule no. 14, but also rules belonging to the realm of customary international law and general principles recognized by civilized nations. In principle, if establishing an agreement on the basis of a practice calls for value judgment on the part of the applier, so does the establishment of a customary international law and a general principle, for the very same reason. With regard to the establishment of the contents of an in international agreement – once again principally speaking – it too will leave scope for subjectivities. From a more practical point of view, it seems that using Rule no. 14, appliers will typically fall back on rules, the contents and existences of which are beyond all serious doubt. To that extent, determining the contents of this means of interpretation will not really be a point of dispute. On the other hand, value judgment will often be required for other reasons. As stated in the above Chapter 6, in choosing between the rules applicable between the parties at the time of the interpreted treaty's conclusion and the rules applicable at the time of interpretation, the applier will sometimes have to determine whether or not the thing interpreted is a generic referring expression with a referent assumed by the treaty parties to be alterable.[25] And – let me repeat – this requires a separate process of interpretation, and one that cannot be justified invoking VCLT Articles 31–33.

Invoking Rule no. 15 or Rule no. 30, appliers draw on the fact that a certain *telos* has been conferred on the interpreted treaty.[26] For the purpose of Rules nos. 15 and 30, the *telos* of a treaty means the state-of-affairs, which according to the parties, should be attained by applying the interpreted provision.[27] Depending on whether or not the thing interpreted is a generic referring expression with a referent assumed by the treaty parties to be alterable, the *telos* of a treaty is determined based upon the intentions held by the parties either at the time of interpretation, or at the time of the interpreted treaty's conclusion.[28] Obviously, *for two reasons*, in order to determine the *telos* of a treaty, appliers will often need to have recourse to a separate process of interpretation. As indicated in the above Chapter 7, in the justification of this process, VCLT Articles 31–33 are of no help.[29]

Invoking Rule no. 16 or Rule no. 31,[30] or any one of Rules nos. 32–37,[31] appliers draw on the normative contents – the meaning – of some particular provision included in the interpreted treaty. In principle, as we know, the meaning of a treaty will often have to be established through interpretation. In other words, in order to determine the contents of the means of interpretation exploited, appliers will need to have recourse to the rules of interpretation laid down in VCLT Articles 31–33, which in turn will often insist upon value judgments to be made. In practice – like in the case of Rule no. 14 – it seems that the applier using any of the rules referred to above will typically fall back on the treaty, only to the extent that its meaning can be considered clear. As long as this is the case, determining the contents of this means of interpretation will not really be a point of dispute.

Invoking Rules nos. 19 and 20, appliers would have to be prepared to identify a state of affairs as a circumstance of the interpreted treaty's conclusion.[32] For the purpose of Rules nos. 19 and 20, a circumstance of a treaty's conclusion means a state of affairs, whose existence at least partially caused the conclusion of the interpreted treaty.[33] Obviously, in order for an applier to determine whether some certain state of affairs fits this description or not, he has to make an assumption about the states of mind of the treaty parties at the time preceding the conclusion. By share necessity, such an assumption calls for value judgement.

Invoking Rules nos. 25 and 26, appliers once again draw on the existence of an element coming within the scope of application of VCLT Article 31 § 2 or § 3.[34] Consequently, for the very same reason as value judgments are required in the application of Rules nos. 6–14, such judgments will be required in the application of Rules nos. 25 and 26 as well.

2 ESTABLISHING RELATIONSHIPS ASSUMED IN THE RULES OF INTERPRETATION

Considering the way many rules of interpretation are constructed, their use will require the applier to make an assumption. In the case of the first-order rules of interpretation, the assumption concerns the relationship held between on the one hand the means of interpretation exploited, and on the other hand either the interpreted provision or the two possible ordinary meanings earlier established. In the case of the second-order rules of interpretation, the assumption concerns the relationship held between two conflicting interpretations. In both cases, the assumption will often insist on value judgment.

In some cases, value judgments are required because the assumption made concerns the meaning of some particular expression or provision contained in a treaty. To facilitate reference, I will refer to this as a type-B assumption. In principle, when appliers confer meaning on a treaty, they will have to be prepared to defend their understanding on the basis of the rules of interpretation laid down in VCLT Articles 31–33. As repeatedly stated, these rules are not capable of always offering sufficient justification for the understanding of a treaty. Hence, it cannot be excluded that partly a type-B assumption will have to be based on reasons beyond international law. In practice, however, it seems that an applier drawing on a type-B assumption will typically fall back on the meaning of a treaty only to the extent that it can be considered clear. As long as this is the case, type-B assumptions will not be a point of dispute. In other cases, value judgments are required because the assumption made concerns matters that fall entirely outside the scope of VCLT Articles 31–33. Since, obviously, the justification of such assumptions poses a greater problem for appliers, I will refer to them as type-A assumptions.

Recapitulating the contents of the various first- and second-order rules of interpretation laid down in international law, I will now put down in clear writing to what extent they insist on type-A and type-B assumptions being made.

Rule no. 2 invites appliers to compare the meanings of two words or phrases used in the interpreted treaty. Drawing upon the result of this comparison, they arrive at the conclusion that, considering the provision interpreted, in one of its two possible ordinary meanings, the usage of the word or phrase will be consistent, whereas in the other possible ordinary meaning it will not.[35] The conclusion turns on a type-B assumption about the meaning given in the treaty to the word or phrase that provides the basis for comparison relative to the two existing interpretation alternatives.

Rule no. 3 calls upon appliers to compare two norms contained in the interpreted treaty. Drawing upon the results of this comparison, they arrive at the conclusion that considered the provision interpreted, in one of its two possible ordinary meanings, the treaty will entail a logical contradiction, whereas in the other possible ordinary meaning it will not.[36] The conclusion turns on a type-B assumption about the contents and existence of the norm that provides the basis for comparison relative to the two existing interpretation alternatives.

Rule no. 4 invites appliers to compare the meaning of two expressions used in the interpreted treaty. Drawing upon the results of this comparison, they arrive at the conclusion that considered the provision interpreted, in one of its two possible ordinary meanings, the treaty will entail a pleonasm, whereas in the other possible ordinary meaning it will not.[37] The conclusion turns on a type-B assumption about the meaning given in the treaty to the expression that provides the basis for comparison relative to the two existing interpretation alternatives.

Rule no. 5 invites appliers to compare the meanings of two words or phrases used in the interpreted treaty. Drawing upon the result of this comparison, they arrive at the conclusion that, considering the provision interpreted, in one of its two possible ordinary meanings, the usage of the word or phrase will differ, whereas in the other possible ordinary meaning it will not.[38] The conclusion turns on a type-B assumption about the meaning given in the treaty to the word or phrase that provides the basis for comparison relative to the two existing interpretation alternatives.

Rule no. 6 calls upon appliers to compare two norms contained in the interpreted treaty. Drawing upon the results of this comparison, they arrive at the conclusion that considered the provision interpreted, in one of its two possible ordinary meanings, the treaty will entail a logical tautology, whereas in the other possible ordinary meaning it will not.[39] The conclusion turns on a type-B assumption about the contents and existence of the norm that provides the basis for comparison relative to the two existing interpretation alternatives.

Rules nos. 7–8 and 11–12 invite appliers to compare the contents of the interpreted treaty provision with the contents of an agreement. Drawing upon the results of this comparison, in the case of Rules nos. 7 and 11, they arrive at the conclusion that in one of its two possible ordinary meanings, the interpreted provision logically contradicts the agreement, whereas in the other possible ordinary meaning it does not.[40] In the case of Rules nos. 8 and 12, they arrive at the conclusion that in one of its two possible ordinary meanings, the interpreted provision expresses a norm, which is also contained in the agreement – so that one of them will appear superfluous – whereas in the other possible ordinary meaning the tautology does not occur.[41] The conclusion turns on an assumption about the contents of the agreement relative to the two existing interpretation alternatives. Depending on the form of the agreement – written or non-written – the assumption will either be of type B or type A.

Rules nos. 9 and 10 invite appliers to compare the contents of the interpreted treaty provision with the contents of an instrument made in connection with the conclusion of said treaty, one or more parties made an instrument, which was later accepted by the other parties as related to the treaty. Drawing upon the results of this comparison, in the case of Rule no. 9, they arrive at the conclusion that in one of its two possible ordinary meanings, the interpreted provision logically contradicts the instrument, whereas in the other possible ordinary meaning it does not.[42] In the case of Rule no. 10, they arrive at the conclusion that in one of its two possible ordinary meanings, the interpreted provision expresses a norm, which is also contained in the instrument – so that one of them will appear superfluous – whereas in the other possible ordinary meaning the tautology does not occur.[43] Depending on the kind of instrument – forming a treaty or not – the assumption will either be of type B or type A.

Rule no. 13 calls upon appliers to compare the contents of the interpreted treaty provision with the contents of an agreement developed between the treaty parties in the application of the treaty. Drawing upon the results of this comparison, they arrive at the conclusion that in one of its two possible ordinary meanings, the interpreted provision logically contradicts the agreement, whereas in the other possible ordinary meaning it does not.[44] The conclusion turns on a type-A assumption about the contents of the agreement relative to the two existing interpretation alternatives.

Rule no. 14 calls upon appliers to compare the contents of the interpreted treaty provision with the contents of a rule of international law. Drawing upon the results of this comparison, they arrive at the conclusion that in one of its two possible ordinary meanings, the interpreted provision logically contradicts the rule, whereas in the other possible ordinary meaning it does not. The conclusion turns on an assumption about the contents of the rule that provides the basis for comparison relative to the two existing interpretation alternatives.[45] Depending on whether the rule is one contained in a treaty, or one belonging to the realm of customary international law or to the general principles, the assumption will either be of type B or type A.

Rule no. 15 invites appliers to compare the contents of the interpreted treaty provision with one of the treaty's *teloi*. Drawing upon the results of this comparison, they arrive at the conclusion that depending on in which of its two possible ordinary meanings the interpreted provision is applied, the *telos* will be realised to a greater or lesser extent.[46] The conclusion turns on a type-A assumption about the instrumental relationship held between the interpreted treaty provision and its *telos* relative to the two existing interpretation alternatives.

Rule no. 16 calls upon appliers to compare two norms contained in the interpreted treaty. Drawing upon the results of this comparison, they arrive at the conclusion that considered the interpreted provision, in one of its two possible ordinary meanings, the other norm will be emptied of all practical contents, whereas in the other possible ordinary meaning it will not.[47] The conclusion turns on a type-A assumption about the significance of the two possible meanings for the application of the norm that forms the basis of comparison in all future cases.

Rules nos. 17–26 invite appliers to compare the contents of the interpreted treaty provision with a concordance established using a supplementary means of interpretation, being either the *travaux préparatoires*, the circumstances of the interpreted treaty's conclusion, a ratification work, a treaty *in pari materia*, or an element belonging to the context as defined in VCLT Article 31 §§ 2–3. Drawing upon the results of this comparison, they arrive at the conclusion that depending on in which of several possible meanings the interpreted provision is applied, the provision will logically either be compatible with the concordance or not.[48] The conclusion turns on a type-A assumption about the significance of the supplementary means of interpretation as indicator of a concordance between the treaty parties relative to the meaning of the interpreted provision.

Rules nos. 27–29 invites appliers to compare the different effects that the two possible ordinary meanings will have for the extension of the interpreted treaty provision. Drawing upon the result of this comparison, they arrive at the conclusion that, that depending on in which of the two ordinary meanings the provision is applied, its extension will be greater or lesser.[49] The conclusion turns on a type-A assumption about the significance of the two possible ordinary meanings for the application of the interpreted treaty provision in all future cases.

Rule no. 30 calls upon appliers to compare the contents of the interpreted treaty provision with one of the treaty's *teloi*. Drawing upon the results of this comparison, they arrive at the conclusion that depending on whether a meaning is implicitly read into the provision or not, the *telos* will be either be realised to some extent, or not at all.[50] The conclusion turns on a type-A assumption about the instrumental relationship held between the interpreted treaty provision and its *telos* relative to the two existing interpretation alternatives.

Rule no. 31 calls upon appliers to compare the contents of the interpreted treaty provision with yet another norm contained in the interpreted treaty. Drawing upon the results of this comparison, they arrive at the conclusion that depending on whether a meaning is implicitly read into the interpreted treaty provision or not, the norm that provides the basis for comparison will either be emptied of all practical contents or not.[51] The conclusion turns on a type-A assumption about the significance of the two possible meanings for the application of this other norm in all future cases.

Rules nos. 32–37 invite appliers to compare two states of affairs (S_1 and S_2), the one of which (S_1) comes within the scope of application of the interpreted treaty provision. Drawing upon the results of this comparison, they arrive at the conclusion that depending on in which of the several possible meanings the interpreted provision is applied, the other state of affairs (S_2) will either come within its scope of application or not.[52] The conclusion turns on a type-B assumption about the meaning of the interpreted provision relative to the state of affairs that provides the basis for comparison (S_1).

Rule no. 39 calls upon appliers to compare two expressions (E_1 and E_2). Drawing upon the results of this comparison, they arrive at the conclusion that depending on in which of several possible meanings the interpreted provision is applied, all referents of the one expression (E_1) will either be limited to the generically defined class referred to by the other expression (E_2), or not.[53] The conclusion turns on a type-B assumption about the meaning given in the treaty to this latter expression (E_2) relative to the possible meaning given to the former expression (E_1).

Rule no. 40 invites appliers to compare the different results obtained by interpreting a treaty provision applying two first-order rules of interpretation. Drawing upon the results of this comparison, they arrive at the conclusion that the communicative assumption underlying the application of the former rule is significantly weaker than the communicative assumption underlying the application of the latter.[54] The conclusion turns on a type-A assumption about the relative weight of the two communicative assumptions.

3 RESOLVING CONFLICTS OCCURRING IN THE APPLICATION OF THE FIRST-ORDER RULES OF INTERPRETATION

Invoking the first-order rules of interpretation laid down in international law, appliers will often be left with conflicting results. One way or another, such conflicts need to be resolved. Of course, the natural way for the applier to proceed would be to exhaust the possibilities offered in international law, drawing on some possible second-order rule of interpretation. As noted in the above Chapter 10, Rules nos. 40 and 41 will resolve the conflict where two first-order rules of interpretation are involved, the one belonging to the group ranging from no. 1 to no. 16, the other to the group ranging from no. 17 to no. 39. Rule no. 42 will resolve the conflict where two first-order rules of interpretation are involved, the one being rule no. 1, the other belonging to the group ranging from no. 2 to no. 16. The problem is that by invoking Rules nos. 40–42, appliers will not be able to resolve all possible conflicts occurring in the application of the various first-order rules of interpretation. So will they not be able to resolve conflicts occurring between any two rules in the group ranging from no. 2 to no. 16; and the same applies to conflicts occurring between any two rules in the group ranging from no. 17 to no. 39. Faced with such a situation, having no second-order rule of interpretation to resolve the conflict confronted, appliers will have to decide themselves which alternative is the weightier. Value judgments will then be called for.

To make the picture complete, it should be observed that invoking the second-order rules of interpretation laid down in international law, neither will appliers be able to resolve a conflict where only one first-order rule of interpretation is involved. Due to the construction of some first-order rules of interpretation, single rules may sometimes be invoked in support of two conflicting results. The obvious example would be Rule no. 1. When conventional language is ambiguous, applying Rule no. 1 may lead to conflicting results depending on the specific meaning drawn upon. The same applies to other rules of interpretation, as for instance Rule no. 15 – considering that more than *telos* may be conferred on a treaty, and considering that the use of different *teloi* may sometimes lead to different interpretation results.

Some such conflicts are less of a problem. This is because the one application of the rule nullifies the justificatory force of the other application, and vice versa.[55] One good example of this would be Rule no. 2:

> If it can be shown that the interpretation of a treaty provision in accordance with interpretation rule no. 1 leads to conflicting results, and that not only in the provision interpreted, but also in some other part of the text of said treaty, a word or phrase is included, the usage of which in one of the two possible ordinary meanings can be considered consistent, while in the other it cannot, then the former meaning shall be adopted.[56]

Suppose that the ordinary meaning of a word (W) used in a treaty provision has been found to be ambiguous: it can be interpreted in the sense of M_1, but it can also be interpreted in the sense of M_2. Furthermore, suppose that an applier shows that in another provision of the treaty the word W is used in the sense of M_1. Obviously, Rule no. 2 would be good reason for adopting M_1. But, of course, things would be different if the applier would go on to show that throughout the treaty the word W actually occurs more than twice, and that in a third provision of the treaty the word W bears the meaning M_2. Then the usage of the word W cannot any more be considered consistent. Rule no. 2 would not any more be good reason for adopting M_1. Neither would it be good reason for adopting M_2. The validity of the one application of Rule no. 2 can be said to have cancelled the validity of the other.

In other cases, conflicts of this kind cannot be resolved. Whether this is because the construction of the first-order rule of interpretation does not invite conflicts of the kind just described, or because the interpretative situation is simply different, the fact remains that once again value judgements will be called for.

NOTES

1. 1 See supra, Chapter 1, Section 1.
2. Ibid.
3. Ibid.
4. Ibid.
5. Ibid.
6. See supra, Chapter 2, Section 5.
7. See supra, Chapter 3, Sections 3–5.
8. Cf. VCLT Article 31 § 2.
9. See supra, Chapter 4, Section 1.
10. Ibid.
11. Cf. VCLT Article 31 § 2(a).
12. See supra, Chapter 5, Section 1.
13. Ibid.
14. See supra, Chapter 5, Sections 1–2.
15. Cf. VCLT Article 31 § 2(b).
16. See supra, Chapter 5, Section 3.
17. Ibid.
18. Cf. VCLT Article 31 § 3(a).
19. See supra, Chapter 6, Section 1.
20. Ibid.
21. Cf. VCLT Article 31 § 3(b).
22. See supra, Chapter 6, Section 2.
23. Cf. VCLT Article 31 § 3(c).
24. See supra, Chapter 6, Section 4.

25. Ibid., Sections 4–5.
26. Cf. VCLT Article 31 § 1 (object and purpose) and the Rule of necessary implication (Article 32), respectively.
27. See supra, Chapter 7, Section 1.
28. Ibid., Section 2.
29. Ibid., Sections 1 and 2.
30. Cf. VCLT Article 31 § 1 (object and purpose) and the Rule of necessary implication (Article 32), respectively.
31. Cf. VCLT Article 32 (interpretation *per analogiam* and *per argumentum a fortiori*).
32. Cf. VCLT Article 32.
33. See supra, Chapter 8, Section 3.
34. Cf. VCLT Article 32 (using the context as a supplementary means of interpretation).
35. See supra, Chapter 4.
36. Ibid.
37. Ibid.
38. Ibid.
39. Ibid.
40. See supra, Chapter 5 and 6, respectively.
41. Ibid.
42. See supra, Chapter 5.
43. Ibid.
44. See supra, Chapter 6.
45. Ibid
46. See supra, Chapter 7.
47. Ibid.
48. See supra, Chapter 8.
49. See supra, Chapter 9, Sections 1–3.
50. See supra, Chapter 9, Section 4.
51. Ibid.
52. Ibid., Sections 5–6.
53. See supra, Chapter 9, Section 8.
54. See supra, Chapter 10.
55. Cf. McCormick and Summers, p. 528.
56. See supra, Chapter 4, Section 5.

ANNEX

Rule no. 1

§ 1. If it can be shown that in a treaty provision, there is an expression whose form corresponds to an expression of conventional language, then the provision shall be understood in accordance with the rules of that language.

§ 2. For the purpose of this rule, CONVENTIONAL LANGUAGE means the language employed at the time of the treaty's conclusion, except for those cases where § 3 applies.

§ 3. For the purpose of this rule, CONVENTIONAL LANGUAGE means the language employed at the time of interpretation, on the condition that it can be shown that th e thing interpreted is a generic referring expression with a referent assumed by the parties to be alterable.

§ 4. For the purpose of this rule, PARTIES means any and all states for which the treaty is in force at the time of interpretation.

Rule no. 2

§ 1. If it can be shown that the interpretation of a treaty provision in accordance with interpretation rule no. 1 leads to conflicting results, and that not only in the provision interpreted, but also in some other part of the text of said treaty, a word or phrase is included, the usage of which in one of the two possible ordinary meanings can be considered consistent, while in the other it cannot, then the former meaning shall be adopted.

§ 2. For the purpose of this rule, the TEXT of a treaty means any and all instruments, of which – considered from the point of view of the parties and with good reason – the treaty can be considered comprised.

§ 3. For the purpose of this rule, PARTIES means any and all states for which the treaty is in force at the time of interpretation.

Rule no. 3

§ 1. If it can be shown that the interpretation of a treaty provision in accordance with interpretation rule no. 1 leads to conflicting results, and that somewhere in the text of said treaty a norm is expressed, which – in light of the provision interpreted – in one of the two possible ordinary meanings can be considered to involve a logical contradiction, while in the other it cannot, then the latter meaning shall be adopted.

§ 2. For the purpose of this rule, the TEXT of a treaty means any and all instruments, of which – considered from the point of view of the parties – the treaty can be considered comprised.

§ 3. For the purpose of this rule, the TEXT of a treaty means not only textual representations but also non-textual ones.

§ 4. For the purpose of this rule, PARTIES means any and all states for which the treaty is in force at the time of interpretation.

Rule no. 4

§ 1. If it can be shown that the interpretation of a treaty provision in accordance with interpretation rule no. 1 leads to conflicting results, and that somewhere in the text of said treaty there is an expression, which – in light of the provision interpreted – in one of the two possible ordinary meanings can be considered a pleonasm, while in the other it cannot, then the latter meaning shall be adopted.

§ 2. For the purpose of this rule, the TEXT of a treaty means any and all instruments, of which – considered from the point of view of the parties – the treaty can be considered comprised.

§ 3. For the purpose of this rule, PARTIES means any and all states for which the treaty is in force at the time of interpretation.

Rule no. 5

§ 1. If it can be shown that the interpretation of a treaty provision in accordance with interpretation rule no. 1 leads to conflicting results, and that in the provision interpreted, as well as in some other part of the text of said treaty, words or phrases are included, the usage of which in one of the two possible ordinary meanings can be considered to differ, while in the other meaning the usage does not, then the latter meaning shall be adopted, provided that the words or phrases, if not identical, can nevertheless be considered to be parts of the same lexical field.

§ 2. For the purpose of this rule, the TEXT of a treaty means any and all instruments, of which – considered from the point of view of the parties – the treaty can be considered comprised.

§ 3. For the purpose of this rule, PARTIES means any and all states for which the treaty is in force at the time of interpretation.

Rule no. 6

§ 1. If it can be shown that the interpretation of a treaty provision in accordance with interpretation rule no. 1 leads to conflicting results, and that somewhere in the text of said treaty a norm is expressed, which – in light of the provision interpreted – in one of the two possible ordinary meanings can be considered to involve a logical tautology, while in the other it cannot, then the latter meaning shall be adopted.

§ 2. For the purpose of this rule, the TEXT of a treaty means any and all instruments, of which – considered from the point of view of the parties – the treaty can be considered comprised.

§ 3. For the purpose of this rule, PARTIES means any and all states for which the treaty is in force at the time of interpretation.

Rule no. 7

§ 1. If it can be shown that the interpretation of a treaty provision in accordance with interpretation rule no. 1 leads to conflicting results, and that in connection with the conclusion of said treaty, the parties made an agreement, which relates to the treaty, and – in light of the provision interpreted – in one of two possible ordinary meanings can be considered to involve a logical contradiction, while in the other it cannot, then the latter meaning shall be adopted.

§ 2. For the purpose of this rule, AGREEMENT means any agreement governed by international law, whether written or not.

§ 3. For the purpose of this rule, the CONCLUSION of a treaty means the point in time when the treaty was established as definite.

§ 4. For the purpose of this rule, PARTIES means any and all states for which the treaty is in force at the time of interpretation.

§ 5. For the purpose of this rule, saying that an agreement RELATES TO a treaty is tantamount to saying that in the view of the parties, the agreement and the treaty are exceptionally closely connected.

Rule no. 8

§ 1. If it can be shown that the interpretation of a treaty provision in accordance with interpretation rule no. 1 leads to conflicting results, and that in connection with the conclusion of said treaty, the parties made an agreement, which relates to the treaty, and – in light of the provision interpreted – in one of two possible ordinary meanings can be considered to involve a logical tautology, while the other cannot, then the latter meaning shall be adopted.

§ 2. For the purpose of this rule, AGREEMENT means any agreement governed by international law, whether written or not.

§ 3. For the purpose of this rule, the CONCLUSION of a treaty means the point in time when the treaty was established as definite.

§ 4. For the purpose of this rule, PARTIES means any and all states for which the treaty is in force at the time of interpretation.

§ 5. For the purpose of this rule, saying that an agreement RELATES TO a treaty is tantamount to saying that in the view of the parties, the agreement and the treaty are exceptionally closely connected.

Rule no. 9

§ 1. If it can be shown that the interpretation of a treaty provision in accordance with interpretation rule no. 1 leads to conflicting results, and that in connection with the conclusion of said treaty, one or more parties made an instrument, which was later accepted by the other parties as related to the treaty, and – viewed in the light of the provision interpreted – in one of two possible ordinary meanings can be considered to involve a logical contradiction, while the other cannot, then the latter meaning shall be adopted.

§ 2. For the purpose of this rule, PARTIES means any and all states for which the treaty is in force at the time of interpretation.

Rule no. 10

§ 1. If it can be shown that the interpretation of a treaty provision in accordance with interpretation rule no. 1 leads to conflicting results, and that in connection with the conclusion of said treaty, one or more parties made an instrument, which was later accepted by the other parties as related to the treaty, and – viewed in the light of the provision interpreted – in one of two possible ordinary meanings can be considered to involve a logical tautology, while the other cannot, then the latter meaning shall be adopted.

§ 2. For the purpose of this rule, PARTIES means any and all states for which the treaty is in force at the time of interpretation.

Rule no. 11

§ 1. If it can be shown that the interpretation of a treaty provision in accordance with interpretation rule no. 1 leads to conflicting results, and that subsequent to the conclusion of the treaty the parties made an agreement regarding the interpretation of the treaty or the application of its provisions, and the agreement – in light of the provision interpreted – in one of the two possible ordinary meanings can be considered to involve a logical contradiction, while in the other it cannot, then the latter meaning shall be adopted.

§ 2. For the purpose of this rule, AGREEMENT means any agreement governed by international law, whether written or not.

§ 3. For the purpose of this rule, an agreement was made SUBSEQUENT to the conclusion of a treaty, if (and only if) it was made after the point in time when the interpreted treaty was established as definite.

§ 4. For the purpose of this rule, PARTIES means any and all states for which the treaty is in force at the time of interpretation.

§ 5. For the purpose of this rule, an agreement is one REGARDING the interpretation of a treaty or the application of its provisions, if (and only if) the agreement was made with the purpose of either clarifying the meaning of said treaty, or of serving in some other manner as a guide for its application.

Rule no. 12

§ 1. If it can be shown that the interpretation of a treaty provision in accordance with interpretation rule no. 1 leads to conflicting results, and that subsequent to the conclusion of the treaty the parties made an agreement regarding the interpretation of the treaty or the application of its provisions, and the agreement – in light of the provision interpreted – in one of the two possible ordinary meanings can be considered to involve a logical tautology, while in the other it cannot, then the latter meaning shall be adopted.

§ 2. For the purpose of this rule, AGREEMENT means any agreement governed by international law, whether written or not.

§ 3. For the purpose of this rule, an agreement was made SUBSEQUENT to the conclusion of a treaty, if (and only if) it was made after the point in time when the interpreted treaty was established as definite.

§ 4. For the purpose of this rule, PARTIES means any and all states for which the treaty is in force at the time of interpretation.

§ 5. For the purpose of this rule, an agreement is one REGARDING the interpretation of a treaty or the application of its provisions, if (and only if) the agreement was made with the purpose of either clarifying the meaning of said treaty, or of serving in some other manner as a guide for its application.

Rule no. 13

§ 1. If it can be shown that the interpretation of a treaty provision in accordance with interpretation rule no. 1 leads to conflicting results, and that subsequent to the conclusion of the treaty a practice has developed, which with good reason can be said to establish the agreement of the parties regarding the interpretation of said treaty, so that the practice – in light of the provision interpreted – in one of the two possible ordinary meanings can be considered to a logical contradiction, while in the other it cannot, then the latter meaning shall be adopted.

§ 2. For the purpose of this rule, PRACTICE means any number of applications, one or many.

§ 3. For the purpose of this rule, the APPLICATION of a treaty means any and all measures based on the treaty.

§ 4. For the purpose of this rule, a practice is considered SUBSEQUENT to the conclusion of a treaty, if (and only if) it developed after the point in time when the interpreted treaty was established as definite.

§ 5. For the purpose of this rule, PARTIES means any and all states for which the treaty is in force at the time of interpretation.

§ 6. For the purpose of this rule, AGREEMENT means not only the concordance upon which the treaty was originally concluded, but also any possible concordance arrived at after the conclusion of the treaty, excluding, however, interpretative agreements governed by international law.

§ 7. For the purpose of this rule, a practice establishes agreement with regard to the INTERPRETATION of a treaty, only on the condition that practice agrees with the treaty, when interpreted in accordance with rule no. 1.

Rule no. 14

§ 1. If it can be shown that the interpretation of a treaty provision in accordance with interpretation rule no. 1 leads to conflicting results, and that a relevant rule of international law is applicable in the relationship between the parties, and the rule – considered in light of the provision interpreted – in one of the two possible ordinary meanings can be considered to involve a logical contradiction, while in the other it cannot, then the latter meaning shall be adopted.

§ 2. For the purpose of this rule, RULE OF INTERNATIONAL LAW means any and all rules whose origin can be traced to a formal source of international law.

§ 3. For the purpose of this rule, PARTIES means any and all states for which the treaty is in force at the time of interpretation.

§ 4. For the purpose of this rule, whether a rule of law is APPLICABLE or not is determined based upon the legal state-of-affairs that prevailed at the time when the treaty was concluded, unless otherwise applies according to § 5.

§ 5. For the purpose of this rule, whether a rule of law is APPLICABLE or not is determined based upon the legal state-of-affairs prevailing at the time of interpretation, provided that it can be shown that what is being interpreted is a generic referring expression with a referent assumed by the parties to be alterable.

Rule no. 15

§ 1. If it can be shown that the interpretation of a treaty provision in accordance with interpretation rule no. 1 leads to conflicting results, and that the treaty has a certain *telos*, which in one of the two possible ordinary meanings, by applying the provision, will be realised to a greater extent than in the other, then the former meaning shall be adopted.

§ 2. For the purpose of this rule, TELOS means any state-of-affairs, which according to the parties should be attained by applying the interpreted provision.

§ 3. For the purpose of this rule, the TELOS of a treaty is determined based upon the intentions held by the parties at the time of the treaty's conclusion, except for those cases where §4 applies.

§ 4. For the purpose of this rule, the TELOS of a treaty is determined based upon the intentions held by the parties at the time of interpretation, provided it can be shown that the thing interpreted is a generic referring expression with a referent assumed by the parties to be alterable.

§ 5. For the purpose of this rule, PARTIES means any and all states for which the treaty is in force at the time of interpretation.

Rule no. 16

If it can be shown that the interpretation of a treaty provision in accordance with interpretation rule no. 1 leads to conflicting results, and that somewhere in the text of that treaty a norm is expressed, which – in light of the provision interpreted – in one of the two possible ordinary meanings can be considered in practice normatively useless, while in the other it cannot, then the latter meaning shall be adopted.

Rule no. 17

§ 1. If it can be shown that the interpretation of a treaty provision in accordance with interpretation rule no. 1 leads to conflicting results, and by using the preparatory work of the treaty a concordance can be shown to exist, as between the parties to the treaty, and with regard to the norm content of the interpreted treaty provision, so that the provision – in light of the preparatory work – in one of the two possible ordinary meanings can be considered to involve a logical contradiction, while in the other it cannot, then the latter meaning shall be adopted.

§ 2. For the purpose if this rule, THE PREPARATORY WORK of a treaty means any representation produced in the process of drafting the treaty, whether textual or not.

§ 3. For the purpose of this rule, PARTIES means any and all states for which the treaty is in force at the time of interpretation.

Rule no. 18

§ 1. If, by using the preparatory work of a treaty, a concordance can be shown to exist, as between the parties to said treaty, and with regard to the norm content of an interpreted treaty provision, then the provision shall be understood in such a way that it logically agrees with the concordance.

§ 2. For the purpose if this rule, THE PREPARATORY WORK of a treaty means any representation produced in the process of drafting the treaty, whether textual or not.

§ 3. For the purpose of this rule, PARTIES means any and all states for which the treaty is in force at the time of interpretation.

Rule no. 19

§ 1. If it can be shown that the interpretation of a treaty provision in accordance with interpretation rule no. 1 leads to conflicting results, and by using the circumstances of the treaty's conclusion a concordance can be shown to exist, as between the parties to the treaty, and with regard to the norm content of the interpreted treaty provision, so that the provision – in light of the circumstances of the treaty's conclusion – in one of the two possible ordinary meanings can be considered to involve a logical contradiction, while in the other it cannot, then the latter meaning shall be adopted.

§ 2. For the purpose of this rule, a CIRCUMSTANCE OF THE TREATY'S CONCLUSION means any state-of-affairs, whose existence at least partially can be said to have caused the conclusion, except for those cases where this state-of-affairs can be taken into account already for the application of the interpretation rules nos. 7–14 or 17–18.

§ 3. For the purpose of this rule, the CONCLUSION of a treaty means the point in time when the treaty was established as definite.

§ 4. For the purpose of this rule, PARTIES means any and all states for which the treaty is in force at the time of interpretation.

Rule no. 20

§ 1. If, by using the circumstances of a treaty's conclusion, a concordance can be shown to exist, as between the parties to said treaty, and with regard to the norm content of an interpreted treaty provision, then the provision shall be understood in such a way that it logically agrees with the concordance.

§ 2. For the purpose of this rule, a CIRCUMSTANCE OF THE TREATY'S CONCLUSION means any state-of-affairs, whose existence at least partially can be said to have caused the conclusion, except for those cases where this state-of-affairs can be taken into account already for the application of the interpretation rules nos. 7–14 or 17–18.

§ 3. For the purpose of this rule, the CONCLUSION of a treaty means the point in time when the treaty was established as definite.

§ 4. For the purpose of this rule, PARTIES means any and all states for which the treaty is in force at the time of interpretation.

Rule no. 21

§ 1. If it can be shown that the interpretation of a treaty provision in accordance with interpretation rule no. 1 leads to conflicting results, and by using any ratification work of the treaty, a concordance can be shown to exist, as between the parties to the treaty, and with regard to the norm content of the interpreted treaty provision, so that the provision – in light of the ratification work used – in one of the two possible ordinary meanings can be considered to involve a logical contradiction, while in the other it cannot, then the latter meaning shall be adopted.

§ **2**. For the purpose of this rule, RATIFICATION WORK means any representation unilaterally produced by a state in the process of deciding whether to ratify the treaty.

§ **3**. For the purpose of this rule, PARTIES means any and all states for which the treaty is in force at the time of interpretation.

Rule no. 22

§ **1**. If, by using any ratification work of a treaty, a concordance can be shown to exist, as between the parties to said treaty, and with regard to the norm content of an interpreted treaty provision, then the provision shall be understood in such a way that it logically agrees with the concordance.

§ **2**. For the purpose of this rule, RATIFICATION WORK means any representation unilaterally produced by a state in the process of deciding whether to ratify the treaty or not.

§ **3**. For the purpose of this rule, PARTIES means any and all states for which the treaty is in force at the time of interpretation.

Rule no. 23

§ **1**. If it can be shown that the interpretation of a treaty provision in accordance with interpretation rule no. 1 leads to conflicting results, and by using a treaty *in pari materia* a concordance can be shown to exist, as between the parties to the treaty, and with regard to the norm content of the interpreted treaty provision, so that the provision – in light of the treaty *in pari materia* – in one of the two possible ordinary meanings can be considered to involve a logical contradiction, while in the other it cannot, then the latter meaning shall be adopted.

§ **2**. For the purpose of this rule, a TREATY IN PARI MATERIA means a treaty whose subject matter is identical – at least partly – with the subject matter covered by the treaty interpreted.

§ **3**. For the purpose of this rule, PARTIES means any and all states for which the treaty is in force at the time of interpretation.

Rule no. 24

§ **1**. If, by using a treaty *in pari materia*, a concordance can be shown to exist, as between the parties to the interpreted treaty, and with regard to the norm content of the interpreted treaty provision, then the provision shall be understood in such a way that it logically agrees with the concordance.

§ **2**. For the purpose of this rule, PARTIES means any and all states for which the treaty is in force at the time of interpretation.

Rule no. 25

§ **1**. If it can be shown that the interpretation of a treaty provision in accordance with interpretation rule no. 1 leads to conflicting results, and by using the context of the provision a concordance can be shown to exist, as between the parties to the treaty, and with regard to the norm content of the interpreted treaty provision, so that the provision – in light of the context – in one of the two possible ordinary meanings can be considered to involve a logical contradiction, while in the other it cannot, then the latter meaning shall be adopted.

§ **2**. For the purpose of this rule, the CONTEXT of an interpreted treaty provision means any element that fits the description provided in article 31 §§2 and 3 of the 1969 Vienna Convention on the Law of Treaties.

§ **3**. For the purpose of this rule, PARTIES means any and all states for which the treaty is in force at the time of interpretation.

Rule no. 26

§ **1**. If, by using the context of an interpreted treaty provision, a concordance can be shown to exist, as between the parties to said treaty, and with regard to the norm content of the interpreted provision, then the provision shall be understood in such a way that it logically agrees with the concordance.

§ **2**. For the purpose of this rule, the CONTEXT of an interpreted treaty provision means any element that fits the description provided in article 31 §§2 and 3 of the 1969 Vienna Convention on the Law of Treaties.

§ **3**. For the purpose of this rule, PARTIES means any and all states for which the treaty is in force at the time of interpretation.

Rule no. 27

If it can be shown that the interpretation of a treaty provision in accordance with interpretation rule no. 1 leads to conflicting results, and that the provision contains an obligation, whose extension in one of the two possible ordinary meanings is comparably greater than it is in the other, then the latter meaning shall be adopted.

Rule no. 28

§ 1. If it can be shown (i) that the interpretation of a treaty provision in accordance with interpretation rule no. 1 leads to conflicting results, (ii) that the content of the treaty has a two-sided nature, (iii) that the treaty was concluded through one of the negotiating parties unilaterally proffering the treaty for acceptance by the other(s), and (iv) that the provision, in one of the two possible ordinary meanings, is of greater disadvantage for this active party than it is in the other, then the former meaning shall be adopted.

§ 2. For the purpose of this rule, saying that the content of a treaty has a TWO-SIDED NATURE is tantamount to saying that the treaty has two parties only, or – should there be more than two parties – that the treaty has been constructed in such a way, that one of the parties has rights and obligations toward each and every one of the others, and vice versa, but these other parties do not have corresponding rights and obligations toward each other.

§ 3. For the purpose of this rule, PARTIES means any and all states for which the treaty is in force at the time of interpretation.

Rule no. 29

If it can be shown (i) that the interpretation of a treaty provision in accordance with interpretation rule no. 1 leads to conflicting results, (ii) that the provision contains an exception to a right or an obligation laid down in said treaty, and (iii) that the extension of the exception in one of the two possible ordinary meanings is comparably greater than it is in the other, then the latter meaning shall be adopted.

Rule no. 30

§ 1. If it can be shown that according to linguistics a meaning can be read into a treaty provision by implication, and that such an implication is necessary to avoid a situation where, by applying the provision a result is attained which is not among the *teloi* conferred on the treaty, then this meaning shall be adopted.

§ 2. For the purpose of this rule, TELOI means the state or states of affairs, which according to the parties should be attained by applying the interpreted provision.

§ 3. For the purpose of this rule, the TELOI of a treaty are determined based upon the intentions held by the parties at the time of the treaty's conclusion, except for those cases where § 4 applies.

§ 4. For the purpose of this rule, the TELOI of a treaty are determined based upon the intentions held by the parties at the time of interpretation, granted it can be shown that the thing interpreted is a generic referring expression with a referent assumed by the parties to be alterable.

§ 5. For the purpose of this rule, PARTIES means any and all states for which the treaty is in force at the time of interpretation.

Rule no. 31

If it can be shown that according to linguistics a meaning can be implicitly read into a treaty provision, and that such an implication is necessary to avoid a situation where, by applying the provision, another part of the treaty will be normatively useless, then this meaning shall be adopted.

Rule no. 32

§ 1. If it can be shown (i) that the interpretation of a treaty provision in accordance with interpretation rule no. 1 leads to conflicting results, (ii) that two states-of-affairs are analogous to one another, (iii) that the one state-of-affairs is governed by the interpreted treaty provision, and (iv) that in one of the two possible ordinary meanings the other state-of-affairs comes within the scope of application of the provision, whereas in the other meaning it does not, then the former meaning shall be adopted.

§ 2. For the purpose of this rule, saying that two states-of-affairs are ANALOGOUS to one another is tantamount to saying that in some significant respect they can be thought of as similar or comparable.

Rule no. 33

§ 1. If it can be shown that of two states-of-affairs, which are analogous to one another, the one comes within the scope of application of an interpreted treaty provision, then the provision shall be understood in such a way that the other comes within that scope of application, too.

§ 2. For the purpose of this rule, saying that two states-of-affairs are ANALOGOUS to one another is tantamount to saying that in some significant respect they can be thought of as similar or comparable.

Rule no. 34

§ 1. If it can be shown that a treaty provision permits an act or a state-of-affairs, which – from the point of view of the parties – can be considered less tolerable than another generically identical act or state-of-affairs, then the provision shall be understood to permit this second act or state-of-affairs, too.

§ 2. For the purpose of this rule, PARTIES means any and all states for which the treaty is in force at the time of interpretation.

Rule no. 35

§ 1. If it can be shown (i) that the interpretation of a treaty provision in accordance with interpretation rule no. 1 leads to conflicting results, (ii) that the provision permits an action or a state-of-affairs, which – from the point of view of the parties – can be considered less tolerable than another generically identical action or state-of-affairs, and (iii) that in one of the two possible ordinary meanings, this other action or state-of-affairs comes within the scope of application of the interpreted provision, whereas in the other meaning it does not, then the former meaning shall be adopted.

§ 2. For the purpose of this rule, PARTIES means any and all states for which the treaty is in force at the time of interpretation.

Rule no. 36

§ 1. If it can be shown that a treaty provision prohibits an act or a state-of-affairs, which – from the point of view of the parties – can be considered more tolerable than another generically identical act or state-of-affairs, then the provision shall be understood to prohibit this second act or state-of-affairs, too.

§ 2. For the purpose of this rule, PARTIES means any and all states for which the treaty is in force at the time of interpretation.

Rule no. 37

§ 1. If it can be shown (i) that the interpretation of a treaty provision in accordance with interpretation rule no. 1 leads to conflicting results, (ii) that the provision prohibits an action or a state-of-affairs, which – from the point of view of the parties – can be considered more tolerable than another generically identical action or state-of-affairs, and (iii) that in one of the two possible ordinary meanings, this other action or state-of-affairs comes within the scope of application of the interpreted provision, whereas in the other meaning it does not, then the former meaning shall be adopted.

§ 2. For the purpose of this rule, PARTIES means any and all states for which the treaty is in force at the time of interpretation.

Rule no. 38

If it can be shown that in a treaty provision there is an expression, which according to conventional language is used to refer to a smaller part of a larger, generically defined class, then the provision shall be understood in such a way that the extension of the expression comprises this smaller part only, and not any other part of the class.

Rule no. 39

If it can be shown (i) that in a treaty provision two expressions are included, of which the one (expression A), according to conventional language, can be considered related to the other (expression B), (ii) that all the referents of the former expression (A) can be considered to be members of a certain, generically defined class, and (iii) that, according to conventional language, all the members of this class are referents of the latter expression (B), then the provision shall be understood under the assumption that no referents to this second expression (B) belong to any other class.

Rule no. 40

§ 1. If it can be shown that the interpretation of a treaty provision in accordance with any one of interpretation rules nos. 1–16 leads to a result, which is different from that obtained by interpreting the provision in accordance with any one of interpretation rules nos. 17–39, and that the application of the former rule either leaves the meaning of the interpreted treaty provision ambiguous or obscure, or amounts to a result which is manifestly absurd or unreasonable, then the provision shall not be understood in accordance with this former rule.

§ 2. For the purpose of this rule, the meaning of a treaty provision shall be considered AMBIGUOUS OR OBSCURE, if interpreting the provision in accordance with any one of interpretation rules nos. 2–16 leads to a result, which is different than that obtained by interpreting the provision in accordance with any other of those fifteen rules.

§ 3. For the purpose of this rule, saying that the application of a rule of interpretation LEADS TO A RESULT WHICH IS MANIFESTLY ABSURD OR UNREASONABLE is tantamount to saying that the application of the two conflicting rules – the first being one among rules numbered 1 to 16, the other being one among the rules numbered 17 to 39 – is based on communicative assumptions, of which the assumption underlying the application of the former rule can be considered significantly weaker than the assumption underlying the application of the latter.

Rule no. 41

If it can be shown that the interpretation of a treaty provision in accordance with any one of interpretation rules nos. 1–16 leads to a result, which is different from that obtained by interpreting the provision in accordance with any one of interpretation rules nos. 17–39, then, rather than being understood in accordance with the latter of the two rules, the provision shall be understood in accordance with the former, except for those cases where interpretation rule no. 40 applies.

Rule no. 42

If it can be shown that the interpretation of a treaty provision in accordance with interpretation rule no. 1 leads to a result, which is different from that obtained by interpreting the provision in accordance with any one of interpretation rules nos. 2–16, then the provision shall not be understood in accordance with interpretation rule no. 1.

Rule no. 43

If it can be shown (i) that a treaty has been authenticated in two or more languages, (ii) that two of the authenticated texts, by applying interpretation rules nos. 1–42, will still have to be understood in two different meanings, and (iii) that by applying the treaty in the one meaning, the object and purpose of the treaty will be realised to a greater extent than in the other, then the former meaning shall be adopted, except for those cases where interpretation rule no. 44 applies.

Rule no. 44

If it can be shown (i) that a treaty has been authenticated in two or more languages, (ii) that two of the authenticated texts, by applying interpretation rules nos. 1–42, will still have to be understood in two different meanings, and (iii) that the parties have agreed that in such cases a particular text shall prevail, then the treaty shall be understood in accordance with the meaning conveyed by that text.

LIST OF SOURCES

1 DOCUMENTS AND REPORTS

(In reverse chronological order)

International Law Commission, "Fragmentation of International Law: Difficulties Arising from the Diversification and Expansion of International Law", Report of the Study Group of the International Law Commission, Chaired by Martti Koskenniemi, 13 April 2006 (UN Doc. A/CN.4/L.682)

Sixth Report on the Law of Treaties, by Sir Humphrey Waldock, Special Rapporteur (UN Doc. A/CN.4/186 and Add. 1–7), *ILC Yrbk*, 1966, Vol. 2, pp. 51 , cit. "Waldock, Sixth Report on the Law of Treaties", United Nations Conference on the Law of Treaties, First session, Vienna, 26 March-24 May 1968, *Official Records*, Summary records of the plenary meetings and of the meetings of the Committee of the Whole

United Nations Conference on the Law of Treaties, Second session, Vienna, 9 April-22 May 1969, *Official Records*, Summary records of the plenary meetings and of the meetings of the Committee of the Whole

United Nations Conference on the Law of Treaties, First and Second sessions, Vienna, 26 March–24 may 1968 and 9 April–22 may 1969, *Official Records*, Documents of the Conference

United Nations General Assembly, Report of the Sixth Committee, 24 November 1967 (UN Doc. A/6913), *Official Records*, 22nd session, Agenda item 86, Annexes

United Nations General Assembly, Report of the Sixth Committee, 21 November 1966 (UN Doc. A/6516), *Official Records of the United Nations General Assembly*, 21st session, Annexes, Agenda item 84

United Nations General Assembly, Comments on the final draft articles on the law of treaties prepared by the International Law Commission at its eighteenth session, Report of the Secretary General (UN Doc. A/6827 and Add. 1 and 2), *Official Records*, 22nd session, Annexes, Agenda item 86

International Law Commission, Report to the United Nations General Assembly, on the work of the second part of its seventeenth session and on its eighteenth session (UN Dec. A/6309/Rev. 1), *ILC Yrbk*, 1966, Vol. 2, pp. 169

International Law Commission, Summary records of the eighteenth session, 4 May–19 July 1966, *ILC Yrbk*, 1966, Vol. 1, Part 2

International Law Commission, Sixth Report on the Law of Treaties, by Sir Humphrey Waldock, Special Rapporteur (UN Doc. A/CN.4/186 and Add. 1–7), *ILC Yrbk*, 1966, Vol. 2, pp. 51 et seq., cit. "Waldock, Sixth Report on the Law of Treaties"

United Nations General Assembly, Report of the Sixth Committee, 4 November 1965 (UN Doc. A/6090), *Official Records*, 20th session, Annexes, Agenda item 87

International Law Commission, Summary records of the first part of the seventeenth session, 3 May–9 July 1965, *ILC Yrbk*, 1965, Vol. 1

International Law Commission, Fourth Report on the Law of Treaties, by Sir Humphrey Waldock, Special Rapporteur (UN Doc. A/CN.4/177 and Add. 1 and 2), *ILC Yrbk*, 1965, Vol. 2, pp. 3 et seq., cit. "Waldock, Fourth Report on the Law of Treaties"

International Law Commission, Report to the United Nations General Assembly, covering the work of its sixteenth session, 11 May-24 July 1964 (UN Doc. A/5809) , *ILC Yrbk*, 1964, Vol. 2, pp. 173

International Law Commission, Summary records of the sixteenth session, 11 May–24 July 1964, *ILC Yrbk*, 1964, Vol. 1

International Law Commission, Third Report on the Law of Treaties, by Sir Humphrey Waldock, Special Rapporteur (UN Doc. A/CN.4/167 and Add. 1–3), *ILC Yrbk*, 1964, Vol. 2, pp. 5 et seq., cit. "Waldock, Third Report on the Law of Treaties"

2 ARTICLES AND MONOGRAPHS

Aarnio, Aulis, "On the Semantic Ambiguity of Legal Interpretation", *Festskrift till Stig Strömholm*, Vol. 1 (Uppsala: Iustus, 1997), pp. 25–33

Aceves, William J., "Ambiguities in Plurilingual Treaties: A Case Study of Article 22 of the 1982 Law of the Sea Convention", *Ocean Development and International Law Journal*, Vol. 27 (1996), pp. 187–233

Agge, Ivar, *Huvudpunkter i den allmänna rättsläran*, 2nd ed. (Stockholm: Juridiska föreningens förlag, 1969)

Akehurst, Michael, "The Hierarchy of the Sources of International Law", *British Yearbook of International Law*, Vol. 47 (1974/1975), pp. 273–285

—- *A Modern Introduction to International Law*, 6th ed. (London et al.: Unwin Hyman, 1987)

Alexy, Robert, *A Theory of Legal Argumentation. The Theory of Rational Discourse as Theory of Legal Justification*, translated from the German by Adler, Ruth and McCormick, Neil (Oxford: Clarendon, 1989)

—- *Theorie der Grundrechte*, 2nd ed. (Frankfurt am Main: Surkamp, 1994)

—- *Recht, Vernunft, Diskurs* (Frankfurt am Main: Surkamp, 1995)

Amerasinghe, C.F., "Interpretation of Texts in Open International Organizations", *British Yearbook of International Law*, Vol. 65 (1994), pp. 175–209

American Law Institute, *Restatement of the Foreign Relations Law of the United States*, As Adopted and Promulgated at Washington, D.C., 14 May 1986, Vol. 1 (St. Paul, Minn.: American Law Institute Publishers, 1986)

Anscombe, G.E.M., "Intention", *The Philosophy of Action*, ed. White, Alan R. (Oxford: Oxford University Press, 1968), pp. 144–152

Anzilotti, Dionisio, *Cours de droit international public*, translated from the Italian by Gidel, Gilbert (Paris: Sirey, 1929)

Aust, Anthony, "The Theory and Practice of Informal International Treaties", *International and Comparative Law Quarterly*, Vol. 35 (1986), pp. 787–812

—- *Modern Treaty Law and Practice* (Cambridge: CUP, 2000)

Bach, K. and Harnish, R., *Linguistic Communication and Speech Acts* (Cambridge, Mass.: MIT Press, 1979)

Barile, Guiseppe, "La structure de l'ordre juridique international", *Recueil des Cours de l'Académie de droit international* , Vol. 161 (1978:3), pp. 9–126

Bennion, Francis, *Statutory Interpretation* (London: Butterworths, 1984)

Berlia, G., "Contribution à l'interprétation des traités", *Recueil des Cours de l'Académie de droit international*, Vol. 114 (1965:1), pp. 287–331

Berman, Frank, "Treaty 'Interpretation' in a Judicial Context", *Yale Journal of International Law*, Vol. 29 (2004), pp. 315–322

Bernhardt, Rudolf, *Die Auslegung völkerrechtlicher Verträge*, Beiträge zum ausländischen öffentlichen Recht und Völkerrecht, Vol. 40 (Köln, Berlin: Carl Heymanns, 1963)

—- "Interpretation and Implied (Tacit) Modification of Treaties: Comments on Art pp. 27, 28, 29 and 38 of the ILC's 1966 Draft Articles on the Law of Treaties", *Zeitschrift für ausländische öffentliche Recht und Völkerrecht*, Vol. 27 (1967), pp. 491–506

—- "Interpretation in International Law", *Encyclopedia of Public International Law*, ed. Bernhardt, Rudolf, Vol. 7 (Amsterdam et al.: North Holland, 1984), pp. 318–327

—- "Evaluative Treaty Interpretation, Especially of the European Court of Human Rights", *German Yearbook of International Law*, Vol. 42 (1999), pp. 11–25

Berman, Frank, "Treaty Interpretation in a Judicial Context", *Yale Journal of International Law*, Vol. 29 (2004), p. 315–322

Bin Cheng, *General Principles of Law as Applied by International Courts and Tribunals* (London: Stevens & Sons, 1953)

Blakemore, Diane, *Understanding Utterance: Introduction to Pragmatics*, Blackwell Textbooks in Linguistics, Vol. 6 (Oxford: Blackwell, 1992)

Blass, Regina, *Relevance Relations in Discourse* (Cambridge: CUP, 1990)

Bleckmann, Albert, "Analogie im Völkerrecht", *Archiv des Völkrerrechts*, Vol. 17 (1977/1978), pp. 161–180
Bonnard, Roger, "Le pouvoir discrétionnaire des autorités administratives et le recours pour excès de pouvoir", *Revue du droit public et de la science politique en France et à l'étranger* (1923), pp. 363–393
Bos, Maarten, "The Recognized Manifestations of International Law: A New Theory of 'Sources'", *German Yearbook of International Law*, Vol. 25 (1977), pp. 9–76
—- *A Methodology of International Law* (Amsterdam et al.: North-Holland, 1984)
Briggs, Herbert W., "The *Travaux Préparatoires* of the Vienna Convention on the Law of Treaties", Review Article, *American Journal of International Law*, Vol. 65 (1971), pp. 705–712
Brownlie, Ian, *Principles of Public International Law*, 4th ed. (Oxford: Clarendon, 1990)
Bydlinski, Franz, *Juristische Methodenlehre und Rechtsbegriff*, 2nd ed. (Wien, New York: Springer, 1991)
Bynon, Theodora, *Historical Linguistics*, Cambridge Textbooks in Linguistics (Cambridge: CUP, 1977)
Capotorti, F., "Sul valore della prassi applicativa dei trattati secundo la convenzione di Vienna", *Le Droit international a l'heure de sa codification. Études en l'honneur de Roberto Ago*, Vol. 1 (Milano: Giuffrè, 1987), pp. 197–218
Cavaré, L., *Le Droit international public posit if*, Vol. 2, 3rd ed. (Paris: Pédone, 1969)
Chaumont, Charles, "Cours général de droit international public", *Recueil des Cours de l'Académie de droit international*, Vol. 129 (1970:1), pp. 333–528
Cheng, C.H., *Essai critique sur l'interprétation des traités* (Diss. Université de Paris; Paris: Tepac, 1941)
Christie, Gordon, "Justifying Principles of Treaty Interpretation", *Queens Law Journal*, Vol. 26 (2000), p. 143 et seq.
Coccia, M., "Reservations to Human Rights Treaties", *California Western International Law Journal*, Vol. 15 (1985), pp. 1–51
Cot, Jean-Pierre, "La conduite subséquente des parties à un traité", *Revue générale de droit international public*, Vol. 70 (1966), pp. 632–666
Criddle, Evan, "The Vienna Convention on the Law of Treaties in U.S. Interpretation", Virginia Journal of International Law Vol. 44 (2004), pp. 431–500
Czaplinski, W. and Danilenko, G., "Conflicts of Norms in International Law", *Netherlands Yearbook of International Law*, Vol. 21 (1990), pp. 3–42
Dahl, K.N., "The Application of Successive Treaties Dealing With the Same Subject-Matter", *Indian Yearbook of World Affairs*, Vol. 17 (1974), pp. 279–318
Dahm, Georg, *Völkerrecht*, Vol. 3 (Stuttgart: W. Kohlhammer, 1961)
Danilenko, G.M., *Law-Making in the International Community*, Developments in International Law, Vol. 15 (Dordrecht et al.: Martinus Nijhoff, 1993)
Dascal, Marcelo and Wróblewski, Jerzy, "Transparency and Doubt: Understanding and Interpretation in Pragmatics and in Law", *Law and Philosophy*, Vol. 7 (1988), pp. 203–224
Davidson, Scott, *The Inter-American Court of Human Rights* (Aldershot et al.: Dartmouth, 1992)
Degan, V.D., *L'interprétation des accords en droit international* (La Haye: Martinus Nijhoff, 1963)
—- "Attempts to Codify Principles of Treaty Interpretation and the South-West Africa Case", *Indian Journal of International Law*, Vol. 8 (1968), pp. 9–32
Dehaussy, J., "Les actes juridiques unilatéraux en droit international: A propos d'une théorie restrictive", *Journal de droit international (Clunet)*, Vol. 92 (1965), pp. 41–66
De Visscher, Charles, *Theory and Reality in Public International Law*, translated from the French by Corbett, P.E. (Princeton, New Jersey: Princeton Univ. Press, 1957)
—- "Remarques sur l'interprétation dite textuelle des traités internationaux", *Nederlands Tijdschrift voor Internationaal Recht*, Vol. 6 (1959), pp. 383–390
—- *Problèmes d'interprétation judiciaire en droit international public* (Paris: Pédone, 1963)
Dickerson, Reed, *The Interpretation and Application of Statutes* (Boston and Toronto: Little, Brown and Co., 1975)
Di Stefano, Giovanni, "La pratique subséquante des états parties à un traité", *Annuaire français de droit international*, Vol. 40 (1994), pp. 41–71
Duguit, Léon, *Traité de droit constitutionnel*, Vol. 1, 3rd ed. (Paris: Ancienne Librairie Fontemoing, 1927)

Dupuy, Pierre-Marie, *Droit international public* (Paris: Dalloz-Sirey, 1992)

Ehrlich, Ludwik, "L'interprétation des traités", *Recueil des Cours de l'Académie de droit international*, Vol. 24 (1928:4), pp. 1–145

Ekelöf, Per Olof, *Rättegång*, fjärde häftet, 5th ed., Institutet för rättsvetenskaplig forskning, Vol. 38 (Lund: Norstedts, 1982)

Elias, T.O., *The Modern Law of Treaties* (Dobbs Ferry, N.Y.: Oceana, 1974)

—- "The Doctrine of Intertemporal Law", *American Journal of International Law*, Vol. 74 (1980), pp. 285–307

Endicott, Timothy A.O., "Putting Interpretation in Its Place", *Law and Philosophy*, Vol. 13 (1994), pp. 451–479

Farer, Tom J., "The Humanitarian Laws of War in Civil Strife: Towards a Definition of 'International Armed Conflict'", *Revue belge de droit international*, Vol. 7 (1971:1), pp. 20–55

Favre, Antoine, "L'interprétation objectiviste des traités internationaux", *Schweizerisches Jahrbuch für internationales Recht*, Vol. 17 (1960), pp. 75–98

—- *Principes du drot international* (Fribourg, Suisse: Editions Universitaires, 1974)

Fenwick, Charles G., *International Law* (New York: 1924)

Ferrajoli, L., "Interpretazione dottrinale e interpretazione operativa", *Rivista internazionale di filosofia del diritto*, Vol. 1 (1966)

FitzGerald, Gerald F., "The Development of the Authentic Trilingual Text of the Convention of International Civil Aviation", *American Journal of International Law*, Vol. 64 (1970), pp. 364–371

Fitzmaurice, Gerald, "The Law and Procedure of the International Court of Justice: Treaty Interpretation and Other Treaty Points", *British Yearbook of International Law*, Vol. 28 (1951), pp. 1–28

—- "The Law and Procedure of the International Court of Justice: International Organizations and Tribunals", *British Yearbook of International Law*, Vol. 29 (1952), pp. 1 et seq.

—- "The Law and Procedure of the International Court of Justice 1951–1954: General Principles and Sources of Law, *British Yearbook of International Law*, Vol. 30 (1953), pp. 1 et seq.

—- "The Law and Procedure of the International Court of Justice 1951–1954: Treaty Interpretation and Other Treaty Points", *British Yearbook of International Law*, Vol. 33 (1957), pp. 205 et seq.

—- "The Law and Procedure of the International Court of Justice 1951–1954: Questions of Jurisdiction, Competence and Procedure", *British Yearbook of International Law*, Vol. 34 (1958), pp. 1 et seq.

—- "Hersch Lauterpacht: The Scholar as Judge. Part III", *British Yearbook of International Law*, Vol. 39 (1963), pp. 133–188

—- "Vae Victis or Woe To the Negotiators! Your Treaty or Our 'Interpretation' of It", Review Article, *American Journal of International Law*, Vol. 65 (1971), pp. 358–373

Fitzmaurice, Gerald G. and Vallat, F.A., "Sir (William) Eric Becket, K.C.M.G., Q.C. (1896–1966): An Appreciation", *International and Comparative Law Quarterly*, Vol. 17 (1968), pp. 267–313

Fitzmaurice, Malgosia, "The Optional Clause System and the Law of Treaties: Issues of Interpretation in Recent Jurisprudence of the International Court of Justice", *Australian Yearbook of International Law*, Vol. 20 (1999), p. 127 et seq.

Ganshof van der Meersch, W. J., "Réflexions sur les méthodes d'interprétation de la Cour européenne des droits de l'homme", *Documentação e direito comparado*, Vol. 11 (1982), pp. 107–132

Gazdar, G., *Pragmatics. Implicature, Presupposition and Logical Form* (New York: Academic Press, 1979)

Germer, Peter, "Interpretation of Plurilingual Treaties: A Study of Article 33 of the Vienna Convention on the Law of Treaties", *Harvard International Law Journal*, Vol. 11 (1970), pp. 400–427

Glahn, Gerhard von, *Law Among Nations. An Introduction to International Law*, 5th ed. (New York: MacMillan, 1986)

Golding, Martin P., "A Note on Discovery and Justification in Science and Law", *Legal Reasoning*, Vol. 1, ed. Aarnio, Aulis and McCormick, Neil D. (Aldershot et al.: Dartmouth, 1992), pp. 109–125, originally published in *Justification*, Nomos, Vol. 27 (1986), pp. 124–140

Golsong, Heribert, "Interpreting the European Convention on Human Rights Beyond the Confines of the Vienna Convention on the Law of Treaties?", *The European System for the Protection of Human Rights*, ed. McDonald, R. St. J. et al. (Dordrecht: Nijhoff, 1993), pp. 147–162

Gordon, Edward, "The World Court and the Interpretation of Constitutive Treaties", *American Journal of International Law*, Vol. 59 (1965), pp. 794–833

Gottlieb, Gideon, "The Interpretation of Treaties by Tribunals", *Proceedings of the American Society of International Law*, at its 63rd Annual Meeting, Held at Washington, D.C., 24–26 April 1969, pp. 122–131

Green, G.M., *Pragmatics and Natural Language Understanding* (Hillsdale, New Jersey: Lawrence Erlbaum, 1989)

Greig, D.W., *International Law*, 2nd ed. (London: Butterworths, 1976)

Grice, H. P., *Logic and Conversation. William James Lectures* (Manuscript, Harvard University, 1967)

—- *Studies in the Way of Words* (Cambridge, MA: Harvard Univ. Press, 1989)

Gross, Leo, "Treaty Interpretation: The Proper Rôle of an International Tribunal", *Proceedings of the American Society of International Law*, at its 63rd Annual Meeting, Held at Washington, D.C., 24–26 April 1969, pp. 108–122

Grossen, Jacques-Michel, *Les présomptions en droit international public* (Dispp. Université de Neuchâtel; Neuchâtel: 1954)

Guggenheim, Paul, *Lehrbuch des Völkerrechts*, Vol. 1 (Basel: Verlag für Recht und Gesellschaft, 1948)

Gutiérrez Posse, Hortensia, "La maxime *ut res magis valeat quam pereat* (Interprétation en fonction de l''effet utile'): Les interprétations 'extensives' et 'restictives'", *Österreichische Zeitschrift für öffentliches Recht*, Vol. 23, NF (1972), pp. 229–254

Hambro, Edward, "The Interpretation of Multilateral Treaties by the International Court of Justice", *Transactions of the Grotius Society*, Vol. 39 (1953), pp. 235–256

Hamzeh, Fuad S., "Agreements in Simplified Form: A Modern Perspective", *British Yearbook of International Law*, Vol. 43 (1968/1969), pp. 178–189

Hannikainen, Lauri, *Peremptory Norms (Jus Cogens) in International Law. Historical Development, Criteria, Present Status* (Diss. Univ. of Lappland; Helsinki: Finnish Lawyers, 1988)

Haraszti, György, *Some Fundamental Problems of the Law of Treaties* (Budapest: Akadémiai Kiadó, 1973)

Harvard Law School, *Research in International Law under the Auspices of the Faculty of the Harvard Law School*, Drafts of Conventions Prepared for the Codification of International Law, Part 3. Law of Treaties, Article 19, *Supplement to the American Journal of International Law*, Vol. 29 (1935), pp. 937–977, cit. "Harvard Law School Research"

Hexner, Ervin P., "Teleological Interpretation of Basic Instruments of Public International Organizations", *Law, State, and International Legal Order. Essays in Honour of Hans Kelsen*, ed. Engel, Salo (Knoxville: Univ. of Tennessee Press, 1964), pp. 119–138 Wolfke

Higgins, Rosalyn, *Problems and Procespp. International Law and How We Use It* (Oxford: Clarendon, 1994)

—- "Some Observations on the Inter-Temporal Rule in International Law", *Theory of International Law at the Threshold of the 21st Century. Essays in Honour of Krzystof Skubiszewski*, ed. Makarczyk, Jerzy (The Hague: Kluwer Law International, 1996)

Hilf, Meinhard, *Die Auslegung mehrsprachiger Verträge*, Beiträge zum ausländischen öffentlichen Recht und Völkerrecht, Vol. 61 (Berlin et al.: Springer, 1973)

Hirsch, E.D., Jr., *Validity in Interpretation*, New Haven and London: Yale University Press, 1967)

Hjelmslev, L., *Essais linguistiques* (Copenhagen: Akademisk Forlag, 1959)

Hogg, James F., "The International Court: Rules of Treaty Interpretation", *Minnesota Law Review*, Vol. 43 (1959), pp. 369–441, cit. "Hogg (I)"

—- "The International Court: Rules of Treaty Interpretation II", *Minnesota Law Review*, Vol. 44 (1959), pp. 5–73, cit. "Hogg (II)"

Holmes, Janet, *An Introduction to Sociolingustics*, Learning About Language (London and New York: Longman, 1992)

Horn, Frank, *Reservations and Interpretative Declarations to Multilateral Treaties*, Studies in International Law, Vol. 5 (The Hague: T.M.C. Asser Institute, 1988)

Hudson, Richard Anthony, *Sociolingustics*, Cambridge Textbooks in Linguistics (Cambridge: CUP, 1980)

Hudson, Manley O., *The Permanent Court of International Justice. A Treatise* (New York: MacMillan, 1934)

Hummer, Waldemar, "'Ordinary' versus 'Special' Meaning", *Österreichische Zeitschrift für öffentliches Recht*, Vol. 26, NF (1975), pp. 87–163

Hurd, Heidi M., "Sovereignty in Silence", *Yale Law Journal*, Vol. 99 (1990), pp. 945–1028

Institut de droit international, Session de Bath, *Annuaire de l'Institut de droit international*, Vol. 43:1 (1950), pp. 367–460

—- Session de Sienne, *Annuaire de l'Institut de droit international*, Vol. 44:1 (1952), pp. 196–223

—- Session de Sienne, *Annuaire de l'Institut de droit international*, Vol. 44:2 (1952), pp. 359–406

—- Session d'Aix-en-Provence, *Annuaire de l'Institut de droit international*, Vol. 45:1 (1954), pp. 225–230

—- Session de Grenade, *Annuaire de l'Institut de droit international*, Vol. 46 (1956), pp. 317–368

—- Session de Centenaire, *Annuaire de l'Institut de droit international*, Vol. 55 (1973), pp. 1–116

—- Session de Wiesbaden, *Annuaire de l'Institut de droit international*, Vol. 56 (1975), pp. 339–374, 536–541

Jacobs, Francis G., "Varieties of Approach to Treaty Interpretation: With Special Reference to the Draft Convention on the Law of Treaties Before the Vienna Diplomatic Conference", *International and Comparative Law Quarterly*, Vol. 18 (1969), pp. 318–346

Jacqué, Jean-Paul, *Élément pour une théorie de l'acte juridique en droit international public*, Bibliotéque de droit international, Vol. 69 (Paris: LGDJ, 1972)

—- "Acte et norme en droit international public", *Recueil des Cours de l'Académie de droit international*, Vol. 227 (1991:2), pp. 357–418

Jennings, R.Y., "General Course on Principles of International Law", *Recueil des Cours de l'Académie de droit international*, Vol. 121 (1967:2), pp. 327–605

Jiménez de Aréchaga, Eduardo, "International Law in the Past Third of a Century", *Recueil des Cours de l'Académie de droit international*, Vol. 159 (1978:1), pp. 1–344

Jokl, M., *De l'interprétation des traités normatifpp. D'aprés la doctrine et la jurisprudence internationales* (Paris: Pédone, 1936)

Karl, Wolfram, "Vetragsauslegung – Vetragsänderung", *Autorität und internationale Ordnung. Aufsätze zum Völkerrecht*, ed. Schreuer, Christoph (Berlin: Duncker & Humblot, 1979), pp. 9–34

—- *Vertrag und spätere Praxis im Völkerrecht*, Beiträge zum ausländischen öffentlichen Recht und Völkerrecht, Vol. 84 (Berlin et al.: Springer, 1983)

Kelsen, Hans, *The Law of the United Nations* (London: Stevens and Sons, 1950)

Kittang, Atle, "Text and tolkning", *En introduktion till den moderna litteraturteorin* (Stockholm, Stehag: Symposion, 1997), pp. 79–106

Klabbers, Jan, Review of Anthony Aust: Modern Treaty Law and Practice, *Nordic Journal of International Law*, Vol. 71 (2002), p. 203–205

—- "International Legal Histories: The Declining Importance of *Travaux Préparatoires* in Treaty Interpretation", *Netherlands International Law review*, Vol. 50 (2003), p. 267–288

Kuner, Christopher B., "The Interpretation of Multilingual Treaties: Comparison of Texts Versus the Presumption of Similar Meaning", *International and Comparative Law Quarterly*, Vol. 40 (1991), pp. 953–964

Köck, Heribert Franz, *Vetragsinterpretation und Vetragsrechtskonvention. Zur Bedetung der Artikel 31 und 32 der Wiener Vertragsrechtskonvention 1969*, Schriften zum Völkerrecht, Vol. 51 (Berlin: Duncker & Humblot, 1976)

Lang, Wienfried, "Les règles d'interprétation codifiées par la Convention de Vienne sur le Droit des Traités et les divers types de traités", *Österreichische Zeitschrift für öffentliches Recht*, Vol. 24, NF (1973), pp. 113–173

Larenz, Karl, *Methodenlehre der Rechtswissenschaft*, 6th ed. (Berlin et al.: Springer, 1991)

Laubadère, André de, *Traité élémentaire de droit administratif*, 3 ed. (Paris: LGDJ, 1963)

Lauterpacht, Elihu, "The Development of the Law of International Organization by the Decisions of International Tribunals", *Recueil des Cours de l'Académie de droit international*, Vol. 152 (1976:4), pp. 381–478

Lauterpacht, Hersch, "Les travaux préparatoires et l'interprétation des traités", *Recueil des Cours de l'Académie de droit international*, Vol. 48 (1934:2), pp. 713–815
—- "Some Observations on Preparatory Work in the Interpretation of Treaties", *Harvard Law Review*, Vol. 48 (1935), pp. 549–591
—- "Restrictive Interpretation and the Principle of Effectiveness in the Interpretation of Treaties", *British Yearbook of International Law*, Vol. 26 (1949), pp. 48–85
—- "De l'interprétation des traités", Report, translated into the French by Lalive, J.-F., *Annuaire de l'Institut de droit international*, Vol. 43:1 (1950), pp. 366–460
Leech, G., *Principles of Pragmatics* (London: Longman, 1983)
Lefeber, René, "The Provisional Application of Treaties", *Essays on the Law of Treatiepp. A Collection of Essays in Honour of Bert Vierdag*, eds. Klabbers, Jan and Lefeber, René (The Hague et al.: Martinus Nijhoff, 1998), pp. 81–95
Leonetti, Antoine-Jean, "L'intérpretation des traités et règles impératives du droit international général (jus cogens)", *Österreichische Zeitschrift für öffentliches Recht*, Vol. 24, NF (1973), pp. 91–111
Levinson, Stephen C., "Minimization and Conversational Inference", *The Pragmatic Perspective*, utg. Verschueren, J. and Bertucelli-Papi, N. (Amsterdam: John Benjamins, 1987)
Lewis, David, *Convention* (Cambridge MA: Harvard University Press, 1969)
—- "Scorekeeping in a Language Game", *Semantics from Different Points of View*, ed. Bauerle, R. et al. (Berlin: Springer, 1979), pp. 172–187
Lijnzaad, Liesbeth, *Reservations to UN-Human Rights Treatiepp. Ratify and Ruin?*, International Studies in Human Rights, Vol. 38 (Dordrecht et al.: Martinus Nijhoff, 1995)
Linderfalk, Ulf, "Is the Hierarchical Structure of Articles 31 and 32 of the Vienna Convention Real or Not? Interpreting the Rules of Interpretation", *Netherlands International Law Review*, Vol. 65 (2007), pp. 133–154, cit. "Linderfalk, 2007(a)"
—- "Treaty Interpretation as a Matter of Art or Science", 2007, forthcoming, cit. "Linderfalk, 2007(b)"
Loftus, E., *Eyewitness Testimony* (Cambridge, MA: Harvard University Press, 1979)
Lyons, John, *Semantics*, Vol. 1–2 (Cambridge: CUP, 1977)
—- *Linguistic Semanticpp. An Introduction* (Cambridge: CUP, 1995)
Malanczuk, Peter, *Akehurst's Modern Introduction to International Law*, 7th ed. (London and New York: Routledge, 1997)
Maluwa, Tiyanjana, "Treaty Interpretation and the Exercise of Prudential Discretion by the International Court of Justice: Some Reflections on the *PLO Mission Case*", *Netherlands International Law Review*, Vol. 37 (1990), pp. 330–346
Marceau, Gabrielle, "Conflicts of Norms and Conflicts of Jurisdiction: The Relationship Between the WTO Agreement and MEAs and Other treaties", *Journal of World Trade*, Vol. 35 (2001), p. 1081 et seq.
Marmor, Andrei, *Interpretation and Legal Theory*, Clarendon Law Series (Oxford: Clarendon Press, 1992)
Matscher, F., "Vertragsauslegung durch Vetragsrechtsvergleichung in der Judikatur internationaler Gerichte, vornehmlich vor den Organen der EMRK", *Völkerrecht als Rechtordnung. Internationale Gerichtsbarkeit Menschenrechte. Festschrift für Hermann Mosler*, utg. Bernhardt, Rudolf et al., Beiträge zum ausländischen öffentlichen Recht und Völkerrecht, Vol. 81 (Berlin et al.: Springer, 1983), pp. 545–566
—- "Methods of Interpretation of the Convention", *The European System for the Protection of Human Rights*, ed. McDonald, R. St. J. et al. (Dordrecht: Nijhoff, 1993), pp. 63–81
McCallum, Gerald C., "Legislative Intent", *Essays in Legal Philosophy*, ed. Summers, Robert S. (Oxford: Basil Blackwell, 1968), pp. 237–273
McCormick, D. Neil and Summers, Robert PP., "Interpretation and Justification", *Interpreting Statutepp. A Comparative Study*, ed. McCormick, D. Neil and Summers, Robert S. (Aldershot et al.: Dartmouth, 1991), pp. 511–551
McDade, Paul V., "The Effect of Article 4 of the Vienna Convention on the Law of Treaties 1969", *International and Comparative Law Quarterly*, Vol. 35 (1986), pp. 499–511
McDougal, Myres, "The International Law Commssion's Draft Articles Upon Interpretation: Textuality Redivivus", *American Journal of International Law*, Vol. 61 (1967), pp. 992 et seq.

McDougal, M., Laswell, H., and Miller, J., *The Interpretation of International Agreements and World Public Order* (Dordrecht: Nijhoff, 1967)
McGinley, Gerald, "Practice as a Guide to Treaty Interpretation", *The Fletcher Forum*, Vol. 9 (1985), pp. 211–230
McLachlan, Campbell, "The Principle of Systemic Integration and Article 31(3)(C) of the Vienna Convention", *International and Comparative Law Quarterly*, Vol. 54 (2005), pp. 279–320
McNair, Arnold, "The Functions and Differing Legal Character of Treaties", *British Yearbook of International Law*, Vol. 11 (1930), pp. 100–118
—- *The Law of Treaties* (Oxford: Clarendon, 1961)
McRae, D.M., "The Legal Effect of Interpretative Declarations", *British Yearbook of International Law*, Vol. 49 (1979), pp. 155–173
McRae, Peter, "The Search for Meaning: Continuing Problems with the Interpretation of Treaties", *Victoria University Wellington Law Review*, Vol. 33 (2002), pp. 209–260
McWhinney, Edward, "The Time Dimension in International Law, Historical Relativism and Intertemporal Law", *Essays in International Law in Honour of Judge Manfred Lachs*, ed. Makarczyk, Jerzy (The Hague et al.: Martinus Nijhoff, 1984), pp. 179–199
Mehrish, B.N. "Travaux Préparatoires as an Element in the Interpretation of Treaties", *Indian Journal of International Law*, Vol. 11 (1971), pp. 39–88
Merrills, J.G., *The Development of International Law by the European Court of Human Rights*, Melland Schill Monographs in International Law (Manchester: MUP, 1993)
Morrisson, Clovis, "Restrictive Interpretation of Sovereignty-Limiting Treaties: The Practice of the European Human Rights Convention System", *International and Comparative Law Quarterly*, Vol. 19 (1970), pp. 361–375
Müller, Jörg P., *Vertrauensschutz im Völkerrecht*, Beiträge zum ausländischen öffentlichen Recht und Völkerrecht, Vol. 56 (Köln, Berlin: Carl Heymanns, 1971)
Mus, Jan B., "Conflicts Between Treaties in International Law", *Netherlands International Law Review*, Vol. 45 (1998), pp. 208–232
Mössner, Jörg Manfred, "Die Auslegung mehrsprachiger Staatsverträge", *Archiv des Völkerrechts*, Vol. 15 (1971/1972), pp. 273–302
Nahlik, Stanislaw E., "La Conférence de Vienne sur le droit des traités: Une vue d'ensemble", *Annuaire français de droit international*, Vol. 15 (1969), pp. 24–53
Naigen, Zhang, "Dispute Settlement under the TRIPS Agreement from the Perspective of Treaty Interpretation", *Temple International and Comparative Law Journal*, Vol. 17 (2003), pp. 199 et seq.
Neisser, U. (ed.), *Memory Observed. Remembering in Natural Contexts*, (San Fransisco: H. Freeman, 1982)
Neuhold, Hanspeter, "Die Wiener Vertragsrechtskonvention 1969", *Archiv des Völkrerrechts*, Vol. 15 (1971/1972), pp. 1–55
—- "The 1968 Session of the United Nations Conference on the Law of Treaties", *Österreichische Zeitschrift für öffentlisches Recht*, Vol. 19 (1969), pp. 59 et seq.
Nowak, Manfred, *UN Covenant on Civil and Political Rightpp. CCPR Commentary* (Kehl et al.: N.P. Engel, 1993)
O'Connell, D.P., *International Law*, Vol. 1, 2nd ed. (London: Stevens and Sons, 1970)
Ogden, Charles Kay and Richards, I.A., *The Meaning of Meaning. A Study of the Influence of Language Upon Thought and the Science of Symbolism* (New York: Harcourt and Brace, 1923)
Oppenheim's International Law, eds. Jennings, Robert and Watts, Arthur, Vol. 1, 9th ed. (Harlow: Longman, 1992)
Orakhelashvili, Alexander, "Restrictive Interpretation of Human Rights in the Recent Jurisprudence of the European court of Human Rights", European Journal of International Law, Vol. 14 (2003), pp. 529–568
Ost, François, "The Original canons of Interpretation of the European Court of Human Rights", *The European Convention for the Protection of Human Rightpp. International Protection versus National Restrictions*, ed. Delmas-Marty, Mireille, International Studies in Human Rights, Vol. 19 (Dordrecht and Boston: Kluwer Academic Publishers, 1992)
Ost, François and Van der Kerchove, Michel, *Entre la lettre et l'ésprit. Les Diréctives d'interprétation en droit* (Bruxelles: Bruylant, 1989)

Pan, Eric J., "Authoritative Interpretation of Agreements: Developing More Responsive International Administrative Regimes", *Harvard International Law Journal*, Vol. 35 (1997), pp. 503–535

Pauwelyn, Joost, *Conflict of Norms in Public International Law* (Cambridge: CUP, 2003)

Peczenik, Aleksander, *Rättsnormer* (Stockholm: Norstedts, 1987)

—- *Vad är rätt? Om Demokrati, rättssäkerhet, etik och juridisk argumentation*, Institutet för rättsvetenskaplig forskning, Vol. 155 (Stockholm: Fritzes, 1995)

Radin, Max, "Statutory Interpretation", *Law and Language*, ed. Schauer, Frederick (Aldershot et al.: Dartmouth, 1993), pp. 189–211, originally published in *Harvard Law Review*, Vol. 43 (1930), pp. 863–885

Ress, G., "The Interpretation of the Charter", *The Charter of the United Nations: A Commentary*, ed. Simma, Bruno (Oxford: Oxford Univ. Press, 1994), pp. 25–44

Rest, Alfred, *Interpretation von Rechtsbegriffen in internationalen Verträgen. Verschiedene Lösungsmöglichkeiten* (Diss. Universität zu Köln, 1971)

Reuter, Paul, *La Convention de Vienne du 29 Mai 1969 sur le Droit des traités* (Paris: Armand Colin, 1970)

—- "Traités et transactions: Réflexions sur l'identification de certains engagements conventionnels", *Le Droit international à l'heure de sa codification. Études en l'honneur de Roberto Ago*, Vol. 1 (Milano: Giuffrè, 1987), pp. 399–415

—- *Introduction to the Law of Treaties*, translated from the French by Mico, José and Haggenmacher, Peter (London and New York: Pinter, 1989)

Review of the Multilateral Treaty-Making Process, United Nations Legislative Series ST/LEG/SER.B/21 (New York: United Nations, 1985)

Ris, Martin, "Treaty Interpretation and ICJ Recourse to *Travaux Préparatoires*: Towards a Proposed Amendment of Articles 31 and 32 of the Vienna Convention on the Law of Treaties", *Boston College International and Comparative Law Review*, Vol. 14 (1991), pp. 111–136

Robertson and Merrills, *Human Rights in Europé*, 3rd ed. (Manchester: MUP, 1993)

Rosenne, Shabtai, "Travaux Préparatoires", *International and Comparative Law Quarterly*, Vol. 12 (1963), pp. 1378–1383

—- *The Law of Treaties. A Guide to the Legislative History of the Vienna Convention* (Leyden: A.W. Sijthoff, 1970), cit. "Rosenne, 1970(a)"

—- "The Temporal Application of the Vienna Convention on the Law of Treaties", *Cornell International Law Journal*, Vol. 4 (1970), pp. 1–24, cit. "Rosenne, 1970(b)"

—- "The Election of Five Members of the International Court of Justice in 1981", *American Journal of International Law*, Vol. 76 (1982), pp. 364–370

—- "The Meaning of 'Authentic Text' in Modern Treaty Law", *Völkerrecht als Rechtordnung. Internationale Gerichtsbarkeit Menschenrechte. Festschrift für Hermann Mosler*, ed. Bernhardt, Rudolf et al., Beiträge zum ausländischen öffentlichen Recht und Völkerrecht, Vol. 81 (Berlin et al.: Springer, 1983), pp. 759–784

—- "Conceptualism as a Guide to Treaty-Interpretation", *Le Droit international à l'heure de sa codification. Études en l'honneur de Roberto Ago*, Vol. 1 (Milano: Giuffrè, 1987), pp. 417–431

—- *Developments in the Law of Treaties 1945–1986*, Cambridge Studies in International and Comparative Law, NS (Cambridge et al.: CUP, 1989)

Rousseau, Charles, *Droit international public*, Vol. 1 (Paris: Sirey, 1970)

Saussure, F. de, *Course in General Linguistics*, translated from the French edition from 1916 by Baskin, Peter (London: Peter Owen, 1974)

Schiffer, S., *Meaning* (Oxford: Clarendon, 1972)

Schröder, Meinhard, "Gedanken zu einer Hierarchie der Interpretationsregeln im Völkerrecht", *Revue hellénique de droit international*, Vol. 21 (1968), pp. 122–132

Schwarzenberger, Georg, "The Fundamental Principles of International Law", *Recueil des Cours de l'Académie de droit international*, Vol. 87 (1955:1), pp. 195–383

—- *International Law*, Vol. 1, 3rd ed. (London: Stevens and Sons, 1957)

—- "Myths and Realities of Treaty Interpretation: Article 27–29 of the Vienna Convention on the Law of Treaties", *Current Legal Problems*, Vol. 22 (1969), pp. 205–227

Schwebel, Stephen M., "May Preparatory Work be Used to Correct Rather than Confirm the 'Clear' Meaning of a Treaty Provision", *Svensk Juristtidning* (1997), pp. 797–804

—- "May Preparatory Work be Used to Correct Rather than Confirm the 'Clear' Meaning of a Treaty Provision", *Theory of International Law at the Threshold of the 21st Century. Essays in Honour of Krzysztof Skubiszewski*, ed. Makarczyk, J. (The Hague: Kluwer, 1996), pp. 541–547
Searle, J., *Speach Acts* (Cambridge: CUP, 1969)
Seidl-Hohenveldern, Ignaz, *Völkerrecht*, 7th ed. (Köln et al.: Carl Heymanns, 1992)
—- "Hierarchy of Treaties", *Essays on the Law of Treaties. A Collection of Essays in Honour of Bert Vierdag*, eds. Klabbers, Jan and Lefeber, René (The Hague m.fl.: Martinus Nijhoff, 1998), pp. 7–18
Shannon, C. and Weaver, W., *The Mathematical Theory of Communication* (Urbana: Univ. of Illinois Press, 1949)
Sharma, "The ILC Draft and Treaty Interpretation With Special Reference to Preparatory Works", *Indian Journal of International Law*, Vol. 8 (1968), pp. 367–398
Shaw, Malcolm N., *International Law*, 3rd ed. (Cambridge: Grotius Publ., 1991)
Shelton, Dinah, "Reconcilable Differences? The Interpretation of Multilingual Treaties", *Hastings International and Comparative Law Review*, Vol. 20 (1997), pp. 611–638
Simon, Denys, *L'interprétation judiciaire des traités d'organisations internationales*, Publication de la Revue générale de droit international public, Vol. 37, NS (Paris: Pédone, 1981)
Sinclair, Ian, "Vienna Conference on the Law of Treaties", *International and Comparative Law Quarterly*, Vol. 19 (1970), pp. 47–69
—- *The Vienna Convention on the Law of Treaties*, 2nd ed. (Manchester: MUP, 1984)
Skubiszewski, Krzysztof, "Remarks on the Interpretation of the United Nations Charter", *Völkerrecht als Rechtordnung. Festschrift für Hermann Mosler*, ed. Bernhardt, Rudolf et al., Beiträge zum ausländischen öffentlichen Recht und Völkerrecht, Vol. 81 (Berlin et al.: Springer, 1983), pp. 891–902
—- "Implied Powers of International Organizations", *International Law at a Time of Perplexity. Essays in Honour of Shabtai Rosenne*, eds. Dinstein, Yoram and Tabory, Mala (Dordrecht et al.: Martinus Nijhoff, 1989), pp. 855–868
Soubeyrol, Jacques, "The International Interpretation of Treaties and the Consideration of the Intention of the Parties", translatd from the French by Kcenig, Michael, *Journal du droit international (Clunet)*, Vol. 85 (1958), pp. 687–759
Spencer, John H., *L'interprétation des traités par les travaux préparatoires* (Diss. Université de Paris; Paris: Éditions internationales, 1935)
Sperber, Dan and Wilson, Deirdre, *Relevance. Communication and Cognition* (Oxford: Basil Blackwell, 1986)
Starke's International Law, utg. Shearer, I.A., 11th ed. (London et al.: Butterworths, 1994)
Stone, Julius, "Fictional Elements in Treaty Interpretation: A Study in the International Judicial Process", *Sydney Law Review*, Vol. 1 (1953/1955), pp. 344–368
Summers, Robert, "Naïve Instrumentalism and the Law", *Law, Morality and Society. Essays in Honour of H.L.A. Hart*, eds. Hacker, P.M.S. and Raz, J. (Oxford: Clarendon, 1977), pp. 119–131
—- *Instrumentalism and American Legal Theory* (Ithaca and London: Cornell Univ. Press, 1982)
Sur, Serge, *L'interprétation en droit international public*, Bibliothéque de droit international, Vol. 75 (Paris: LGDJ, 1974)
Sztucki, Jerzy, *Jus Cogens and the Vienna Convention on the Law of Treaties. A Critical Appraisal* (Wien and New York: Springer, 1974)
Sørensen, Max, *Les Sources du droit international* (Copenhague: Einar Munksgaard, 1946)
—- "Le problème dit du droit intertemporel dans l'ordre international", Rapport provisoire, et Rapport définitif, *Annuaire de l'Institut de droit international*, Vol. 55 (1973), pp. 1–68, 85–98
Tabory, Mala, *Multilingualism in International Law and Institutions* (Alphen aan den Rijn: Sijthoff & Noordhoff, 1980)
Tammelo, Ilmar, *Treaty Interpretation and Practical Reason. Towards a General Theory of Legal Interpretation*, Studies in Legal Method Series, Vol. 1 (Sidney et al.: The Law Book Company, 1967)
Tchivounda, Guillaume Pambou, "Le droit international de l'interprétation des traités à l'épreuve de la jurisprudence", *Journal du Droit international (Clunet)*, Vol. 113 (1986), pp. 627–650
Teboul, Gérard, "Remarques sur les réserves aux conventions de codification", *Revue générale de droit international public*, Vol. 86 (1982), pp. 679–717
Thirlway, Hugh, *International Customary Law and Codification* (Leiden: A.W. Sijthoff, 1972)

—- "The Law and Procedure of the International Court of Justice: 1960–1989, Part One", *British Yearbook of International Law*, Vol. 60, (1989), pp. 1
—- "The Law and Procedure of the International Court of Justice: 1960–1989, Part Three", *British Yearbook of International Law*, Vol. 62, (1991), pp. 1–75
Torres Bernárdez, Santiago, "Interpretation of Treaties by the International Court of Justice Following the Adoption of the 1969 Vienna Convention on the Law of Treaties", *Liber Amoricum. Professor Ignaz Seidl-Hohenveldern in Honour of His 80th Birthday*, ed. Hafner, Gerhard et al. (The Hague et al.: Kluwer Law International, 1998), pp. 721–748
Trudgill, Peter, *Språk och social miljö. En introduktion till sociolingvistike*n (Stockholm: Pan/Norstedts, 1974)
Tunkin, Grigory, "International Law in the International System", *Recueil des Cours de l'Académie de droit international*, Vol. 147 (1975:4), pp. 1–218
Uibopuu, Henn-Jüri, "Interpretation of Treaties in the Light of International law: Art. 31, para. 3(c) of the Vienna Convention on the Law of Treaties", *Annuaire de l'A.A.A.*, Vol. 40 (1970), pp. 1–42
Urueña, Rafaela, "El problema de la interpretación de tratados redactados en diversos idiomas, según el derecho internacional", *Language Problems and Language Planning*, Vol. 14 (1990), pp. 209–223
Vallat, Sir Francis, "The Vienna Convention on the Law of Treaties, 1969", *Annuaire de l'A.A.A.*, Vol. 40 (1970), pp. xi-xxviii
Van Hoof, G.J.H., *Rethinking the Sources of International Law* (Deventer et al.: Kluwer Law and Taxation Publishers, 1983)
Vedel, *Droit administratif* (Paris: Presses Universitaires de France, 1968)
Verdross, Alfred and Simma, Bruno, *Universelles Völerrecht: Theorie und Praxis*, 3rd ed. (Berlin: Duncker & Humblot, 1984)
Verzijl, J.H.W., *International Law in Historical Perspective*, Vol. 6 (Leiden: A.W. Sijthoff, 1973)
Vierdag, E.W., "The Law Governing Treaty Relations Between Parties to the Vienna Convention on the Law of Treaties and States Not Party to the Convention", *American Journal of International Law*, Vol. 76 (1982), pp. 779–801
—- "The Time of the 'Conclusion' of a Multilateral Treaty: Article 30 of the Vienna Convention on the Law of Treaties and Related Provisions, *British Yearbook of International Law*, Vol. 59 (1988), pp. 75–111
Villiger, Mark E., *Customary International Law and Treaties*, Developments in International Law (Dordrecht et al.: Martinus Nijhoff, 1986)
Vitányi, Béla, "Treaty Interpretation in the Legal Theory of Grotius and Its Influence on Modern Doctrine", *Netherlands Yearbook of International Law*, Vol. 14 (1983), pp. 41–67
Voïcu, Ioan, *De l'interprétation authentique des traités internationaux* (Paris: Pédone, 1968)
Waldock, Sir Humphrey, "The Evolution of Human Rights Concepts and the Application of the European Convention of Human Rights", *Le Droit International: Unité et Diversité. Mélanges Offerts à Paul Reuter*, ed. Gross, André (Paris: Pédone, 1981), pp. 535–547
Wasserstom, Richard A., *The Judicial Decision* (Stanford, Calif.: Stanford University Press, 1961)
Weissberg, Guenter, "Maps as Evidence in International Boundary Disputes: A Reappraisal", *American Journal of International Law*, Vol. 57 (1963), pp. 781–803
Wessel, Jared, "Relational Contract Theory and Treaty Interpretation: End-Game Treaties", *New York University Annual Survey of American Law*, Vol. 60 (2004), pp. 149 et seq.
White, Gillian, "Treaty Interpretation: The Vienna Convention 'Code' as Applied by the World Trade Organization Judiciary", *Australian Yearbook of International Law*, Vol. 20 (1999), pp. 319–339
Williams, Glanville L., "The Origin and Logical Implications of the *Ejusdem Generis* Rule", *Conveyancer and Property Law*, Vol. 7, NS (1943), pp. 119–128
—- "Language and the Law", *Law and Language*, ed. Schauer, Frederick (Aldershot et al.: Dartmouth, 1993), pp. 97–184, Originally partly published in *Law Quarterly Review*, Vol. 61 (1946), pp. 71–86, 179–195, 293–303, 384–406, and Vol. 62 (1947), pp. 387–406
Wolf, James C., "The Jurisprudence of Treaty Interpretation", *University of California Davis Law Review*, Vol. 21 (1988), pp. 1023–1071

Wolfke, Karol, "Treaties and Custom: Aspects of Interrelation", *Essays on the Law of Treaties. A Collection of Essays in Honour of Bert Vierdag*, eds. Klabbers, Jan and Lefeber, René (The Hague et al.: Martinus Nijhoff, 1998), pp. 31–39

Wright, Quincy, "The Interpretation of Multilateral Treaties", *American Journal of International Law*, Vol. 23 (1929), pp. 94–107

Wróblewski, Jerzy, "Semantic Basis of the Theory of Legal Interpretation", *Logique et Analyse*, Vol. 21–24, NS (1963), pp. 397–416

—- "Legal Reasoning in Legal Interpretation", *Logique et Analyse*, Vol. 45, NS (1969), pp. 3–31

—- "Legal Language and Legal Interpretation", *Law and Philosophy*, Vol. 4 (1985), pp. 239–255

—- *The Judicial Application of Law*, eds. Bankowski, Zenon and McCormick, Neil, Law and Philosophy Library, Vol. 15 (Dordrecht et al.: Kluwer Academic Publishers, 1992)

Yasseen, Mustafa Kamil, "L'interprétation des traités d'après la Convention de Vienne sur le droit des traités", *Recueil des Cours de l'Académie de droit international*, Vol. 151 (1976:3), pp. 1–114

Yü, Tsune-Chi, *The Interpretation of Treaties* (Diss. Columbia University; New York, 1927)

Ziembinski, Z., "Analogia legis et interprétation extensive", *Annales de la Faculté de Droit et des Sciences économiques de Toulouse*, Vol. 15 (1967)

Zoller, Elisabeth, *La bonne foi en droit international public*, Publication de la Revue générale de droit international public, Vol. 28, NS (Paris: Pédone, 1977)

Zuleeg, M., "Vertragskonkurrenz im Völkerrecht. Teil I: Verträge zwischen souveränen Staaten", *German Yearbook of International Law*, Vol. 20 (1977), pp. 246–276

INDEX

Law and Philosophy Library

1. E. Bulygin, J.-L. Gardies and I.Niiniluoto (eds.): *Man, Law and Modern Forms of Life.* With an Introduction by M.D. Bayles. 1985 ISBN 90-277-1869-5
2. W. Sadurski: *Giving Desert Its Due. Social Justice and Legal Theory. 1985* ISBN 90-277-1941-1
3. N. MacCormick and O. Weinberger: *An Institutional Theory of Law.* New Approaches to Legal Positivism. 1986 ISBN 90-277-2079-7
4. A. Aarnio: *The Rational as Reasonable.* A Treatise on Legal Justification. 1987 ISBN 90-277-2276-5
5. M.D. Bayles: *Principles of Law.* A Normative Analysis. 1987 ISBN 90-277-2412-1; Pb: 90-277-2413-X
6. A. Soeteman: *Logic in Law.* Remarks on Logic and Rationality in Normative Reasoning, Especially in Law. 1989 ISBN 0-7923-0042-4
7. C.T. Sistare: *Responsibility and Criminal Liability.* 1989 ISBN 0-7923-0396-2
8. A. Peczenik: *On Law and Reason.* 1989 ISBN 0-7923-0444-6
9. W. Sadurski: *Moral Pluralism and Legal Neutrality.* 1990 ISBN 0-7923-0565-5
10. M.D. Bayles: *Procedural Justice.* Allocating to Individuals. 1990 ISBN 0-7923-0567-1
11. P. Nerhot (ed.): *Law, Interpretation and Reality.* Essays in Epistemology, Hermeneutics and Jurisprudence. 1990 ISBN 0-7923-0593-0
12. A.W. Norrie: *Law, Ideology and Punishment.* Retrieval and Critique of the Liberal Ideal of Criminal Justice. 1991 ISBN 0-7923-1013-6
13. P. Nerhot (ed.): *Legal Knowledge and Analogy.* Fragments of Legal Epistemology, Hermeneutics and Linguistics. 1991 ISBN 0-7923-1065-9
14. O. Weinberger: *Law, Institution and Legal Politics.* Fundamental Problems of Legal Theory and Social Philosophy. 1991 ISBN 0-7923-1143-4
15. J. Wróblewski: *The Judicial Application of Law.* Edited by Z.Bańkowski and N. MacCormick. 1992 ISBN 0-7923-1569-3
16. T. Wilhelmsson: *Critical Studies in Private Law.* A Treatise on Need-Rational Principles in Modern Law. 1992 ISBN 0-7923-1659-2
17. M.D. Bayles: *Hart's Legal Philosophy.* An Examination. 1992 ISBN 0-7923-1981-8
18. D.W.P. Ruiter: *Institutional Legal Facts.* Legal Powers and their Effects. 1993 ISBN 0-7923-2441-2
19. J. Schonsheck: *On Criminalization.* An Essay in the Philosophy of the Criminal Law. 1994 ISBN 0-7923-2663-6
20. R.P. Malloy and J. Evensky (eds.): *Adam Smith and the Philosophy of Law and Economics.* 1994 ISBN 0-7923-2796-9
21. Z. Bańkowski, I. White and U. Hahn (eds.): *Informatics and the Foundations of Legal Reasoning.* 1995 ISBN 0-7923-3455-8
22. E. Lagerspetz: *The Opposite Mirrors.* An Essay on the Conventionalist Theory of Institutions. 1995 ISBN 0-7923-3325-X
23. M. van Hees: *Rights and Decisions.* Formal Models of Law and Liberalism. 1995 ISBN 0-7923-3754-9
24. B. Anderson: *"Discovery" in Legal Decision-Making.* 1996 ISBN 0-7923-3981-9
25. S. Urbina: *Reason, Democracy, Society.* A Study on the Basis of Legal Thinking. 1996 ISBN 0-7923-4262-3
26. E. Attwooll: *The Tapestry of the Law.* Scotland, Legal Culture and Legal Theory. 1997 ISBN 0-7923-4310-7

Law and Philosophy Library

27. J.C. Hage: *Reasoning with Rules.* An Essay on Legal Reasoning and Its Underlying Logic. 1997 ISBN 0-7923-4325-5
28. R.A. Hillman: *The Richness of Contract Law.* An Analysis and Critique of Contemporary Theories of Contract Law. 1997 ISBN 0-7923-4336-0; 0-7923-5063-4 (Pb)
29. C. Wellman: *An Approach to Rights.* Studies in the Philosophy of Law and Morals. 1997 ISBN 0-7923-4467-7
30. B. van Roermund: *Law, Narrative and Reality.* An Essay in Intercepting Politics. 1997 ISBN 0-7923-4621-1
31. I. Ward: *Kantianism, Postmodernism and Critical Legal Thought.* 1997 ISBN 0-7923-4745-5
32. H. Prakken: *Logical Tools for Modelling Legal Argument.* A Study of Defeasible Reasoning in Law. 1997 ISBN 0-7923-4776-5
33. T. May: *Autonomy, Authority and Moral Responsibility.* 1998 ISBN 0-7923-4851-6
34. M. Atienza and J.R. Manero: *A Theory of Legal Sentences.* 1998 ISBN 0-7923-4856-7
35. E.A. Christodoulidis: *Law and Reflexive Politics.* 1998 ISBN 0-7923-4954-7
36. L.M.M. Royakkers: *Extending Deontic Logic for the Formalisation of Legal Rules.* 1998 ISBN 0-7923-4982-2
37. J.J. Moreso: *Legal Indeterminacy and Constitutional Interpretation.* 1998 ISBN 0-7923-5156-8
38. W. Sadurski: *Freedom of Speech and Its Limits.* 1999 ISBN 0-7923-5523-7
39. J. Wolenski (ed.): *Kazimierz Opalek Selected Papers in Legal Philosophy.* 1999 ISBN 0-7923-5732-9
40. H.P. Visser 't Hooft: *Justice to Future Generations and the Environment.* 1999 ISBN 0-7923-5756-6
41. L.J. Wintgens (ed.): *The Law in Philosophical Perspectives.* My Philosophy of Law. 1999 ISBN 0-7923-5796-5
42. A.R. Lodder: *DiaLaw.* On Legal Justification and Dialogical Models of Argumentation. 1999 ISBN 0-7923-5830-9
43. C. Redondo: *Reasons for Action and the Law.* 1999 ISBN 0-7923-5912-7
44. M. Friedman, L. May, K. Parsons and J. Stiff (eds.): *Rights and Reason.* Essays in Honor of Carl Wellman. 2000 ISBN 0-7923-6198-9
45. G.C. Christie: *The Notion of an Ideal Audience in Legal Argument.* 2000 ISBN 0-7923-6283-7
46. R.S. Summers: *Essays in Legal Theory.* 2000 ISBN 0-7923-6367-1
47. M. van Hees: *Legal Reductionism and Freedom.* 2000 ISBN 0-7923-6491-0
48. R. Gargarella: *The Scepter of Reason.* Public Discussion and Political Radicalism in the Origins of Constitutionalism. 2000 ISBN 0-7923-6508-9
49. M. Iglesias Vila: *Facing Judicial Discretion.* Legal Knowledge and Right Answers Revisited. 2001 ISBN 0-7923-6778-2
50. M. Kiikeri: *Comparative Legal Reasoning and European Law.* 2001 ISBN 0-7923-6884-3
51. A.J. Menéndez: *Justifying Taxes.* Some Elements for a General Theory of Democratic Tax Law. 2001 ISBN 0-7923-7052-X

Law and Philosophy Library

52. W.E. Conklin: *The Invisible Origins of Legal Positivism.* A Re-Reading of a Tradition. 2001 ISBN 0-7923-7101-1
53. Z. Bańkowski: *Living Lawfully.* Love in Law and Law in Love. 2001 ISBN 0-7923-7180-1
54. A.N. Shytov: *Conscience and Love in Making Judicial Decisions.* 2001 ISBN 1-4020-0168-1
55. D.W.P. Ruiter: *Legal Institutions.* 2001 ISBN 1-4020-0186-X

Volumes 56–63 were published by Kluwer Law International.

56. G. den Hartogh: *Mutual Expectations.* A Conventionalist Theory of Law. 2002 ISBN 90-411-1796-2
57. W.L. Robison (ed.): *The Legal Essays of Michael Bayles.* 2002 ISBN 90-411-1835-7
58. U. Bindreiter: *Why Grundnorm?* A Treatise on the Implications of Kelsen's Doctrine. 2002 ISBN 90-411-1867-5
59. S. Urbina: *Legal Method and the Rule of Law.* 2002 ISBN 90-411-1870-5
60. M. Baurmann: *The Market of Virtue.* Morality and Commitment in a Liberal Society. 2002 ISBN 90-411-1874-8
61. G. Zanetti: *Political Friendship and the Good Life.* Two Liberal Arguments against Perfectionism. 2002 ISBN 90-411-1881-0
62. W. Sadurski (ed.): *Constitutional Justice, East and West.* 2002 ISBN 90-411-1883-7
63. S. Taekema: *The Concept of Ideals in Legal Theory.* 2003 ISBN 90-411-1971-X
64. J. Raitio: *The Principle of Legal Certainty in EC Law.* 2003 ISBN 1-4020-1217-9
65. E. Santoro: *Autonomy, Freedom and Rights.* A Critique of Liberal Subjectivity. 2003 ISBN 1-4020-1404-X
66. S. Eng: *Analysis of Dis/agreement – with particular reference to Law and Legal Theory.* 2003 ISBN 1-4020-1490-2
67. D. González Lagier: *The Paradoxes of Action.* (Human Action, Law and Philosophy). 2003 ISBN Hb-1-4020-1661-1
68. R. Zimmerling: *Influence and Power.* Variations on a Messy Theme. 2004 ISBN Hb-1-4020-2986-1
69. A. Stranieri and J. Zeleznikow (eds.): *Knowledge Discovery from Legal Databases.* 2005 ISBN 1-4020-3036-3
70. J. Hage: *Studies in Legal Logic.* 2005 ISBN 1-4020-3517-9
71. C. Wellman: *Medical Law and Moral Rights.* 2005 ISBN 1-4020-3751-1
72. T. Meisels: *Territorial Rights.* 2005 ISBN 1-4020-3822-4
73. G.W. Rainbolt: *The Concept of Rights.* 2005 ISBN 1-4020-3976-X
74. O. Ezra: *Moral Dilemmas in Real Life.* Current Issues in Applied Ethics. 2006 ISBN 1-4020-4103-9
75. N.T. Casals: *Group Rights as Human Rights.* A Liberal Approach to Multiculturalism. 2006 ISBN 1-4020-4208-6
76. C. Michelon Jr.: *Being Apart from Reasons.* The Role of Reasons in Public and Private Moral Decision-Making. 2006 ISBN 1-4020-4282-5
77. A.J. Menendez and E.O. Eriksen (eds): *Arguing Fundamental Rights.* 2006 ISBN 1-4020-4918-8
78. J. Stelmach and B. Brozek: *Methods of Legal Reasoning.* 2006 ISBN 1-4020-4936-6

79. M. La Torre: *Constitutionalism and Legal Reasoning*. 2006 ISBN 1-4020-5594-3
80. P. Costa and D. Zolo (eds): *The rule of Law*. History, Theory and Criticism. 2007 ISBN 978-1-4020-5744-1
81. H. Avila: *Theory of Legal Principles*. 2007 ISBN 978-1-4020-5878-3
82. C. Deniz: *Law as Symbolic Form Ernst Cassirer and the anthropocentric view of law Series Law and Philosophy Library,* 2007, ISBN: 978-1-4020-6255-1
83. U. Linderfalk: *On the Interpretation of Treaties*. The Modern International Law as Expressed in the 1969 Vienna Convention on the Law of Treaties. 2007 ISBN 978-1-4020-6361-9